# SAP SuccessFactors Talent: Volume 2

## A Complete Guide to Configuration, Administration, and Best Practices: Succession and Development

Susan Traynor
Michael A. Wellens
Venki Krishnamoorthy

Apress®

***SAP SuccessFactors Talent: Volume 2***

Susan Traynor
Coronado, CA, USA

Michael A. Wellens
Davidson, NC, USA

Venki Krishnamoorthy
Coraopolis, PA, USA

ISBN-13 (pbk): 978-1-4842-6994-7
ISBN-13 (electronic): 978-1-4842-6995-4
https://doi.org/10.1007/978-1-4842-6995-4



Managing Director, Apress Media LLC: Welmoed Spahr
Acquisitions Editor: Divya Modi
Development Editor: Matthew Moodie
Coordinating Editor: Divya Modi

Cover designed by eStudioCalamar

Cover image designed by Freepik (www.freepik.com)

Distributed to the book trade worldwide by Springer Science+Business Media New York, 1 New York Plaza, New York, NY 10004. Phone 1-800-SPRINGER, fax (201) 348-4505, e-mail orders-ny@springer-sbm.com, or visit www.springeronline.com. Apress Media, LLC is a California LLC and the sole member (owner) is Springer Science + Business Media Finance Inc (SSBM Finance Inc). SSBM Finance Inc is a **Delaware** corporation.

For information on translations, please e-mail booktranslations@springernature.com; for reprint, paperback, or audio rights, please e-mail bookpermissions@springernature.com.

Apress titles may be purchased in bulk for academic, corporate, or promotional use. eBook versions and licenses are also available for most titles. For more information, reference our Print and eBook Bulk Sales web page at http://www.apress.com/bulk-sales.

Any source code or other supplementary material referenced by the author in this book is available to readers on GitHub via the book's product page, located at www.apress.com/978-1-4842-6994-7. For more detailed information, please visit http://www.apress.com/source-code.

Printed on acid-free paper

*Jeffrey S. Kob and Randall M. Kob with gratitude*

*and*

*Sheila McGovern who gave Michael the opportunity to jump into the world of SAP SuccessFactors.*

*and*

*To Venki's mom Thiripurasundari who was his guide and dear friend. Dedicated with gratitude.*

# Table of Contents

# About the Authors

**Susan Traynor, M.A.** is an SAP SuccessFactors Certified Professional with more than 21 years of progressive experience in SAP HCM and SuccessFactors. She has considerable experience working on full lifecycle project implementations as well as supporting upgrades and integration projects You can follow her on LinkedIn.

**Michael A. Wellens, M.S.** is a certified SAP SuccessFactors consultant with over 15 years of human resources information systems implementation experience.
He has successfully launched a variety of core HR and talent management solutions across a variety of fortune 500 companies around the world. You can follow him on LinkedIn or on Twitter at @mike_wellens.

**Venki Krishnamoorthy** is an SAP SuccessFactors consultant. Venki has over 15 years of experience as a functional lead, project manager, and program manager in HCM transformation projects. Venki has completed over 35 full lifecycle implementations of SuccessFactors projects across multiple modules. You can follow Venki on LinkedIn or on Twitter at @venki_sap.

# About the Technical Reviewer

**Gaye Bowles**, is an SAP SuccessFactors Certified consultant with 16+ years' technical and functional experience in SuccessFactors and HR Applications. With over 25 full lifecycle global implementations including large transformation and conversion projects for Fortune 500 companies; she has also supported both commercial and national security (NS2) clients. You can follow her on LinkedIn.

# Introduction

Welcome to Volume 2 of SAP SuccessFactors Talent! In Volume 2, we continue the logical progression of building a comprehensive SAP SuccessFactors Talent solution we started in Volume 1 by diving into the details of Development and Succession.

In Chapter 1, we begin with learning how to configure development plans, how these are similar to the goal plans we created in Volume 1, and how they integrate into other parts of the system. In Chapter 2, we continue with the Career Worksheet, discussing what a career worksheet is, how to configure it, and how it integrates into other modules. This chapter also covers the Career Explorer. In Chapter 3, we then walk through the Career Worksheet as an end user. Chapter 4 then dives into configuring and using Mentoring. The next three chapters cover Succession Management. In Chapter 5 we introduce Succession Management and guide you through the configuration and usage of the 9-box and the Talent Review Form. Chapter 6 then jumps into core Succession Management with talent cards, setting up nominations, and configuring and using the Succession Org Chart. Chapter 7 wraps up Succession Management covering additional features like the Talent Search, Talent Pools, the Position Tile View, and Lineage Chart. We then complete Volume 2 with a conclusion that reviews the content we've covered and looks ahead to realizing business value and maintaining the system long-term.

# Introduction

[illegible]

# CHAPTER 1

# Development Plans

Career Development Planning is an ongoing process used to help an individual assess their strengths, weaknesses, skills, interests, and priorities to plan their career growth and prepare for future opportunities. A career development plan is used to set actionable goals to help an individual determine where they are heading and what steps are needed to get there. It is a blueprint used by an employee to capture short- and long-term actionable goals needed to grow in their current role and to prepare for future roles. The plan can be based on the skills, competencies, education, training, or behaviors required for the employee to achieve personal and professional growth. The plan may include the steps or activities and the time frame needed to accomplish these goals. Setting personal and professional development goals gives an employee a road map to future success.

SAP SuccessFactors has a bundle of tools within the Career Development Planning (CDP) module that an employee may use to manage personal and professional development goals, do career planning, view career paths, and participate in mentoring programs.

In this chapter, we will walk through the steps to setting up Career Development Planning. We start by turning on the module in Provisioning and assigning configuration permissions. We will then demonstrate how to use the online editor to create and modify a development plan template. We will learn about the use of role competencies with development goals and learning activities. Then we highlight the details of editing the XML generated by that online editor with sample code. We will also see how a development plan may integrate with Performance Management, Calibration, Continuous Performance Management, Succession, and Career Worksheet. We will finish by taking a tour of the end-to-end development plan process as an end user. Following this chapter, we will dive into other features of CDP: Career Worksheet, Career Paths, and Mentoring.




S. Traynor et al., *SAP SuccessFactors Talent: Volume 2*, https://doi.org/10.1007/978-1-4842-6995-4_1

## Goal Plans vs. Development Plans

As we go through this chapter, we will see that goal and development plans have similar templates, permissions, and functionality. Before we begin, we will review the commonalities and the differences between the two plan types. It is best practice to have just one goal and one development plan template.

A development plan is like a goal plan in many ways:

- Similarly structured with the same look and feel
- Plan access being role based
- Use of the plan template XML to identify what a permission role may see and do
- May link to activities and achievements in Continuous Performance Management (CPM)
- May appear in a performance review form
- May be configured to copy goals from another goal plan

A development plan differs from a goal plan in the following ways:

- A goal library is not accessed.
- Development goals may be linked to competencies.
- Development goals may be linked to learning activities.
- Development goals may be linked to competencies in Career Worksheet.
- Development plans are ongoing and not limited to a year.
- Cannot cascade or align development goals.
- Development plans are usually private with access only to the employee and their manager hierarchy.

# Basic Configuration of Development Plans

In this section, we will cover all the steps needed to configure a basic development plan from beginning to end. The result will be a simple plan that a user may access to create and manage development goals. Like the goal plan discussed in Volume 1, Chapter 4, this type of plan is a good start for a first iteration review with real-life customers.

We will be working with Development Plan V12, which is the newest version of the UI and leverages the Fiori design standards. And to use the current versions of Career Worksheet (v12) and Career Path (v2), this latest version is required.

# Provisioning Configuration Prerequisites

Before we can configure a development goal plan, there are some preliminary steps to perform in Provisioning.

## Enable Career Development Planning

We will begin by editing Provisioning settings so that the Career Development Planning screens and permissions become available in SAP SuccessFactors. Log into Provisioning and select the appropriate company id. We will head to Company Settings to make our updates. In order to use the Career Development Planning module and its features, there are some underlying features that must be enabled.

We will start by verifying the settings listed in the following have been enabled:

- Version 12 UI Framework (Revolution)
- Enable Generic Objects
- Enable the Attachment Manager
- Role-Based Permission
- JDM v2.0/Skills Management
- SuccessFactors 2.1 Competency Library
- LMS (optional)

Once confirmed, we will enable the features to make the Career Development Planning module available. Within the Goal Frameworks section of Company Settings, find Career & Development Planning as shown in Figure 1-1.

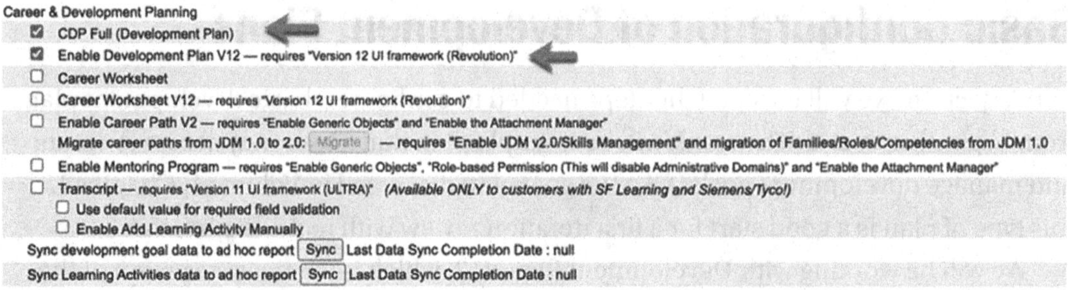

Career & Development Planning
☑ CDP Full (Development Plan)
☑ Enable Development Plan V12 — requires "Version 12 UI framework (Revolution)"
☐ Career Worksheet
☐ Career Worksheet V12 — requires "Version 12 UI framework (Revolution)"
☐ Enable Career Path V2 — requires "Enable Generic Objects" and "Enable the Attachment Manager"
Migrate career paths from JDM 1.0 to 2.0: Migrate — requires "Enable JDM v2.0/Skills Management" and migration of Families/Roles/Competencies from JDM 1.0
☐ Enable Mentoring Program — requires "Enable Generic Objects", "Role-based Permission (This will disable Administrative Domains)" and "Enable the Attachment Manager"
☐ Transcript — requires "Version 11 UI framework (ULTRA)" *(Available ONLY to customers with SF Learning and Siemens/Tyco!)*
☐ Use default value for required field validation
☐ Enable Add Learning Activity Manually
Sync development goal data to ad hoc report Sync Last Data Sync Completion Date : null
Sync Learning Activities data to ad hoc report Sync Last Data Sync Completion Date : null

***Figure 1-1.*** *Career & Development Planning Permissions*

We recommend enabling CDP Full (Development Plan) to have access to the full version of Career Development Planning which includes Development Plan, Career Worksheet, and Career Path. Even if you do not use Career Worksheet and Career Path, CDP Full allows for development plan customization and links to SAP SuccessFactors Learning.

Table 1-1 details the Career & Development Planning options that are available within Goal Frameworks.

***Table 1-1.*** *Career & Development Planning Settings*

| Option | Description |
| --- | --- |
| CDP Full (Development Plan) | Enables Development Goals V11 with Learning Activity integration. |
| Enable Development Plan V12 | Enables Development Goals V12, must also enable CDP Full. |
| Career Worksheet | Enables Career Worksheet V11, must also enable CDP Full. |
| Career Worksheet V12 | Enables Career Worksheet V12, must also enable CDP Full. |
| Enable Career Path V2 | Enables Career Path V2, must also enable Career Worksheet V12. |
| Enable Mentoring Program | Enables Mentoring Program. |
| Transcript | Enable only if integrated with SAP SuccessFactors Learning. |
| Use default value for required field validation | Do not use. |
| Enable Add Learning Activity Manually | Allows users to manually add a learning activity to a development goal; also enable Transcript. |

We will cover permissions and functionality of Career Worksheet, Career Path, and Mentoring in later chapters.

## Enable Learning Activities

SAP SuccessFactors Learning (LMS) may be integrated with CDP. The development plan may be configured to allow users to add learning activities to development goals and track actions and training being done toward achieving the goals. When enabled, users can add learning activities directly from the LMS learning catalog. Users may also be able to manually add custom learning activities to development goals.

To integrate with Learning, these features, also within the Career & Development Planning section of Goal Frameworks, may be enabled as seen in Figure 1-2.

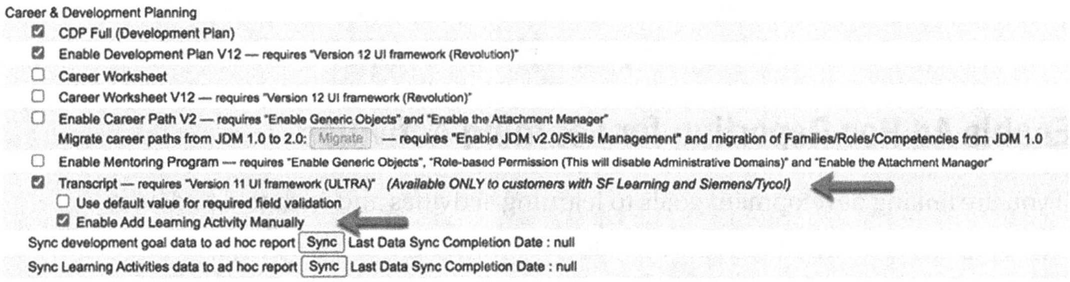

Career & Development Planning
- [x] CDP Full (Development Plan)
- [x] Enable Development Plan V12 — requires "Version 12 UI framework (Revolution)"
- [ ] Career Worksheet
- [ ] Career Worksheet V12 — requires "Version 12 UI framework (Revolution)"
- [ ] Enable Career Path V2 — requires "Enable Generic Objects" and "Enable the Attachment Manager"
  Migrate career paths from JDM 1.0 to 2.0: Migrate — requires "Enable JDM v2.0/Skills Management" and migration of Families/Roles/Competencies from JDM 1.0
- [ ] Enable Mentoring Program — requires "Enable Generic Objects", "Role-based Permission (This will disable Administrative Domains)" and "Enable the Attachment Manager"
- [x] Transcript — requires "Version 11 UI framework (ULTRA)" *(Available ONLY to customers with SF Learning and Siemens/Tyco!)*
  - [ ] Use default value for required field validation
  - [x] Enable Add Learning Activity Manually

Sync development goal data to ad hoc report Sync Last Data Sync Completion Date : null
Sync Learning Activities data to ad hoc report Sync Last Data Sync Completion Date : null

***Figure 1-2.*** *LMS-Related Permissions for CDP Integration*

To allow adding manual learning activities to a development goal, enable the following:

- Transcript
- Enable Add Learning Activity Manually

## Enable Development Goal Copy

There is a setting also under Goal Frameworks that you may enable if you opt to allow users to copy development goals from another development plan. This is the same functionality that is available on goal plans. To do so, enable TGM/CDP Goal Transfer Wizard as shown in Figure 1-3. Since development plans may span several years, this feature may not be of great use.

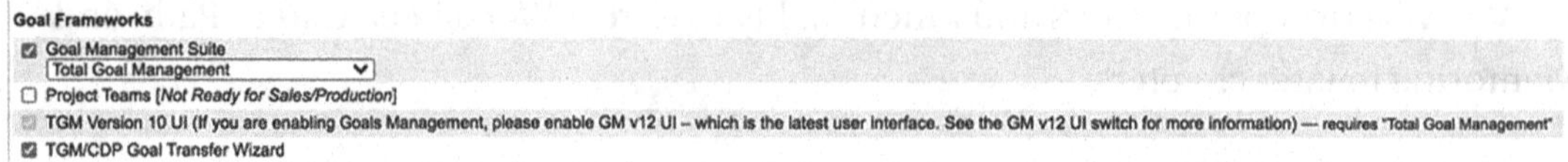


***Figure 1-3.*** *Option to Copy Development Goals from Another Plan*

## Enable Ad Hoc Reporting for Development Goals

In order do ad hoc reporting on Career Development data as either the admin or a user, enable the following in Company Settings:

- Analytics and Dashboard Tabs & Misc Reporting ➤ Additional Adhoc Sub domain Schemas Configuration ➤ Development Goal
- Analytics and Dashboard Tabs & Misc Reporting ➤ Enable INCLUDE STARTING FROM USER in people pill ➤ Development Goal

## Enable Ad Hoc Reporting for Learning Activities

If you are linking development goals to learning activities and wish to do ad hoc reporting on learning activity data, enable the following:

- Analytics and Dashboard Tabs & Misc Reporting ➤ Additional Adhoc Sub domain Schemas Configuration ➤ Learning Activities
- Analytics and Dashboard Tabs & Misc Reporting ➤ Enable INCLUDE STARTING FROM USER in people pill ➤ Learning Activities

## Summary of Provisioning Updates

Shown in the following is a summary of the features that we have enabled.

Development Plan:

- Goal Frameworks ➤ Career & Development Planning ➤ CDP Full (Development Plan)
- Goal Frameworks ➤ Career & Development Planning ➤ Development Plan V12

Development goals linked to learning activities (optional):

- Goal Frameworks ➤ Career & Development Planning ➤ Transcript

- Goal Frameworks ➤ Career & Development Planning ➤ Enable Add Learning Activity Manually

Development goal copy from another development plan (optional):

- Goal Frameworks ➤ TGM/CDP Goal Transfer Wizard

Ad hoc development goal reporting (optional):

- Analytics and Dashboard Tabs & Misc Reporting ➤ Additional Adhoc Sub domain Schemas Configuration ➤ Development Goal
- Analytics and Dashboard Tabs & Misc Reporting ➤ Enable INCLUDE STARTING FROM USER in people pill ➤ Development Goal

Ad hoc Learning Activities reporting (optional):

- Analytics and Dashboard Tabs & Misc Reporting ➤ Additional Adhoc Sub domain Schemas Configuration ➤ Learning Activities
- Analytics and Dashboard Tabs & Misc Reporting ➤ Enable INCLUDE STARTING FROM USER in people pill ➤ Learning Activities

After saving the new features, back out of Company Settings, return to the main screen of Provisioning, and log out.

## Assign Permissions to Configure and Administer Career Development Planning

We will now head into the instance to assign role-based permissions which will enable you to configure and administer the Career Development Planning module. Permissions for Development Plans work similarly to goal plan permissions. For questions on how to assign permissions, refer back to Volume 1, Chapter 4 which detailed the steps to edit permission roles.

To assign admin role-based permissions, go to the action search bar, and type and select "Manage Permission Roles". Find the admin role that you wish to modify, open it, and then click "Permission...:" Under Administrator Permissions on the left, click "Manage Career Development"; then click the box next to "Development Admin," as shown in Figure 1-4.

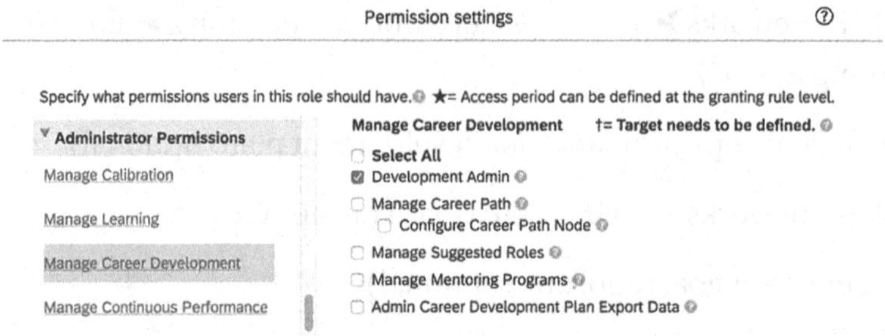

*Figure 1-4.* *Manage Career Development Permissions*

The administrator role now can manage the features of Career Development Planning.

Table 1-2 describes the Manage Career Development permissions that are available.

***Table 1-2.*** *Summary of Manage Career Development Permissions*

| Permission | Description |
| --- | --- |
| Development Admin | To manage all development plan settings. |
| Manage Career Path | To define and manage career paths. |
| Configure Career Path Node | To define what appears on the node within a career path; only for Career Path V2. |
| Manage Suggested Roles | To configure Suggested Roles settings. |
| Manage Mentoring Programs | To manage mentoring programs. |
| Admin Career Development Plan Export Data | To export Career Development Plan data via Data Subject Information |

Additionally, grant the admin access to run companywide development reports using the paths noted in the following:

- User Permissions ➤ Reports Permission ➤ Create Report ➤ Development Goal
- User Permissions ➤ Reports Permission ➤ Run Report ➤ Development Goal

If using learning activities and wish to report on them, add the following access as well:

- User Permissions ➤ Reports Permission ➤ Create Report ➤ Learning Activities
- User Permissions ➤ Reports Permission ➤ Run Report ➤ Learning Activities

If the standard development plan or custom tiles/dashboards are going to be used, these permissions are needed as well. They may be found using the following path:

- User Permissions ➤ Reports Permission ➤ Analytics Tiles and Dashboards

# Primary Configuration of Development Goal Management

Now that we have the Career Development Planning module activated and we have permissions to the needed screens to conduct our configurations, let's get started! This section will walk you through the basic steps of configuring a simple development plan, as well as covering the screens to modify the primary template and administer the process.

## Development Template Configuration

Here, we will take a look at how to create and edit a development template. The configuration of the development plan template in Career Development Planning relies on most of the same template configuration options done for Goal Management. Any differences will be noted.

Development templates are commonly referred to as development or career development plans. Unlike a goal plan that is created annually, a development plan may span multiple years. It is advisable to use one development plan in your instance. This is especially important when using Career Worksheet because it may only be linked to a single Career Development Planning template. We will cover this feature in depth in the next chapter.

In our example, we will use the "Manage Templates" online editor screen. There are some features of development plan templates that are not available for editing in the online editor that must be done directly in the development plan template's underlying XML and then uploaded into the system via Provisioning. We will cover this process later in the chapter. To get started, follow these steps.

In the search bar, type and select "Manage Templates." The screen will appear with multiple tabs representing the various template types. Click the Development tab to see any development templates as seen in Figure 1-5.

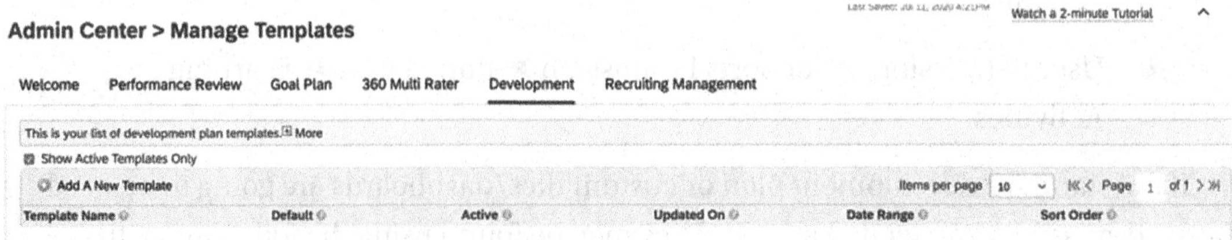


***Figure 1-5.** Manage Templates View of Development Templates*

Let's look at the features found on this screen. The column headings are identical to those in the Goal Plan tab.

- **Show Active Templates Only:** When checked, the inactive templates will not appear in the listing. Inactive plans will also not be accessible by employees or in performance forms.
- **Add a New Template:** Download a template from SuccessStore to use as a starting point when building your plan.
- **Default:** Identify which plan is the default. This is the development plan that a user sees when they access Development.
- **Sort Order:** For active plans, shows the order in which plans are listed in the user's dropdown list.
- **Active:** Available for use. If permitted, users will have access to the plan.
- **Updated On:** The last time the template was modified.
- **Date Range:** Time frame of the plan.

Now let's create a template. A development plan cannot be created from scratch. It must be created from a template in SuccessStore or copied from an existing development plan:

1. Click "Add A New Template." In the popup, select a development plan template from SuccessStore. This will be a starter template for you to edit. Select a plan and click "Add to my Instance" as seen in Figure 1-6.

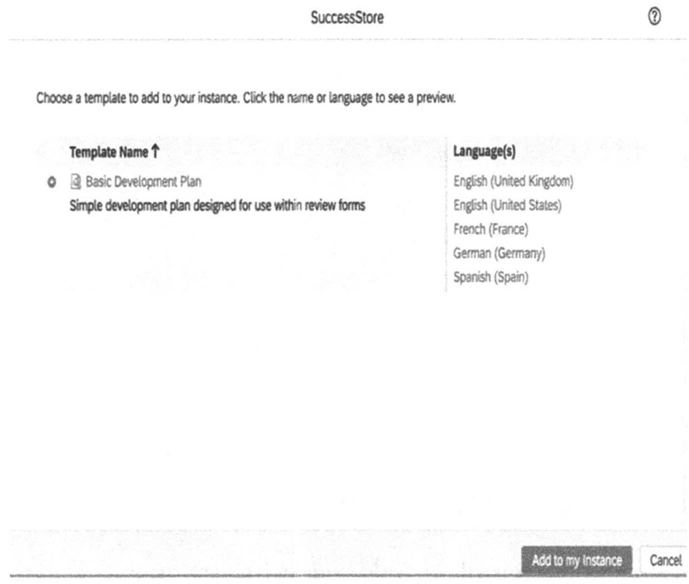


***Figure 1-6.*** *Adding a Template from SuccessStore*

2. You will be prompted to name your template as seen in Figure 1-7. Type a name for your template such as "Career Development Plan" and click "Save."

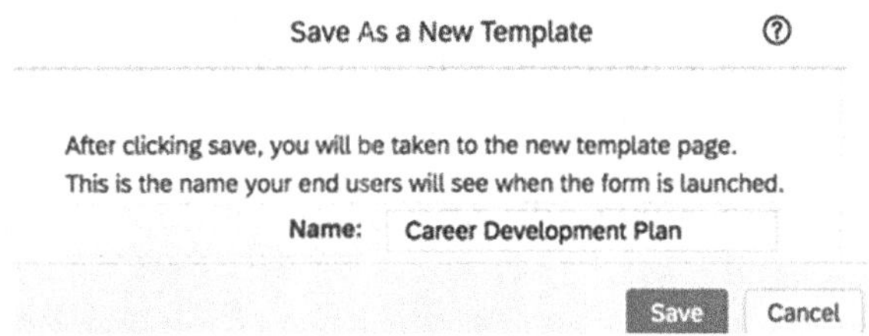


***Figure 1-7.*** *Naming a New Development Plan Template*

Once named and saved, the online editor will appear as seen in Figure 1-8 showing the Preview page for the template.

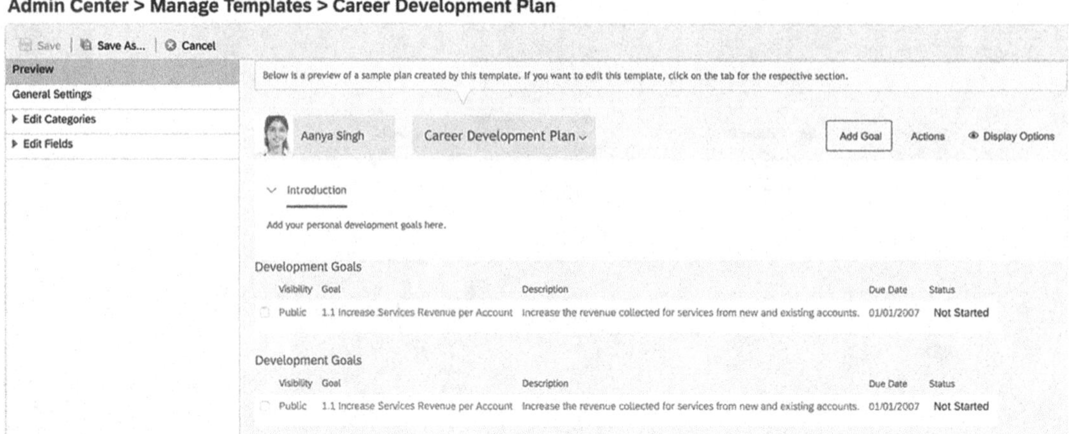


***Figure 1-8.** Development Plan Editor Preview*

Before we start to edit the template, let's review its sections:

- **Preview:** View only. Provides a glimpse of how the plan will appear to a user. The layout of the fields is not a 100% true representation of how the form will look on-screen.
- **General Settings:** Used to edit the top section of the plan: plan name, an introduction, and plan dates.
- **Edit Categories:** Used to create, edit, and delete categories of development goals. Can reorder and relabel.
- **Edit Fields:** Used to create, edit, and delete development goal plan fields.

Now let's go through the steps to modify the template. Please note that this process is identical to editing a goal plan:

1. Click "General Settings" on the left panel. The screen will update with the General Settings page as shown in Figure 1-9. Start by making sure you are on the default language in the "Change Language" dropdown at the top of the screen. If you are performing a global implementation, you can choose a language from the dropdown to provide needed translations.

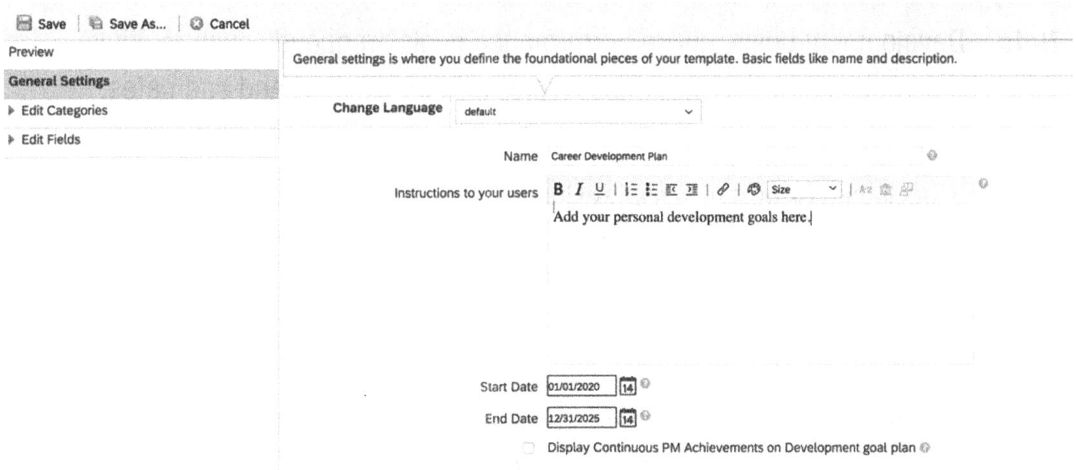


*Figure 1-9. General Settings for a Development Plan Template*

---

**Note** We recommend always configuring the form first using the default language on every page of the online editor. This will automatically fill in the values for the remaining languages active for your system (if you need to edit the available languages, these are activated in Provisioning under Company Settings). If you only use US English (en_US) and fill in all of the default values in US English, you will not have to change languages at all.

---

2. Use the Name field to change the title of your development plan as needed.

3. Enter any instructions you would like to provide in the "Instructions to your users" field.

---

**Note** We find that some customers like to provide links to technical help documentation and policy documents that provide context of creating development goals.

---

4. Enter a start and end date.

---

**Note** Development goals, unlike performance goals, frequently span multiple years, so do not use a calendar or fiscal year for the plan start and end dates.

---

5. Check the box next to "Display Continuous PM Achievements on Development goal plan" if desired. This will add a column to the development goal plan showing any CPM achievements related to the goal.

---

**Note** We recommend using this feature as it can be helpful to remind users of their achievements. You must have implemented Continuous Performance Management (CPM) for this feature to work. Refer to Volume 1, Chapter 13 for more details.

---

Now, we will move on the "Edit Categories" section of the template:

1. Click "Edit Categories." This will expand the section to show the standard categories that come with the template you downloaded. Unlike the goal plan template, there is only one standard category. However, you may add additional categories if you like.
    a. To add a category, click "Add a New Category," and the category will appear on the list.
    b. To edit the name of a category, click the category and type the new name of the category in the field that appears to the right (after making a language selection).
    c. To delete a category, click the trash can icon.

---

**Note** We do not recommend deleting a category after the form is put to use by end users as this can corrupt data!

---

Next, we will review the Edit Fields section of the template.

Click "Edit Fields." The area will expand showing the fields included in the template you downloaded from SuccessStore as shown in Figure 1-10. You can mouse over a field and click the trash can icon to delete it. You can drag and drop fields to change the order the fields appear in the development goal plan.

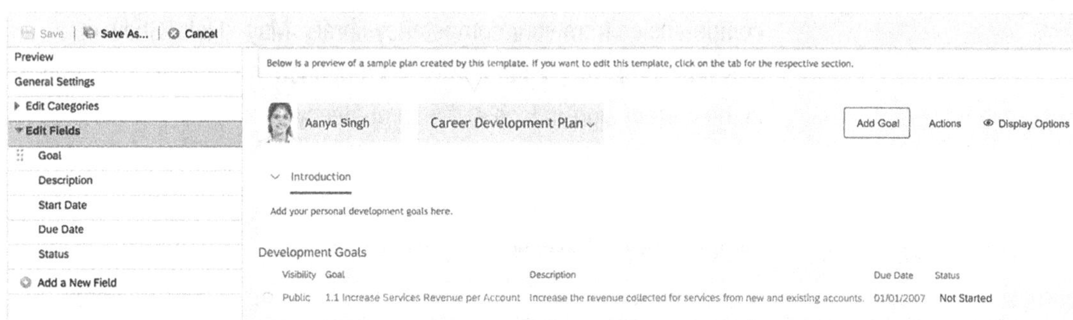


***Figure 1-10.*** *Edit Fields*

Click an existing field to edit it. When editing a field, edit the label (be sure to choose your desired language first) and indicate if the field is required. If you would like to show this field in the People Profile block, check the corresponding box as well. See Volume 1, Chapter 2 for more information on this block, and see Volume 1, Chapter 4 to reference the tables of standard fields and options along with custom fields and types. When adding a new field to your plan, the only options that appear are Competencies, Purpose, and Custom Field as seen in Figure 1-11.

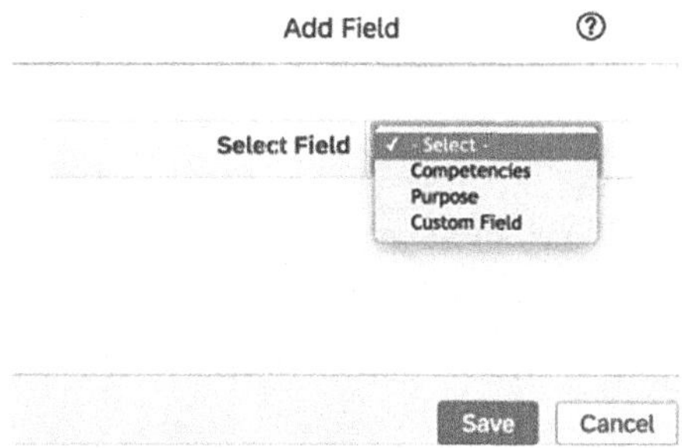


***Figure 1-11.*** *Add Fields to a Development Plan*

Review Table 1-3 for additional fields specific to development goals that may be added to the template.

*Table 1-3. Development Fields to Add to the Plan*

| Technical Field Name | Field Type | Description | Configuration Options |
|---|---|---|---|
| competency | competencies | Used to link development goal to one or more competencies from your competency library. May only link competencies that have been defined in the current sign-in locale. If a competency is defined in English only, and when a user signs in the system with another language, that competency isn't available for linking. | Label, Required Field, Show in People Profile Block |
| purpose | enum | Dropdown listing for items such as "current role," "future role," or "general skillset." | Label, Required Field, Show in People Profile Block |

To add additional fields to the plan, click "Add a New Field." An example of adding a field to the plan is shown in Figure 1-12.

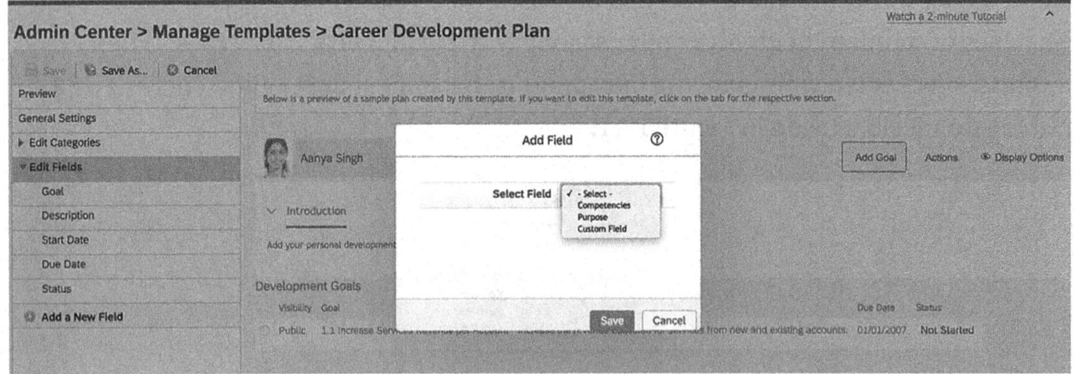


*Figure 1-12. Adding a Field to the Development Goal Plan*

In the preceding example, there are some standard fields that may be added along with a custom field. If you plan on allowing users to tie development goals to competencies, a competency library is required, and the competency field has to be added to the plan. Competencies may identify and communicate information about the behaviors expected to perform a job. Competencies are important because they can be used in performance management, career development, compensation, succession management, 360 surveys, recruiting, and workforce planning. Competencies are mapped to job roles and can be used as part of an employee's development path.

This is an optional field to add to the development plan. However, if you plan on implementing Career Worksheet, a competency library is necessary. We recommend you use the SuccessFactors 2.1 Competency Library since it contains associated teasers, tunings, and behaviors. This library can be modified, or you may create your own competency library to be imported.

The other standard field that you may add is "Purpose." It uses a list as shown in Figure 1-13.

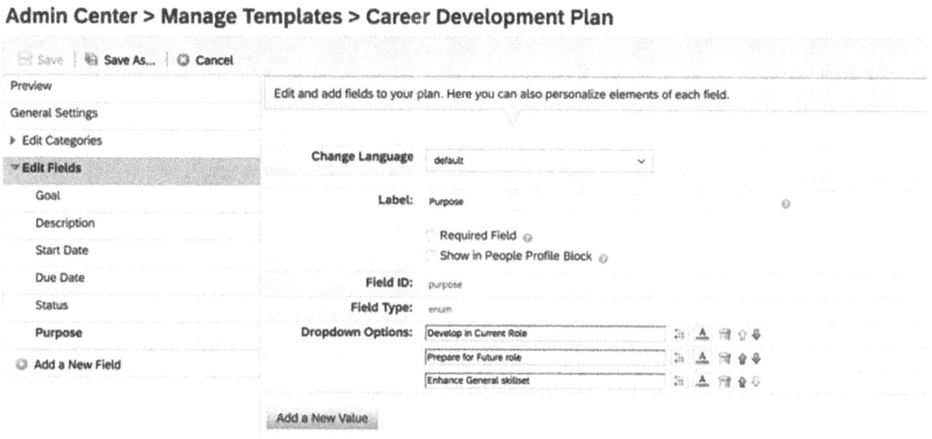

***Figure 1-13.*** *View of the Purpose Field with Dropdown Options*

For "Purpose," you may add or delete dropdown options, change the sort order, rename the labels, or change the text and background color for each label. Click "Add a New Value" in order to create a new value for the field.

The development plan may use custom fields just as the goal plan allows. It is best to add the custom fields here rather than adding them directly in the development plan XML.

After naming the custom field, providing a custom field id and label, and identifying the field type, save your updates.

The remaining standard fields, which are also available for goal plans, may not be shown when trying to add a new field. So these would have to be added in the development plan template XML which we will cover shortly.

Congratulations! You have now configured your development plan! This template can record development goal data using a variety of fields that can be added, removed, and configured to suit the needs of the organization. We've also shown you which fields can be used to integrate with competencies and Continuous Performance Management.

## Email Notifications

The goal email notifications that were discussed in Volume 1, Chapter 4 are applicable to development goals as well. These notifications are available for goal creation, deletion, and modification and goal comments as noted in Figure 1-14. Refer to Volume 1, Chapter 4 to review the list of goal plan notification descriptions and the process to enable them.

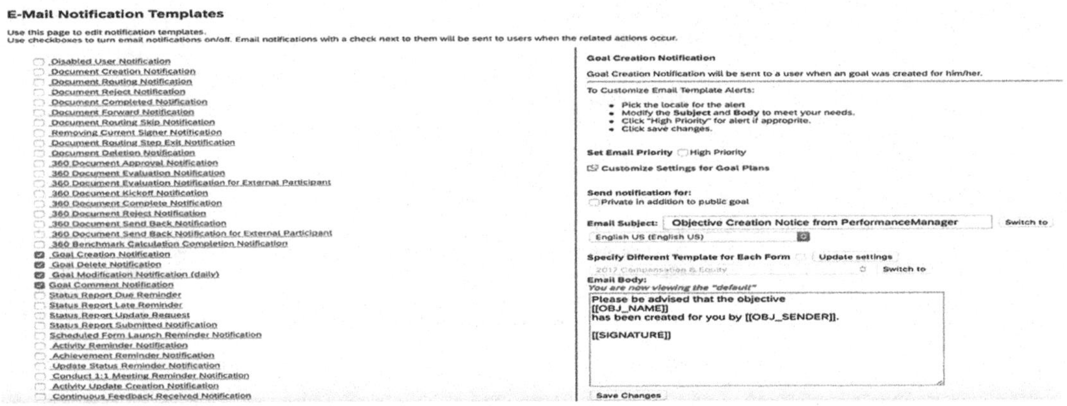

***Figure 1-14.*** *"E-Mail Notification Templates" Screen*

It is possible to regulate which goal plans send notifications. That means that you can have any of the goal plan notifications turned on but only sent for specific goal plans. You may wish to have a notification sent when a goal is added to a user's goal plan but not sent when a development goal is added to their development plan. When a notification is enabled, click its name, and you will see the notification details on the right side of the screen. You will see a link "Customize Settings for Goal Plans" as seen in Figure 1-15.

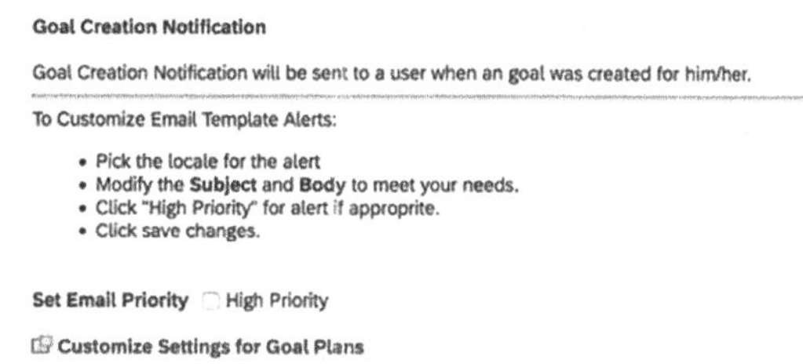

Goal Creation Notification
Goal Creation Notification will be sent to a user when an goal was created for him/her.
To Customize Email Template Alerts:
• Pick the locale for the alert
• Modify the Subject and Body to meet your needs.
• Click "High Priority" for alert if approprite.
• Click save changes.
Set Email Priority High Priority
Customize Settings for Goal Plans


***Figure 1-15.*** *Customize Settings for Goal Plans*

Click the link to see all of the active goal and development plans available for the notification. Uncheck plans to disable their notification. Any plan that is still checked will generate an email. An example is shown in Figure 1-16.

**Customize Settings for Goal Plans**

| Goal Plan | Enabled |
| --- | --- |
| 2019 Goal Plan Extended | ☑ |
| 2019 Goal Plan | ☑ |
| 2020 Goal Plan | ☑ |
| Career Development Plan | ☑ |

***Figure 1-16.*** *Selection of Goal Plans for Email Notification*

## Enable Mobile Career Development Plan

The development plan may be accessed on the mobile app (iOS and Android). Similar to mobile goal plans, mobile development goal plans may be viewed and edited. It is possible to add development goals.

---

**Note** Due to the simplistic nature of the mobile app, we will not cover using the app. You may go to the Apple App Store or Android Market and search for "SuccessFactors" to download the app. Once it is downloaded, you can click "Demo" in the upper right-hand corner to take a tour of the app. If you want to associate your app with a specific user on your instance to use real data, you will need to walk through the on-screen registration process. To see the list of features supported and not supported, please reference SAP note #2475032.

---

To enable mobile features, follow these steps:

1. Type and select "Enable Mobile Features" in the search bar. The Mobile Settings screen will appear.

2. Click "Modules" on the left. Then click the checkbox next to "Career Development Planning" as shown in Figure 1-17. The changes will take effect immediately.

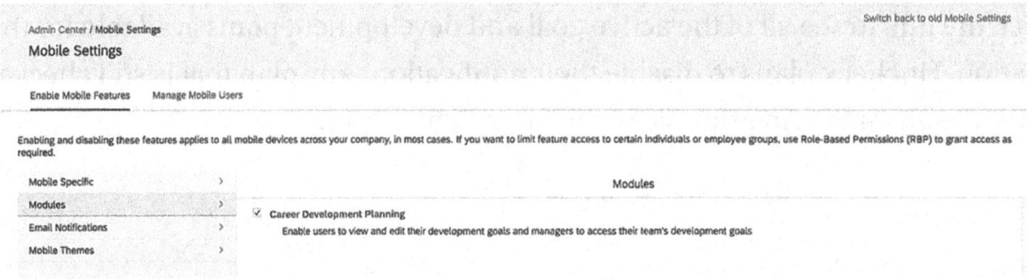

***Figure 1-17.*** *Activating Career Development Planning in Mobile Settings*

We have now created a development plan and seen how to enable email notifications and how to turn on mobile features for development goals.

## Assigning Development Plan Permissions to End Users

Before we dive into configuring our development plan further by editing the plan template XML, we can assign permissions to end users (e.g., just a test user) in our test instance so that we can see the results of our XML configurations and troubleshoot as needed.

Setting up the role-based permissions for end users follows the same steps as those followed for the admin role. The end user permissions are similar to goal plan permissions. You may refer to Volume 1, Chapter 4 to review the discussion on end user roles and targeted roles.

There are two permission types that control access to a career development plan:

1. Access to the Development Plan tab within the Development module

2. Access to the development plan templates for a specific target population

We will now modify the role-based permissions for the employee, manager, and HR manager roles. We will set permissions for Career Development to identify which users' plans each role may access. The roles will need Career Development Plan (CDP) Access Permission and Goal Plan Permissions for the specific development plan. This gives each role access to the Career Development tab and permission to access the specific development plan. The difference between the permission roles is the granted and targeted populations defined on these roles which will determine whose plan they may see. We will call out additional permissions for the manager and HR manager roles.

## Access to the Development Tab

Within Manage Permission Roles, open the role that you wish to edit. Under the User Permissions section of the settings, click "Career Development Planning" on the left-hand side of the popup and click the checkbox next to "Career Development Plan (CDP) Access Permission." This gives the role access to the Development tab. The permission is shown in Figure 1-18.

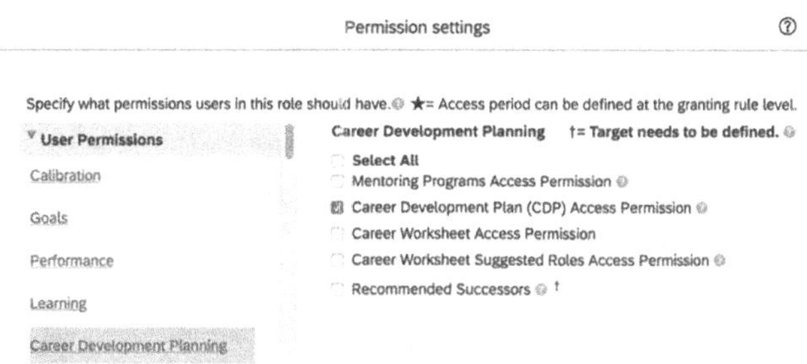


***Figure 1-18.*** *Access to the Development Tab*

## Access to Development Plans

Next, grant permissions so that a role can access the specific development plan. Also found under "User Permissions," on the left, click "Goals". Here, you will need to grant access to the Career Development Plan found under Goal Plan Permissions as seen in Figure 1-19.

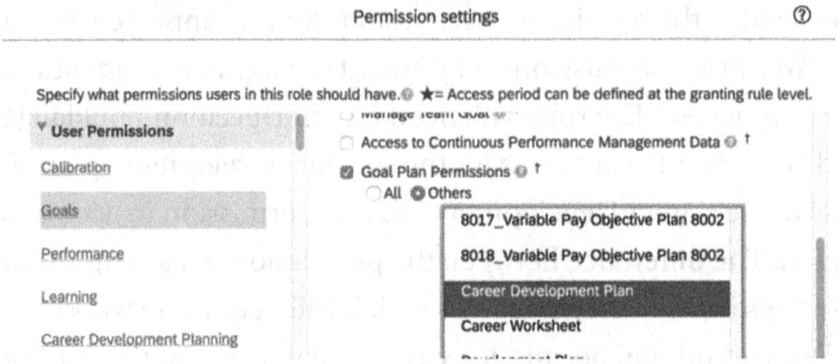

*Figure 1-19. Permission for Career Development Plan Access*

Users can add learning activities to a development goal if they have learning access permission. This requires an additional goal plan permission to allow the user to have access to see and add learning activities to a development goal. The role will require access to the Learning Activity List/Detail View template as seen in Figure 1-20.

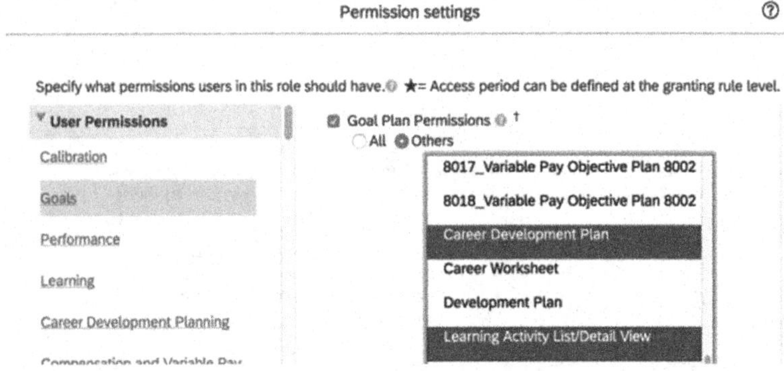


*Figure 1-20. Learning Activity List/Detail View Permission*

If the role already has CPM permissions and you wish to display CPM achievements on the development plan, add "Access to Continuous Performance Management Data" also found within Goals. Permissions for the development plan, Learning Activity List/Detail View template, and CPM data access are displayed in Figure 1-21.

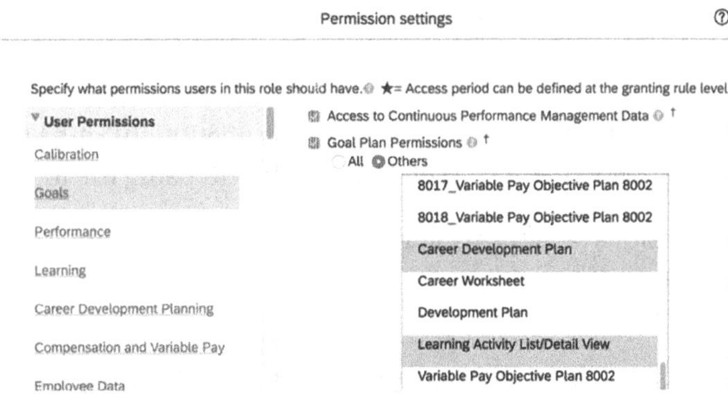


***Figure 1-21.*** *Development Plan and CPM Access*

# Role-Based Permissions for Learning

If users will be able to add learning activities to their development plan, they will need access to the learning activities content defined in the Learning Activity List/Detail View template XML. We have not discussed this template yet, but the role-based permissions will need to be updated for the same roles that have Career Development permissions (employee, manager, and HR manager roles). Users can add or view learning activities tied to a development goal only if they have learning access permission defined in the Learning Activity List/Detail View template XML.

# Manager and HR Manager Reporting Role-Based Permissions

In order to allow managers and HR managers to run reports on development plans and associated learning activity data, the permission roles will need the following additions:

- User Permissions ➤ Reports Permission ➤ Create Report ➤ Development Goal
- User Permissions ➤ Reports Permission ➤ Run Report ➤ Development Goal

If using learning activities and wish to report on them, add the following:

- User Permissions ➤ Reports Permission ➤ Create Report ➤ Learning Activities

- User Permissions ➤ Reports Permission ➤ Run Report Learning Activities

If the standard development plan or custom tiles/dashboards are going to be used, these permissions are needed as well. They may be found using the following path:

- User Permissions ➤ Reports Permission ➤ Analytics Tiles and Dashboards

## Role-Based Permissions to View Others' Plans

The role-based permissions required to allow access to anyone's plan would need to be added to a permission role used for employee search which allows Organization Chart Navigation Permission and Company Info Access and User Search as seen in Figure 1-22. We will discuss the corresponding permissions to define in the development plan template XML in the next section of this chapter.

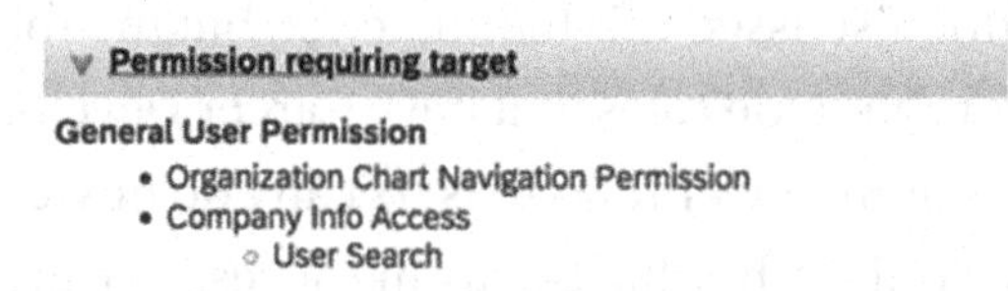


***Figure 1-22.*** *Permission to Allow User Search*

This is granted to "Everyone" for a target population of "Everyone" as seen in Figure 1-23.

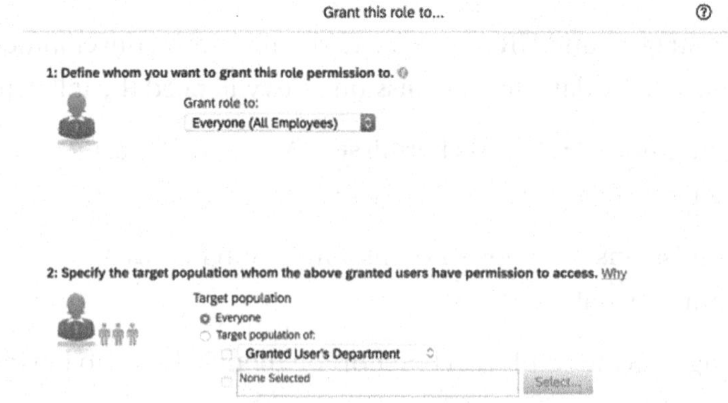


***Figure 1-23.*** *Target Population for Name Search*

If you add the access to the Development tab (Career Development Plan (CDP) Access Permission) and to the development plan (Goal Plan Permissions ➤ Career Development Plan), this will allow any user to see the development goal plan and its content for anyone.

These are the permissions required for the employee, manager, and HR manager roles. The difference lies in the target population. The employee is usually granted access to "self," which means they can only see and edit their own development goal plan. Managers typically have access to their direct reports, and you may also choose how far down the hierarchy you would like the manager to have access. The HR manager role would have access to their HR reports.

To reiterate, development goal plan permissions must specify a target population. This means that you identify the plan the role has access to (goal plan permissions) and then identify whose plans they may see (target population).

Table 1-4 identifies which users have the permission granted to see the target population.

***Table 1-4.*** *Roles and Target Populations*

| Role | Permission Group or Users to Grant the Permission to | Target Population |
|---|---|---|
| Employee | Employees | Granted user (self). |
| Manager | Managers | Granted user's direct reports; specify levels and exclude self. |
| HR manager | HR manager | Granted user's HR reports; specify levels and exclude self. |

# Basic Development Plan Features Requiring XML Configuration

We now have a basic development plan built and have granted access to the employee, manager, and HR manager permission roles. Now we can look at the development plan template XML configuration.

As we just saw, role-based permissions define which type of plan a user has access to and which users' plans they can view. As we will see now, access to the content and actions of the development plan is restricted by the permissions defined in the development plan template XML.

The template permissions identify which roles can perform certain tasks such as creating development goals, deleting development goals, and editing development goals. Field permissions identify what development goal plan fields a role may view or edit. Access to the content and actions of the development plan is restricted by the permissions defined in the development plan template XML.

## Downloading, Editing, and Uploading the XML

An XML is automatically created when you create the development plan template using the online tool shown in the prior sections of this chapter. There are modifications that cannot be made in the online tool, so we will need to edit the XML. You can export the career development plan template XML to make updates to the fields that cannot be made via Managing Templates in the UI, specifically around attributes and permissions. You may also add standard fields that are not available from the basic template in the instance. This would also require "Read" and "Write" permissions granted to the fields and adding the fields to the plan layout so they will display on the plan.

Before we can edit, we need to download the development plan template XML from Provisioning. Plan templates are found under Managing Plan Template as shown in Figure 1-24. Here, you will find links to the various templates. We will be working with the Development Plan template.

**Managing Plan Template**

Import/Update/Export Objective Plan Template
Import/Update/Export Variable Pay Objective Plan Template
Import/Update/Export Development Plan Templates
Import/Update/Export Learning Activities Templates
Import/Update/Export Career Worksheet Templates

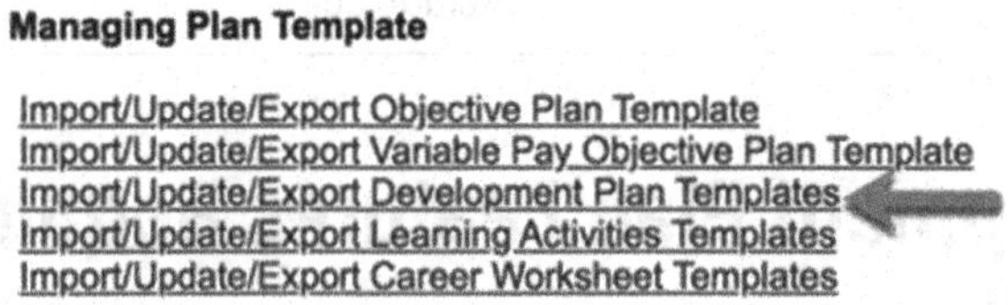

***Figure 1-24.*** *Plan Templates in Provisioning*

Click the link "Import/Update/Export Development Plan Templates." In Figure 1-25, you will now see the screen where you download and upload the development plan template XML.

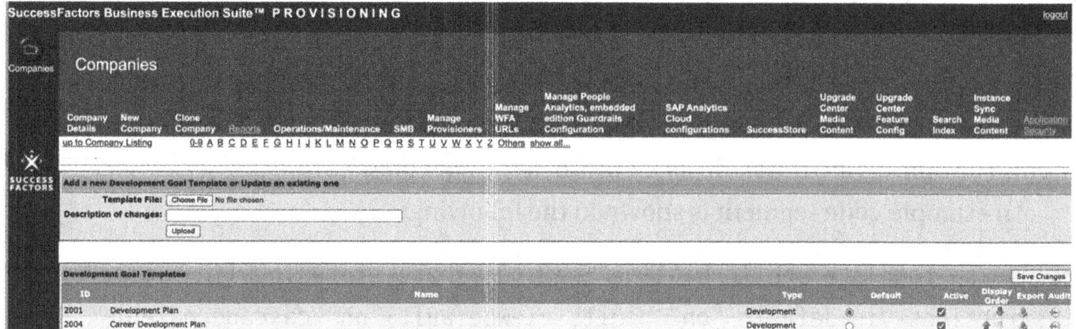

*Figure 1-25.* *Development Plan Template Screen*

Here, you will see the Career Development plan templates for your instance. Find the development plan template that you created in the instance. Click the icon beneath the Export column as shown in the following figure. Your web browser will download the file to your local machine. We will make any necessary edits and then upload the modified XML.

Now let's look at the XML to better understand what it contains and how it works. The development goal plan is similar to the goal plan except

- A Development Plan is ongoing and isn't limited to a one-year span.
- Development goal template IDs must be in the range 2001–2999.
- The obj-plan-type should be "Development."
- Development goals may be linked to competencies.
- Learning activities may be linked to development goals, using learning catalog or custom activities.
- You cannot include a goal library in the development plan.
- You cannot cascade and align development goals.

## Development Plan Template XML

The development plan template uses the majority of the template configuration options as the goal plan template. In this section, we touch briefly on the sections that are identical to those in the goal plan XML. Please refer to Volume 1, Chapter 4 to review the standard fields and options along with custom field types and configuration options. The configuration options that are particular to development plans will be explained in detail.

## Template Attribute Updates

The *<obj-plan-template>* tag is the highest-level tag in the XML structure. It defines a series of options that can be turned on or off or adjusted to turn on/off features or adjust them. The options are the same as for those in the goal plan XML.

An example code segment is shown in the following:

```
<obj-plan-template spellchk="true" new-obj-share-status-public="false"
instructions-viewdefault="on" alerts-viewdefault="on" cascade-parent-
viewdefault="on" cascade-child-viewdefault="on" pager-max-objs-per-
page="10" pager-max-page-links="9" pager-max-children-per-parent="3"
display-alignment-format="goals" more-details-child-format="goal-plan"
share-confirm="true" unshare-confirm="true" allow-group-goal="false"
goal-tree-link="true" expand-collapse-categories="false" use-text-for-
privacy="true" cws-people-role="true" overwrite-target-population="false"
swap-goal-link="false" learning-activity-deep-link="false" show-total-
goalscore="false" show-goal-id="false">
```

Refer to Table 4-4 in Volume 1, Chapter 4 that details the *<obj-plan-template>* attributes.

There are two attributes worth noting that pertain to privacy:

1. new-obj-share-status-public: When true, all goals default to public.
2. use-text-for-privacy: When true, text (private, public) displays in the Visibility column on the plan icon; when false, the icon (sunglasses) is used to indicate if the goal is private. The Visibility column found on both the goal plan and the development plan may contain an icon or text.

Table 1-5 contains a portion of the development plan template XML with certain features highlighted with a brief explanation. We will go into more depth shortly.

*Table 1-5. Description of Object Elements*

| Element | Description | Code |
|---|---|---|
| obj-plan-id | Unique numeric identifier of the development goal plan. Range must be within 2001–2999. | <obj-plan-id>2001 </obj-plan-id> |
| obj-plan-type | Defines the plan type: goal plan, development plan, learning activity, or career worksheet. | <obj-plan-type>Development </obj-plan-type> |
| obj-plan-name | Title of the goal plan as you set it using the online tool that appears for end users. The first line defines the default. You can set the name for each active locale in your instance below that. | <obj-plan-name>Career Development Plan </obj-plan-name> <obj-plan-name lang="en_US"> Career Development Plan </obj-plan-name |
| obj-plan-desc | The description is shown only to those configuring the development plan in the XML or the online tool. The last modified is updated automatically when you save in the online tool or when you upload the XML in Provisioning. | <obj-plan-desc><![CDATA [ Career Development Plan]]> </obj-plan-desc> |
| obj-plan-lastmodified | The last modified is shown only to those configuring the development plan in the XML or the online tool. The last modified is updated automatically when you save in the online tool or when you upload the XML in Provisioning. | <obj-plan-lastmodified> 5/29/20 6:54 PM </obj-plan-lastmodified> |
| obj-plan-start | The start date defines the period for which the development goals are achieved. Also acts as the default start date when the user creates a development goal. | <obj-plan-start> 01/01/2020</obj-plan-start> |

(*continued*)

***Table 1-5.*** *(continued)*

| Element | Description | Code |
|---|---|---|
| obj-plan-due | The end date defines the period for which the development goals are achieved. Also acts as the default end date when the user creates a development goal. A development plan is ongoing and isn't limited to a one-year span. | <obj-plan-due>12/31/2023 </obj-plan-due> |

A sample code segment for these elements is shown in the following:

```
<obj-plan-id>2001</obj-plan-id>
<obj-plan-type>Development</obj-plan-type>
<obj-plan-name>Career Development Plan</obj-plan-name>
<obj-plan-desc><![CDATA[Development Goals]]></obj-plan-desc>
<obj-plan-lastmodified>5/29/20 6:54 PM</obj-plan-lastmodified>
<obj-plan-start>01/01/2020</obj-plan-start>
<obj-plan-due>12/31/2023</obj-plan-due>
```

**Switches**

The "switches" element is used to turn features on or off for the development goal plan. The default value is "off" which means you will only need to insert switches into the template if you don't wish to use the defaults. The switches specific to the development plan template are shown in Table 1-6.

***Table 1-6.*** *Development Plan Switches*

| Switch | Description |
|---|---|
| show-competency-browser | To add a competency on a development goal. |
| continuouspm-integration | To show CPM achievement related to a development goal on the plan. |
| development-scorecard-show-all-goals | To include development goals in the scorecard. |

Switches are added in the XML following *"<obj-plan-due>" or "<obj-plan-numbering>"* if used.

A switches example code segment is shown in the following:

```
<switches>
        <switch for="show-competency-browser" value="on" />
        <switch for="continuouspm-integration" value="on" />
        <switch for="development-scorecard-show-all-goals" value="on" />
</switches>
```

Let's look at each switch more closely to see what it controls.

### <switch for="show-competency-browser" value="on" />

This switch is only applicable if your development plan will contain competencies. This switch enables a user to add a competency to a development goal as shown in Figure 1-26. While a competency may be added to a development goal from the designated competency library, the switch enables a link "Add Competencies" in the competency browser containing all competencies.

***Figure 1-26.** Switch That Enables Adding an Additional Competency to a Development Goal*

### *<switch for="continuouspm-integration" value="on" />*

This switch allows the Continuous Performance Management (CPM) column to appear on the development goal plan which indicates the number of achievements tied to a development goal. This is the same functionality available on a goal plan. Instead of adding this option within the XML, you may enable the checkbox "Display Continuous PM Achievements on Development goal plan" within the development plan template in the instance.

Either method will enable the achievements on the development plan. Setting the switch in the XML will set the checkmark in the template. Similarly, setting the checkbox in the template will create the switch in the XML. In either case, be sure you your instance is using CPM data before you set this switch.

### <switch for="development-scorecard-show-all-goals" value="on" />

This switch is used to include the Development Plan Portlet in People Profile. Setting this switch will display all of the user's development goals in the Development Plan Portlet in People Profile. Turning this switch on removes the employee's ability to hide any of the goals from their development plan in the portlet. It also removes the ability to manually add development goals to the portlet directly from their development plan.

This switch is only viable if the Development Plan Portlet is configured in the Succession Data Model, the portlet is configured in People Profile, and role-based permissions are set to view the portlet. We will cover this in more depth later in the chapter.

## Linking Competencies to Development Goals: Competency Filters

To use competencies within a development goal plan, there are some additions to make to the XML:

- Create a competency field on the plan (if this field was not added when creating the template in the instance).
- Identify which competencies may be used.
- Optionally allow the competency browser to add additional competencies from any available competency library.

To enable a user to link competencies to a development goal, a competency field must be added to the development plan XML. When we were creating our development goal plan template, we saw that the competency field could be added in the template. However, we will still need to add permissions in the XML. When using this field, a competency library also needs to be identified in the XML. This defines which competency library a user may select competencies from to add to a development goal.

Use the *<competency-filters>* tag to define the sources (type) of competencies that the development plan may reference. Valid types include roles, forms, categories, and libraries. This is used in conjunction with "exclude" and "include" values. An "exclude" type identifies the competency type to exclude. An "include" type identifies the type (forms, roles, category, library) with a match. This identifies which specific role, form, category, or library may be used.

In the example code segment shown in the following, only competencies from a specific category of a specific library may be added to a development goal. These are the only competencies that a user will have the option of adding to their development goal:

```
default-category id="Goals">
    <category-name>Development Goals</category-name>
    <category-name lang="en_US">Development Goals</category-name>
  </default-category>
  <competency-filters>
    <exclude type="forms"/>
    <exclude type="roles"/>
    <include type="category" match="SuccessFactors Premium Library"
    library="SuccessFactors 2.1 Competency Library"/>
  </competency-filters>
```

The *<competency-filters>* tag follows *<default-category>* and is before *<field-definition>*.

To allow users to add a learning activity to a development goal, a reference is needed to the learning activities template. The template ID should be "4201," and the code segment is shown in the following:

```
<learning-activities template-id="4201"/>
```

This should follow text replacements and appear before the default category ID as seen in the code segment sample that follows:

```
<text-replacement for="category">
    <text lang="en_US"><![CDATA[Category]]></text>
      </text-replacement>
  <learning-activities template-id="4201"/>
  <default-category id="Goals">
```

## Development Plan Fields

The field-definition element defines the fields in the development plan template. The same standard fields found in the goal plan are available in a development goal plan with the exception of the competency field. Shown in Table 1-7 are the fields that may be used in a development plan.

***Table 1-7.*** *Standard Development Goal Plan Fields*

| Field | Description |
|---|---|
| Name | Development goal name. |
| Description | What the development goal is. |
| Metric | How the development goal is being measured. |
| Start | Begin date of the goal. Default value of <obj-date-start>. |
| Due | Completion date of the goal. Default value of <obj-date-due>. |
| State | Status of the goal. |
| Done | Percentage complete. |
| Weight | Usually a percentage; if the development plan is used in the PM form, the weight auto-populates. |
| Category | May identify the type of development goal. |
| Tasks | Table with actions associated with the development goal: multiple actions for a goal. |
| Milestones | Table of milestones toward achieving the development goal: multiple milestones for a goal. |
| Competency | Link the development goal to a competency; may tie multiple competencies to a goal. |

Note that when we downloaded the template from SuccessStore, several of these fields were not on the plan. In order to use any of these (Metric, Tasks, Milestones, Weight, Done), they would need to be added to the XML.

The State field is often used as the development goal Status field. It is defined as a text value that displays in color, usually as a dropdown listing with a background and font color associated with each value. The final value in the list denotes completion of the development goal. When a goal is completed, no more learning activities may be added to the goal.

A code segment displays an example of how to create the state definition:

```
<field-definition id="state" type="enum" required="false" detail="false"
viewdefault="on" showlabel="false" field-show-coaching-advisor="false"
cascade-update="push-down">
    <field-label>Status</field-label>
    <field-label lang="en_US">Status</field-label>
    <field-description>Status</field-description>
    <field-description lang="en_US">Status</field-description>
    <enum-value value="Not Started" style="background:white;color:black">
      <enum-label>Not Started</enum-label>
      <enum-label lang="en_US">Not Started</enum-label>
    </enum-value>
    <enum-value value="On Track" style="background:yellow;color:black">
      <enum-label>On Track</enum-label>
      <enum-label lang="en_US">On Track</enum-label>
    </enum-value>
    <enum-value value="At Risk" style="background:blue;color:white">
      <enum-label>At Risk</enum-label>
      <enum-label lang="en_US">At Risk</enum-label>
    </enum-value>
    <enum-value value="Behind" style="background:red;color:black">
      <enum-label>Behind</enum-label>
      <enum-label lang="en_US">Behind</enum-label>
    </enum-value>
```

```
    <enum-value value="Completed" style="background:green;color:white">
      <enum-label>Completed</enum-label>
      <enum-label lang="en_US">Completed</enum-label>
    </enum-value>
  </field-definition>
```

When adding or editing a goal, the Status field will appear as a dropdown listing as shown in Figure 1-27.

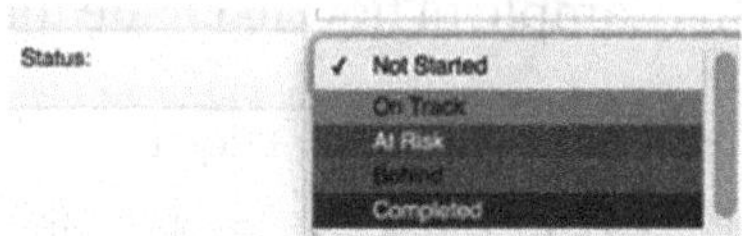


***Figure 1-27.** Status Field Options*

## Competencies

As mentioned earlier in this chapter, it is possible to link development goals to one or more competencies that the employee is trying to develop. To accomplish this, a field definition with a field type of "competencies" needs to be added to the development plan template in the instance or here in the XML. This is in addition to identifying the competency library to reference when adding competencies to development goals within the development plan.

There may only be one competency field added to the plan, but it is possible to tie a development goal to multiple competencies.

Sample code is shown in the following:

```
<field-definition id="competency" type="competencies" required="false"
detail="false" viewdefault="on" showlabel="false" field-show-coaching-
advisor="true" cascade-update="push-down">
    <field-label>Competencies</field-label>
    <field-label lang="en_US">Competencies</field-label>
    <field-description>Competencies</field-description>
    <field-description lang="en_US">Competencies</field-description>
  </field-definition>
```

The default when adding competencies to a development goal is a list with checkboxes as shown in Figure 1-28. It is the option to select multiple competencies.

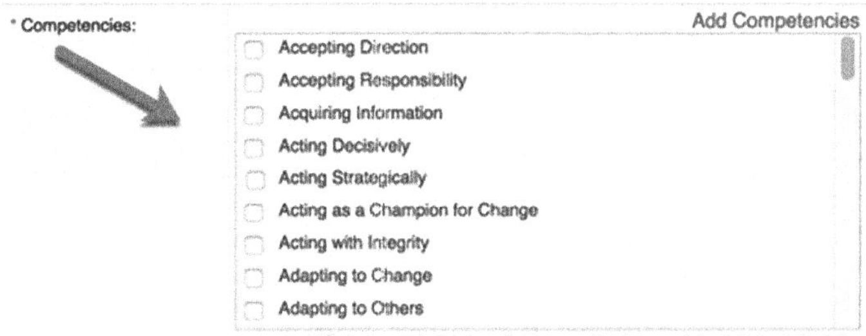

***Figure 1-28.** Add Competencies to a Development Goal*

It is possible to allow only one competency to be added to a development goal. Add the *<field-format>* tag within the field-definition block:

```
<field-format>use-competencies-single</field-format>
```

The competency field code segment to incorporate this tag is shown in the following:

```
<field-definition id="competency" type="competencies" required="true"
detail="false" viewdefault="on" showlabel="false" field-show-coaching-
advisor="true" cascade-update="push-down">
    <field-label>Competencies</field-label>
    <field-description>Competencies</field-description>
    <field-format>use-competencies-single</field-format>
  </field-definition>
```

This will make the competency field a dropdown list to select just one value as shown in Figure 1-29.

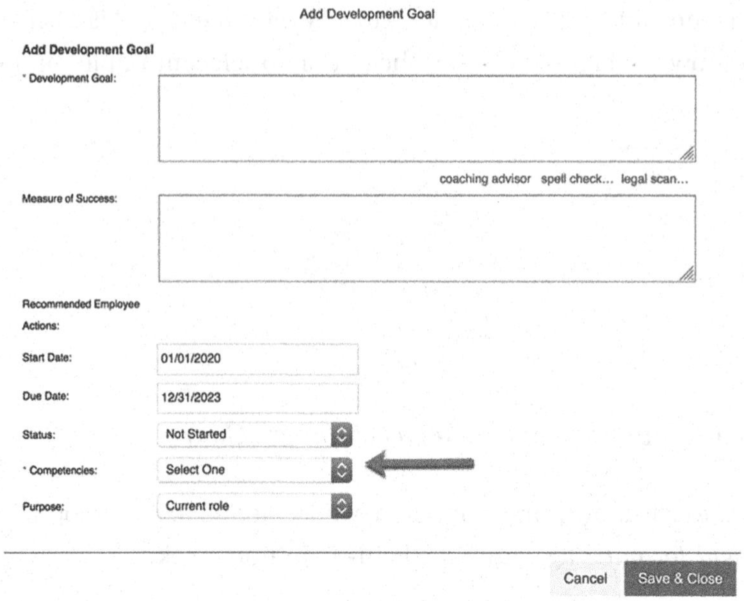

*Figure 1-29.* *Add a Single Competency to a Development Goal*

It is possible to use behaviors in this field instead of competencies. However, your competencies must include behaviors in order for this to work. If you are using the SuccessFactors 2.1 Competency Library, behaviors are included. It is also possible to add behaviors to the competencies via Manage Job Profile Content. To use behaviors, set the field-format tag as shown in the following:

```
<field-format>use-behaviors</field-format>
```

When using this tag, only the competencies that have behaviors are then shown to users. They can select behaviors under the competency when creating a development goal. The competency field will then list the selected behaviors. Please note that the single select option is not available for use with behaviors.

The field definition containing these tags is shown in the following code segment:

```
<field-definition id="competency" type="competencies" required="false"
detail="false" viewdefault="on" showlabel="false" field-show-coaching-
advisor="true" cascade-update="push-down">
    <field-label>Competencies</field-label>
    <field-label lang="en_US”>Competencies</field-label>
    <field-description>Competencies</field-description>
```

```
    <field-format>use-competencies-single</field-format>
    <field-description lang="en_US">Competencies</field-description>
  </field-definition>
```

If Writing Assistant is enabled in Provisioning and the competency library has teasers associated with the competencies, you may use Coaching Advisor for any textarea field.

The Coaching Advisor content is based on competency teasers as is defined by "field-show-coaching-advisor"="true".

A code segment sample is shown in the following:

```
<field-definition id="metric" type="textarea" required="false"
detail="false" viewdefault="on" showlabel="false" field-show-coaching-
advisor="true" cascade-update="push-down">
    <field-label>Measure of Success</field-label>
    <field-label lang="en_US">Measure of Success</field-label>
    <field-description>Measure of Success</field-description>
    <field-description lang="en_US">Measure of Success</field-description>
  </field-definition>
```

Shown in the following is an example of a custom field added through "Manage Templates" in the online editor:

```
<field-definition id="custom01" type="textarea" required="false"
detail="false" viewdefault="on" showlabel="false" field-show-coaching-
advisor="true" cascade-update="push-down">
    <field-label>Recommended Employee Actions</field-label>
    <field-label lang="es_US">Recommended Employee Actions</field-label>
    <field-description>Recommended Employee Actions</field-description>
    <field-description lang="es_US">Recommended Employee Actions
    </field-description>
  </field-definition>
```

And just to note, like the goal plan, it is not possible to add custom fields to a table field.

We have now looked at the fields that may be used on a development goal plan. Next, we will discuss the content permissions.

## Content Permissions

The content permissions control the visibility of the fields of a development goal plan and the actions that a user is allowed to take. Action permissions control the actions that the users can take on the development plan. "View" and "Write" permissions control the fields which a given role can view and write for when creating or editing the development goal.

Public and private goals are both supported on the development plan, so based on your organization's needs, you may configure role permissions for these types of goals differently.

## Action Permissions

As seen in Table 1-8, actions that the users can take on the development plan are described.

***Table 1-8.*** *Actions with the Development Template XML*

| Action | Description |
|---|---|
| Private-access | Access to private goals. |
| Create | Ability to create a development goal. |
| Delete | Ability to delete a development goal. |
| Move | Ability to move a development goal up and down in the development plan. |
| Share | Ability to make a private goal public. |

Typical action permissions are as follows:

- The employee and manager can create, delete, and move development goals.
- Make goals private.
- The manager's manager and HR manager hierarchy may go into the employee's development goal plan to view it.

Since cascade and alignment of development goals are not supported, you may remove all cascade and unalign actions from the template which include cascade-push, cascade-pull, cascade-align, unalign-parent, and unalign-child.

,Next you will need to identify which roles may perform the actions and update the template accordingly.

The role-based permissions in the instance define which roles can access the development plan, but without the permissions in the development plan XML, plan data will not be visible.

When creating or editing a goal, the user could set the goal as private. The "private-access" permission identifies which roles may see the private goals on a goal plan. Identify the roles that may see private goals using the "private-access" action as shown in the following code segment sample:

```
<permission for="private-access">
    <description><![CDATA[Employees, and their HR reps and managers up the
    reporting chain may view unshared/private goals.]]></description>
    <role-name><![CDATA[E]]></role-name>
    <role-name><![CDATA[EM+]]></role-name>
    <role-name><![CDATA[EH]]></role-name>
  </permission>
```

This action permission will enable a user to identify goals as private which limits which permitted roles will see these goals on the plan. In this example, only the employee, their manager hierarchy, and HR manager will be able to see private goals on the employee's plan.

Development plans often are considered private between an employee and their manager, so all goals would be private. Because of this, you may decide to eliminate the Visibility column on the plan entirely.

There are four steps required to eliminate this column:

1. Eliminate the "Share" permissions from the template:

```
<permission for="share">
    <description><![CDATA[Only the employee may share and
    unshare goals in his/her own plan.]]></description>
    <role-name><![CDATA[E]]></role-name>
  </permission>
```

2. Remove the private-access permission:

```
<permission for="private-access">
    <description><![CDATA[Employees, and their HR reps and
    managers up the reporting chain may view unshared/
    private goals.]]></description>
    <role-name><![CDATA[E]]></role-name>
    <role-name><![CDATA[EM+]]></role-name>
    <role-name><![CDATA[EH]]></role-name>
  </permission>
```

3. Change attribute *new-obj-share-status-public* to "*false*." Or remove the attribute from the template.

4. Change *use-text-for-privacy* attribute to "false."

Figure 1-30 shows the plan without the Visibility column.

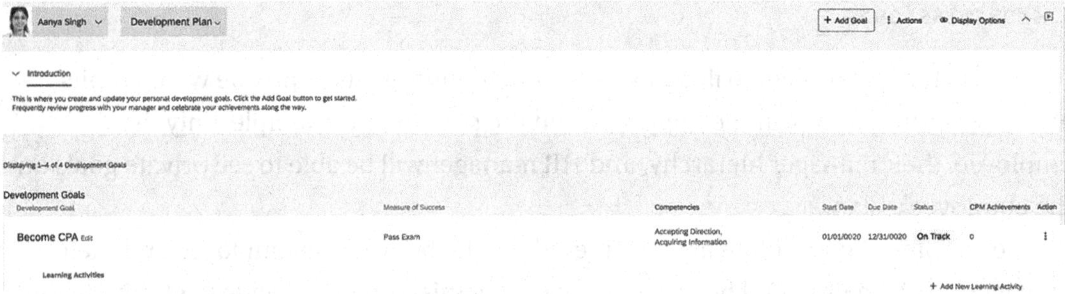


***Figure 1-30.*** *Plan Without the Visibility Column*

Now that we have identified which roles may perform which actions, next, we will look at the development goal field permissions.

## View/Write Field Permissions

The "View/Write" permissions control the fields that a role can view and write when creating or editing a development goal.

Permissions need to be assigned to each goal plan field. The permissions are

- **None:** Role has no access to the field.
- **Read:** Role can read the field.
- **Write:** Role can read and write the field.

Within the development plan template XML, use field permission types of "Read" and "Write" to identify which roles have access to which development plan content. The "Read" and "Write" field permissions define if a role may view or write when creating or updating a goal. Field permissions are scanned in XML source order. Identify the fields used in the development plan and determine which roles may read or write the fields.

Shown in the following is a code segment sample of an employee and their manager being able to write certain fields in a development goal plan:

```
<field-permission type="write">
     <description><![CDATA[Employees, and their managers may read the
     fields. ]]></description>
     <role-name><![CDATA[E]]></role-name>
     <role-name><![CDATA[EM]]></role-name>
      <field refid="desc"/>
     <field refid="start"/>
     <field refid="due"/>
     <field refid="state"/>
     <field refid="comments"/>
</field-permission>
```

If your development goal plan allows users to add learning activities, which we will discuss later in this chapter, conditional permissions may also be added to the XML. Identified by the tag "*<condition>*," a condition must be met in order to allow a role to see a field on the plan.

In the code segment seen in the following, a manager may only read a development goal's purpose when the status of the goal is completed:

```
<field-permission type="read">
   <description><![CDATA[Only Managers may read purpose when Completed]]>
   </description>
   <condition><![CDATA[status eq Completed]]></condition>
```

```
    <role-name><![CDATA[EM]]></role-name>
    <field refid="purpose"/>
</field-permission>
```

Goal plans are often accessible to view by others, but it is highly unlikely that a user's development plan would be available for viewing by anyone within the organization.

Based on the transparency of the organization, however, you may decide to allow a user to view anyone's development plan. The development plan template XML would have to grant access to all roles ("*") to read the fields in the development goal plan as shown in following sample code segment:

```
<field-permission type="read">
    <description><![CDATA[Everyone may read name and metric.]]>
    </description>
    <role-name><![CDATA[*]]></role-name>
    <field refid="name"/>
    <field refid="metric"/>
    <field refid="start"/>
    <field refid="due"/>
    <field refid="state"/>
    <field refid="competency"/>
    <field refid="purpose"/>
    <field refid="custom01"/>
  </field-permission>
```

This permission requires some updates to role-based permissions for the user search role that we discussed earlier in this chapter.

Like the goal plan, the development plan layout needs to be defined in the *<plan-layout>* section of the template. This will determine the order of the development goal fields on the development plan.

If you are going to have development goals appear on a performance form, use the *<form-layout>* section in the XML to identify which development goal fields will appear in the development plan section of a performance form. Refer to Volume 1, Chapter 4 for more information on how to configure these sections.

After the development plan template XML has been modified, save and import in Provisioning.

# Learning Activities XML

Learning activities are stored within the context of development goals. The template can support catalog learning from LMS and manual learning.

To use with the development plan, the learning activities template XML will need revisions. Within Provisioning, find "Managing Plan Template" as shown in Figure 1-31.

**Managing Plan Template**

Import/Update/Export Objective Plan Template
Import/Update/Export Variable Pay Objective Plan Template
Import/Update/Export Development Plan Templates
Import/Update/Export Learning Activities Templates
Import/Update/Export Career Worksheet Templates

***Figure 1-31.*** *Link to Learning Activities Templates*

Click the link to see the Learning Activity List/Detail View template as seen in Figure 1-32.

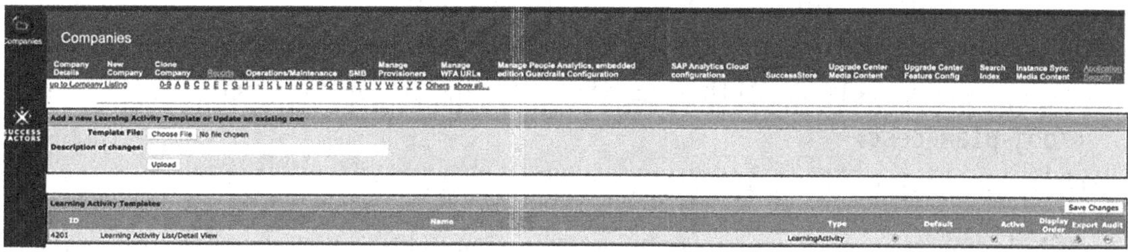


***Figure 1-32.*** *Learning Activities Templates Screen*

Export the template in order to make modifications. Open the XML and we can begin.

You may create a deep link to a learning activity from the LMS catalog with the parameter shown in the following:

```
learning-activity-deep-link=true
```

The following code segment sample shows the placement of this parameter:

```
<?xml version="1.0" encoding="UTF-8"?><!DOCTYPE obj-plan-template PUBLIC
"-//SuccessFactors, Inc.//DTD Objective Template 4.0//EN" "objective-
template_4_0.dtd">
```

```
<obj-plan-template spellchk="true" new-obj-share-status-public="true"
instructions-viewdefault="on" alerts-viewdefault="on" cascade-parent-
viewdefault="on" cascade-child-viewdefault="on" pager-max-objs-per-
page="8" pager-max-page-links="9" pager-max-children-per-parent="0"
display-alignment-format="names" more-details-child-format="goal-plan"
share-confirm="true" unshare-confirm="true" allow-group-goal="false"
goal-tree-link="true" expand-collapse-categories="false" use-text-for-
privacy="false" cws-people-role="true" overwrite-target-population="true"
swap-goal-link="false" learning-activity-deep-link="true" show-total-
goalscore="false" show-goal-id="false">
```

The template ID should be "4201" with the obj-plan-type "LearningActivity." You may only have one learning activities template active at a time. A sample code segment is shown in the following:

```
<obj-plan-id>4201</obj-plan-id>
<obj-plan-type>LearningActivity</obj-plan-type>
<obj-plan-name>Learning Activity List/Detail View</obj-plan-name>
 <obj-plan-desc><![CDATA[This is the Learning Activity template.]]>
 </obj-plan-desc>
<obj-plan-lastmodified>5/23/19 5:39 PM</obj-plan-lastmodified>
```

In order for development goals to have learning activities, the learning template ID needs to be referenced in the development plan template XML as discussed earlier in this chapter.

A switch may be added to the learning activities template XML to control the UI on the popup of manually added transcript learning:

```
<switch for="transcript-disable-fancy-pod" value="on"/>
```

Fancy Pod "on" enables a fancy layout for Name, Status, and Description fields as shown in Figure 1-33.

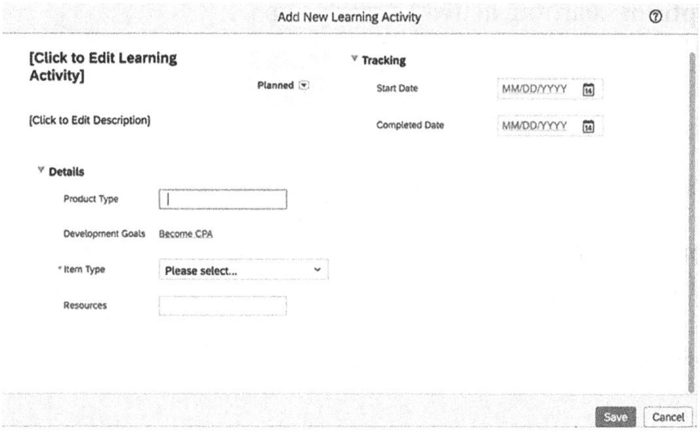

*Figure 1-33.* *View of Adding a Learning Activity Using Fancy Pod*

Including this switch disables the "fancy" pod layout in order. Instead, the standard layout for the Name, Status, and Description fields would display. Figure 1-34 shows the appearance of the "Adding New Learning Activity" popup when Fancy Pod is disabled.

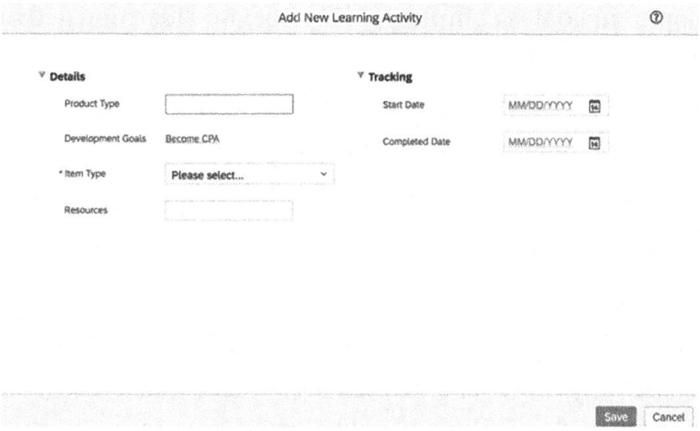

*Figure 1-34.* *Adding New Learning Activity Using Standard Layout*

Private-access, cascade-pull, cascade-push, and cascade-align actions are not used and may be removed from the Learning Activity List/View Detail template XML.

For catalog learning, the following fields are required:

**assigned:** Owner of the learning activity

**completed_date:** Learning activity completion date

**name:** Learning activity name

**description:** Learning activity description

**status:** Status of the learning activity

**guid:** Learning activity unique ID

**type:** Product type, reserved and may only be text

**dev-goals:** Learning activity associated with a goal; must have a "Write" permission

Default statuses are

- Planned
- Locked
- Deleted
- Failed
- Completed

When a development goal is completed, all associated learning activities are set to "Completed" or "Locked."

Conditional permissions may also be added to the XML. Identified by the tag "*<condition>*," a condition must be met in order to allow a role to see fields on the plan.

It is possible for roles to read fields based on conditions as seen in the following code segment:

```
<field-permission type="read">
    <description><![CDATA[Employee, and their HR reps, managers up the
    reporting chain may read the following fields when the learning
    activity status is Completed.]]></description>
    <condition><![CDATA[status eq Completed]]></condition>
    <role-name><![CDATA[E]]></role-name>
    <role-name><![CDATA[EM+]]></role-name>
    <role-name><![CDATA[EH]]></role-name>
     <field refid="start_date"/>
    <field refid="completed_date"/>
    <field refid="assignee"/>
    <field refid="name"/>
    <field refid="description"/>
```

```
    <field refid="status"/>
    <field refid="type"/>
    <field refid="dev_goals"/>
    <field refid="source_type"/>
    <field refid="customtext4"/>
  </field-permission>
```

Shown in the following is a code segment sample for a custom learning type:

```
<field-definition id="customtext4" type="enum" required="true"
detail="false" viewdefault="on" showlabel="false" field-show-coaching-
advisor="false" cascade-update="push-down">
    <field-label>Item Type</field-label>
    <field-label lang="en_US">Item Type</field-label
    <field-description>Item Type</field-description>
    <field-description lang="es_US">Item Type</field-description>
    <enum-value value="External Course">
      <enum-label>External Course</enum-label>
      <enum-label lang="en_US">External Course</enum-label>
    </enum-value>
    <enum-value value="Project">
      <enum-label>Project</enum-label>
       <enum-label lang="en_US">Project</enum-label>
    </enum-value>
    <enum-value value="On-the-Job Training (OJT)">
      <enum-label>On-the-Job Training (OJT)</enum-label>
      <enum-label lang="en_US">On-the-Job-Training (OJT)</enum-label>
    </enum-value>
    <enum-value value="Job Rotation">
      <enum-label>Job Rotation</enum-label>
      <enum-label lang="en_US">Job Rotation</enum-label>
    </enum-value>
    <enum-value value="E-Learning/Webinars">
      <enum-label>E-Learning/Webinars</enum-label>
      <enum-label lang="en_US">E-Learning/Webinars</enum-label>
    </enum-value>
```

```
    <enum-value value="Conference / Seminar">
      <enum-label>Conference / Seminar</enum-label>
      <enum-label lang="en_US">Conference/Seminar</enum-label>
      </enum-value>
    <enum-value value="Assignment">
      <enum-label>Assignment</enum-label>
      <enum-label lang="en_US">Assignment</enum-label>
      </enum-value>
    <enum-value value="Self-Learning">
      <enum-label>Self-Learning</enum-label>
      <enum-label lang="en_US">Self-Learning</enum-label>
     </enum-value>
    <enum-value value="Others">
      <enum-label>Others</enum-label>
      <enum-label lang="en_US">Others</enum-label>
    </enum-value>
  </field-definition>
```

The plan-layout defines how the fields for the learning activity will display in the development goals. The form-layout, pdf-layout, and details-layouts sections are not used. A sample of the plan-layout is displayed in the following:

```
<plan-layout>
    <column weight="40.0">
      <field refid="name"/>
      <field refid="description"/>
    </column>
    <column weight="7.0">
      <field refid="status"/>
    </column>
    <column weight="10.0">
      <field refid="type"/>
    </column>
    <column weight="5.0">
      <field refid="start_date"/>
    </column>
```

```
    <column weight="5.0">
      <field refid="completed_date"/>
    </column>
  </plan-layout>
```

All of the fields that should display when creating a learning activity will need "Read" and "Write" permissions granted. Fields are defined and permissions granted similar to the goal and development plan templates.

Roles that can read development goal fields on the development plan should have the same Read permissions for the learning activity fields. Otherwise, when viewing the development plan, the user would not see any fields for learning activities. You may decide that a manager may add development goals to a direct report's development plan but can only read the learning activity fields. This means the development plan XML should have "Write" permissions for the manager and the learning activities XML should have "Read" permissions.

You will need to thoughtfully plan what each role should be able to do and what they should see because you have to correctly configure the permissions in the template XML and the role-based permissions.

# Setup for the Development Goals Portlet to Appear in People Profile

A switch in the development template XML was mentioned earlier in the chapter, and it permits development goals to appear in People Profile in a portlet. There is additional configuration needed in the Succession Data Model to add the Development Objective Portlet background element.

Log into Provisioning and go to Company Settings. Find the "Succession Management" section and click the link "Import/Export Data Model" as seen in Figure 1-35.

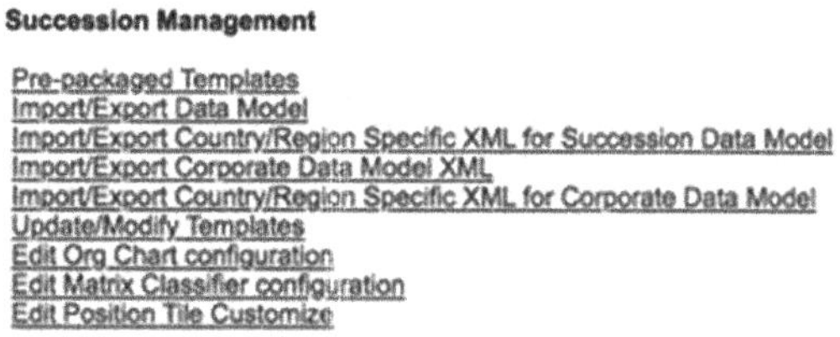

**Succession Management**

Pre-packaged Templates
Import/Export Data Model
Import/Export Country/Region Specific XML for Succession Data Model
Import/Export Corporate Data Model XML
Import/Export Country/Region Specific XML for Corporate Data Model
Update/Modify Templates
Edit Org Chart configuration
Edit Matrix Classifier configuration
Edit Position Tile Customize

***Figure 1-35.*** *Succession Management Access*

On the Import/Export Data Model screen as seen in Figure 1-36, download the data model in order to make modifications.

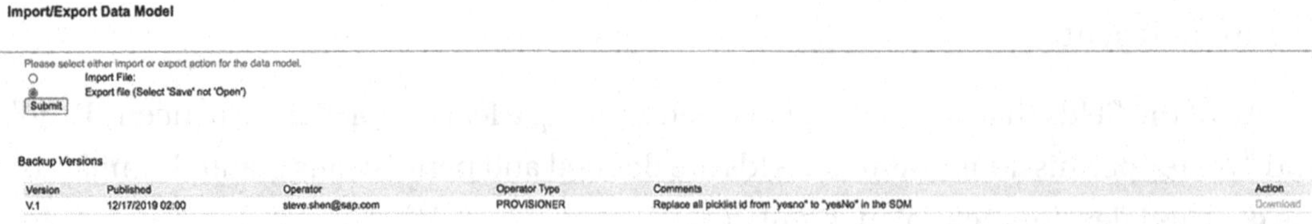


***Figure 1-36.*** *Import/Export Data Model*

Add the background element "sysScoreCardDevelopmentObjectivesPortlet" as shown in the following code segment:

```
<background-element id="sysScoreCardDevelopmentObjectivesPortlet"
type-id="101">
    <label>Development Goals Portlet</label>
    <label xml:lang="en-US">Development Goals Portlet</label>
    <data-field id="title" field-name="vfld1" required="true" hidden="true"
    max-length="999" max-file-size-KB="1000">
      <label>Development Goal</label>
      <label xml:lang="en-US">Development Goal</label>
    </data-field>
  </background-element>
```

Also add the background element portlet to "view-template for employeeScoreCard" as shown in the following code segment:

```
<view-template id="employeeScoreCard" visibility="none" pdf-printing-
enabled="true">
    <label>View Template for Employee Scorecard</label>
    <description>This view Template for Employee Scorecard should have only
    1 edit template</description>
    <edit-template id="scorecardEditTemplate">
      <label>Edit Template for Employee Scorecard</label>
      <description>Edit Template for Employee Scorecard</description>
      <background-element-ref refid="sysScoreCardOverviewPortlet"/>
      <background-element-ref refid="sysScoreCardContactPortlet"/>
```

```
    <background-element-ref refid="sysScoreCardOrgProfilePortlet"/>
    <background-element-ref refid="sysScoreCardExpSnapshotPortlet"/>
    <background-element-ref refid="sysScoreCardPerfHistoryPortlet"/>
    <background-element-ref refid="sysScoreCardCompetenciesPortlet"/>
    <background-element-ref refid="sysScoreCardCompBehaviorPortlet"/>
    <background-element-ref refid="sysScoreCardObjRatingsPortlet"/>
    <background-element-ref refid="sysScoreCardNominationPortlet"/>
    <background-element-ref refid="sysScoreCardSuccessorPortlet"/>
    <background-element-ref refid="sysScoreCardDevelopmentObjectives
    Portlet"/>
  </edit-template>
</view-template>
```

After making the updates, save and import the Succession Data Model.

---

**Note** The name of the background element is Development Objective Portlet, but in our examples, we are using "Goal" for labels in place of "Objective." We will reference the background element portlet using its standard name, but it will appear in our instance as "Development Goals Portlet."

---

## Development Portlet Setup in People Profile

Back in the instance, the portlet needs to be configured in People Profile.

Go to "Configure People Profile" to add the Development Goals Portlet.

Find the block and drag it to a section where you would like to display it as seen in Figure 1-37.

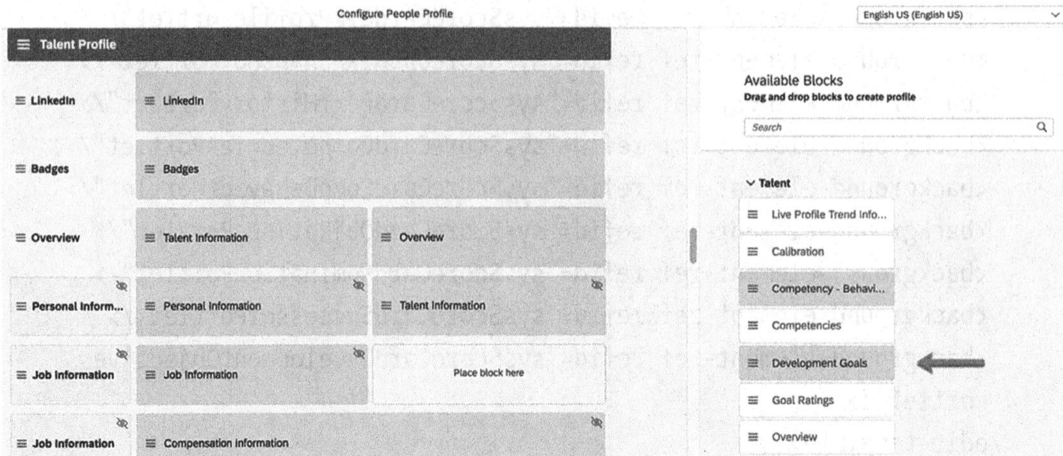


***Figure 1-37.** Adding a Development Plan Block in People Profile*

Label the subsection, and add a block title and description as seen in Figure 1-38. Local labels may also be created.

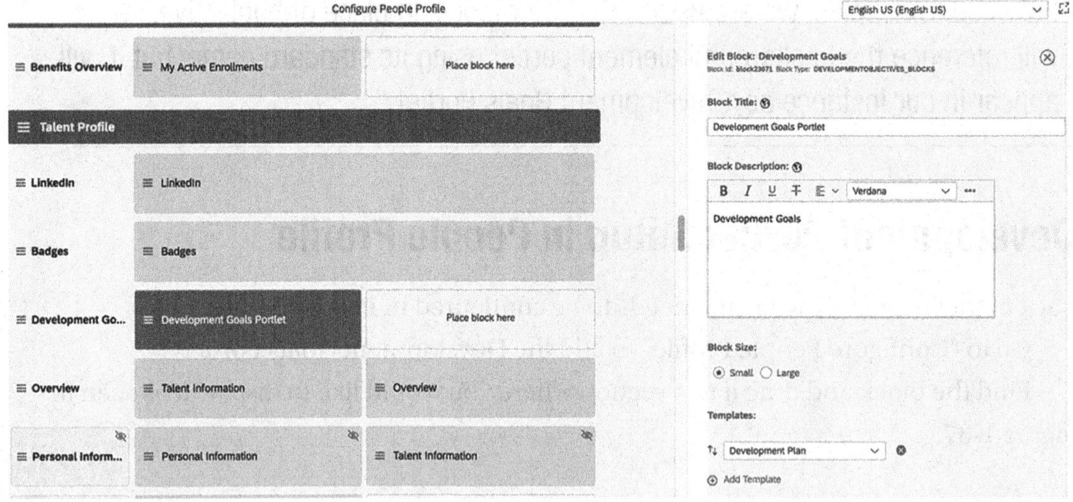


***Figure 1-38.** Identifying the Development Plan Template*

Save the profile after adding the block. Role-based permissions will need to be granted to access this data in People Profile. Type and select "Manage Permission Roles" in the search bar.

For each role that should have access to the portlet, click the "Permissions" button, find the User Permissions section, and select "Employee Data." Grant "View" access to the Development Goals Portlet within the Background section as seen in Figure 1-39.

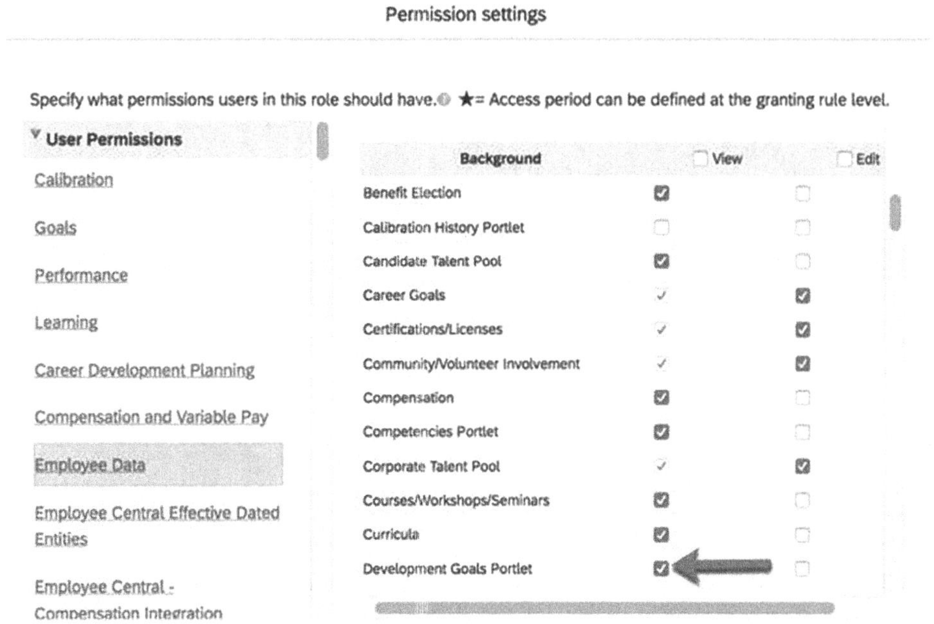

***Figure 1-39.** Permission to Access the Development Goals Portlet*

We learned earlier in this chapter about the switch to set in the development plan XML as seen in the following:

```
<switch for="development-scorecard-show-all-goals" value="on" />
```

When this switch is on, all of the user's development goals would appear in the Development Goals Portlet in People Profile. When this switch is not used, the default setting allows the user to select which development goals to add to the portlet in their profile. In this situation, the "Edit" permission for this portlet would be required as well. An example is shown in Figure 1-40.

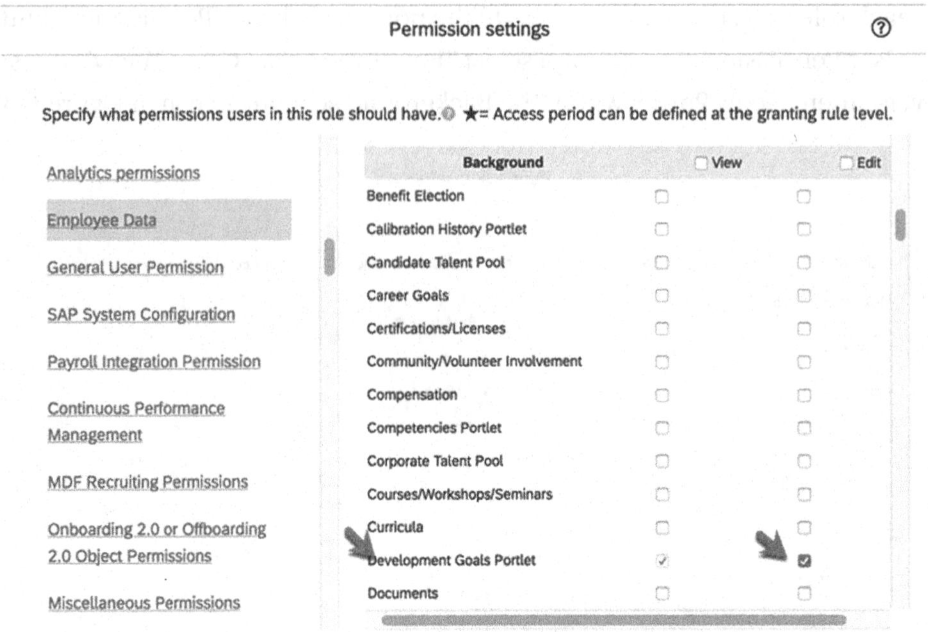

*Figure 1-40.*

We will see how this works when we walk through the development plan as an employee.

## Importing Development Goals

There is a development goals import tool that may be used to upload employee development goals in mass. This works in the same manner as the goal import but uses a different screen with a different template. You may have granted access to the admin permission role to perform this task if you have imported employee goals; the permission applies to both. Within the role-based permissions for the admin role, go the Administrator Permissions section. Find "Manage Goals" and add "Import Goals".

There may be a situation where you are converting from another development goal tracking system to SAP SuccessFactors Career Development. In that case, you may wish to copy the development goals from the other system to the users' new development plans. Another use for the import is assign a division or companywide development goal to select users.

To start the process, type and select "Import Development Goals" in the search bar, and the import screen will display as seen in Figure 1-41.

**Admin Center**

Back to Admin Center

**Import Development Goals**

Import Goals by uploading CSV fileThe limit for the total number of goals in a CSV file is up to 30,000. Please don't upload a CSV file containing more than 30,000 goals.

Available List of Templates: Development Plan Generate CSV Header

Import File: Browse... No file selected.

Character Encoding: Western European (Windows/ISO)

Read-only goals ☐ Yes (Check only if you wish to set the imported goals to be read-only)

Allow Duplicate Assignment of Group Goals ☐

Import

***Figure 1-41.*** *Import Development Goals Screen*

From the Available List of Templates, select the development plan template used for your development plan and click "Generate CSV Header". The import template will contain the fields specific to your development plan. When you download the CSV header file, "OBJ_PLAN_ID" and "OBJ_PLAN_NAME" contain your development plan name and ID.

Open the template to see its layout. An example is shown in Figure 1-42.

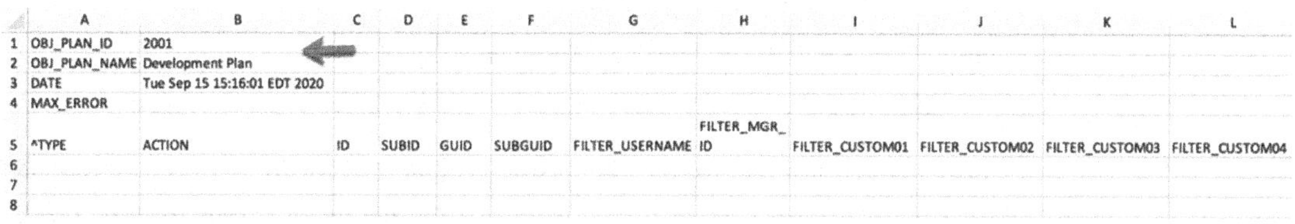

| | A | B | C | D | E | F | G | H | I | J | K | L |
|---|---|---|---|---|---|---|---|---|---|---|---|---|
| 1 | OBJ_PLAN_ID | 2001 | | | | | | | | | | |
| 2 | OBJ_PLAN_NAME | Development Plan | | | | | | | | | | |
| 3 | DATE | Tue Sep 15 15:16:01 EDT 2020 | | | | | | | | | | |
| 4 | MAX_ERROR | | | | | | | | | | | |
| 5 | ^TYPE | ACTION | ID | SUBID | GUID | SUBGUID | FILTER_USERNAME | FILTER_MGR_ ID | FILTER_CUSTOM01 | FILTER_CUSTOM02 | FILTER_CUSTOM03 | FILTER_CUSTOM04 |
| 6 | | | | | | | | | | | | |
| 7 | | | | | | | | | | | | |
| 8 | | | | | | | | | | | | |

***Figure 1-42.*** *Development Plan Import Template*

The first four rows should not be altered. They identify the development plan.

Row 5 contains the headers for the development goal plan fields. The header rows define the values needed for each field of a development goal. If there are standard development goal plan fields that you aren't populating, those columns may be deleted.

You will create a row for each development goal that you wish to import.

The ^TYPE (column A) field is always required. Each row should have "OBJECTIVE" in the ^TYPE column.

The ACTION (column B) field is always required. Each row should have "OBJECTIVE" in the ACTION column. Valid action types are "ADD," "DELETE," and "UPDATE."

For adding goals to an employee's goal plan, use "ADD."

Any field that is required when creating a development goal must be populated on the file.

## Field Descriptions for Import File

Refer to Table 1-9 for the development goal plan field descriptions.

***Table 1-9.*** *Development Plan Import Fields*

| Field | Description | Value |
|---|---|---|
| ^TYPE | Type of plan used in upload. | OBJECTIVE. |
| ACTION | What to do with the goal. | ADD, DELETE, or UPDATE. |
| ID | System generated when importing the goal. | Leave blank for the *ADD* action. |
| SUBID | Not supported. | Leave blank. |
| GUID | An identifier used as reference when updating or deleting a goal. | May be any value that you want as long as each goal GUID is unique. |
| FILTER_USERNAME | Username of the employee whom you are adding a goal for. May mass assign a goal by entering multiple usernames. | May use multiple usernames separated by a semicolon. To give the goal to everyone: ALL. |
| FILTER_ CUSTOM01-15 | Custom fields that are filter options (custom-filters within the "default" module of the data model). | May delete these columns if not needed. |
| FILTER_DEPT | Filtered against the username's department. | List a department and everyone in the department will get the goal. |
| FILTER_DIV | Filtered against the username's division. | List a division and everyone in the division will get the goal. |
| FILTER_JOBCODE | Not supported. | Leave blank or delete column. |
| FILTER_LOC | Filtered against the username's location. | List a location and everyone in the location will get the goal. |
| OBJECTVEter_ CATEGORY | Default category ID from the goal template. | Goals. |
| OBJECTIVE_ PARENTID | Not used. | Leave blank. |

(*continued*)

***Table 1-9.*** *(continued)*

| Field | Description | Value |
|---|---|---|
| OBJECTIVE_PUBLIC | Indicator if the goal is public. | Use 1 or Y for public and 0 or N for private goal. |
| OBJECTIVE_name | Name of the development goal. | Use the development goal name that you wish to see on the plan. |
| OBJECTIVE_metric | Development goal measure if used in the plan. | May use any text if defined as text or textarea in the template. |
| OBJECTIVE_start | Development goal start date if used in the plan. | If entered, date must be in MM/DD/YYYY format. |
| OBJECTIVE_due | Development goal due date if used in the plan. | If entered, date must be in MM/DD/YYYY format. |
| OBJECTIVE_state | Development goal status if used in the plan. | If status is a dropdown list, use the enum-value for the status. |
| OBJECTIVE_competency | If development goal has associated competencies. | In JPB, locate the competency to get the GUID; list each competency GUID separated by a comma. |
| OBJECTIVE_purpose | Purpose of the development goal if used in the plan. | If purpose is a dropdown list, use the enum-value for the status. |

Any FILTER columns may be used to mass assign a goal based on the value entered in the column.

FILTER_USERNAME, FILTER_MGR_ID, FILTER_DEPT, FILTER_DIV, and FILTER_LOC are default columns. The username filter is the only filter which supports multiple entries in a single row (separated by a semicolon).

Custom fields to be used as filters must be defined in the data model under <custom-filters>.

If you don't wish to mass assign a goal using any of these filters, these columns may be deleted from the file.

The field headings that contain "OBJECTIVE" correspond to the fields on the development goal plan. An example is shown in Figure 1-43.

| A | B | C | D | E | F | AB | AC | AD | AE | AF | AG | AH | AI | AJ | AK |
|---|---|---|---|---|---|---|---|---|---|---|---|---|---|---|---|
| OBJ_PLAN_ID | 2001 | | | | | | | | | | | | | | |
| OBJ_PLAN_NAME | Development Plan | | | | | | | | | | | | | | |
| DATE | Tue Sep 15 15:16:01 EDT 2020 | | | | | | | | | | | | | | |
| MAX_ERROR | | | | | | | | | | | | | | | |
| ^TYPE | ACTION | ID | SUBID | GUID | SUBGUID | OBJECTIVE_ CATEGORY | OBJECTIVE_ PARENTID | OBJECTIVE_ PUBLIC | OBJECTIVE_ name | OBJECTIVE_ metric | OBJECTIVE_ start | OBJECTIVE_ due | OBJECTIVE_ state | OBJECTIVE_ competency | OBJECTIVE_ purpose |

***Figure 1-43.*** *Development Goal Import Headings*

If your development plan includes competencies and you wish to import development goals with competencies, a reference to the competency is needed in the file. This reference is the competency GUID.

To find competency GUIDs, type and select "Manage Job Profile Content" in the search bar. Then select "Competency", and you will see the GUID associated with each competency. An example is shown in Figure 1-44.

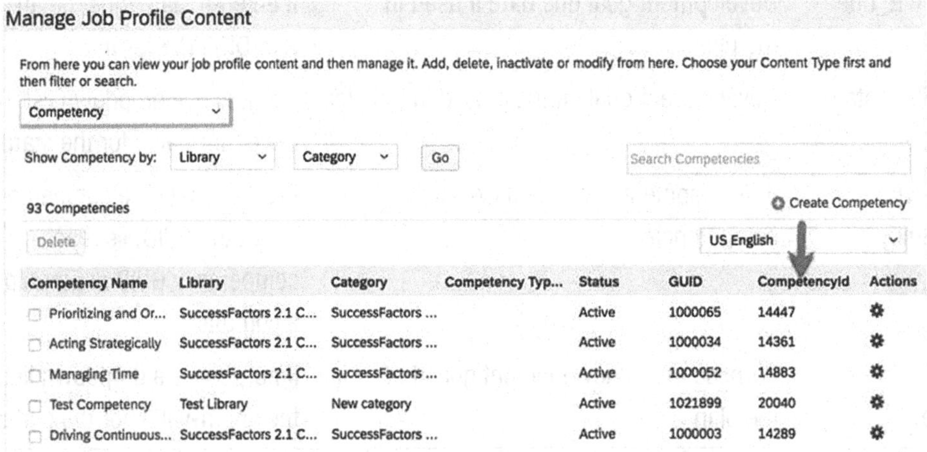


***Figure 1-44.*** *Manage Job Profile Content for Competencies*

For a development goal with multiple competencies, populate the OBJECTIVE_competency field and list each competency ID separated by a comma. Make sure the format of the cell is text in order to use the comma separator as seen in Figure 1-45.

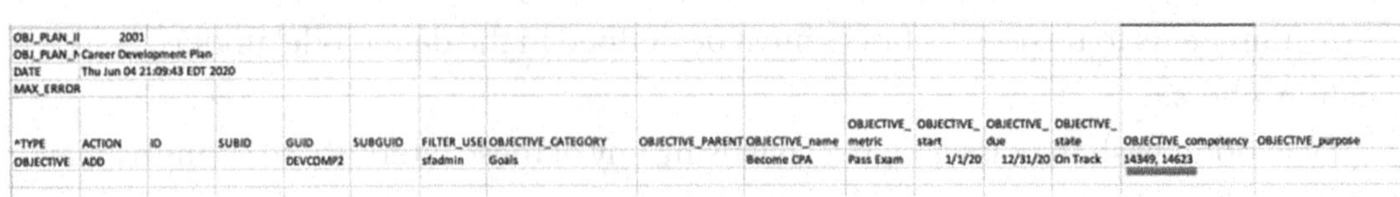

| OBJ_PLAN_II | 2001 | | | | | | | | | | | | | | |
|---|---|---|---|---|---|---|---|---|---|---|---|---|---|---|---|
| OBJ_PLAN_N | Career Development Plan | | | | | | | | | | | | | | |
| DATE | Thu Jun 04 21:09:43 EDT 2020 | | | | | | | | | | | | | | |
| MAX_ERROR | | | | | | | | | | | | | | | |
| *TYPE | ACTION | ID | SUBID | GUID | SUBGUID | FILTER_USEI | OBJECTIVE_CATEGORY | OBJECTIVE_PARENT | OBJECTIVE_name | OBJECTIVE_ metric | OBJECTIVE_ start | OBJECTIVE_ due | OBJECTIVE_ state | OBJECTIVE_competency | OBJECTIVE_purpose |
| OBJECTIVE | ADD | | | DEVCOMP2 | | sfadmin | Goals | | Become CPA | Pass Exam | 1/1/20 | 12/31/20 | On Track | 14349, 14623 | |

***Figure 1-45.*** *Competency Column on the Import File*

Use CSV file format and import the file with character encoding Unicode (UTF-8) as shown in Figure 1-46.

Admin Center

Back to Admin Center

Import Development Goals

Import Goals by uploading CSV fileThe limit for the total number of goals in a CSV file is up to 30,000. Please don't upload a CSV file containing more than 30,000 goals.

Available List of Templates: Development Plan Generate CSV Header

Import File: Browse... Import_Career_Development_Plan_with_comp.csv

Character Encoding: Unicode (UTF-8)

Read-only goals Yes (Check only if you wish to set the imported goals to be read-only)

Allow Duplicate Assignment of Group Goals

Import

***Figure 1-46.*** *Development Goal Import*

After the upload completes, the admin will receive an email with the import status. An example is shown in Figure 1-47.

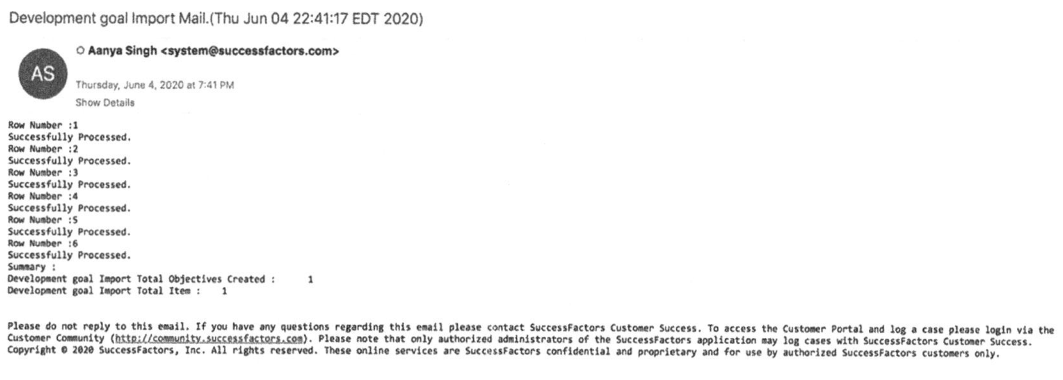

Development goal Import Mail.(Thu Jun 04 22:41:17 EDT 2020)

AS

Aanya Singh <system@successfactors.com>

Thursday, June 4, 2020 at 7:41 PM

Show Details

Row Number :1
Successfully Processed.
Row Number :2
Successfully Processed.
Row Number :3
Successfully Processed.
Row Number :4
Successfully Processed.
Row Number :5
Successfully Processed.
Row Number :6
Successfully Processed.
Summary :
Development goal Import Total Objectives Created : 1
Development goal Import Total Item : 1

Please do not reply to this email. If you have any questions regarding this email please contact SuccessFactors Customer Success. To access the Customer Portal and log a case please login via the Customer Community (http://community.successfactors.com). Please note that only authorized administrators of the SuccessFactors application may log cases with SuccessFactors Customer Success. Copyright © 2020 SuccessFactors, Inc. All rights reserved. These online services are SuccessFactors confidential and proprietary and for use by authorized SuccessFactors customers only.

***Figure 1-47.*** *Development Goal Import Status Email*

The file will show any errors detected during the import. Make any file corrections and reimport the file.

After a successful import, the user's development plan contains the newly uploaded development goal with the associated competencies as seen in Figure 1-48.

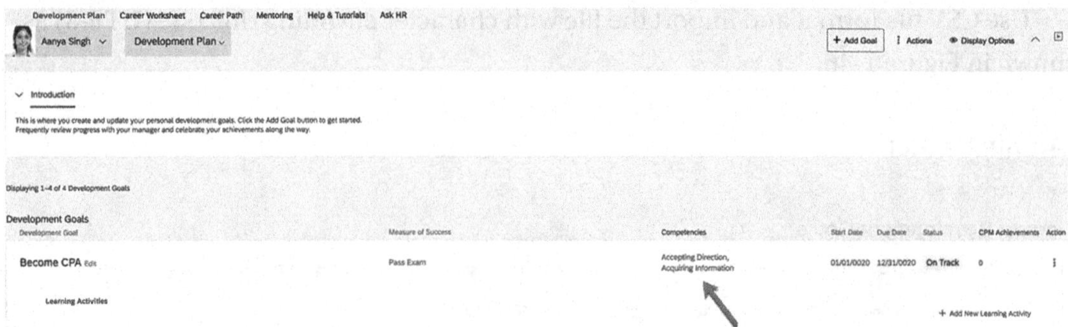


*Figure 1-48.* *Development Goal Added via Import*

## Development Goal Update or Deletion

In order to mass update or delete any existing goals on users' development plans, the system-generated goal ID is needed. Create an ad hoc report using the development plan template and include the development goal ID field as output as shown in Figure 1-49.

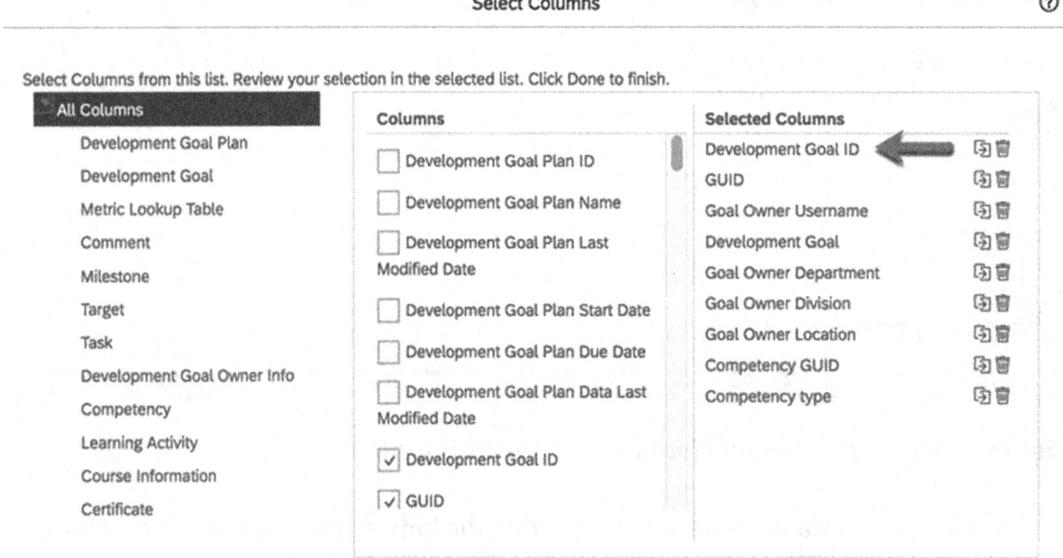


*Figure 1-49.* *Development Goal ID in Ad Hoc Creation*

As seen in Figure 1-50, to update any existing goals, use "OBJECTIVE" for ^TYPE and "UPDATE" for ACTION. Use the development goal ID from the ad hoc report in column C. Populate just the fields that are changing for the development goal.

| A | B | C | D | E | F | G | H | I | J | K | L | M |
|---|---|---|---|---|---|---|---|---|---|---|---|---|
| OBJ_PLAN_ID | 2001 | | | | | | | | | | | |
| OBJ_PLAN_NAME | Career Development Plan | | | | | | | | | | | |
| DATE | Thu Jun 04 21:09:43 EDT 2020 | | | | | | | | | | | |
| MAX_ERROR | | | | | | | | | | | | |
| ^TYPE | ACTION | ID | SUBID | GUID | SUBGUID | FILTER_USERNAM | OBJECTIVE_( | OBJECTIVE_I | OBJECTIVE_I | OBJECTIVE_name | OBJECTIVE_metric | OBJECT |
| OBJECTIVE | UPDATE | 9050 | | | | | | | | | Completion of coursework | |

***Figure 1-50.*** *Fields for Development Goal Update*

To delete any existing goals, use "OBJECTIVE" for ^TYPE, "DELETE" for ACTION, and the goal ID in column C. No other fields are populated. An example is shown in Figure 1-51.

| | | | | | | | | | | | | | | | | |
|---|---|---|---|---|---|---|---|---|---|---|---|---|---|---|---|---|
| OBJ_PLAN_ID | 5 | | | | | | | | | | | | | | | |
| OBJ_PLAN_NAME | 2018 Performance Goals | | | | | | | | | | | | | | | |
| DATE | Fri Jul 06 11:59:40 EDT 2018 | | | | | | | | | | | | | | | |
| MAX_ERROR | | | | | | | | | | | | | | | | |
| ^TYPE | ACTION | ID | SUBID | GUID | SUBGUID | FILTER_USER | FILTER_MGR | FILTER_CUST | FILTER_CUST | FILTER_CUST | FILTER_CUST | FILTER_CUST | FILTER_CUST | FILTER_CUST | FILTER_CUST | FILTE |
| OBJECTIVE | DELETE | 6804 | | | | | | | | | | | | | | |

***Figure 1-51.*** *Fields for Development Goal Delete*

## Import Development Goals with Learning Activities

As noted earlier, to import learning activities with development goals, you need to enable the Transcript feature in Provisioning. On the import file, you may add, delete, and update custom learning activities; but you cannot add catalog learning activities.

It is not possible to include learning activities when importing new development goals for a user. Instead, two imports are needed. First, load the new development goals. Once the development goals are added, get the development goal GUIDs. Now you are ready to load the learning activities associated with the development goals. Download a fresh header template for the file. Here we will just populate the learning activity-specific fields. We will also need to identify the development goal user and the development goal to add the learning activities to. For each row, populate ^TYPE with "LEARNING" and use "ADD" for ACTION. Include the GUID for the development goal, the required learning fields, and any other learning activity fields.

An example of the file is seen in Figure 1-52.

| A | B | C | D | E | F | G | T | U | V | W | X | Y | Z | AA | AB | AC |
|---|---|---|---|---|---|---|---|---|---|---|---|---|---|---|---|---|
| OBJ_PLAN_ID | 2001 | | | | | | | | | | | | | | | |
| OBJ_PLAN_NAME | Development Plan | | | | | | | | | | | | | | | |
| DATE | Tue Sep 15 17:20:13 EDT 2020 | | | | | | | | | | | | | | | |
| MAX_ERROR | | | | | | | | | | | | | | | | |
| ^TYPE | ACTION | ID | SUBID | GUID | SUBGUID | FILTER_USEI | LEARNING_start_date | LEARNING_completed_date | LEARNING_name | LEARNING_description | LEARNING_status | LEARNING_guid | LEARNING_type | LEARNING_dev_goals | LEARNING_source_type | LEARNING_customtext4 |
| LEARNING | ADD | 9070 | | | | sfadmin | 1/1/20 | | Time Management Course | Learn to manage time | Planned | | Project | | | Self-Learning |

***Figure 1-52.*** *Development Plan Import File with Learning Activities*

Follow the same development goal process. An example of the updated development goal which includes a learning activity is shown in Figure 1-53.

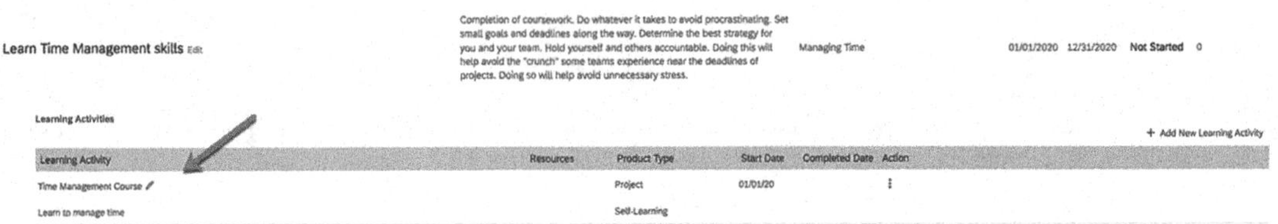


***Figure 1-53.*** *Adding a Learning Activity on Import File*

---

**Note** To learn more about importing learning activities, see SAP note #2472229.

---

# Using Career Development from the Employee Perspective

We have discussed how to set up Career Development in Provisioning and in the instance. We have reviewed role-based permissions and have seen how to mass import development goals, configure the Development Goals Portlet, and configure learning activities.

Now we will demonstrate a scenario of an employee using the Development Plan.

An employee may access the Development module from the Home menu listing as shown in Figure 1-54.

***Figure 1-54.*** *Home Menu with the Development Tab*

The Development Plan will display. An example is shown in Figure 1-55.

***Figure 1-55.*** *Blank Development Plan*

Before any goals have been added, the user will see an empty plan containing an introduction, if configured, and some options across the top of the plan. The development plan has the same look and feel as the goal plan. Template configuration will determine the layout, permissions, and actions available in the plan. Refer to Volume 1, Chapter 4 for any additional details.

We will first review the options available in the top-right section of the screen. The user will have the option to add a new development goal as seen in Figure 1-56. Unlike the goal plan, there is no goal library to reference.

***Figure 1-56.*** *Add a Goal*

The user will be able to print the plan as shown in the Actions menu in Figure 1-57.

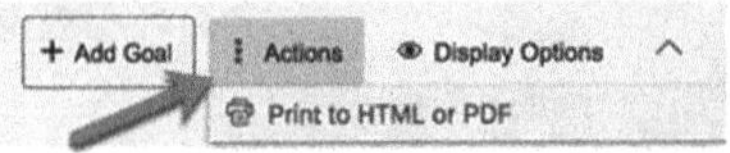


***Figure 1-57.*** *Print Action*

As seen in Figure 1-58, the Display Options feature allows the user to select which goal plan fields to display on the plan. Some fields may be hidden to make the plan look less cluttered.

***Figure 1-58.*** *Development Plan Display Options*

The user may add a development goal as seen in Figure 1-59. The popup will display all of the fields that were configured in the template. All required fields will need to be populated in order to save the goal.

Add Development Goal

**Add Development Goal**

Fields marked with * are required.

coaching advisor spell check... legal scan...

* Development Goal:

coaching advisor spell check... legal scan...

Measure of Success:

Recommended Employee Actions:

Start Date: 01/01/2020

Due Date: 12/31/2023

Status: Not Started

* Competencies: Select One

Purpose: Current role

Cancel Save & Close

***Figure 1-59.*** *Adding a Development Goal to the Plan*

If the development plan was configured to add competencies to a development goal, this option will appear as well. An example is shown in Figure 1-60.

Add Development Goal

**Add Development Goal**

Fields marked with * are required.

| | |
|---|---|
| Visibility: | Public |
| * Development Goal: | coaching advisor spell check... legal scan... |
| Measure of Success: | coaching advisor spell check... legal scan... |
| Recommended Employee Actions: | |
| Start Date: | 01/01/2018 |
| Due Date: | 12/31/2020 |
| Status: | Not Started |
| * Competencies: | Add Competencies<br>☐ Accepting Direction<br>☐ Accepting Responsibility<br>☐ Acquiring Information<br>☐ Acting Decisively<br>☐ Acting Strategically<br>☐ Acting as a Champion for Change<br>☐ Acting with Integrity<br>☐ Adapting to Change<br>☐ Adapting to Others |
| Purpose: | Current role |

Cancel Save & Close

***Figure 1-60.*** *Add Competencies to a Development Goal*

Based on the default competency field configuration, the user may select several competencies to attach to the development goal.

There is also the "Add Competencies" option which allows the user to add additional competencies from the competency library as seen in Figure 1-61.

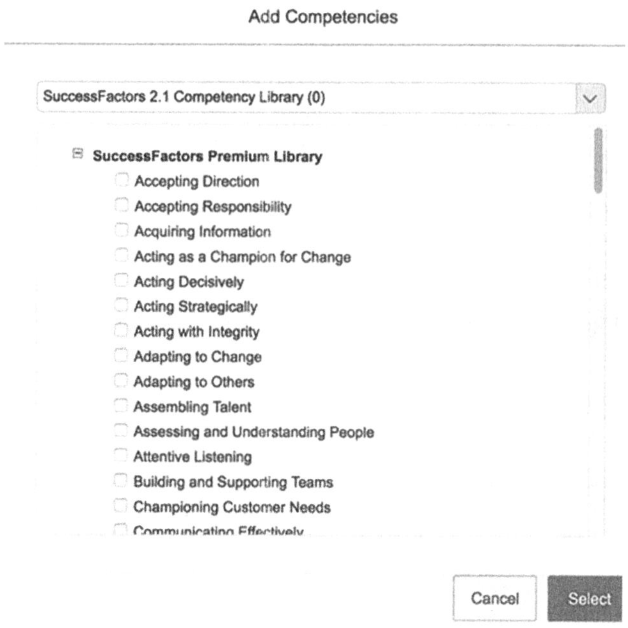

*Figure 1-61. Adding Competencies from the Competency Library to a Development Goal*

If configured, the user will see "Coaching Advisor" for the field as seen in Figure 1-62.

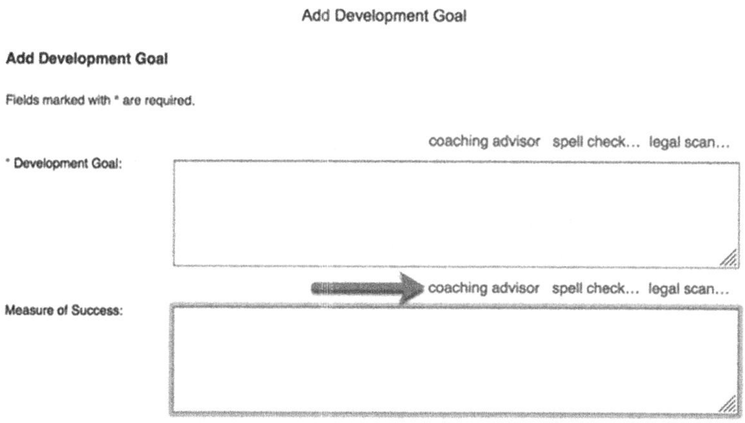

*Figure 1-62. Coaching Advisor*

As seen in Figure 1-63, a popup window will appear which enables the user to select the competency set to view.

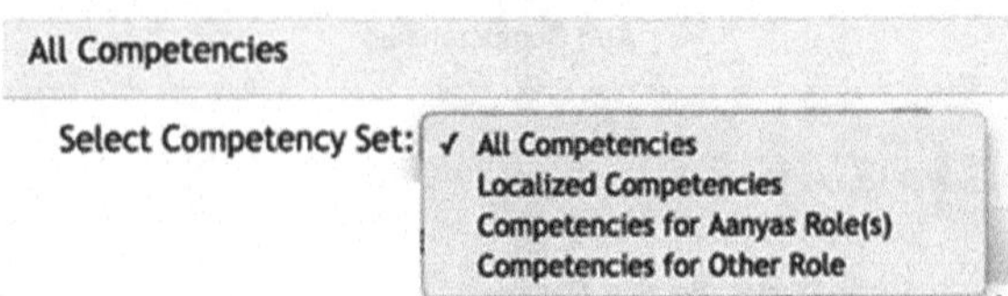


***Figure 1-63.*** *Select Competencies for Coaching Advisor*

When the competency set is selected, the appropriate competencies display. In this example, shown in Figure 1-64, the competencies tied to the user's job role appear.

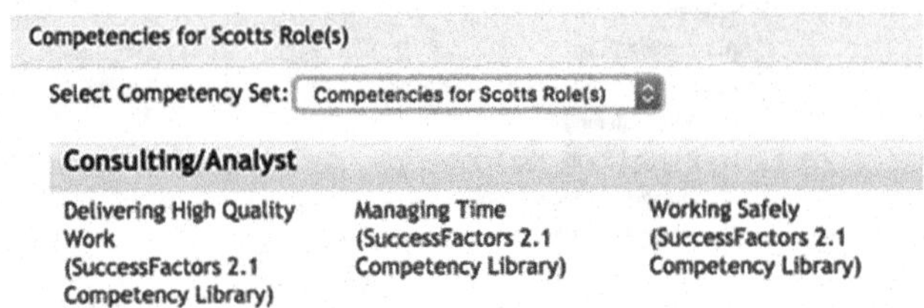


***Figure 1-64.*** *Job Role Competencies*

The user may then drill down into a competency to see the coaching advice. An example is seen in Figure 1-65. After selecting a competency teaser, the user scrolls down to see the corresponding coaching advice.

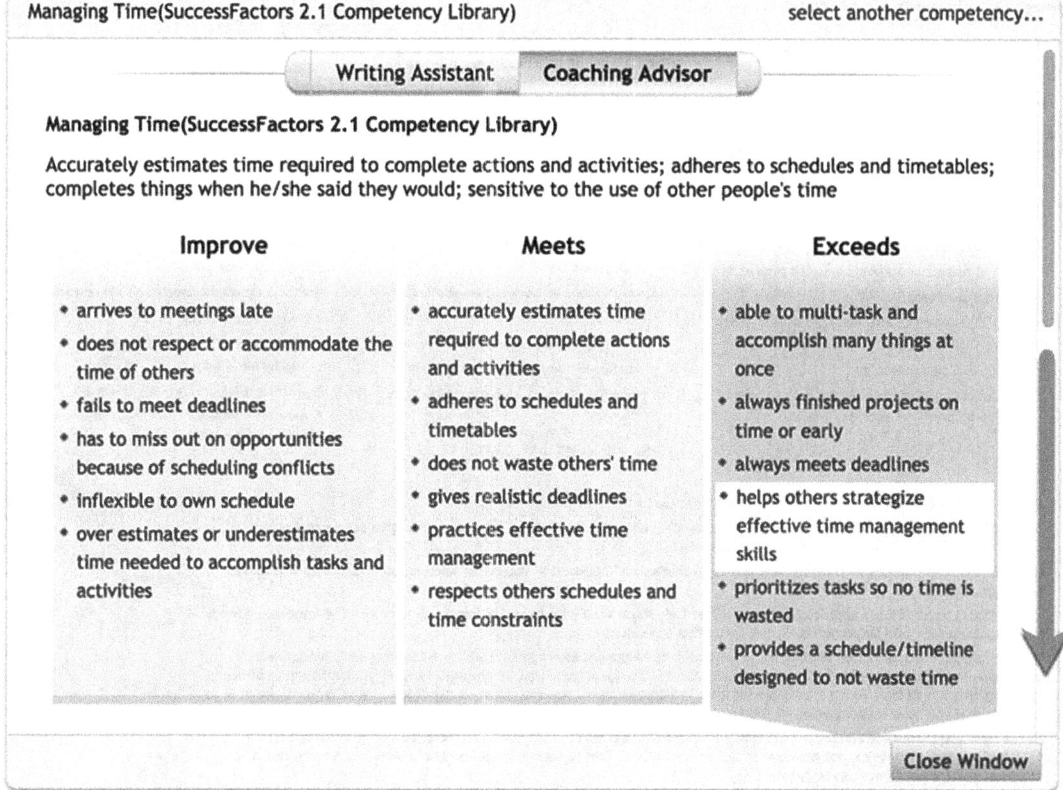


***Figure 1-65.*** *Coaching Advice*

The user may add coaching advice by clicking the “Place Text” button as shown in Figure 1-66.

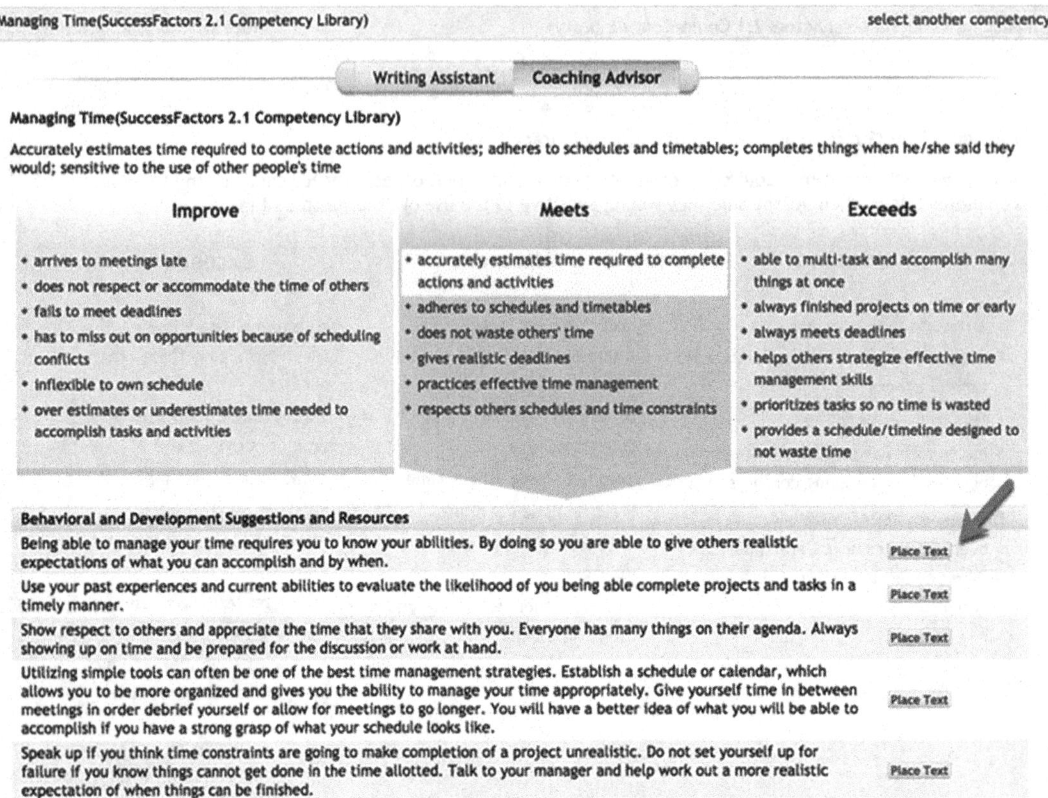


***Figure 1-66.*** *Select Text to Add to a Development Goal*

There will be a confirmation message that the text was added to the field in the development goal as seen in Figure 1-67.

Text placed successfully in comment box | Close Window

***Figure 1-67.*** *Confirmation Message*

The user would then close the popup window, and the text would appear in the goal plan field as shown in Figure 1-68.

Add Development Goal

**Add Development Goal**

Fields marked with * are required.

coaching advisor spell check... legal scan...

* Development Goal:

coaching advisor spell check... legal scan...

Measure of Success:

Being able to manage your time requires you to know your abilities. By doing so you are able to give others realistic expectations of what you can accomplish and by when.

***Figure 1-68.*** *Coaching Advice Added to a Development Goal*

The user may edit the coaching advice verbiage added to the development goal Updated development goal is shown in Figure 1-69.

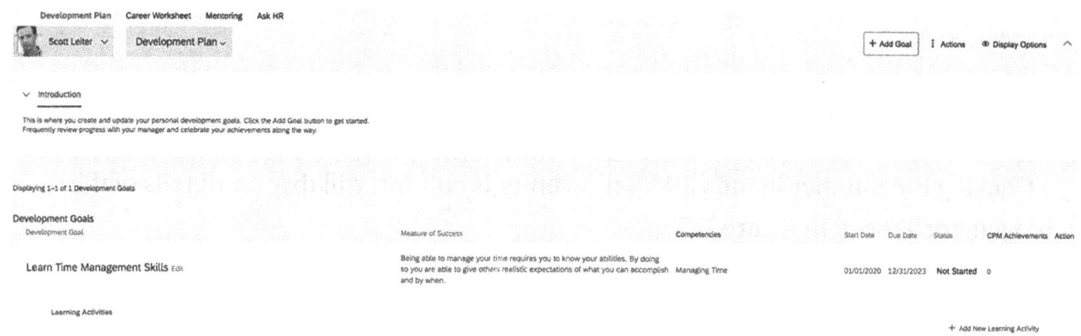


***Figure 1-69.*** *Development Goal After Adding Coaching Advice*

# CPM Achievements on the Development Plan

If development goals are tied to Continuous Performance Management achievements, the user may reference the development plan to link to an activity or achievement. As seen in Figure 1-70, the user may tie development goals to CPM activities and achievements.

Add Achievement

*Achievement Name

Completed Online Course

*Achievement Date

September 15, 2020

Development Goal

Learn Time Management Skills

Save Cancel

***Figure 1-70.*** *Tie Development Goals to CPM Activity or Achievement*

If the user has attached a development goal to a CPM achievement, there will be a count that displays in the CPM Achievements column. An example is shown in Figure 1-71.

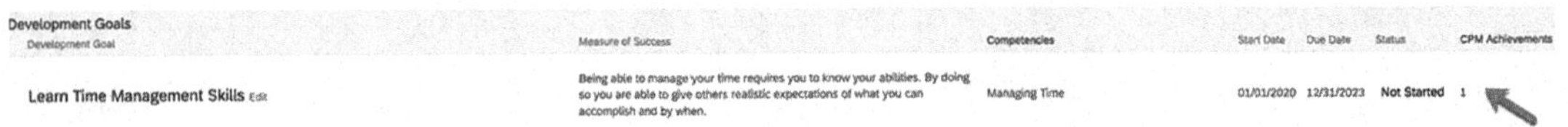


***Figure 1-71.*** *CPM Achievement Detail on a Development Goal*

Clicking the number in the CPM Achievements column will display details of the achievement as seen in Figure 1-72.

Continuous Performance Management achievements

Search

Completed Online Course

Created on: 9/15/20
Linked to Activity:
Linked to Development Goal: Learn Time Management Skills

> Feedback (0)

***Figure 1-72.*** *CPM Achievement Detail*

Based on the action permissions configured in the development plan template XML, the user may edit or delete a goal, add a learning activity, or add to the Development Goal Portlet in their profile. The options will display under the Action column as seen in Figure 1-73.

***Figure 1-73.*** *Actions Available for the Development Goal*

## Learning Activities Tied to Development Goals

If learning activities are configured to be part of the development plan, the user will be able to add learning activities. An example is shown in Figure 1-74.

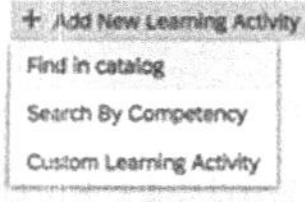


***Figure 1-74.*** *Add a Learning Activity to a Development Goal*

If the LMS catalog is configured to be available for the user in their development plan, the user may go to the LMS catalog to find a course. An example is seen in Figure 1-75.

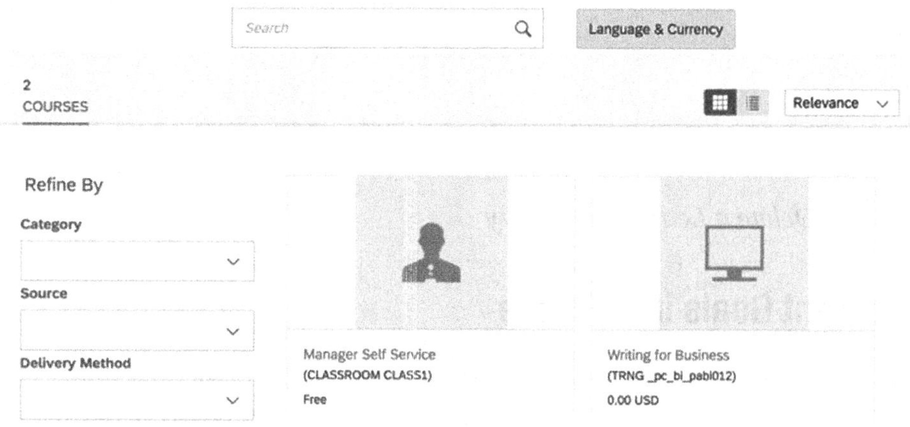


***Figure 1-75.*** *Search the LMS Catalog for a Course*

The user may have the option to add a custom learning activity to a development goal as seen in Figure 1-76.

Add New Learning Activity

Details

Learning Activity

Description

Legal Scan

Development Goals Learn Time Management Skills

Start Date MM/DD/YYYY

* Status Planned

* Product Key

Product Type

Tracking

Start Date MM/DD/YYYY

Completed Date MM/DD/YYYY

Save Cancel

***Figure 1-76.** Adding a Learning Activity to a Development Goal*

The layout of the custom learning activity is based on the learning activities template XML.

Multiple learning activities may be added to a development goal.

The user may edit, view, or delete goals all based on the permissions configured in the development plan template XML.

A user may delete a custom learning activity via "Action" or clicking the pencil icon to edit.

Details are shown in Figure 1-77.

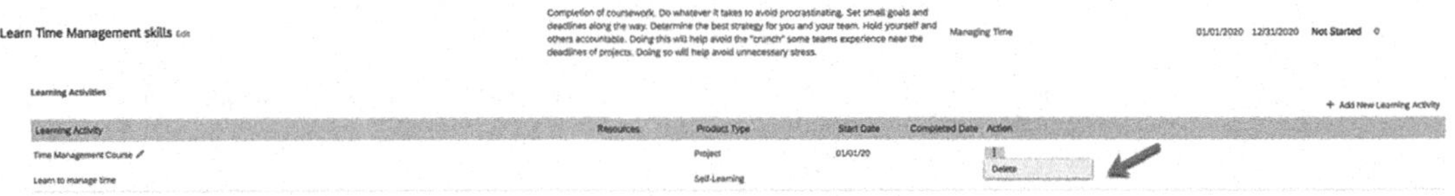


***Figure 1-77.** Delete a Learning Activity*

## Development Goals in a Profile

Depending on the Development Plan Portlet configuration, the user may add a development goal to their profile, or it will be automatically added to the portlet. Action options are seen in Figure 1-78. In the example shown in the following, the user may select a development goal to add to the portlet.

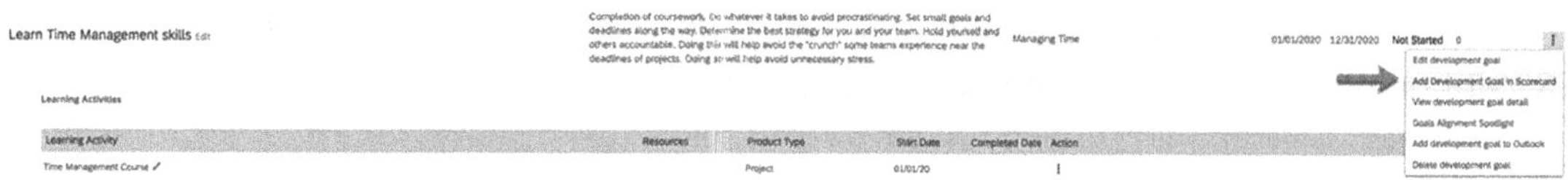


*Figure 1-78. Add a Development Goal to the Development Plan Portlet*

When the switch was added to the development plan template XML as discussed earlier, the user will not be able to choose which development goals to display in the Development Goals Portlet in the profile. All development goals added to their plan will automatically get added to the portlet in their profile. The "Add Development Goal in Scorecard" option will no longer display as an action for a development goal.

Shown in Figure 1-79 is an example of the portlet appearing in People Profile.

Alison Mahoney (amahoney) Planning & Scheduling Manager, Middlesex (0200-0006), Manufacturing (MANU) Actions Header As of Today

ME EMPLOYMENT COMPENSATION PAYROLL TIME BENEFITS TALENT PROFILE

Development Goals Portlet

Development Goals Portlet

Development Plan

Development Goals

Improve Public Speaking Skills

Become PMP Certified

*Figure 1-79. Development Goals Portlet*

If the switch was not set and users could add development goals directly in this portlet, the Development Goals Portlet does not support adding custom learning activities or searching by competencies.

## Viewing Development Plans of Others

If the development plan template XML granted read access to all roles for the goal plan fields, the user would be able to view others' plans provided the role-based permissions allowed it. When the user is viewing their own development plan, they may do a name search to find another user in order to view their plan.

In this example as seen in Figure 1-80, a user would be able to go into their own development plan, do a name search, and view the contents of someone's plan.

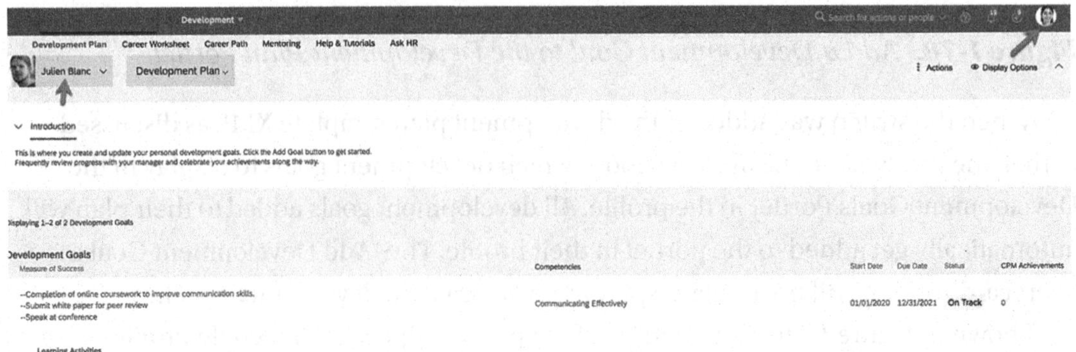


*Figure 1-80. Employee View of Another User's Development Plan*

## Using Career Development from a Manager's Perspective

The manager will be able to access their direct reports' goal plans via name search as seen in Figure 1-81.

*Figure 1-81. Manager Searching for a Direct Report*

The development plan template XML permissions determine what a manager will see and what actions may be performed. It is possible to allow a manager to create, edit, and delete goals. The permissions may allow them to only edit certain fields or not allow them to add learning activities.

If the manager permission role has access to all levels, an upper-level manager would have access to the goal plan as well.

If the HR manager role was updated to allow access to anyone they support, they would have access to those users' plans. Based on permission in the XML, the HR manager may be able to edit, delete, or add development goals or may only have "Read" permission and a limitation on what fields they may see.

Now that we have reviewed the configuration of development goal plans and walked through how a development plan works, we will briefly look at reporting options.

# Reporting: Standard Reports

Development goal reporting is available in "Standard Reporting" under "Classic View." Select "Development Goals" as shown in Figure 1-82.

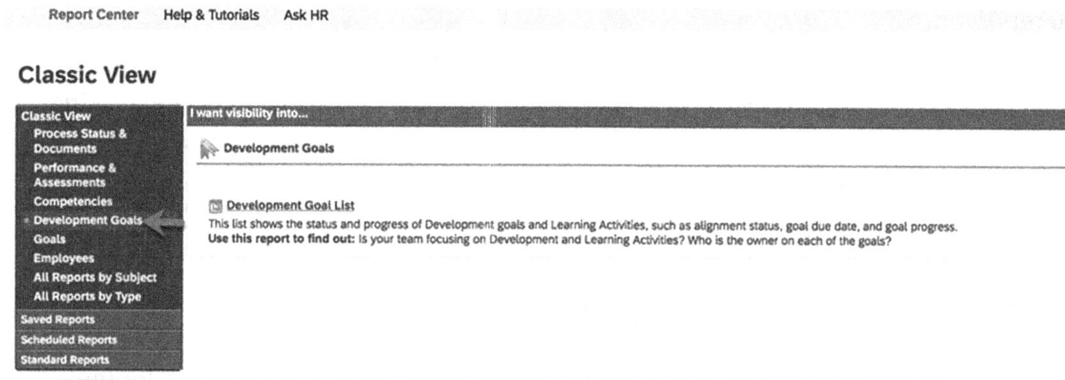


*Figure 1-82. Development Goal List in Classic View*

Here you will find the lone standard development plan-related report.

Now click "Goals" as shown in Figure 1-83.

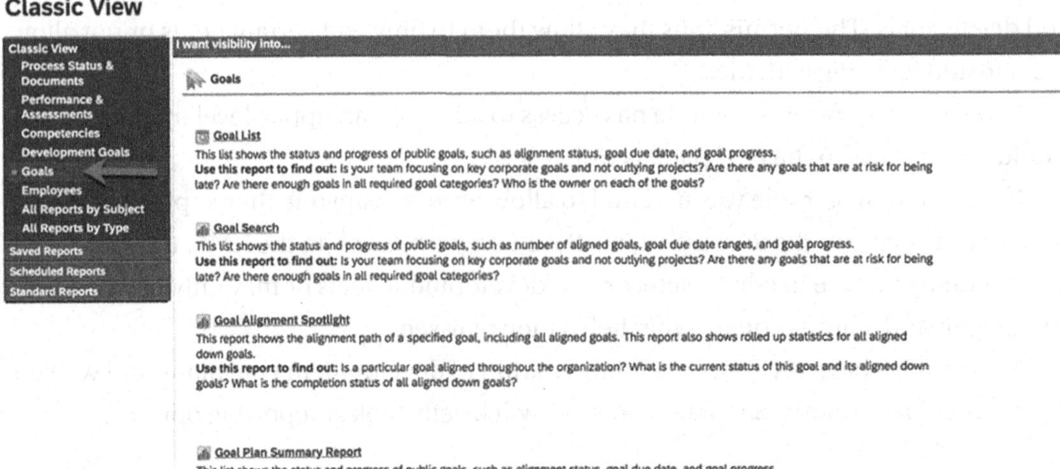


***Figure 1-83.*** *Goal List*

Many of the standard Goal Management reports may be used for development goal reporting. Within the report's filter options, select your development plan that you wish to report on.

Use the Goal Search report to report on learning activities. Select your development goal plan which contains learning activities and make sure your export options include activity-level data. However, when the Transcript feature is enabled, classic reports do not support reporting on learning activities.

# Reporting: Ad Hoc Reports

Ad hoc reporting can include learning activities and competencies with development goal plan data.

Use the Development Goal domain when creating ad hoc reports as shown in Figure 1-84.

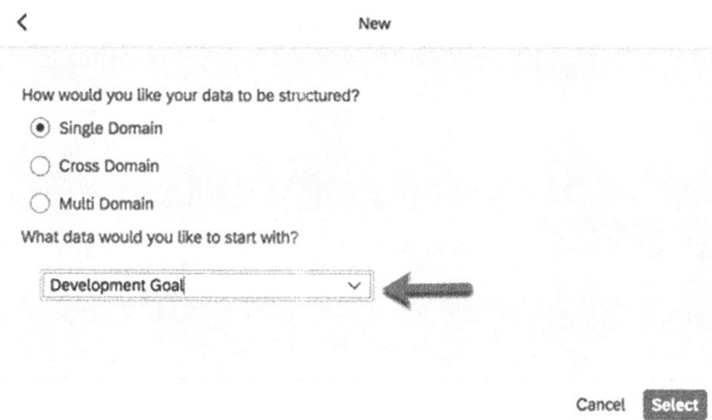


***Figure 1-84.** Ad Hoc Creation with the Development Goal Domain*

If ad hoc create permissions are granted for development goal data, HR managers or managers could create or run development plan ad hoc reports for their target groups.

As the admin, you could create ad hoc reports that would be available to HR managers and managers so they could run the development reports for their target groups. When walking through the wizard to create an ad hoc report, in the People tab, select "Logged In User" and the number of levels that the manager should have access to. An example is shown in Figure 1-85.

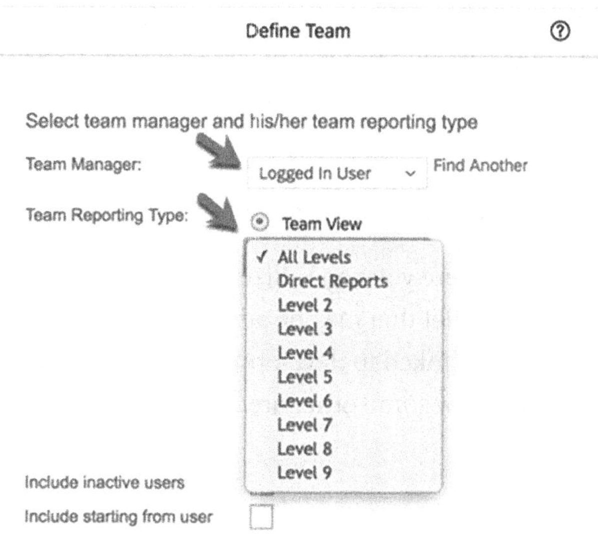


***Figure 1-85.** Select Reporting Type*

When a manager runs this report, the only results would be for the employees in their team.

There are many fields that may be reported on as seen in Figure 1-86.

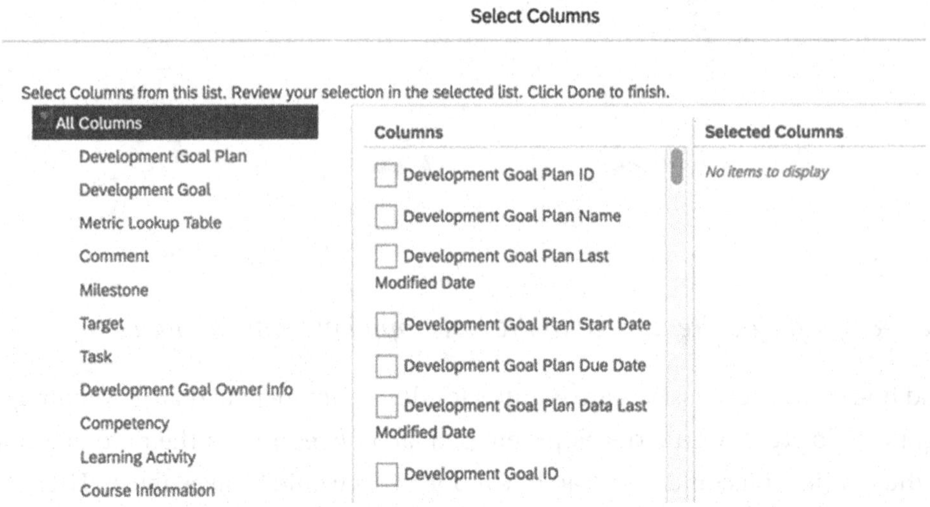

Select Columns

Select Columns from this list. Review your selection in the selected list. Click Done to finish.

All Columns
Development Goal Plan
Development Goal
Metric Lookup Table
Comment
Milestone
Target
Task
Development Goal Owner Info
Competency
Learning Activity
Course Information

Columns
Development Goal Plan ID
Development Goal Plan Name
Development Goal Plan Last Modified Date
Development Goal Plan Start Date
Development Goal Plan Due Date
Development Goal Plan Data Last Modified Date
Development Goal ID

Selected Columns
No items to display

***Figure 1-86.*** *Development Plan Fields*

Having ad hoc reports available to managers gives them an easy way to see which of their employees have created development goals and also to track the goal progress.

---

**Note** To learn more about ad hoc reporting, see SAP note #2536445.

---

# Additional Uses for Development Plans

There are many touchpoints where you can utilize development plan goal data. We have seen the Development Plan Portlet that may be added to People Profile and have seen how CPM achievements can be linked to development goals and appear on the user's development plan. We will review some other areas of integration.

# Integration with Performance Management Forms

Performance forms may be configured to include development goals. The inclusion would create a development plan section on the performance form. Development goals are not rated, but it can be helpful to incorporate this section into the performance form for planning. The user may add a development goal on their performance form, and it will flow to their development plan as well. An example is shown in Figure 1-87.

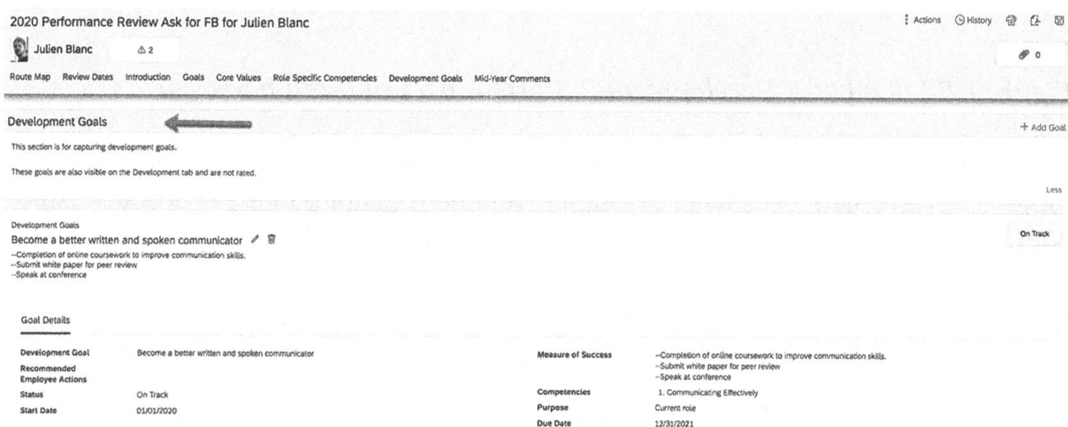


***Figure 1-87.*** *Performance Form with a Development Goals Section*

Refer back to Volume 1, Chapter 7 to review the setup required to incorporate development goals into the performance review template.

# Development Plan Integration with 360 Forms

360 forms can generate reports with references and links to development goals. When enabled in the form, the link will use the default development plan. The links are available for Rank View and Summary View. This functionality is not available for Blind Spots, Hidden Strengths, and Gap Analysis Views. For further information, refer to the Volume 1, Chapter 12.

# Development Plan Integration with Calibration

An employee's development plan may be viewed within a calibration session. In the List View as shown in Figure 1-88, clicking the "More" icon for an employee will display the options available.

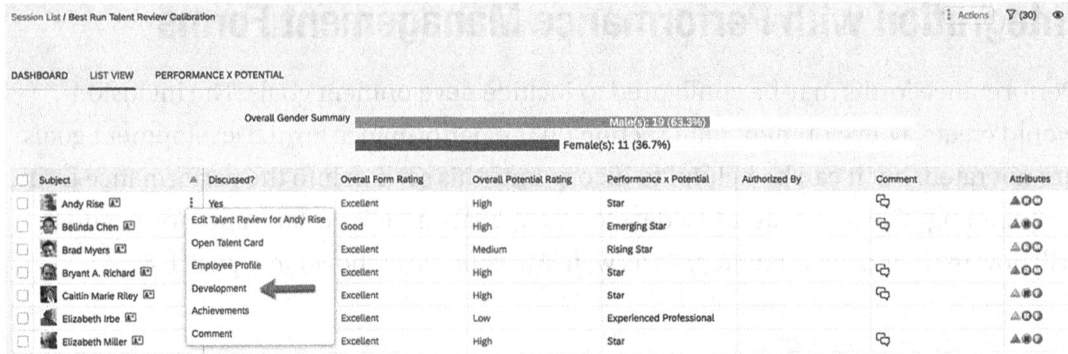


***Figure 1-88.*** *Link to a Development Plan Within a Calibration Session*

Clicking "Development" will create a popup window that displays the calibration subject's development plan. Refer to Chapter Volume 1, Chapter 14 to see how to enable this option.

# Career Development Plan Integration with Succession

Within the Succession module, the development plan may be viewed in the Successor card as shown in Figure 1-89.

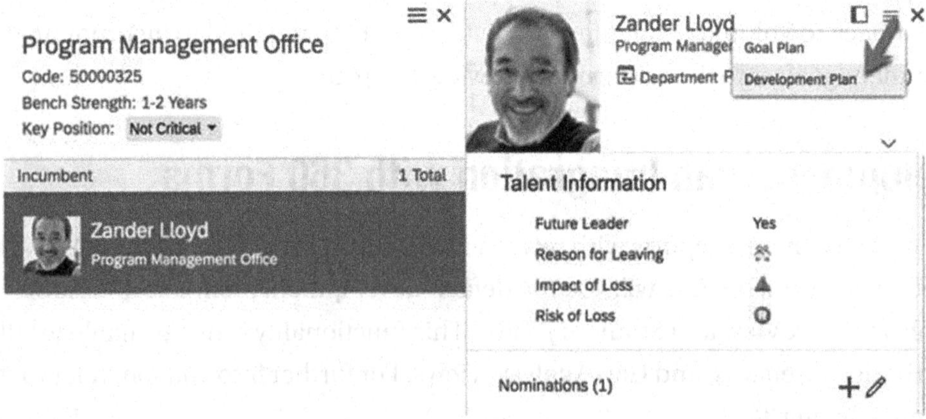


***Figure 1-89.*** *Link to a Development Plan from the Successor Card*

Refer to Chapter 6 to learn more about the configuration of the Successor card.

## Development Goals Tied to Competencies in Career Worksheet

As long as your development goal plan uses competencies, it is possible to add development goals to job role competencies found on a user's career worksheet as seen in Figure 1-90.

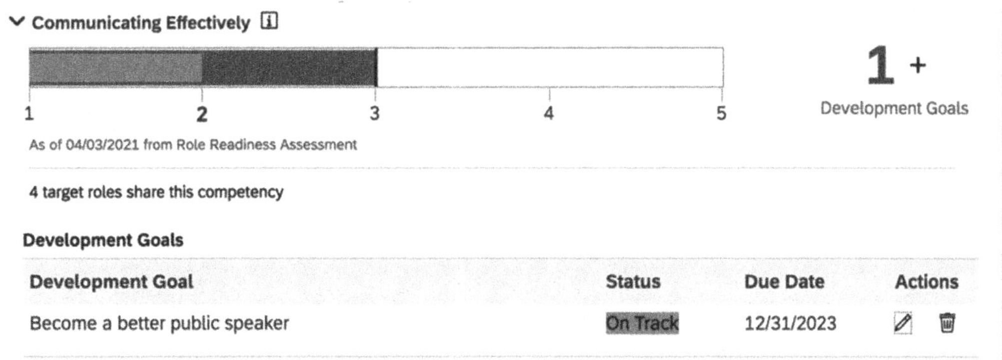


***Figure 1-90.*** *Development Goal Linked to a Competency on Career Worksheet*

A development goal added to a competency on the worksheet may then appear as a development goal on the user's plan with the competency associated with it.

You will learn more about this functionality in the Chapters 2 and 3.

# Conclusion

We hope you have enjoyed our journey through development plan creation. You should now know how to activate Career Development Planning in Provisioning, set up permissions to configure and administer development plans, create a basic development plan template, and directly edit the plan template XML. We have also seen how to use the development plan as a manager and employee. We have learned how to link competencies to development goals and create custom learning activities. We saw how the LMS catalog may be used to create learning activities tied to development goals. We saw how development plans may be integrated within other areas of Performance Management, including Continuous Performance Management, Calibration, People Profile, and Succession. We reviewed the standard reports available for development plan reporting and saw how to create ad hoc reports for development plans. In the next chapter, we will step into another feature of Career Development Planning which utilizes development goals to help plan for future roles.

CHAPTER 2

# Configuring Career Worksheets

In the previous chapter, we briefly touched upon the features available within the SAP SuccessFactors Career Development module. Development Plan, Career Worksheet, Career Path, and mentoring are available when CDP Full is enabled in Provisioning.

In this chapter, we will first learn what a career worksheet is and what its interdependencies are, and then we will focus on the administrative tasks for Career Worksheet. We will enable Career Worksheet and create the necessary configuration and permissions for this career planning tool. We will learn how to create career paths and explore the settings for suggested job roles. We will review the process to add expected ratings to job role competencies. We will look at how to create the Role Readiness Assessment form. We will explore the use of job role competencies with development goals and how they interact with the career worksheet. We will also learn what is needed to evaluate an employee's readiness for future roles. Finally, we will touch briefly on Career Explorer. This new feature is only available in the Early Adopter Care (EAC) program at this time.

## What Is a Career Worksheet?

Career Worksheet is a tool which provides users with a view of career progression opportunities by looking at job roles, suggested roles, and career paths. This tool helps an employee proactively plan for and be ready for future roles. It is a vehicle to view job roles and the competencies required to perform these job roles. An employee may target job roles to grow into and focus their development efforts on preparing for these future roles. Easy to implement and manage, the use of Career Worksheet may boost employee engagement and retention.




S. Traynor et al., *SAP SuccessFactors Talent: Volume 2*, https://doi.org/10.1007/978-1-4842-6995-4_2

Career Worksheet is heavily dependent upon job roles with mapped competencies. Competencies can be mapped to job roles by using Job Profile Builder or via legacy Families and Roles. A job role may have multiple competencies, and for Career Worksheet, each competency must have an expected rating. The expected rating for each competency identifies the score that constitutes mastery of a competency.

The career worksheet calculates employee readiness for a role by evaluating the employee's rated competencies against the competencies mapped to the future role. Competency ratings may come from the most recent completed PM or 360 form or from a role readiness form which an employee may launch from the worksheet. Based on a calculation using actual ratings against expected ratings, a readiness meter displays a percentage of how ready an employee is to step into the future role.

The worksheet also identifies competency gaps which highlight development areas that the employee needs to work on. Based on the gaps, the employee may create development goals aimed at attaining proficiency for the competencies needed for a new role.

A sample career worksheet is shown in Figure 2-1.

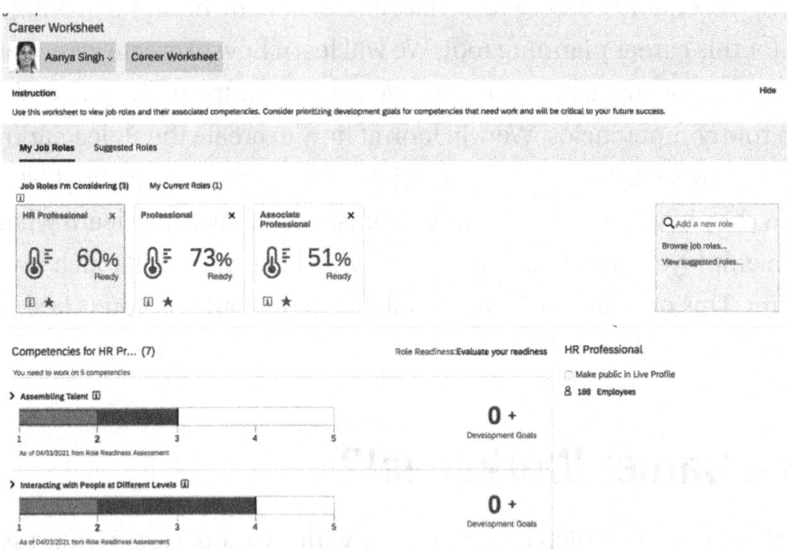


***Figure 2-1.*** *Sample Career Worksheet*

On the career worksheet, the employee may browse job roles, view suggested roles, or view career paths. Regardless of the method, the employee will be able to see the job description and the competencies linked to the job roles. This will give them a glimpse of the job responsibilities and skills to determine if this a role they may wish to strive for.

In the coming pages, we will walk through the settings to enable in Company Settings. Next, we will set up the role-based permissions for the admin role. We will also learn how to create career paths, add a Career Goals block to People Profile, create a role readiness form, and add expected ratings to competencies.

# Provisioning Settings

There are some settings to enable in Provisioning in order to use Career Worksheet and Career Path. In order for Career Worksheet to function properly, there are some Company Settings prerequisites that we need to check first:

1. A competency library is required since Career Worksheet relies on competencies mapped to job roles. You may use the SuccessFactors 2.1 Competency Library as shown in Figure 2-2, or you may create a custom competency library.

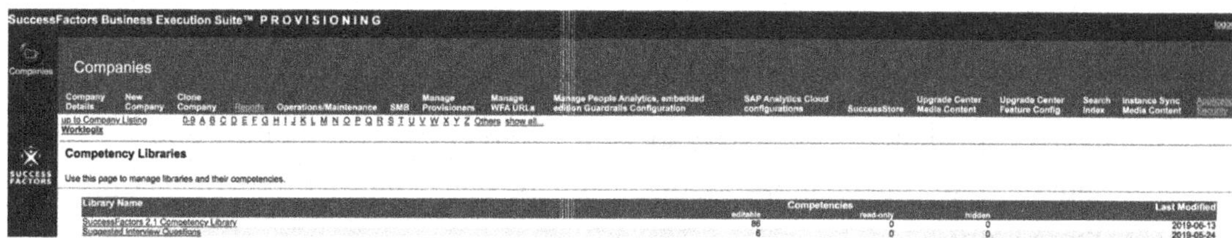

***Figure 2-2.** Competency Libraries in Provisioning*

Next, we will go into Company Settings to verify some settings are enabled.

2. The Development Plan settings should already be enabled. Within Company Settings, find the Goal Frameworks section to verify.

   Under Career & Development Planning, "CDP Full (Development Plan)" and "Development Plan V12" should be enabled. "Transcript" would have been enabled as well if you are using learning activities in your development plans.

   The Development Plan Settings are shown in Figure 2-3.

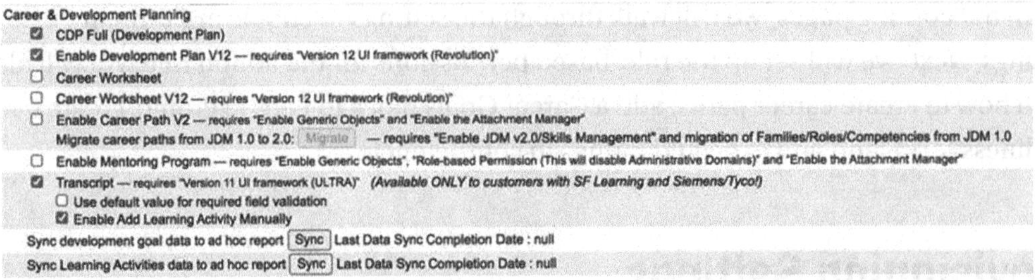

***Figure 2-3.*** *Career & Development Planning Features in Company Settings*

3. Verify "Enable the Attachment Manager," "Enable Generic Objects," "Version 12 UI Framework (Revolution)," and "JDM v.2/ Skills Management" are enabled as well.

4. Check to see if "Employee Directory" is enabled. If it is, this may help you decide on a setting in the Career Worksheet template XML that we will discuss later in this chapter.

## Company Settings to Enable

Now we are ready to enable Career Worksheet and Career Path within the Career Development module. Shown in the following are the paths within Company Settings to enable them both:

- Goal Frameworks ➤ My Goals Tab
- Goal Frameworks ➤ Career & Development Planning ➤ Career Worksheet V12
- Goal Frameworks ➤ Career & Development Planning ➤ Career Worksheet
- Goal Frameworks ➤ Career & Development Planning ➤ Enable Career Path V2
- Goal Frameworks ➤ Career & Development Planning ➤ Enable Career Path

Enabling "Career Worksheet V12" will also enable "Career Worksheet." Similarly, enabling "Career Path V2" will enable "Career Path."

We will also need to enable "My Goals Tab" also found with the Goal Frameworks section of Company Settings.

If you are using ad hoc reporting in your instance, there are some limited Career Worksheet reporting capabilities. To allow reporting on the targeted roles users have on their career worksheets, go to "Analytics and Dashboard Tabs & Misc Reporting" and enable the following:

- Additional Adhoc Sub domain Schemas Configuration ➤ Career Worksheet Targeted Roles
- Enable INCLUDE STARTING FROM USER in people pill ➤ Career Worksheet Targeted Roles

Once these settings have been updated and saved, back out of Company Settings. Next, we will need to head to another area in Provisioning to download the Career Worksheet template.

# Career Worksheet XML

Because the Career Worksheet template is not available in the instance, we will need to download the template XML in order to make updates such as selecting features to turn on, changing labels, and setting action and field permissions. Once the updates are made, the file will be imported back into Provisioning.

Go to "Managing Plan Template" as seen in Figure 2-4. This is where the goal and development goal plan templates are found, and most recently discussed in Chapter 1.

**Managing Plan Template**

Import/Update/Export Objective Plan Template
Import/Update/Export Variable Pay Objective Plan Template
Import/Update/Export Development Plan Templates
Import/Update/Export Learning Activities Templates
Import/Update/Export Career Worksheet Templates

***Figure 2-4.*** *Plan Templates in Provisioning*

Locate and click the link "Import/Update/Export Career Worksheet Templates." Here, you will find the starter Career Worksheet template XML.

As seen in Figure 2-5, the screen to download and upload the Career Worksheet template XML displays. You will need to export the template XML. Your web browser will download the file to your local machine.

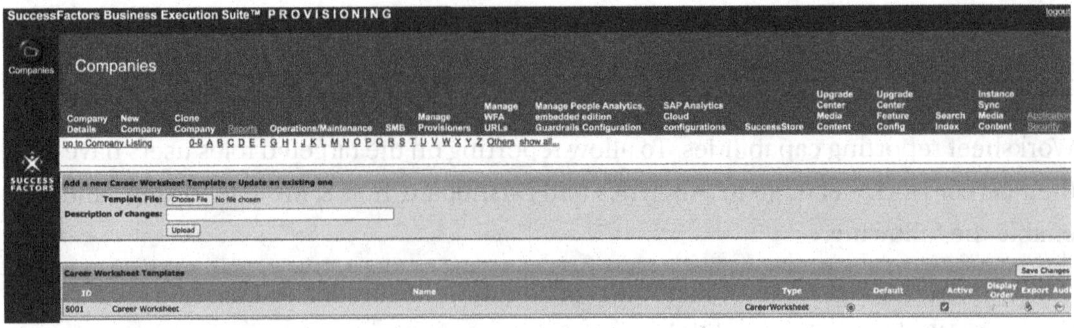

***Figure 2-5.*** *Screen to Export and Import the Career Worksheet Template XML*

It is unlikely, but if the Career Worksheet template is not displayed here, go to the CDP Implementation Guide which contains starter template samples. The guide contains a Career Worksheet template XML that you may copy into your XML editor. From there, you can make updates to the file and then import the XML into Provisioning. Another method to access a starter template would be to export the Career Worksheet template XML in Provisioning from a sales demo system and then import it into Provisioning for your environment.

Now that the template is downloaded, let's open it in the XML editor and take a look at the components of Career Worksheet and learn what options can be modified.

These are the elements that may be updated in the Career Worksheet template XML:

- Removal of fields (gap_graph in particular)
- Field labels
- Function and field permissions
- Rating scale id
- Limit on the number of targeted roles that a user may select
- Switches

Before we get too far in our discussion, here are some points to note when using Career Worksheet:

- There can only be one active Career Worksheet template.
- Field ids on the Career Worksheet template may not be modified.
- Categories cannot be used on the Career Worksheet template XML.

- Custom fields cannot be created on the Career Worksheet template XML.
- No "Write" permissions may be granted on the Career Worksheet template XML.
- Only ratings from completed forms are displayed in the career worksheet.
- Development goals may be used on the career worksheet to add goals to competencies and to provide a count of the number of development goals tied to a competency.
- Career Worksheet may only be linked to a single Career Development Planning template.
- The career worksheet uses the default development plan to list the development goals associated with a competency.
- Development goal permissions are based on the action and role permissions on the development goal plan XML.

Take a look at the first section of the XML. The <obj-plan-template> tag is the highest-level tag in the XML structure. It defines a series of options that can be turned on or off. This is the same tag you will find in the XML for goal and development plan templates, but there is one attribute specific to the worksheet that may be modified.

An example code segment is shown in the following:

```
<?xml version="1.0" encoding="UTF-8"?>
<!DOCTYPE obj-plan-template PUBLIC "-//SuccessFactors, Inc.//DTD Objective
Template 4.0//EN" "objective-template_4_0.dtd">
<obj-plan-template spellchk="false" new-obj-share-status-public="false"
instructions-viewdefault="on" alerts-viewdefault="on" cascade-parent-
viewdefault="off" cascade-child-viewdefault="off" pager-max-objs-per-
page="0" pager-max-page-links="0" pager-max-children-per-parent="-1"
display-alignment-format="names" more-details-child-format="original"
share-confirm="false" unshare-confirm="false" allow-group-goal="false"
goal-tree-link="true" expand-collapse-categories="false" use-text-for-
privacy="false" cws-people-role="true" overwrite-target-population="true"
swap-goal-link="false" learning-activity-deep-link="true" show-total-
goalscore="false" show-goal-id="false">
```

Within the tag, the "cws-people-role" attribute is set to "true" by default. This setting allows an indicator to show the number of employees who hold a targeted role on the career worksheet. If Employee Directory is enabled in Company Settings, there will be a link in the worksheet to show the names of the employees who hold the targeted role.

If you do not wish to show the names of the job role holders on the worksheet, change "cws-people-role" to "false". You will still see the employee count but will not see the names of those who hold the job role.

There should not be any other attribute changes needed for the <obj-plan-template> tag.

Just like the goal and development plan template XML, there are a series of elements that follow the tag. The template ID for the Career Worksheet template must fall within the range 5001–5099 and is typically 5001. The plan type must be CareerWorksheet. The only changes that you may wish to make are to the plan start date <obj_plan_start> and due date <obj_plan_due>.

An example code segment is shown in the following:

```
<obj-plan-id>5001</obj-plan-id>
 <obj-plan-type>CareerWorksheet</obj-plan-type>
 <obj-plan-name>Career Worksheet</obj-plan-name>
 <obj-plan-desc><![CDATA[Example Career Worksheet]]></obj-plan-desc>
 <obj-plan-lastmodified>5/23/19 5:38 PM</obj-plan-lastmodified>
 <obj-plan-start>01/01/2019</obj-plan-start>
 <obj-plan-due>12/31/2021</obj-plan-due>
```

Since development plans typically span years, it is recommended to use the same start and due dates as the development goal plan.

There are some additional tags that may be added to the Career Worksheet template XML.

If behaviors are defined for your job role competencies, you may use a behavior readiness rating in the calculation in the career worksheet. Shown in the following is the behavior tag to use:

```
<behaviors hide="false" hide-ratings="false" use-in-readiness="true"/>
```

Here is an example of the behavior tag when behavior readiness is not used in the calculation and not showing in the career worksheet:

```
<behaviors hide="true" hide-ratings="true" use-in-readiness="false"/>
```

This tag may follow *<text-replacement>* tags and precedes the field-definition tags.

## Data Source for Role Readiness Calculation

Competency ratings for a job role are the driver of Career Worksheet and indicate how ready an employee is to step into their next role. The data source for the ratings must be defined for Career Worksheet to calculate readiness for the targeted role.

The default source for the employee's current competency ratings is a completed performance review form or 360 review form. However, you may identify a specific form or forms as the source of the existing competency ratings. Additionally, there is an option within the career worksheet that enables an employee to select a targeted role and then launch a Role Readiness Assessment form which is used to rate the user's proficiency of competencies for a targeted role.

In either case, to identify the rating source, the *<assessment-filter>* filter should be added to the Career Worksheet template XML if you are using ratings from a form. The form template ID must be referenced. You may find the form IDs in Provisioning under Form Template Administration as shown in Figure 2-6.

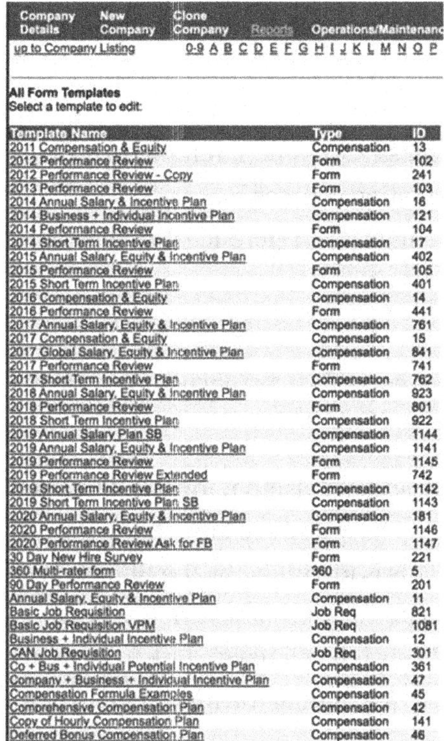


**All Form Templates**
Select a template to edit:

| Template Name | Type | ID |
|---|---|---|
| 2011 Compensation & Equity | Compensation | 13 |
| 2012 Performance Review | Form | 102 |
| 2012 Performance Review - Copy | Form | 241 |
| 2013 Performance Review | Form | 103 |
| 2014 Annual Salary & Incentive Plan | Compensation | 16 |
| 2014 Business + Individual Incentive Plan | Compensation | 121 |
| 2014 Performance Review | Form | 104 |
| 2014 Short Term Incentive Plan | Compensation | 17 |
| 2015 Annual Salary, Equity & Incentive Plan | Compensation | 402 |
| 2015 Performance Review | Form | 105 |
| 2015 Short Term Incentive Plan | Compensation | 401 |
| 2016 Compensation & Equity | Compensation | 14 |
| 2016 Performance Review | Form | 441 |
| 2017 Annual Salary, Equity & Incentive Plan | Compensation | 761 |
| 2017 Compensation & Equity | Compensation | 15 |
| 2017 Global Salary, Equity & Incentive Plan | Compensation | 841 |
| 2017 Performance Review | Form | 741 |
| 2017 Short Term Incentive Plan | Compensation | 762 |
| 2018 Annual Salary, Equity & Incentive Plan | Compensation | 923 |
| 2018 Performance Review | Form | 801 |
| 2018 Short Term Incentive Plan | Compensation | 922 |
| 2019 Annual Salary Plan SB | Compensation | 1144 |
| 2019 Annual Salary, Equity & Incentive Plan | Compensation | 1141 |
| 2019 Performance Review | Form | 1145 |
| 2019 Performance Review Extended | Form | 742 |
| 2019 Short Term Incentive Plan | Compensation | 1142 |
| 2019 Short Term Incentive Plan SB | Compensation | 1143 |
| 2020 Annual Salary, Equity & Incentive Plan | Compensation | 181 |
| 2020 Performance Review | Form | 1146 |
| 2020 Performance Review Ask for FB | Form | 1147 |
| 30 Day New Hire Survey | Form | 221 |
| 360 Multi-rater form | 360 | 5 |
| 90 Day Performance Review | Form | 201 |
| Annual Salary, Equity & Incentive Plan | Compensation | 11 |
| Basic Job Requisition | Job Req | 821 |
| Basic Job Requisition VPM | Job Req | 1081 |
| Business + Individual Incentive Plan | Compensation | 12 |
| CAN Job Requisition | Job Req | 301 |
| Co + Bus + Individual Potential Incentive Plan | Compensation | 361 |
| Company + Business + Individual Incentive Plan | Compensation | 47 |
| Compensation Formula Examples | Compensation | 45 |
| Comprehensive Compensation Plan | Compensation | 42 |
| Copy of Hourly Compensation Plan | Compensation | 141 |
| Deferred Bonus Compensation Plan | Compensation | 46 |

***Figure 2-6.*** *Form Templates with IDs*

To use multiple competency rating sources, the form IDs should be listed separated by commas. In the cases where multiple forms are included, the system will use the ratings from the most recently completed form:

```
<assessment-filters>
        <include-form-ids lang="en_US">5,1146,1147</include-form-ids>
</assessment-filters>
```

For each language your form uses, you will need a separate *<include-form-ids>* filter ID. Shown in the following is an example segment of code where ratings from multiple forms are being used and for multiple languages:

```
<assessment-filters>
        <include-form-ids lang="en_US">5,1146,1147</include-form-ids>
        <include-form-ids lang="en_GB">5,1146,1147</include-form-ids>
        <include-form-ids lang="fr_FR">5,1146,1147</include-form-ids>
</assessment-filters>
```

If you plan to allow users to self-assess using the Role Readiness Assessment form, include the *<self-assessment>* tag with the form template ID. We have not discussed the Role Readiness template yet, but if Career Worksheet is enabled in Provisioning, you will see the standard Role Readiness Assessment template in Form Template Administration just like the IDs for the form rating sources.

An example code segment used to reference the Role Readiness Assessment form ID is shown in the following:

```
<self-assessment>
  <each-assessment lang="en_US">101</each-assessment>
</self-assessment>
```

Normally the Role Readiness Assessment form is launched for a targeted role. However, it is now possible to allow users to launch the Role Readiness Assessment form for their current role. This is identified by the filter *<current-self-assessment>*. It will reference the same form IDs as the <self-assessment> filter.

The "My Current Roles" sub-tab will have a link to evaluate readiness based on the employee's current job role when adding the filter seen in the following code segment:

```
<current-self-assessment>
   <current-each-assessment lang="en_US">101</current-each-assessment>
 </current-self-assessment>
```

The correct order for these tags is contained in the following code example:

```
<text-replacement for="Instructions">
    <text><![CDATA[Use this worksheet to view job roles and their
associated competencies. Consider prioritizing development goals
for competencies that need work and will be critical to your future
success.]]></text>
</text-replacement>
<behaviors hide="true" hide-ratings="true" use-in-readiness="false"/>
<self-assessment>
  <each-assessment lang="en_US">101</each-assessment>
</self-assessment>
<current-self-assessment>
   <current-each-assessment lang="en_US">101</current-each-assessment>
</current-self-assessment>
```

## Switches

There are a series of switches that may be added after these elements in the XML. Switches are used to turn features off or on. The switches that may be used in the Career Worksheet template are shown in Table 2-1.

***Table 2-1.*** *Summary of Career Worksheet XML Switches*

| Switch | Description | Default |
|---|---|---|
| cws-dispoption-competency-desc | To display the competency description for each role. Set as "on." | Off |
| disable-jpb-profile-in-cws | Set as "off "in order to see the job profile description for a role. | On |
| hide-position-count | To hide the open position count for a role. Only applicable when True Position Hierarchy is turned on in Provisioning. | Off |
| new-role-readiness-calculation | To identify how role readiness is calculated: sum or average. When "on," readiness is based on average. | Off |
| show-self-assessment-in-current-role-tab | To allow employees to launch Role Readiness Assessment forms for their current roles in their career worksheets. | Off |

An example code segment for switches in the Career Worksheet template XML is shown in the following:

```
<switches>
    <switch for="cws-dispoption-competency-desc" value="on" />
    <switch for="disable-jpb-profile-in-cws" value="off" />
    <switch for="hide-position-count" value="on" />
    <switch for="new-role-readiness-calculation" value="on" />
     <switch for="show-self-assessment-in-current-role-tab" value="on" />
 </switches>
```

Now we will look closer at each switch and what feature it controls.

```
<switch for="cws-dispoption-competency-desc" value="on" />
```

This switch regulates whether or not the details for a targeted role's competency will display. If you wish to turn on the switch to see the competency descriptions, you need to have the descriptions created for each competency. You could manually add descriptions to each competency or use a mass upload of competencies with their descriptions. This may be done using Manage Job Profile Contents Import/Export which will be explained later in this chapter.

When the switch is set to "on," the description for each competency may be viewed by mouse hovering over the info icon on the career worksheet.

```
<switch for="disable-jpb-profile-in-cws" value="off" />
```

This switch is used when Job Profile Builder is enabled with defined job profiles. When this switch is set to "off," the job profile details for the targeted role display.

```
<switch for="hide-position-count" value="on" />
```

This switch shows how many open positions exist for a targeted role.

By default, the open position count displays. The openings are linked to Succession positions, not RCM requisitions. However, the open position count only works for the legacy position nomination method and when True Position Hierarchy is turned on in Provisioning. It is not supported for MDF positions.

To hide the open position count, the switch should be included with the value set to "on." If the switch is not set and you are not using the legacy position nomination method, the open position count will be visible with 0 openings.

```
<switch for="new-role-readiness-calculation" value="on" />
```

This switch is used to define how to calculate readiness for a role. Readiness may be calculated as the sum of the ready competencies or by averaging competency readiness. When this switch is set to "yes," the readiness calculation is proportional (average). If no switch is defined, the default value is "off" which uses summing as the calculation type.

## Types of Readiness Calculations

Since we just introduced the switch used to identify the role readiness calculation type, let's dig deeper.

Both summing and averaging use the employee's latest competency ratings which may come from a performance review form or the average rating from 360 reviews, a specified form or forms, or the Role Readiness Assessment form.

We will look at both types of readiness calculations so you may decide which to use. We will start with summing.

## Summing

The system first checks an employee's readiness rating for each competency for the targeted role. An employee is "ready" for a targeted role's competency if their current competency rating is equal to or greater than the expected rating. If the employee does not have a competency that is needed for the targeted role, the employee is "not ready" for the competency.

Then readiness is calculated as (number of competencies the employee is ready for)/(total number of required competencies) %.

## Averaging

Readiness is based on the calculation of an employee's readiness for each of the targeted role's competencies. Then an average of these ratings is calculated to determine readiness. The calculations use the rating scale defined in the XML:

- If the rating for a competency meets or exceeds the expected competency rating, the competency readiness is 100%.
- If the employee's current rating on the targeted role's competency is lower than the expected rating, the competency readiness is calculated using the following formula:

  (Current rating - lowest rating in the rating scale)/(Expected competency rating - lowest rating in the rating scale) %.

- If a competency doesn't have an expected rating or the employee doesn't have a rating for the competency, the readiness for that competency is 0.

Next, the percentages are added up and divided by the total number of competencies for the targeted role to arrive at the role readiness percentage.

This method may not be the most accurate because if a competency doesn't have an expected rating or the employee doesn't have a rating for the competency, the average calculation will be skewed.

```
<switch for="show-self-assessment-in-current-role-tab" value="on" />
```

Prior to the Q4 2019 release, if an employee wanted to launch a Role Readiness Assessment form for their current role, it was done in Performance Management. Now an employee may launch the Role Readiness Assessment form for their current role directly in their career worksheet. Turning the switch on will create a link in the My Current Roles tab to evaluate readiness.

This switch has to be used in conjunction with the *<current-self-assessment>* tag which identifies the Role Readiness Assessment form to launch.

Now that we have reviewed the switches available for the career worksheet, let's look at one additional option.

Following the switches, you may limit the number of targeted roles that a user may consider. This is done using the *<max-per-category>* attribute within *<category-config>* and follows the switches as seen in the example code segment shown in the following:

```
<switches>
    <switch for="cws-dispoption-competency-desc" value="on" />
    <switch for="disable-jpb-profile-in-cws" value="off" />
    <switch for="show-self-assessment-in-current-role-tab" value="on" />
  </switches>
<category-config>
  <max-per-category>5</max-per-category>
</category-config>
```

If an employee tries to add more targeted roles than the maximum allowed, an error message will display, and the user will not be able to proceed unless removing some existing targeted roles before trying to add another.

For performance reasons, it is best to limit the number of roles that an employee may select as future roles to no more than 20.

## Permissions on the Career Worksheet Template XML

Access to Career Worksheet and specific career worksheet plans is controlled by role-based permissions in the instance. Permissions to view, add, or remove targeted job roles in the career worksheet along with the Read permissions of certain fields in the career worksheet are controlled within the Career Worksheet template XML .

Let's review the permissions and field definitions section of the Career Worksheet template XML. We will start by looking at the actions/roles to define which apply to the "Job Roles I'm Considering" sub-tab as seen in Figure 2-7.

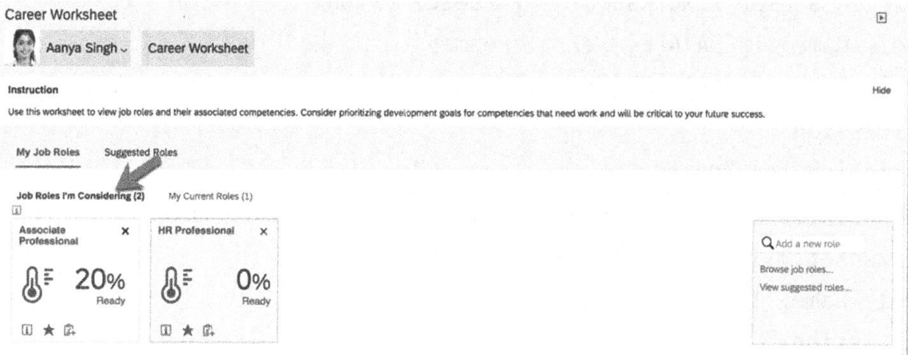


***Figure 2-7.** Job Roles I'm Considering View of Career Worksheet*

Action permissions define what functions a role may perform in the career worksheet. The actions are described in the following:

- **Private-access** grants permissions to view the targeted roles in the Job Roles I'm Considering section of the career worksheet.
- **Create** grants permission to add targeted roles and is needed to have access to the Suggested Roles tab.
- **Delete** grants permission to delete any selected targeted role from the Job Roles I'm Considering sub-tab.

Shown in the following example code segment, an employee, their manager hierarchy, and HR manager may view the targeted roles. Only the employee and their manager may add targeted roles, and only the employee may delete a targeted role:

```
<permission for="private-access">
    <description><![CDATA[Employees, and their managers up the reporting
chain and HR reps may view unshared/private roles.]]></description>
    <role-name><![CDATA[E]]></role-name>
    <role-name><![CDATA[EM+]]></role-name>
    <role-name><![CDATA[EH]]></role-name>
  </permission>
  <permission for="create">
    <description><![CDATA[Only the employee, and their manager may add a
    role in a user's worksheet.]]></description>
    <role-name><![CDATA[E]]></role-name>
    <role-name><![CDATA[EM]]></role-name>
  </permission>
  <permission for="delete">
    <description><![CDATA[Only the employee may delete role in his/her
    worksheet.]]></description>
    <role-name><![CDATA[E]]></role-name>
  </permission>
```

In the example seen in Figure 2-8, there is an option to allow an employee to make their targeted role visible in People Profile.

Associate Professional

View Career Path

Make public in Live Profile

0 Employees

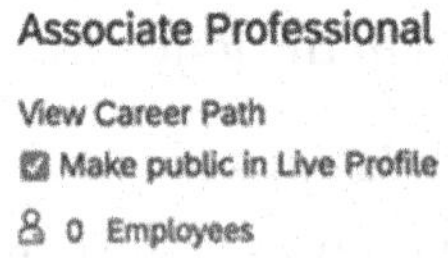

***Figure 2-8.*** *Checkbox to Make a Targeted Role Visible in People Profile*

The Share permissions must be enabled for at least the employee role. The "Share" permission is shown in the following sample code segment:

```
<permission for="share">
    <description><![CDATA[Only the employee may copy targeted roles to
    their live profile page.]]></description>
    <role-name><![CDATA[E]]></role-name>
  </permission>
```

If no roles are granted "share" access, the "Make public in Live Profile" link will not appear on the career worksheet. A sample code segment is shown in the following:

```
<permission for="share">
    <description><![CDATA[No roles may copy targeted roles to employee 's
    live profile page.]]></description>
    <role-name><![CDATA[ ]]></role-name>
  </permission>
```

Later in this chapter, we will review the additional steps to configure the Career Goals block in People Profile.

The "Move" permission is not applicable in the worksheet, so you may remove it from the template XML.

There are standard fields in the Roles I'm Considering sub-tab that we will review. Table 2-2 details the fields found in the template that define the detailed permissions for the targeted job roles. As mentioned earlier, the XML identifies the roles that can view, add, or remove targeted job roles of a user. With the exception of the readiness meter, all the fields are required. These fields are essential for what the worksheet is designed to do and should not be removed.

***Table 2-2.*** *Fields to Permit in the Job Roles I'm Considering Sub-tab*

| Field | Description |
|---|---|
| competency_name | Name of the competency associated with the job role. |
| last_rated_form | Name of the performance (or 360) form where the competency was last rated. |
| last_rated_date | Date of last competency rating. |
| last_rating | Latest rating of a competency on a job role. |
| gap_graph | Representation of expected competency rating vs. actual. May be removed from the XML. |
| development_goals | Development goals (if any) associated with the competency. |
| readiness_meter | Percentage ready for the targeted job role. |

We have made mention of the Role Readiness Assessment form, and if used, there is an additional update made to the last_rating field. The rating scale used in the career worksheet to calculate role readiness must be the same rating scale used in the Role Readiness Assessment form. If the rating scales do not match, the readiness meter will not populate.

An example code segment shown in the following displays the rating scale id field which needs to be identical to the rating scale id used in the PM template associated with the role readiness form:

```
<field-definition id="last_rating" type="number" required="true"
detail="true" viewdefault="on" showlabel="false" field-show-coaching-
advisor="false" cascade-update="push-down">
    <field-label>Last Rating</field-label>
    <field-format>#.#</field-format>
    <rating-scale rate-on-form-option="false" default="true">
      <rating-scale-id>Performance Rating Scale</rating-scale-id>
    </rating-scale>
  </field-definition>
```

The Role Readiness Assessment template XML must reference the same rating scale in the competency section as seen in the following code segment:

```
 <fm-sect-scale show-value="true">
    <scale-source>1</scale-source>
    <scale-id><![CDATA[Performance Rating Scale]]></scale-id>
    <scale-type><![CDATA[HORIZONTAL_RADIO]]></scale-type>
  </fm-sect-scale>
  <meta-grp-label><![CDATA[Group]]></meta-grp-label>
</competency-sect>
```

We will look at the Role Readiness Assessment form template XML later in this chapter.

# Template Fields on the Career Worksheet XML

We have now looked at the fields on the career worksheet. Things will make more sense with a view of portions of the career worksheet and where these fields are used. Refer back to Table 2-2 to review the template fields. Figure 2-9 shows where on the worksheet these fields are found.

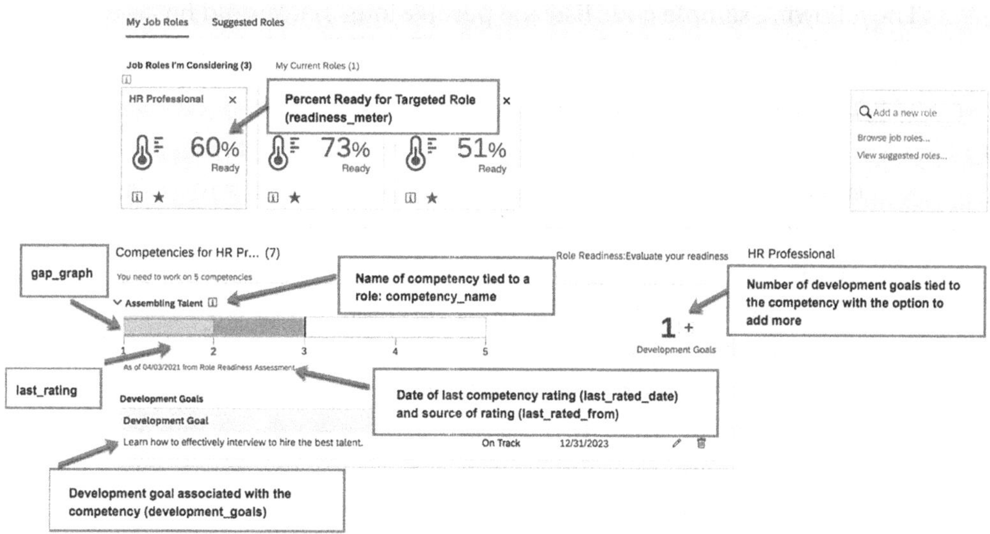


***Figure 2-9.*** *Overview of Career Worksheet Template Fields and Their Sources*

In addition to defining the template fields in the XML, you also need to identify which role(s) has visibility of these fields. "Write" permission is not supported in the worksheet, so you will only have to define "Read" permissions. The standard template permissions are probably very close to what you will need. Just make any modifications based on the permissions specific to your organization.

The following are some things to consider:

- Role-based career worksheet permissions do not work with a target population. If the user has access to Career Worksheet, the user will be able to search for other employees based on the User Search permission. This means a user in their own career worksheet could do a name search to access another employee's worksheet. In order to prevent this, grant "Read" permissions in the Career Worksheet template XML only to roles that should be able to view the employee's career worksheet.
- "Read" permissions should only be granted to the roles that should view any employee's career worksheet such as the employee, manager, and HR manager.

The following sample code lists the permissions that should be used for these fields:

```
<field-permission type="read">
    <description><![CDATA[Only the employee, and their
    managers up the reporting chain and HR reps may read
    any public field]]></description>
    <role-name><![CDATA[E]]></role-name>
    <role-name><![CDATA[EM+]]></role-name>
    <role-name><![CDATA[EH]]></role-name>
    <field refid="competency_name"/>
    <field refid="last_rated_form"/>
    <field refid="last_rated_date"/>
    <field refid="last_rating"/>
    <field refid="gap_graph"/>
    <field refid="development_goals"/>
    <field refid="readiness_meter"/>
  </field-permission>
```

- Since the succession planners usually will not have any kind of relationship to the successors they are nominating, it's recommended to allow visibility over the "readiness_meter" field for all roles (*). A sample code segment is shown in the following:

```
<field-permission type="read">
    <description><![CDATA[Everyone may read the
    readiness_meter field]]></description>
    <role-name><![CDATA[*]]></role-name>
    <field refid="readiness_meter"/>
  </field-permission>
```

- No one should be able to write to any career worksheet fields as seen in the following sample code segment:

```
<field-permission type="write">
  <description><![CDATA[No one can write to any fields]]>
  </description>
  <role-name><![CDATA[]]></role-name>
  <field refid="competency_name"/>
</field-permission>
```

# Adding a Development Goal to a Targeted Job Role Competency

If you are allowing a user to add a development goal to a targeted job role or current job role competency, the "development_goal" field must be included in the field definitions with Read permissions. The development plan must have the competency field defined as well.

The inclusion of the development_goal field in the Career Worksheet template XML will also enable the development goal count shown for each role competency as seen in Figure 2-10.

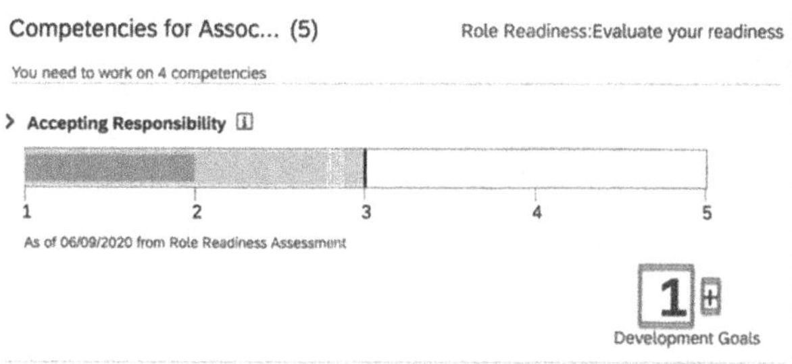


***Figure 2-10.*** *Adding a Development Goal a to Competency*

The plus sign icon allows the employee to add a development goal to a competency. The employee may create a development goal associated with a competency that they need to strengthen. For this to work, the development plan template must contain the competency field with permission to create a competency for a goal.

Any development goal added to a competency on the worksheet will then appear on the development plan along with the competency.

By default, the user "Read" and "Write" permissions for the development goal are derived from the development plan template configuration. You must make sure all roles that can see a user's career worksheet also have Read permissions for the development goal fields in the development plan XML. Without this permission, the role will not see the development goals on the career worksheet.

It is also possible to link development goals to behaviors on the career worksheet instead of using competencies. To do so, the development plan must be configured to use behaviors in the competency field. Refer to Chapter 1 to learn more.

Since a development goal can be linked to more than one competency, the same development goal may be counted more than once in the career worksheet. And the same development goal can be represented in more than one job role.

Once the Career Worksheet template XML updates are complete, save and import the file in Provisioning within Managing Plan Template ➤ Import/Update/Export Career Worksheet Templates.

We discussed the "Share" permission in the Career Worksheet template XML that allows the user to identify the targeted role as a career interest in People Profile. In order for this to work, an update is needed in the Succession Data Model. We will need to add the "preferredNextMove" background element in the data model. Go back into Provisioning to download the data model. Under Succession Management, click the link Import/Export Data Model as seen in Figure 2-11.

**Succession Management**

Pre-packaged Templates
Import/Export Data Model
Import/Export Country/Region Specific XML for Succession Data Model
Import/Export Corporate Data Model XML
Import/Export Country/Region Specific XML for Corporate Data Model
Update/Modify Templates
Edit Org Chart configuration
Edit Matrix Classifier configuration
Edit Position Tile Customize

***Figure 2-11.** Location of Data Models Within Provisioning Company Settings*

Download the data model file as seen in Figure 2-12.

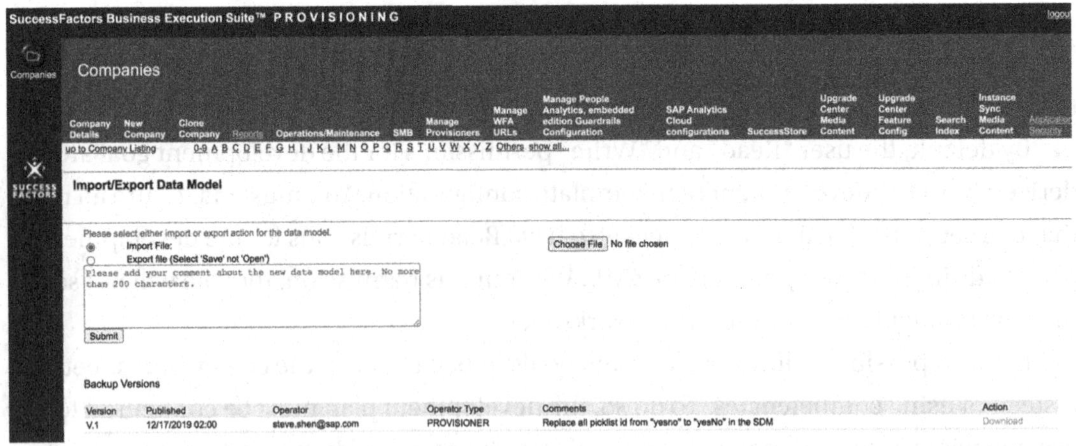


***Figure 2-12.** Import/Export Data Model Screen*

Open the file in an XML editor and look to see if the "preferredNextMove" background element is being used. If it is already in the data model, it may contain several fields that will not populate from the worksheet into the profile.

An example code segment for the background element is shown in the following:

```
<background-element id="preferredNextMove" type-id="40">
    <label>Preferred Next Move</label>
    <label xml:lang="en-US">Preferred Next Move</label>
    <data-field id="title" field-name="vfld1" required="true"
    max-length="4000" max-file-size-KB="1000">
      <label>Title</label>
      <label xml:lang="en-US">Title</label>
    </data-field>
    <data-field id="level" field-name="vfld5" max-length="4000"
    max-file-size-KB="1000">
      <label>Level</label>
      <label xml:lang="en-US">Level</label>
      <picklist id="lead_level"/>
    </data-field>
    <data-field id="function" field-name="vfld2" max-length="4000"
    max-file-size-KB="1000">
      <label>Function</label>
      <label xml:lang="en-US">Function</label>
      </data-field>
    <data-field id="timeframe" field-name="vfld3" max-length="4000"
    max-file-size-KB="1000">
      <label>Timeframe</label>
      <label xml:lang="en-US">Timeframe</label>
      <picklist id="lead_ready"/>
    </data-field>
    <data-field id="comments" field-name="vfld4" display-size="100"
    max-length="4000" max-file-size-KB="1000">
      <label>Comments</label>
      <label xml:lang="en-US">Comments</label>
    </data-field>
  </background-element>
```

There needs to be a "title" data-field defined within the background element. This is the only field used from the career worksheet to populate in the career interest block in People Profile.

If there are other fields included in the background element, they will not populate when clicking the checkbox on the career worksheet. These fields will appear empty in the block. The additional fields would only populate if the user added them within the profile. However, if you are allowing a user to update the block in the profile, you may include additional fields in the background element. For our purposes, we will just use the title field.

In either case, make sure title is a required field.

If this background element is in the data model but not being used, you may remove any other data fields as shown in the code segment sample. If it is not in the data model, you will need to add it and can use this same version.

An example code segment for the background element is shown in the following:

```
<background-element id="preferredNextMove" type-id="40">
    <label>Preferred Next Move</label>
    <label xml:lang="en-US">Preferred Next Move</label>
    <data-field id="title" field-name="vfld1" required="true" max-
    length="4000" max-file-size-KB="1000">
      <label>Title</label>
      <label xml:lang="en-US">Title</label>
    </data-field>
  </background-element>
```

An <element-template> for the background element needs to be included in the data model as well. A sample code element is shown in the following:

```
<edit-template id="preferredNextMove">
      <label>Preferred Next Move</label>
      <label xml:lang="en-US">Preferred Next Move</label>
      <description>Career Goals.</description>
      <background-element-ref refid="preferredNextMove"/>
</edit-template>
```

As mentioned earlier, when discussing action permissions in the Career Worksheet template XML, the share permission must be enabled for at least the employee role to add targeted roles to their profile.

Once the additions have been made, import the updated data model XML. When we get into the instance, we will review the role-based permissions for this background element and the People Profile updates to make.

We have now enabled Career Worksheet and Career Path in Provisioning. We have made updates to the Career Worksheet template XML to define the features, data sources, rating calculation type, and the action permissions for fields within the career worksheet. We have also updated the Succession Data Model XML in order to display targeted roles in People Profile. We are now ready to jump into the instance to set up role-based permissions.

## Role-Based Permissions for Career Worksheet and Career Path

In addition to the action and Read permissions that are set in the Career Worksheet template XML, role-based permissions are needed to grant users access to the Career Worksheet tab within Career Development and access to career worksheet plans. If you have decided to use Career Path, Suggested Roles, and the Role Readiness Assessment form, role-based permissions are needed for those as well. Our discussion will assume all of these features will be used because these give Career Worksheet all of its functionality.

We will start by granting administrator permissions to configure and manage the features of Career Worksheet. In Chapter 1, we discussed the admin role that will manage all Career Development–related features. This may be an HR admin role that handles everything Performance Management related or an admin permission role specific to managing Career Development. You may also consider allowing HR managers to create and manage career paths. We will discuss the HR manager role permissions later in this chapter.

# Assigning Permissions to Configure and Administer Career Worksheet

Go to "Manage Permission Roles" and select the admin role that you are adding these permissions to. Under the Administrator Permissions section of permission settings, find "Manage Career Development" as shown in Figure 2-13.

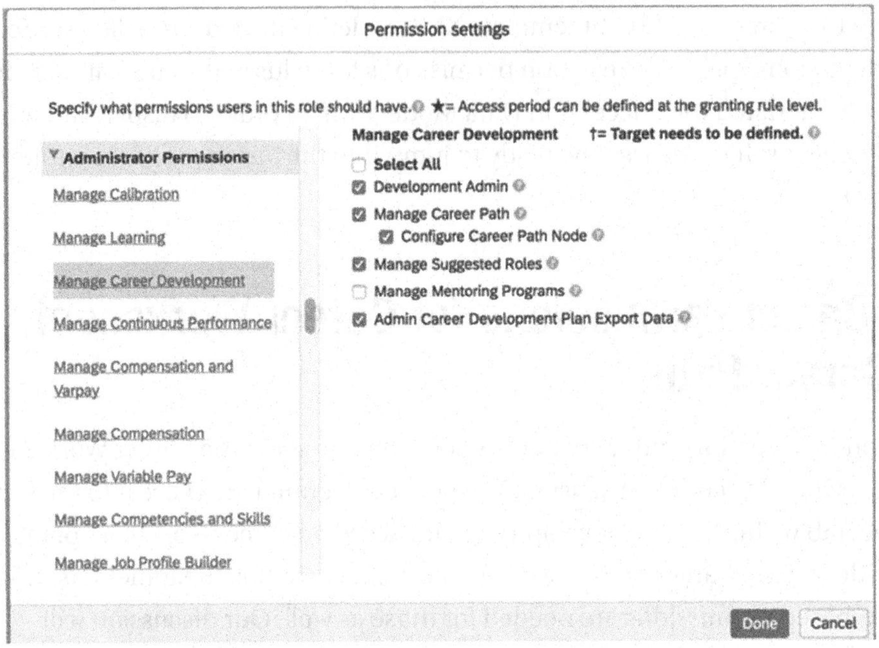

***Figure 2-13.** Manage Career Development Permissions*

"Development Admin" should already be enabled from our discussion in the previous chapter. We are now adding permission to "Manage Career Path," "Configure Career Path Node," and "Manage Suggested Roles."

Table 2-3 contains the Manage Career Development permissions. The highlighted permissions should be added to the admin role.

***Table 2-3.** Manage Career Development Permissions*

| Permission | Description |
|---|---|
| Development Admin | To manage all development plan settings. |
| Manage Career Path | To define and manage career paths. |
| Configure Career Path node | To define what appears on the node within a career path, only for Career Path V2. |
| Manage Suggested Roles | To configure Suggested Roles settings. |
| Manage Mentoring Programs | To manage mentoring programs. |
| Admin Career Development Plan Export Data | To export Career Development Plan data. |

We will need to add permissions found under the User Permissions section within Career Development Planning. Figure 2-14 shows the permissions in this section.

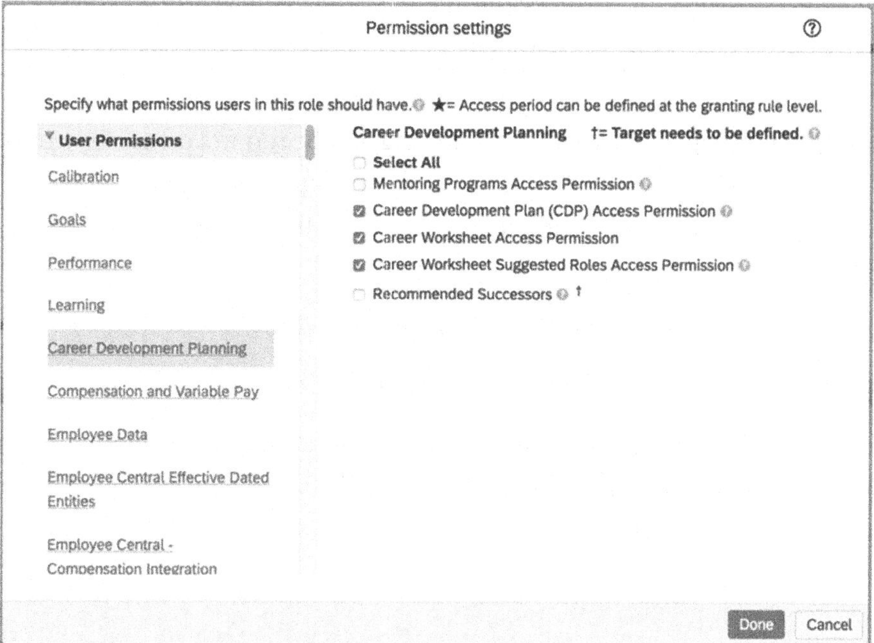


***Figure 2-14.** Career Development Planning Permissions*

The admin role should already have Career Development Plan (CDP) Access Permission. Now we will add Career Worksheet Access Permission and Career Worksheet Suggested Roles Access Permission to the role.

Table 2-4 highlights the additional permissions to grant within User Permissions ➤ Career Development Planning.

***Table 2-4.** Summary of Career Development Planning User Permissions*

| Permission | Description |
| --- | --- |
| Mentoring Programs Access Permission | Access to the Mentoring tab in Development. |
| Career Development Plan (CDP) Access Permission | Access to the Development module. |
| Career Worksheet Access Permission | Access to the Career Worksheet tab in Development. |
| Career Worksheet Suggested Roles Access Permission | Access to Suggested Roles within Career Worksheet in Development. |
| Recommended Successors | Allows access to the Recommended Successor section of the Succession Org Chart. |

If the admin is going to be creating or running ad hoc reports on career worksheet–related data, permission will be needed to create and run these reports.

Go to "Reports Permission" found in the User Permissions section and enable the following:

- Create Report ➤ Career Worksheet Targeted Role
- Run Report ➤ Career Worksheet Targeted Role

The role will also need access to the CDP Dashboard. Also found within Reports Permission, under Analytics Tiles and Dashboards, enable "CDP Dashboard".

Figure 2-15 shows the report access to add.

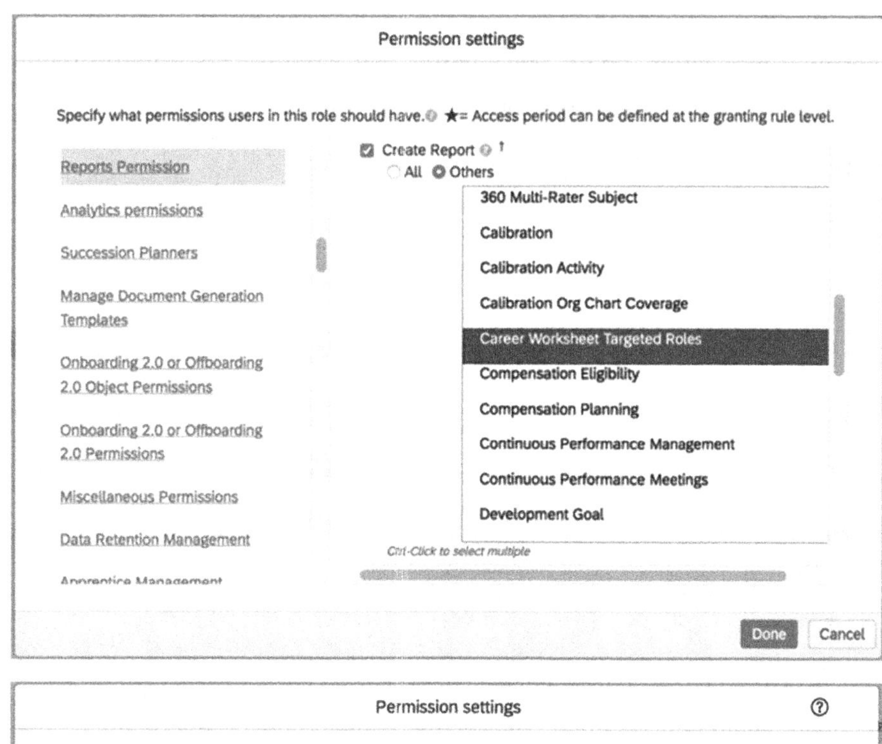


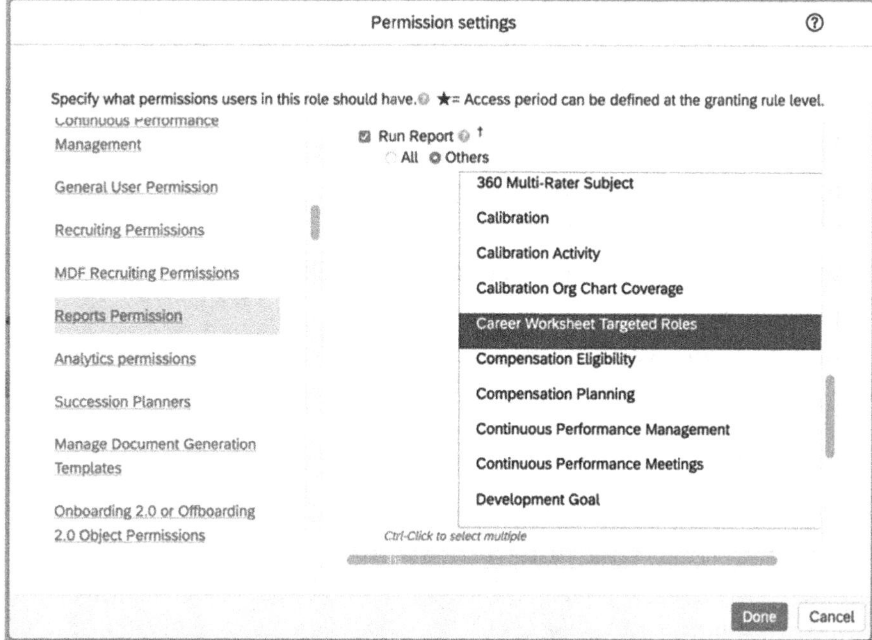


***Figure 2-15.*** *Create and Run Ad Hoc Reports Permissions*

The admin will also need access to create and view career paths. Found under the User Permissions section, go to "Miscellaneous Permissions". Scroll through the permissions to find "Career Path" as shown in Figure 2-16.

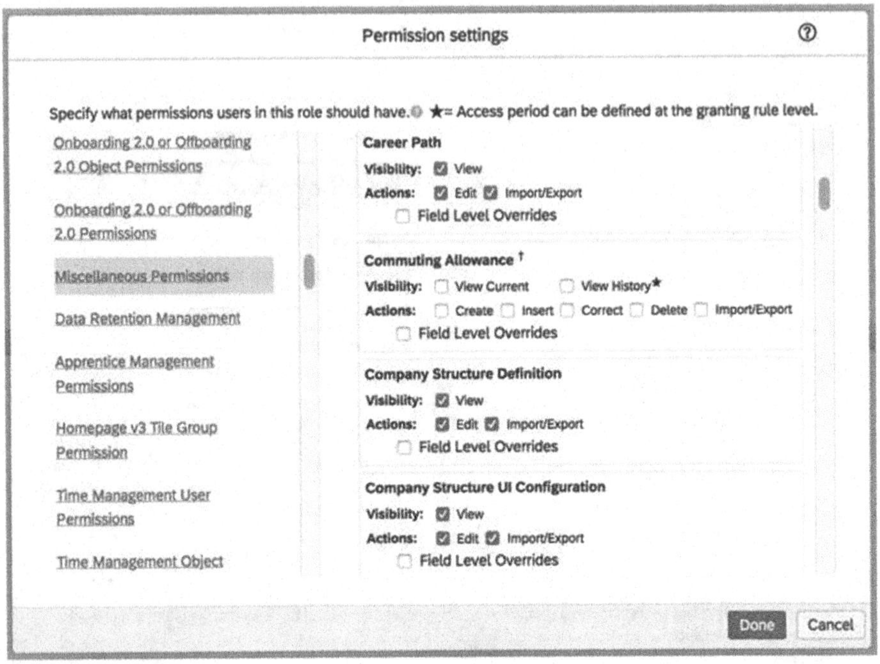

***Figure 2-16.*** *Miscellaneous Permissions to View and Edit Career Paths*

For Career Path, enable the "View" option for Visibility. Enable "Edit" and "Import/Export Actions" options.

Finally, add the Career Worksheet goal plan permissions as seen in Figure 2-17.

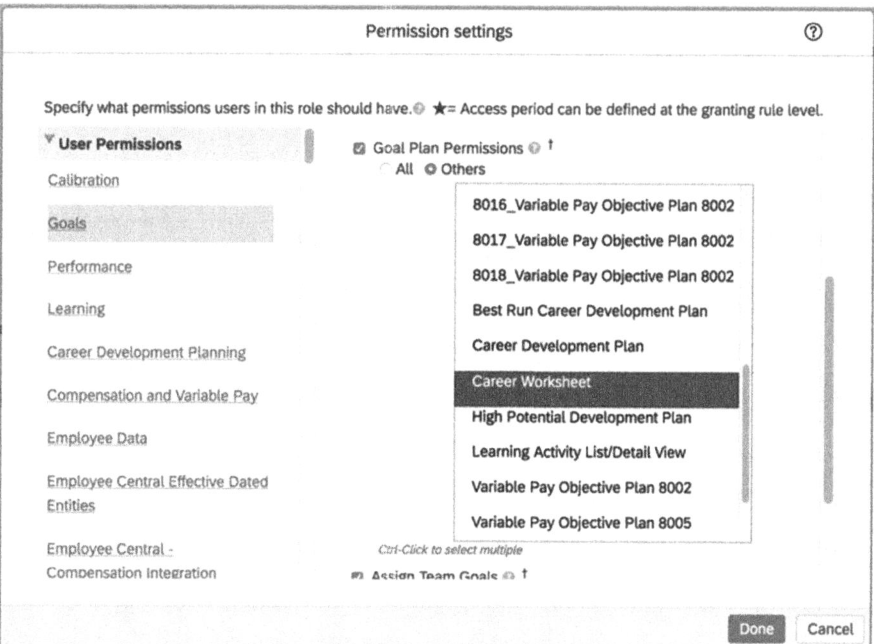


***Figure 2-17.** Goal Permissions for Career Worksheet*

In our Provisioning discussion, we talked about the option to add a targeted role to appear in a Career Goals block in People Profile. We added the "Share" permission on the Career Worksheet template XML. We also added the "nextPreferredMove" background element to the data model.

In order for the admin to create the Career Goals block used in People Profile, the background element must be enabled in the permission role. As seen in Figure 2-18, go to "Employee Data" found in the User Permissions section. Scroll down to find the background element "preferredNextMove" in the data model and grant "Edit" permission.

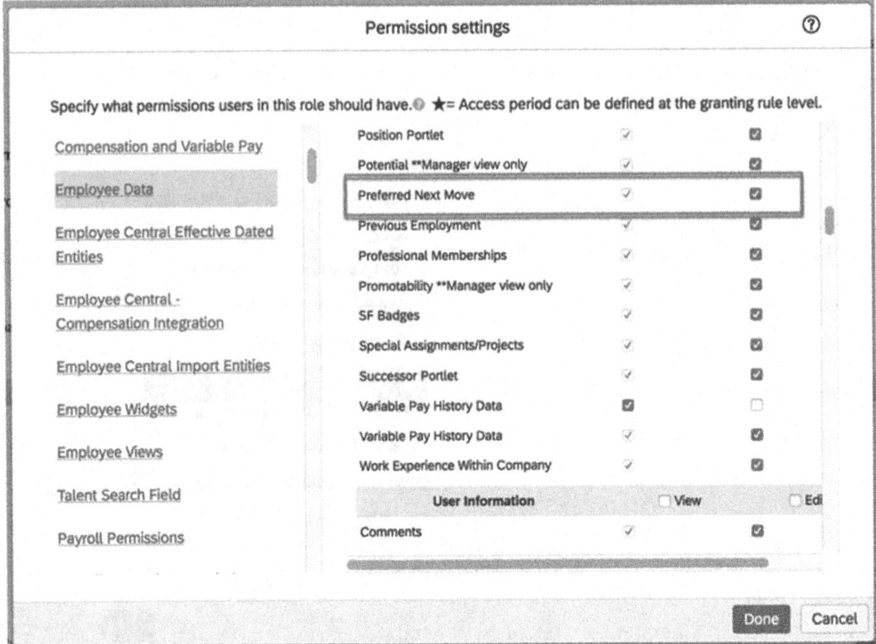


*Figure 2-18.* *Permission for the Preferred Next Move Background Element*

We have now granted the admin permission role access to manage the features of Career Worksheet. Save the permission role.

# Career Worksheet Setup

We will now walk through all of the features that the admin will enable for Career Worksheet.

## People Profile Update

If you are not currently using the block to represent Career Goals, go to "Configure People Profile" to add the block as seen in Figure 2-19.

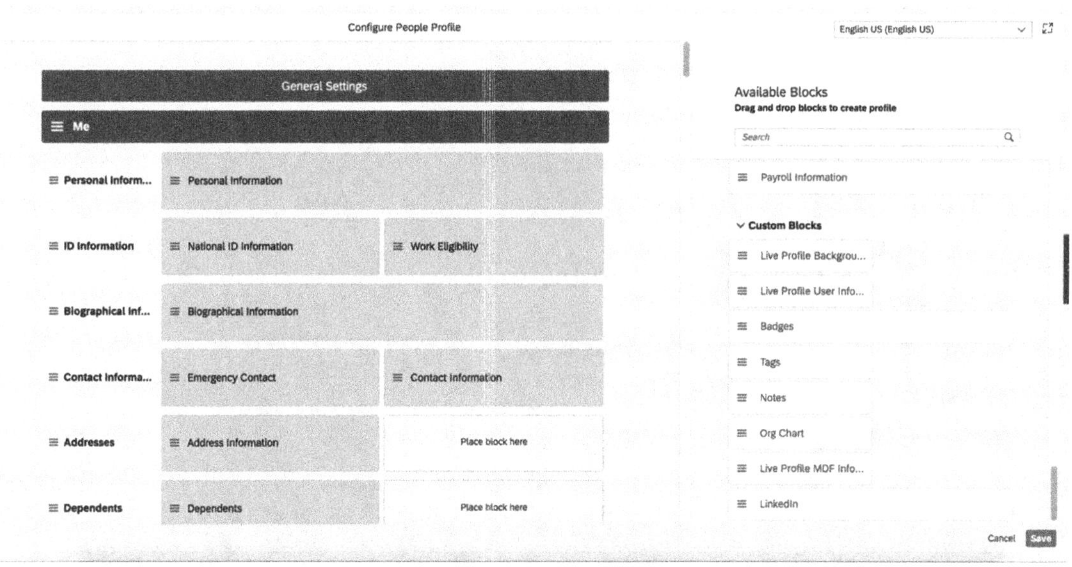

***Figure 2-19.*** *Configure People Profile Add New Block*

Find a section where you would like to place the block. You can add the block to an existing section that has similar types of blocks. Typically, this would be a Talent Profile section that is visible to the employee, manager, and HR manager. On the right side of the screen under Custom Blocks, select "Live Profile Background Information" and drag it to a new block within a section.

Name the block and give it a description. As seen in Figure 2-20, the section and block are labeled "Career Goals."

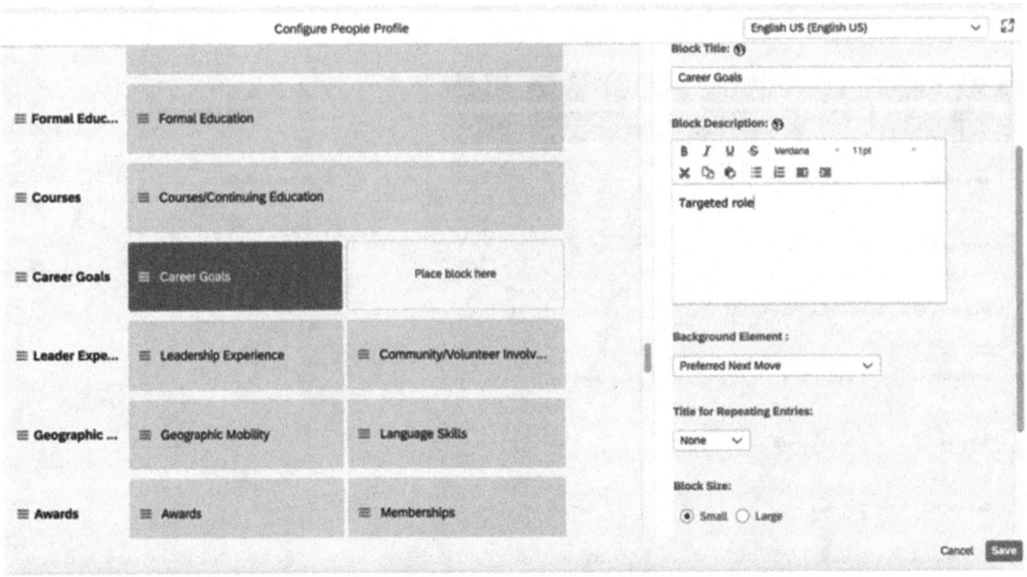

*Figure 2-20. Adding and Labeling the Career Goals Block*

Under the description section, there is a background element dropdown list. Select the background element "preferredNextMove" as seen in Figure 2-21.

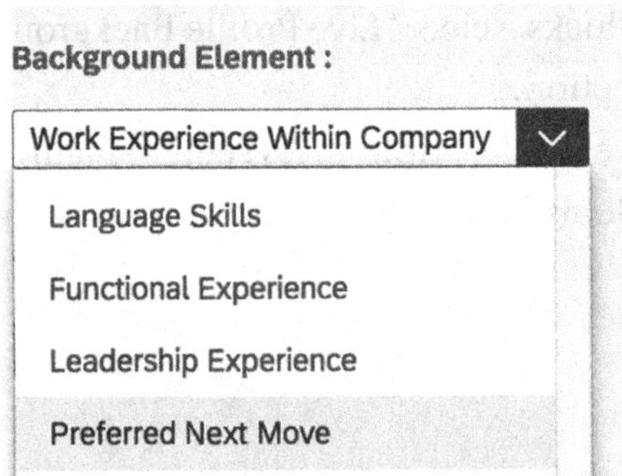


*Figure 2-21. Selection of a Background Element*

Save the block, and we will move on to the tasks the admin will need to perform before the career worksheet is ready for use.

## Role Competency Expected Ratings

A critical component of Career Worksheet is job role competencies; it is the backbone of Career Worksheet since readiness is based on a role's competencies. In order to use Career Worksheet as intended, all of the job roles need mapped competencies. Each competency linked to a job role must also have an expected rating. The expected ratings will be measured against an employee's actual competency ratings. This will determine how role-ready the employee is.

Use Job Profile Builder (JPB) to make sure each job role has competencies. We will also need to verify that there are expected ratings for each job role competency. If you are not using JPB, you may use Families and Roles.

The admin may manually add the expected ratings to job roles. To do this, go to Job Profile Contents ➤ Families and Roles ➤ Competencies as seen in Figure 2-22.

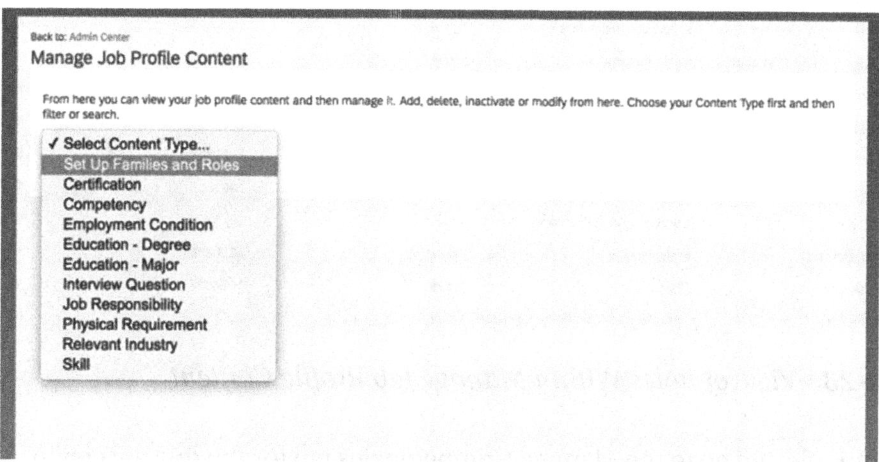


***Figure 2-22.** Accessing Families and Roles Using Job Profile Builder*

Go to Manage Job Profile Content ➤ Set Up Families and Roles.

Go to the Roles tab and select a role to edit as seen in Figure 2-23.

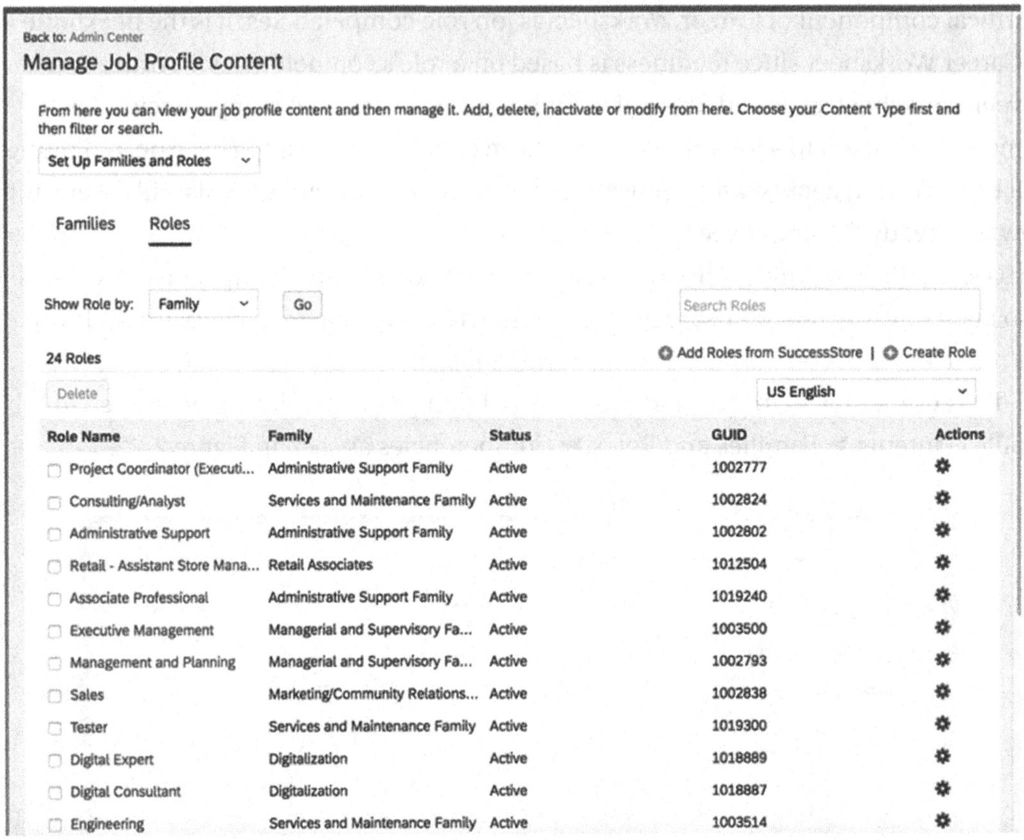

Back to: Admin Center

Manage Job Profile Content

From here you can view your job profile content and then manage it. Add, delete, inactivate or modify from here. Choose your Content Type first and then filter or search.

Set Up Families and Roles

Families Roles

Show Role by: Family Go Search Roles

24 Roles Add Roles from SuccessStore | Create Role

Delete US English

| Role Name | Family | Status | GUID | Actions |
|---|---|---|---|---|
| Project Coordinator (Executi... | Administrative Support Family | Active | 1002777 | |
| Consulting/Analyst | Services and Maintenance Family | Active | 1002824 | |
| Administrative Support | Administrative Support Family | Active | 1002802 | |
| Retail - Assistant Store Mana... | Retail Associates | Active | 1012504 | |
| Associate Professional | Administrative Support Family | Active | 1019240 | |
| Executive Management | Managerial and Supervisory Fa... | Active | 1003500 | |
| Management and Planning | Managerial and Supervisory Fa... | Active | 1002793 | |
| Sales | Marketing/Community Relations... | Active | 1002838 | |
| Tester | Services and Maintenance Family | Active | 1019300 | |
| Digital Expert | Digitalization | Active | 1018889 | |
| Digital Consultant | Digitalization | Active | 1018887 | |
| Engineering | Services and Maintenance Family | Active | 1003514 | |

***Figure 2-23.** View of Roles Within Manage Job Profile Content*

Select a role and go to the Mapped Competencies tab for the role as seen in Figure 2-24. If needed, first, map competencies to the job role.

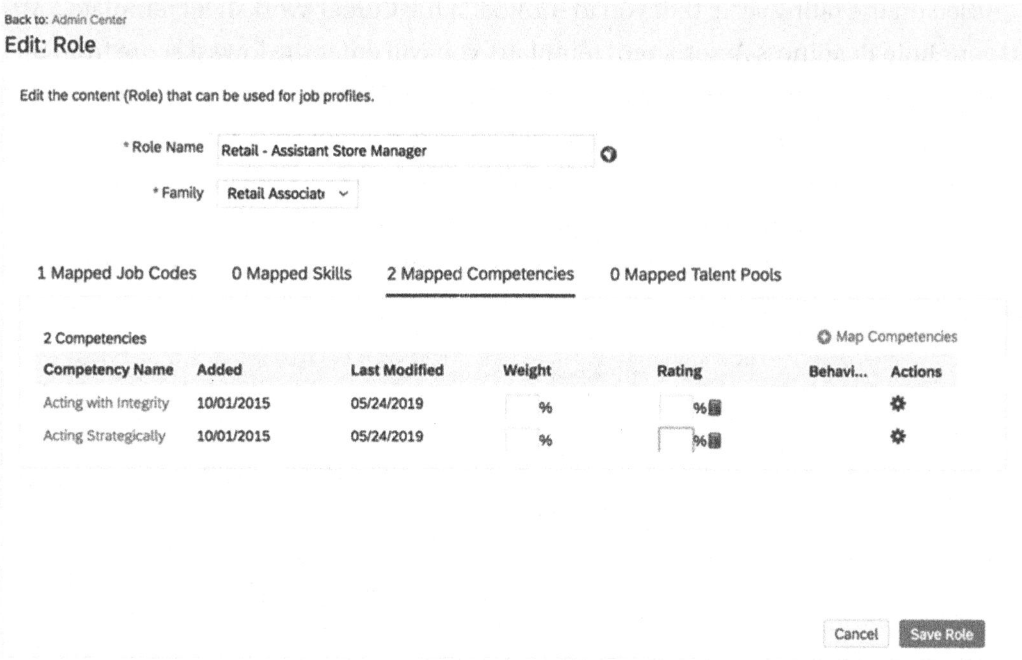

***Figure 2-24.*** *Mapped Competencies for a Job Role*

We need to focus on the Rating column. Click the calculator icon for a competency. A popup will display as seen in Figure 2-25.

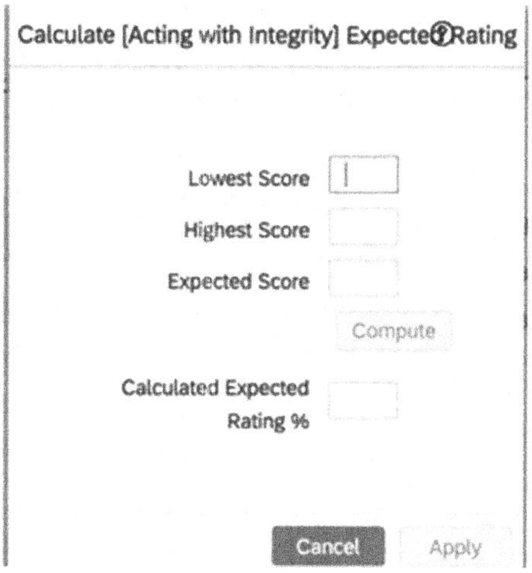

***Figure 2-25.*** *Calculator for Expected Rating*

Based on the rating scale that you identified in the Career Worksheet template XML and your Role Readiness Assessment template, you will enter the lowest score from the rating scale, the highest score, and then the expected rating score for the competency. The expected score would be a rating that would be acceptable for competency proficiency. You may need to confer with a Compensation or Talent Management individual within your organization to identify these ratings.

After entering the three scores, the "Compute" button becomes active as seen in Figure 2-26.

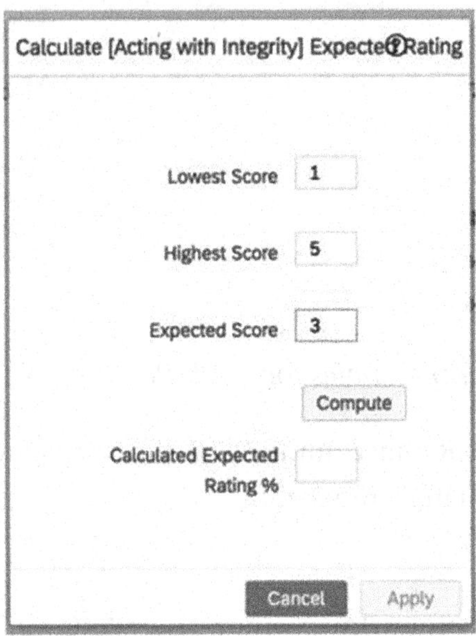


***Figure 2-26.*** *Compute Button Active Once Scores Are Entered*

The calculated expected rating % will then display. The hardcoded system equation to calculate this competency expected rating is (x – 1)/(rating scale – 1) = expected rating in percentage, where x is the expected rating of a competency in Career Worksheet.

Click the "Apply" button as shown in Figure 2-27.

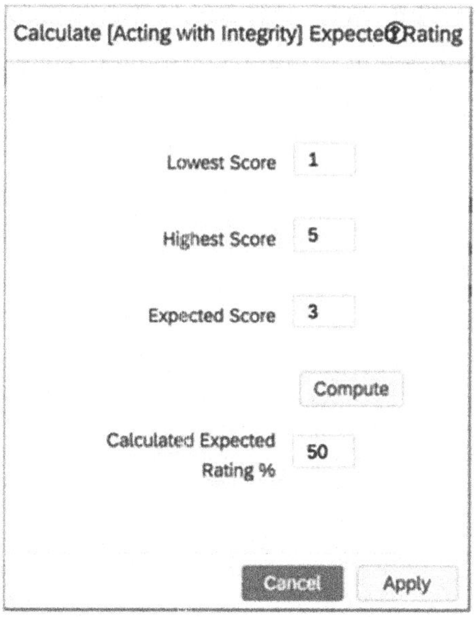

***Figure 2-27.** Applying the Rating for the Competency*

The calculated rating field is now populated for the competency as seen in Figure 2-28.

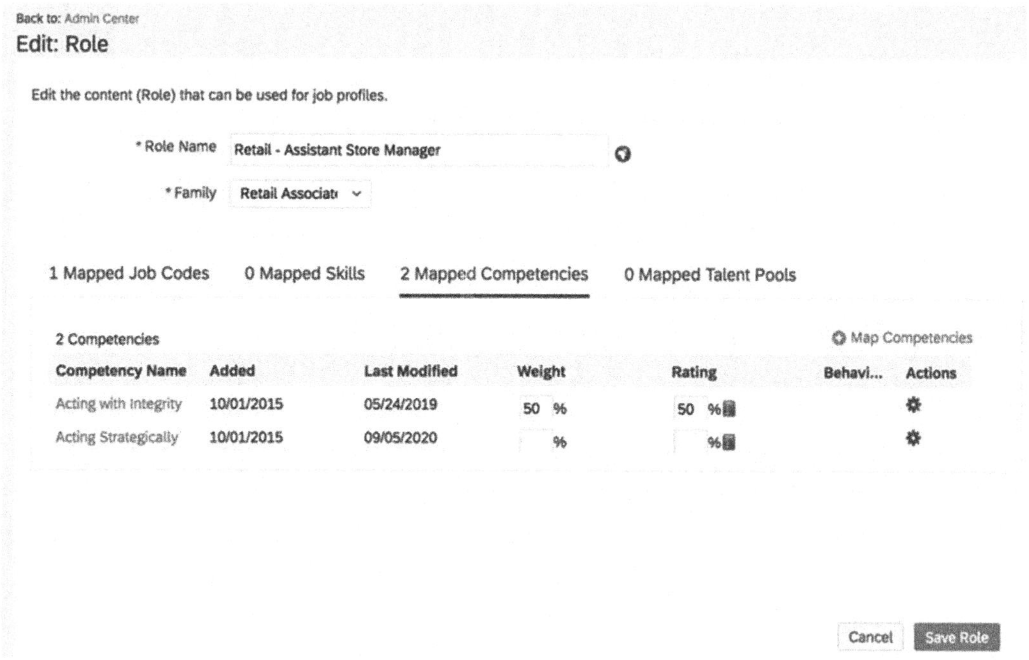

***Figure 2-28.** Competency with Rating %*

Perform the same process for each competency mapped to the role. You may also provide a weight for each competency. When completed, click the "Save Role" button as seen in Figure 2-29.

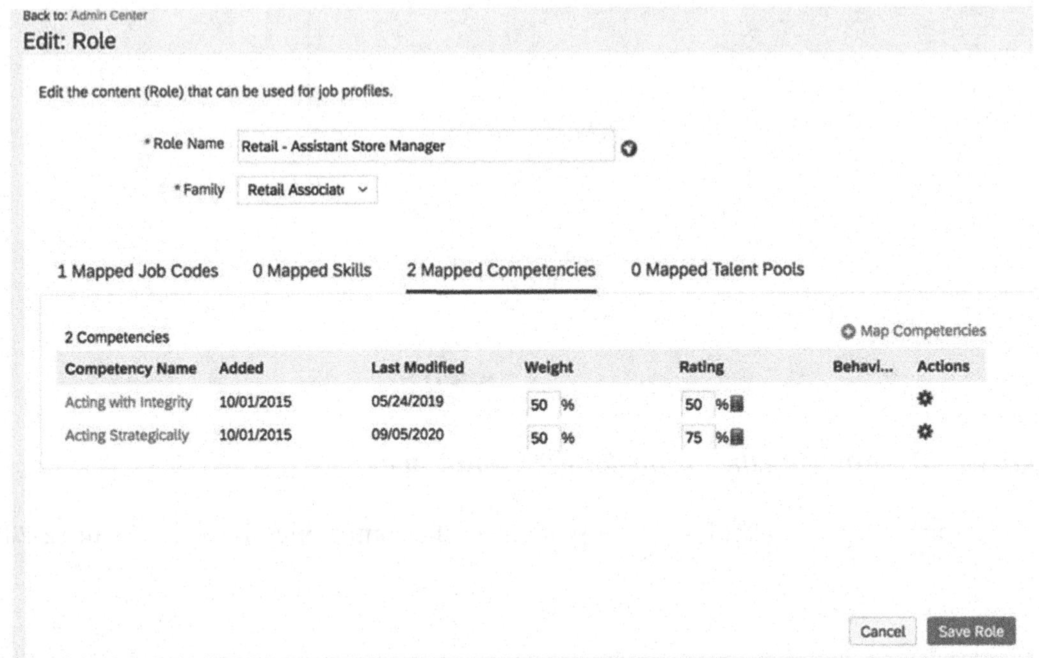


***Figure 2-29.*** *Save Role for Ratings to Take Effect*

This needs to be done for each competency on each job role. To streamline the process, you may use an import to update job role competencies in mass.

## Mass Update of Job Role Competencies

Assuming your job roles have mapped competencies, we would just need to add the weight (optional) and expected rating to each competency on each job role. This is done on the Role-Mapped Competencies template.

Type and select "Manage Job Profile Contents Import/Export" in the search bar. We will download the Role-Mapped Competencies template as seen in Figure 2-30.

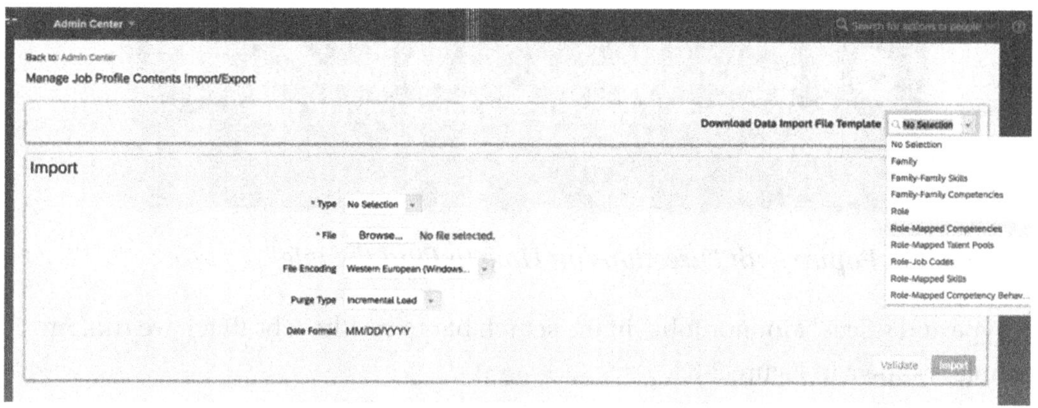


***Figure 2-30.*** *Download the Role-Mapped Competencies File*

When prompted, you will want the template to include existing data as seen in Figure 2-31.

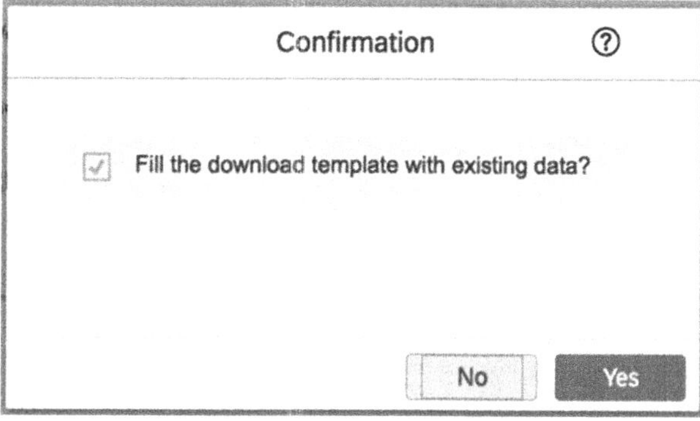


***Figure 2-31.*** *Confirmation to Include Data with Download*

A message will appear that directs you to go to "Monitor Job" to retrieve the downloaded file. The message is seen in Figure 2-32.

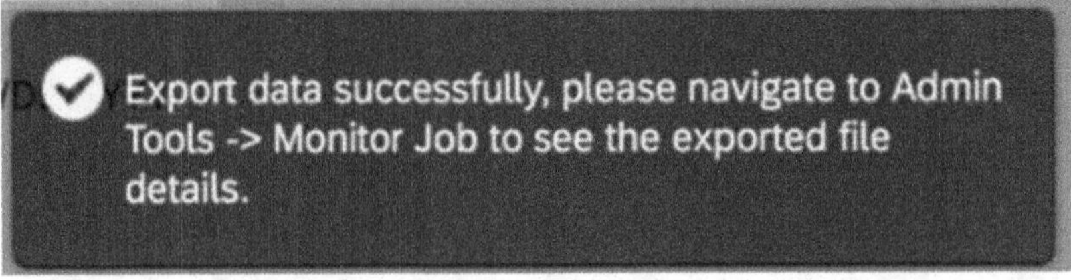


*Figure 2-32. Popup with Directions on How to Find the File*

Type and select "Monitor Jobs" in the search bar to see the jobs that have run. An example is shown in Figure 2-33.

Back to: Admin Center
Monitor Jobs

Items per page 25 Page 1 of 81

| Job Name | Job Description | Job Type | Job Status | Submitted By | Submission Time | Com |
|---|---|---|---|---|---|---|
| RoleEntity-roleCompetencyBehaviorMappin...... | | MDF Data Export | Completed | sfadmin | 2020-07-01 22:58:... ... | 20 |
| RoleEntity-roleCompetencyMappings_MDF...... | | MDF Data Export | Completed | sfadmin | 2020-07-01 22:58:... ... | 20 |
| CompetencyEntity_MDFExport_07/01/2020 | | MDF Data Export | Completed | sfadmin | 2020-07-01 22:39:... ... | 20 |
| RoleEntity_MDFExport_07/01/2020 | | MDF Data Export | Completed | sfadmin | 2020-07-01 22:29:... ... | 20 |
| RoleEntity-roleCompetencyMappings_MDF...... | | MDF Data Export | Completed | sfadmin | 2020-07-01 22:28:... ... | 20 |
| RoleEntity-jobCodeMappings_MDFExport_0..... | | MDF Data Export | Completed | sfadmin | 2020-07-01 22:24:1..... | 20 |
| RoleEntity-roleCompetencyMappings_MDF...... | | MDF Data Export | Completed | sfadmin | 2020-07-01 22:22:... ... | 20 |
| timeAccountChangeCalendar_8769602_14...... | | Time Account Calendar Run | Completed | v4admin | 2020-07-01 03:21:... ... | 20 |
| timeAccountChangeCalendar_813631_144...... | | Time Account Calendar Run | Completed | v4admin | 2020-07-01 03:21:... ... | 20 |
| timeAccountChangeCalendar_8769602_14...... | | Time Account Calendar Run | Completed | v4admin | 2020-06-30 06:41:... ... | 20 |
| timeAccountChangeCalendar_8769602_14...... | | Time Account Calendar Run | Completed | v4admin | 2020-06-29 06:51:... ... | 20 |
| timeAccountChangeCalendar_8769602_14...... | | Time Account Calendar Run | Completed | v4admin | 2020-06-28 04:26:... ... | 20 |
| timeAccountChangeCalendar_8769602_14...... | | Time Account Calendar Run | Completed | v4admin | 2020-06-27 04:31:... ... | 20 |
| timeAccountChangeCalendar_8769602_14...... | | Time Account Calendar Run | Completed | v4admin | 2020-06-26 04:01:... ... | 20 |
| timeAccountChangeCalendar_8769602_14...... | | Time Account Calendar Run | Completed | v4admin | 2020-06-25 02:31:... ... | 20 |

*Figure 2-33. Jobs That Have Run*

Use the scroll bar at the bottom of the screen to move to the right to see the Download Status column as seen in Figure 2-34.

Back to: Admin Center
Monitor Jobs

Items per page 25 | Page 1 of 81

| Job Type | Job Status | Submitted By | Submission Time | Completion Time | Job Details | Download Status |
|---|---|---|---|---|---|---|
| MDF Data Export | Completed | sfadmin | 2020-07-01 22:58:... ... | 2020-07-01 22:58:... ... | | Download Status |
| MDF Data Export | Completed | sfadmin | 2020-07-01 22:58:... ... | 2020-07-01 22:58:... ... | | Download Status |
| MDF Data Export | Completed | sfadmin | 2020-07-01 22:39:... ... | 2020-07-01 22:39:... ... | | Download Status |
| MDF Data Export | Completed | sfadmin | 2020-07-01 22:29:... ... | 2020-07-01 22:29:... ... | | Download Status |
| MDF Data Export | Completed | sfadmin | 2020-07-01 22:28:... ... | 2020-07-01 22:28:... ... | | Download Status |
| MDF Data Export | Completed | sfadmin | 2020-07-01 22:24:1.... | 2020-07-01 22:24:... ... | | Download Status |
| MDF Data Export | Completed | sfadmin | 2020-07-01 22:22:... ... | 2020-07-01 22:22:... ... | | Download Status |

***Figure 2-34.*** *Monitor Jobs View with Download Status*

Click "Download Status" to be prompted to save or open the file. An example is shown in Figure 2-35.

Opening jobResponse160089.csv

**You have chosen to open:**

**jobResponse160089.csv**

which is: CSV file (2.5 KB)

from: **https://salesdemo4.successfactors.com**

**What should Firefox do with this file?**

Open with Microsoft Excel (default)

Save File

Do this automatically for files like this from now on.

Cancel OK

***Figure 2-35.*** *Popup Screen to Open or Save the File*

This is the file that we will need to update. When opened, you will see that there are multiple language columns; these are the labels for different languages. Figure 2-36 shows the layout of the file.

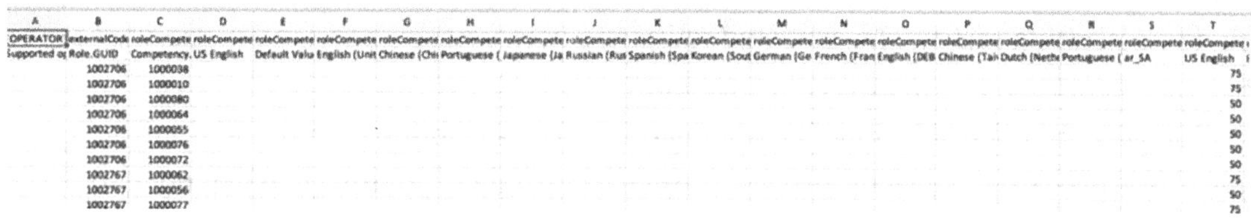

***Figure 2-36.*** *Role-Mapped Competencies File*

To make the file more manageable, you can delete any language columns that are not used in your instance. In the example shown in Figure 2-37, Default Value and US_ English are the only language columns that remain.

| [OPERATOR] | externalCode | roleCompetencyMappings.competency.externalCode | roleCompetencyMappings.weight.en_US | roleCompetencyMappings.weight.defaultValue | roleCompetencyMappings.rating.en_US | roleCompetencyMappings.rating.defaultValue | roleCompetencyMappings.status | roleCompetencyMappings.externalCode | roleCompetencyMappings.subModule |
|---|---|---|---|---|---|---|---|---|---|
| Supported o | Role.GUID | Competency. | US English | Default Value | US English | Default Valu | Status(Valid | GUID | subModule |
| | 1002706 | 1000038 | | | | | A | 1002710 | |
| | 1002706 | 1000010 | | | | | A | 1002711 | |
| | 1002706 | 1000080 | | | | | A | 1002712 | |
| | 1002706 | 1000064 | | | | | A | 1002713 | |
| | 1002706 | 1000055 | | | | | A | 1002714 | |
| | 1002706 | 1000076 | | | | | A | 1002715 | |
| | 1002706 | 1000072 | | | | | A | 1002716 | |
| | 1002767 | 1000062 | | | | | A | 1007110 | |
| | 1002767 | 1000056 | | | | | A | 1007111 | |
| | 1002767 | 1000077 | | | | | A | 1007112 | |
| | 1002767 | 1000063 | | | | | A | 1007113 | |
| | 1002767 | 1000055 | | | | | A | 1007114 | |
| | 1002767 | 1000076 | | | | | A | 1007115 | |
| | 1002767 | 1000078 | | | | | A | 1007116 | |
| | 1012504 | 1000031 | | | | | A | 1021720 | |
| | 1012504 | 1000034 | | | | | A | 1021721 | |
| | 1018887 | 1000011 | | | | | A | 1018904 | |

***Figure 2-37.** Role-Mapped Competencies File with Extraneous Language Columns Removed*

To add the expected rating percentage for each job role competency, we will be adding values in the following columns:

- roleCompetencyMappings.rating.en_US
- roleCompetencyMappings.rating.defaultValue

Use the following calculation to determine the expected rating % value to put in these columns:

(x - 1)/(rating scale - 1) = expected rating in percentage, where x is the expected rating of a competency in Career Worksheet

Weights are not used when calculating role readiness, but you may add them for any future use. To add weight to each competency for each job role, you will need to populate the following columns:

- roleCompetencyMappings.weight.en_US

- roleCompetencyMappings.weight.defaultValue

If you are using any other languages, you would include a column for each locale.

You may include weights for some competencies and none for others. Expected rating percentages are needed for all competencies. The numbers you see are the percentages and not the ratings based on the calculation shown earlier. A sample file is shown in Figure 2-38.

| A | B | C | D | E | F | G | H | I | J |
|---|---|---|---|---|---|---|---|---|---|
| [OPERATOR] | externalCode | roleCompetencyMappings.competency.externalCode | roleCompetencyMappings.weight.en_US | roleCompetencyMappings.weight.defaultValue | roleCompetencyMappings.rating.en_US | roleCompetencyMappings.rating.defaultValue | roleCompetencyMappings.status | roleCompetencyMappings.externalCode | roleCompetencyMappings.subModule |
| Supported o[ | Role.GUID | Competency. | US English | Default Value | US English | Default Valu | Status(Valid | GUID | subModule |
| | 1002706 | 1000038 | 10 | 10 | 75 | 75 | A | 1002710 | |
| | 1002706 | 1000010 | 10 | 10 | 75 | 75 | A | 1002711 | |
| | 1002706 | 1000080 | 20 | 20 | 50 | 50 | A | 1002712 | |
| | 1002706 | 1000064 | 10 | 10 | 50 | 50 | A | 1002713 | |
| | 1002706 | 1000055 | 10 | 10 | 50 | 50 | A | 1002714 | |
| | 1002706 | 1000076 | 20 | 20 | 50 | 50 | A | 1002715 | |
| | 1002706 | 1000072 | 20 | 20 | 50 | 50 | A | 1002716 | |
| | 1002767 | 1000062 | | | 75 | 75 | A | 1007110 | |
| | 1002767 | 1000056 | | | 50 | 50 | A | 1007111 | |
| | 1002767 | 1000077 | | | 75 | 75 | A | 1007112 | |
| | 1002767 | 1000063 | | | 50 | 50 | A | 1007113 | |

***Figure 2-38.*** *Role-Mapped Competencies File with Weights and Ratings*

To import the template, you will need to include these columns:

- externalCode
- roleCompetencyMappings.competency.externalCode
- roleCompetencyMappings.weight.en_US
- roleCompetencyMappings.weight.defaultValue
- roleCompetencyMappings.weight.en_DEBUG
- roleCompetencyMappings.rating.en_US
- roleCompetencyMappings.rating.defaultValue
- roleCompetencyMappings.rating.en_DEBUG
- roleCompetencyMappings.status
- roleCompetencyMappings.externalCode
- roleCompetencyMappings.subModule

Import the file from Manage Job Profile Contents Import/Export as shown in Figure 2-39. First, run to validate; and if successful, then do the import. Be sure to select "Unicode (UTF-8)" in the File Encoding field.

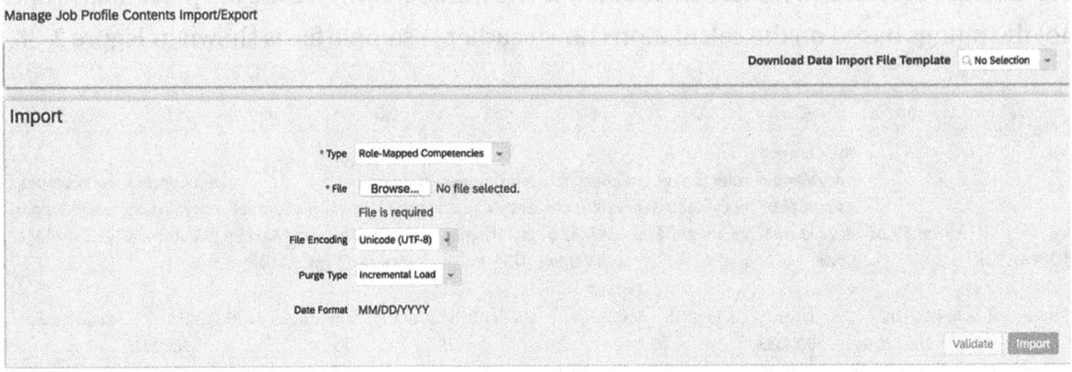

***Figure 2-39.*** *Import of the Updated Role-Mapped Competencies File*

We have now seen the file and what needs to be added. But the job role names and competency names are not included in the file. This will make it tricky to figure out which job role/competency mapping you are adding the fields to. So we are going to backtrack so you may create a file to use as reference to identify the roles and competencies you are working with.

Go back to "Manage Job Profile Contents Import/Export". We will download the Role template with data to get the job role names and the associated external codes that are used on the Role-Mapped Competencies file. Next, we will have to download the Competency template with data to see the competency names with the associated external codes. You can combine the two files to act as a reference when updating the Role-Mapped Competencies file. For more details, you may reference Volume 1, Chapter 3.

# Manage Career Paths

The use of career paths provides a visual representation of job progression and enables an employee to get a sense of which roles act as a stepping-stone to the next. A career path is comprised of a group of like jobs that are mapped to show movement from entry-level to management positions.

You may set up multiple career paths. The career paths created are instance-wide.

For example, you may create paths that are specific to departments such as finance, sales, and HR. And you may limit which career paths an employee may view. The career worksheet may include a link to career paths so that an employee can see the various paths to find roles they aspire to. They may select any of the roles to view on their career worksheet to see the competencies needed to be successful in the role and how ready they are.

As seen in Figure 2-40, there is a link within the worksheet to view the career paths of any targeted role.

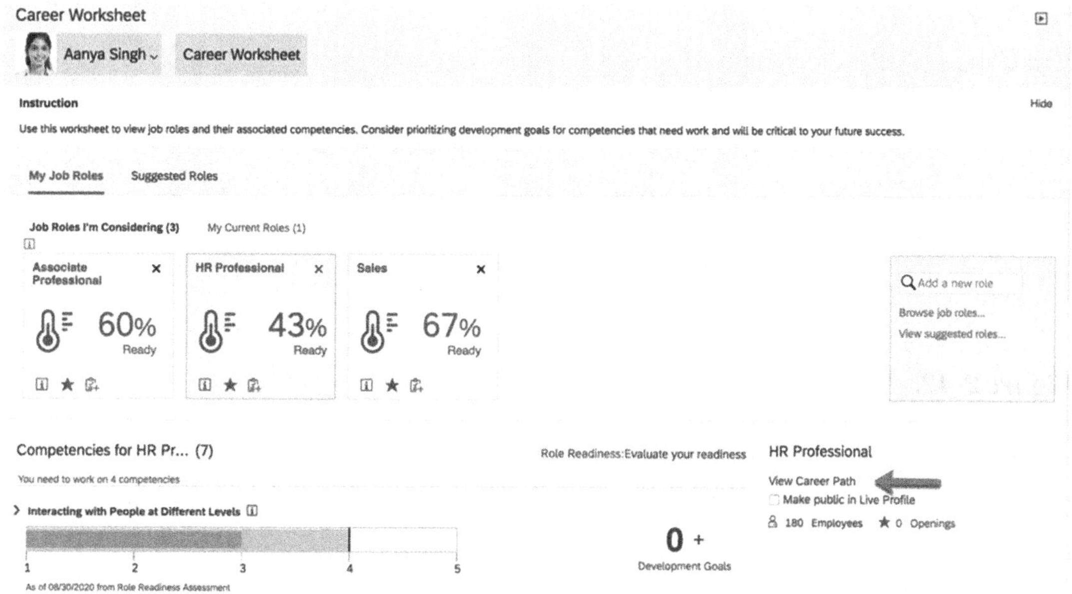


***Figure 2-40.** Access to a Career Path for a Targeted Role*

The career path for the role will display with the targeted role highlighted as seen in Figure 2-41.

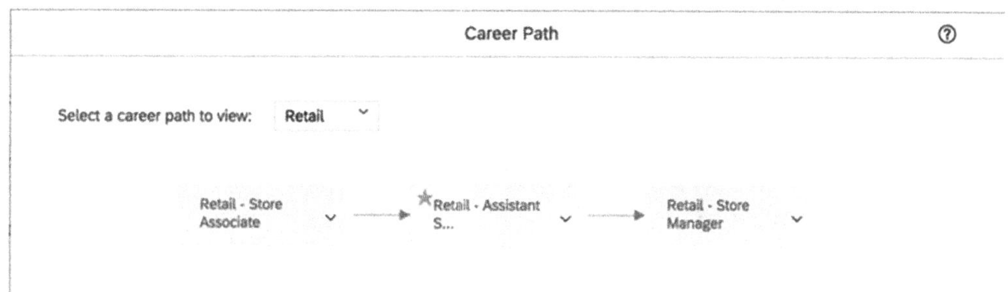


***Figure 2-41.** Career Path for a Targeted Role*

The admin will need to create career paths for the job roles to be referenced in the career worksheet.

The admin will have a tab for Career Paths within Development as shown in Figure 2-42. It is here where career paths are managed. This tab is only visible to the role that has Manage Career Path permission in their role-based permissions.

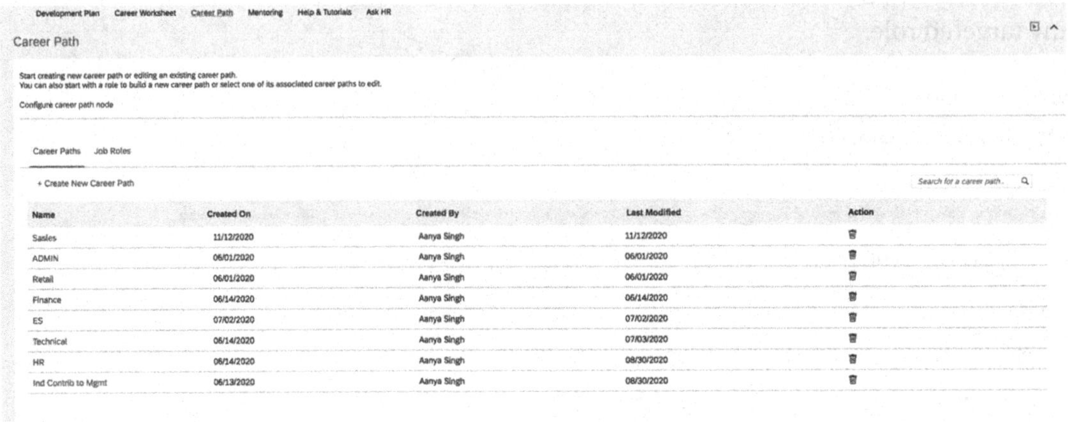

***Figure 2-42.*** *Manage Career Path*

The Manage Career Path screen contains two tabs: Career Paths and Job Roles. Permission to access Manage Career Path grants access to both tabs which cannot be permitted separately.

The Career Paths tab is used to configure the career path node and create, edit, and delete career paths. Click the link "Configure career path node" which is seen beneath the introductory text. It is here where the elements to display on a role node are determined. The tab is seen in Figure 2-43.

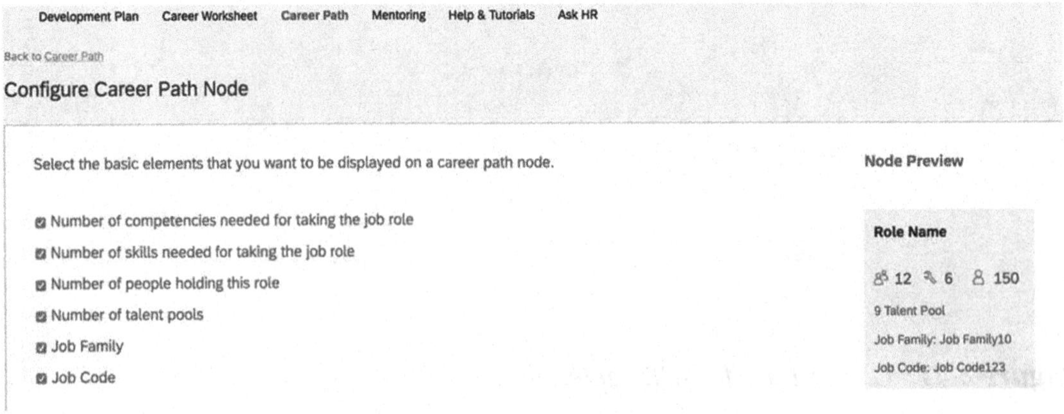

***Figure 2-43.*** *Configure Career Path Node*

Use this screen to decide what information should display for each role (node) within a career path. Figure 2-44 identifies the options that you may choose from.

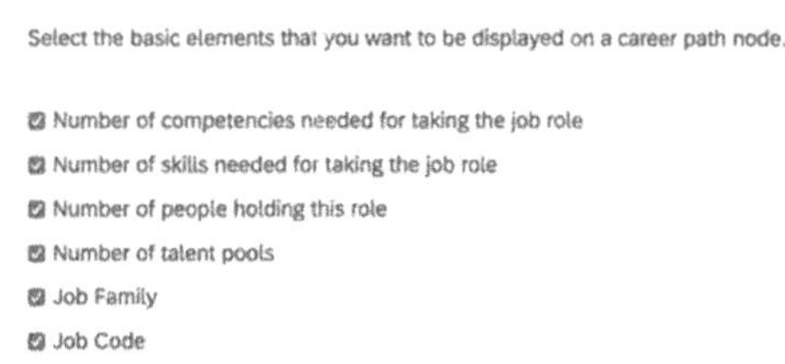


***Figure 2-44.*** *Career Path Node Options*

After deciding which elements to display for a node, you may look at the node preview which will show what the node will look like based on your choices. Figure 2-45 uses all of the elements.

***Figure 2-45.*** *Preview of a Career Path Node*

The selections made will reflect on career nodes for every path that you create. Save the selections and return to the Career Path screen.

Clink "Create a New Career Path". A popup displays as seen in Figure 2-46.

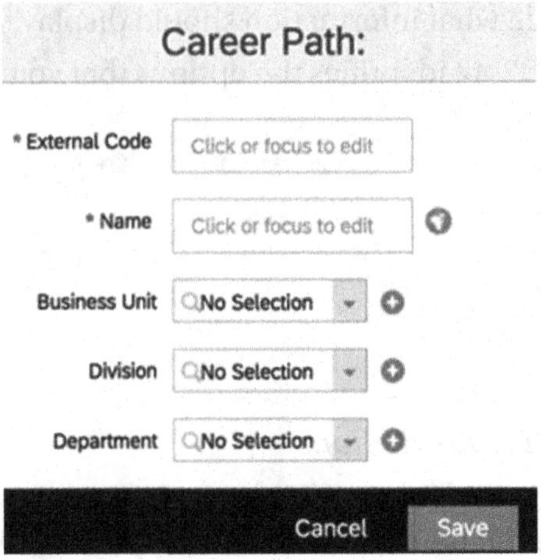

***Figure 2-46.*** *Create a Career Path*

You will need to give your career path a meaningful name. The External Code and Name fields are required; Business Unit, Division, and Department are optional. The optional fields can be used to restrict employee access to specific career paths.

Figure 2-47 shows an example of a career path using only the required fields.

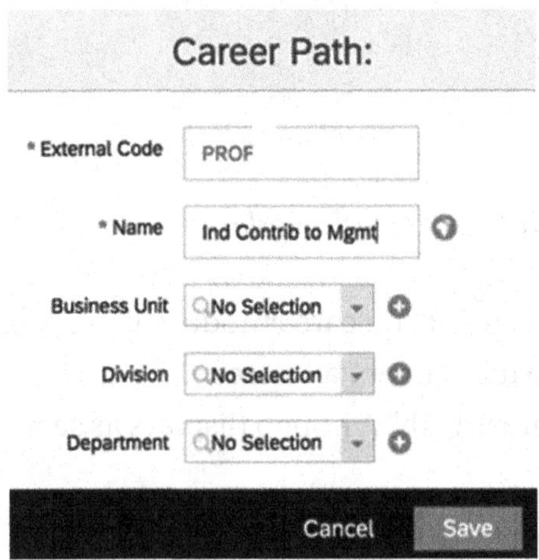


***Figure 2-47.*** *Career Path Creation with Required Fields*

Upon saving, a screen will display where you will build the career path as seen in Figure 2-48.

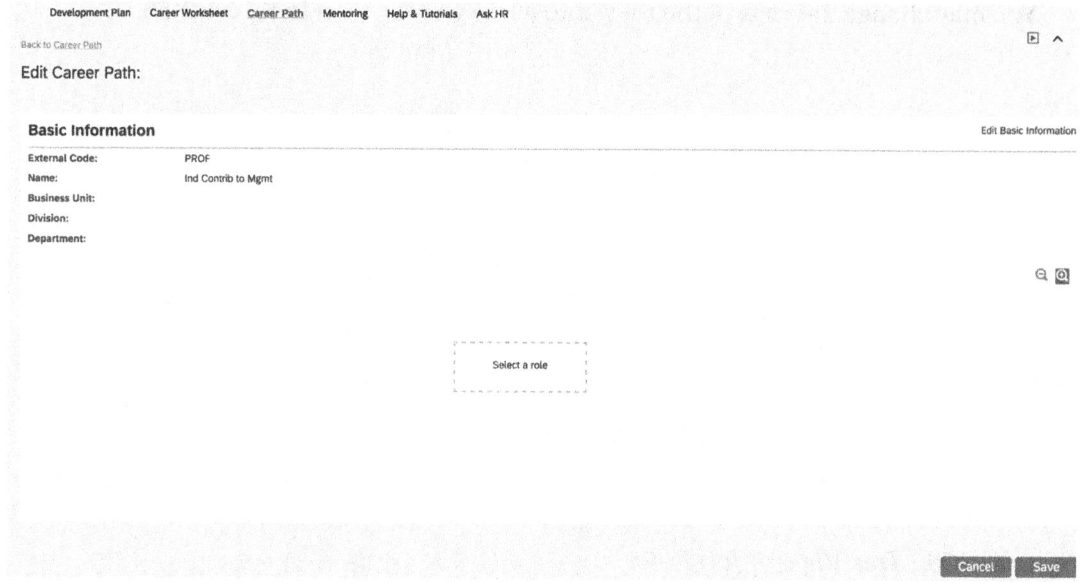


***Figure 2-48.** Building the Career Path*

Click "Select a role" found in the middle of the screen to start to build the path as seen in Figure 2-49. A popup will display the roles you may select from. A list view is the default, and roles display in family/role name order.

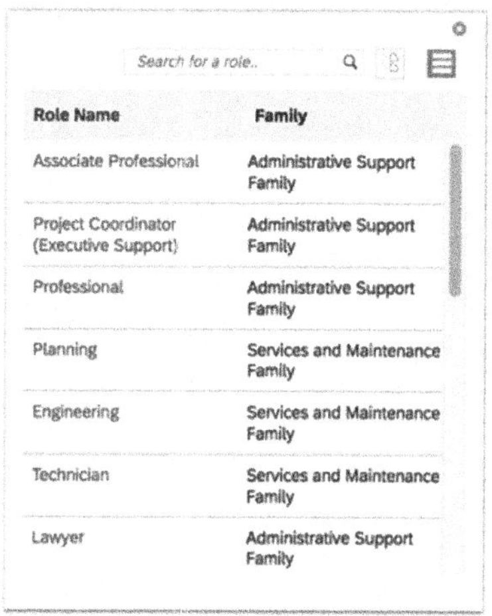


***Figure 2-49.** Roles Available to Add to the Career Path*

You may change the view of the roles into a tree view as seen in Figure 2-50.

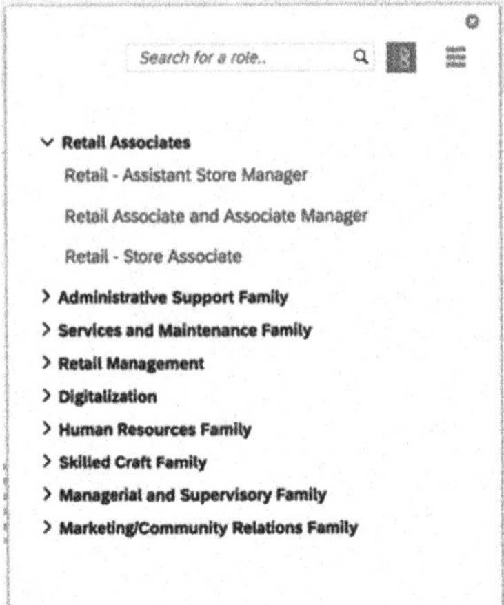


***Figure 2-50.*** *Tree View of Job Roles*

Select a role, and it will then appear on the Career Path screen as seen in Figure 2-51.

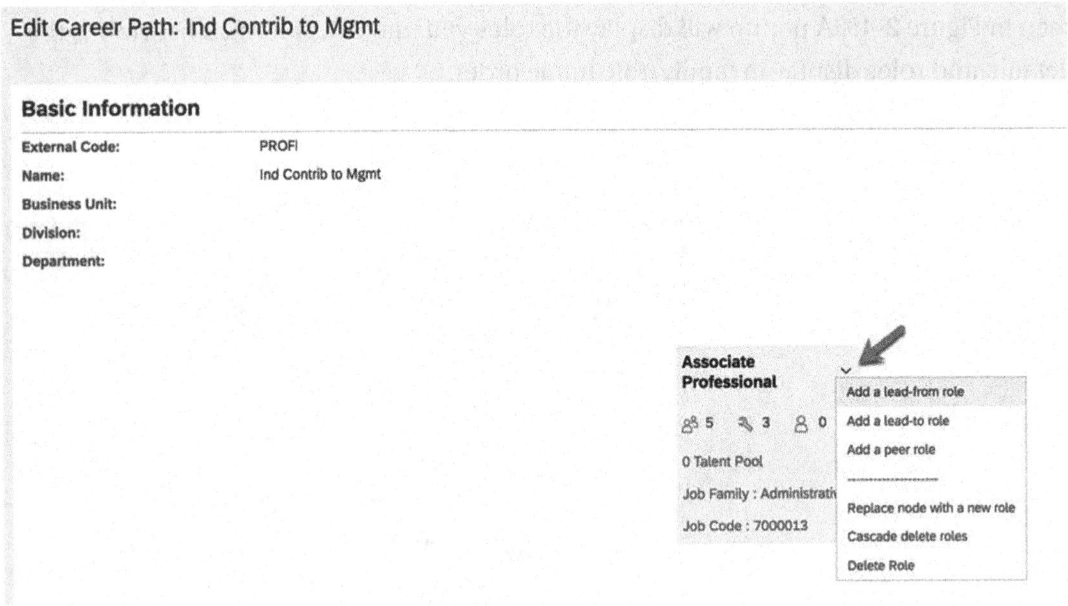

Edit Career Path: Ind Contrib to Mgmt

Basic Information

External Code: PROFI

Name: Ind Contrib to Mgmt

Business Unit:

Division:

Department:

Associate Professional

5 3 0

0 Talent Pool

Job Family : Administrati

Job Code : 7000013

Add a lead-from role

Add a lead-to role

Add a peer role

Replace node with a new role

Cascade delete roles

Delete Role

***Figure 2-51.*** *Adding a Job Role to a Career Path*

There are several actions available for a career path node:

- Add a lead-from role which adds a preceding role to the current role.
- Add a lead-to role which adds a role after the current role.
- Add a peer role which adds a lateral role above the current role – maximum of two lateral roles for a node.
- Replace the node with a new role. Remove a node and you may select a replacement node.
- Cascade delete roles. Remove the current role and any roles that follow.
- Delete a role. Remove a role and connect the lead-from role to the lead-to role.

The node will appear in the path based on the action selected. In the following example in Figure 2-52, a lead-to role is being added to the path.

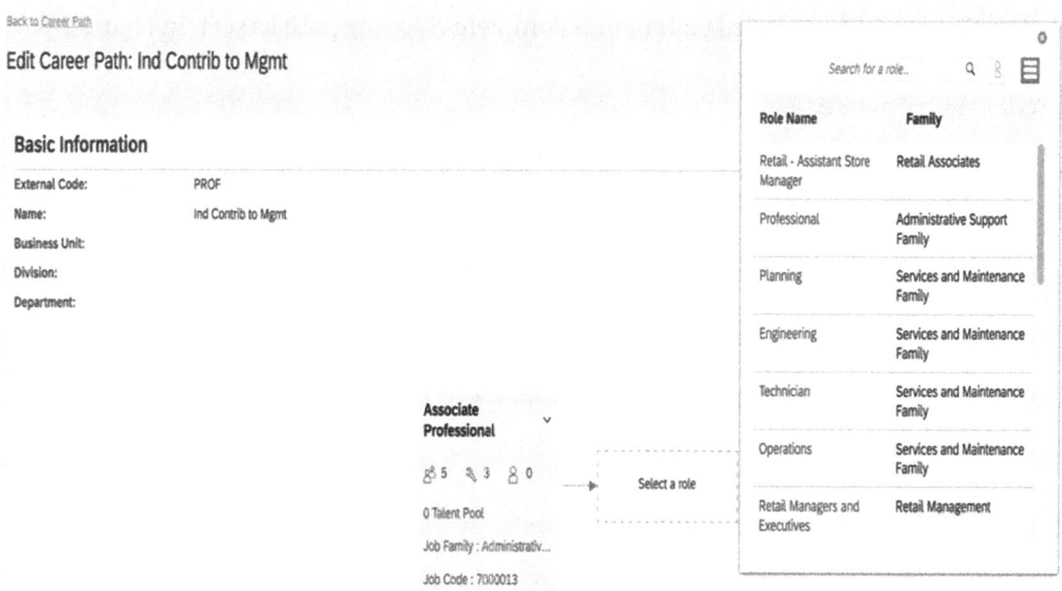


***Figure 2-52.** Addition of a Lead-To Role*

Figure 2-53 shows adding a peer role. This puts a role on the same level in the path.

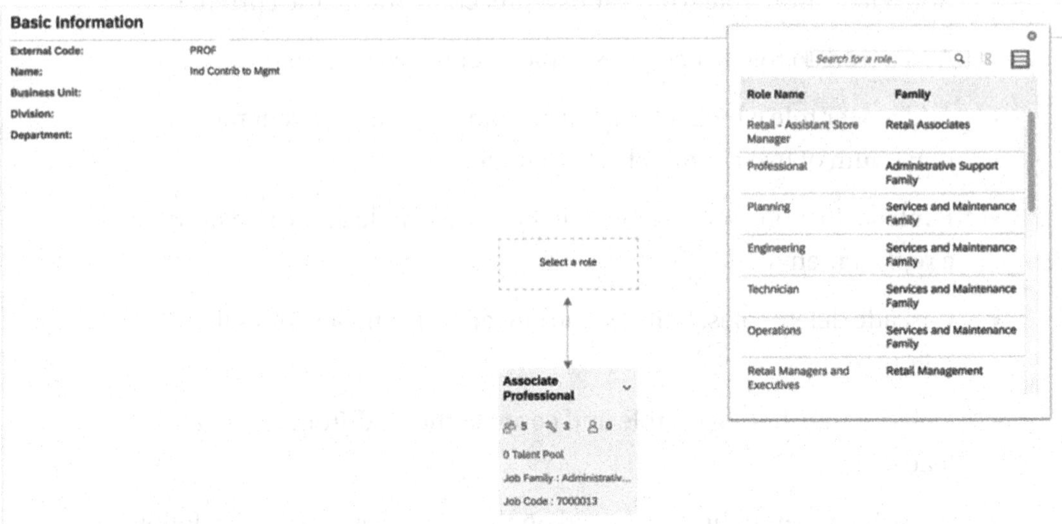


*Figure 2-53.* *Addition of a Peer Role*

Continue to add roles until your path is complete. Save the path as seen in Figure 2-54.

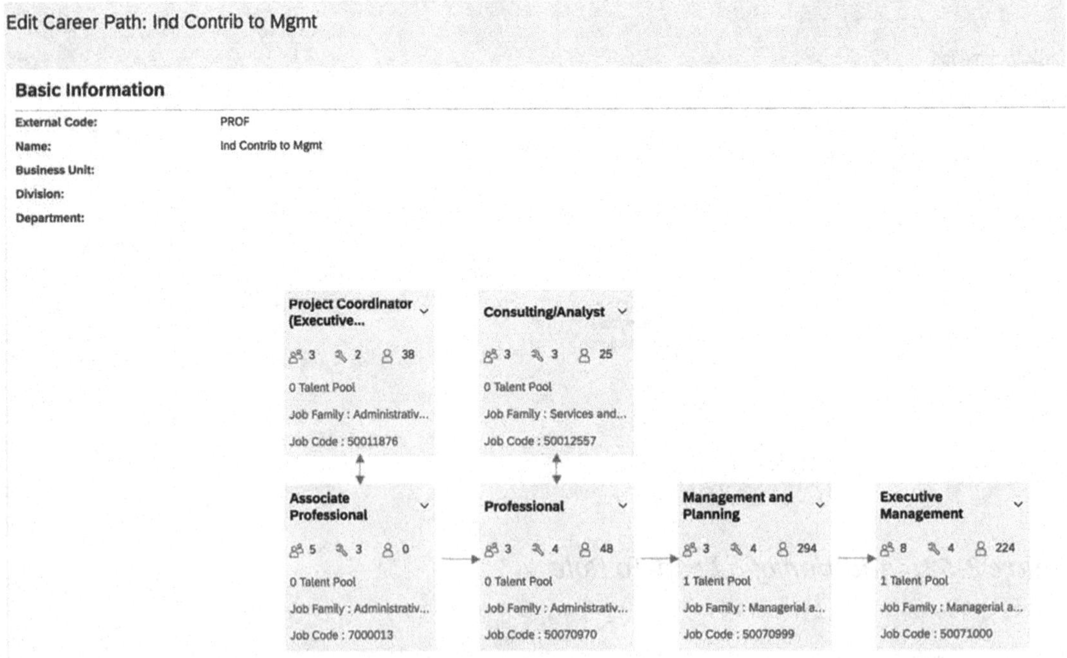


*Figure 2-54.* *Saving the Newly Built Career Path*

Go back to Career Path to see your newly added career path listed.

You may continue to create paths, and you may edit and delete paths. To edit a path, click a path name. Here, you are able to modify the path or edit basic information as seen in Figure 2-55.

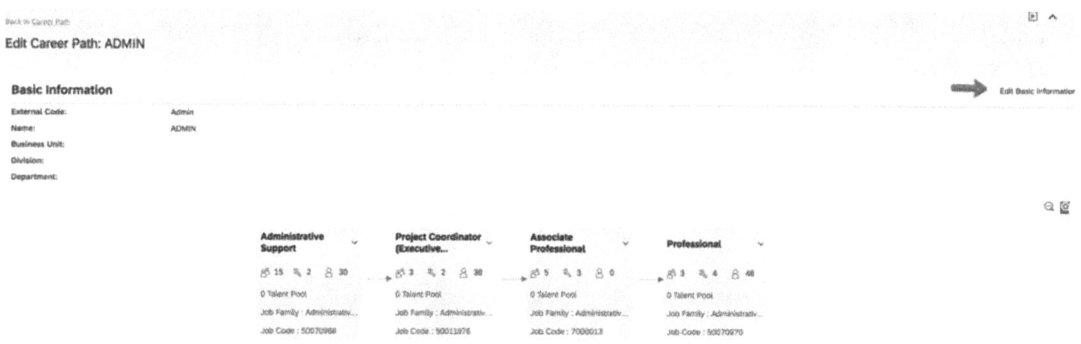


***Figure 2-55.** Edit Basic Information on a Career Path*

Click "Edit Basic Information" to add filters as seen in Figure 2-56. You may add a business unit, division, and/or department which enables you to restrict access to the career path to employees belonging to these areas.

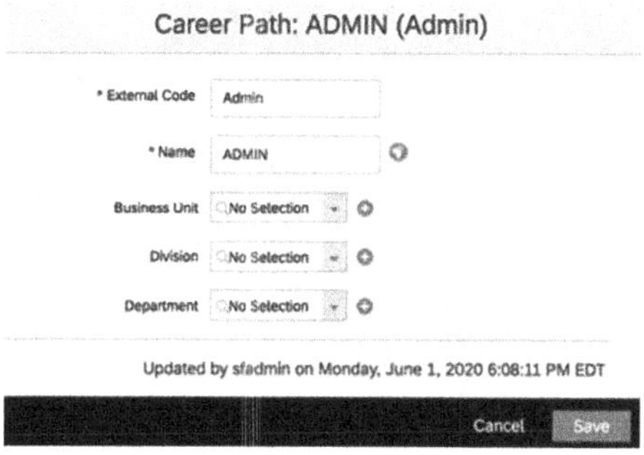

***Figure 2-56.** Editing a Career Path*

Back on the Career Path home screen, you may go to the Job Roles tab as seen in Figure 2-57.

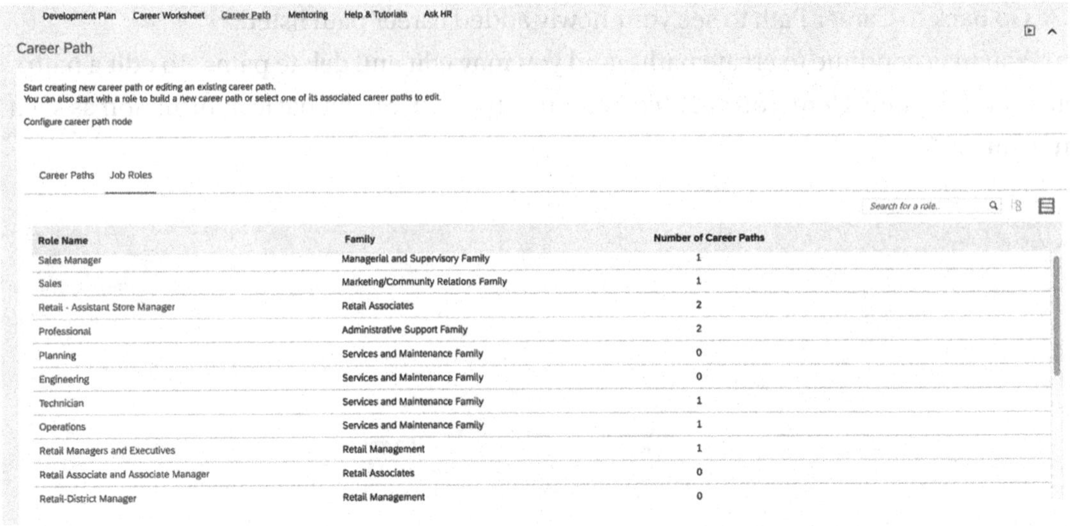

***Figure 2-57.*** *Job Roles Tab*

This view lets you see how many career paths a role is a part of. Click a role name, and the career path will display. The role you selected will be highlighted in the path as seen in Figure 2-58.

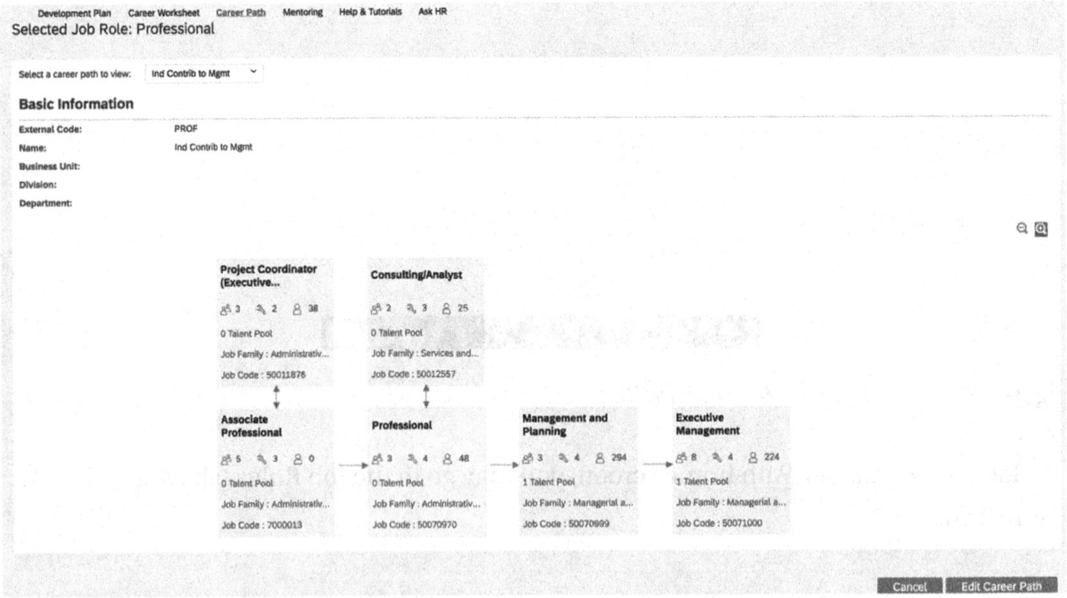

***Figure 2-58.*** *Selected Role Within a Career Path*

From this screen, you may edit the career path by clicking the "Edit Career Path" button found on the lower-right side of the screen. This will take you back to the screen where you may edit basic career path information or edit the path itself as seen in Figure 2-59.

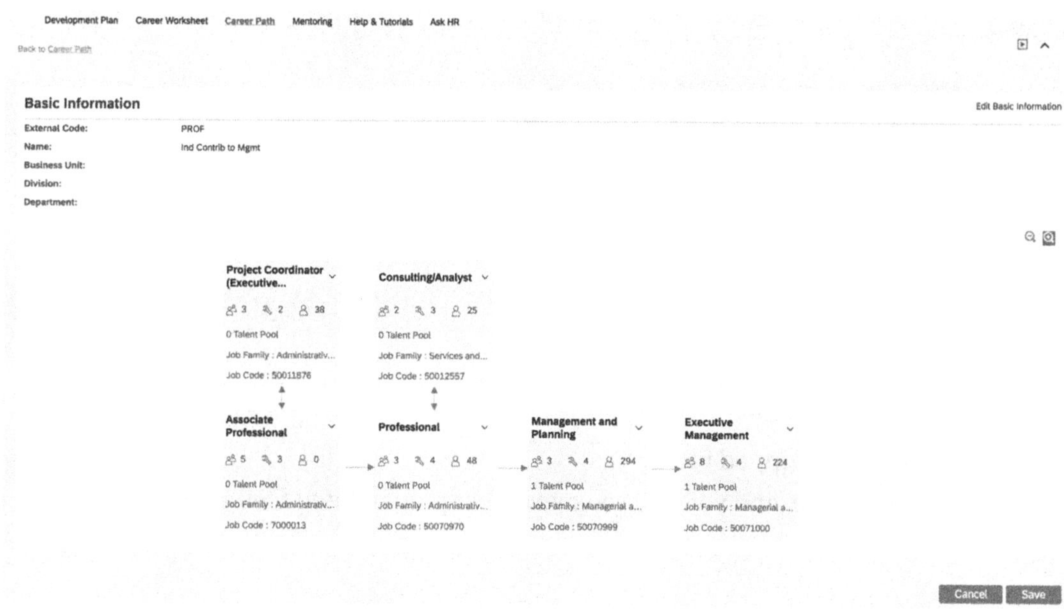


*Figure 2-59.* *Screen Where Career Paths May Be Edited*

You will need to perform these steps to create each career path.

## Import Career Path V2

If you have a very large organization and need to build a large number of career paths, creating each manually can be very time consuming. To avoid this manual process, it is possible to import career paths.

There are two files that we will reference:

- **Career Path** which contains external code and locale-specific translations.
- **Career Path-Career Path Details** which contains the career path external code in relation to the job roles.

Type and select "Import and Export Data" in the search bar and select "Download Template" as the action to perform. Using the "Select Generic Object" dropdown listing, choose "Career Path". Then download the template as seen in Figure 2-60.

Back to: Admin Center
Import and Export Data
* Select the action to perform Download Template
* Select Generic Object Career Path
* Include dependencies Yes
* Include Immutable IDs No
* Exclude reference objects No
* Key Preference Business Key
* Hide External Code No
* Identity Type User ID
Download

***Figure 2-60.*** *Download Career Path*

This will produce a zipped file.

Open the zipped file, and you will see two career path–related files as seen in Figure 2-61.

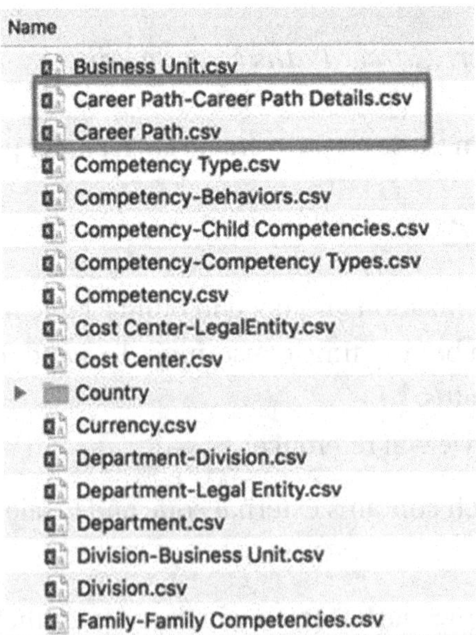


***Figure 2-61.*** *Downloaded Career Path Files*

As shown in Figure 2-62, the Career Path template will contain the same fields available when manually creating a career path: external code, career path name, business unit, division, and department. There will also be columns for locale-specific translations of career path name for the languages enabled in your instance.

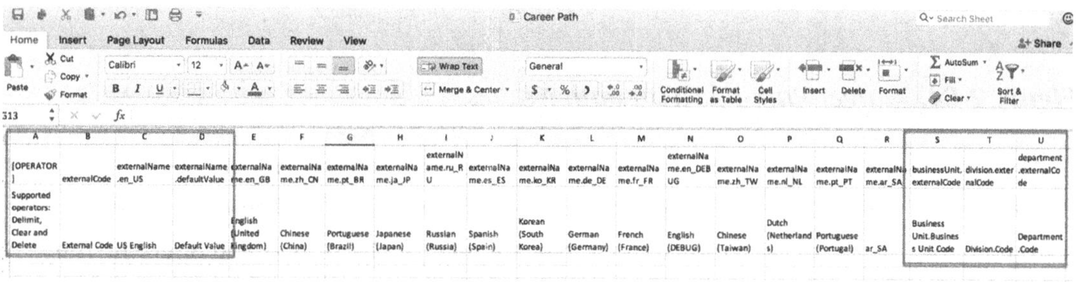

***Figure 2-62.*** *Career Path Template*

You may delete external name columns for languages not used in your instance as seen in Figure 2-63. In this example, only the "externalName column en_US" will remain.

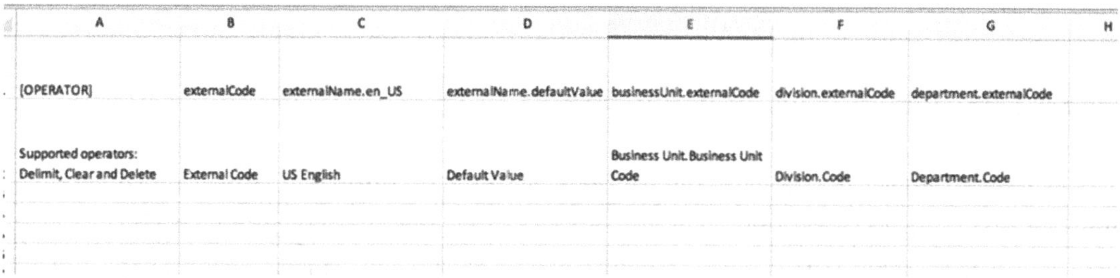

| A | B | C | D | E | F | G | H |
|---|---|---|---|---|---|---|---|
| [OPERATOR] | externalCode | externalName.en_US | externalName.defaultValue | businessUnit.externalCode | division.externalCode | department.externalCode | |
| Supported operators: Delimit, Clear and Delete | External Code | US English | Default Value | Business Unit.Business Unit Code | Division.Code | Department.Code | |

***Figure 2-63.*** *Career Path Template After Extraneous Language Columns Removed*

When you build the career path file, you will only need to populate the required External Code and Name fields. You will also need a unique external code for each path. You may use whatever naming convention that is meaningful to you.

Save the file that contains all of the career paths you are creating. In Figure 2-64 is a sample of creating three new career paths.

| A | B | C | D | E | F | G | H |
|---|---|---|---|---|---|---|---|
| [OPERATOR] | externalCode | externalName.en_US | externalName.defaultValue | businessUnit.externalCode | division.externalCode | department.externalCode | |
| Supported operators: Delimit, Clear and Delete | External Code | US English | Default Value | Business Unit.Business Unit Code | Division.Code | Department.Code | |
| | CPTECH | Technical | Technical | | | | |
| | CPFIN | Finance | Finance | | | | |
| | CPHR | HR | HR | | | | |

***Figure 2-64.*** *Career Path File with Path Names*

Type and select "Import and Export Data" in the search bar to import the newly created career path file. Be sure to use file encoding type of UTF-8. Import by first validating the file. Go to "Monitor Jobs" to see the results. Download and open the file found in the Download Status column as seen in Figure 2-65.

| A |
|---|
| Company: SFPART050144 |
| Total Records: 3 |
| Number of failed records: 0 |
| There are no error(s) found in the import file. |

***Figure 2-65.*** *Results of Validation Import*

If there are no errors, the career path file is ready to be imported. Type and select "Import and Export Data" in the search bar and import the career path file. Again, go to "Monitor Jobs" to check the status of the import and ensure the import was successful as seen in Figure 2-66.

| |
|---|
| Company: SFPART050144 |
| Total Records: 3 |
| Number of failed records: 0 |
| The Import was successfully completed. |

***Figure 2-66.*** *Results of Career Path Import*

If successful, when you go back to "Career Path" in Development, you will see the newly created career paths.

Next, you will need to build the career nodes for each career path. You will need the GUID of each job role that you are including. The role GUIDs can be found via "Manage Job Profile Contents Import/Export Data" downloading "Role" with data as shown in Figure 2-67.

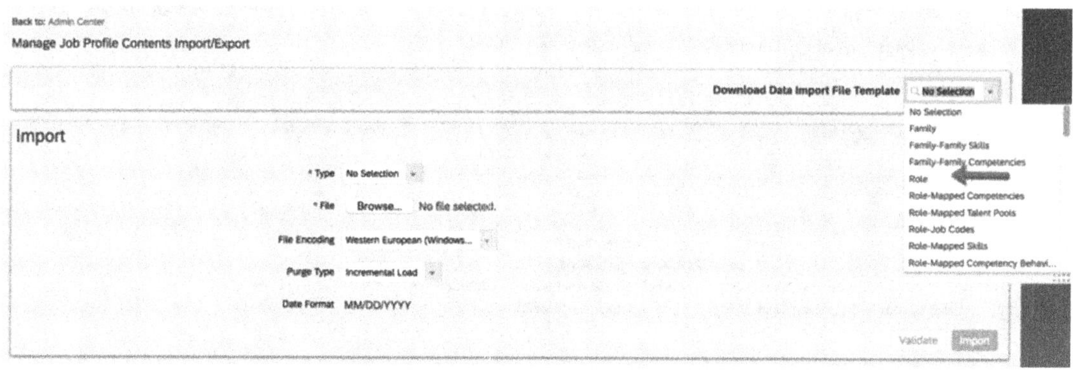


*Figure 2-67.* *Downloading the Role Template*

After downloading the file, go to "Monitor Jobs" to download the file. This file will be used as a reference when building the career path details file. The external role GUID column is what is needed on the career path details file as shown in Figure 2-68.

Role

G1 | *fx* externalCode

| | A | B | C | D | E | F | G | H |
|---|---|---|---|---|---|---|---|---|
| 1 | [OPERATOR] | name.en_US | name.defaultValue | family.externalCode | createdLocale | status | externalCode | subModule |
| 2 | Supported or | US English | Default Value | Family.GUID | createdLocale | Status(Valid Values | GUID | subModule |
| 3 | | HR Professional | HR Professional | 1002704 | en_US | A | 1002706 | |
| 4 | | Lawyer | Lawyer | 1002702 | en_US | A | 1002767 | |
| 5 | | Project Coordinator (Executive Suppc | Project Coordinator (I | 1002702 | en_US | A | 1002777 | |
| 6 | | Operations | Operations | 1002701 | en_US | A | 1002783 | |
| 7 | | Management and Planning | Management and Pla | 1002700 | en_US | A | 1002793 | |
| 8 | | Administrative Support | Administrative Suppc | 1002702 | en_US | A | 1002802 | |
| 9 | | Professional | Professional | 1002702 | en_US | A | 1002809 | |
| 10 | | Craft Worker | Craft Worker | 1002703 | en_US | A | 1002818 | |
| 11 | | Consulting/Analyst | Consulting/Analyst | 1002701 | en_US | A | 1002824 | |
| 12 | | Technician | Technician | 1002701 | en_US | A | 1002831 | |
| 13 | | Sales | Sales | 1002705 | en_US | A | 1002838 | |
| 14 | | Executive Management | Executive Manageme | 1002700 | en_US | A | 1003500 | |
| 15 | | Engineering | Engineering | 1002701 | en_US | A | 1003514 | |
| 16 | | Planning | Planning | 1002701 | en_US | A | 1003531 | |
| 17 | | Retail Managers and Executives | Retail Managers and | 1012421 | en_US | A | 1012422 | |
| 18 | | Retail Associate and Associate Mana | Retail Associate and | 1012420 | en_US | A | 1012427 | |
| 19 | | Retail-District Manager | Retail-District Manag | 1012421 | en_US | A | 1012500 | |
| 20 | | Retail - Store Manager | Retail - Store Manag | 1012421 | en_US | A | [illegible] | |

*Figure 2-68.* *Role GUIDs*

When building the career path details file, you will need a record for each role in the path. The record will include the career path external code, the role GUID for the job role you are adding to the path, the role GUID for the next role in the path, and if the role being added is a peer role ("TRUE" or "FALSE"). A sample file is shown in Figure 2-69.

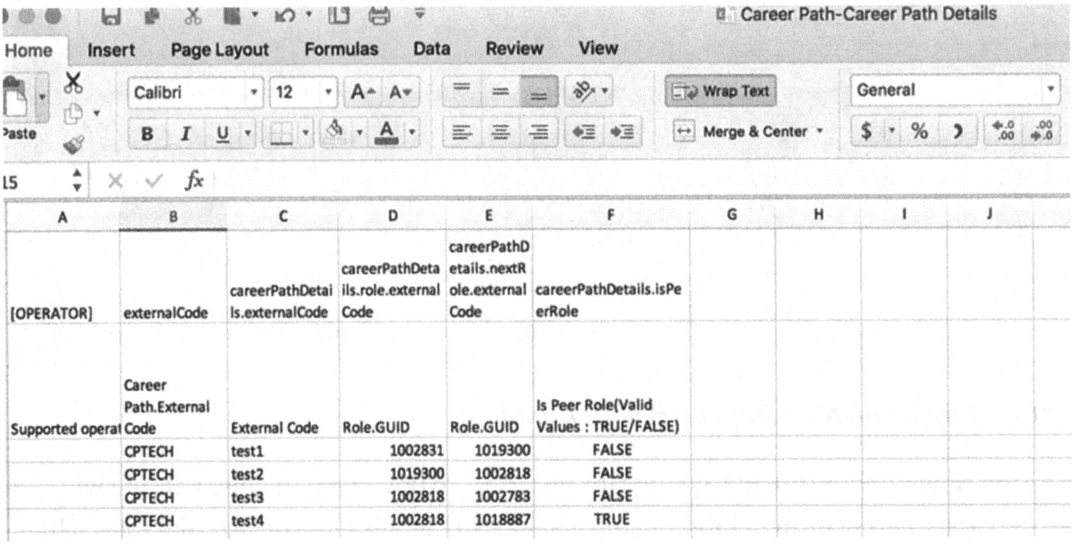

Career Path-Career Path Details

| A | B | C | D | E | F |
|---|---|---|---|---|---|
| [OPERATOR] | externalCode | careerPathDetails.externalCode | careerPathDetails.role.externalCode | careerPathDetails.nextRole.externalCode | careerPathDetails.isPeerRole |
| Supported operat | Career Path.External Code | External Code | Role.GUID | Role.GUID | Is Peer Role(Valid Values : TRUE/FALSE) |
| | CPTECH | test1 | 1002831 | 1019300 | FALSE |
| | CPTECH | test2 | 1019300 | 1002818 | FALSE |
| | CPTECH | test3 | 1002818 | 1002783 | FALSE |
| | CPTECH | test4 | 1002818 | 1018887 | TRUE |

***Figure 2-69.*** *Career Path Details File*

You will need to plan out the career path referencing the role GUIDs from the Role file to identify each role and which role it leads to. The path will be built based on whatever role GUID is listed in the nextRole column of the Career Path-Career Path Details file along with the value of the isPeerRole column.

## Career Path-Career Path Details File Layout

The file is used to map associations to lead-to and lead-from roles.

The columns for the file are explained in the following:

- **OPERATOR** (column A) will be blank for new career paths. Other values are Clear, Delimit, and Delete.
- **externalCode** (column B) will contain the career path name. This is the name you assigned in column B of the career path file.
- **careerPathDetails.externalCode** (column C) is where, for a new career path, you can assign a unique external code. If you are updating details within an existing career path, you need to find the code from an export of the career path details file.
- **careerPathDetails.role.externalCode** (column D) should contain the role GUID for the role that you are adding to the path.

- **nextRole.externalCode** (column E) should contain the role GUID of the next role in the path.
- **careerPathDetails.isPeerRole** (column F) identifies if the role is a peer role (TRUE or FALSE).

When mapping "lead-to" and "lead-from" roles, "careerPathDetails.role.externalCode" and "careerPathDetails.nextRole.externalCode" are used to associate the next role in the path. By identifying a role in column D and the next role in column E, the system will know if the next role is already in the path. If so, the role you are adding is the "lead-to" role rather than the "lead-from" role.

When mapping peer roles, "careerPathDetails.role.externalCode" and "careerPathDetails.nextRole.externalCode" may contain either of the two roles because "careerPathDetails.isPeerRole" = "TRUE" defines if the mapping is a peer role.

After the paths are built, save the file, and validate it in "Import and Export Data" with generic object type of "Career Path-Career Path Details". After checking the results in "Monitor Jobs", if the validation was successful, go back to "Import and Export Data" and import the file.

After the import, you can return to the Career Paths tab in Development, and the career path has been built.

You have now created the career paths that employees will be able to reference in their career worksheets.

# Suggested Roles

Another feature of Career Worksheet enables the employee to see suggested roles. There is a tab on the worksheet called "Suggested Roles" as seen in Figure 2-70. Here, an employee will see roles suggested for them based on configuration by the admin. The Suggested Roles tab is only visible to an employee and not to their managers or HR managers.

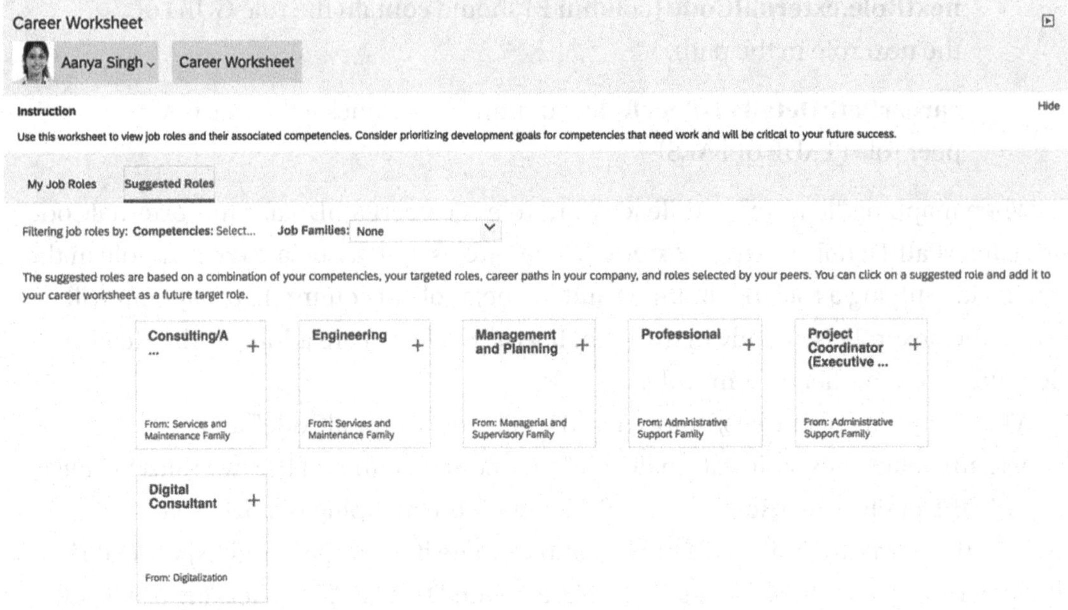


***Figure 2-70.*** *Suggested Roles*

Suggested roles can be based on career paths or a defined set of criteria. The suggested roles can be a combination of competencies, targeted roles, career paths, and roles selected by peers. The suggested roles are based on configuration done by the admin. Go to Tools ➤ Manage Suggested Roles as seen in Figure 2-71.

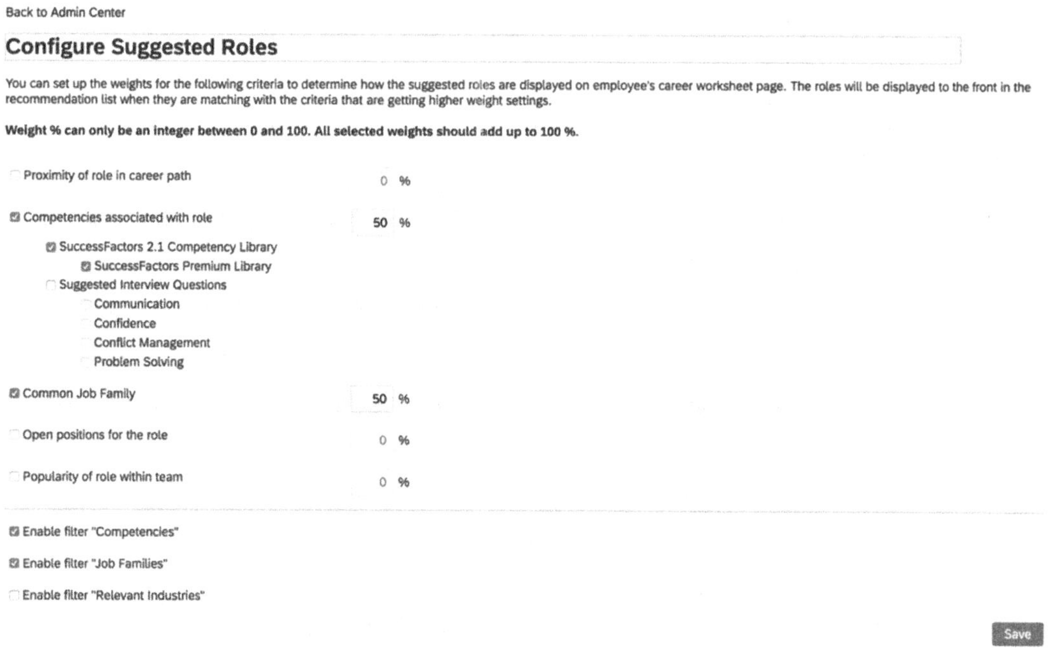

Back to Admin Center

**Configure Suggested Roles**

You can set up the weights for the following criteria to determine how the suggested roles are displayed on employee's career worksheet page. The roles will be displayed to the front in the recommendation list when they are matching with the criteria that are getting higher weight settings.

**Weight % can only be an integer between 0 and 100. All selected weights should add up to 100 %.**

- [ ] Proximity of role in career path 0 %
- [x] Competencies associated with role 50 %
  - [x] SuccessFactors 2.1 Competency Library
    - [x] SuccessFactors Premium Library
  - [ ] Suggested Interview Questions
    - [ ] Communication
    - [ ] Confidence
    - [ ] Conflict Management
    - [ ] Problem Solving
- [x] Common Job Family 50 %
- [ ] Open positions for the role 0 %
- [ ] Popularity of role within team 0 %

- [x] Enable filter "Competencies"
- [x] Enable filter "Job Families"
- [ ] Enable filter "Relevant Industries"

Save

***Figure 2-71.*** *Configure Suggested Roles*

An algorithm based on the criteria selected on this screen will create suggested roles for a user to choose a targeted role on their career worksheet.

There are a series of checkboxes to identify the criteria to use for suggesting roles. A weight percentage must be assigned for each criterion enabled. Weights must add up to 100 and can only be integers between 0 and 100.

The criteria to select from are

- Proximity in the career path
- Competencies
- Job family
- Open positions
- Popularity within the team

The description and scoring for each criterion are shown in Table 2-5.

***Table 2-5.*** *Suggested Roles Criteria and Scoring*

| Criteria | Description | Scoring |
|---|---|---|
| Proximity in the career path* | The closer the role is in the career path, the higher the assigned score. | For each role in the career path, calculate proximity as 1/(number of roles between current role and each role in the path). |
| Competencies associated with targeted role | Based on computed match score using Career Worksheet readiness calculation. Compared against expected competency rating. | Uses Career Worksheet role readiness %. Converts from percentage. For example, a readiness % of 70% would be a score of 0.7. |
| Job family | If the role is in the same job family as the user's role. | 0=role in a different job family as the user's role.<br>1= role in the same job family as the user's role. |
| Open positions | Only applicable for legacy positions. | 0=no open positions.<br>1=open positions. |
| Popularity within the team | Employees with the same manager who have selected the same targeted role. | Score is based on calculation: Number of peers who have selected the same targeted/the number of peers. |

As of this writing, there is a limitation when using the proximity factor. It only works on instances using Job Description Manager (JDM1.0). The date for a code enhancement for use with Job Profile Builder (JPB or JDM2.0) has not yet been announced.

Using the selected factors, a score is calculated for each role and then weighted. The roles display from highest score to lowest in the Suggested Roles tab. Up to 60 roles may be displayed.

There are three filter options seen at the bottom of the Suggested Roles configuration page: Competencies, Job Families, and Relevant Industries. These filters will be available to users when they see their suggested roles, and it allows them to filter out roles that are not aligned with their career interests. Relevant Industries is a filter available only when you use Job Profile Builder and you have added Relevant Industries as a section on your job profile template.

# Role Readiness Assessment Form

Before we get into the mechanics of the Role Readiness Assessment form, let's talk about what the form is and how it fits into the career worksheet.

The Role Readiness Assessment form is launched from the career worksheet by the employee and is used to rate how proficient they are in the competencies needed for the future role that they selected. The form is used to help employees plan their career development and identify areas of development needed for the future roles.

The Role Readiness Assessment template is a PM template, so it uses a rating scale and a route map. If Career Worksheet is enabled, a standard Role Readiness Assessment template should be found in Provisioning. It can be found under Form Template Administration.

The template should not use an overall performance rating and should only contain individual ratings for job role competencies.

The competency section of a template is shown in Figure 2-72.

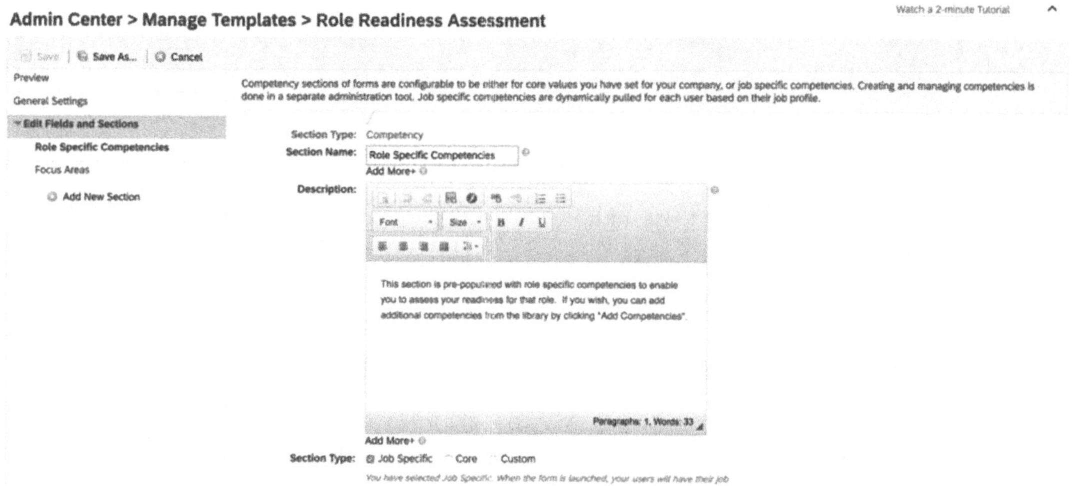


***Figure 2-72.** Role Readiness Assessment Template*

Check the template's advanced settings so that "Only create for users who don't have an existing form with an End Date between {date} and {date}" is not enabled as shown in Figure 2-73.

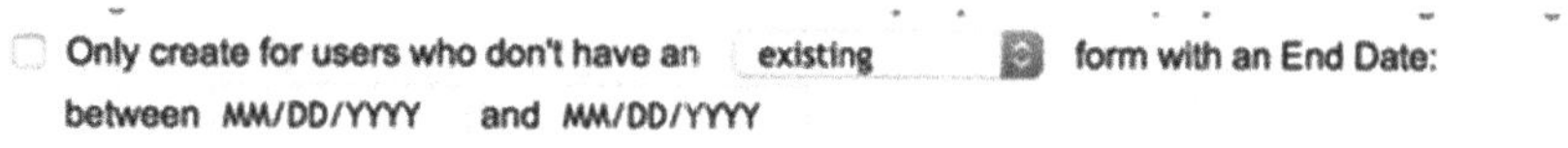

Only create for users who don't have an existing form with an End Date:
between MM/DD/YYYY and MM/DD/YYYY

***Figure 2-73.** Advanced Settings*

The template uses a very simple route map using only employee and manager roles. The employee launches the form to self-rate on the targeted role competencies. After self-rating, the form then routes to the manager who will have a Performance To-Do item on their home page and will access the form like any other PM form. The manager will rate each competency on the form. The manager's competency ratings are used to compare against the expected ratings to determine role readiness. The form then goes back to the employee to set it to completed. Having that last step in the route map enables the employee to know that the can then check the role readiness in their career worksheet. A sample route map is seen in Figure 2-74.

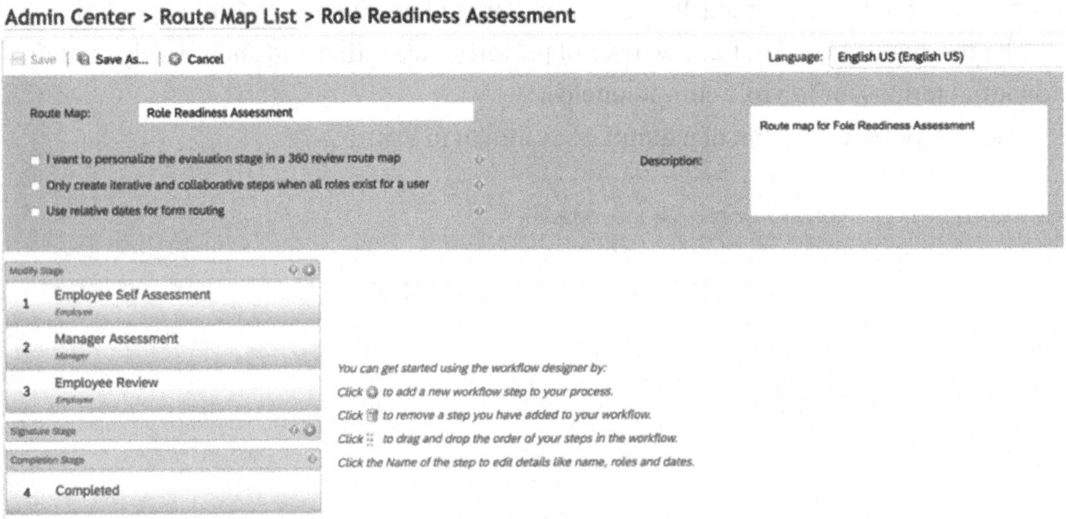

***Figure 2-74.*** *Route Map for the Role Readiness Assessment Template*

There is one additional feature that the admin may configure for Career Worksheet that will be discussed next.

# Creating a Deep Link to My Current Roles on the Career Worksheet

A deep link can be added to the Quick Links tile on a user's home page.

To set this up, type and select "Manage Home Page" in the search and find the Quick Links tile as seen in Figure 2-75.

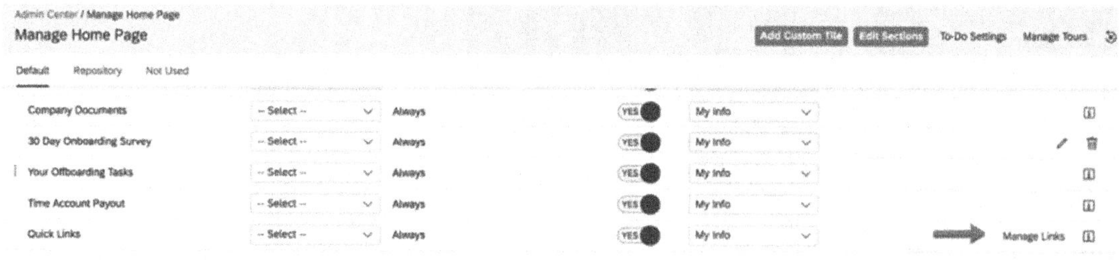

*Figure 2-75.* *Manage Home Page*

Click "Manage Links" in order to add the URL as seen in Figure 2-76.

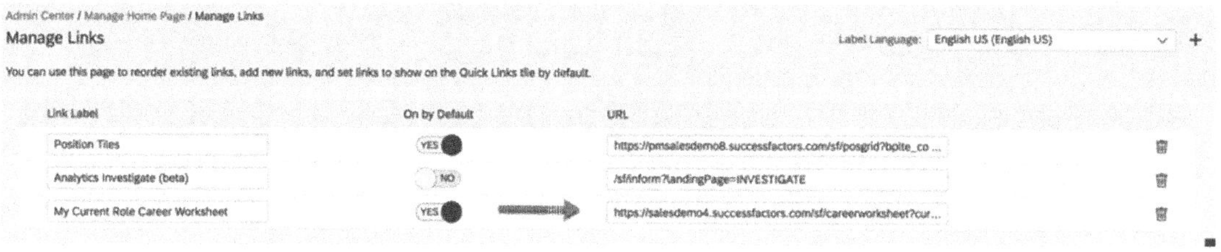

*Figure 2-76.* *Manage Links*

Provide a name for the label and enter the base URL followed by sf/careerworksheet?currentrole=true.

To find your base URL, look at the URL for your login page. An example is shown in the following:

`https://performancemanager4.successfactors.com/login#/companyEntry`

Remove "login#/companyEntry" and add "/sf/careerworksheet?currentrole=true" as seen in the following example:

`https://performancemanager4.successfactors.com/sf/careerworksheet?currentrole=true`

Make the link appear as a default and save.

The new deep link will now be available in the Quick Links tile on the home Page. The link will take the employee to the My Current Roles tab on their career worksheet as seen in Figure 2-77.

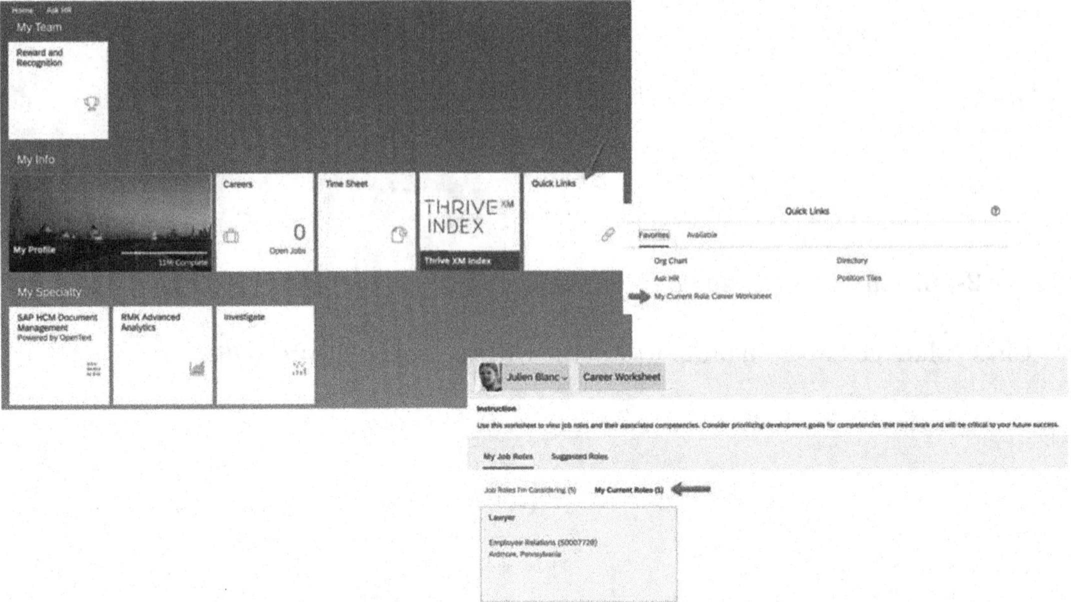

*Figure 2-77. Quick Link Tile on the Home Page*

# Recap

We have now reviewed the Career Worksheet and Career Path settings required in Provisioning. We have modified the Career Worksheet template XML. We have looked at the role-based permissions for the admin. We have learned how to create career paths and how to configure suggested roles. We have viewed Job Profile Builder to map expected ratings to job role competencies. We discussed the Role Readiness Assessment form and how to set it up. Career Worksheet is now ready to be used. In the next chapter, we will set up user role-based permissions and walk through Career Worksheet from the user perspective.

Let's now look at Career Worksheet integration.

# Career Worksheet Integration with Suggested Successors in the Succession Org Chart

Career Worksheet is integrated with Succession. The readiness calculation from Career Worksheet is used to display ten potential successors in the v12 Succession Org Chart as seen in Figure 2-78.

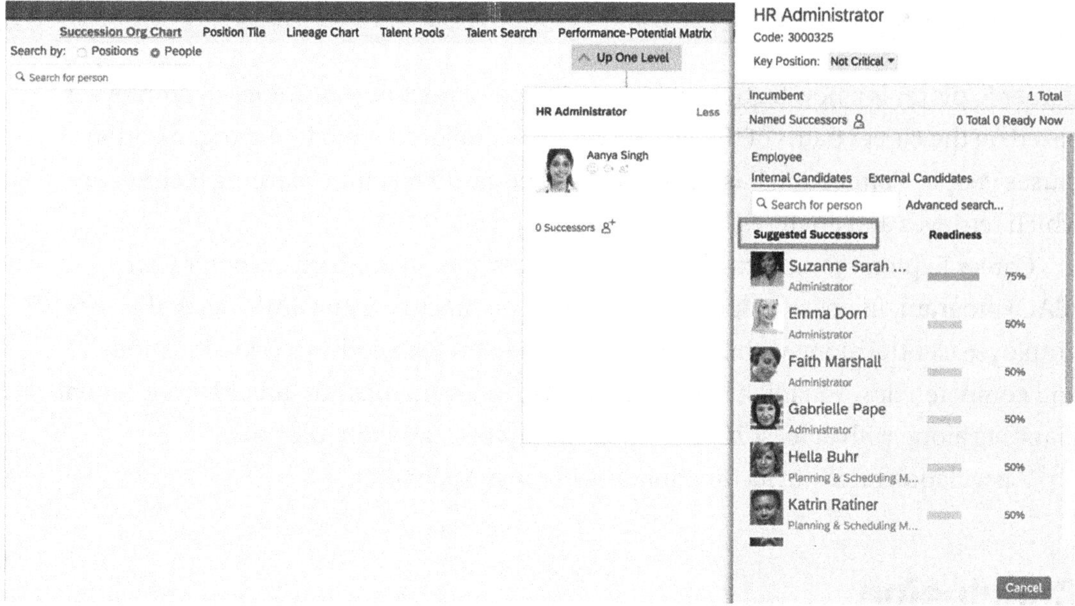


***Figure 2-78.*** *Suggested Successors*

The successor's readiness is based on the job role competencies of the target position and the competency ratings of the potential successor.

In order for this to work

- The readiness calculation switch needs to be set to "on" in the Career Worksheet template XML:

```
<switch for="new-role-readiness-calculation" value="on"/>
```

- JDM 2.0 must be used.
- The Career Worksheet template XML has "Read" permission for readiness_meter for all roles "*".
- Job role competencies are defined, and users are associated with job roles.
- Succession planners' permission role has Recommended Successors permission.

If a user does not have a competency rating for any of the competencies needed for the role, they will not be listed as a possible successor.

# Career Explorer

Career Explorer is a new feature that recommends career opportunities to employees based on the career paths of the people who are similar to them in the organization. It uses People Connection based on the SAP Leonardo machine learning technology which retrieves and analyzes Employee Central data.

Career Explorer is currently available only to those in the Early Adopter Care (EAC) program. In order to apply, at the least, you must be using SAP SuccessFactors Employee Central along with Job Profile Builder using job code, job classifications, and competencies. You must have Succession Management and Career Development Planning along with at least 1000 records of employee and job role pairs.

We will look briefly at its functionality in the next chapter.

# Conclusion

Career Worksheet is enabled, the Career Worksheet template XML has been configured, and permissions to manage the features of Career Worksheet have been granted. The admin has created career paths, determined the criteria for suggested roles, and configured the Role Readiness Assessment template.

In the next chapter, we will set up the role-based permissions that the employee, manager, and HR manager roles need to access Career Worksheet and its components.

We will then walk through the functionality available to an employee and their manager when accessing Career Worksheet.

# CHAPTER 3

# Using Career Worksheet

In Chapter 2, we enabled and configured Career Worksheet. We granted admin permissions and learned how to create career paths. We saw how to choose the settings for suggesting roles. We viewed the process to add expected ratings to job role competencies, and we looked at the Role Readiness Assessment form. Now, we are ready to see how Career Worksheet is used by an employee and their manager.

We will gain insight on how an employee uses Career Worksheet to explore job roles within the organization. We will also see how career paths provide an employee with a glimpse of job role progression to move forward within the organization. We will also learn how to evaluate an employee's readiness for future roles.

In this chapter, we will walk through the tabs within the career worksheet. We will see how the readiness meter works when selecting a targeted role. We will discuss the components in each tab and how to browse career paths, view suggested roles, and launch a Role Readiness Assessment form. We will look at the features available to an employee, their manager, and their HR manager. We will also touch briefly on the new Career Explorer.

The following are just a few reminders from the previous chapter:

- Career Worksheet is dependent on job roles and their job role definitions, mapped competencies, and expected competency proficiency ratings.
- Competencies must be mapped to job roles either by using Job Profile Builder or via legacy Families and Roles. We suggest using JDM v2.0 which supports the use of job profile descriptions. If you are not using EC with MDF position nomination which has job code on the position object, the job codes have to be assigned in the user data file (UDF) which are then used in your role/job code mapping. You may refer to Volume 1, Chapter 3 for more information on how to map job codes to roles and assign competencies to roles. You may also map behaviors to competencies.




S. Traynor et al., *SAP SuccessFactors Talent: Volume 2*, https://doi.org/10.1007/978-1-4842-6995-4_3

- The development goal plan must include a competency field if you want a user to tie career development goals to a targeted job role's competency.
- Competency ratings used in Career Worksheet may come from a completed performance or 360 form or the Role Readiness Assessment form.

---

**Note** For information on upgrading to Job Profile Builder, see SAP note #2383059. For more information on upgrading to Career Path V2, see SAP note #2485992.

---

# Role-Based Permissions for User Roles

Before we begin, we will need to set up the role-based permissions for the employee, manager, and HR manager roles. Differences between any of these role permissions will be highlighted.

## Career Worksheet Permission

Grant the role-based permission so roles can access the Career Worksheet tab under Development.

There is a permission difference for employee, manager, and HR manager roles of access within Career Development Planning.

The employee role will need access to the career worksheet and suggested roles. The suggested roles are only accessible to the employee; managers cannot view the suggested roles of their direct reports. Even if permitted, the manager and HR manager do not have access to suggested roles.

Type and select "Manage Permission Roles" in the search bar. Let's start with the employee role. Open the role, click "Permissions," and use the following paths to grant permission:

User Permissions ➤ Career Development Planning ➤ Career Worksheet Access Permission

User Permissions ➤ Career Development Planning ➤ Career Worksheet Suggested Roles Access Permission

The permissions are shown in Figure 3-1. Make sure the Career Development Plan (CDP) Access Permission is already granted. This provides access to the Development tab from the Home menu.

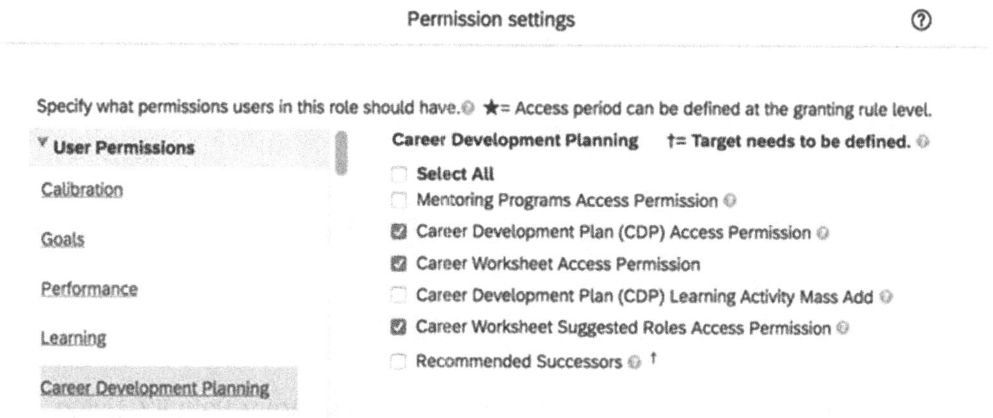

***Figure 3-1.*** *Career Development Planning Permissions*

Save the role. For the manager and HR manager roles, use the following path to grant the permission:

User Permissions ➤ Career Development Planning ➤ Career Worksheet Access Permission.

In the previous chapter, we learned how to configure career paths. If the HR manager role will be creating and managing career paths, there is an additional permission needed. The role-based permission needed for the HR role is found in Administrator Permissions ➤ Manage Career Development. Grant access to "Manage Career Path" as shown in Figure 3-2. Configuring career path nodes is optional.

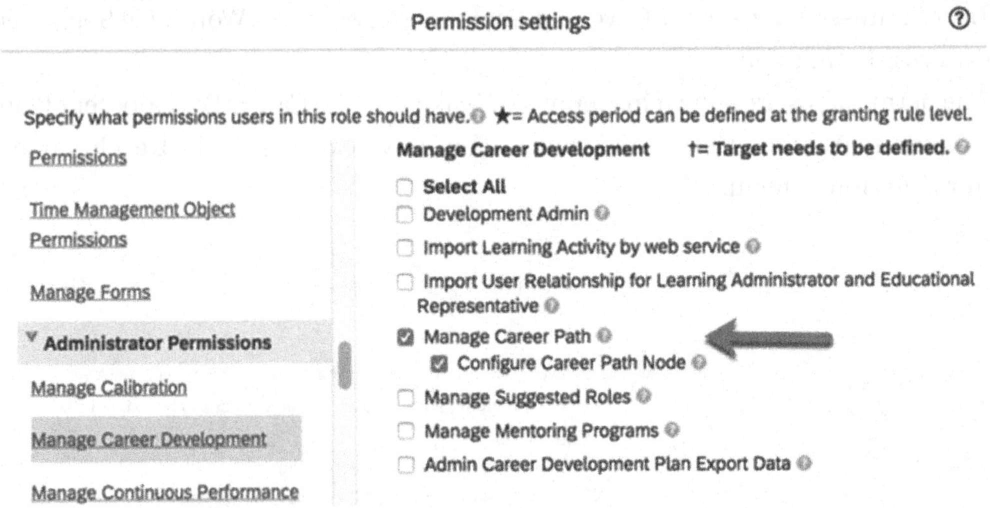

Permission settings

Specify what permissions users in this role should have. ★= Access period can be defined at the granting rule level.

Permissions

Time Management Object Permissions

Manage Forms

Administrator Permissions

Manage Calibration

Manage Career Development

Manage Continuous Performance

Manage Career Development †= Target needs to be defined.

- [ ] Select All
- [ ] Development Admin
- [ ] Import Learning Activity by web service
- [ ] Import User Relationship for Learning Administrator and Educational Representative
- [x] Manage Career Path
  - [x] Configure Career Path Node
- [ ] Manage Suggested Roles
- [ ] Manage Mentoring Programs
- [ ] Admin Career Development Plan Export Data

***Figure 3-2.*** *Manage Career Path Permission*

---

**Note** A career path node is only available when using Career Path V2. Using career path nodes provides additional information for a role, such as job code, job family, number of employees in the role, and number of role competencies.

---

## Career Worksheet Template Access

Grant permission to the Career Worksheet template so that the role may access the career worksheet plan. Permissions are defined by target population. Since the employee role has access to "self," the employee will see only their plan. When the manager role has the template permission, they can view the career worksheet plans of their direct reports. Similarly, when the HR manager role has this access, the target population will be all of the employees the HR manager supports.

Use the following path to grant permission for the employee, manager, and HR manager roles:

User Permissions ➤ Goals ➤ Goal Plan Permissions ➤ Others ➤ Career Worksheet

The permission setting to access the career worksheet plan is shown in Figure 3-3.

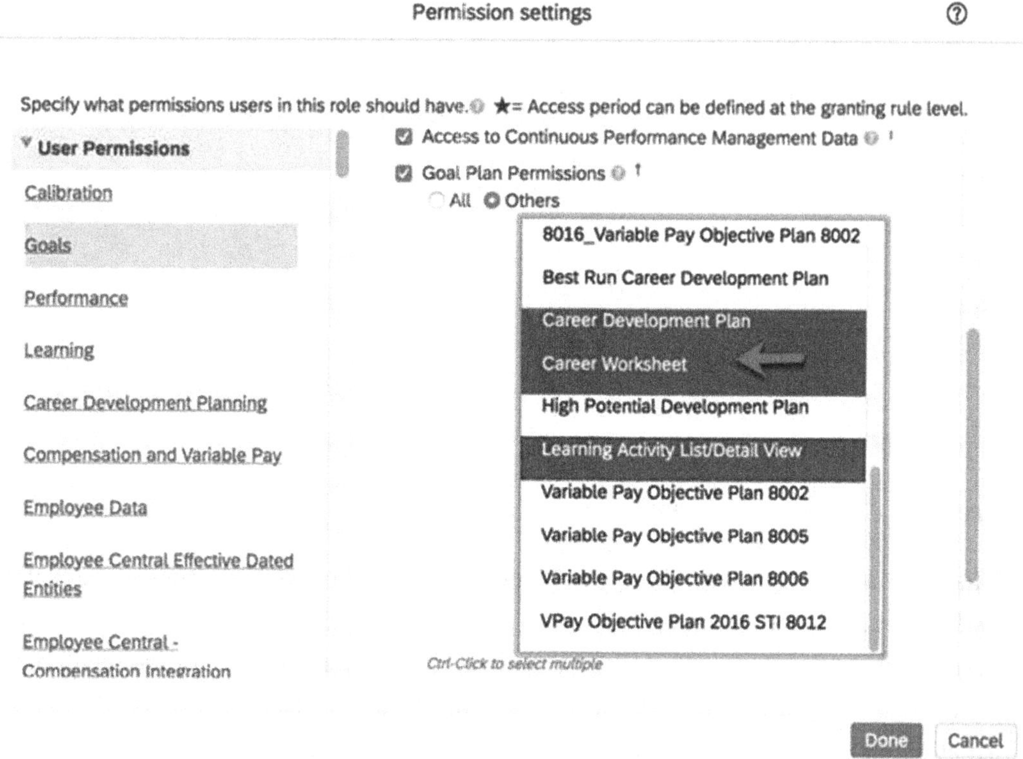


***Figure 3-3.** Goal Plan Permissions for Career Worksheet*

This is in addition to the Career Development Plan access granted earlier and the Learning Activity List/Detail View if using learning activities with the development plan.

# Career Path Permission

Career path access for all of the roles is needed. If the HR manager role will be creating career paths, the permissions will differ.

For the employee and manager roles, within the User Permissions section, go to Miscellaneous Permissions ➤ Career Path ➤ View Visibility. The permission is shown in Figure 3-4.

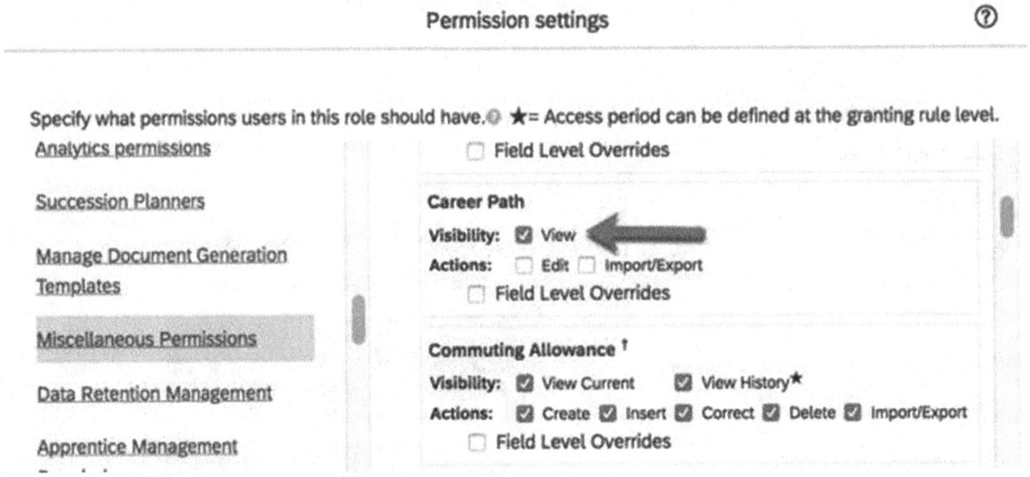

**Figure 3-4.** *Career Path Permissions*

The HR manager role would require "View" and "Edit" career path permissions if the role will be creating career paths.

A sidenote on this permission: For "View" and "Edit" permissions, the role will have access to all career paths. The Field Level Overrides option is used to choose which basic information elements to display or hide for a career path definition.

The override fields are shown in Figure 3-5.

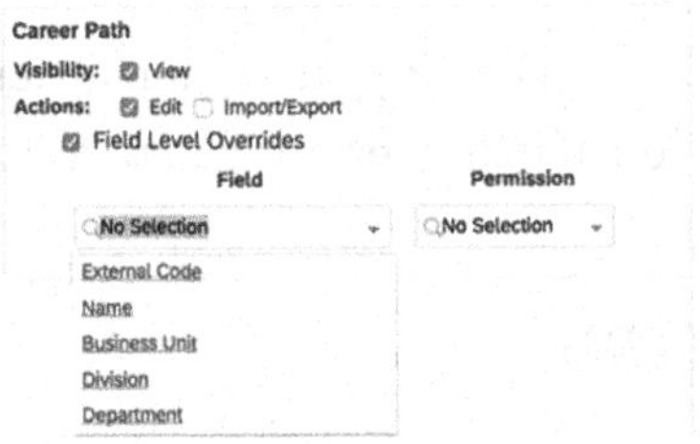

**Figure 3-5.** *Career Path Override Fields*

The permission types are "No Access" or "Read Only" as seen in Figure 3-6.

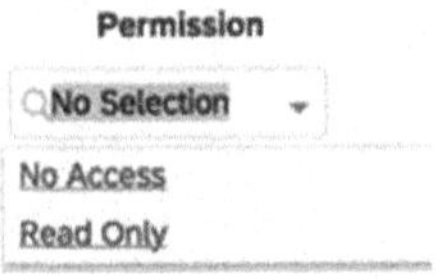

**Figure 3-6.** *Override Permissions*

When "*No Access*" is selected for a field, the field will be hidden. If "Read Only" is selected, the role will not be able to use this field when creating or editing a career path.

If you wish to restrict user access to specific career paths, this is done in the Edit Granting section of a permission role as seen in Figure 3-7.

Admin Center

Back to Admin Center

Permission Role Detail

Page 1 of 1

| | Permission Groups or Users | Target population | Active | Action |
|---|---|---|---|---|
| | Employees | everyone in self | ✔ | Edit Granting |

***Figure 3-7.*** *Restrict Access*

Within Edit Granting, under step 3, "Specify the target population for the other objects" as seen in Figure 3-8, scroll down to find Career Path.

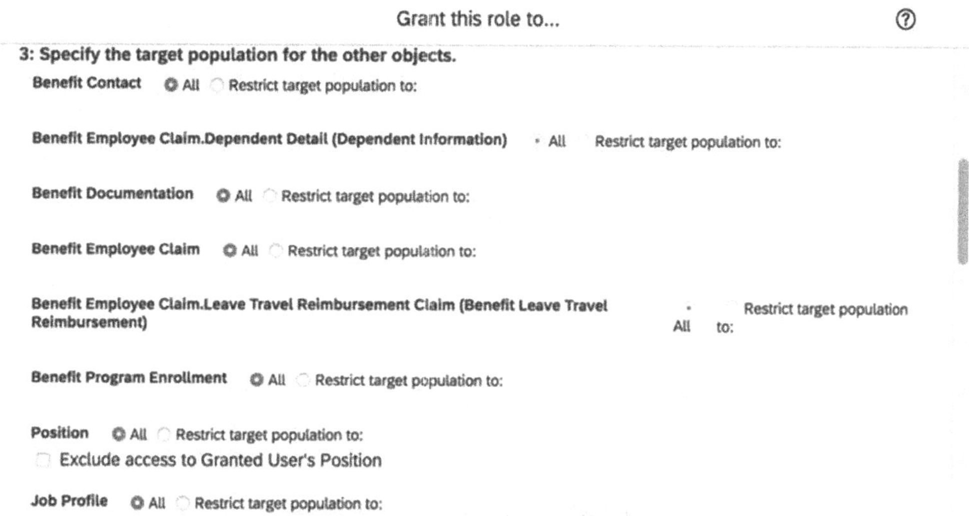


***Figure 3-8.*** *Specify the Career Path Target Population*

There is an option to restrict the target population to selected career paths. Select the restrictions in the dropdown menus. The options are visible in the dropdown list as seen in Figure 3-9.

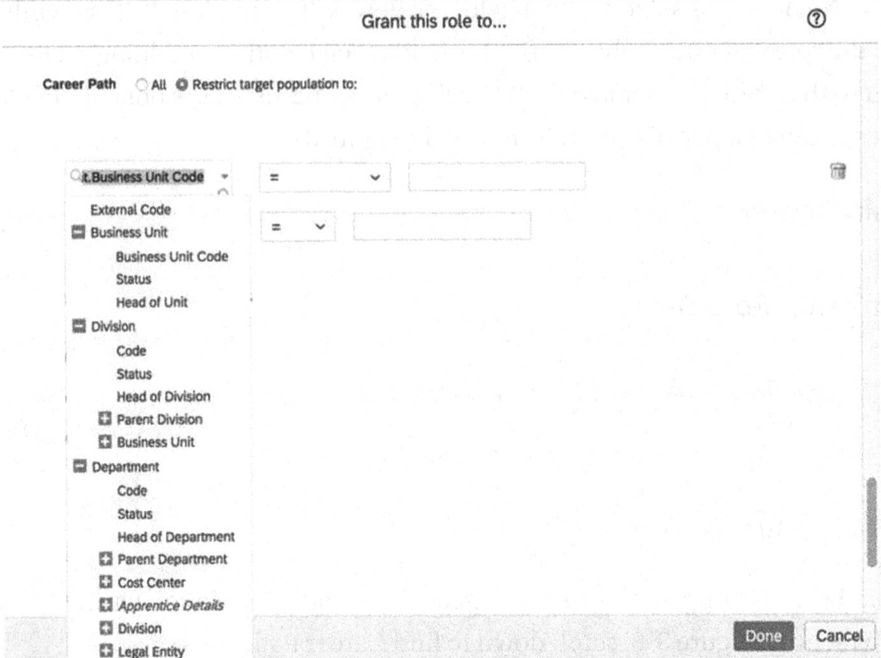


*Figure 3-9.* Restriction Options

Access may be restricted by external code, business unit, department, or division. These are the same filters seen when creating a career path, as seen in Figure 3-10.

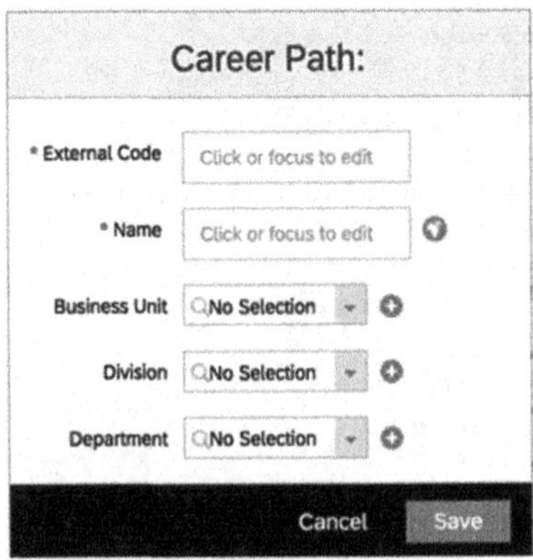


*Figure 3-10.* Career Path Fields to Restrict By

Next, select the criteria and the values to identify the career paths the role is restricted to as seen in Figure 3-11.

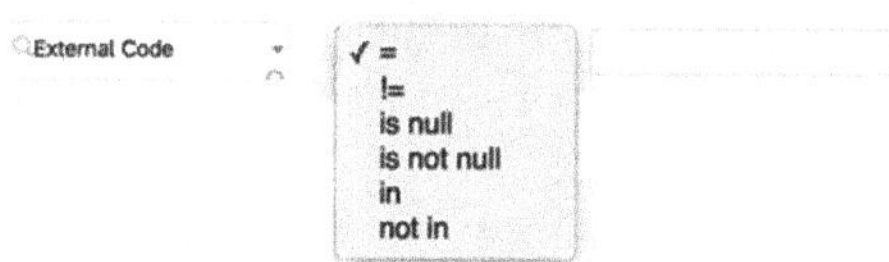


*Figure 3-11.* *Value to Restrict By*

## Employee Permissions for Role Readiness

The employee and manager roles will need Performance Management Access within Performance under the User Permissions section of permission settings as seen in Figure 3-12. This allows access to the Role Readiness Assessment form. Most likely, this permission has already been granted.

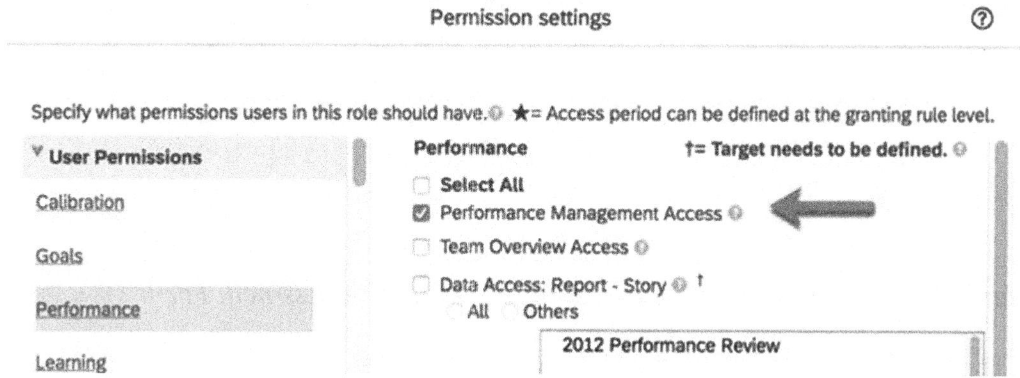


*Figure 3-12.* *Performance Management Access*

The employee role will also need to be able to launch the Role Readiness Assessment form, so grant permission to Create Forms under General User Permission and select Role Readiness Assessment as seen in Figure 3-13.

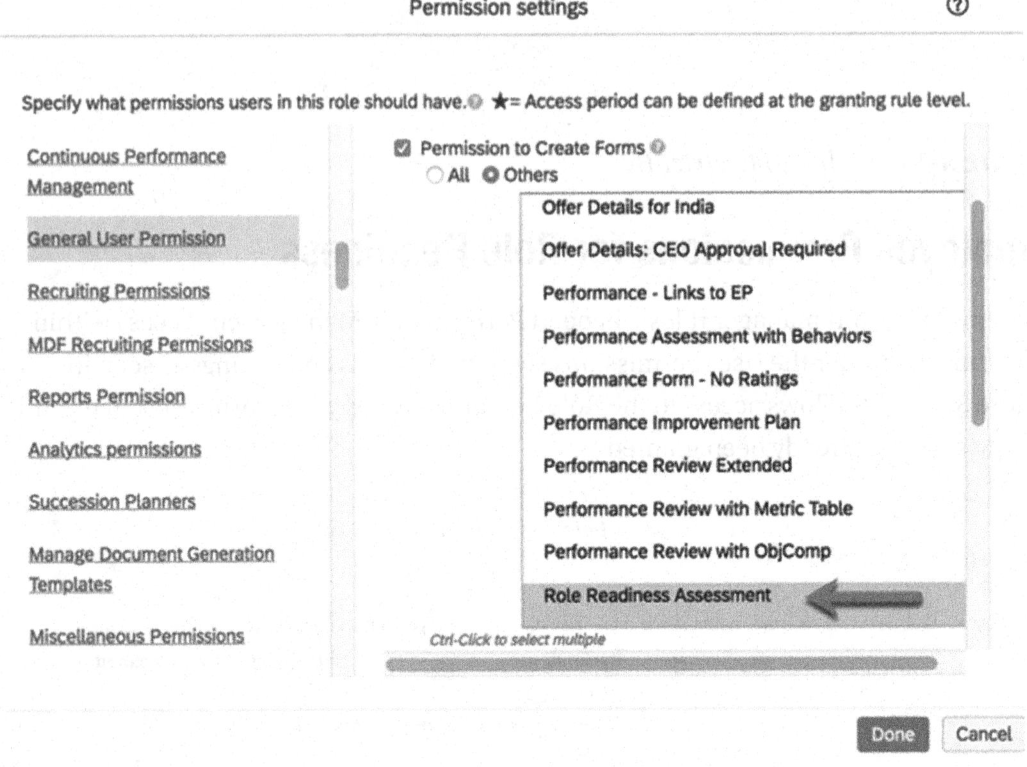


***Figure 3-13.** Permission to Create the Role Readiness Assessment Form*

The manager and HR manager roles do not require permission to create the Role Readiness Assessment form because only employees may launch this form from their career worksheets.

# Reporting Permissions for Manager and HR Manager Roles

If managers and HR managers are going to be creating or running ad hoc reports on Career Worksheet targeted role data, permission will be needed to create and run these reports.

For these roles, go to Reports Permission found in the User Permissions section and enable the following:

- Create Report ➤ Career Worksheet Targeted Role
- Run Report ➤ Career Worksheet Targeted Role

These roles will also need access to the CDP Dashboard. Also found within Reports Permission, under Analytics Tiles and Dashboards, enable CDP Dashboard.

These permissions will allow a manager report access to their direct reports. The HR manager role will have access to all employees whom they support.

The role-based permissions are summarized in Table 3-1.

***Table 3-1.*** *Permissions Needed by Role*

| **Permission/Role** | **Employee Role** | **Manager Role** | **HR Manager Role** |
|---|---|---|---|
| Career Development Planning ➤ Career Worksheet Access Permission | X | X | X |
| Career Development Planning ➤ Career Worksheet Suggested Roles Access Permission | X | | |
| Manage Career Development ➤ Manage Career Path | | | X optional |
| Permission to Create Forms ➤ Role Readiness Assessment | X | | |
| Performance Management Access | X | X | |
| Miscellaneous Permissions ➤ Career Path | X | X | X |
| Goals ➤ Goal Plan Permissions ➤ Career Worksheet | X | X | X |
| Reports Permission ➤ Create Report ➤ Career Worksheet Targeted Role | | X | X |
| Reports Permission ➤ Run Report ➤ Career Worksheet Targeted Role | | X | X |
| Reports Permission ➤ Analytics Tiles and Dashboards ➤ CDP Dashboard | | X | X |

We have now granted Career Worksheet access to the employee, manager, and HR manager permission roles. We will now look at the features within Career Worksheet.

## Career Worksheet Features Available to an Employee

Features and functionality available to an employee in Career Worksheet include the following:

- Browse job roles
- View suggested roles
- See job profiles when browsing roles
- Add a targeted role
- See competencies needed for a targeted role
- See all the roles that have a competency of a targeted role
- Launch the Role Readiness Assessment form
- View the career path for targeted roles
- View the career path for the current role
- Make the targeted role visible on Employee Profile
- Add development goals to targeted role competencies
- Add development goals to current role competencies
- View names of employees in a targeted role
- See the readiness meter for each targeted role
- See competencies met for a targeted role
- See gap analysis for a targeted role

## Using Career Worksheet

Now that we have seen what is available for an employee, let's begin!

Career Worksheet is contained within the Career Development module. An employee will have access to Career Worksheet from the Home main menu by clicking the dropdown and selecting Development. Development Plan is the default view as seen in Figure 3-14. Click the tab to "Career Worksheet".

***Figure 3-14.** View of the Development Module from the Home Menu*

Career Worksheet, as shown in Figure 3-15, is comprised of two tabs: My Job Roles and Suggested Roles. The view shown in the following displays the My Job Roles tab.

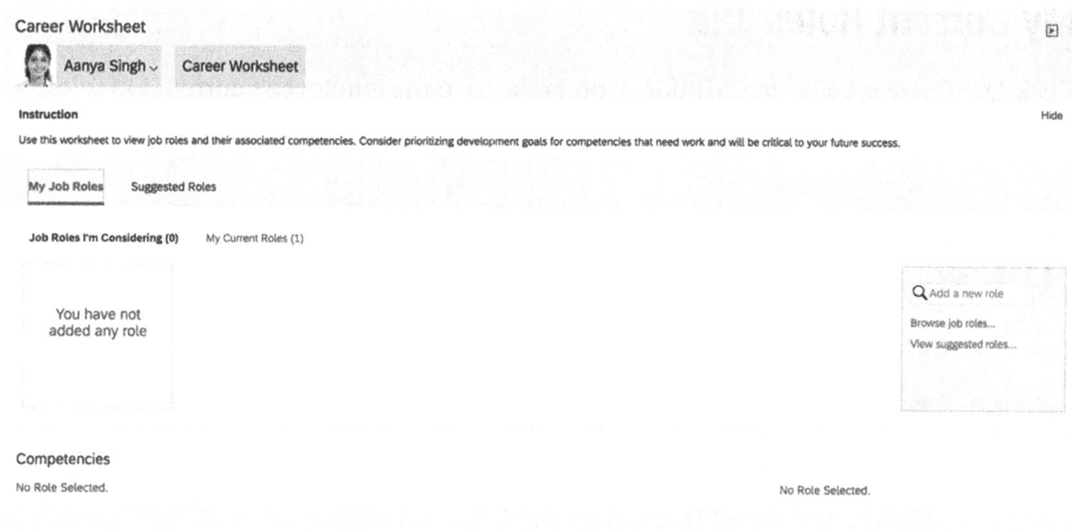


***Figure 3-15.** Employee's Initial View of Career Worksheet*

# My Job Roles

We will walk through each tab of the worksheet. We will review what appears in each tab and how each tab works. First, we will look at the My Job Roles tab.

My Job Roles contains two sub-tabs: Job Roles I'm Considering and My Current Roles. The label for each tab includes a job role count.

Job Roles I'm Considering will display each job role that the employee selects as a targeted role. This can be thought of as a potential future role. Until the employee selects a targeted role, there will be no job roles displaying here. In this case, "You have not added any role" displays in this tab as shown in Figure 3-15.

Once a targeted role is selected, an employee will see how ready they are to step into the role. The readiness is based on the mastery of the job role competencies for the targeted role and is displayed in a readiness meter. The Readiness Meter shows a percentage of how ready the employee is.

Before we look at the functionality available on this screen, how to browse job roles, view suggested roles or career paths, and select targeted roles, let's switch over to the My Current Roles sub-tab. This will give us a chance to familiarize ourselves with some of the components found in each sub-tab. We will return to Job Roles I'm Considering once we understand the basics.

## My Current Roles Tab

Click "*My Current Roles*" to see information related to the employee's current job role. The screen is shown in Figure 3-16.

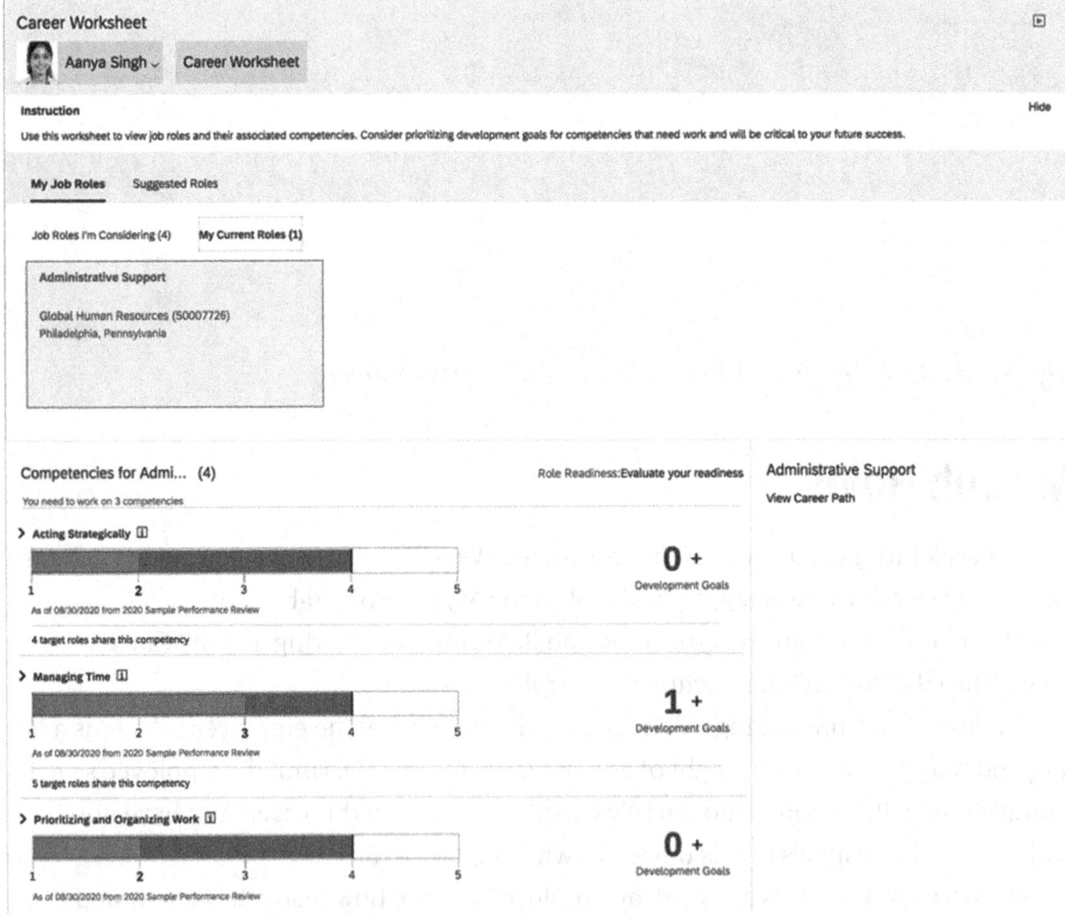


***Figure 3-16.*** *My Current Roles Tab*

My Current Roles contains the job role that the employee is associated with based on the job code field. The current job title is listed in a box above the competencies for the job role. As a reminder, a job code may only be mapped to one job role, but you may have multiple job codes mapped to a job role. The job role has mapped competencies with expected ratings. It is the expected ratings for the job role competencies that we will be focusing on. We discussed defining the expected competencies in the prior chapter. Volume 1, Chapter 3 describes the process of mapping job codes to job roles, so you may refer back to that chapter for any questions as well.

The job role competencies and any associated development goals for the employee's current job role are seen in this sub-tab. If the employee has completed a performance review that rated job role competencies, the worksheet will use the competency ratings from the form and display the actual competency rating against the expected competency rating for the job role.

If that doesn't make sense yet, we will get there. We are setting the stage to understand the Job Roles I'm Considering tab by looking at the current job role first.

This page is structured so that all of the job role competencies are listed and will include any core competencies mapped to the job role. The competencies where the employee did not meet or exceed the expected rating will display first. These will appear under the heading "You need to work on n competencies" where "n" is the number of competencies as seen in Figure 3-17.

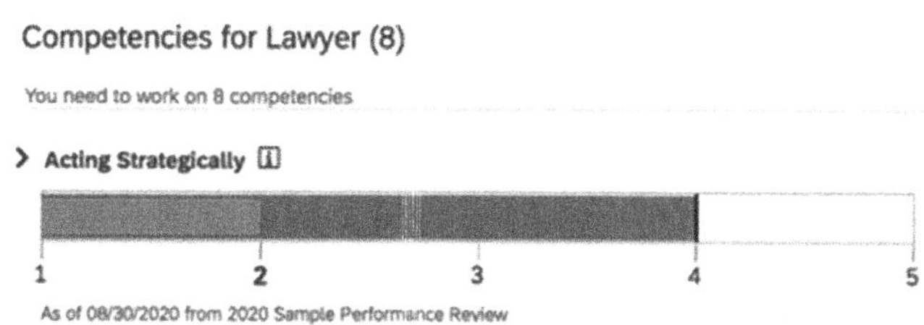


***Figure 3-17.** Current Role Where Competencies Have Not Been Met*

The job role's competencies where the employee's competency rating meets or exceeds the expected rating will display under the heading "You have met n competencies" as seen in Figure 3-18. These competencies will follow the unmet competencies.

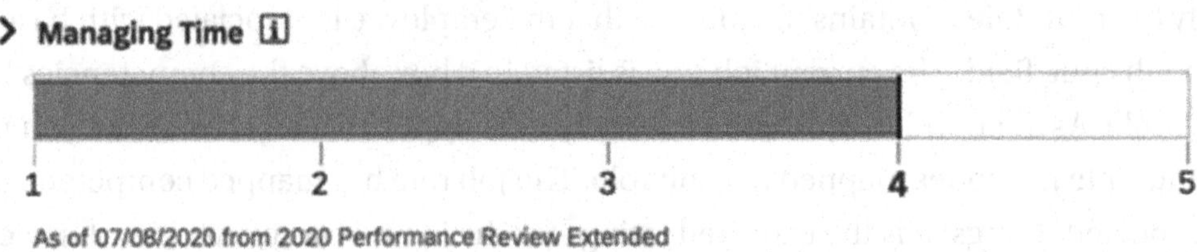


***Figure 3-18.*** *View of a Job Role Competency Where the Actual Rating Meets or Exceeds the Expected Rating*

Figure 3-19 shows the details for a competency.

Click the information icon to the right of the competency name to see the competency details.

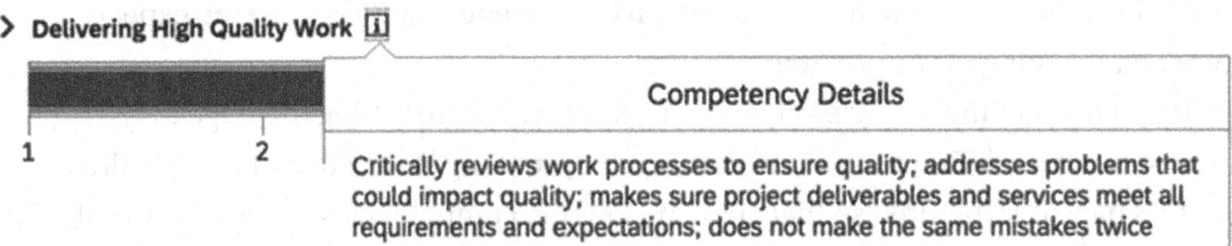


***Figure 3-19.*** *Competency Details*

The competency details come from the competency description as seen in Figure 3-20. This can be found using the path Manage Job Profile Content ➤ Competency ➤ Competency Name.

Back to: Admin Center

Edit: Competency

Edit the content (Competency) that can be used for job profiles.

* Competency Name: Communicating Effectively

* Library: SuccessFactors 2.1 Competency Library

* Category: SuccessFactors Premium Library

Description: Expresses ideas and information in a clear and concise manner; tailors message to fit the interests and needs of the audience; delivers information in a manner that is interesting and compelling to the listener

Paragraphs: 1, Words: 34

* Core: Yes No

***Figure 3-20.*** *Competency Description*

Back on My Job Roles, there is a gap graph under each competency. This is a visual representation of the gap in an employee's mastery of a competency against the expected competency rating. The graph identifies the difference between the employee's last rating of record for the competency and the expected rating for the competency. It uses the rating scale that was identified in the Career Worksheet template XML and the performance template where the ratings are coming from. We looked at both in the previous chapter and pointed out that the same rating scale must be used in order for the gap graphs and readiness meters to work.

Mouse over the graph to see the actual rating vs. the expected rating as seen in Figure 3-21.

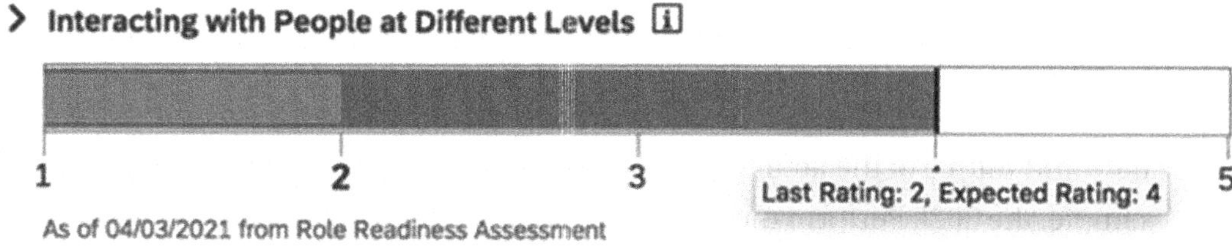


***Figure 3-21.** Gap Graph with Ratings*

The expected rating seen on the graph comes from the job role competency expected rating as shown in Figure 3-22. Refer to the prior chapter to review the setup of the expected competency ratings.

Back to: Admin Center

Edit: Role

Edit the content (Role) that can be used for job profiles.

* Role Name Lawyer

* Family Administrative

1 Mapped Job Codes 1 Mapped Skills 8 Mapped Competencies 0 Mapped Talent Pools

8 Competencies

Map Competencies

| Competency Name | Added | Last Modified | Weight | Rating | Behavi... | Actions |
|---|---|---|---|---|---|---|
| Critical Thinking | 10/01/2015 | 05/24/2019 | % | 75 % | | |
| Composing and ... | 10/01/2015 | 05/24/2019 | % | 50 % | | |
| Making Convincin... | 10/01/2015 | 05/24/2019 | % | 75 % | | |
| Reading Effectively | 10/01/2015 | 05/24/2019 | % | 50 % | | |
| Communicating E... | 10/01/2015 | 05/24/2019 | % | 75 % | | |
| Working Safely | 10/01/2015 | 05/24/2019 | % | 50 % | | |
| Making Accurate ... | 10/01/2015 | 05/24/2019 | % | 75 % | | |
| Acting Strategically | 10/01/2015 | 09/05/2020 | % | 75 % | | |

Calculate [Communicating Effectively] Expecte...

Lowest Score 1

Highest Score 5

Expected Score 4

Compute

Calculated Expected Rating % 75

Cancel Apply

***Figure 3-22.** Job Role Competency Expected Score*

Every competency where the employee's rating met or exceeded the expected rating will show the green line (last rating) covering the blue line (expected rating) as seen in Figure 3-23. An as mentioned earlier, these competencies will display after all competencies that have not been met.

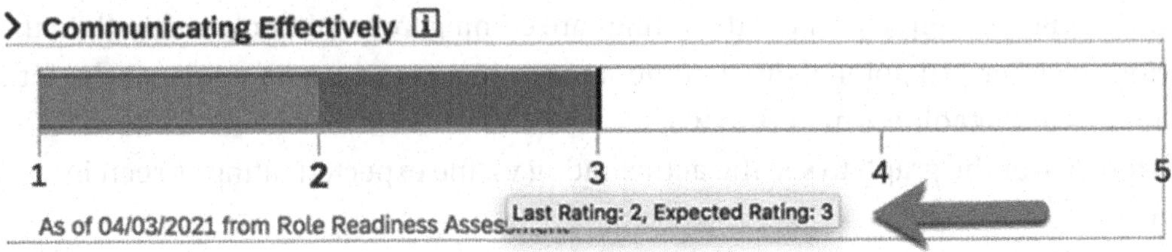


***Figure 3-23.** Actual Competency Rating Exceeding the Expected Competency Rating*

The date and source of the actual rating are seen beneath the graph as in Figure 3-24. In this example, the 2020 Performance Review Ask for FB form completed on 09/14/20 is the competency rating source.

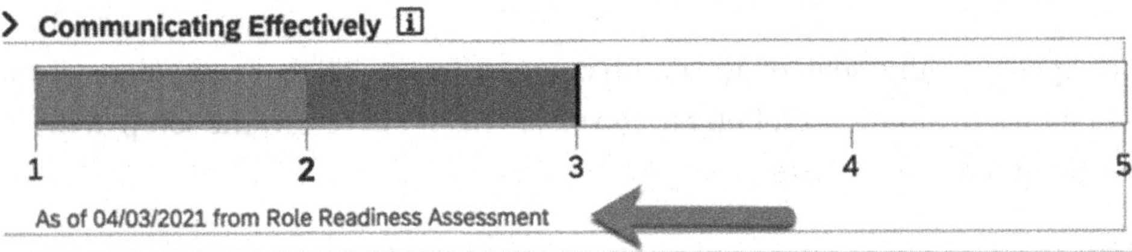


***Figure 3-24.** Date and Source of the Actual Competency Rating*

As a reminder, the most recent rating from a completed performance form is used.

If there are any development goals associated with the competency, they will be reflected in the development goal count to the right of the gap graph. To see the development goal details, expand the competency as shown in Figure 3-25. Here, you may edit or delete the competency. Any changes made here will reflect in the employee's development plan.

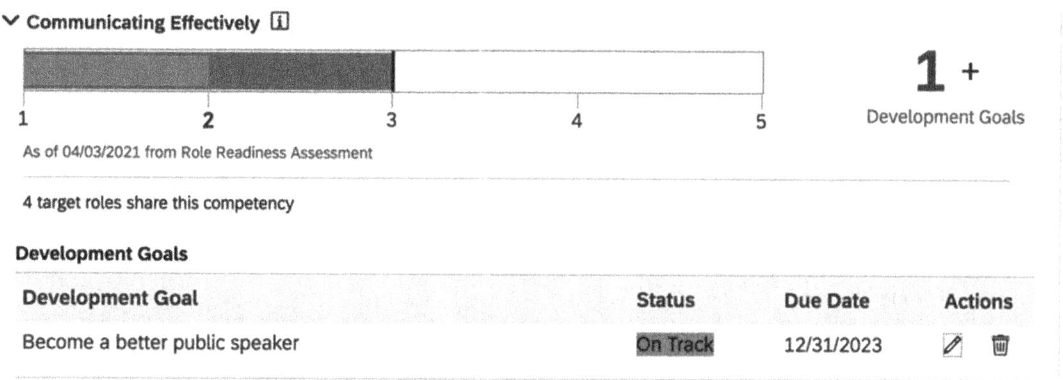


*Figure 3-25.* *Development Goals Associated with a Job Role Competency*

Click the plus sign as seen in Figure 3-26 to add a development goal to the competency.

1 +

Development Goals

*Figure 3-26.* *Development Goal Count for a Competency*

Adding the goal will increment the development goal count for the competency and will also add the goal to the development goal plan with the associated competency as seen in Figure 3-27.

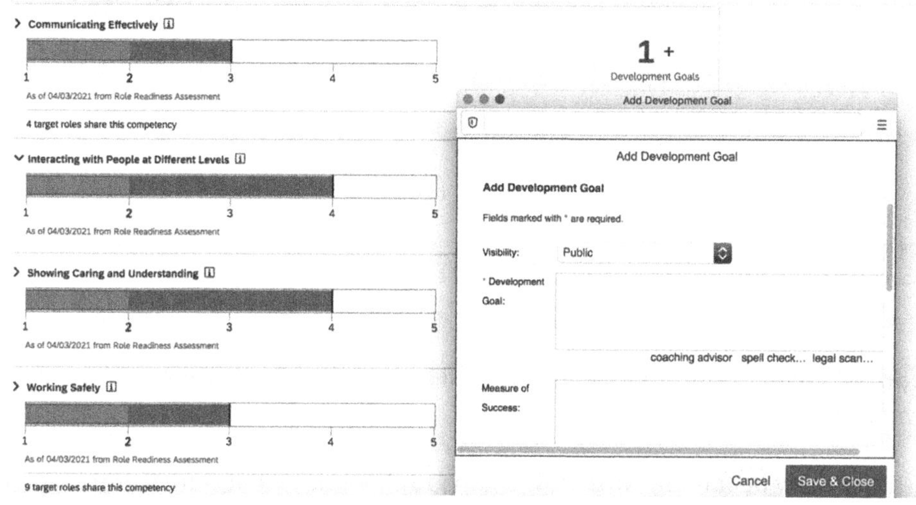


*Figure 3-27.* *Adding a Development Goal to a Competency*

The development goal is now associated with the competency on the worksheet as seen in Figure 3-28.

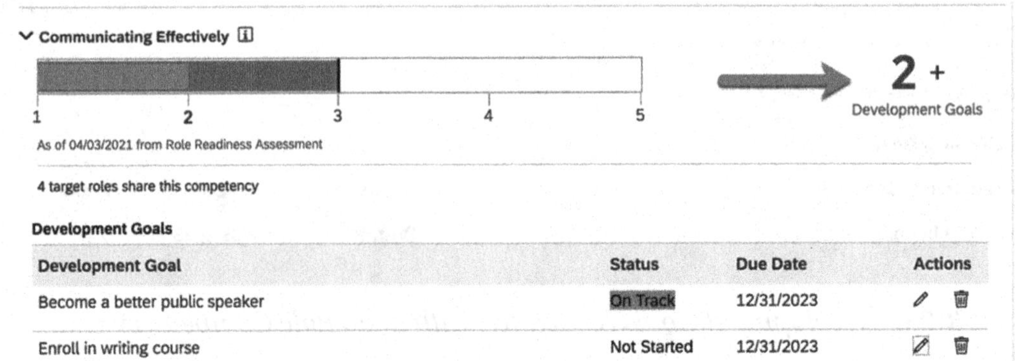


*Figure 3-28. New Development Goal Added to a Job Role Competency*

The development goal has been added to the development plan and has the competency associated with it as seen in Figure 3-29.

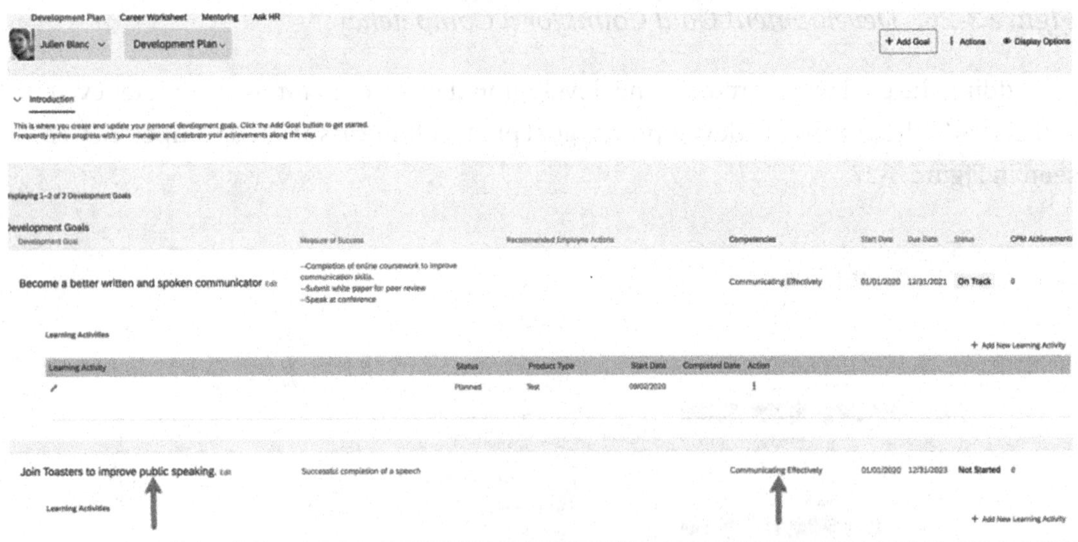


*Figure 3-29. Development Plan with the New Development Goal and Associated Competency*

We should now be familiar with how a gap graph works, what is measured, and how job role competencies are seen for My Current Roles. This is the same layout used in the Job Roles I'm Considering tab with additional features that we will explore next.

## Job Roles I'm Considering

The Job Roles I'm Considering sub-tab will not contain any roles or competencies until the employee selects a future role as seen in Figure 3-30. As mentioned earlier, a future role is also called a targeted role, and the terms may be used interchangeably.

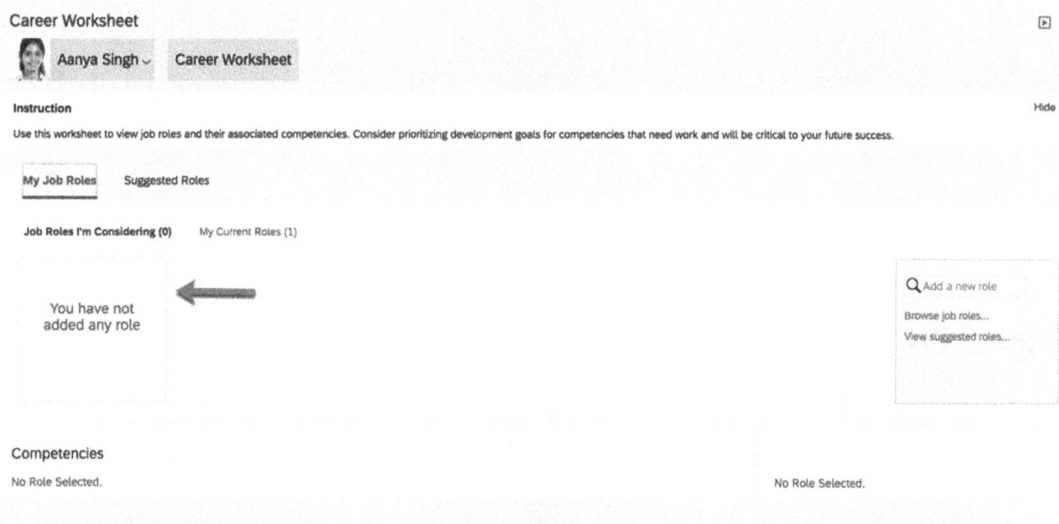


***Figure 3-30.*** *Job Roles I'm Considering Tab Without Any Roles*

Once a job role is selected, it will display in this sub-tab, and the competencies associated with the role will be included.

Initially, there are two ways for an employee to select a targeted role: browsing job roles or viewing suggested roles. Once a role is selected, there will be an additional option through the targeted role's career path. We will look at each method in detail.

## Browse Job Roles

The employee may view all job roles by clicking the link "Browse job roles..." as seen in Figure 3-31.

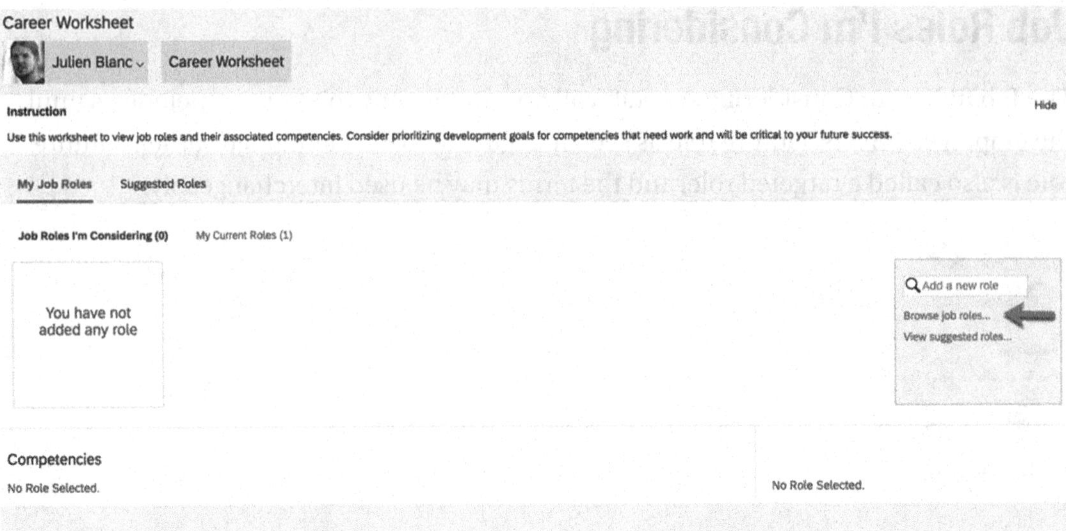


***Figure 3-31.*** *Browse Job Roles*

A popup will display all job roles arranged by job family. The employee may expand any family to see its roles. An example is shown in Figure 3-32.

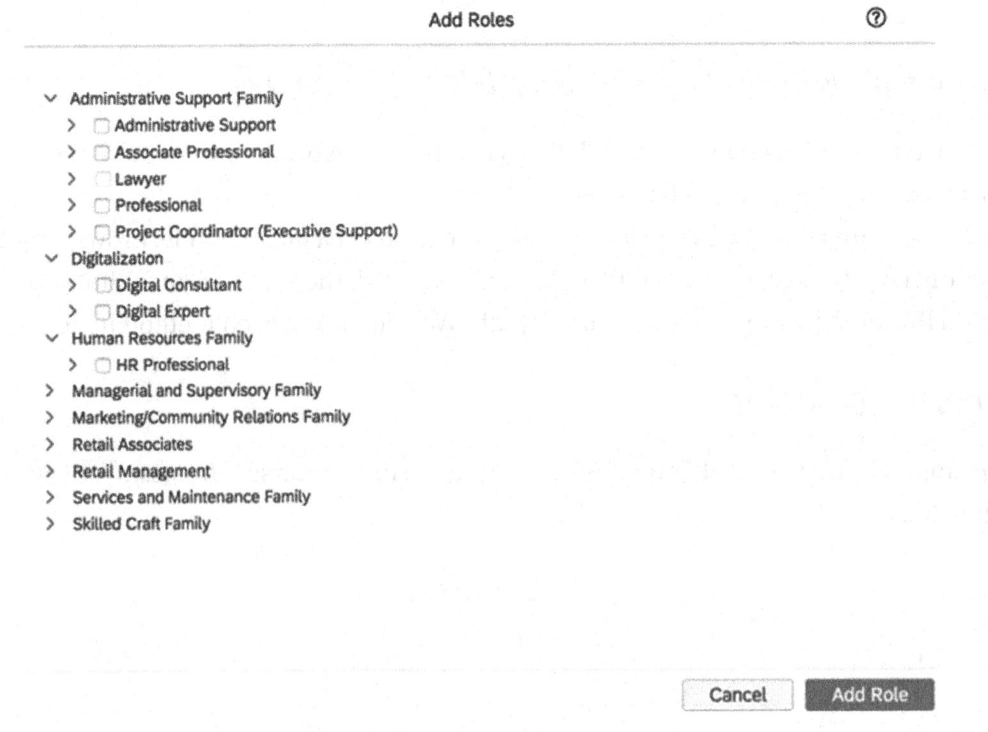


***Figure 3-32.*** *Browse Job Roles by Job Family*

Click the expand icon for a job role to see the job description. This is based on the job profile for the job role. An example is shown in Figure 3-33.

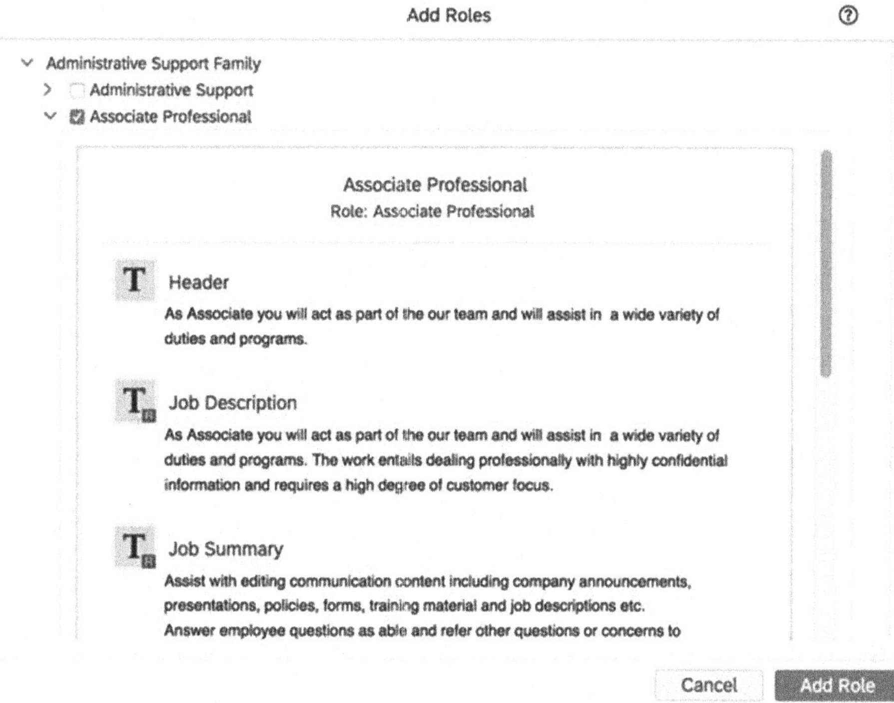


***Figure 3-33.*** *Job Profile*

Select a role and click "Add Role." Any number of roles may be selected to be target roles. However, an attribute may be set in the Career Worksheet XML to limit the number of roles selected. Once the limit has been reached, the employee will not be able to select additional roles as seen in Figure 3-34.

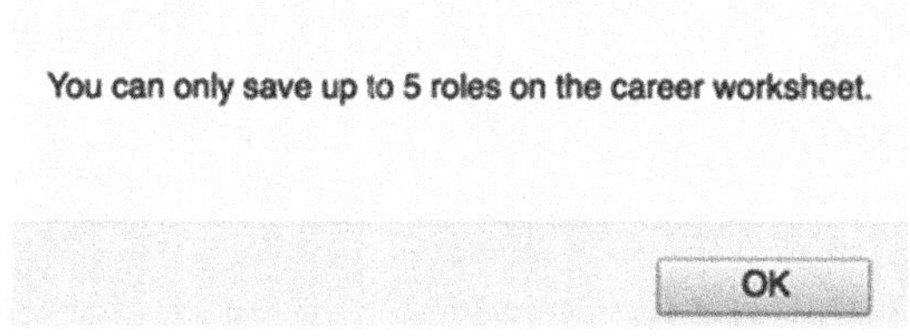


***Figure 3-34.*** *Maximum Roles Met Message*

Refer back to the prior chapter to review how to set this limit in the Career Worksheet XML.

The Job Roles I'm Considering screen will display with the newly selected roles as seen in Figure 3-35.

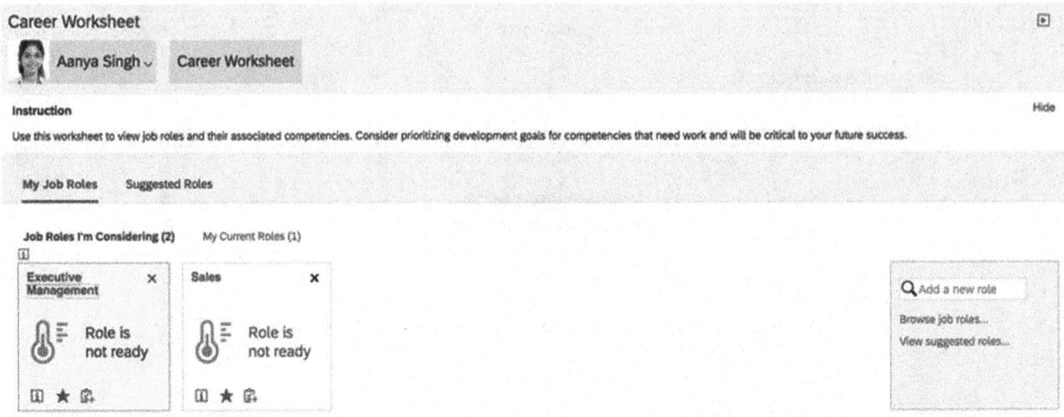


***Figure 3-35.*** *Targeted Roles in the Job Roles I'm Considering Sub-tab*

The other method for selecting targeted roles in this sub-tab is using "View suggested roles...".

## Suggested Roles

There are two ways to access Suggested Roles. From Job Roles I'm Considering, you may click "View suggested roles...". The other option is to click the "Suggested Roles" tab. Both options are highlighted in Figure 3-36.

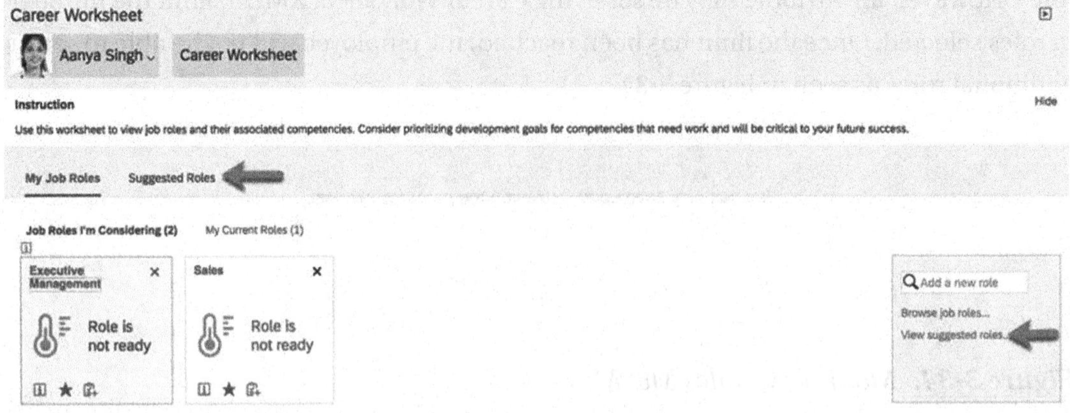


***Figure 3-36.*** *Options to View Suggested Roles*

The Suggested Roles tab permission is not role based. In other words, you cannot select which permitted roles may view this tab. However, this tab is only available for an employee when viewing their career worksheet. If the role-based permission for the manager or HR manager role grants access to Suggested Roles, this option would not be visible to either role when viewing the employee's career worksheet.

We have discussed Suggested Roles configuration in the prior chapter. Suggested Roles may be based on career paths created by the system admin or an algorithm based on a set of criteria.

Figure 3-37 shows an example of what an employee would see in the Suggested Roles tab of their career worksheet.

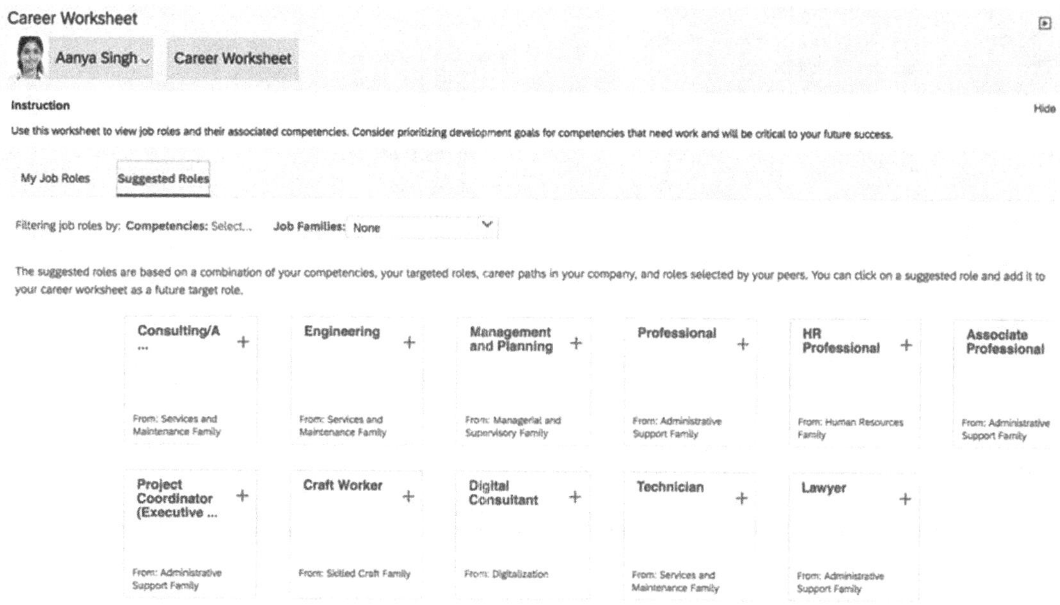


*Figure 3-37.* *Suggested Roles*

The employee may narrow down the roles using the Competencies or Job Families filters as seen in Figure 3-38.

My Job Roles Suggested Roles

Filtering job roles by: **Competencies:** Select... **Job Families:** None

*Figure 3-38.* *Suggested Roles Filters*

The employee may select to view suggested roles based on the competencies of these suggested roles as seen in Figure 3-39.

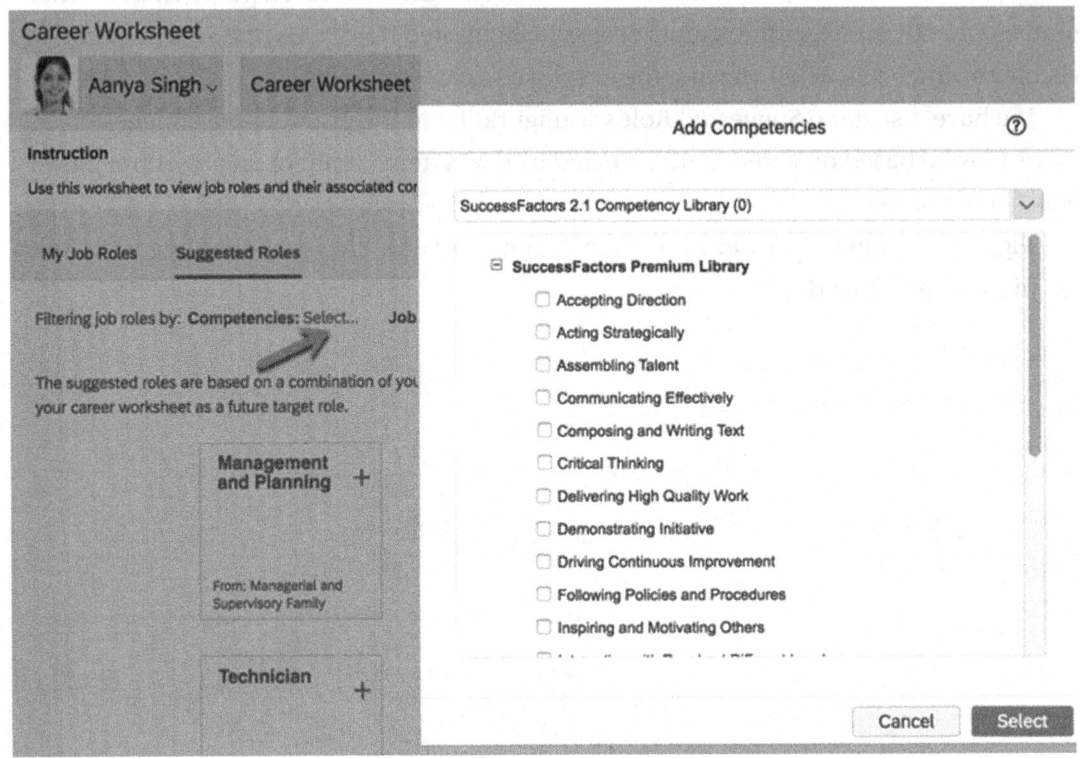


***Figure 3-39.*** *Filter Based on Suggested Roles Competencies*

The employee may filter by any of the job families of the suggested roles as seen in Figure 3-40.

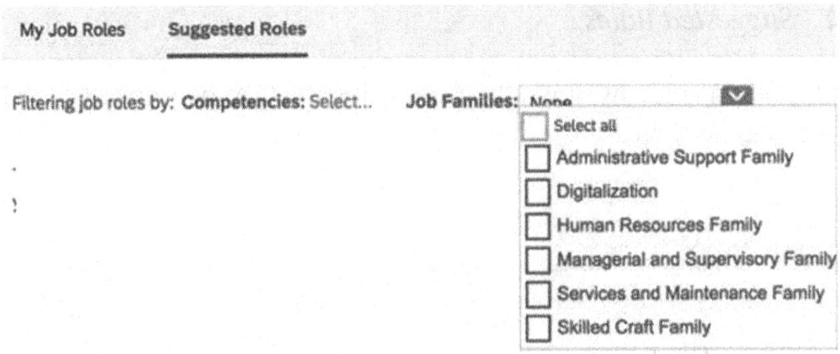

***Figure 3-40.*** *Suggested Job Roles by Job Families*

An example of the Job Families filter is shown in Figure 3-41. Based on the filter selected, only four suggested roles display.

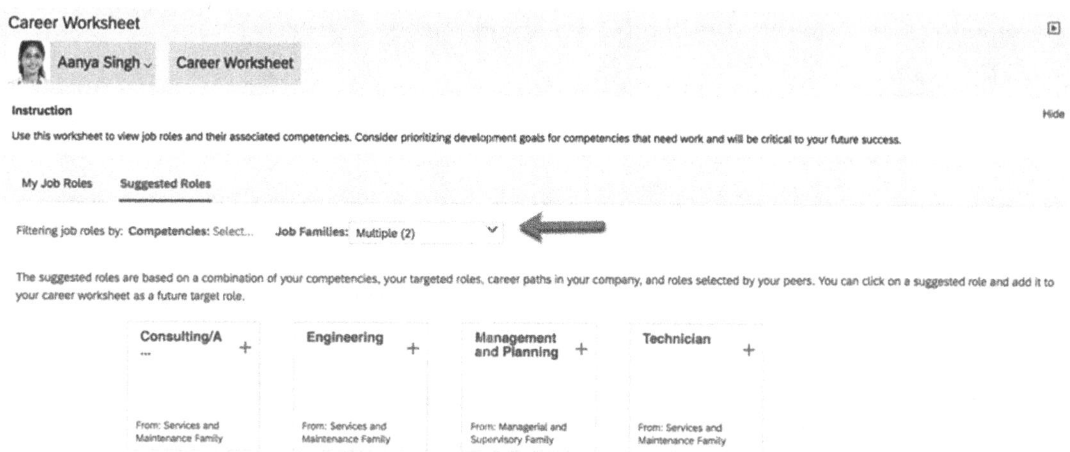


***Figure 3-41.*** *Suggested Roles Based on Job Families Filter*

It is possible that an employee will see no suggested roles. An example is shown in Figure 3-42.

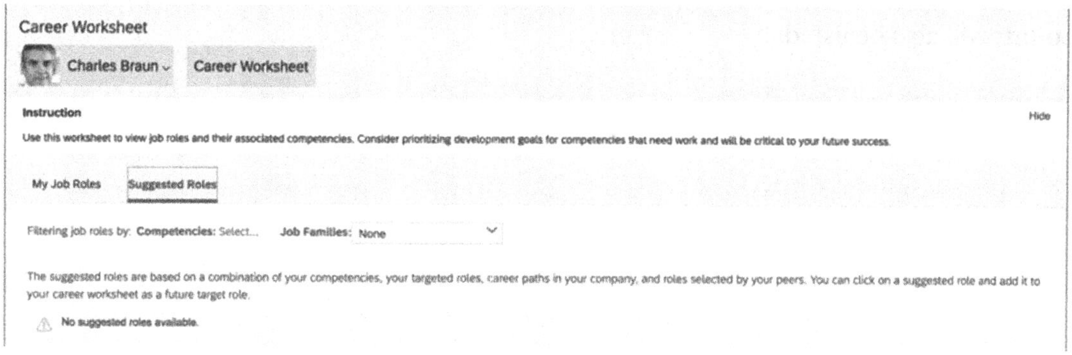

***Figure 3-42.*** *No Suggested Roles Available*

This may occur if the employee has not selected any targeted roles yet, does not have a completed performance form with competencies, or does meet any of the suggested roles' criteria. Often, once the employee selects a role and returns to this page, suggested roles will display.

Any or all of the suggested roles may be selected by clicking the plus sign for each role. A confirmation message will display as seen in Figure 3-43. In addition, the add icon for that role is now inactive.

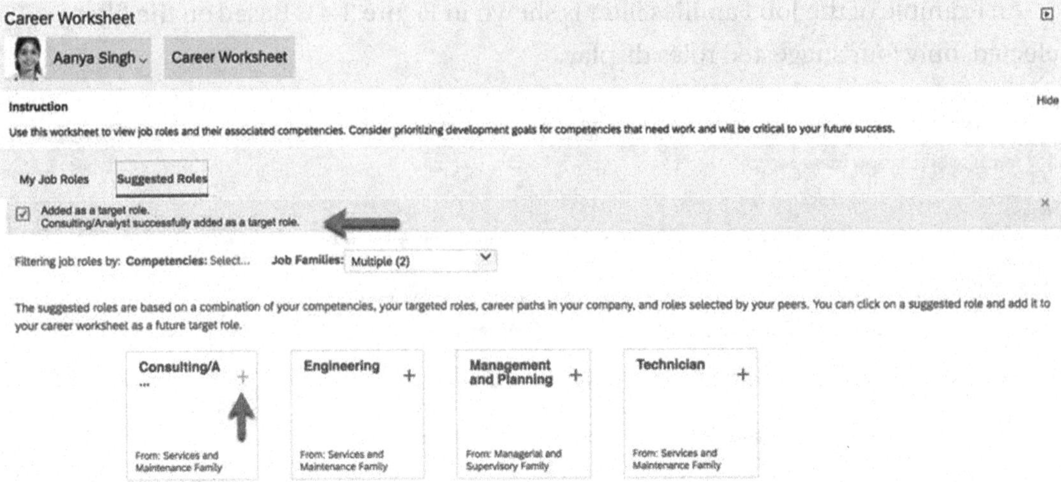


***Figure 3-43.*** *Suggested Roles Added Message*

The targeted roles now display in the Job Roles I'm Considering sub-tab as seen in Figure 3-44.

The competencies needed for the job role will be listed as well. If the employee's current role contains any of the same competencies, the gap graphs may populate; and if they have development goals linked to the competencies, the development goals and counts will also be listed.

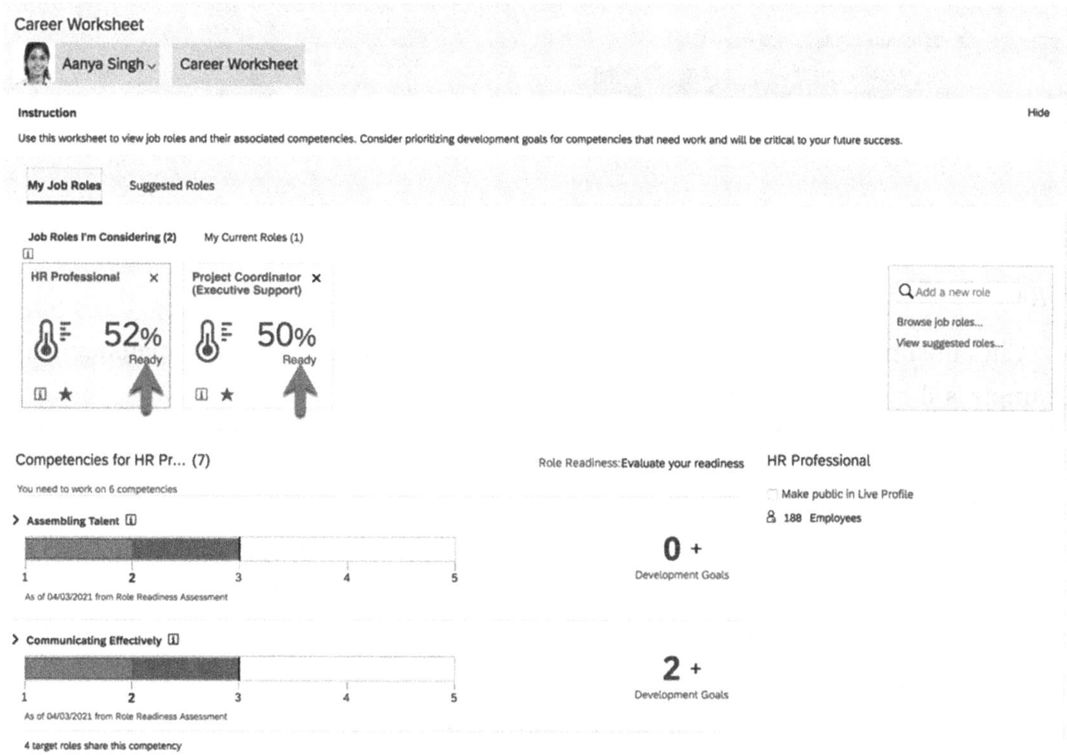


***Figure 3-44.** Targeted Role in the Job Roles I'm Considering Sub-tab*

You will notice that the readiness meters contain readiness percentages for these targeted roles. That is due to the employee's current role containing some of the same competencies as the targeted roles. The employee has competency ratings from their current role that are used to calculate the readiness percentage. You will also notice that only two of the five competencies have gap graphs. That is because the employee only has two of those competencies in their current role and has ratings for these. We will see later in this chapter that using the Role Readiness Assessment form is a way to get these other competencies populated because the employee is being rated on the targeted role's competencies instead.

For each of the targeted role's competencies, there will be a count of the roles that also have this competency linked to them as seen in Figure 3-45. All job roles mapped to a competency in Families and Roles will be included in the gap graph section as roles that have that competency.

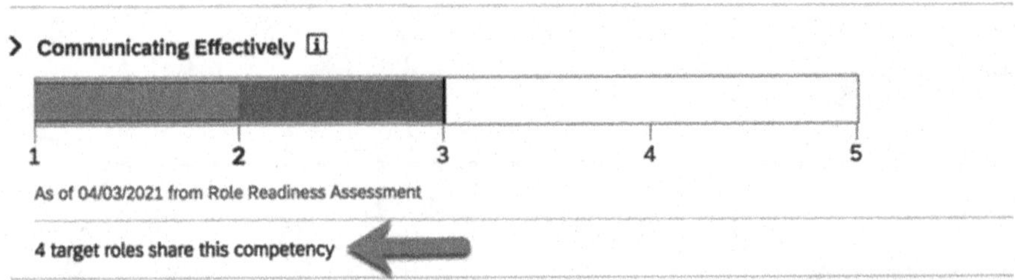


***Figure 3-45.*** *Other Roles That Share the Competency*

Click the link to see the names of the target roles that also have this competency. An example is shown in Figure 3-46.

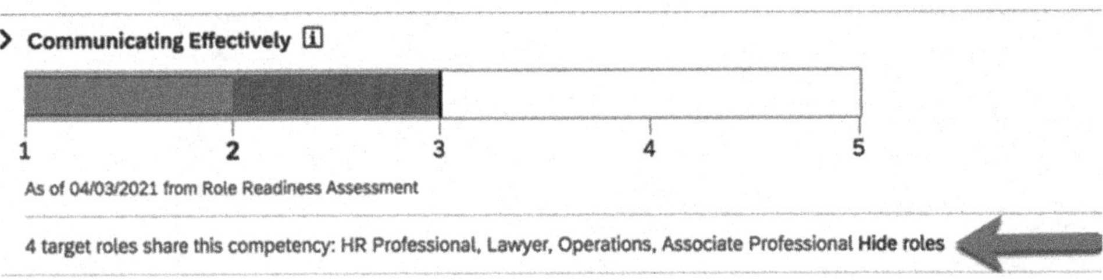


***Figure 3-46.*** *Other Job Roles with the Competency*

## Career Paths

Now that the employee has selected targeted roles, there is an option to view career paths. The employee may view the career path of the targeted roles. An example is as seen in Figure 3-47.

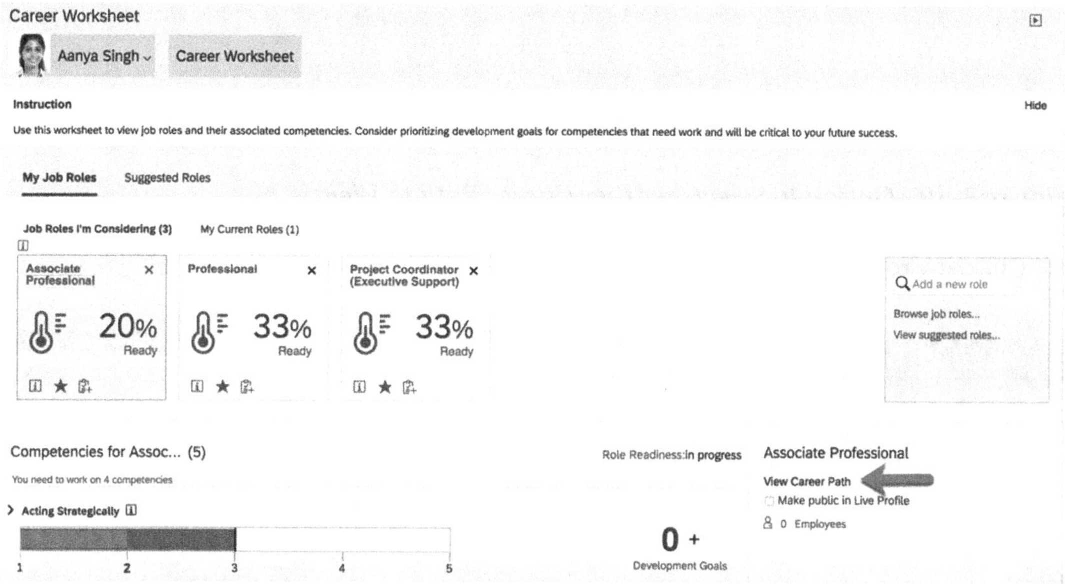


*Figure 3-47. Option to View the Targeted Role Career Path*

The career path will display. An example is shown in Figure 3-48.

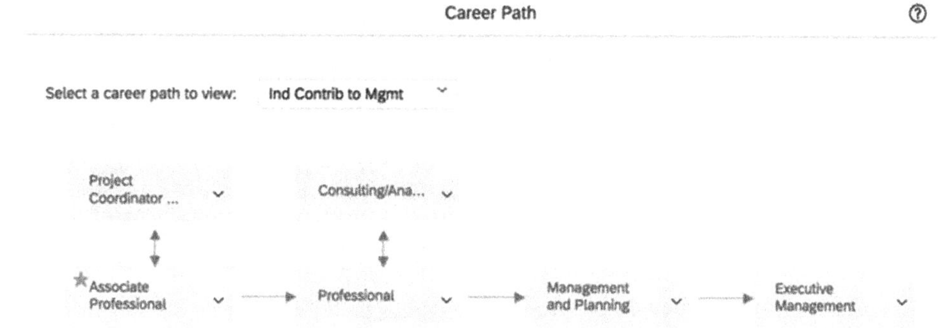


*Figure 3-48. Career Path for a Targeted Role*

The targeted role will be starred and will display in a different color, usually blue.

If the employee's current role is in the career path, it will be starred as well. If the employee has selected multiple target roles, it is possible to view those career paths from this screen as well. Click the "Select a career path to view:" dropdown listing to see the path names for the other targeted roles as seen in Figure 3-49.

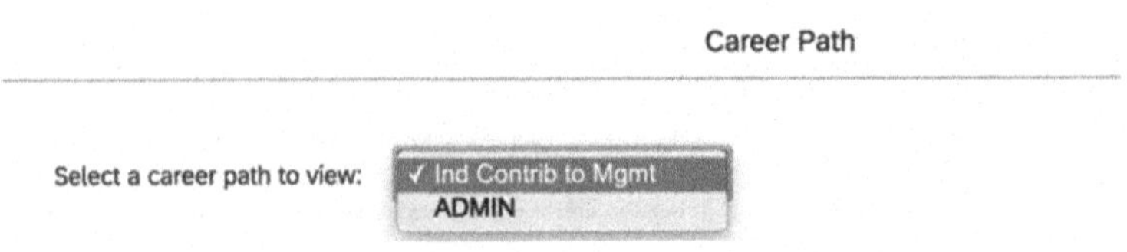


***Figure 3-49.** Option to Select Another Career Path to View*

Click any role in the career path to see its job profile as seen in Figure 3-50.

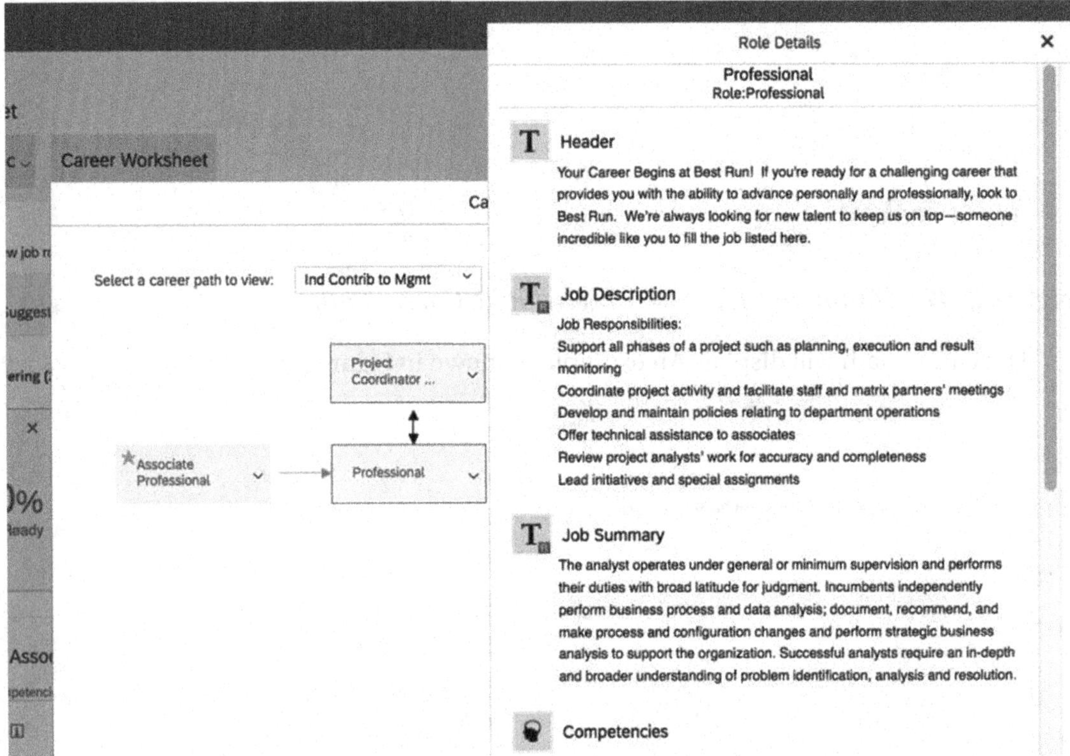


***Figure 3-50.** Targeted Role Job Profile*

It is also possible to add another targeted role from the career path. Click the downward arrow for a role as seen in Figure 3-51.

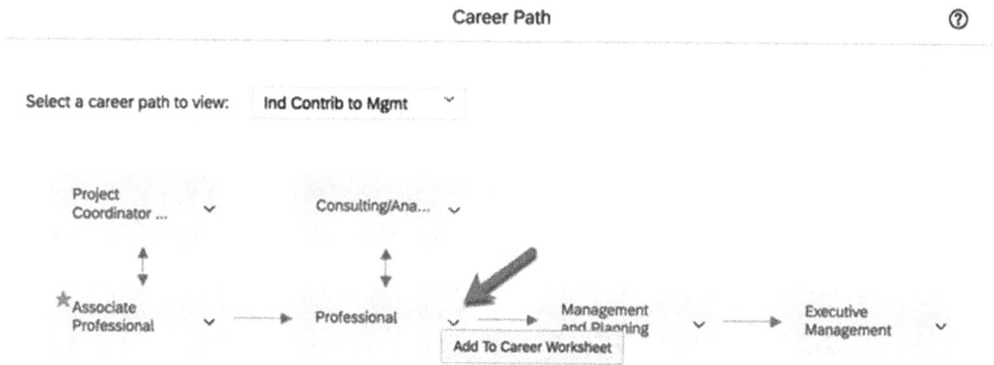


*Figure 3-51.* *Adding a Targeted Role*

It is also possible to remove an existing targeted role from the career worksheet. Click the dropdown icon to see the removal option. An example is seen in Figure 3-52.

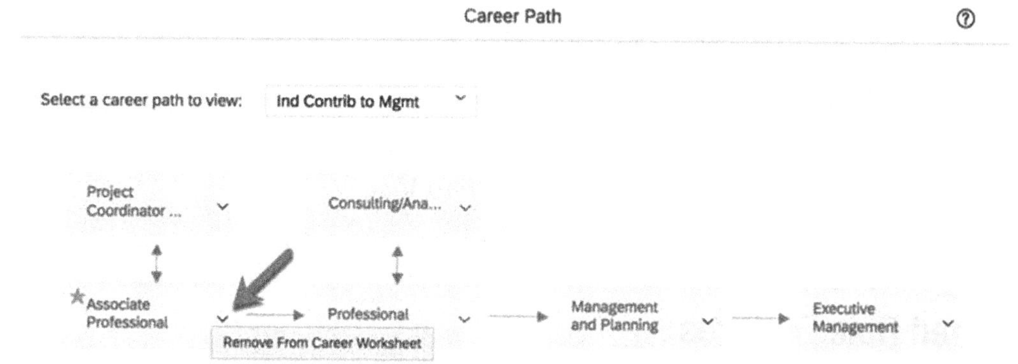


*Figure 3-52.* *Deselecting a Targeted Role*

The changes made here will be reflected in the Job Roles I'm Considering sub-tab.

If a targeted role is not in a career path, there will be no option to view the career path as seen in Figure 3-53.

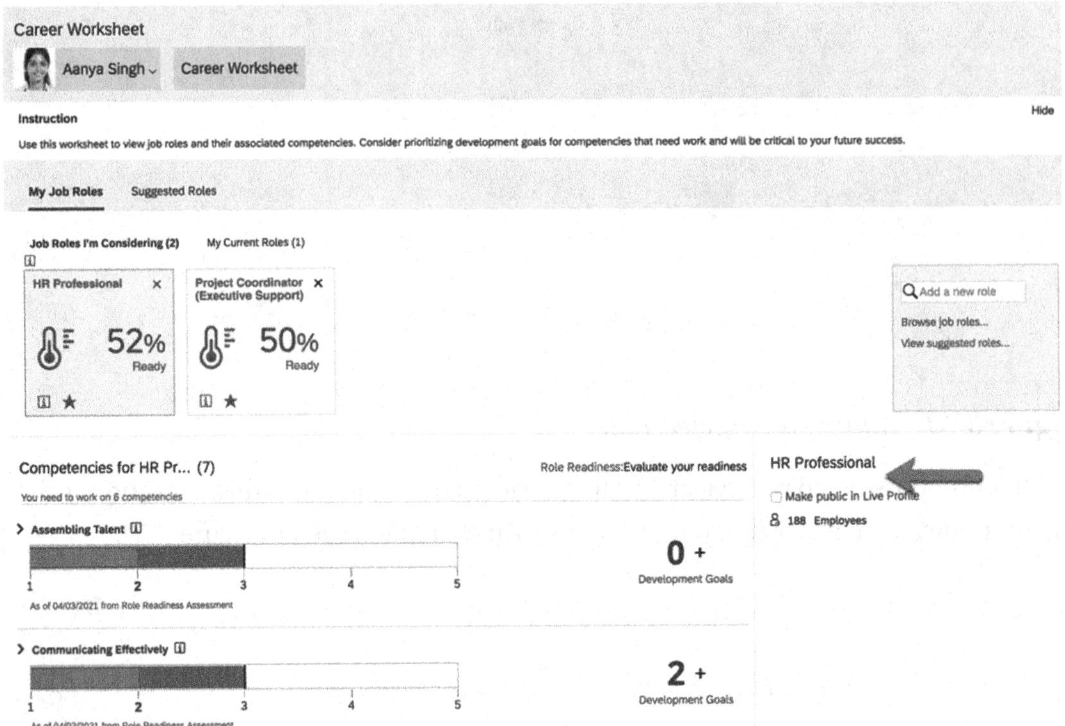


*Figure 3-53.* *Target Role with No Career Path to View*

Now that targeted roles have been selected, let's look at them more closely.

# Targeted Role Features

Each targeted role will have a readiness meter with three icons: Role Details, Make this the default target role, and Add New Learning Activity. An example is shown in Figure 3-54.

*Figure 3-54.* *Readiness Meter Icons*

## Role Details

Mouse over the info icon for any of the targeted roles to see the job profile as seen in Figure 3-55.

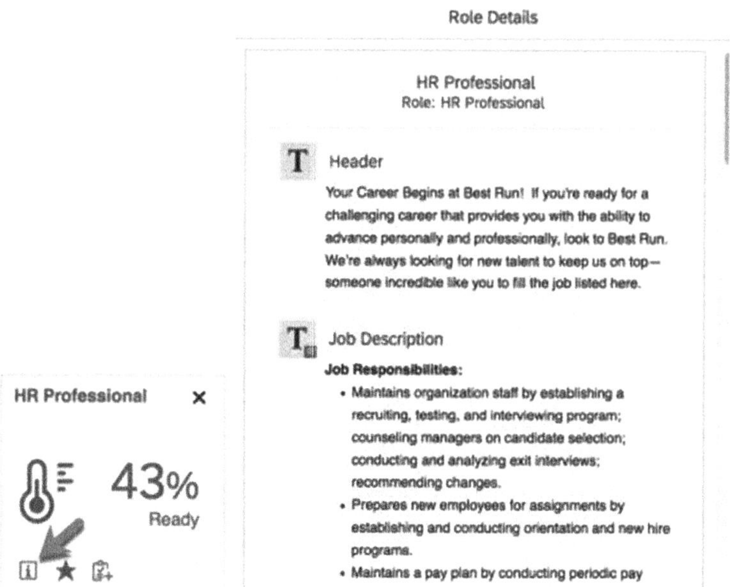


***Figure 3-55.*** *Targeted Role Job Profile*

## Default Role

Click the star icon for any of the targeted roles to make the role the default as seen in Figure 3-56. The star will change color for the targeted role when it becomes the default targeted role.

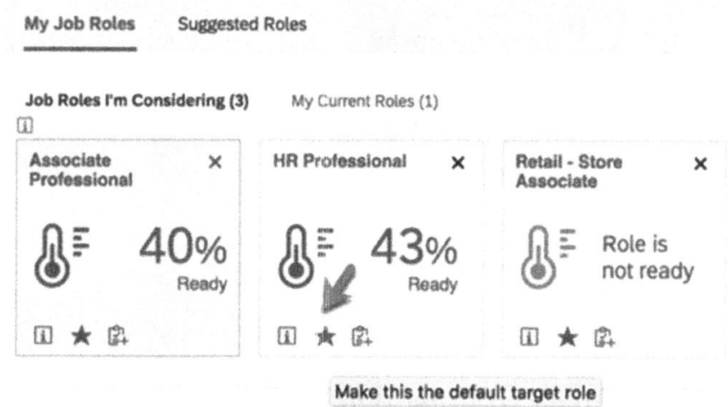


***Figure 3-56.*** *Click the Star Icon to Make the Role the Default Target Role*

## Add Learning Activity

The Add New Learning Activity icon as seen in Figure 3-57 will display when LMS is enabled.

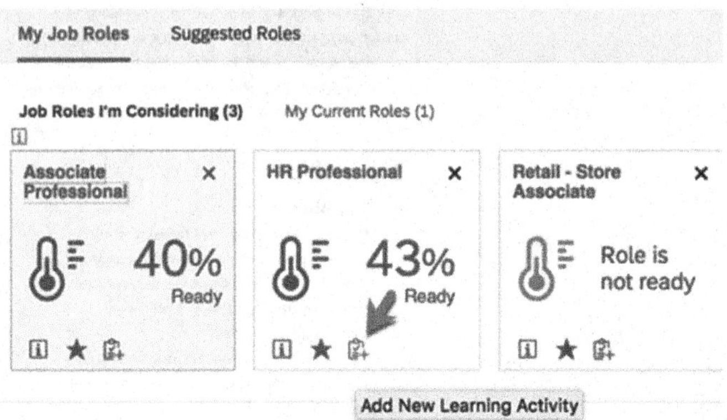


***Figure 3-57.*** *Add New Learning Activity Icon*

If LMS is integrated with the Development module and you are allowing users to add learning activities to development goals, the employee may assign learning activities to their LMS To-Do list.

As seen in Figure 3-58, the employee may find activities in the learning catalog or by searching for activities by competency. Please be aware that the readiness meter updates when the user receives a competency rating from a completed learning item from LMS.

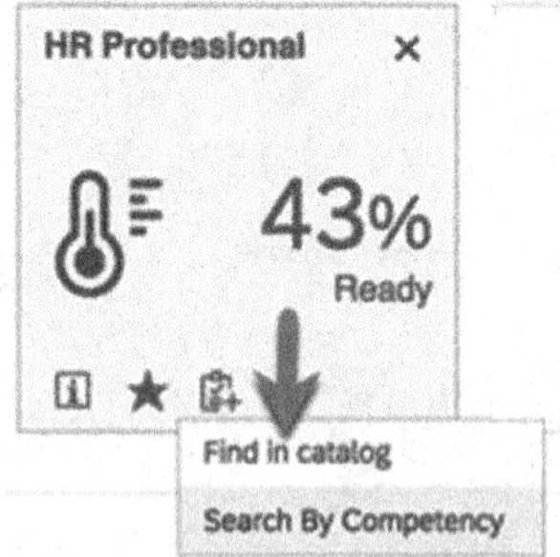


***Figure 3-58.*** *Learning Activity Options When LMS Is Enabled*

You may have LMS turned on but not being used in the Development module. In that case, you will see this icon, but it won't link to anything. There is no option within the Career Worksheet template XML to hide this.

## Targeted Role Options

To delete a targeted role from the Job Roles I'm Considering sub-tab, click the "X" icon in the top-right corner of the targeted role as seen in Figure 3-59.

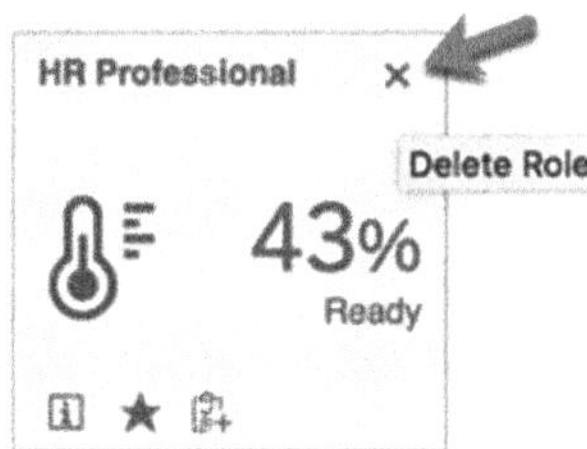


***Figure 3-59.*** *Removing a Target Role*

This will remove the targeted role from the Job Roles I'm Considering sub-tab.

## Readiness Meter

As mentioned in early sections, competencies mapped to job roles are the sole source of competencies listed on the career worksheet. An employee's readiness for a role is determined by evaluating the employee's rated competencies against the targeted role's expected competency ratings. The graph always uses the most recent competency ratings regardless of the source.

The Readiness Meter will display a percentage, 0%, or "Role is not ready" based on the circumstances. The Readiness Meter for a targeted role will contain a percentage if the user has a completed performance form with any of the targeted role's competencies. However, the percentage may be 0% if the employee's competency ratings for the targeted role are very low and calculate readiness to 0%. The employee may only have one of the competencies needed for the targeted role, so the readiness calculates to 0% as well.

In the example shown in Figure 3-60, the employee only has one of the targeted role's competencies, and the rating is below the expected rating.

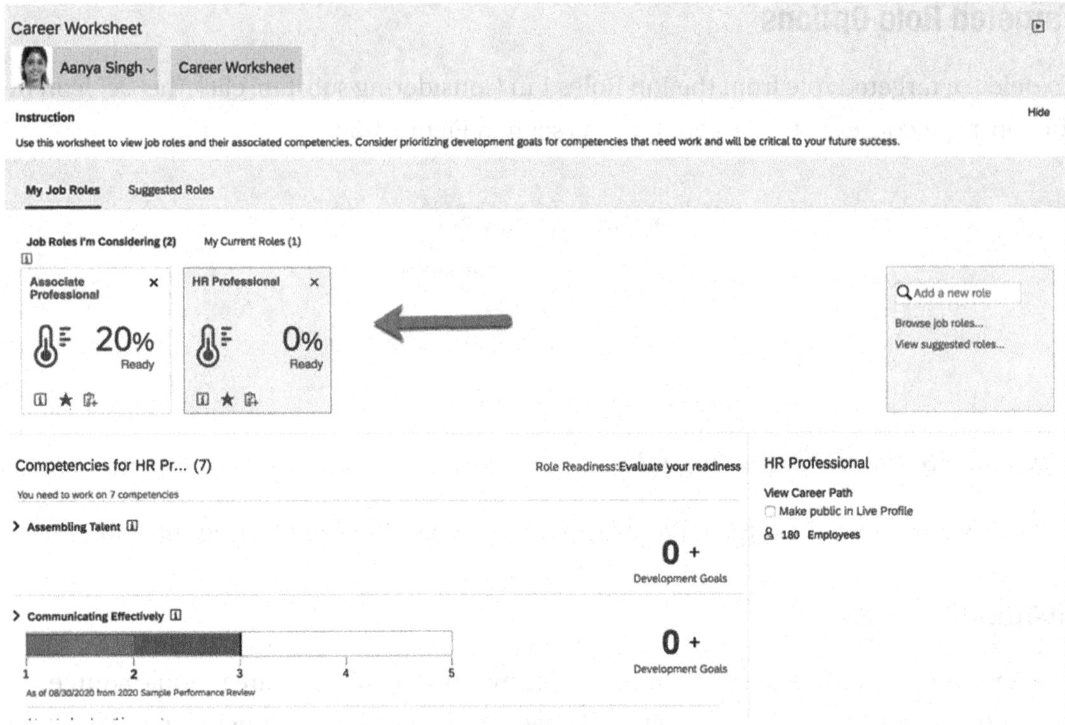


***Figure 3-60.** 0% Targeted Role Readiness*

If the employee has no ratings for any of the competencies in the targeted role, the readiness meter will display "Role is not ready" as seen in Figure 3-61.

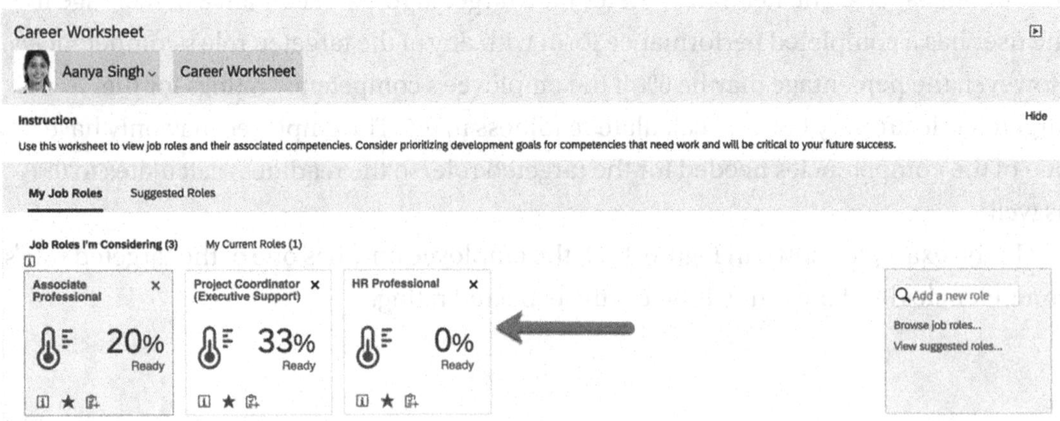


***Figure 3-61.** Targeted Role with No Matched Competencies*

## Career Goals on Employee Profile

The employee may add any or all targeted roles to their People Profile in the Career Goals block. This is done by clicking the checkbox "Make public in Live Profile" on a targeted role as seen in Figure 3-62.

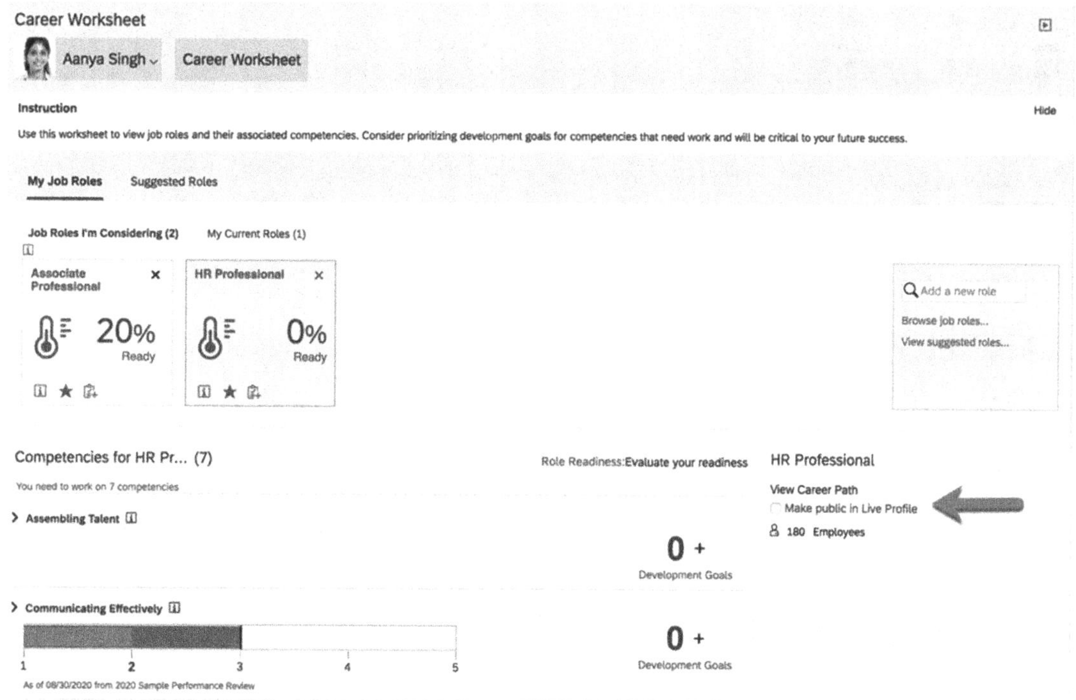


*Figure 3-62. Adding a Target Role to the Profile*

When the employee views their profile, this role will now display as seen in Figure 3-63.

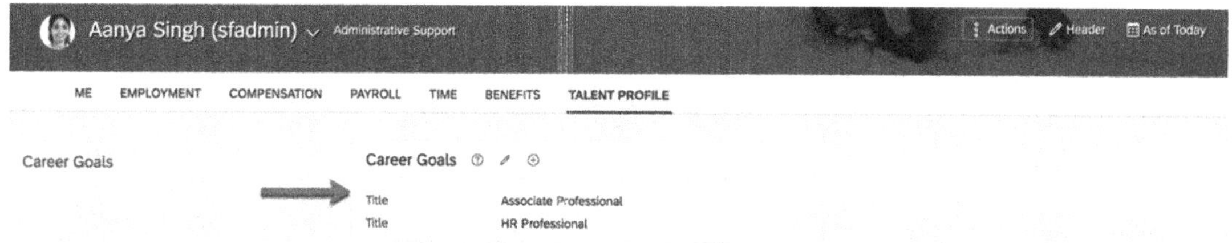


*Figure 3-63. Targeted Role in the Profile*

Based on the permissions, the employee may view the targeted role or edit the goal within their profile. Permissions may also be granted for other roles to see this block when viewing the employee's profile.

Back on the Job Roles I'm Considering sub-tab of the career worksheet, the employee may see the count of the employees in a targeted role as seen in Figure 3-64.

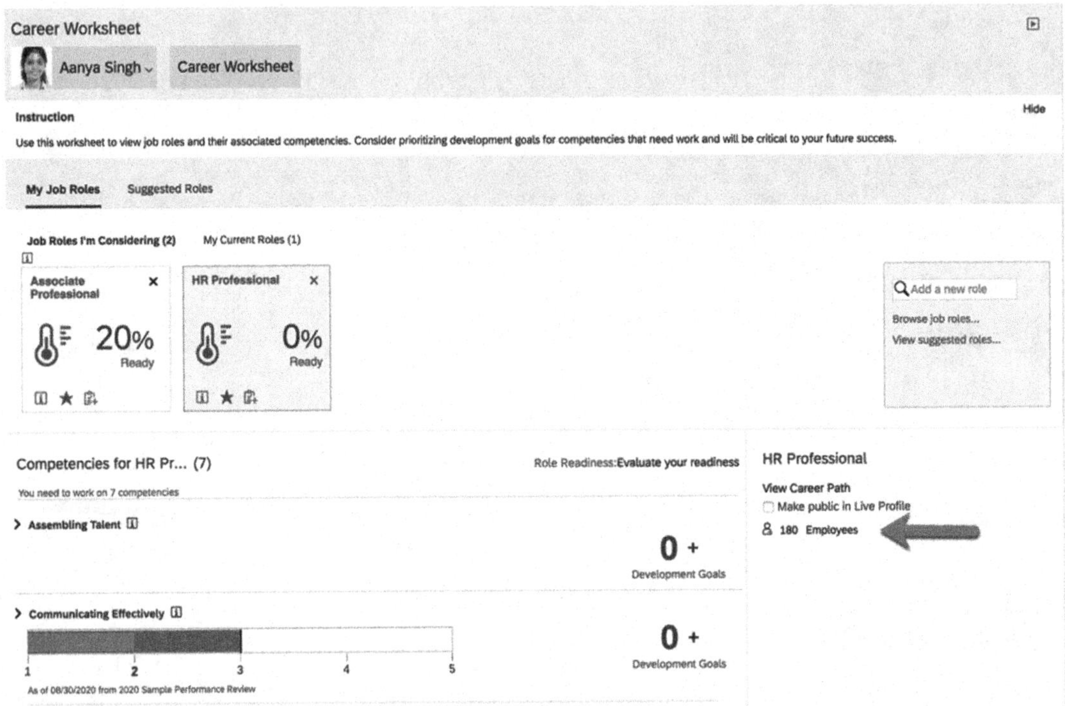


*Figure 3-64.* *Number of Employees in the Targeted Role*

Click the count to see the employee names associated with the role as seen in Figure 3-65.

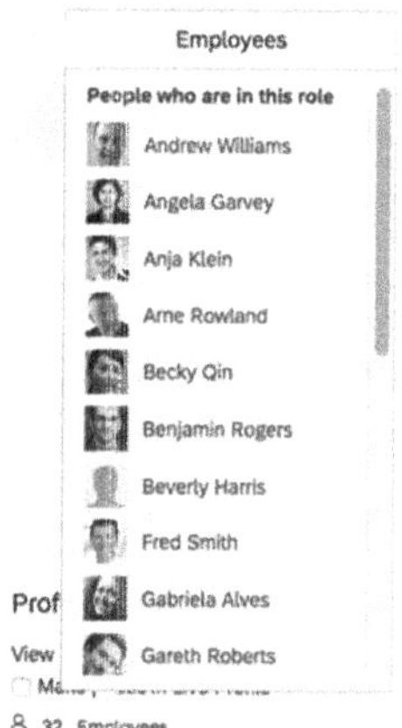


***Figure 3-65.*** *Names of Employees Holding the Targeted Role*

# Role Readiness Assessment

In addition to evaluating an employee's readiness to move into a targeted role based on their existing role currently rated competencies, it is also possible to evaluate solely on the target role's competencies. This method uses the Role Readiness Assessment form. The employee highlights a targeted role and then clicks the link to launch the Role Readiness Assessment form. An example is shown in Figure 3-66.

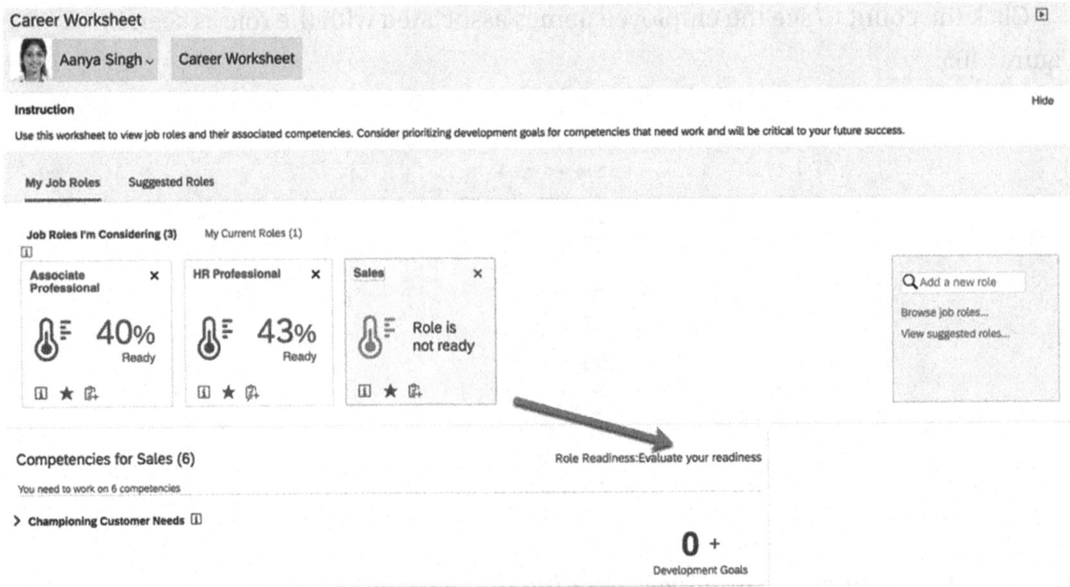


*Figure 3-66. Launching Role Readiness Assessment*

The benefit of launching the Role Readiness Assessment form is that the employee and ultimately their manager rate readiness based on the competencies of the targeted role rather than relying on current competency ratings which may not be applicable to the new role. Or the employee may be missing competencies needed for the targeted role, so the readiness calculation may be skewed.

Only the employee role can launch the Role Readiness Assessment form within the career worksheet. The manager or HR manager cannot launch the form, and the proxy function does not allow a user to launch the form on an employee's behalf.

When using the Role Readiness Assessment form, the gap graph rating for each competency is based on the manager's competency rating and the expected competency rating.

For any of the targeted roles in the Jobs Roles I'm Considering sub-tab, there is a link to "Evaluate your readiness." This directly opens the Role Readiness Assessment form, bypassing the usual form creation steps. The form is configured to auto-populate the targeted job role competencies. An example is shown in Figure 3-67.

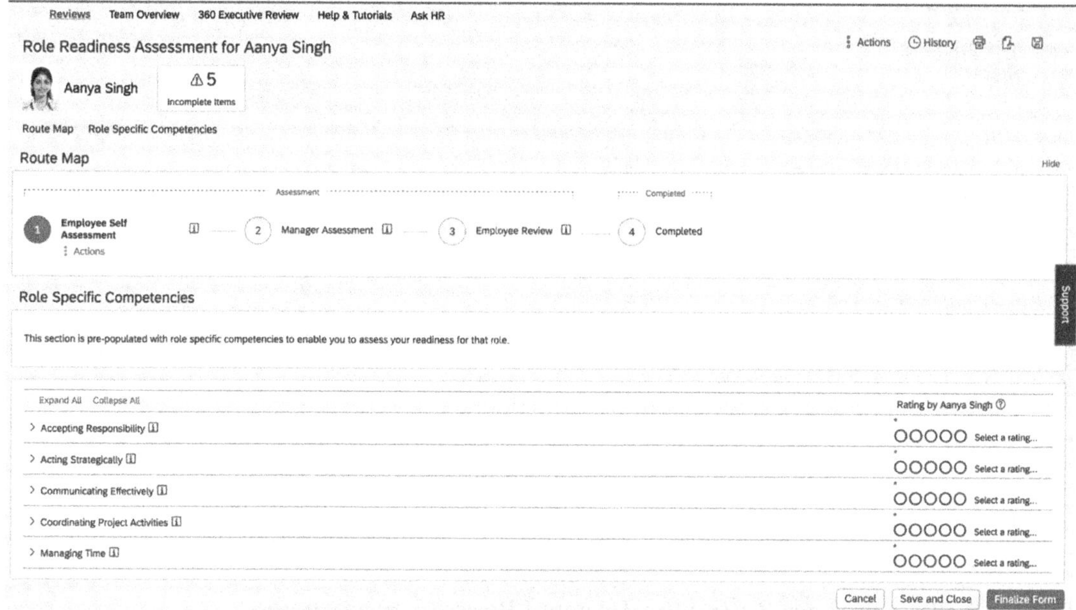


***Figure 3-67.** Launching the Role Readiness Assessment Form from Career Worksheet*

The employee will self-rate on each of the targeted role's competencies. Upon completion, the form will be routed to their manager to rate.

The manager will receive the Role Readiness Assessment form in their Performance Inbox. The manager will provide a rating for each competency based on how well they think the employee has mastered the competency as seen in Figure 3-68.

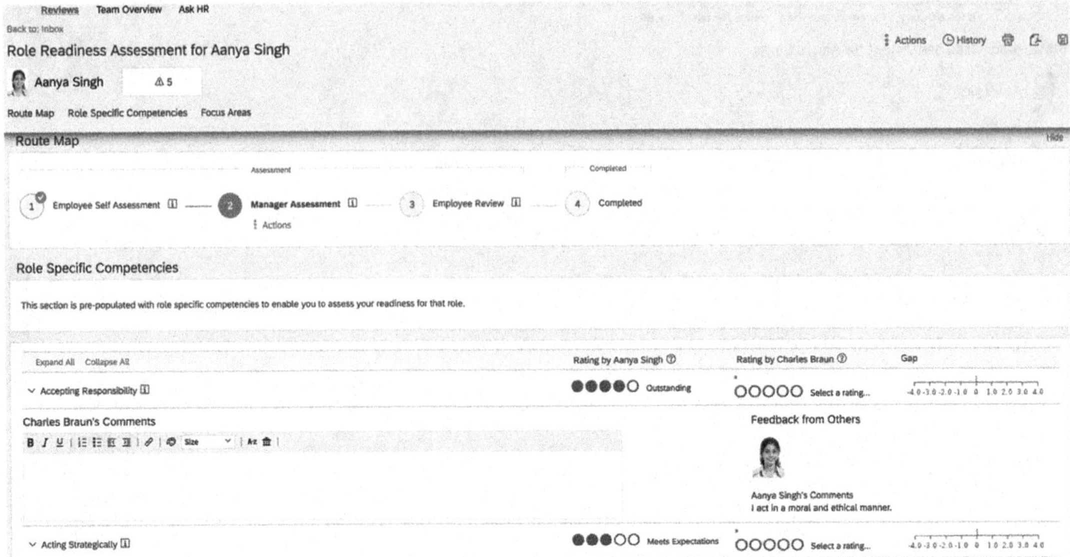


***Figure 3-68.*** *Manager Rating the Targeted Role's Competencies*

The form goes back to the employee to view the manager's ratings and set the form to completed. The employee may access the form from their Performance Inbox or by going back to their career worksheet. For the targeted role, there will be a link "Role Readiness in progress" as seen in Figure 3-69.

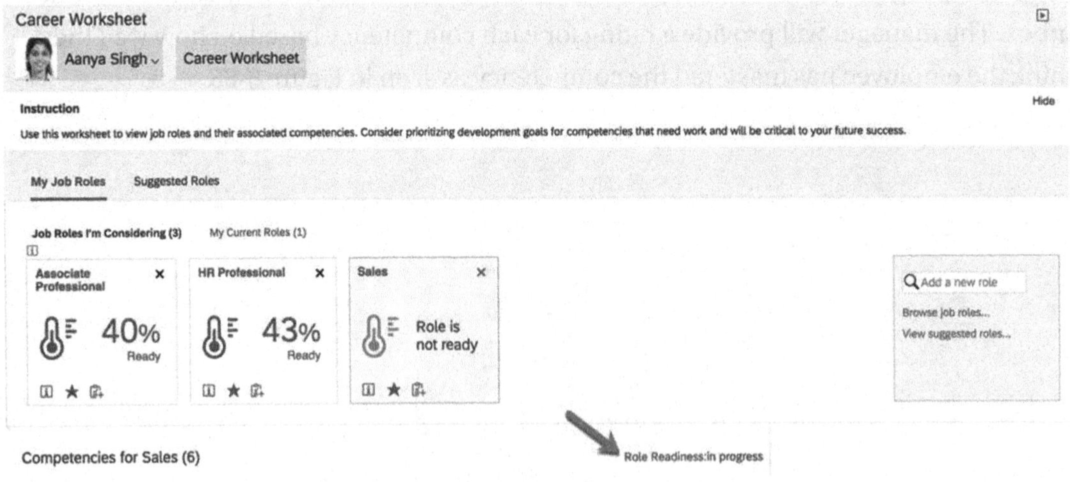


***Figure 3-69.*** *Form in Progress*

Clicking the link will take the employee into the form to set it to complete as seen in Figure 3-70.

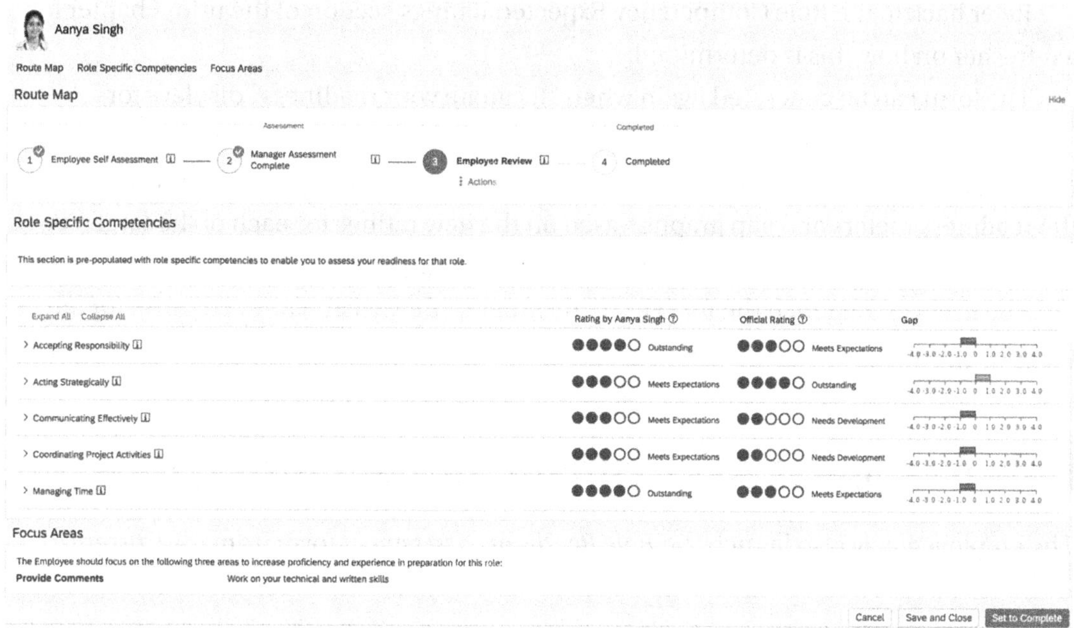

**Figure 3-70.** *View of the Form Set to Completed*

The completed form will appear in the employee and manager's Performance Completed folder. When the employee goes back into the worksheet, the Readiness Meter will show the percentage based on the ratings as seen in Figure 3-71.

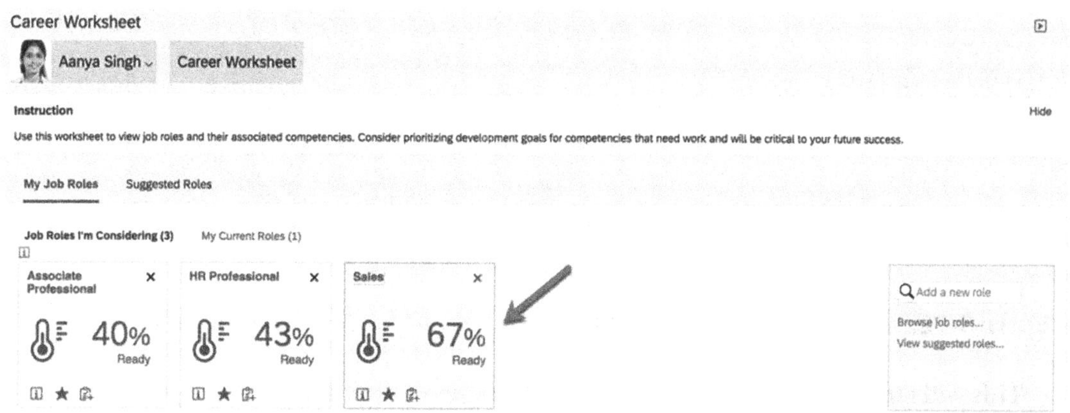

**Figure 3-71.** *Readiness Meter Updated After Assessment Is Complete*

The Readiness Meters for the other targeted roles may show different readiness percentages now if those roles have any of the same competencies of the targeted role that were just rated.

Refer back to the Role Competency Expected Ratings section of the prior chapter for a refresher on how this is determined.

The form can be generated again when "Evaluate your readiness" displays for a targeted role. The form also may be launched for any of the other targeted roles. Relaunching and completing another Role Readiness Assessment form will recalculate the readiness meters and gap graphs based on the new ratings for each of the targeted roles. It is also possible to add more roles to consider and run the form for the new roles.

The user can relaunch the form as many times as they wish. They can rerun for any of the targeted roles that they select.

## Role Readiness Assessment for the Current Role

The employee may also launch the *Role Readiness Assessment* form from My Current Roles as seen in Figure 3-72.

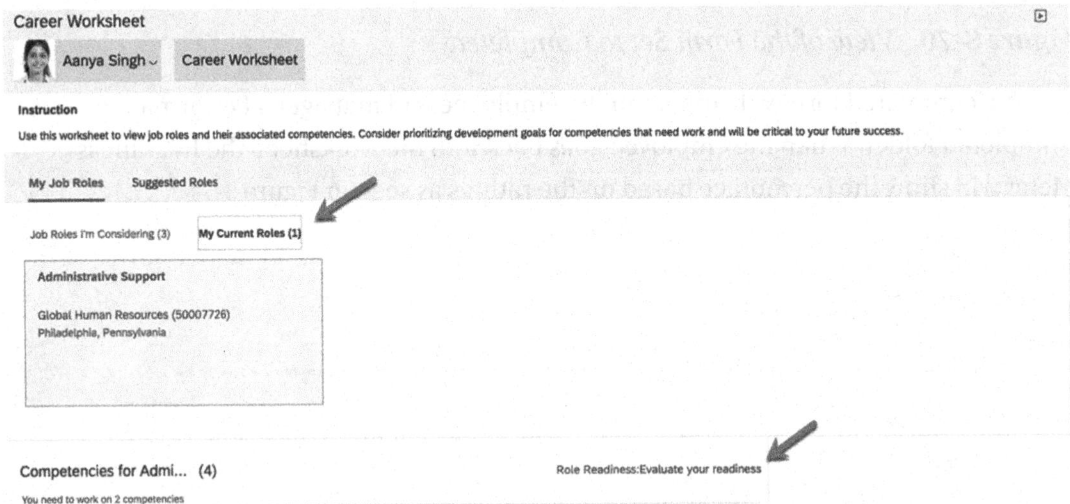


***Figure 3-72.*** *Launching Role Readiness Assessment for the Current Role*

This will launch the form using the competencies of their current role as shown in Figure 3-73.

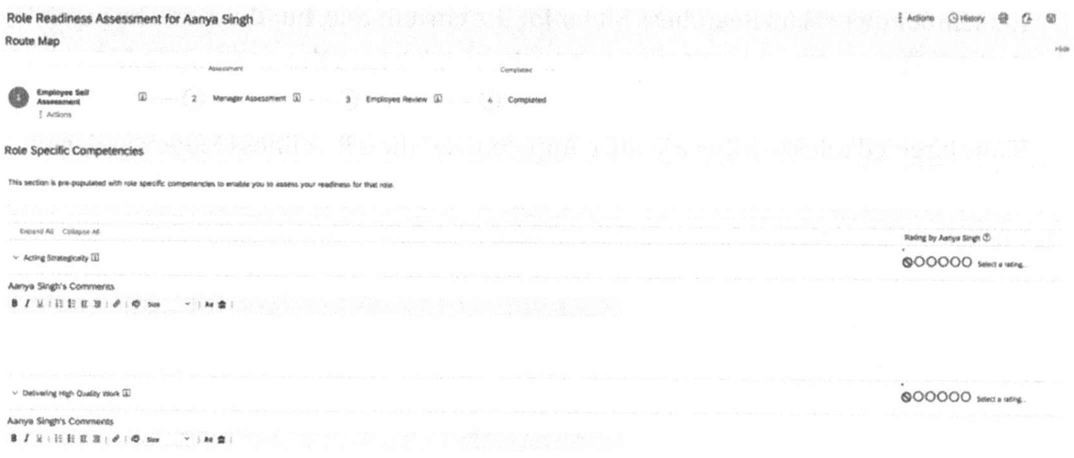

Role Readiness Assessment for Aanya Singh
Route Map
Role Specific Competencies
Aanya Singh's Comments
Aanya Singh's Comments

*Figure 3-73.* *Role Readiness Assessment Form for the Current Role*

The form will go through the same steps as when launching the form for a targeted role.

As shown in Figure 3-74, upon completion, the current role will show the updated competency ratings in each gap graph, and the form name and form completion date will appear.

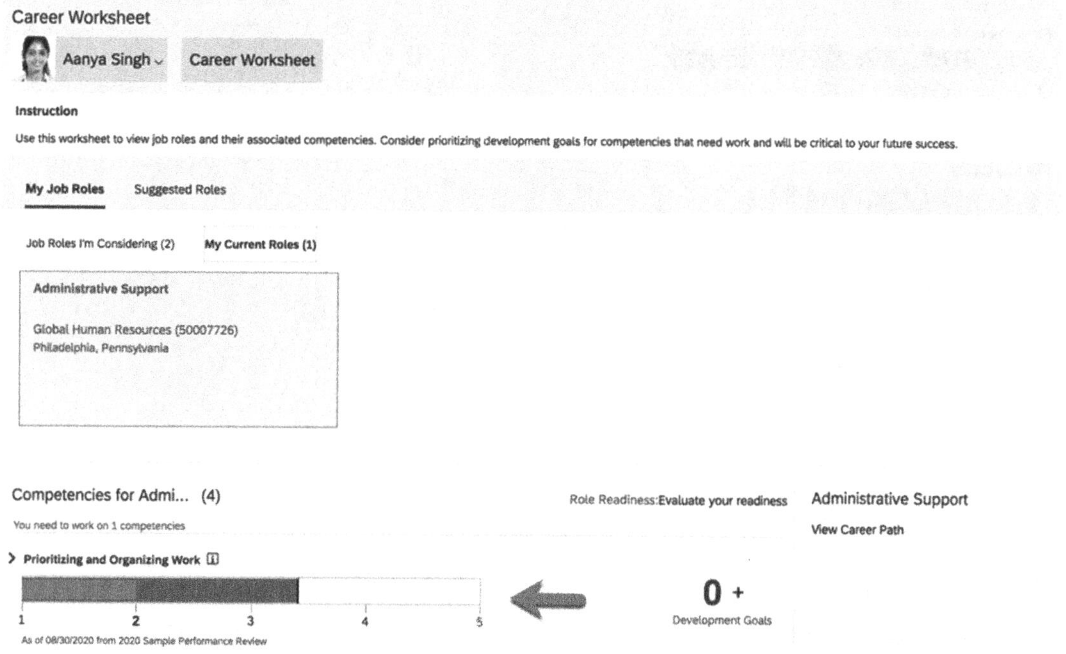


*Figure 3-74.* *Updated Gap Graphs Based on Role Readiness Assessment*

Remember there is no Readiness Meter for the current role, but there will be gap graphs for each competency. This is useful to the employee so that they may add development goals targeted around these competencies.

If any targeted roles use these same competencies, their Readiness Meters and gap graphs will be updated in the Job Roles I'm Considering sub-tab. An example is shown in Figure 3-75.

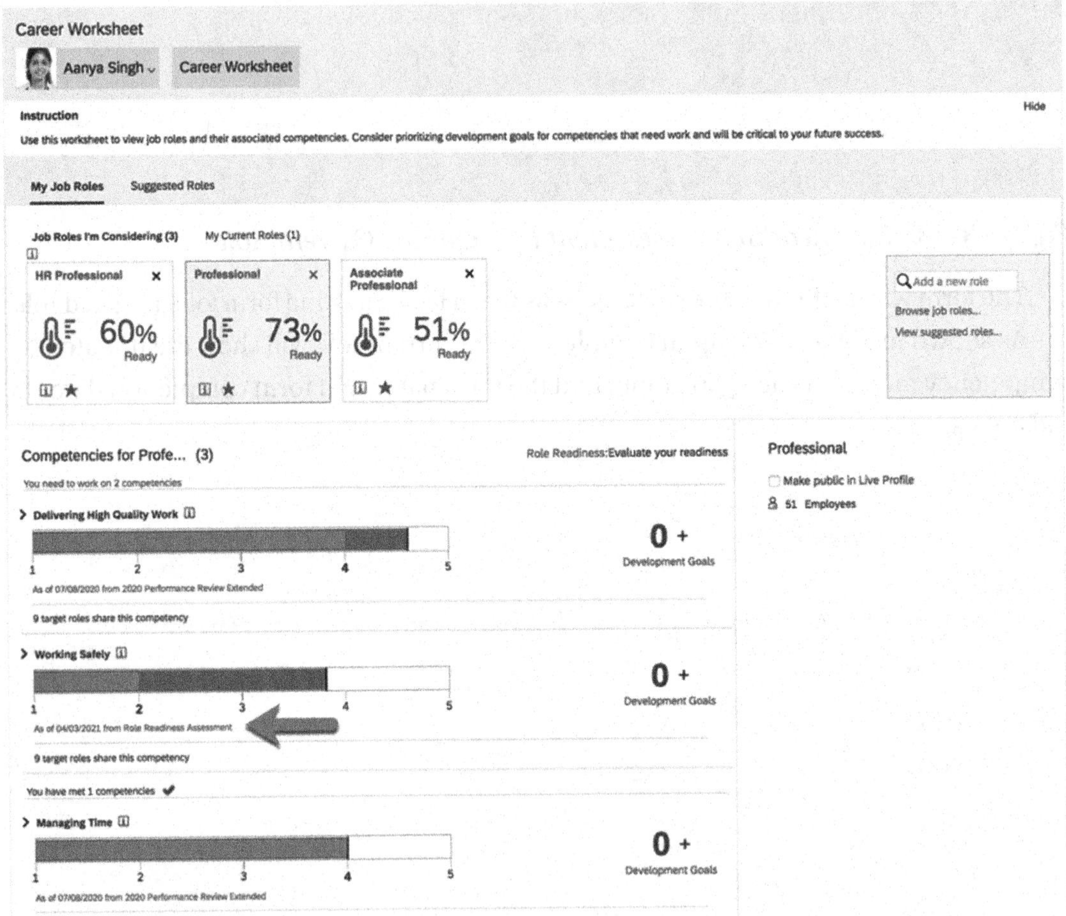


***Figure 3-75.** Targeted Roles' Updated Gap Graphs Based on Role Readiness Assessment Completed*

The rated competencies for the current role will also reflect for any targeted roles that have those competencies along with the form name and form completion date.

That is something to keep in mind; if you are not running the Role Readiness Assessment form for a targeted role, the readiness rating for a targeted role may be derived from ratings from different sources on different dates.

# Deep Link to My Current Roles on the Career Worksheet

Prior to the H1 2020 Release, if an employee wanted to view their current role on their career worksheet, they would have to go into the Development module, open Career Worksheet, and change the My Job Roles sub-tab from Job Roles I'm Considering to My Current Roles as seen in Figure 3-76.

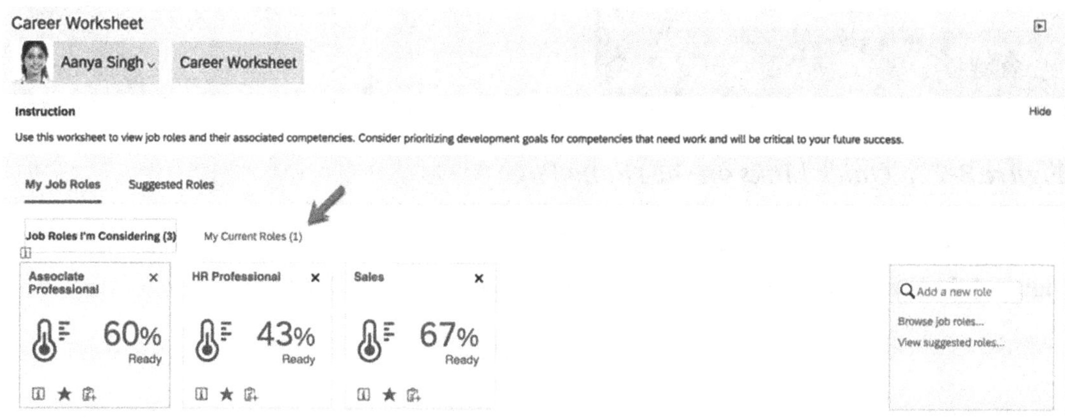


***Figure 3-76.*** *View of the Current Role Within Career Worksheet*

Now an employee may go to the My Current Roles sub-tab in Career Worksheet directly from a dedicated home page Quick Links tile as seen in Figure 3-77.

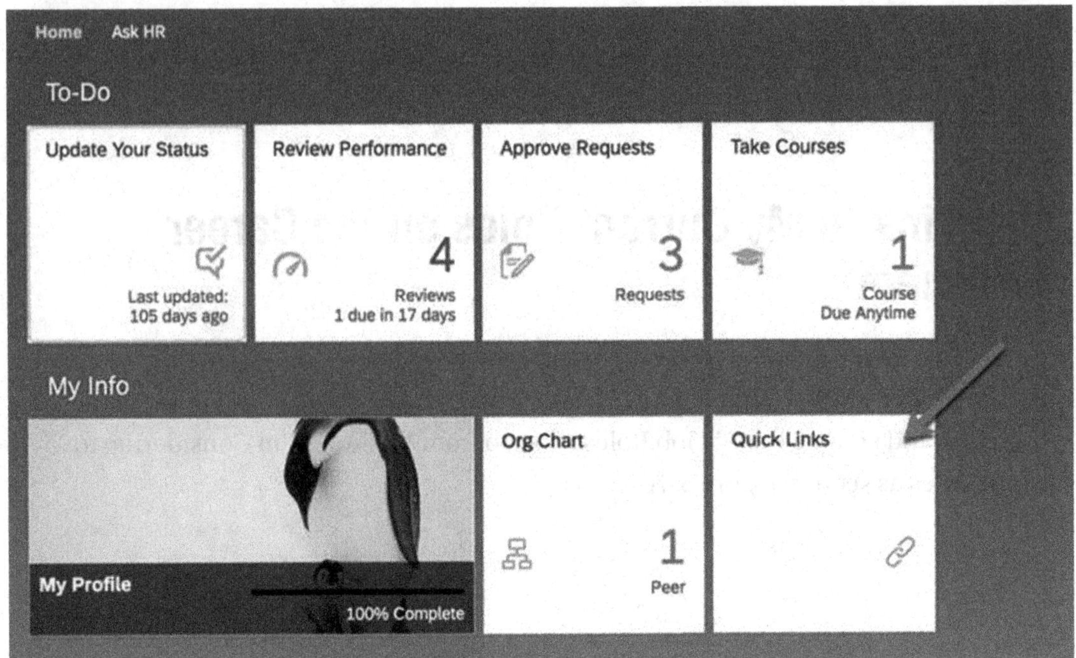


*Figure 3-77. Quick Links on the Home Page*

The user would click the Quick Links tile to see all of the available links as seen in Figure 3-78 to be taken directly to their current role in Career Worksheet.

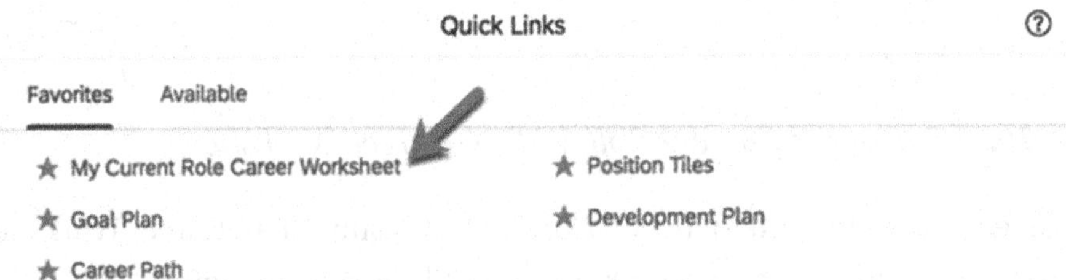


*Figure 3-78. Quick Link to the Current Role*

Clicking the My Current Role Career Worksheet link will take the employee directly to their career worksheet as seen in Figure 3-79.

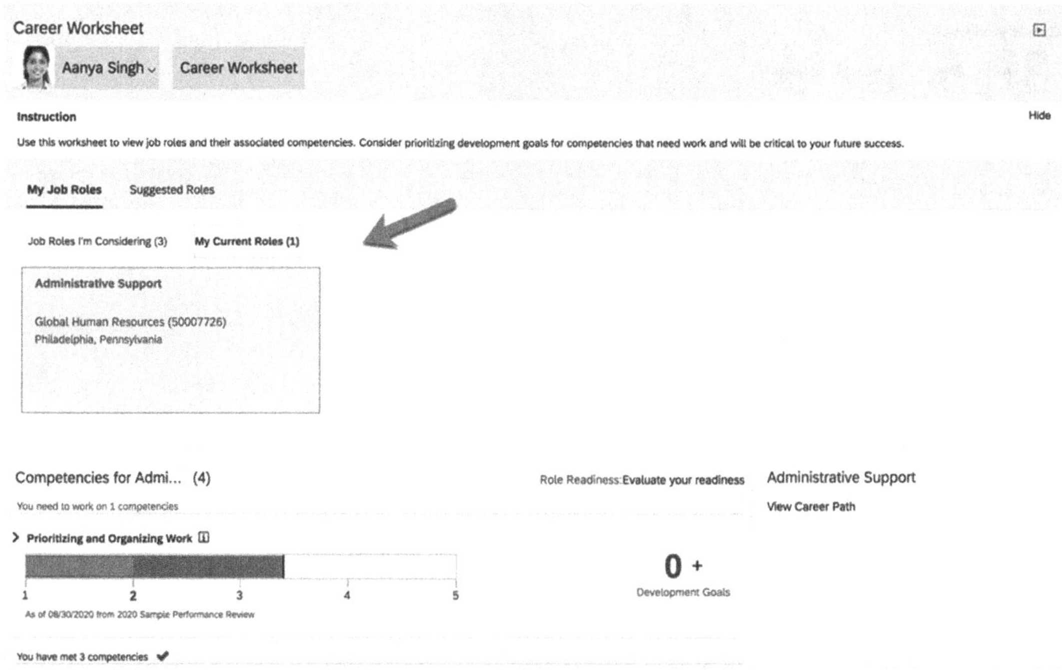


*Figure 3-79.* *Link to the Current Role*

# Manager View of Career Worksheet

Now that we have seen what an employee can do in Career Worksheet, let's look at the manager's view.

Based on configuration in the Career Worksheet template XML and role-based permissions, the manager and HR manager roles can access an employee's career worksheet.

Either role would go into their own career worksheet and do a name search to access the employee's plan. The manager may view the career path for a targeted role, browse roles, and see employees in the targeted role as seen in Figure 3-80.

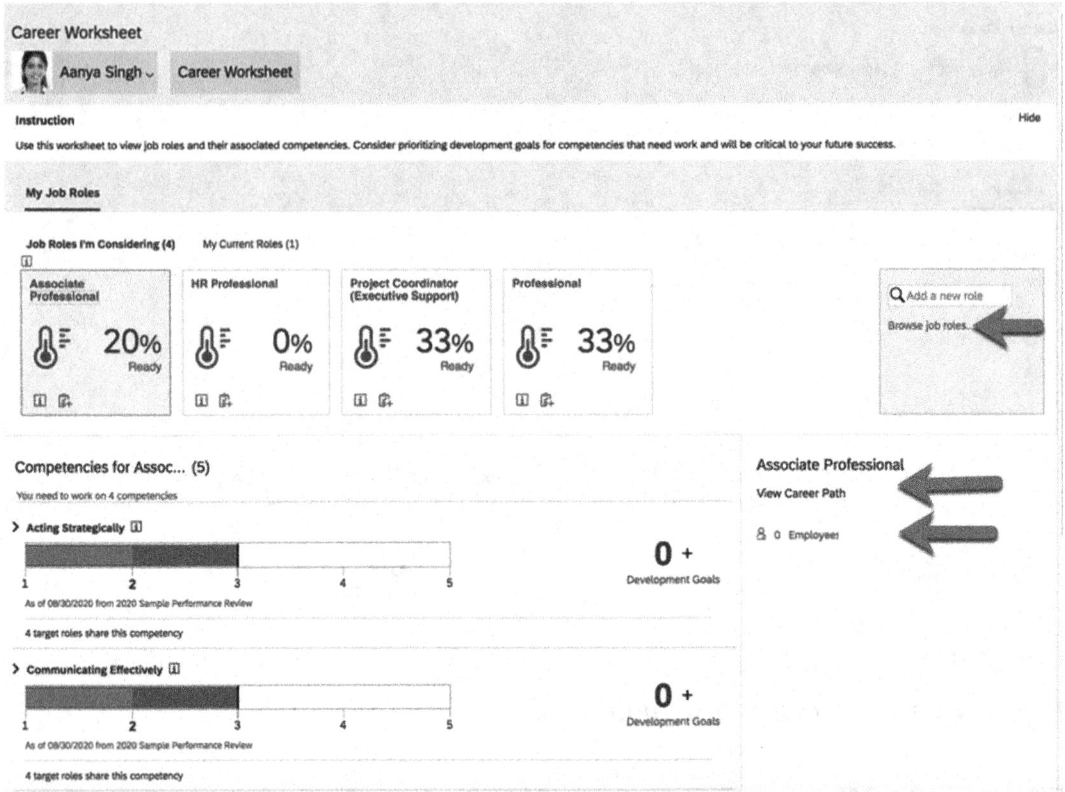


***Figure 3-80.** Manager View of the Employee's Job Roles I'm Considering Sub-tab*

The manager will also have access to the employee's My Current Roles sub-tab as shown in Figure 3-81.

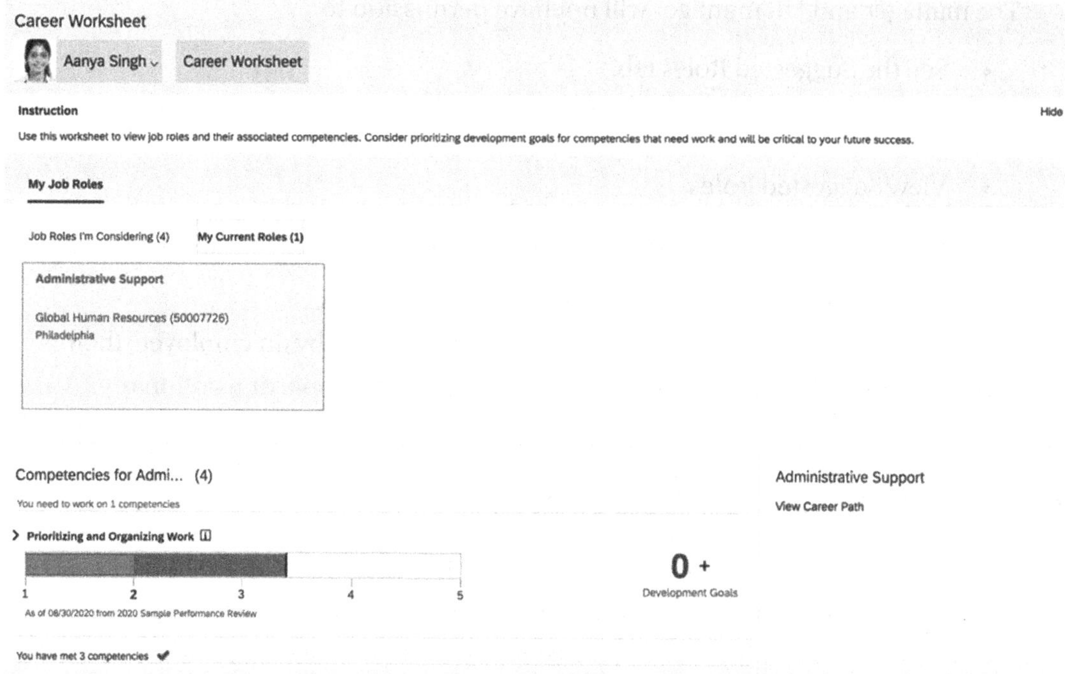


***Figure 3-81.*** *Manager's View of the Employee's Current Role*

Based on permissions, the manager will be able to see roles under consideration and current roles along with gap graphs and readiness meters. They will also have access to view career paths for the roles, browse job roles, and add jobs to consider. But the manager will not see the Suggested Roles tab for the employee, and they will be unable to launch the Role Readiness Assessment form.

Manager and HR manager access to the employee's career worksheet may include the following:

- Browse job roles.
- See targeted roles with readiness meters and gap analysis.
- Add a targeted role.
- View career paths and add roles.
- Add development goals to a competency on a targeted role or current role.

The manager and HR manager will not have permission to

- See the Suggested Roles tab.
- Delete targeted roles.
- View Suggested Roles.
- Launch a Role Readiness Assessment (on behalf of the employee).

If permitted, the HR manager may also create career paths.

We have now seen what can be done in Career Worksheet by an employee, their manager, and their HR manager. Next, we will look briefly at reporting options.

# Career Worksheet Reporting

Career Worksheet ad hoc reporting is very limited. Targeted roles are the only component of the career worksheet that is reportable. The report may display all of the targeted roles that an employee has selected on their career worksheet. However, it also displays the current role, and there is no way to distinguish current from targeted roles.

## Ad Hoc Reporting

To create an ad hoc report for Career Worksheet targeted roles, the report type is "Table" as shown in Figure 3-82.

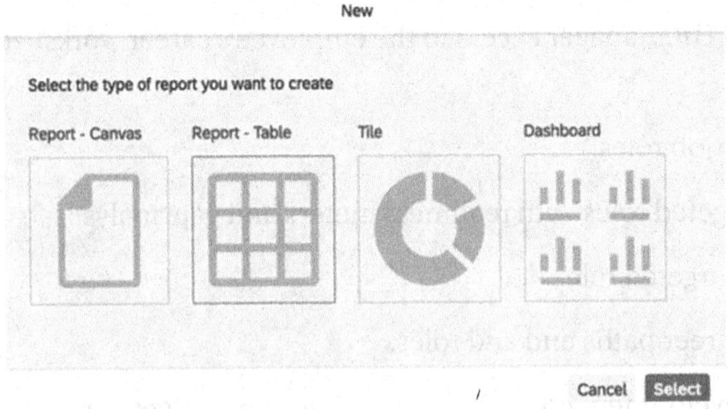


***Figure 3-82.** Report Type to Create an Ad Hoc Report*

The domain to select is Career Worksheet Targeted Roles as seen in Figure 3-83.

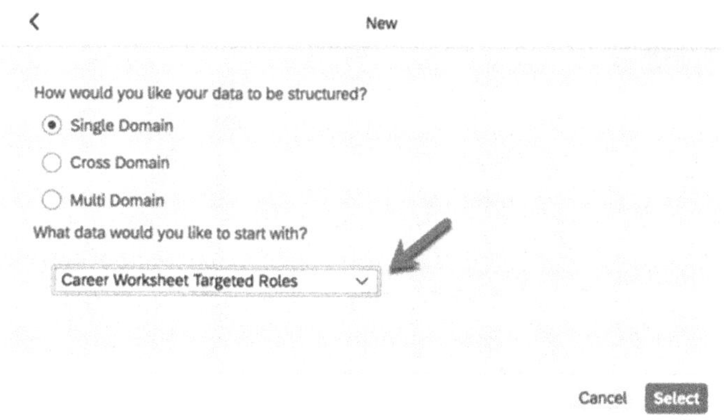

***Figure 3-83.*** *Data Source*

A wizard walks you through the steps to create the report. First, name the report, and select the people to include. In the Data Sets tab, the template to select is "Career Worksheet" as seen in Figure 3-84.

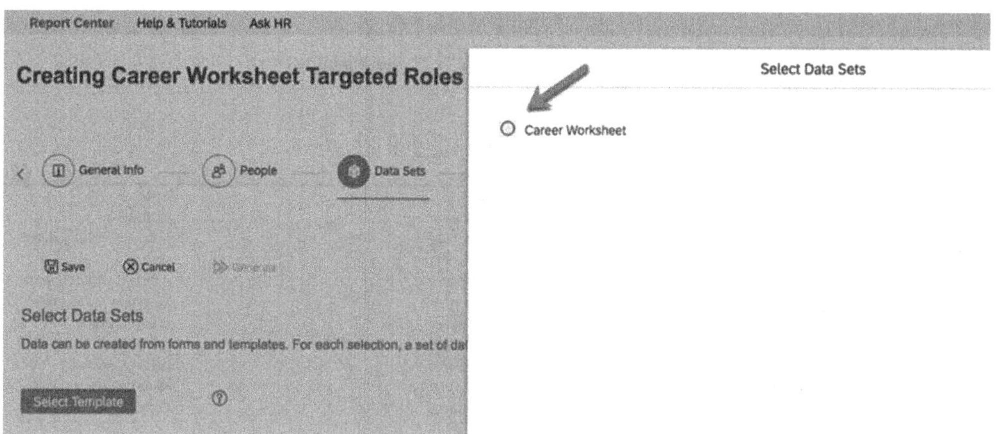


***Figure 3-84.*** *Template to Select*

From the Columns tab, select the fields to display as seen in Figure 3-85.

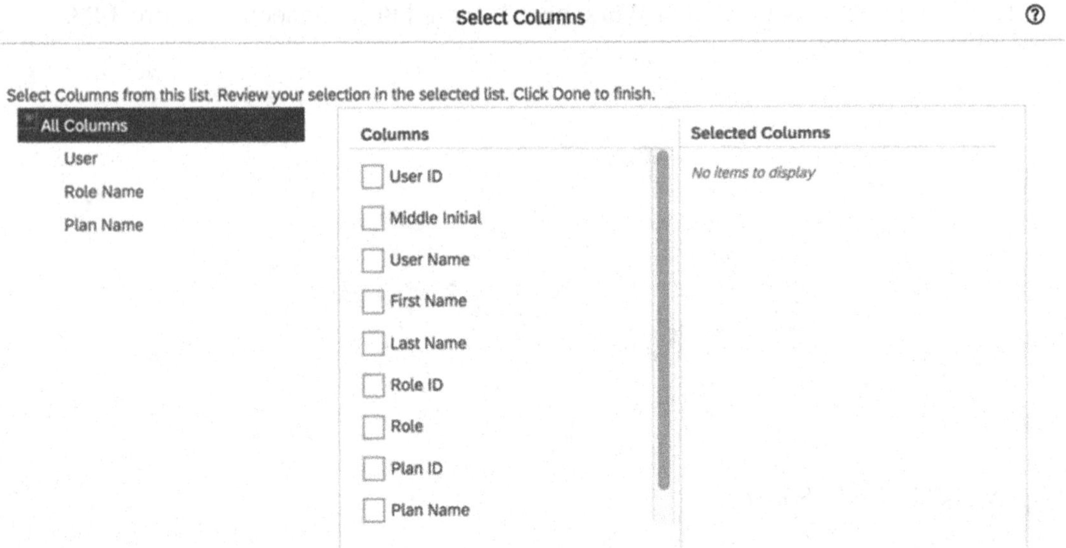

Select Columns

Select Columns from this list. Review your selection in the selected list. Click Done to finish.

All Columns
User
Role Name
Plan Name

Columns
User ID
Middle Initial
User Name
First Name
Last Name
Role ID
Role
Plan ID
Plan Name

Selected Columns
No items to display

***Figure 3-85.*** *Output Fields for Report*

After selecting fields and any filters, run the report. The report will display the employee's current role along with the targeted roles as seen in Figure 3-86.

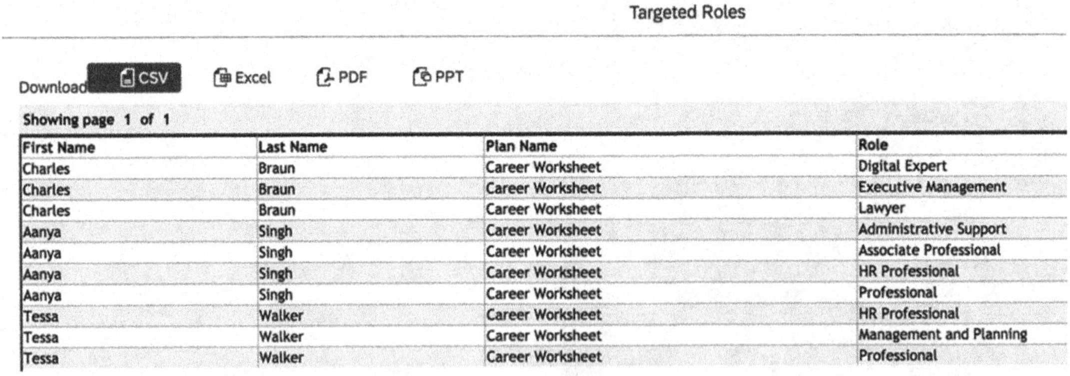

Targeted Roles

Download CSV Excel PDF PPT

Showing page 1 of 1

| First Name | Last Name | Plan Name | Role |
|---|---|---|---|
| Charles | Braun | Career Worksheet | Digital Expert |
| Charles | Braun | Career Worksheet | Executive Management |
| Charles | Braun | Career Worksheet | Lawyer |
| Aanya | Singh | Career Worksheet | Administrative Support |
| Aanya | Singh | Career Worksheet | Associate Professional |
| Aanya | Singh | Career Worksheet | HR Professional |
| Aanya | Singh | Career Worksheet | Professional |
| Tessa | Walker | Career Worksheet | HR Professional |
| Tessa | Walker | Career Worksheet | Management and Planning |
| Tessa | Walker | Career Worksheet | Professional |

***Figure 3-86.*** *Report Results*

# Dashboard

There is also a standard CDP Dashboard that may be enabled. It allows managers to see targeted roles for employees in their team and the competency readiness for each role.

The dashboard may be added from SuccessStore. Type and select "Manage Dashboards" in the search bar. As seen in Figure 3-87, click "Manage Standard Dashboards and YouCalc Files."

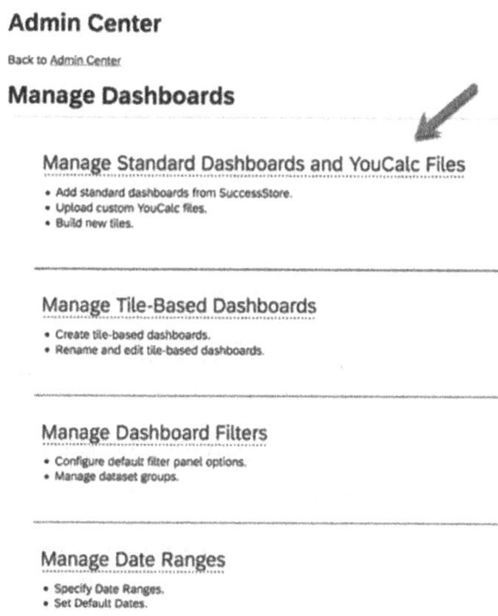


• Build new tiles.

• Create tile-based dashboards.
• Rename and edit tile-based dashboards.

• Configure default filter panel options.
• Manage dataset groups.
Manage Date Ranges
• Specify Date Ranges.
• Set Default Dates.

***Figure 3-87.*** *Manage Dashboards*

Click "Add From SuccessStore" as shown in Figure 3-88.

Admin Center
Back to Admin Center
Manage Dashboards > Manage Standard Dashboards and YouCalc Files
Build Tile
Add From SuccessStore
Upload Custom YouCalc File
Restore Deleted Models
ID | Dashboard Name | Product | Type
12 | Recruiting Metrics Bar | Recruiting | Custom
221 | Recruiting Model | Recruiting | Standard
161 | Employee Central Embedded Tile | Employee Central | Standard


***Figure 3-88.*** *Adding Standard CDP Dashboard in Manage Dashboards*

Scroll through the list, find CDP Dashboard, and click "Add to instance" as shown in Figure 3-89.

Standard Dashboards and Tiles

| | | | |
|---|---|---|---|
| Competency Dashboard | Overview of most common competencies, competency gaps and competency rating More.. | Jul 11, 2016 4:26AM | Add to Instance |
| Objective Dashboard | Overview of objectives status, objective alignment and objective distribution. | Jul 11, 2016 4:27AM | Add to Instance |
| Performance Dashboard | Overview of form status, rating distribution and performance vs. potential. | Mar 06, 2020 3:34AM | Add to Instance |
| Performance and Competencies Dashboard | Overview of performance form status, rating distribution and most common More.. | Sep 30, 2019 3:46AM | Add to Instance |
| Performance Form Status | Get an overview of the Performance form status. | Feb 22, 2017 2:43AM | Add to Instance |
| Objective Status | See the status of the goals in your team. | Oct 22, 2015 3:55AM | Add to Instance |
| CDP Dashboard | See targeted roles among people in your team and the competency readiness for More.. | Nov 28, 2016 7:05AM | Add to Instance |

***Figure 3-89.*** *Adding Standard CDP Dashboard in Manage Dashboards*

As mentioned in the role-based permissions at the start of the chapter, be sure that the manager and HR roles have access to this dashboard. In the role-based permissions for the manager and HR manager roles, add Reports Permission ➤ Analytics Tils and Dashboards ➤ Others ➤ CDP Dashboard as shown in Figure 3-90.

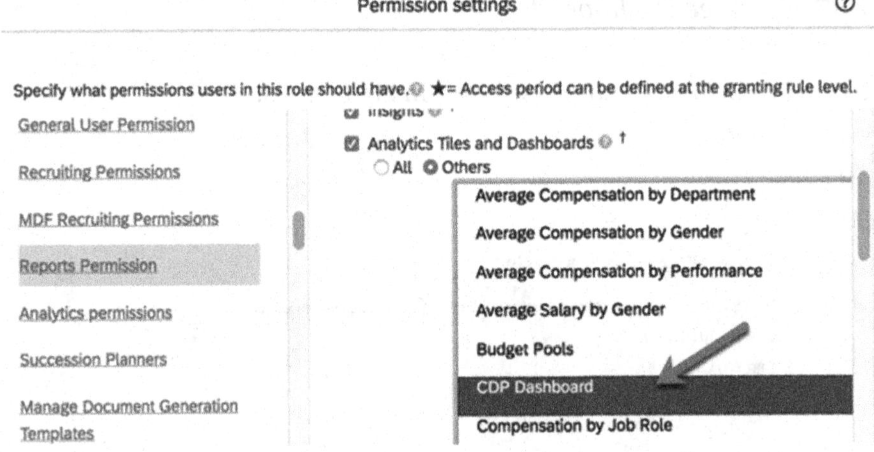


***Figure 3-90.*** *Permission to Access CDP Dashboard*

When the dashboard is generated by a manager, the Dashboard Overview displays the targeted role counts as seen in Figure 3-91.

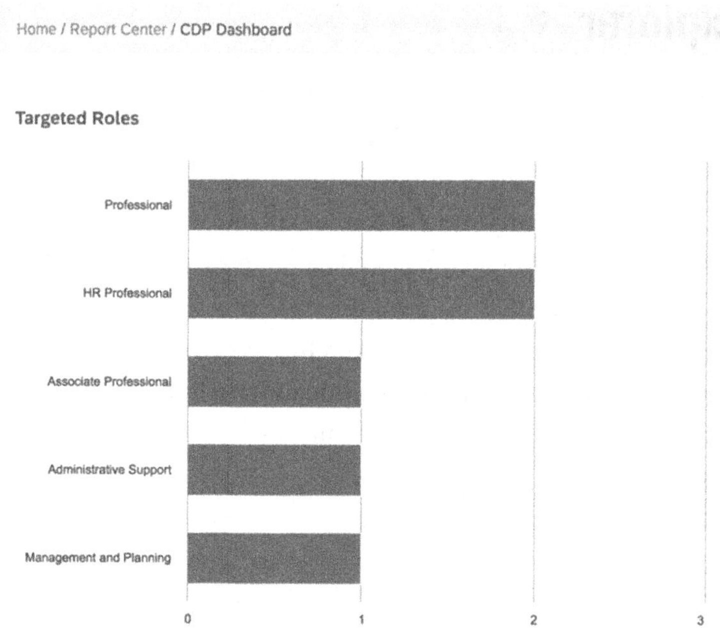


***Figure 3-91.** Targeted Role Counts on the Dashboard*

The manager can drill into any role to see the readiness for each employee as seen in Figure 3-92.

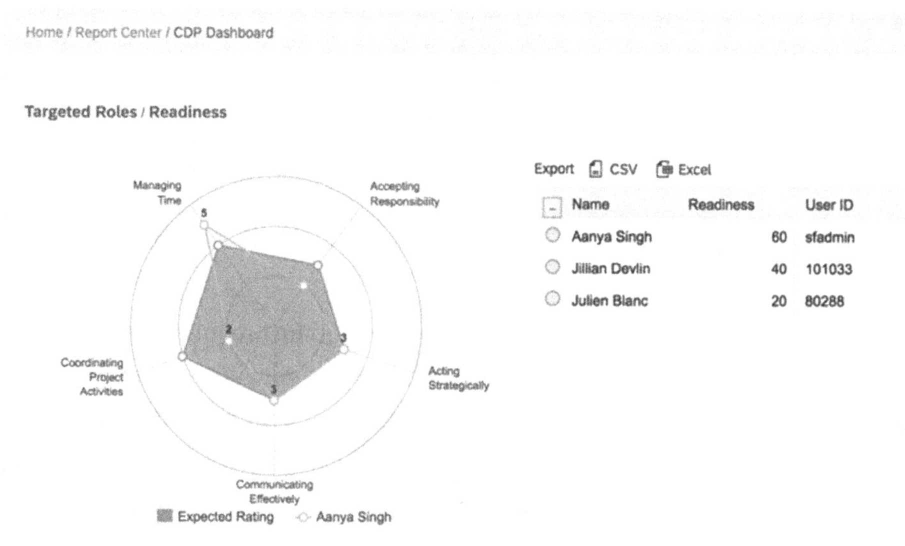


***Figure 3-92.** Drill Down for the Targeted Role*

## Career Explorer

A new component of Career Development is Career Explorer. It uses a machine learning algorithm to make recommendations for future job roles based on users "like me." Career Explorer recommends career opportunities based on the career paths of the people who are similar to the employee in the organization. This allows an employee to find possible future roles outside of traditional career paths and set those roles as targets for their career development.

An employee can see the career paths taken by users who used to hold their job role or who have similar skills, previous roles, or education to help them identify their next move. This provides personalized guidance unlike using the predefined career paths to determine one's next role.

Career Explorer is shown in Figure 3-93.

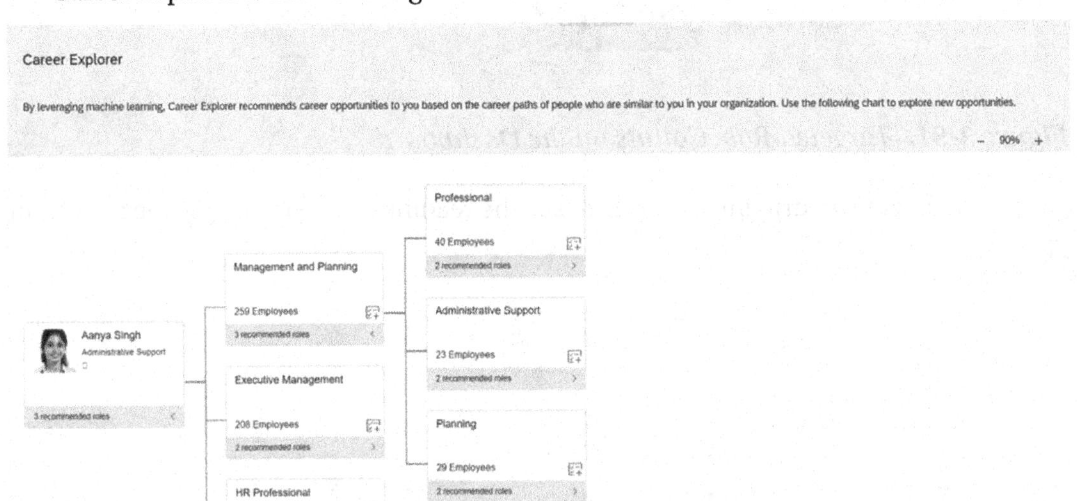


***Figure 3-93.*** *Career Explorer*

An employee uses Career Explorer to see customized future job roles to consider. Competencies, skills, and other job profile details may be viewed for each role. An employee may select a future role which gets added to their career worksheet. On the worksheet, the employee will see the competencies required to be successful in the targeted role which helps them identify competency gaps and needed areas of development.

With that said, Career Explorer is only available in an Early Adopter Care (EAC) program in H1 2020.

## Conclusion

We have granted user permissions to Career Worksheet. We have seen how an employee can use the features of Career Worksheet based on the configuration decisions made by the HR admin. The employee can use this tool to explore career paths, see roles they may wish to attain in the future, find gaps in skills and competencies to reach those roles, and strategically plan how to overcome those deficiencies through development goals. We have seen how a manager and HR manager may access an employee's career worksheet and run reports on their targeted roles. We briefly saw Career Explorer and how it integrates with Career Worksheet.

# CHAPTER 4

# Mentoring

A mentoring program is a valuable tool to aid in an employee's personal growth and career development. A mentorship establishes a relationship between an experienced employee who provides guidance, advice, and role modeling and a more junior-level employee. A mentor can share insight from their own career and help a mentee set development goals, identify areas of interest, and provide network opportunities.

The mentoring solution in SAP SuccessFactors is twofold. The mentoring administrator will create, maintain, and track mentoring programs outside of the Development module using the Manage Mentoring Programs tool. The admin will create the mentoring programs, identify participants, define criteria used to match mentors and mentees, invite users to participate, assign and reassign matches, and change the status of a program. We will talk more about these functions in detail. This module works in conjunction with the Development module to support development for employees.

## Overview of the Mentoring Process

Once the admin creates a mentoring program, an email invitation is sent to the selected employees asking them to join. The email contains a link which directs the invitee to a new tab in the Career Development module called Mentoring. All user-based mentoring tasks are performed here and include signing up for a mentoring program, identifying preferences in order to find the perfect match, accepting and rejecting requests, and ending a mentoring relationship. We will walk through mentoring program examples as a mentor and mentee.

Once the programs are established and the mentors and mentees have been matched, the admin may change mentoring relationships, change mentor availability, track and report on the programs, and close programs.




S. Traynor et al., *SAP SuccessFactors Talent: Volume 2*, https://doi.org/10.1007/978-1-4842-6995-4_4

When joining, the mentor and mentee identify what they are looking for in a mentoring relationship. Mentor/mentee matching is done by identifying the preferences and then finding a mentor who meets those needs for a mentee. The type of program created dictates who can join, how matching is done, and if participation approval is needed.

Email notifications are very heavily used in the mentoring programs. There are 24 mentoring notifications that a user may receive during the program. The emails prompt users to take action within the Mentoring overview page. At the end of the chapter, we will look at the emails, what they contain, and what triggers them.

In this chapter, we will cover the following topics:

- Mentoring setup in Provisioning
- Role-based permissions
- Managing mentoring programs
- Creating custom mentoring programs
- Using match programs
- Using mentoring as a participant
- Email notifications
- Ad hoc reporting

# Provisioning Setup

Let's start with the Provisioning features required to enable to use mentoring.

These features should already be enabled in Provisioning if you are using Career Development:

- Metadata Framework (MDF)
- Generic objects
- Attachment Manager
- CDP Full (Development Plan)
- Role-based permissions

## Mentoring Settings

To use mentoring, in Company Settings, under the Career & Development Planning section of Goal Frameworks, click the box next to Enable Mentoring Program as seen in Figure 4-1.

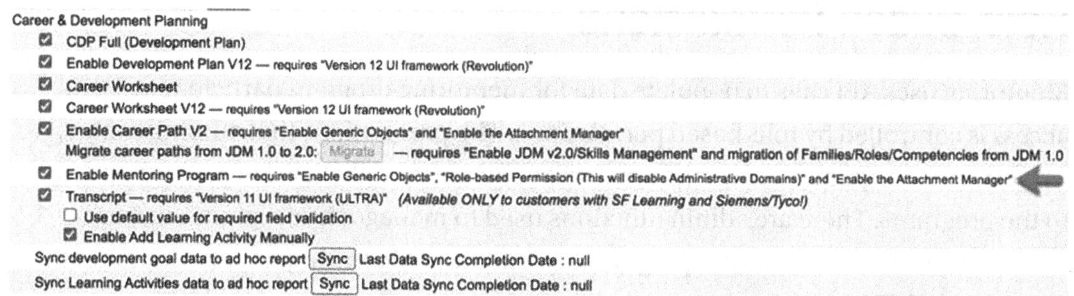


***Figure 4-1.*** *Enabling Mentoring Programs in Company Settings*

## Additional Options to Enable

Based on your organization, there are additional options that you may enable:

- Dynamic Groups V2 (My Groups) should be enabled if you wish to identify mentoring participants through the use of dynamic employee groups.
- SAP Jam may be integrated with Mentoring to create SAP groups. If you wish to use this feature, SAP Jam Integration must be enabled in Company Settings as well.
- For Ad Hoc Mentoring Reporting, make sure "Ad Hoc Report Builder" is enabled, and then enable:
    - "Mentoring Programs" under Additional Adhoc Sub domain Schemas Configuration
    - "Mentoring Programs" under Enable INCLUDE STARTING FROM USER in people pill

Save the updates made.

Dependent on the features that you choose to use in your mentoring programs, there may be additional tasks to perform in Provisioning. These items are related to custom programs and custom picklists. We will explain both later in this chapter.

Once Mentoring is enabled in Provisioning, permissions need to be set in the UI.

# Role-Based Permissions

Mentoring uses API calls to populate data for mentoring program participants. Data access is controlled by role-based permissions. The permissions that administrators, owners, and program participants need will vary based on the level of access needed to the programs. There are admin functions used to manage the programs and user functions to allow access to the programs. In addition, Mentoring uses the Metadata Framework (MDF) which requires all of the roles to have basic Read and Write permissions.

We will now look at the roles that are needed for Mentoring and the permission each requires.

## Mentoring Administrator Role

You may decide to create a new role for an individual within your talent group to administer the mentoring programs. In that case, assign that user to a mentoring permission group tied to this permission role. In very large organizations, you may have multiple mentoring administrators. You may decide to add the mentoring permissions to an existing HR admin role.

## Mentoring Participant Role

If all members of your organization will be eligible to participate in mentoring programs, the mentoring permissions may be added to the employee role.

If only certain segments of the organization will be participating, create a permission group for those users. Assign the new permission group to a new mentoring permission role.

Type and select "Manage Permission Roles" in the search bar. Select the roles to update. Table 4-1 contains the permissions needed for the mentoring admin role and the mentoring user role. Mentors and mentees have the same permissions, so these permissions do not require separate permission roles. You may add permissions to an existing employee permission role. Or as just mentioned, if there is a specific subset of employees that will be using mentoring, you may identify the users to create a permission group and then assign them to a mentoring user role.

***Table 4-1.*** *Role-Based Permissions to Manage and Participate in Mentoring Programs*

| User Permissions Section | Permission | Admin Role | Mentor/Mentee Role |
|---|---|---|---|
| **User Permissions Section** | | | |
| General User Permission | Company Info Access ➤ User Search | X | X |
| | Community Access | X | X |
| Employee Data | Last Name, First Name ➤ View | X | X |
| Career Development Planning | Mentoring Programs Access Permission | X | X |
| Reports Permission | Create/Run Ad hoc reports for Mentoring Program | | X |
| **Administrator Permissions Section** | | | |
| Metadata Framework | Access to non-secured objects | X | X |
| Manage Integration Tools | Allow Admin to Access OData API through Basic Authentication | X | |
| Manage Career Development | Manage Mentoring Programs | X | |
| Manage User | Manage Employee Dynamic Groups | X (optional) | |

As mentioned earlier, Mentoring includes an integration with SAP Jam. When enabled, mentoring administrators can create SAP Jam (community) groups when establishing mentoring programs. This gives participants an additional platform for collaboration, training, and discussions. To take advantage of this integration, be sure that SAP Jam access role-based permissions are enabled for all users who are participating in mentoring programs.

## Picklists

When creating a mentoring program, the mentoring admin designs a sign-up form. The sign-up form includes a series of questions that the mentor and mentee must answer in order to participate. The questions are used to identify the preferences that they are looking for in a mentoring relationship. Based on the responses and the matching rules, the system recommends mentor/mentee pairings. Answers to the questions may be free-form text or based on values from a picklist. The standard picklists that may be used for answering questions are listed in the following:

- Competency
- Department
- Division
- Location
- Gender
- Job Family
- Job Role
- Job Code
- Job Level
- Job Title
- Skill

It is possible to create custom picklists as well. In either case, the standard and custom picklists have to be defined in the data model and have Read permissions granted.

Now that we have enabled Mentoring in Provisioning and set up the admin and mentoring user role-based permissions, let's talk more about the types of programs that may be created and the steps to create them.

# Mentoring Program Types

There are three types of mentoring programs that may be created:

1. **Open Enrollment:** These programs are open to all employees or to defined groups. There are no defined dates for the program, including an end date. Users may sign up as a mentor, a mentee, or both. There is an option so that mentor participation must be approved by either their manager or the mentoring admin. Mentees must select a mentor during sign-up; however, the mentor may decline.

2. **Supervised:** The mentoring admin selects the mentors and mentees to participate in the program. The admin must manually send the invitations based on predefined dates. Mentees may not sign up until after the mentor sign-up period has ended. Mentees may identify mentor preferences, but mentors are not notified to approve or reject the mentee. A matching program identifies the best fit for each mentee. The admin may change any matches, and only then does a matchup confirmation get sent to mentors and mentees.

3. **Unsupervised:** The unsupervised mentoring type is invitation based. The mentoring admin selects the mentors and mentees to participate, and invitations are system generated based on the mentor and mentee sign-up dates. The admin may manually trigger the invitation emails as well. During sign-up, the mentee must select a mentor. The mentor is notified of the request and may approve or reject the offer. The admin may also assign or unassign relationships.

Table 4-2 highlights some of the features that differ by program. These features will be discussed in detail later in the chapter.

*Table 4-2. Features Available for Each Program Type*

| Action/Program Type | Supervised | Unsupervised | Open Enrollment |
|---|---|---|---|
| Invitations automatically sent | | X | |
| Uses a matching program to identify recommended matches | X | | |
| Uses program dates | X | X | |
| Mentor approval to participate | | | X |
| Program requires invitation to participate | X | X | |
| Program open to anyone with access to mentoring | | | X |
| May join the program as mentee, mentor, or both | | | X |
| Mentee may select a mentor | X | X | X |
| When mentee selects a mentor, the mentor receives an email | | X | X |
| Admin may assign and reassign any matches | X | X | X |
| Mentor may reject mentee request | | X | X |
| Mentor may change their availability | X | X | X |
| Sign up only during separate mentor and mentee sign-up periods | X | | |

# Custom Programs

We have now seen the three standard mentoring program types that are available. It is also possible to create up to three custom program types. They have the same features and functionality as the standard programs but with custom labels. Custom programs provide the flexibility to replace all mentoring phrases used in a program with your own labels. You may wish to call a program a "coaching program" rather than a mentoring program. By creating the custom labels, the screens within a custom program will use your labels as will the email notifications.

The system-level Text Replacement tool overwrites default text with custom values. Here, all mentoring terms could be replaced with other labels. This would impact all the labels for all of the standard mentoring programs. Program-level replacement text is used to create custom mentoring programs with custom labels specific only to those programs. Up to three custom programs may be created, each with its own labels. A text replacement pack is created with the custom labels. We will walk through this process shortly.

# Mentoring Admin Functions

We will now learn how to create, track, and update mentoring programs. Type and select "Manage Mentoring Programs" in the search bar. The Mentoring Program overview screen will display as seen in Figure 4-2.

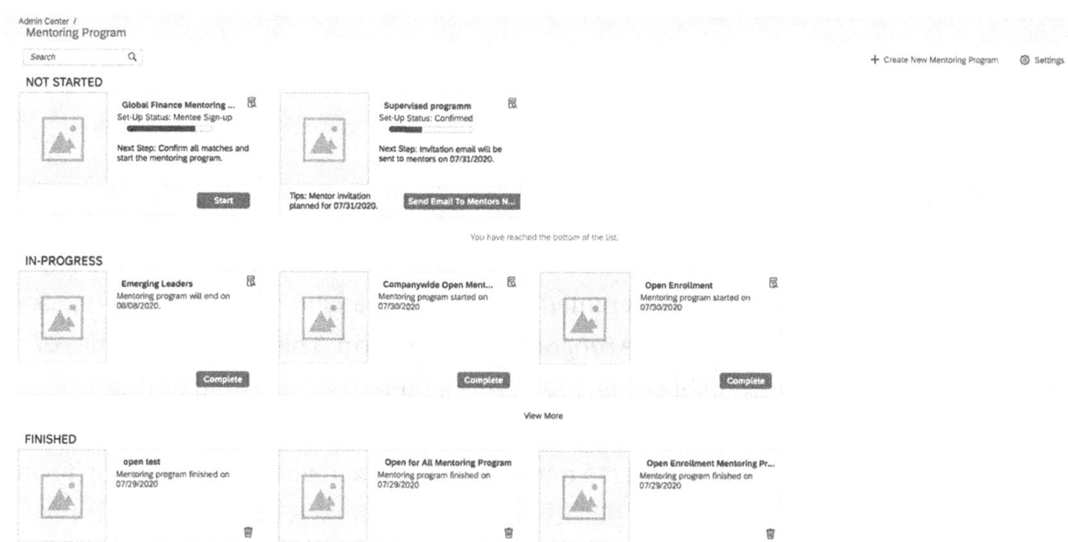


***Figure 4-2.*** *Managing Mentoring Program Overview Page*

All of the mentoring administrative tasks are performed here.

We will review the functionality on this page to create and manage mentoring programs, but let's first look at some optional setting configurations that may be set up prior to creating any programs.

## Mentoring Program Settings

Found in the top-right corner of the screen, click "Settings" to link to the mentoring program configuration. Configuration done here will apply to all mentoring programs.

Two types of configuration may be defined: custom picklists and text replacement. Figure 4-3 displays the default tab for custom picklist configuration.

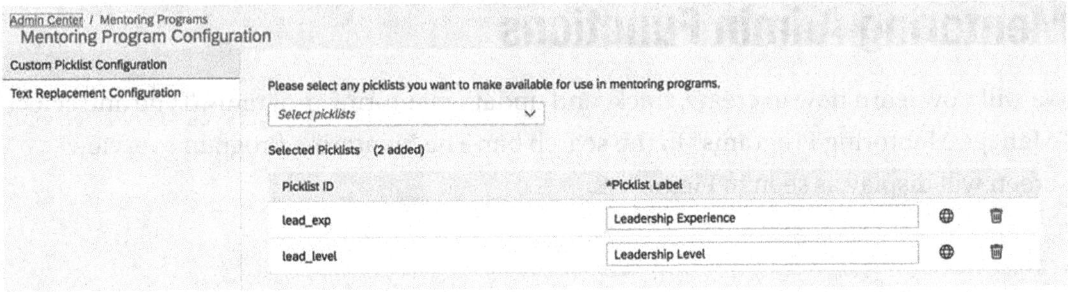

***Figure 4-3.** Mentoring Program Settings*

## Custom Picklists

In addition to the standard picklists, the admin may also use custom picklists for the sign-up questions. Any custom picklists identified here will be available when the admin picks a question category when creating the program's sign-up form. This allows the values of the custom picklists to be available when answering a preference question during sign-up.

From the dropdown listing in the Custom Picklist Configuration tab, the admin would identify any additional picklists to make available when designing a sign-up form. After selecting the picklist, create the picklist label. An example is shown in Figure 4-4. This is the picklist name that will display when selecting the question category during program creation.

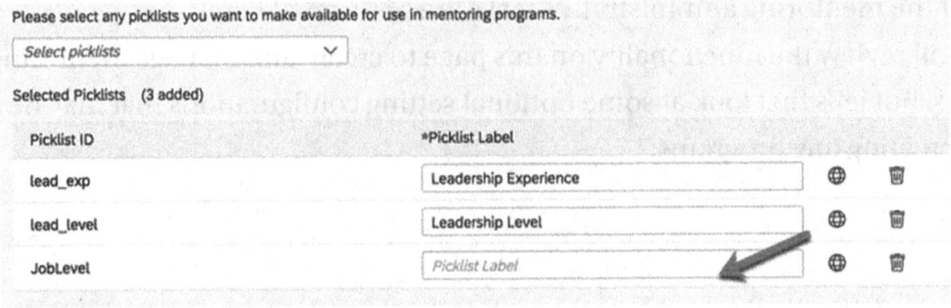

***Figure 4-4.** Adding a Custom Picklist*

Picklist labels may be localized as seen in Figure 4-5.

***Figure 4-5.*** *Localize a Custom Picklist Name*

All of the picklists that are used for a question will appear in the question category selection when designing the sign-up form. In the dropdown list for the question category, the custom picklists will appear alphabetically after the standard picklists.

## Custom Programs

Click the other tab within "Settings". In this tab, the admin would identify the text replacement pack for up to three custom programs. An example is shown in Figure 4-6.

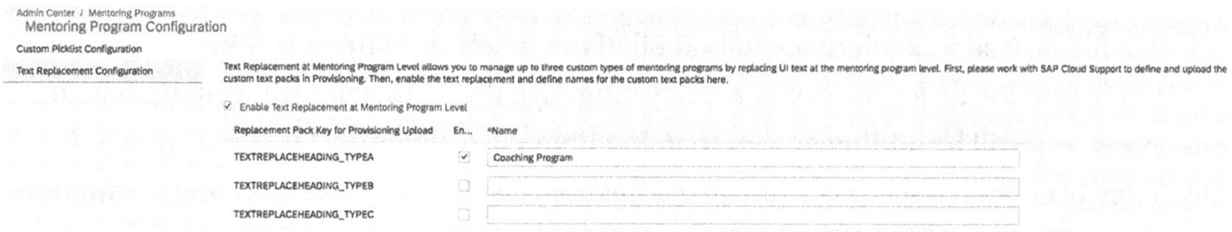

***Figure 4-6.*** *Text Replacement Configuration Tab Used to Identify Custom Mentoring Programs*

If you do not plan on using any custom programs, no entries are needed in this tab. You may skip the following section which details the steps to create the custom language packs.

If you plan on using custom programs, define the replacement text before using the Text Replacement Configuration tab.

Let's go back to Company Settings in Provisioning. Language Packs should be enabled along with "Enable Manage Languages tool." Language packs need to be enabled for each language you are using.

Once the Manage Languages tool is enabled, "Manage Languages" will be available in Company Settings as seen in Figure 4-7.

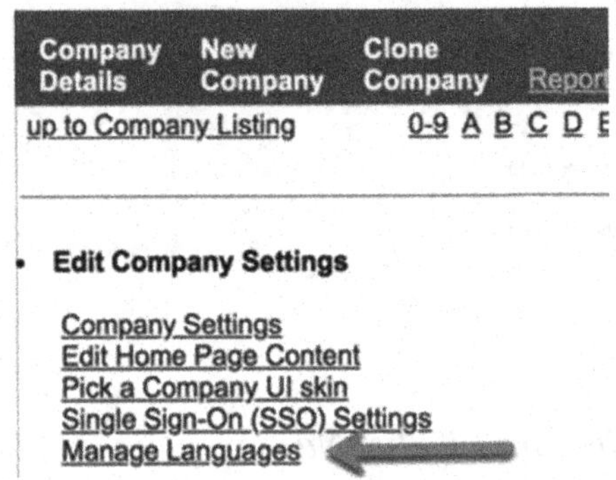


***Figure 4-7.** Access to Manage Languages in Provisioning*

Within Manage Languages, download the default labels for the default active language as seen in Figure 4-8.

| | | | | |
|---|---|---|---|---|
| English SAP SLS | en_SAP_SLS | ☐ | Tue Jul 14 12:40:20 EDT 2020 | |
| English UK (English UK) | en_GB | ☑ | Tue Jul 14 12:40:20 EDT 2020 | Download default labels |
| English US (English US) | en_US | ☑ | Tue Jul 14 12:40:20 EDT 2020 | |

***Figure 4-8.** Download Standard Default Labels*

This file is used as a reference to find all of the labels used in mentoring programs.

If a custom locale for the default active language does not exist, then create one. If one exists, you will be adding entries to it. In either case, download the custom labels file. A newly created file will contain just a header row. We will be populating it with new keys that will contain labels for the new custom programs.

Open the default .csv file with Notepad or any UTF-8 editor.

Sort the file by key (column A) to find all keys that start with "DEVELOPMENT_MENT." These will be all of the mentoring-related labels as seen in Figure 4-9.

| | A | B |
|---|---|---|
| 1 | Key | en_US |
| 2 | DEVELOPMENT_MENTEE_HOME_PAGE_GOAL | Career Development Plan |
| 3 | DEVELOPMENT_MENTEE_HOME_PAGE_HINT | The $(DEVELOPMENT_mentoring_program) will begin on {0} and you will be notified when all matches are finalized. |
| 4 | DEVELOPMENT_MENTEE_HOME_PAGE_MY_MENTOR | My $(DEVELOPMENT_MENTORING_PROGRAM_MENTOR) |
| 5 | DEVELOPMENT_MENTEE_HOME_PAGE_NO_MENTOR | $(DEVELOPMENT_MENTORING_PROGRAM_MENTOR) will be displayed here once confirmed. |
| 6 | DEVELOPMENT_MENTEE_HOME_PAGE_NOPREFERENCE | No available preferences. |
| 7 | DEVELOPMENT_MENTEE_HOME_PAGE_PREFERENCE | Your $(DEVELOPMENT_MENTORING_PROGRAM_Mentoring) Preferences |
| 8 | DEVELOPMENT_MENTOR_HOME_PAGE_MENTEE_INFO_MESSAGE | Your $(DEVELOPMENT_MENTORING_PROGRAM_mentees) will show up here after they sign-up and you accept their $(DEVELOPMENT_MENTORING_PROGRAM_mentoring) requ |
| 9 | DEVELOPMENT_MENTOR_HOME_PAGE_MORE_REQUEST | You have {0} new $(DEVELOPMENT_MENTORING_PROGRAM_Mentoring) Requests |
| 10 | DEVELOPMENT_MENTOR_HOME_PAGE_NO_MENTEE | $(DEVELOPMENT_MENTORING_PROGRAM_MENTEES) will be shown here. |
| 11 | DEVELOPMENT_MENTOR_HOME_PAGE_NO_MENTEE_NOW | You don't have any $(DEVELOPMENT_MENTORING_PROGRAM_mentees) yet |
| 12 | DEVELOPMENT_MENTOR_HOME_PAGE_ONE_REQUEST | You have {0} new $(DEVELOPMENT_MENTORING_PROGRAM_Mentoring) Request |
| 13 | DEVELOPMENT_MENTOR_HOME_PAGE_REVIEW_NEWMENTEE_REQUEST_ | Review Requests |
| 14 | DEVELOPMENT_MENTOR_HOME_PAGE_REVIEW_NEWMENTEE_REQUEST_ | {0} New $(DEVELOPMENT_MENTORING_PROGRAM_Mentoring) Requests |
| 15 | DEVELOPMENT_MENTOR_SWITCH_VALUE_FALSE | FALSE |
| 16 | DEVELOPMENT_MENTOR_SWITCH_VALUE_TRUE | TRUE |
| 17 | DEVELOPMENT_MENTOR_UVAILABILITY_IN_ONE_DAY_BODY | Dear [MENTOR_NAME], This is a reminder that your status in [PROGRAM_NAME] will be set to available tomorrow. This means that, starting tomorrow, you may be selected as |
| 18 | DEVELOPMENT_MENTOR_UVAILABILITY_IN_ONE_DAY_SUBJECT | You will be available as a $(DEVELOPMENT_MENTORING_PROGRAM_MENTOR) tomorrow in [PLAIN_PROGRAM_NAME] |
| 19 | DEVELOPMENT_MENTOR_UVAILABILITY_IN_SEVEN_DAYS_BODY | Dear [MENTOR_NAME], This is a reminder that your status in [PROGRAM_NAME] will be set to available in 7 days. To make changes to your availability status or dates, go to th |
| 20 | DEVELOPMENT_MENTOR_UVAILABILITY_IN_SEVEN_DAYS_SUBJECT | You will be available as a $(DEVELOPMENT_MENTORING_PROGRAM_MENTOR) in [PLAIN_PROGRAM_NAME] in 7 days |
| 21 | DEVELOPMENT_Mentoring | Mentoring |
| 22 | DEVELOPMENT_mentoring | mentoring |
| 23 | DEVELOPMENT_MENTORING__ALL_MENTEES_SLOT_FULL | No $(DEVELOPMENT_MENTORING_PROGRAM_mentees) are available. |
| 24 | DEVELOPMENT_MENTORING__ALL_MENTORS_SLOT_FULL | No $(DEVELOPMENT_MENTORING_PROGRAM_mentors) are available. |

***Figure 4-9.*** *Mentoring-Related Labels in the Default Labels File*

We will need to create custom keys with custom labels for the custom mentoring program types. To start, copy all of mentor-related keys from the default file into the blank custom file or to the existing custom file. The custom file will just contain two columns: Key and the language. In creating our file, we will be using "en_US" in column B.

Go through the labels (column B) for each key to find any that contains a mentor-related word or phrase. You can delete any keys on the custom file that won't need a new label. A more laborious option is the go into the instance, turn on the debug version of the system language, and view each mentoring screen to see the keys and labels used. Make note of all of the keys that will need custom labels and make sure these will be your custom text file.

References to the three custom programs must be identified as TYPEA, TYPEB, or TYPEC. For example, if you are creating a coaching program, all the labels for this custom program should contain TYPEA in the key. If another mentoring program is for a learning group, all the labels for this program should contain TYPEB in the key. The other new program would use labels of TYPEC.

For your first custom program, use TYPEA. On your custom file, you should now have all of the keys that need new text. You will append "_TEXTREPLACEHEADING_TYPEA" to each key on the custom file.

As you will see in Figure 4-10, column A contains all of the regular DEVELOPMENT_MENTORING keys with the added replacement text key (_TEXTREPLACEHEADING_TYPEA). These keys identify all of the labels that will be used in your first custom program (TYPEA).

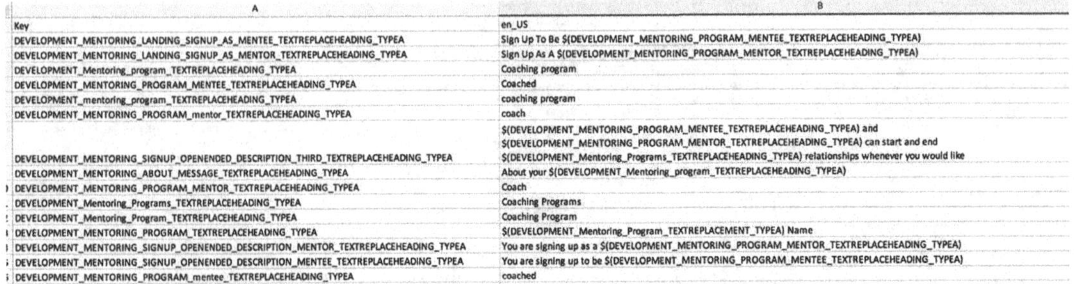

| A | B |
|---|---|
| Key | en_US |
| DEVELOPMENT_MENTORING_LANDING_SIGNUP_AS_MENTEE_TEXTREPLACEHEADING_TYPEA | Sign Up To Be $(DEVELOPMENT_MENTORING_PROGRAM_MENTEE_TEXTREPLACEHEADING_TYPEA) |
| DEVELOPMENT_MENTORING_LANDING_SIGNUP_AS_MENTOR_TEXTREPLACEHEADING_TYPEA | Sign Up As A $(DEVELOPMENT_MENTORING_PROGRAM_MENTOR_TEXTREPLACEHEADING_TYPEA) |
| DEVELOPMENT_Mentoring_program_TEXTREPLACEHEADING_TYPEA | Coaching program |
| DEVELOPMENT_MENTORING_PROGRAM_MENTEE_TEXTREPLACEHEADING_TYPEA | Coached |
| DEVELOPMENT_mentoring_program_TEXTREPLACEHEADING_TYPEA | coaching program |
| DEVELOPMENT_MENTORING_PROGRAM_mentor_TEXTREPLACEHEADING_TYPEA | coach |
| DEVELOPMENT_MENTORING_SIGNUP_OPENENDED_DESCRIPTION_THIRD_TEXTREPLACEHEADING_TYPEA | $(DEVELOPMENT_MENTORING_PROGRAM_MENTEE_TEXTREPLACEHEADING_TYPEA) and $(DEVELOPMENT_MENTORING_PROGRAM_MENTOR_TEXTREPLACEHEADING_TYPEA) can start and end $(DEVELOPMENT_Mentoring_Programs_TEXTREPLACEHEADING_TYPEA) relationships whenever you would like |
| DEVELOPMENT_MENTORING_ABOUT_MESSAGE_TEXTREPLACEHEADING_TYPEA | About your $(DEVELOPMENT_Mentoring_program_TEXTREPLACEHEADING_TYPEA) |
| DEVELOPMENT_MENTORING_PROGRAM_MENTOR_TEXTREPLACEHEADING_TYPEA | Coach |
| DEVELOPMENT_Mentoring_Programs_TEXTREPLACEHEADING_TYPEA | Coaching Programs |
| DEVELOPMENT_Mentoring_Program_TEXTREPLACEHEADING_TYPEA | Coaching Program |
| DEVELOPMENT_MENTORING_PROGRAM_TEXTREPLACEHEADING_TYPEA | $(DEVELOPMENT_Mentoring_Program_TEXTREPLACEMENT_TYPEA) Name |
| DEVELOPMENT_MENTORING_SIGNUP_OPENENDED_DESCRIPTION_MENTOR_TEXTREPLACEHEADING_TYPEA | You are signing up as a $(DEVELOPMENT_MENTORING_PROGRAM_MENTOR_TEXTREPLACEHEADING_TYPEA) |
| DEVELOPMENT_MENTORING_SIGNUP_OPENENDED_DESCRIPTION_MENTEE_TEXTREPLACEHEADING_TYPEA | You are signing up to be $(DEVELOPMENT_MENTORING_PROGRAM_MENTEE_TEXTREPLACEHEADING_TYPEA) |
| DEVELOPMENT_MENTORING_PROGRAM_mentee_TEXTREPLACEHEADING_TYPEA | coached |

***Figure 4-10.*** *Sample File Used for Creating Custom Labels*

For the keys that are replacing a word or phrase such as mentor, mentee, or mentoring, provide the new custom label in column B. For keys to reference the new words, create new keys using "_TEXTREPLACEHEADING_TYPEA" for those as well. The label should reference the new word keys.

In the file that we looked at in the preceding figure, the mentoring program key (DEVELOPMENT_Mentoring_program) will now have a custom key on the file called "DEVELOPMENT__Mentoring_program_TEXTREPLACEHEADING_TYPEA" with a label of "Coaching Program". Any keys that reference "mentoring" program will need to have a new key created also with "_TEXTREPLACEHEADING_TYPEA" in the key name, and the label would need to reference "DEVELOPMENT__Mentoring_program_TEXTREPLACEHEADING_TYPEA" in order to replace "mentoring program" with "coaching program".

After the file is built, upload the custom labels file. To have the custom text replacement working in other system languages, repeat the same procedure for those languages.

Now the mentoring admin can go back into the instance to "Settings" in "Manage Mentoring Programs" to identify the text replacement packs to use. Enable and name each type created as seen in Figure 4-11.

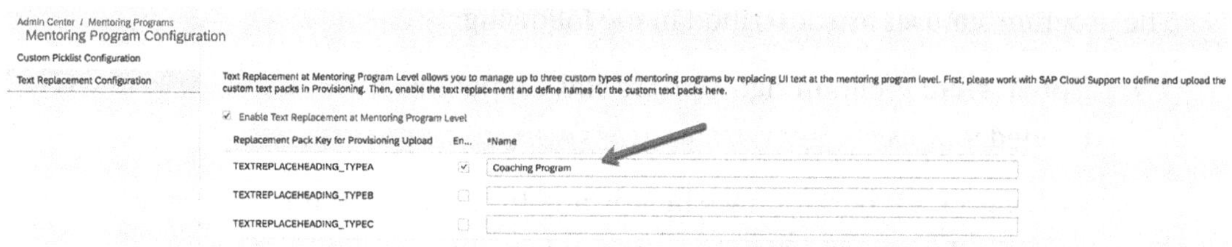


***Figure 4-11.*** *Identifying Custom Language Text Packs to Use for Custom Mentoring Programs*

Just one custom program was created in the example that we walked through. Note that the replacement pack key is the same name as the suffix that was added to the keys on the custom file TEXTREPLACEHEADING_TYPEA.

When creating a new program of any of the standard types, the admin will select the "Program Text Replacement Option" and identify the name of the replacement pack to use. This will make more sense when we create a program.

# Program Overview Page for Admins

After updating program settings, go back to the program overview page. Mentoring programs are grouped by status. The programs will display in Not Started, In-Progress, and Finished sections of the overview page. An example of the overview page is shown in Figure 4-12.

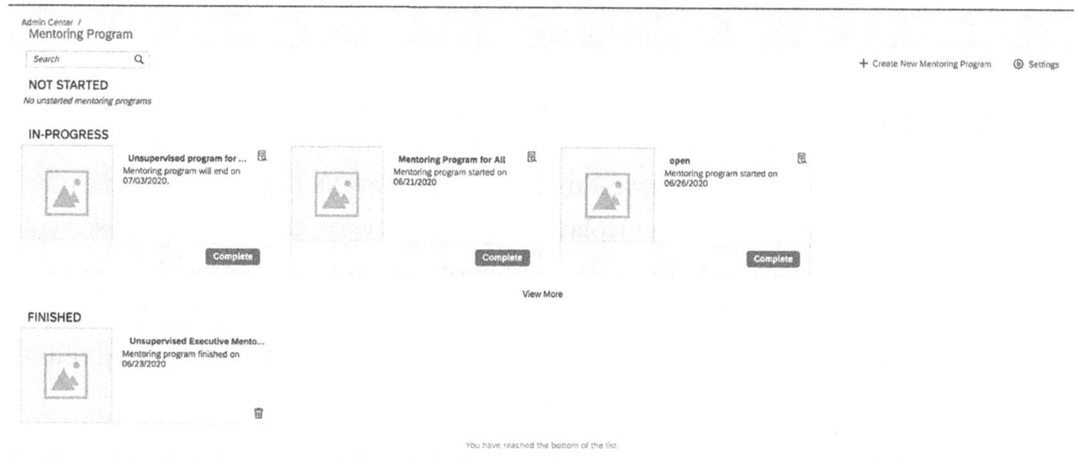


***Figure 4-12.*** *Mentoring Program Overview*

The program statuses are described in the following:

- **Not Started:** Program sign-ups are still happening; input is still needed.
- **In-Progress:** Programs have begun, and for open programs, they stay open until manually closed. Supervised and unsupervised programs run until end dates. Cannot be deleted in this stage. The admin would have to first set the status to Complete.
- **Finished:** Programs reached the end date and are no longer active. Only finished programs may be deleted.

Clicking an existing program will display the Details tab, which is the default tab. Depending on the program type and status, there may also be tabs for Mentors, Mentees, Questions, and Matches. An example is shown in Figure 4-13.

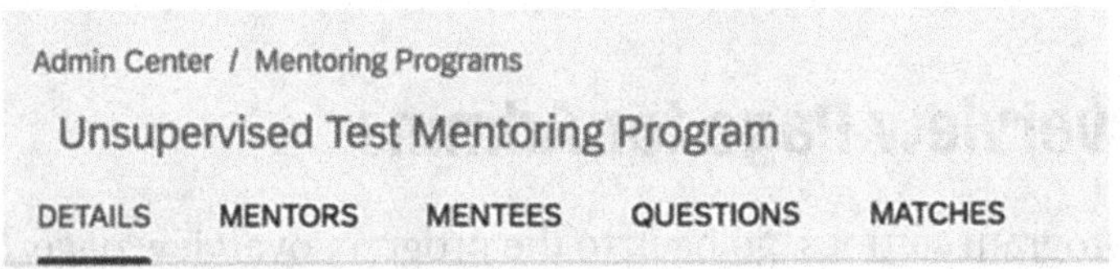


***Figure 4-13.*** *Tabs Within a Mentoring Program*

Now that we have seen the overview page and learned about the settings, let's look at the screens that are used to create a mentoring program.

# Creating a New Mentoring Program

From the overview page, the admin would click "Create New Mentoring Program". As seen in Figure 4-14, a popup screen displays the program types. Once the admin selects the type of program to create, there will be a series of screens to walk through to define the parameters of the program. Based on the program type, there are some differences in the details screen fields and participant screens. After selecting the type, the admin would click the "Continue" button to start to create the mentoring program.

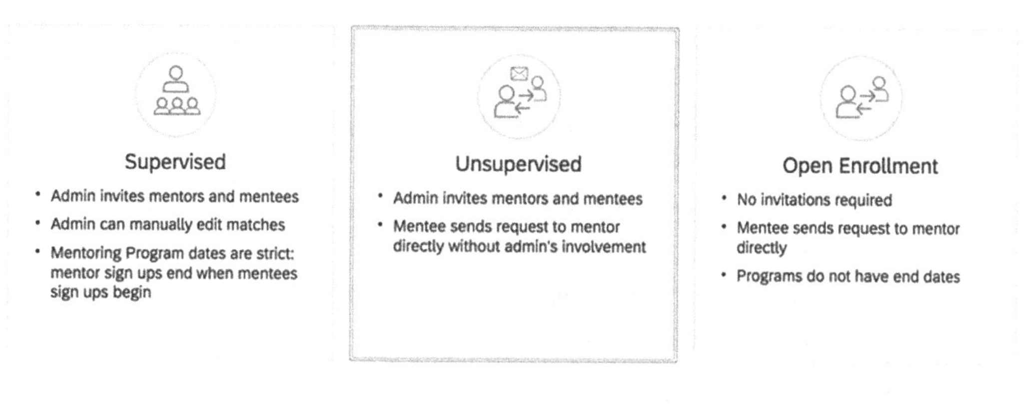

Create New Mentoring Program
First, select the type of mentoring program.
Supervised
Admin invites mentors and mentees
Admin can manually edit matches
Mentoring Program dates are strict: mentor sign ups end when mentees sign ups begin
Unsupervised
Admin invites mentors and mentees
Mentee sends request to mentor directly without admin's involvement
Open Enrollment
No invitations required
Mentee sends request to mentor directly
Programs do not have end dates
Cancel
Continue


***Figure 4-14.*** *Selecting Program Type When Creating a Mentoring Program*

The program type selected defines the audience, if there are invitations, and if program dates are set. You would identify the labels in the Details tab.

Table 4-3 contains the screens that the admin will use when creating a mentoring program. Based on the mentoring program type, there are some differences.

***Table 4-3.*** *Program Screens*

| Program Create Page | Description | Supervised | Unsupervised | Open Enrollment |
|---|---|---|---|---|
| Mentoring Program Details | Used to name and define the program and its settings and set dates if applicable. | X | X | X |
| Mentors | Select the employees who are being invited to participate in the program as mentors. | X | X | |
| Mentees | Select the employees who are being invited to participate in the program as mentees. | X | X | |

*(continued)*

*Table 4-3.* (continued)

| Program Create Page | Description | Supervised | Unsupervised | Open Enrollment |
|---|---|---|---|---|
| Signup Form | Define the questions that participants will need to complete in order to sign up. The matching rules are defined as well. | X | X | X |
| Summary | Contains the contents from each of the pages used to create the form which provides the admin the opportunity to make any updates before launching. | X | X | X |
| Email templates | The standard mentor and mentee invitation email notifications appear on the Summary page to allow the admin to do any customizations. | X | X | |

When creating any type of mentoring program, the Mentoring Program Details page will display. There are just a few minor differences in the fields that will appear for each program type. As an example, the supervised Mentoring Program Details page is displayed in Figure 4-15.

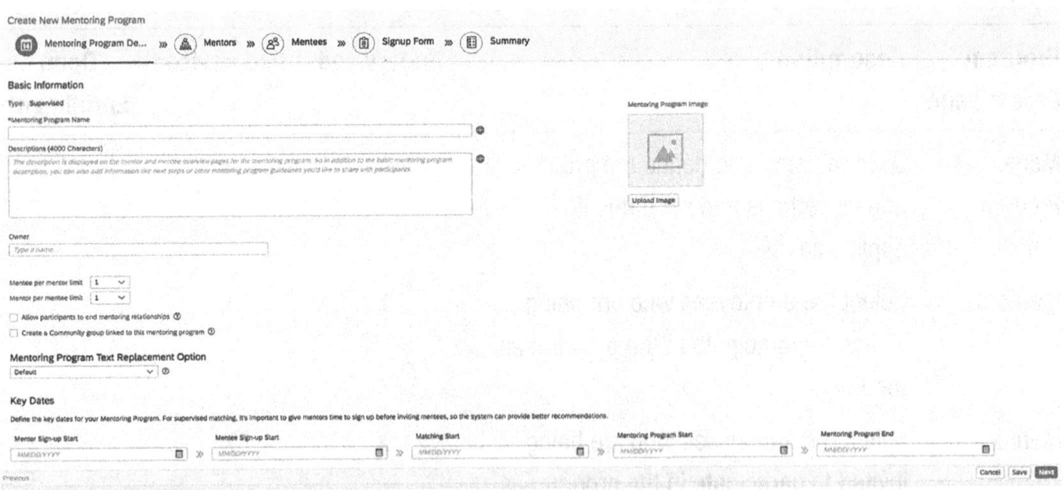


***Figure 4-15.*** *Details Page for a Supervised Mentoring Program*

All of the possible fields found on the Details page are listed in Table 4-4. The description of each field is included as well as the program type that will see each field.

***Table 4-4.** Details Tab Fields*

| Field | Description | Supervised | Unsupervised | Open Enrollment |
|---|---|---|---|---|
| Upload Image | May upload an image for your program. | X | X | X |
| Mentoring Program Name | Name of the mentoring program which will display on emails, the admin mentoring tool, and the mentoring screens for participants. Required field. May be localized. | X | X | X |
| Descriptions | Visible to participants on the program page for each program they are a part of. Also use this field to include any helpful information as next steps or program guidelines. May be localized. | X | X | X |
| Owner | Assigned owner may manage the program once the admin creates it. Any time during the process, the admin may remove the owner or change the owner. | X | X | X |
| Mentee per mentor limit | Define maximum number of mentees a mentor may have; 20 is the limit. Admin will be able to adjust the limit after the program is created. When mentors sign up, they can adjust the number as well, as long as the limit is greater than 1. | X | X | X |

*(continued)*

***Table 4-4.*** *(continued)*

| Field | Description | Supervised | Unsupervised | Open Enrollment |
|---|---|---|---|---|
| Mentor per mentee limit | Define maximum number of mentors a mentee may have; 20 is the limit. Admin will be able to adjust the limit after the program is created. When mentors sign up, they can adjust the number as well, as long as the limit is greater than 1. | X | X | X |
| Allow participants to end mentoring relationships | This option is enabled for open enrollment programs; otherwise, participants may not end a relationship, and the admin would have to intervene. May be enabled for supervised and unsupervised programs. | X | X | X |
| Create a Community group linked to this mentoring program | Links Community group to the program. The mentoring admin and owners are invited to the group and act as administrators of the group. After mentors and mentees match, they are added to the group as well. The SAP Jam group feed is displayed in the mentor and mentee overview pages for the mentoring program. | X | X | X |

*(continued)*

***Table 4-4.*** *(continued)*

| Field | Description | Supervised | Unsupervised | Open Enrollment |
|---|---|---|---|---|
| Mentor Approval Method ➤ Require Mentor Approval (by mentoring program administrators or by managers) | Only applicable for open enrollment programs. If checked, the mentoring program admin or manager must approve the mentor's participation in the program. | | | X |
| Administrator or owner approves mentor | With this option, include text which identifies the documents that must be included with the sign-up request. Mentor submits a sign-up request and uploads documents that the admin or owner must approve. Status of mentor is pending until approved. | | | X |
| Managers approve mentors | When a user signs up as a mentor, email is sent to their manager to approve their participation. Status of mentor is pending until approved. | | | X |
| Target Participants | To limit participation, select a target group. Unless a group is specified, any role with access to mentoring will be eligible to participate. | | | X |
| Mentoring Program Text Replacement Option | Select the text replacement pack if creating a non-mentoring custom program where custom text is created. | X | X | X |

*(continued)*

*Table 4-4.* (*continued*)

| Field | Description | Supervised | Unsupervised | Open Enrollment |
|---|---|---|---|---|
| Mentor Sign-up Start | Required field. Date when mentors can sign up for the program they were invited to. Cannot be current. | X | X | |
| Mentee Sign-up Start | Required field. Date when mentees can sign up for the program they were invited to. Cannot be before or the same date as the mentor sign-up. | X | X | |
| Matching Start | Required field. Date when matching program starts and no more participants can sign up. | X | | |
| Mentoring Program Start | Required field. First day of the mentoring program. | X | X | |
| Mentoring Program End | Required field. Final day of the program. | X | X | |

We learned how to create custom programs earlier in the chapter. Now we will see where to reference them. Select one of these mentoring program types as seen in Figure 4-16.

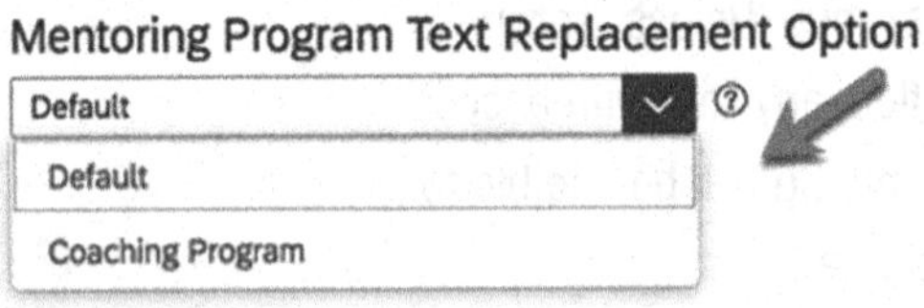

***Figure 4-16.*** *Selection for Custom Program*

By selecting the newly defined text pack from the Mentoring Program Text Replacement Option list, the program will use these labels instead of the system default labels. These labels apply to the mentoring screens as well as system-generated mentoring emails. You can create an open enrollment, supervised, or unsupervised program using the new labels without changing the labels for the standard programs.

Once the custom program is created, when a user goes into Mentoring to enroll, they will see the new program, and it will contain the new labels as seen in Figure 4-17.

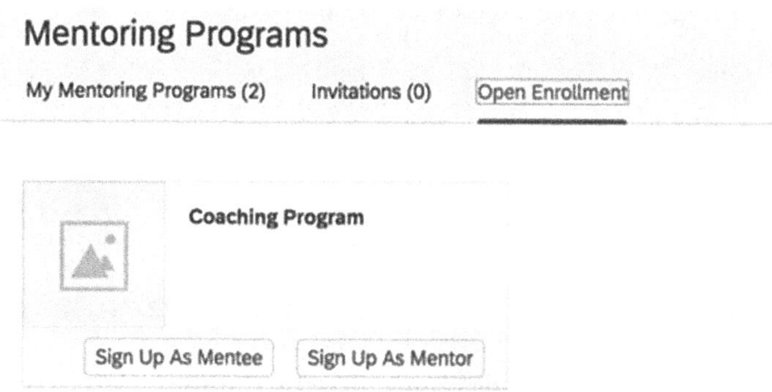


***Figure 4-17.*** *Open Enrollment Program Using Custom Labels*

All prior references to mentor, mentee, or mentoring programs will now reference the new labels.

Now back to the Details page. Based on the type of mentoring program that you are creating, complete the Mentoring Program Details page, save, and move on to the next screen.

As we have seen earlier in Table 4-4, the Mentors and Mentees pages are included for the supervised and unsupervised mentoring programs. These screens are not applicable to open enrollment programs since they are open to anyone and employees can sign up as mentors, mentees, or both.

The Mentors and Mentees pages are used to identify which employees will be invited to participate in the mentoring program.

The Mentors page is shown in Figure 4-18.

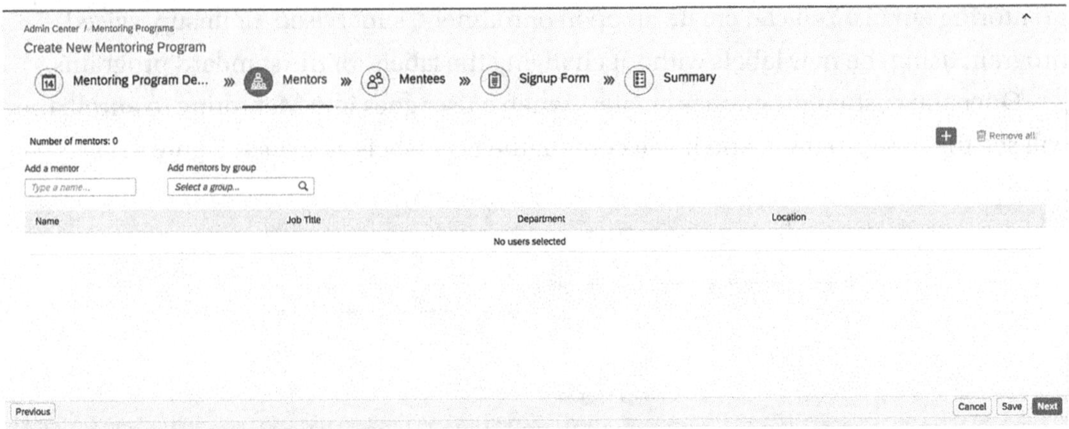

*Figure 4-18.* *Mentors Page Used to Identify Invited Mentors*

On both the Mentors and Mentees pages, use the name search to select individuals or any groups that have been set up.

For the supervised and unsupervised programs, the Mentees page looks identical to and follows the Mentors page. Here, the admin will select the employees who will receive an invitation to join the mentoring program as a mentee.

All mentoring program types have the Signup Form page. This page is used to create the questions the participants will answer during sign-up. Matching rules will be defined here as well. During matching, the system will then make recommended matches based on the rules.

A sample of the screen is shown in Figure 4-19.

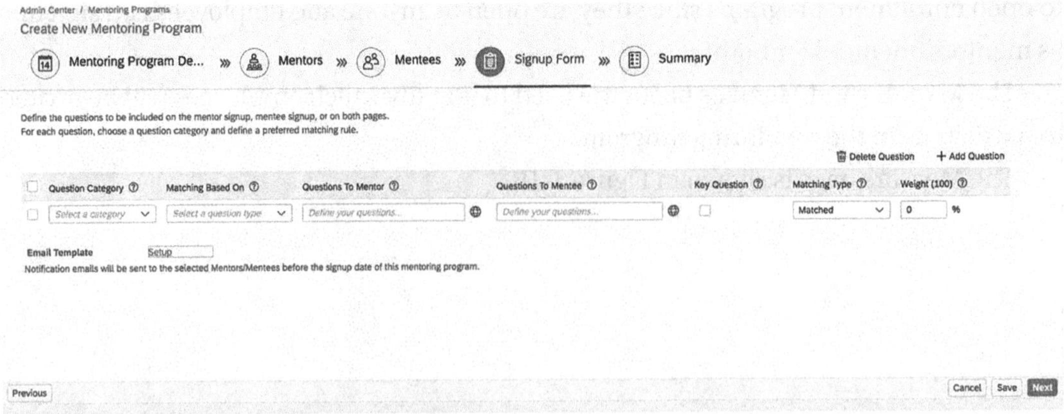

*Figure 4-19.* *Signup Form to Create Questions*

The fields that appear on the Signup Form screen are shown in Table 4-5. Review the descriptions when creating your form to guide you when creating your questions and matching rules.

***Table 4-5.*** *Question Fields on the Sign-Up Form Creation Page*

| Signup Form Fields | Description |
|---|---|
| Question Category | If the question is answered from a picklist, identify the picklist to use. The other option is free-form text. With this option, there is no "Matching Based On" field and no matching type. If you are not using questions, select a category to use with employee profile matching. In order for mentors to be matched to mentees, all of the questions cannot be free-form text. |
| Matching Based On | Preferences, Profiles, Mentee's Preferences, or Mentor's Preferences<br>• Matching Based on Preferences: Mentors and mentees are matched based on their answer to the question.<br>• Mentee's Preferences: Using this match type, the question is only for the mentee. The mentor will not get the question on their sign-up form. Matching is based on the mentee's answers and the mentor's employee profile.<br>• Mentor's Preferences: Using this match type, the question is only for the mentor. The mentee will not get the question on their sign-up form. Matching is based on the mentor's answers and the mentee's employee profile.<br>• Profiles: This match type does not use a question. Matching is done based on mentor and mentee's employee profiles. |
| Questions to Mentor | Provide a question to ask the mentor. This is a text field and may be localized. This question is only seen by mentors when signing up for the program. |
| Questions to Mentee | Provide a question to ask the mentee. This is a text field and may be localized. This question is only seen by mentees when signing up for the program. |
| Key Question | If a question is identified as "key" and mentor and mentee answers to the question don't match, they won't be matched. |

(*continued*)

***Table 4-5.*** *(continued)*

| Signup Form Fields | Description |
|---|---|
| Matching Type | Options are Matched or Not Matched. How matches are made depends on participant answers or employee profiles matched. |
| Weight | If left blank for each question, questions are weighted equally. Otherwise, an integer 1–100 should be entered. Weights must add up to 100. |
| Email Template Setup: Mentor invitation and Mentee invitation | Seen only for supervised and unsupervised programs. The admin may modify the standard text of the email invitations that are sent. |

The fields that must be populated for each question are shown in Figure 4-20.

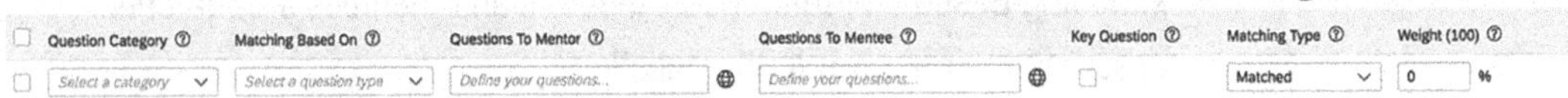


***Figure 4-20.*** *Fields for a Question on a Signup Form Page*

Based on the question category selected, some of the fields will be grayed out. Table 4-6 identifies which fields are available for each text question and picklist. Since there are four matching options for picklists, the fields that must be filled in will differ.

***Table 4-6.*** *Fields to Populate Based on Question Category*

| Question Category | Matching Based On | Question to Mentor | Question to Mentee | Key Question | Matching Type | Weight |
|---|---|---|---|---|---|---|
| Free-form text | N/A | X | X | N/A | N/A | N/A |
| Picklist | Preferences | X | X | X | X | X |
| Picklist | Profiles | N/A | N/A | X | X | N/A |
| Picklist | Mentee's Preferences | N/A | X | X | X | X |
| Picklist | Mentor's Preferences | X | N/A | X | X | X |

Use the question category field to identify the picklist that is used in the question, so those values are shown when the mentor and mentee answer the question. After the picklist is selected, identify the matching criteria. The "Matching Based On" preference will determine which fields will be seen on the sign-up form for that question.

Keep in mind when using free-text questions, the responses are limited to 128 characters. Furthermore, the answers are not used for matching and are not used in the matching algorithm. The answers are primarily informational because the responses may be viewed when looking at a potential mentor/mentee in their mentoring preferences.

Mentors and mentees will answer questions during sign-up. Recommended mentors are defined by the questions used and the matching rule for each question.

Rules for match order include the following:

- Mentee chooses a preferred mentor unless the mentor has maximum number of mentees allowed.
- Mentee chooses multiple preferred mentors; the mentor with the highest match score matches.
- Mentee's preferred mentor is not available; then the mentee is matched with the mentor with the highest match score.
- If mentee does not choose a preferred mentor, the mentee is matched with the mentor with the highest match score.

Supervised programs use a different method to calculate matches. The mapping program will be discussed later in this chapter.

For supervised and unsupervised programs, the admin will have the option to update the email invitations for mentors and mentees. The email template is shown in Figure 4-21. To modify the email template, click "Setup." Here the admin may modify the subject and the email body text for the mentor and mentee invites.

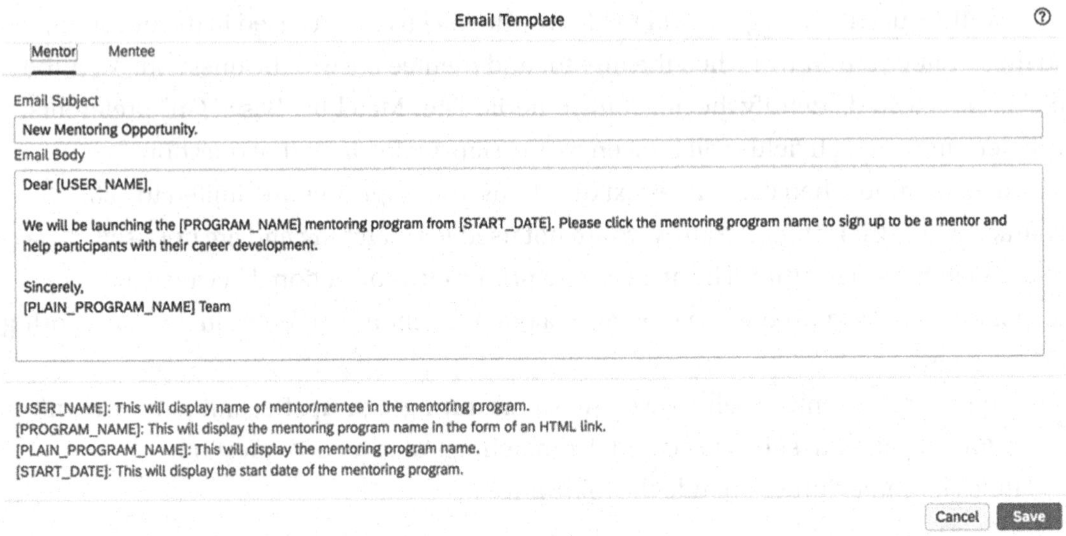

***Figure 4-21.*** *Email Notification to Edit*

After creating the questions and modifying the email invitations if applicable, the admin will go to the Summary screen. The contents of each screen that was used during the creation process will display on the Summary page. Figure 4-22 shows an example of a supervised mentoring program Summary page.

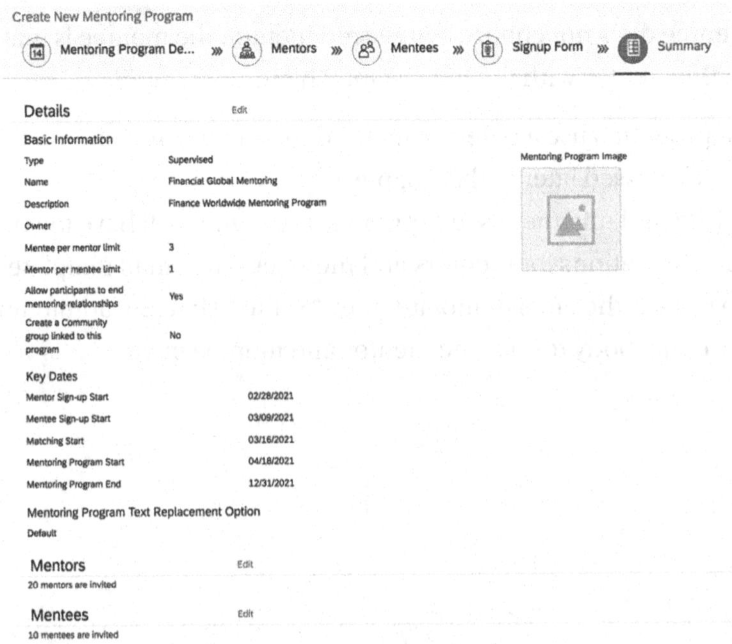

***Figure 4-22.*** *Summary Page of a Supervised Program*

After making any updates, the program may be deleted, saved, or launched. If the form is saved without launching, the program setup status is Draft and remains in the Not Started bucket on the overview page. If launched, invites will go out and the sign-up begins.

Let's have a quick recap of the program creation process highlighting some differences based on program type.

## Open Enrollment Programs

There are three screens in the creation process: Mentoring Program Details, Signup Form, and Summary. No dates are used for these programs, and no mentors or mentees are invited. Program is open to anyone as a mentor, mentee, or both. A group may also be identified if you do not wish to have the program open to anyone. Unique to open enrollment, the admin may choose to make mentor participation approved by the manager or admin.

If you configure the program to require approval by manager, you must be using home page tiles. Go to Manage Home Page ➤ To-Do Settings ➤ Show/Hide To-Do Tiles as seen in Figure 4-23.

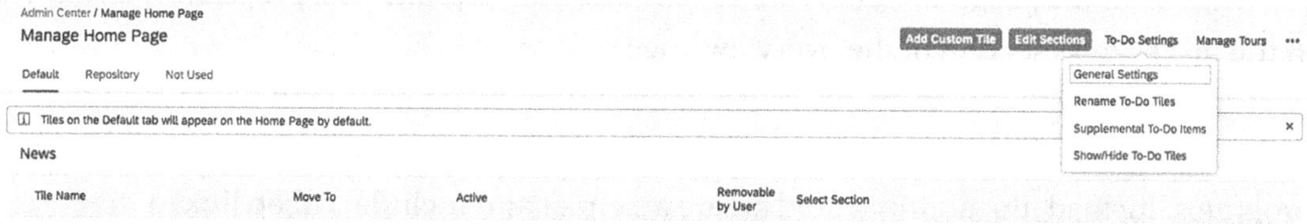

***Figure 4-23.*** *Show/Hide To-Do Tiles*

The Approve Requests To-Do tile must be enabled as seen in Figure 4-24.

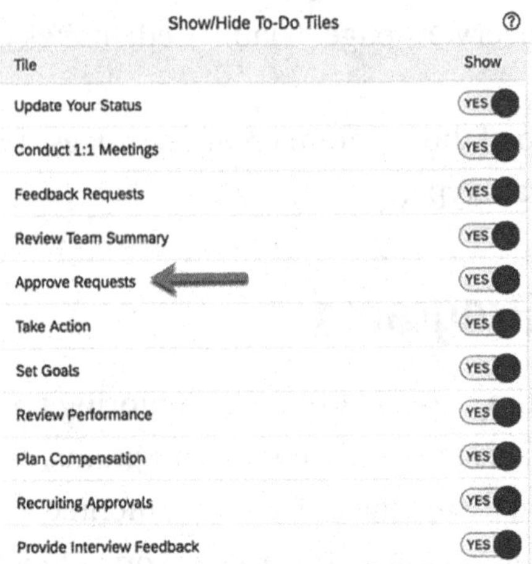


***Figure 4-24.** Approve Requests To-Do Tile to Enable*

Once this is configured, when an employee needs manager approval to participate in an open enrollment program as a mentor, the manager will have a To-Do tile on their home page where they may approve or reject the request.

Once all of the program details are set, launch the program. The program will now be in the In-Progress section of the overview page.

Continuing with the open enrollment launch, the admin may send out invitations to join the program. There are no invitation emails like the supervised and unsupervised programs. Instead, the admin would create an email and include a deep link to the program. To find the deep links, go to the overview page and find the program. Click the program name and look at the Details tab. Scroll down to see the deep links as seen in Figure 4-25.

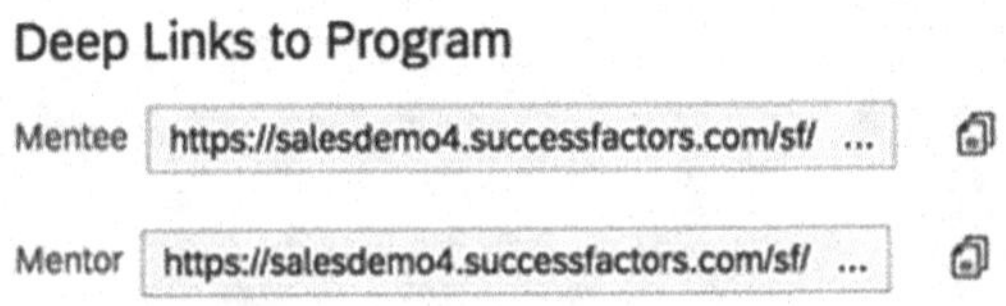

Deep Links to Program

Mentee https://salesdemo4.successfactors.com/sf/ ...

Mentor https://salesdemo4.successfactors.com/sf/ ...

***Figure 4-25.** Deep Links Within an Open Enrollment Program*

There is a different link for mentors and mentees since the questions to answer are based on their viewpoint and there are different steps to perform in the mentoring process. However, if you are going to allow anyone to be a mentor or a mentee, both links can be in the email.

Upon email notification, mentors and mentees may then go to the sign-up page to enroll. If admin approval is needed for a mentor to join, the admin would need to go into the program and accept or reject the request as seen in Figure 4-26.

***Figure 4-26.*** *Notification of a Mentor Participation Request to the Mentoring Admin*

Rejecting the request will send an email to the mentor and remove the program from the mentor's My Mentoring Programs tab. Approving will make the mentor available for matching and remove their pending status.

At any time during the sign-up, the admin may go back into the program and make changes such as adding questions, changing dates, or changing the owner. They will now see Mentors, Mentees, and Matches tabs. The admin may see who has joined and who has a mentor and may also assign or reassign matches. The program will stay open until the admin closes it. This is true for the supervised and unsupervised programs as well.

# Creating Supervised and Unsupervised Mentoring Programs

The admin follows the same initial steps as creating an open enrollment mentoring program. Table 4-7 shows some of the features and how they differ for the two program types.

***Table 4-7.*** *Program Type Comparison*

| Supervised Program | Unsupervised Program |
|---|---|
| Defined start and end dates that strictly identify when mentors and mentees may sign up. Once mentees start to sign up, mentor sign-up closes. | Dates are more flexible so mentees may sign up while mentor sign-up is in progress. |
| Manually push program to the next step. | Based on dates, system moves program to the next step with option to move manually. |
| Invitation emails must be manually initiated by admin. | Invitation emails sent automatically based on the start date defined for the program or may be done manually. |
| After mentee invite goes out, no more invited mentors may sign up. | For both mentors and mentees, the sign-up period ends one day before the programs end. |
| Use of matching start date. | Matching start date not used. |
| May edit questions up until matching. | Questions may be edited as long as program has not ended. |
| Matching based on configuration and preference, but admin may edit matches. | Matching guidance provided, but mentees contact mentors directly. |
| A mentee does not have to select a mentor during sign-up. If they do select a mentor, no email is sent to the mentor until after the matching program run. | When a mentee signs up, they must select a mentor. The request goes to the mentor immediately. |
| There is no mentor approval. After the matching program ends, mentors and mentees will receive their match via email. | Mentors must approve the mentee request for the match to occur. If not, the admin can do the matching manually. |
| Mentor and mentee may opt out during sign-up but can't later decide to sign up. | Mentor and mentee may opt out during sign-up but can't later decide to sign up. |
| Admin may add, edit, and delete sign-up form questions and modify matching rules after the programs are launched. | Admin may add, edit, and delete sign-up form questions and modify matching rules after the programs are launched. |

(*continued*)

*Table 4-7.* (*continued*)

| Supervised Program | Unsupervised Program |
|---|---|
| Mentee enrollment start date cannot be the same date as or earlier than mentor start date. | Mentee enrollment start date cannot be the same date as or earlier than mentor start date. |
| Mentor start date cannot be current date. | Mentor start date cannot be current date. |
| Matching triggers program to move from Not Started to In-Progress. | No matching program. |
| Admin will not see the Matches tab in the program until match program runs. | Admin will see the Matches tab after mentors get invitations. |
| Admins cannot assign or reassign mentors and mentees until the matching program runs. | Admins can assign and reassign once there are mentors and mentees enrolled in the program. |
| Program does not appear as In-Progress until the matching program is complete and the admin makes any reassignments. | Program appears as In-Progress once mentees have signed up and admin has done any match reassignments. |

**Supervised Mentoring Program**

A supervised mentoring program uses defined start and end dates, and the admin must manually send out the invites by clicking a button on the program as seen in Figure 4-27.

***Figure 4-27.*** *Supervised Program on Admin's Mentoring Overview Page*

Upon confirmation, the email is sent to all of the employees who were identified as a mentor during the program creation. Any time during the sign-up, the admin may go back into the program and make changes such as adding questions, changing dates, or changing the owner. However, the mentor start date cannot be changed, and no more mentors may be added.

Once the mentee start date arrives, the admin would have to go back to the overview page to send the mentee invitations on the planned mentee start date. If the admin sends the email before the designated mentee start date, no more mentors may enroll.

Again, during the sign-up, the admin may still make program changes. However, once the mentee invitation has gone out, the mentee start date cannot be changed, and no more mentees may be added.

The mentoring admin waits for the mentors and mentees to sign up for or opt out of the program. There is no overlap of when mentees and mentors may join. For a supervised program, matching will begin based on the configured matching start date. The admin will not see the Matches tab in the program until the matching program is run. The admin will see all of the mentors and mentees who have joined or opted out and may view their preferences.

Once the mentee sign-up is completed, the admin will then manually start the match program as seen in Figure 4-28.

***Figure 4-28.*** *Supervised Program Set to Run Matching Program*

The program will not go into the In-Progress status until the admin looks at the matches and manually makes any adjustments. Once the matches are finalized, the admin will start the program. Emails will go out to the mentors and mentees notifying them of their mentoring partner.

## Unsupervised Mentoring Programs

For an unsupervised program, the system will automatically send the program invitations based on the start dates identified at program creation. However, the admin may manually send out the invitations prior to the system send date. The same process is used for the mentee sign-up. Based on the start date identified when creating the program, the mentee invitations will go out, or the admin may manually send the invites.

During this time, the admin may make program changes and will see the mentors and mentees who have joined, opted out, or not responded. The Matches tab will also be visible, so the admin will see the mentor choices that the mentees have made. The admin will be able to make any matching reassignment as well. Once the admin has reviewed the matching and made any final changes, the program goes to "In-Progress". Anyone with a mentor change will get an email notification.

The programs are now in full swing. The supervised and unsupervised mentoring programs will run until their end date or until the admin ends them. The mentors and mentees may also end their mentoring relationships, if configured.

# Managing Programs

We did touch on what an admin may do once the notifications start to go out. We will look deeper at these functions now. As mentioned earlier, the admin or owner does all of the program management from the program overview screen using the Manage Mentoring Programs tool. The owner may perform all program management functions except creating a program.

Once the programs are created, the mentoring admin may make changes to the programs, view mentors and mentees, view matches, and assign and reassign matches. This will occur at different times based on the mentoring program.

For all program types, the mentoring admin may view the program at any step in the process. Depending on the status of the program, the admin may be able to modify questions, change mentor/mentee limits, make a mentor unavailable, or do matching.

For supervised programs, questions and matching rules may be modified up until the matching program runs. For open enrollment and unsupervised programs, changes may be made up until the program ends.

Once the mentees and mentors are part of the program, the admin may change mentoring relationships and assign mentors to unassigned mentees.

If the admin adds questions after launching, the questions are applicable to those who sign up after questions are added. Existing participants would see the new questions if they edit their preferences.

Deleted questions are not seen by those who sign up after the admin removes a question. Those already signed up will not see the question anymore either.

The ability to do manual matches is available for all of the program types. We will cover the matching program used by the supervised program after reviewing the manual match feature.

## Admin Matches

For open enrollment and unsupervised mentoring programs, once the program invites have gone out, the admin will see the Matches tab in the program. This tab will not be visible in supervised programs until after the matching program has run. The Matches tab has two sub-tabs: Matched and Not Matched. The Matched tab contains assignments based on mentors who approved a request from a mentee. Those who had no recommended matches or had their request declined will appear in the Not Matched tab. Figure 4-29 displays the Not Matched tab.

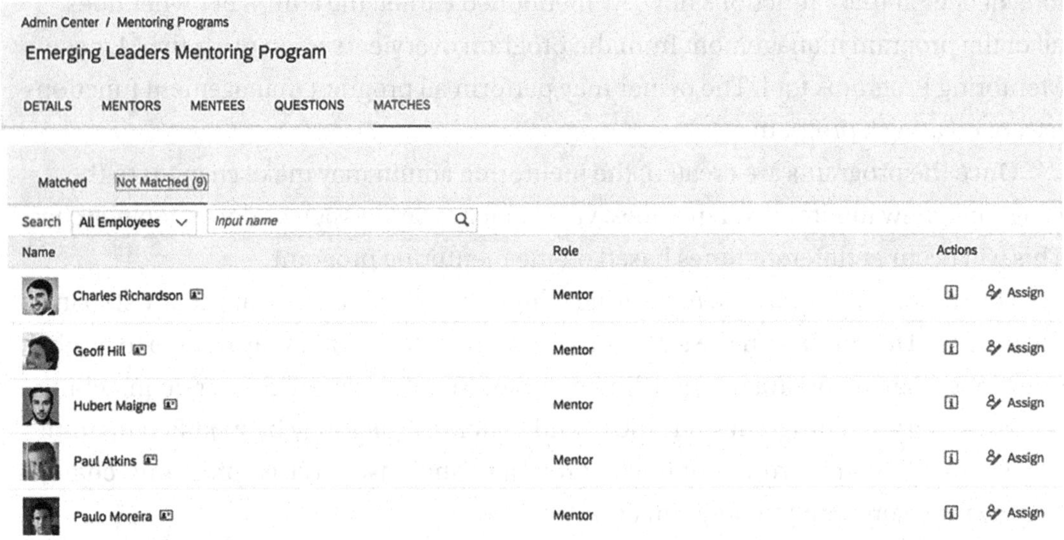

***Figure 4-29.** Mentors and Mentees Without a Match or Not Yet Assigned*

In Figure 4-30, the admin selects a new mentor for a mentee. This is based on the available mentors. If mentors are allowed multiple mentees and haven't reached the limit, they will appear as possible mentors as well.

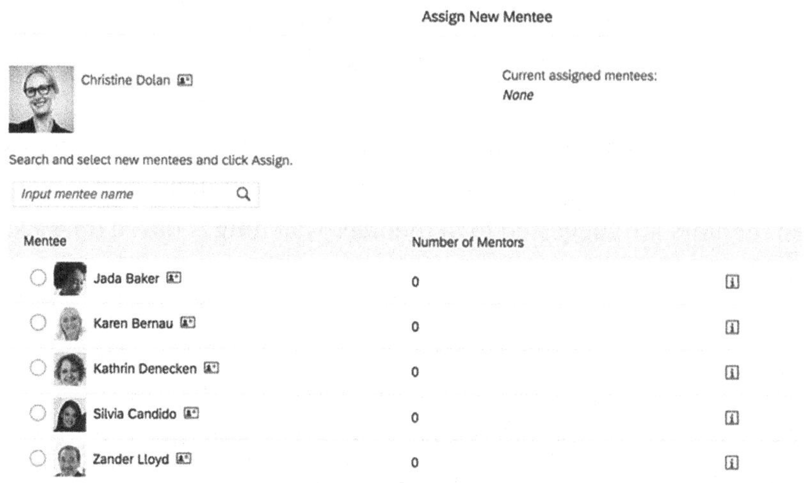

***Figure 4-30.*** *Admin Assigns a Mentor*

The mentoring admin may also change existing mentoring relationships in the Matched tab. This is done by deleting a mentee from a mentor. When the mentee is in the Not Matched tab, the admin may do a new match.

Once the admin moves the program to In-Progress, any mentor changes will result in an email notification. If the admin removes a relationship, the mentee will receive an email notification. If there is a new mentoring relationship, email notifications go out to the mentor and mentee.

The supervised program has a mapped program feature that is not available for the other two mentoring program types. It is explained in detail in the following.

# Matching Program for Supervised Programs

The matching between mentors and mentees is based on the rules set up for the sign-up form questions. Matching rules determine the recommended matches. The matching program first filters by matching rules of key questions, and if the rule is not satisfied, the mentor and mentee are not considered a match. If there is a match based on a rule of a key question, the system keeps matching based on additional question matching rules. For non-key questions, preferences or employee profiles are compared to calculate a match score.

Skill and competency questions do a match based on the number of picklist values matched. The number of matching values divided by the number of mentee's total value is the match score with range 0–100.

The rest of the standard picklist and custom picklist questions use a score of 0 or 100. At least one value has to match between mentor and mentee to have a score of 100 for the question.

All match scores are summed for the mentor. If there are different weights on the questions, weights are part of the calculation for the final match score.

Up to ten mentors are suggested for a mentee. Matching is based on a star system with four matching levels:

1. Preferred (four stars) match based on preferred mentor selected during sign-up

2. Excellent match (three stars) based on 75% or higher match score

3. Good match (two stars) based on 50–74.99% match score

4. Average match (one star) based on 49.99% or lower match score

Once the matching program is completed, the admin may click the program name to view the program details.

It is only after the matching program run that the Matches tab will be visible. The Matched tab may list up to 200 matches. A sample of the Matched tab is shown in Figure 4-31.

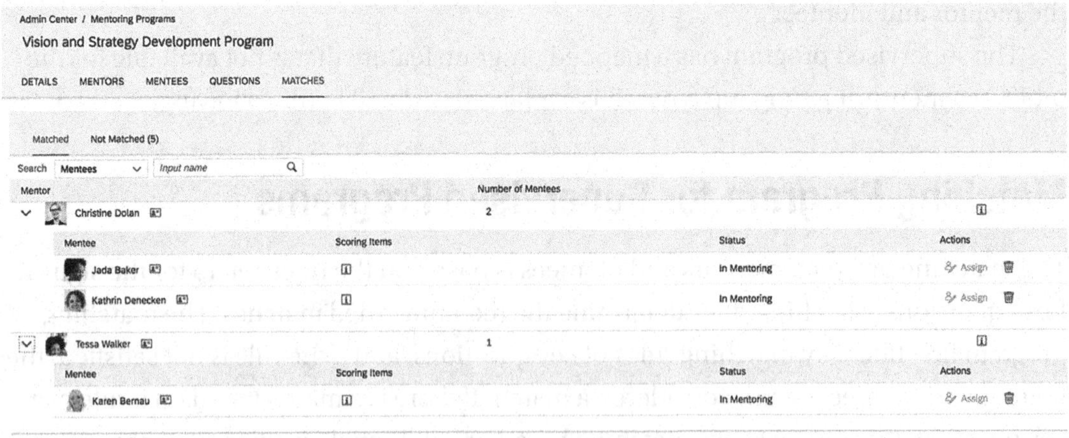

***Figure 4-31.** Matching Program Results in a Supervised Program*

As seen in the example shown in Figure 4-32, the admin may filter by match level to view a more manageable list of matches. If there are hundreds of entries to review, filtering makes it easier to look for changes to make.

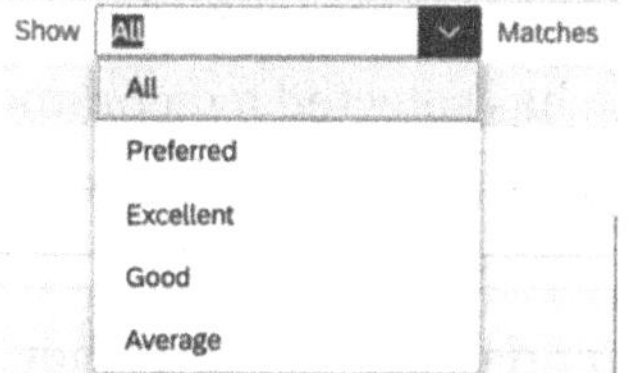


***Figure 4-32.** Filter to Narrow the List of Matches*

The admin may delete any matches which will cause both the mentor and mentee to go to the Not Matched tab. There may be some unassigned mentors or mentees who didn't meet the matching criteria as well that will also appear in the Not Matched tab. The admin will need to assign a mentor to all unmatched mentees. There may be mentors without mentees if multiple mentees can be linked to a mentor or there was an abundance of mentors.

In the Not Matched tab, the first 500 non-matches will display. As relationships are assigned, the list will include additional names that exceed the initial 500 non-matches. Not Matched results will include any remaining mentors due to a lack of mentees or mentees with a lack of mentors in the program.

The admin may filter by mentor or mentee as shown in Figure 4-33.

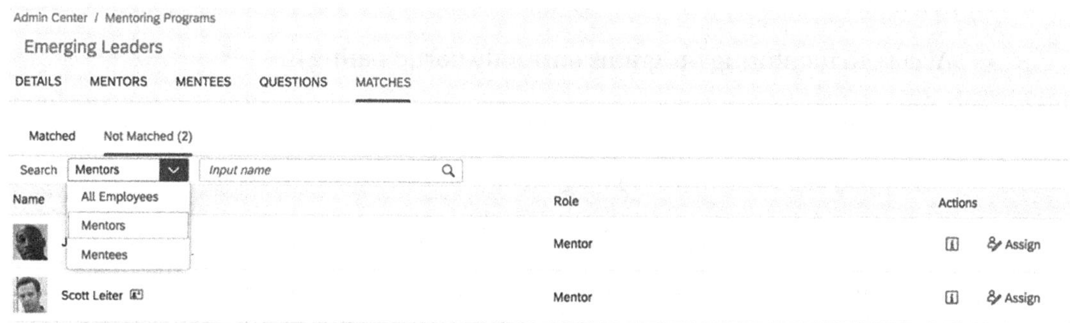


***Figure 4-33.** Viewing Not Matched Participants by Filter*

The admin may assign a user based on the remaining available mentors or mentees. When all of the match decisions have been made, the admin goes back to the overview page and clicks the start button for the program. The program will move from Not Started to In-Progress status.

The mentoring match email is then sent to the mentors and mentees providing them with their matches. If the mentee has selected a recommended mentor during sign-up and the admin or the matching program changed the assignment, the mentee will receive a notification and then be provided with the new mentor's name. Now it is up to the mentor and mentee to meet and figure out what they hope to accomplish through the mentoring process.

The program will appear as In-Progress until the program end date or until the admin manually forces the program to completion, and then the program is in Finished status.

# User Access to Mentoring

Before we walk through the lifecycle of a mentoring program from the participants' perspective, we will look at how an employee accesses the program.

Access to the Mentoring tab within Development requires the user to have Career Development Plan (CDP) Access Permission and Mentoring Programs Access Permission.

All employee mentoring-related functions are accessed through the Mentoring overview page:

- Access to mentoring programs currently participating in
- Signing up for invitation-based programs
- Signing up for open enrollment programs

The Mentoring overview page is composed of three tabs:

1. **My Mentoring Programs** is the default tab and contains all the programs the user is currently participating in.
2. **Invitations** contains invitations to supervised and unsupervised programs. These are programs the user has been invited to join but has not signed up for yet.
3. **Open Enrollment** contains the open enrollment programs that the user is eligible to join.

An example of an employee's Mentoring overview page is shown in Figure 4-34.

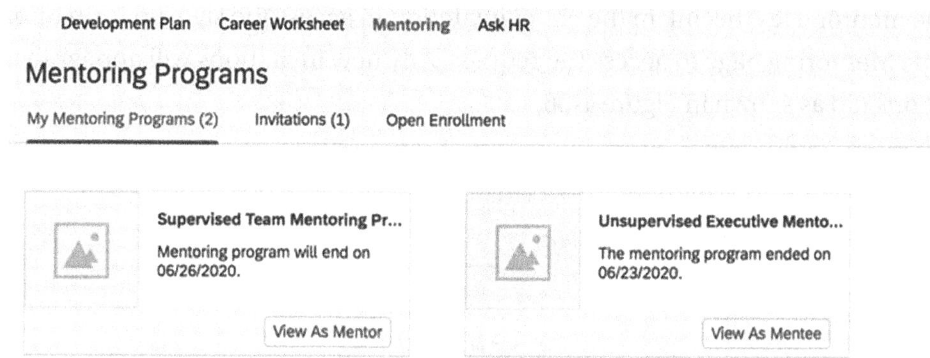


***Figure 4-34.*** *Mentoring Overview Page for Participants*

In this example, the employee is currently enrolled in two programs, one as a mentor and one as a mentee. There is also pending invitation.

Supervised and unsupervised program invitations appear in the Invitations tab, while open enrollment programs display in the Open Enrollment tab.

We will now look at the lifecycle of a mentoring program from the user perspective. Any differences in behavior by program type will be noted.

# Mentor Sign-Up

With all program types, the mentor should be the first to sign up. Mentees make the mentor selection, so there have to be mentors in the program to select from.

After the admin launches a supervised or unsupervised mentoring program, the invitations go out to the mentors. A sample invitation sent to mentors is shown in Figure 4-35.

New Mentoring Opportunity.

AS Aanya Singh <system@successfactors.com>
Friday, June 26, 2020 at 12:04 PM
Show Details

Dear Ann Lau,

We will be launching the Unsupervised program for IT Global mentoring program from 06/30/2020. Please click the mentoring program name to sign up to be a mentor and help participants with their career development.

Sincerely,
Unsupervised program for IT Global Team

***Figure 4-35.*** *Mentor Invitation Email*

The mentor uses the link in the email invitation to access the sign-up form or may go to the Mentoring page to access the request. Any new invitations will appear in the Invitations tab as shown in Figure 4-36.

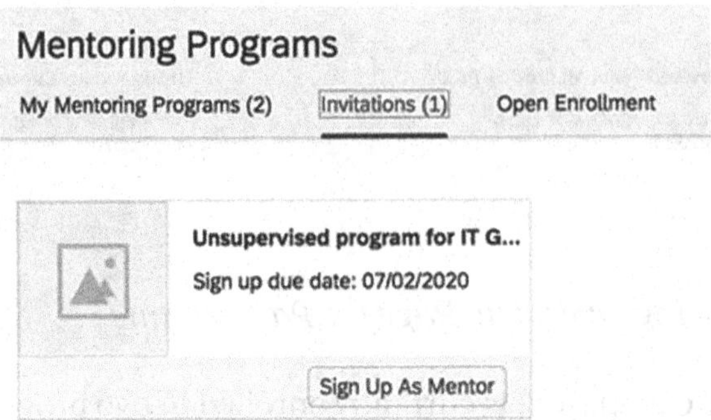


***Figure 4-36.** Invitations Tab with Pending Program Sign-Up*

The mentor will need to click the "Sign Up As Mentor" button to join or opt out:

- For supervised programs, if the mentor does not enroll before the mentee sign-up start date, mentor sign-up is closed and they may not enroll.
- For unsupervised programs, mentors may continue to sign up even while mentee sign-up begins. Both mentors and mentees may sign up until the day before the mentoring program start date.

For open enrollment programs, as seen in Figure 4-37, the invitation is in the Open Enrollment tab and the user may sign up as a mentor, a mentee, or both.

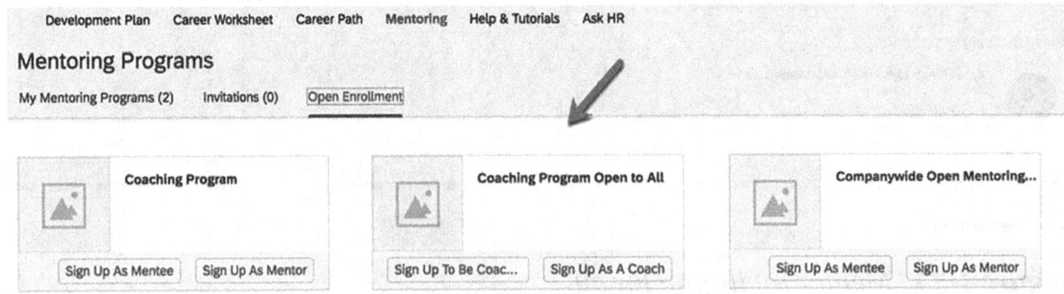


***Figure 4-37.** Open Enrollment Tab with Invitations*

For open enrollment programs, there is no opt-out option. If you don't sign up, you are not in the program. Since the dates are open-ended, the invitee can join at a later date. For open enrollment programs, sign-up may be done as a mentor or mentee.

All three program types use the same three screens during the sign-up process: Welcome, Preference, and Done.

The Welcome page is shown in Figure 4-38.

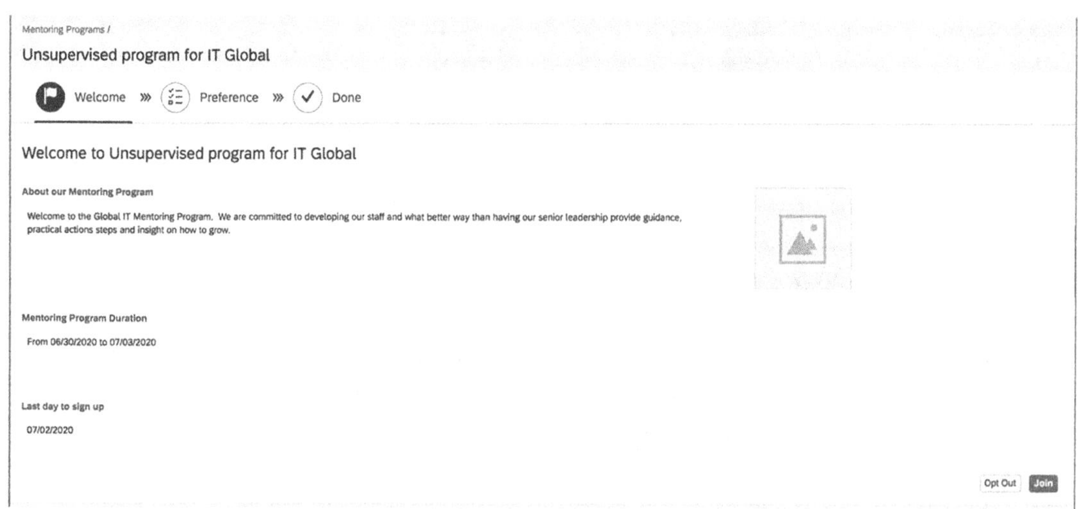
Mentoring Programs /
Unsupervised program for IT Global
Welcome
Preference
Done
Welcome to Unsupervised program for IT Global
About our Mentoring Program
Welcome to the Global IT Mentoring Program. We are committed to developing our staff and what better way than having our senior leadership provide guidance, practical actions steps and insight on how to grow.
Mentoring Program Duration
From 06/30/2020 to 07/03/2020
Last day to sign up
07/02/2020
Opt Out
Join

***Figure 4-38.*** *Welcome Page Used to Join or Opt Out*

The Welcome page shows the program name and description along with the sign-up end dates and the program start and end dates. For open enrollment programs, there are no sign-up dates or program start and end dates listed.

For the supervised and unsupervised programs, there is option to reject the invitation. To opt out of the program, the user will click the "Opt Out" button. After confirming their wish to reject the invitation, the program is removed from the user's Invitations tab. No emails are generated for removal from the program, and the program is no longer seen on the program overview page. If they change their mind later, they may not sign up.

For open enrollment programs, there will be an option to join, but there is no opt-out option. If they do nothing, they will not be part of the program. They may, however, go in at any time to enroll as long as the program has not closed.

The Preference page is used in all programs. This is where the questions are answered in order to find a compatible match. Mentors will answer the questions in order to match with a mentee. Mentors do not make any mentee selections. That is up to the mentees or the matching program.

A sample is shown in Figure 4-39.

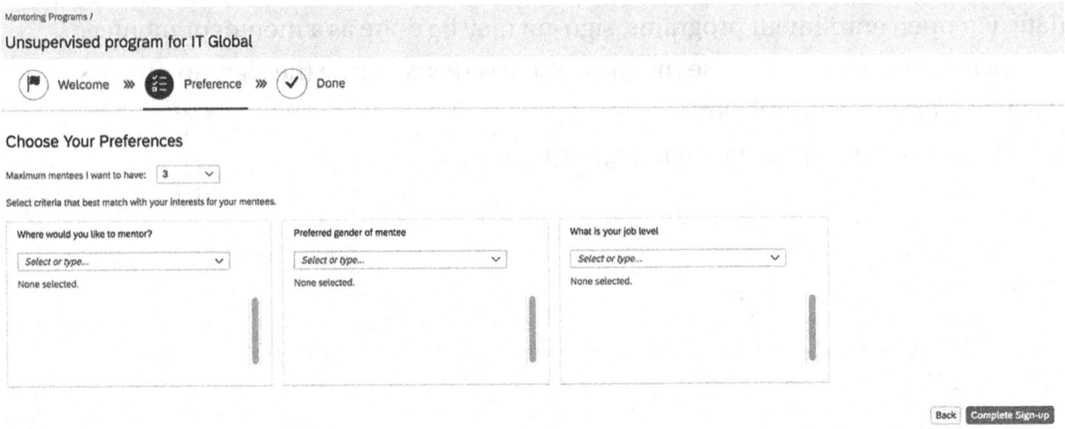

***Figure 4-39.*** *Preference Page for the Mentor*

During sign-up, the mentor may change the number of mentees if the program has been configured to permit more than one.

After answering the questions, the mentor will have completed the sign-up, and the final screen in the enrollment process will display as seen in Figure 4-40.

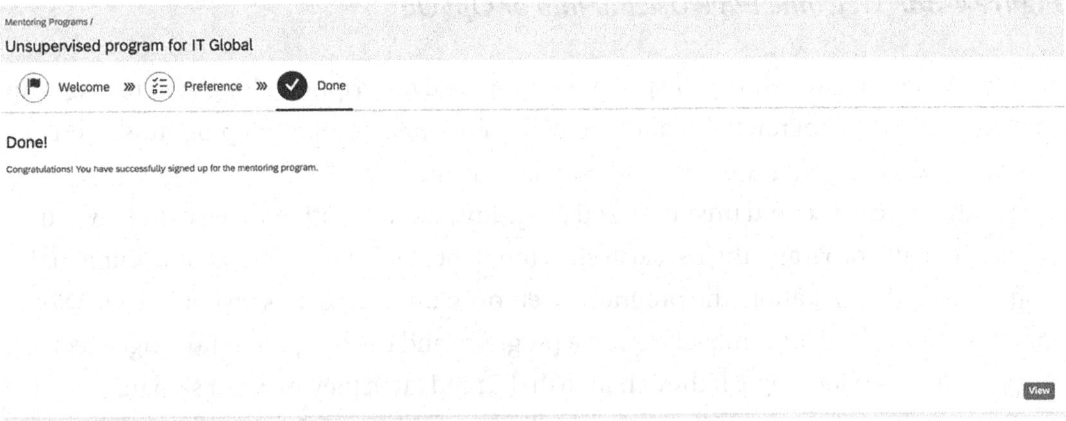

***Figure 4-40.*** *Mentor Sign-Up Complete*

The mentor may view the details of the program, edit the preferences, and change their availability for the program. The program-level overview page is seen in Figure 4-41.

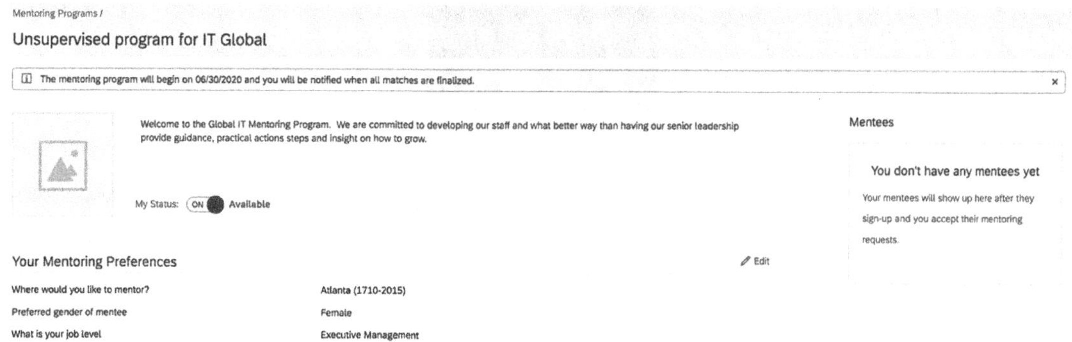
Mentoring Programs /
Unsupervised program for IT Global
The mentoring program will begin on 06/30/2020 and you will be notified when all matches are finalized.
Welcome to the Global IT Mentoring Program. We are committed to developing our staff and what better way than having our senior leadership provide guidance, practical actions steps and insight on how to grow.
My Status: ON Available
Mentees
You don't have any mentees yet
Your mentees will show up here after they sign-up and you accept their mentoring requests.
Your Mentoring Preferences
Edit
Where would you like to mentor?
Atlanta (1710-2015)
Preferred gender of mentee
Female
What is your job level
Executive Management

***Figure 4-41.*** *Program Overview Page for a Mentor*

After enrollment, the program has moved from the Invitations tab to the My Mentoring Programs tab.

# Unique to Open Enrollment Mentor Sign-Up

For open enrollment programs, the program may have been set up to require a mentor to receive manager or admin approval to participate. In these cases, the mentor status is pending. The mentor will not be a part of the program until approval is granted. This means the potential mentor may not change their preferences, change availability, or see program details.

The mentor's manager will receive an email that will direct them to a link to their home page. There will be a To-Do tile to approve the request. The To-Do tile is shown in Figure 4-42.

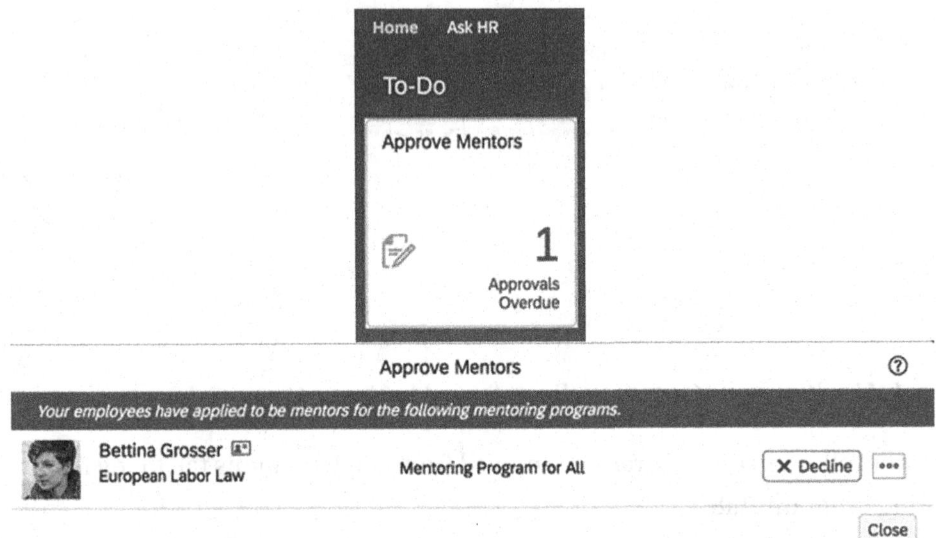


***Figure 4-42.*** *Manager To-Do Tile for Mentor Approval*

If the manager declines the request, there is an option for the manager to add a note that will be included when the mentor receives email notification of the rejection.

Similarly, if the mentor needs to get admin approval to join, the admin will have to approve the request. There are two types of decline: decline the documents or decline the mentor participation. By declining the supporting documents, a note may be added to the notification so that the mentor will know what is needed to resubmit. Mentor status remains pending until approved. If the admin approves, the mentor becomes a part of the program. The mentor now sees the program in their My Mentoring Programs tab and can view as mentor or sign up as mentee.

If rejected, the mentor is then removed from the program, and the program will no longer display in the My Mentoring Programs tab.

The mentor can still join as a mentee by going back to the Open Enrollment tab on the home page and clicking "Sign Up As Mentee".

If approved, the mentor will receive a confirmation email, and they will now be available for a mentee to select. The mentor will now be able to go back into the program-level overview page to change their preferences or change their availability.

Table 4-8 summarizes the differences by program during mentor sign-up.

*Table 4-8. Mentor Sign-Up Options by Program Type*

| Action/Program Type | Supervised | Unsupervised | Open Enrollment |
|---|---|---|---|
| Invites sent to mentors. | X | X | X (optional) |
| Invitation located in the Invitations tab. | X | X | |
| Invitation located in the Open Enrollment tab. | | | X |
| Mentor may opt out of joining the program. | X | X | |
| Manager or admin approves mentor participation. | | | X |
| Mentors can each review their preferences during the sign-up and acceptance processes. Mentors can change their availability. | X | X | X |

# Mentee Sign-Up

After a mentee receives an invitation to join a supervised or unsupervised program, the mentee will use the link in the email invitation or go directly to the Mentoring page to join or opt out. The invitation will appear in the Invitations tab as shown in Figure 4-43.

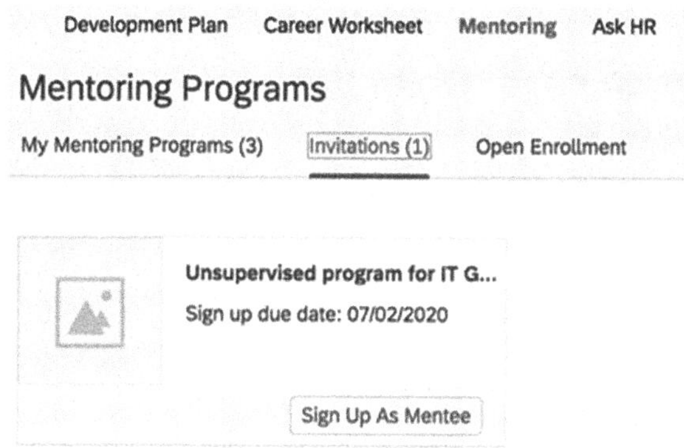


***Figure 4-43.** Mentee Invitation for a Mentoring Program*

## Sign-Up Dates for Mentees

Sign-up dates vary by program type:

- For supervised programs, if the mentee does not enroll before the program matching start date, mentee sign-up is closed and they may not enroll.
- For unsupervised programs, mentees may continue to sign up until the day before the mentoring program start date.
- For open enrollment programs, sign-up may continue until the program is ended by the admin.

The mentee must click "Sign Up As Mentee" to join or opt out. If they do nothing or try to enroll once the program starts, they will not be in the program. If they opt out, the invitation is removed from the Invitations tab.

Identical to the mentor sign-up, the mentee will see the program details and will then be able to opt out or join. For open enrollment programs, the only option is to join. If the mentee does not wish to join, they do nothing. To join, they complete the sign-up form to list their mentor preferences. The mentee sign-up screen has some additional features not found on the mentor sign-up: Show Recommended Mentors and Search for a Mentor. This is applicable to all three program types. A sample sign-up page is shown in Figure 4-44.

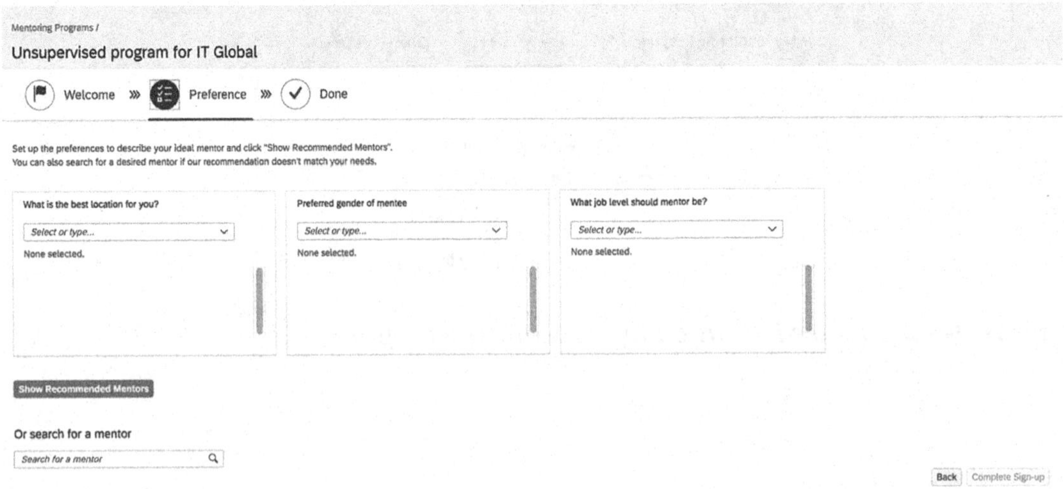

***Figure 4-44.*** *Mentee Preference Page*

To enroll, the mentee must complete the questionnaire. The questions will be tailored to the mentee's perspective but will use the same picklists as the mentor's questions. Free-text questions will be the same for mentors and mentees.

After completing the questions, the mentee clicks the "Show Recommended Mentors" button to see all recommended mentors based on their preferences and the matching rules. If there are no matches, the mentee may perform a name search to find a mentor.

Unsupervised programs do not allow a mentee to sign up without a mentor selection. It is optional for supervised programs because the matching program will find their best match.

Figure 4-45 shows recommended mentors after the mentee enters their preferences.

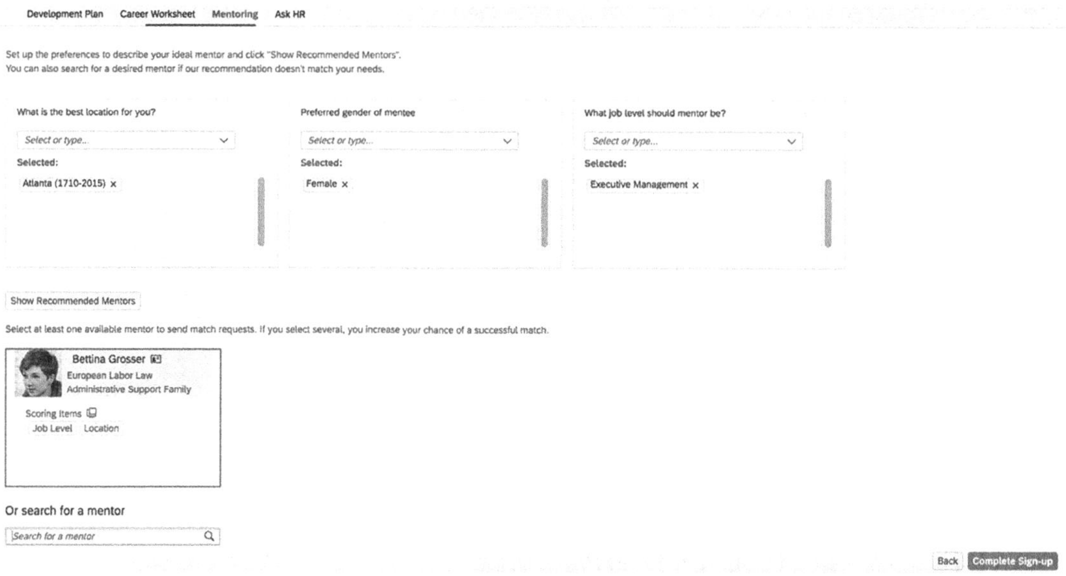

***Figure 4-45.*** *Recommended Match Based on Preferences and Matching Rules*

After making a mentor selection (or multiple selections based on how many recommended mentors there are), the mentee completes the sign-up as seen in Figure 4-46.

Mentoring Programs /
Unsupervised program for IT Global
Welcome
Preference
Done
Done!
Congratulations! You have successfully signed up for the mentoring program.
View

***Figure 4-46.*** *Mentee Sign-Up Completion Page*

The mentee may view the program to see its details and may change their preferences or invite additional mentors as seen in Figure 4-47.

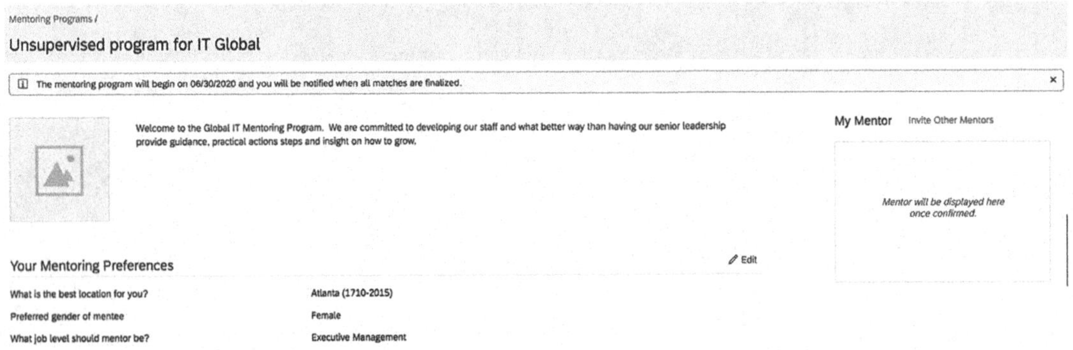
Mentoring Programs /
Unsupervised program for IT Global
The mentoring program will begin on 06/30/2020 and you will be notified when all matches are finalized.
Welcome to the Global IT Mentoring Program. We are committed to developing our staff and what better way than having our senior leadership provide guidance, practical actions steps and insight on how to grow.
My Mentor
Invite Other Mentors
Mentor will be displayed here once confirmed.
Your Mentoring Preferences
Edit
What is the best location for you?
Atlanta (1710-2015)
Preferred gender of mentee
Female
What job level should mentor be?
Executive Management

***Figure 4-47.*** *Mentee Program Overview Page*

Until the mentor approves (for unsupervised and open enrollment programs), the mentor will not display.

The mentee may send additional invites, and they will be prompted to answer the questions again and then select a mentor. A sample is shown in Figure 4-48. As is the case when selecting a mentor during sign-up, if there are no matches when adding additional mentors, the mentee may find a mentor through a name search.

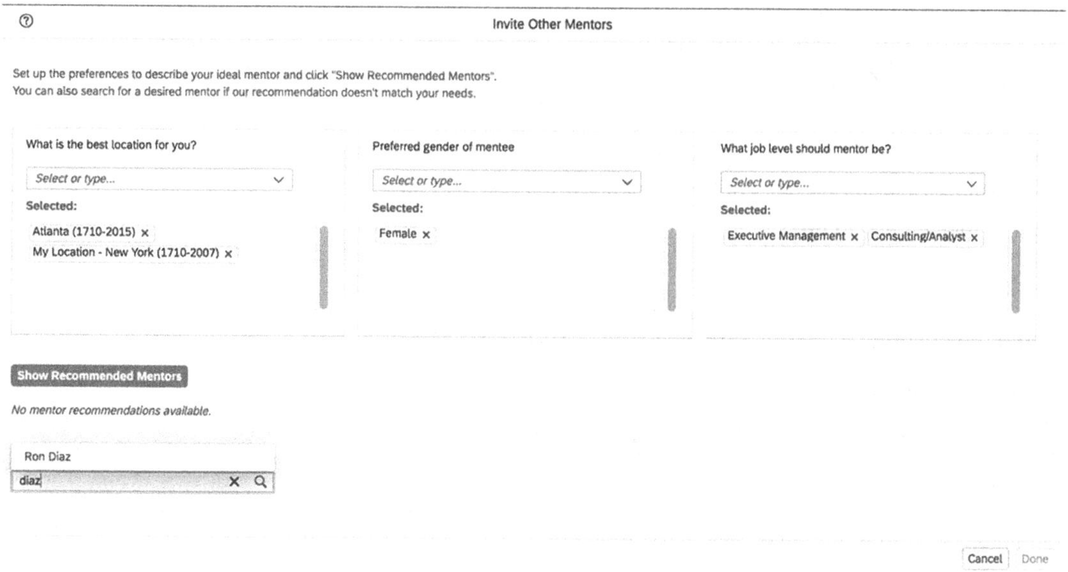

***Figure 4-48.** Mentee Adding Additional Mentors*

If there are no recommended matches based on their responses, the mentee can do a name search to find a mentor.

For open enrollment and unsupervised program, the mentor must approve the mentee's request. The invite will go out to the mentor and will need their approval. For a supervised program, a mentee does not need to select a mentor during sign-up since the matching program will identify the match.

Table 4-9 summarizes the differences by program during mentee sign-up.

***Table 4-9.** Mentee Sign-Up Actions by Program Type*

| Action/Program Type | Supervised | Unsupervised | Open Enrollment |
|---|---|---|---|
| Invites sent to mentees. | X | X | X (optional) |
| Invitation located in the Invitations tab. | X | X | |
| Invitation located in the Open Enrollment tab. | | | X |
| Mentee accepts or declines invitation to join the program. | X | X | |

*(continued)*

***Table 4-9.*** *(continued)*

| Action/Program Type | Supervised | Unsupervised | Open Enrollment |
|---|---|---|---|
| Mentee may view preferences of recommended mentors when signing up. | X | X | X |
| Mentee selects a mentor. | X (optional) | X | X |
| Mentor must approve mentee's request. | | X | X |
| Mentees can add more mentor requests after sign-up. | X | X | X |
| Mentees may view and update their preferences after sign-up. | X | X | X |
| Mentees view the preferences set by the mentors during the sign-up and acceptance processes. | X | X | X |
| Mentors may continue to enroll once mentee sign-up starts. | | X | X |

# Mentor Approval

Once the mentee has signed up and selected their mentor, unsupervised and open enrollment programs require mentor approval for any selection made by a mentee. Selecting a mentor during sign-up causes a system-generated email notification to be sent to the mentor.

A sample mentoring request is shown in Figure 4-49.

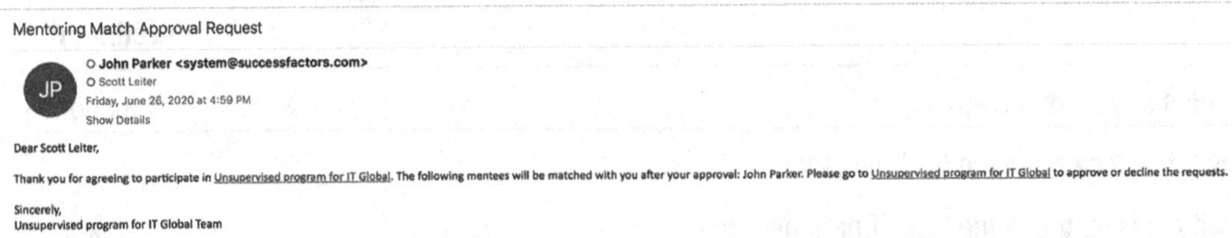

Mentoring Match Approval Request

JP

John Parker <system@successfactors.com>

Scott Leiter

Friday, June 26, 2020 at 4:59 PM

Show Details

Dear Scott Leiter,

Thank you for agreeing to participate in Unsupervised program for IT Global. The following mentees will be matched with you after your approval: John Parker. Please go to Unsupervised program for IT Global to approve or decline the requests.

Sincerely,
Unsupervised program for IT Global Team

***Figure 4-49.*** *Email Request to the Mentor*

This email notification is not used for supervised mentoring programs since this program does not use approvals.

The mentor will click the link in the email to see the request or go directly to the mentoring program-level page as seen in Figure 4-50.

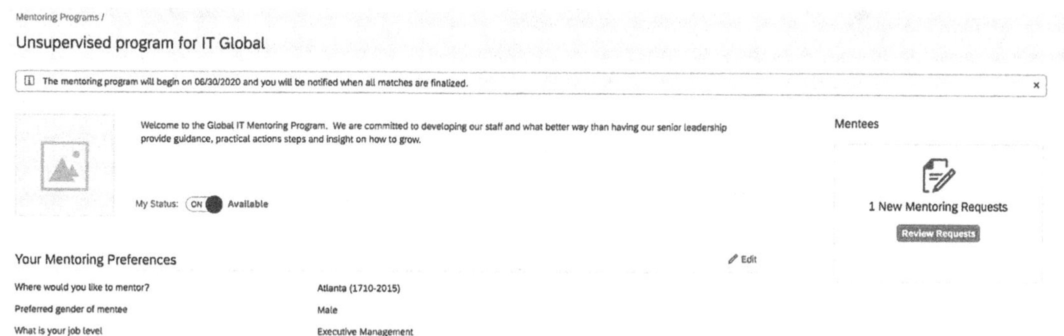
Mentoring Programs /
Unsupervised program for IT Global
The mentoring program will begin on 06/30/2020 and you will be notified when all matches are finalized.
Welcome to the Global IT Mentoring Program. We are committed to developing our staff and what better way than having our senior leadership provide guidance, practical actions steps and insight on how to grow.
My Status: ON Available
Mentees
1 New Mentoring Requests
Review Requests
Your Mentoring Preferences
Edit
Where would you like to mentor?
Atlanta (1710-2015)
Preferred gender of mentee
Male
What is your job level
Executive Management

***Figure 4-50.** Mentor View of the Program Overview Page with Pending Request*

As seen in Figure 4-51, the mentor may view the request, look at the mentee's preferences, and accept or decline the mentorship.

New Mentee Request
You can accept up to 3 mentees. You have 3 mentee slots left.
John Parker has sent a Mentee request.
View Mentoring Preferences
Decline
Accept
Close

***Figure 4-51.** Mentor to Approve or Decline the Mentee Request*

Declining the request will generate an email to the mentee so they may go back into the program to make another selection.

If the mentor accepts the mentee's request, a confirmation email is sent to the mentee, and they are now assigned .

Upon acceptance, the mentee will now display on the mentor's program page as seen in Figure 4-52.

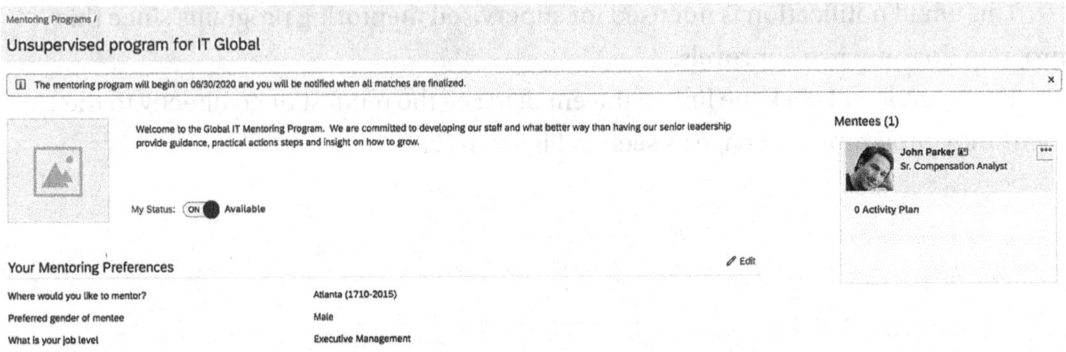

*Figure 4-52.* *Mentor Program Overview Page with the Mentee*

The mentor may view the mentee's details and add activities to the mentee's plan as shown in Figure 4-53.

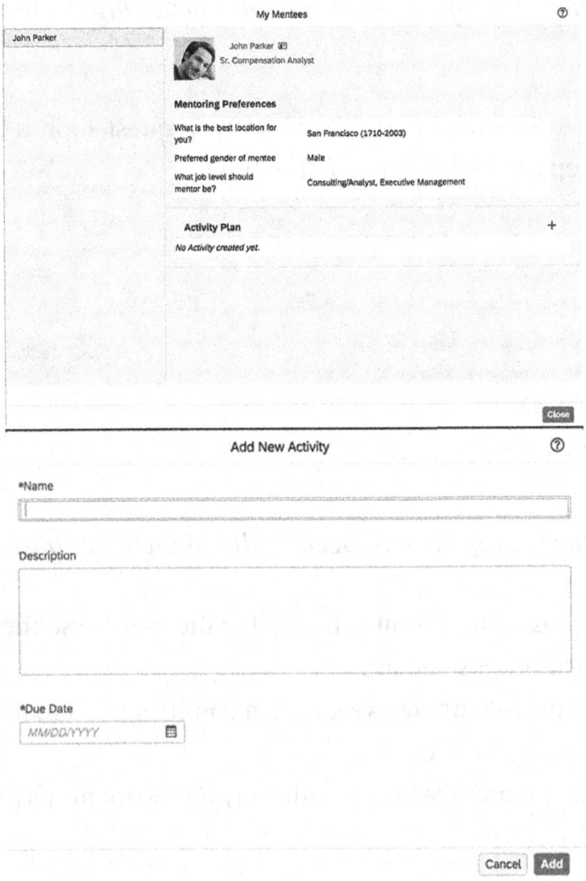

*Figure 4-53.* *Mentor Adding Activity to the Mentee's Plan*

Between the mentor and mentee, five activities may be added.

When the mentee goes back into their program, they will see their mentor has been added, and any activities created by the mentor will display as well. A sample is shown in Figure 4-54.

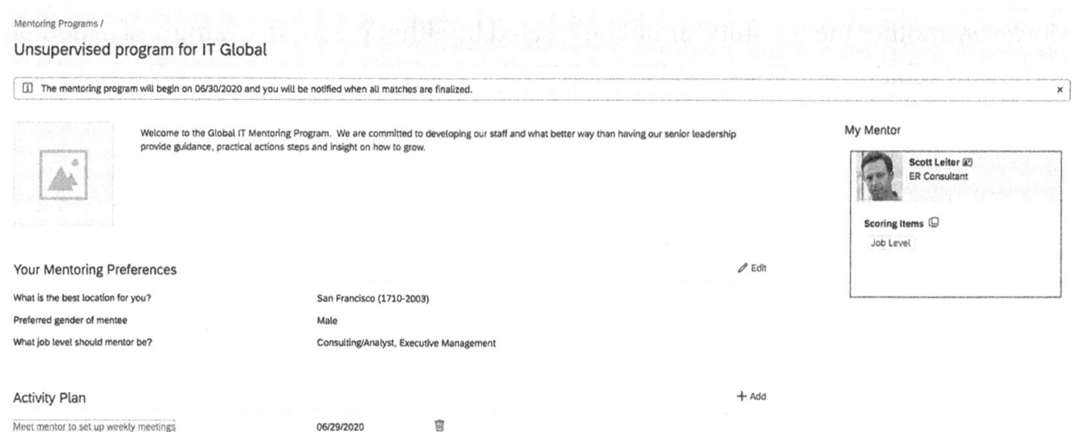
Mentoring Programs /
Unsupervised program for IT Global
The mentoring program will begin on 06/30/2020 and you will be notified when all matches are finalized.
Welcome to the Global IT Mentoring Program. We are committed to developing our staff and what better way than having our senior leadership provide guidance, practical actions steps and insight on how to grow.
My Mentor
Scott Leiter
ER Consultant
Scoring Items
Job Level
Your Mentoring Preferences
Edit
What is the best location for you?
San Francisco (1710-2003)
Preferred gender of mentee
Male
What job level should mentor be?
Consulting/Analyst, Executive Management
Activity Plan
Add
Meet mentor to set up weekly meetings
06/29/2020

***Figure 4-54.*** *Mentee View of the Program Overview Page*

The relationship will continue until the program ends, the admin makes a reassignment, or the mentor and mentee end the relationship.

Before the program starts, any mentors and mentees who have previously been unassigned may be matched manually by the admin. Mentors and mentees will receive mentoring match notifications. The admin may also change assignments, and any mentors or mentees who were reassigned will receive an email notification.

Even after the program starts, the admin may make any mentoring relationship changes, and email notifications will be sent.

# Mentor and Mentee Functionality When the Program Starts

Once the program starts, the functionality available to mentees and mentors is shown in the following:

- Mentors and mentee may add activities for the mentee.
- End and restart mentorships.

- Update preferences.
- Mentors may make themselves unavailable/available.
- View the mentoring program details.

When the program starts, either the mentor or mentee may end their relationship. However, another mentorship cannot be created by either party. An example of a mentee ending the relationship is seen in Figure 4-55.

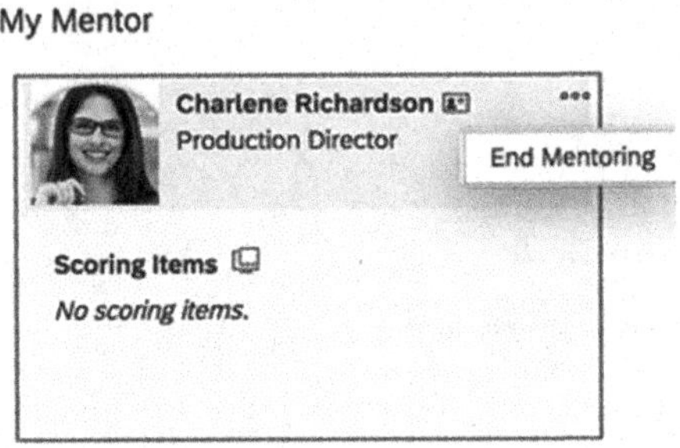


***Figure 4-55.*** *Option to End Mentoring Relationship*

A note may be added to the email that the mentor will receive as seen in Figure 4-56.

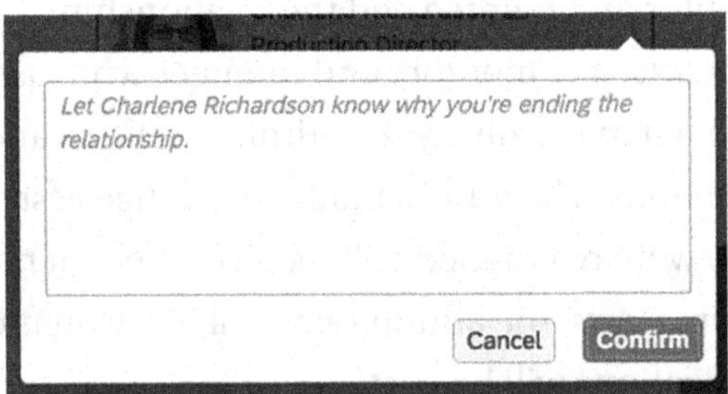


***Figure 4-56.*** *Optional Note to Be Included When Ending a Relationship*

The relationship will now display as ended as seen in Figure 4-57.

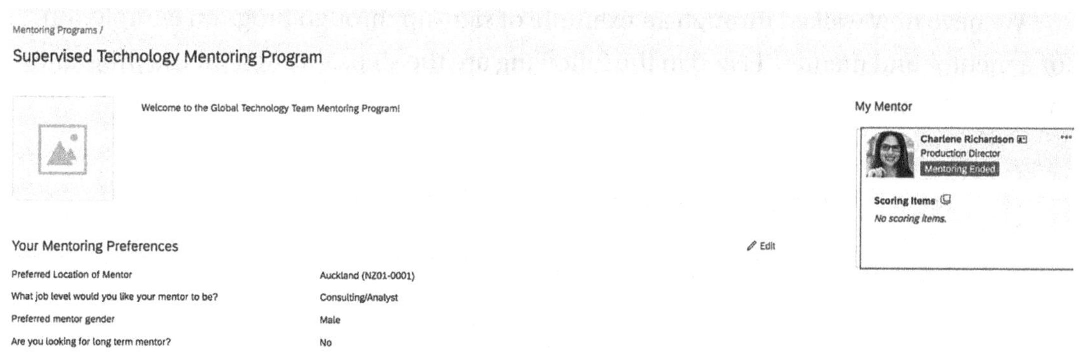


***Figure 4-57.** Ended Mentoring Relationship on the Program-Level Overview Page*

The mentor will receive an email notification. A sample is shown in Figure 4-58.

***Figure 4-58.** Email Notification of End of Mentoring Relationship*

The user that ended the mentorship may restart as seen in Figure 4-59.

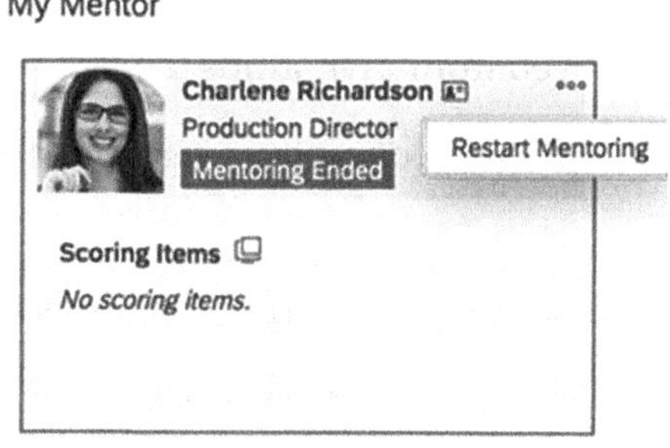


***Figure 4-59.** Restart Mentoring Relationship*

We have now walked through an example of sign-up through program completion for a mentor and mentee. Listed in the following are the steps throughout the programs that include the admin, mentors, and mentees.

## High-Level Steps for Supervised Programs

- Admin creates a supervised mentoring program.
- Program launches and stays in the Not Started status.
- Admin manually sends the mentor invites.
- Mentor sees invitation in the Invitations tab.
- Mentors receive email invitation to join the program:
    - If they join, they complete the sign-up form, and the program is now in the My Mentoring Programs tab.
    - If they opt out, they are removed from the program, and invitation is removed from the Invitations tab.
- Mentoring sign-up period ends:
    - No more mentors may sign up.
    - Admin may add or delete mentees before the invites go out.
- Admin manually sends out mentee invitation emails.
- Mentee receives invitation:
    - Mentee opts out of the program and is removed from the program:
    - Invitation is removed from Invitations tab.
    - Mentee joins the program completes sign-up form to identify preferences:
    - Program is now in the My Mentoring Programs tab.
    - Mentees may select mentors by name search or select from recommendations.

    - No email invite is sent to mentor if mentee made a selection.
    - Mentee may sign up without selecting a mentor.
- Mentee sign-up period ends.
- After all mentors and mentees signed up, admin may edit questions, modify match start date and mentoring program start and end dates, and upload an image.
- Matching period begins, and admin runs the matching program:
    - No more mentees may sign up at this stage.
    - Suggested matches are made based on preferences and employee profiles.
    - Admin may assign any unassigned participants.
    - Admin may unassign any assigned participants.
    - Admin makes final matches and the program is now In-Progress.
    - Emails go out to mentors and mentees with the match.
- During the In-Progress stage:
    - If admin unassigns any relationship, mentee is notified.
    - If admin does reassignment, mentee and mentor are notified.
    - Mentors and mentees arrange to meet to begin mentoring.
- Mentor or mentee may end the relationship.
- Program ends on the designated end date or if admin stops it.

## High-Level Steps for Unsupervised Programs

- Admin creates an unsupervised mentoring program.
- Program launches and stays in the Not Started status.
- Email goes out to mentors automatically based on mentor sign-up start date, or admin may manually trigger the emails.

- Mentors receive email invitation to join the program:
    - Invitation is in the Invitations tab.
    - If they join, they complete the sign-up form to provide their preferences, and the program is now in the My Mentoring Programs tab.
    - If they opt out, they are removed from the program, and invite is removed from the Invitations tab.
- Mentoring sign-up period ends.
- Mentee email goes out automatically on mentee sign-up start date or manually by admin.
- Mentee receives invitation:
    - Mentee opts out of the program and is removed from the program.
    - Mentee joins the program and completes the sign-up form to identify preferences:
    - Mentees must select a mentor either by name search or from recommendations.
    - Email invite is sent to the mentor.
- Mentor receives invitation from mentee.
    - If declined, email is sent to mentee to inform them and to make new selection:
    - Mentee continues to request for a mentor until someone accepts.
    - If the mentor accepts the invitation, email is sent to mentee and a match is made.
- Mentee and mentor can view each other's preferences.
- Admin may unassign or assign matches made by mentees and may make any changes once mentees start making matches.

- Any match changes made by admin will create notifications for mentee and mentor.
- Matches changed by admin don't require manager approval.
- Once assignments are finalized, admin starts the program:
    - Program is now In-Progress.
    - Changes still may be made, and any match changes will generate emails.
- Mentor and mentee decide how and when they will meet.
- Mentor and mentee can add activities for mentee.
- Mentor or mentee may end the relationship at any time if configured.
- Program ends on the designated program end date, or admin manually ends it.

Shown in the following are the steps that occur for an open enrollment mentoring program.

## High-Level Steps for Open Enrollment Programs

- Admin creates the program.
- Admin launches the program; it immediately goes to In-Progress status. Admin will now see Mentors, Mentees, and Matches tabs.
- Admin manually sends out invites with a deep link, with separate emails for mentors and mentees.
- Emails may go to mentees now or after mentors are set.
- Invitations are found in the Open Enrollment tab.
- Mentors may opt to join or may decline.
- If they join, they complete the sign-up form, and the program goes to My Mentoring Programs tab.

- If manager approval is needed, an email goes to the manager:
  - Mentor status is pending until approved or rejected.
  - Manager may approve or reject mentor's participation in the program:
    - If rejected, email is sent to mentor and mentor is removed from the program.
    - If approved, mentor receives email and will wait for a match.
- If admin approval is needed, the mentor must attach documentation to the sign-up form:
  - Mentor status is pending until approved or rejected.
  - If rejected, email is sent to mentor and mentor may resubmit request with proper documentation.
  - If approved, mentor receives email and will wait for a match.
- Mentees respond to invitations.
- Mentees cannot enroll until there is at least one mentor enrolled.
- Mentee may opt to join or decline:
  - If they decline, mentee is removed from the program.
  - If they join, mentee answers questions on the sign-up form:
    - Based on answers, mentee searches for a mentor by recommendations or name search.
    - Mentee submits request for a mentor.
    - Email is sent to mentor to accept or approve.
  - Once joined, the program moves from Open Enrollment to My Mentoring Programs.

- Mentor receives mentee request email:
  - Mentor declines:
    - Email is sent to mentee and they must select and request for a different mentor.
  - Mentor accepts:
    - Mentor and mentee are assigned.
    - Email notification goes to mentee.
- Admin monitors the program to see sign-ups.
- Admin may unassign matches or assign matches.
- Participants are notified when mentor changes.
- Program continues until admin ends it.
- Mentor or mentee may stop participation at any time if configured.

Next, we will review the email notifications that are used in Mentoring.

# E-mail Notifications

From sign-up through program completion, there are 24 email notifications that are used. The system automatically sends email notifications to mentors, mentees, mentor's manager, and mentor admin based on certain actions.

These email notifications are specific to mentoring and are not found within E-Mail Notification Templates. The only email notifications that may be modified are the invitations to participate in a mentoring program as we saw earlier. These mentor and mentee invitations may be modified for supervised and unsupervised programs during the program creation.

The remainder of the notifications cannot be controlled to turn off or to edit.

Table 4-10 identifies the mentoring email notifications that are sent.

***Table 4-10.*** *Email Notifications Throughout the Mentoring Process*

| Trigger to Send Notification | Recipient | Purpose |
|---|---|---|
| Open program starts | Mentor | Invitation to join as mentor. |
| Open program starts | Mentee | Invitation to join as mentee. |
| Supervised program match | Mentor | Supervised program mentee match. |
| Supervised program match | Mentee | Supervised program mentor match. |
| Request mentor | Mentor | Mentee requests mentor to approve. |
| Decline mentor request | Mentee | Mentor does not approve mentee. |
| Mentor not available | Mentee | Mentor not available. |
| Mentor becomes unavailable | Mentor | Mentor status changed to unavailable with end date. Can change status. |
| Current mentor became unavailable | Mentee | Mentor status changed to unavailable with end date. Can request another. |
| Pending mentor approval; mentor becomes unavailable | Mentee | Pending mentor status changed to unavailable. Can request another. |
| Mentor becomes available | Mentor | Mentor status changed to unavailable with end date. Now may be selected as mentor or can change status. |
| Mentor is available again | Mentee | Mentor is available again. |
| Pending mentor is available again | Mentee | Mentor is available. Back to pending approval, or change request. |
| Mentor is available next day | Mentor | Notification to the mentor that tomorrow they will be available as a mentor. Can change status. |
| Mentor is available in 7 days | Mentor | Notification to the mentor that they will be available as a mentor in 7 days. Can change status. |
| Mentor ending mentee relationship | Mentee | No longer mentored. |

(*continued*)

*Table 4-10.* (*continued*)

| Trigger to Send Notification | Recipient | Purpose |
|---|---|---|
| Mentor restarts mentee relationship | Mentee | Mentee is being mentored again by previously unavailable mentor. |
| Mentor needs manager's approval to participate | Mentor's manager | Manager notified of direct report intent to mentor. Manager may approve or decline. |
| Manager approval of mentor request | Mentor | Manager approved request. Mentor is now awaiting a match. |
| Manager rejects mentor request | Mentor | Manager of potential mentor rejects request. No longer in program. |
| Open enrollment participation approval | Mentor | Mentor receives approval by admin or owner to participate in open enrollment program. Pending match. |
| Open enrollment participation rejection | Mentor | Admin or program owner rejects request for mentor to participate in open enrollment program. May resubmit forms to ask for approval again. |
| Match is removed by admin | Mentee | Match is removed, pending rematch. |
| Jam group create failed | Mentoring admin | Program owners did not become group admins for program. |
| Jam group image failed | Mentoring admin | Program image not created for Jam group. |
| Users not invited to Jam group | Mentoring admin | Auto invites not created for Jam group. |

# Ad Hoc Reporting

Although there are no standard Mentoring dashboards available, the admin may create ad hoc mentoring reports. The following data elements may be reported on:

- Mentoring program
- Mentoring participants
- Mentoring program owners

- Mentoring program activity
- Mentoring program matched participants
- Mentoring program mentor requests
- Mentoring program mentor sign-up forms
- Mentoring program mentee sign-up forms
- Mentoring program email templates
- Mentoring program sign-up template
- Status of all invited participants: signed up, matched, not signed up, or pending
- Mentoring preference responses from mentors and mentees
- Jam group associated with a mentoring program
- Participants who can manually end mentoring relationships

This uses data from Mentoring Program as seen in Figure 4-60.

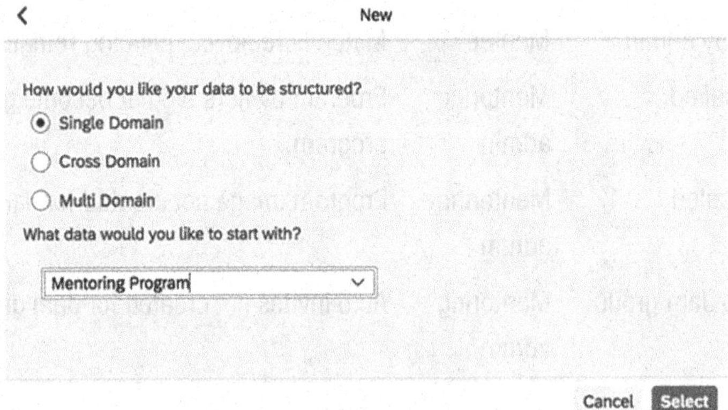


***Figure 4-60.*** *Mentoring Program Domain to Use for Reporting*

Then select the mentoring program(s) to use as your data set(s) as seen in Figure 4-61.

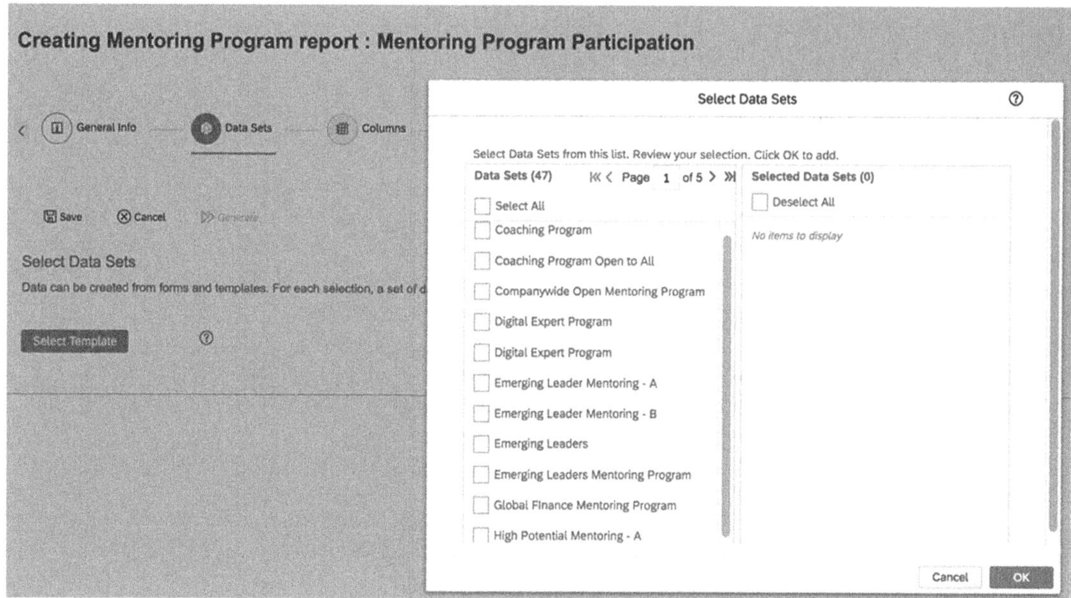


***Figure 4-61.*** *Selection of Mentoring Program(s) to Report On*

There is a fairly extensive list of mentoring fields that may be reported on such as the Program Details page, owner and participant information, mentor requests and approvals, sign-up form fields, emails, and matching results. The admin can run reports to track participation, check to see how many invitations have not resulted in sign-ups, see pending approval requests, and identify participants.

# Conclusion

We have now seen how to configure Mentoring and identify the role-based permissions needed. We have learned how an admin creates and manages mentoring programs and the steps involved to get mentees matched with mentors. The mentoring program acts as the framework to join mentors and mentees together. The programs are created, tracked, and closed by the admin. Once the matches are made, it is up to mentors and mentees to figure what they hope to accomplish with the mentorship. All of this is done outside of the system as each relationship will have unique needs. The benefit of this tool is that it creates a way of matching people based on what the mentees need and what the mentors may offer. The mentoring programs are tracked in one spot; and the admin can control the types of programs used, who participates, and the length of the programs, who has the ability to create the type of mentoring programs that fit their organization's needs.

# CHAPTER 5

# Succession Management Intro, 9-Box, and Talent Review Forms

Succession Management refers to the business process of identifying top talent and flagging them as potentials to take on key positions within an organization. For example, a company conducting sales around the globe may be on a constant lookout for SVP of Sales who oversees regional managers across the United States. For such a company, it would be of the utmost importance to have a list of people who could fill in such a critical role in short notice in the event the SVP of Sales left. However, Succession Management goes beyond simply maintaining lists of potential successors. Indeed, a good Succession Management strategy involves identifying gaps in the succession strategy and actively identifying, recruiting, and developing talented individuals suitable for key positions so that the business not only survives but thrives.

To extrapolate on this more, let's take a look at two examples of companies where an SVP of Sales is leaving their position:

1. A model company which is implementing a fully realized Succession Management strategy using SAP SuccessFactors
2. A company with a minimal Succession Management strategy

In the minimal Succession Management strategy company, the SVP of Sales decides to leave the company. They feel they've reached the peak of their career at the current company and have no hopes of promotion and see no path to advancement other than leaving. The president for the United States has a spreadsheet of potential successors they went over with the senior leadership team last year and contacts the person at the top of the list to see if they are interested in the position. The successor accepts, and




S. Traynor et al., *SAP SuccessFactors Talent: Volume 2*, https://doi.org/10.1007/978-1-4842-6995-4_5

the president arranges a handoff call between the two prior to the transition date. They sends an email accounting the transition, and the successor starts the new position. The daily grind at the company continues with only a slight decrease in sales over a short period of time.

In the model Succession Management strategy company, the president has been conducting continuous performance management meetings with the current SVP of Sales using SAP SuccessFactors. As part of these meetings, the president has proactively identified the SVP of Sales as a high risk of leaving the company and flagged them as such in the system. Prior to this, the president has already had a 9-box calibration session with the senior leadership team where the SVP of Sales was flagged as a high potential. The SVP of Sales has also been nominated as a successor in the system for the president's position. The system has calculated the gaps between their current competency set and what's needed to fulfill the duties of the new position. This has made life for both the SVP of Sales and the president easier since they now have a common goal to work toward. As part of their continuous performance management meetings, they have been working with the SVP of Sales' development plan in the system to get them prepared for their new role. The SVP of Sales has also been matched with another VP as a mentor as part of the SuccessFactors mentoring program to help them prepare for their new role. Being so actively engaged in their career at the current model company, the SVP of Sales hasn't really considered leaving the company at all and is helping to mentor their own successors who are their regional managers. Meanwhile, the president has been doing the same activities for the potential new SVP of Sales. As the transition day for the SVP of Sales position draws near, the president works with the change management team to assess impacts of the transition and how best to communicate the transition. Seeing in the SuccessFactors system that the new SVP of Sales has worked their way up from a small accounts executive, they decide an in-person event celebration of the new SVP of Sales's accomplishments is best. The event is conducted, and the staff's morale is improved with sales levels remaining on target and interest in development plans and employee retention increasing.

While the preceding examples are of course theoretical, it is undeniable that SAP SuccessFactors provides a variety of tools to assist customers in achieving this idealized model. SAP SuccessFactors Succession Management provides perhaps the most integrated solution that builds upon data from other modules to create a comprehensive business solution as outlined in the example. Some of the tools mentioned in the preceding example are already covered in prior chapters from Volumes

1 & 2. This chapter shows the reader how to implement SAP SuccessFactors Succession Management to its fullest potential like the model company example given here. The example model company will be referenced as we dive deeper into the configuration of each of the functions of the Succession Management module.

This and the next two chapters will follow the logical flow of configuring the Succession Management module (also referred to as SCM). We will start with the 9-box or matrix grid configuration in this Chapter. We will then cover the standard Talent Review Form and how it may be adjusted to meet your organization's specific business needs. Then in the next chapter, we will show how the talent cards are configured. We will then walk through nomination setup and the Succession Org Chart. After that, the Lineage Chart feature is examined. Last, in Chapter 6, we will dive into the remaining features including Talent Search, Talent Pools, Position Tile View, Lineage Chart, and then Succession Presentations. Let's get started!

# Basic Settings

Each section in this and the next two chapters will dive into detail about the features and configurations of the different major areas of the Succession module. Each of these assumes the following steps have been taken to turn on the basic Succession Management settings:

1. Log in to provisioning and navigate to your organization and click "Company Settings."
2. Check the box next to "Succession Planning" and "Succession Management."
3. Click "Save."

---

**Note** Throughout this chapter, we also assume role-based permissions and the MDF are turned on.

---

# 9-Box or Matrix Grid

The matrix grid is often referred to as a 9-box because many companies use a 3 × 3 configuration that results in literally nine boxes (some companies use other numbers of boxes such as 2 × 2 or 3 × 4, and SAP SuccessFactors supports such configurations as well). It is a tool to help visually identify how employees are performing across two dimensions at the same time by giving them a placement within one of these boxes. These dimensions are typically performance-potential (most common, shown in Figure 5-1) and objective-competency (also called "How vs. What" and shown in Figure 5-2). SAP SuccessFactors supports configuration of both types of matrix grid simultaneously or use of one or the other.

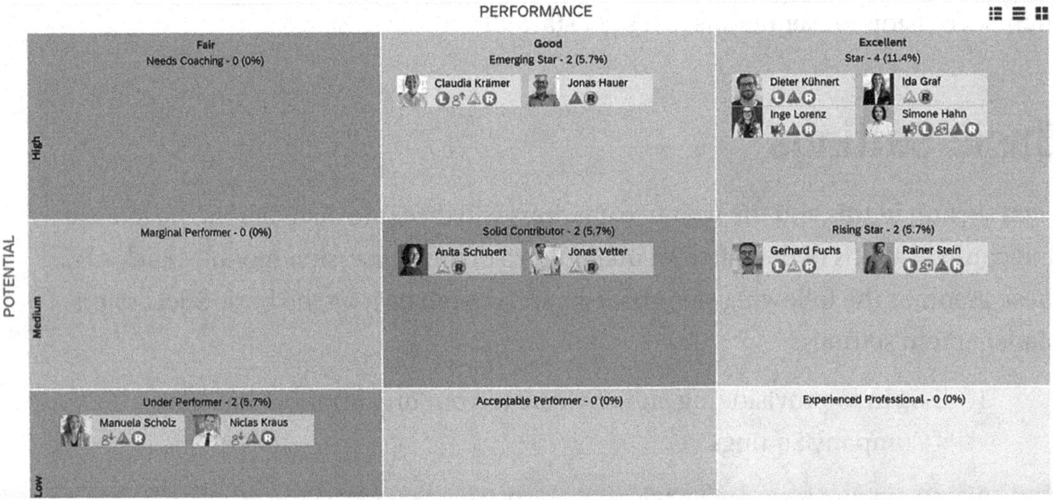


***Figure 5-1.** Example Performance-Potential 9-Box*

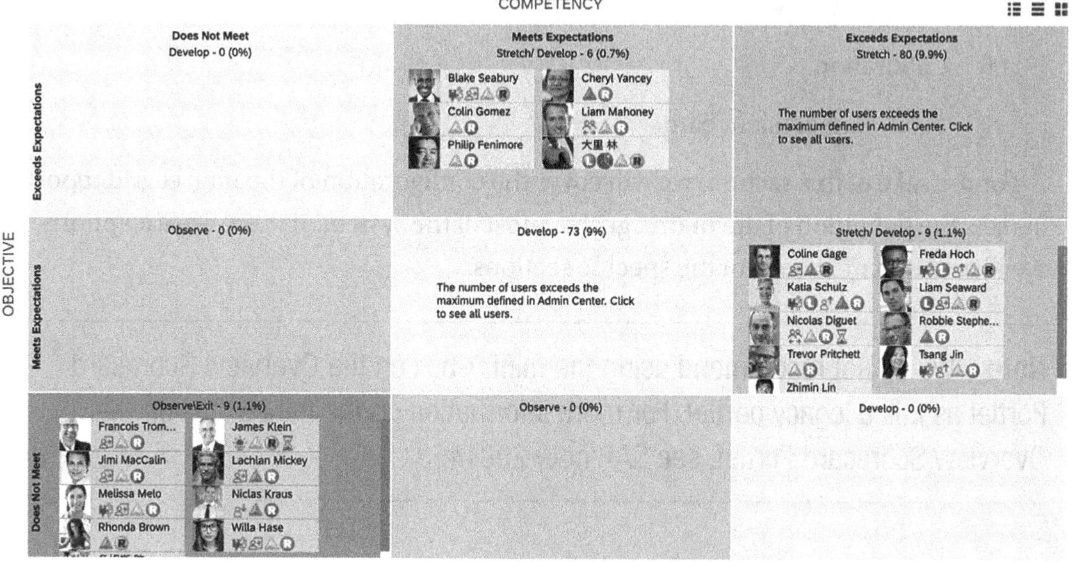


***Figure 5-2.** Example Objective-Competency or "How vs. What" 9-Box*

It is an important business decision to agree upon which dimensions will be used and what scales these dimensions will each take, not only to determine the size of your organization's matrix grid but also to consistently communicate to your talent decision makers. In our experience, we find that one of the biggest risks to a Succession Management implementation project is not having organizational alignment on what the matrix grid will look like or what criteria lead to placement within each square. It is vital to understand these prior to configuration of this area of the system.

There are multiple areas in the system where the matrix grid is displayed and/or used:

1. The matrix grid report
2. The talent card
    a. Within presentations
    b. Within the Succession Org Chart
3. As a presentation slide
4. The employee profile (mini 9-box on the Overview Scorecard, Performance History, Trend Elements, and Matrix Grid Placement History portlets)

5. The Talent Review Form
6. Calibration
7. Pixel-perfect talent cards

For the sake of this section, we will cover the configuration of the matrix grid report. This sets the definition of the matrix grid in most of the system. If there are exceptions, we will cover them in each of the specific sections.

---

**Note** We do not recommend using the mini 9-box on the Overview Scorecard Portlet as it is a legacy portlet. For more information on the mini 9-box on the Overview Scorecard Portlet, see SAP note 2091458.

---

## Prerequisites for Configuring the Matrix Grid

Prior to being able to access the matrix grid configuration screen, the following settings and configurations need to be completed.

### Provisioning

In Provisioning, navigate to "Company Settings" and check the "Matrix Grid Report (9-Box)" and "Matrix Grid How Vs. What Report (9-Box)" as shown in Figure 5-3 and click "Save."

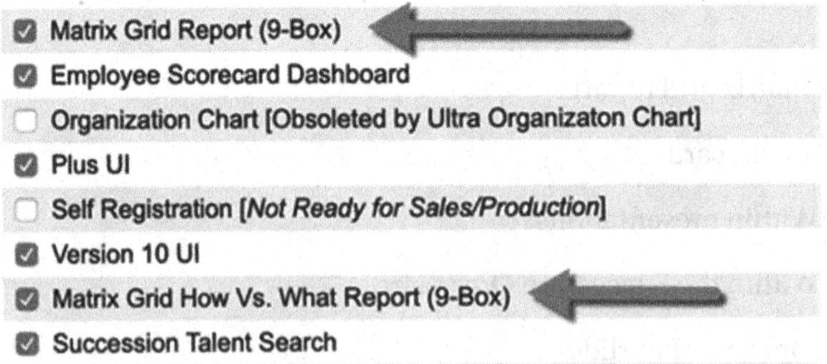


*Figure 5-3. Provisioning Settings Required Prior to Matrix Grid Configuration*

## Permissions

Once the provisioning settings have been configured, permission options will become available to select for roles within the "Manage Permission Roles" screen.

---

**Note** We assume throughout this Chapter that role-based permissions have been turned on in Provisioning. Please also note sometimes it takes time for provisioning settings to take effect in the system. If you do not see the permissions appear immediately, log out and log back in an hour or so later. Changes should not take more than overnight to take effect.

---

1. Type and select "Manage Permission Roles" in the search bar.
2. When the screen loads, click the role you wish to modify. Then click "Permission...:"
3. In order to access the matrix grid reports as an end user, the "Succession Management and Matrix Report Permissions" and "Matrix Report Permissions" need to be selected for the permission role as shown in Figure 5-4.

---

**Note** The "Succession Management and Matrix Report Permissions" requires a target population. This will define the population the end user can see when they run the report.

---

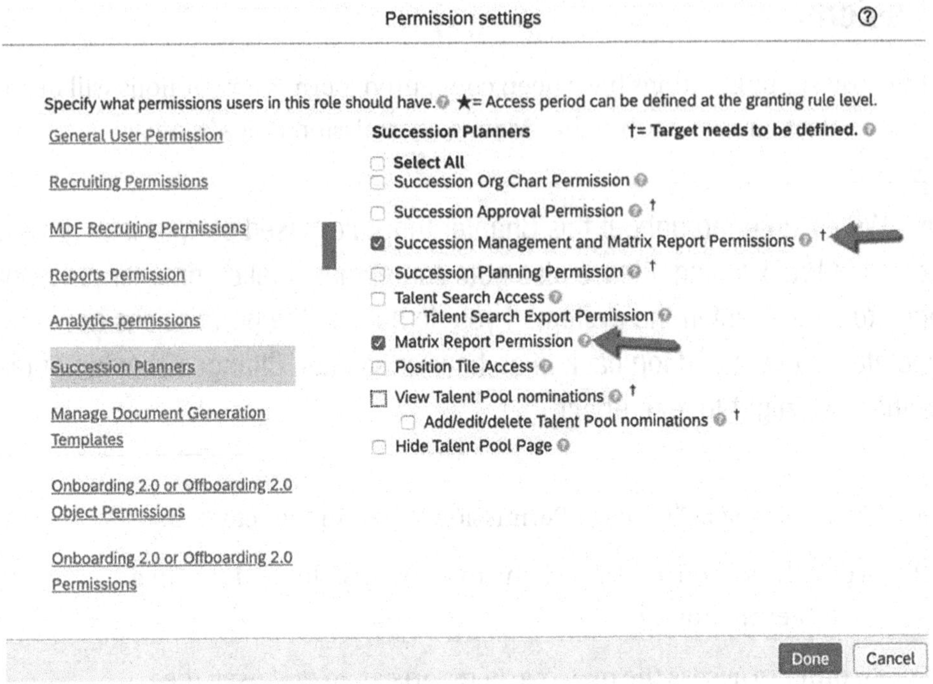

***Figure 5-4.*** *Permissions Required for Accessing the Matrix Grid Reports as an End User*

4. In order to access the screens to configure the matrix grid, the "How vs. What Configuration," "Matrix Grid Rating Scales," and "Performance-Potential Configuration" selections need to be checked under the "Manage Succession" section for the assigned permission role as shown in Figure 5-5. Click "Done." Be sure to save your role on the main screen as well.

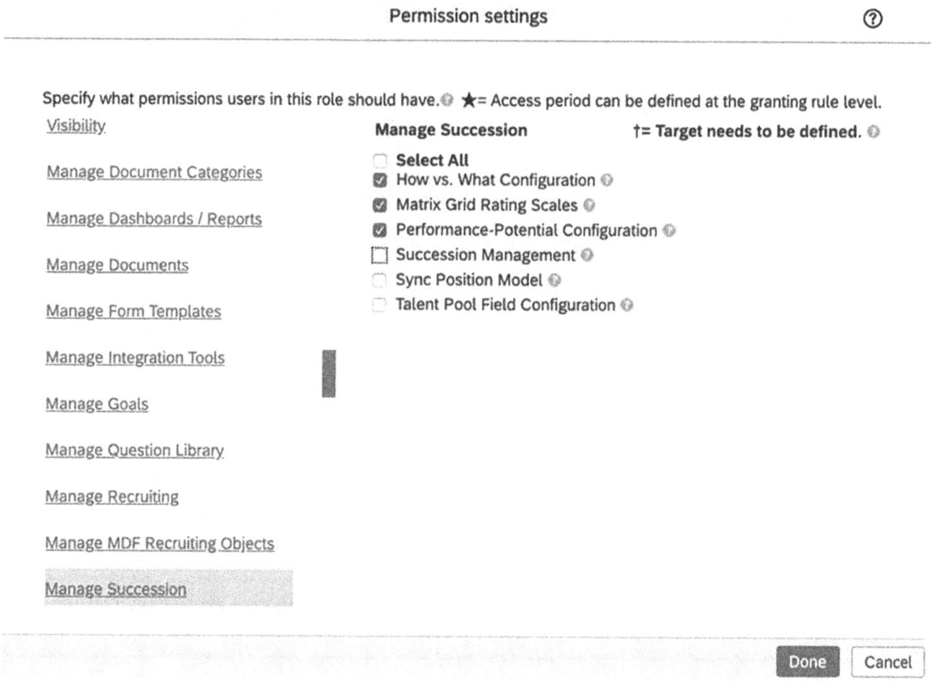

***Figure 5-5.*** *Permissions Required for Configuring the Matrix Grids*

## Processes and Forms Configuration

Many companies organize multiple forms into logical annual process groupings so that only relevant forms are viewable to end users. This is accomplished by utilizing the Processes and Forms configuration screen as shown in Figure 5-6. If you have not done so already, please ensure this configuration is completed prior to matrix grid configuration. For more information on performance review forms and processes, see Volume 1, Chapters 6–10.

Processes and Forms

Process Table

Create New

| Process Name | # of Form Templates | Show/Hide | Default | Action |
|---|---|---|---|---|
| All Forms | | ☑ | ◉ | |
| Employee Scorecard | 11 | ☑ | ○ | |
| 2012 Forms | 2 | ☑ | ○ | |
| 2013 Forms | 1 | ☑ | ○ | |
| 2014 Forms | 1 | ☑ | ○ | |
| 2015 Forms | 1 | ☑ | ○ | |
| 2014 Comp Forms | 2 | ☑ | ○ | |
| 2015 Comp Forms | 3 | ☑ | ○ | |
| 2017 Forms | 1 | ☑ | ○ | |
| 2016 Performance | 1 | ☑ | ○ | |

Form Drilling Visibility: ○ Managers can only drill to see forms after they have been in their inbox at least once.
◉ Managers can drill to see all forms in their team at any point in the process.

Include In-Progress Documents: ☑

Basic Goal Management: ☐ Include Basic Goal Management goals when "All Forms/Goal Plans" is selected

Save

***Figure 5-6.*** *The Processes and Forms Configuration Screen*

# Matrix Grid Configuration

This section details the screens and steps used to configure the matrix grid.

## The Matrix Grid Rating Scale Configuration Screen

Prior to the main configuration of either matrix grid, you should check and modify the rating scale configuration. These scales allow you to control the dimensions of your matrix grid, for example, making it a 9-Box vs. some other size. It also allows you to change the text associated with each rating level in all languages turned on for your system. To access the matrix grid rating scale configuration screen, type and select "Matrix Grid Rating Scales" in the search bar. Figure 5-7 shows the screen.

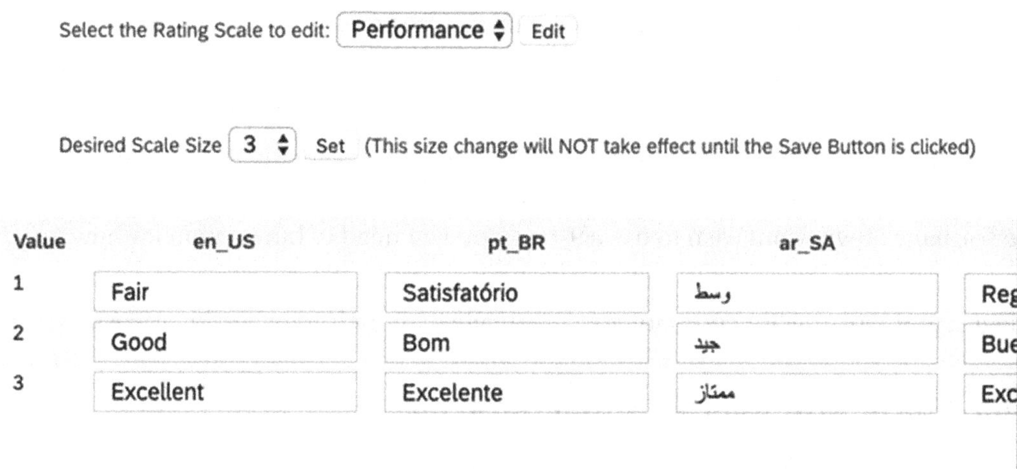

Matrix Grid Rating Scales

Modify the rating scales used for the Matrix Grid Report.

- *Maximum scale label is 128 characters.*
- *When configuring scale labels for a specific locale, a label must be provided for each scale value for that locale.*
- *Reducing the Desired Scale Size value will truncate the scale on save.*
- *Leading and trailing spaces are removed.*

Select the Rating Scale to edit: Performance Edit

Desired Scale Size 3 Set (This size change will NOT take effect until the Save Button is clicked)

| Value | en_US | pt_BR | ar_SA | |
|---|---|---|---|---|
| 1 | Fair | Satisfatório | وسط | Reg |
| 2 | Good | Bom | جيد | Bue |
| 3 | Excellent | Excelente | ممتاز | Exc |

***Figure 5-7.** The Matrix Grid Rating Scale Configuration Screen*

Take the following steps to make your configurations on the screen:

1. When the screen loads, there are six rating scales to choose from in the main dropdown: Performance, Potential, Objective, Competency, Custom1, and Custom2.
2. Choose one of the options and click "Edit."
3. The area below the dropdown will expand to show the number of values in the scale as well as the translations in each language activated for your instance.
4. You can change the scale by selecting a different number in the Desired Scale Size dropdown and clicking "Set."
5. After choosing a scale size, enter the text descriptions.
6. When you are finished, click Save.
7. Repeat the process for the remaining scales.

**Note** The options you choose here will also affect the scales in the employee profile. For example, if you allow managers to choose a potential rating directly in the employee profile, the scale will come from this configuration.

For the sake of our model company, we recommend using a three-point scale for both performance and potential. This will allow for a 9-box configuration. Furthermore, we recommend that this scale match the annual performance review scale so that a three-point scale is used in performance ratings. If a three-point scale is not used for performance ratings, please refer to the next section on steps how to normalize. Similarly, with goal and competency ratings, we recommend three-point scales that match the ratings given for the Goals section and Competency section of the performance review. If you choose to go with scales that are higher or lower than three points for your performance review but wish to use a 9-box, you will need to have a plan for how to translate those scales into a 9-box in a simple and systematic way. This is perhaps the biggest problem area for companies that struggle with their matrix grid process.

## The Matrix Grid Configuration Screens

SAP SuccessFactors allows for two matrix grid reports: one for performance-potential and one for goal-competency. As such, there are two separate configuration screens, one for each report (though the screens look and do the same thing for each report). These are the primary areas where the matrix grid is configured. To access the performance-potential report configuration screen, type and select "Matrix Grid Reports: Performance-Potential" in the search bar. To access the goal-competency report configuration screen, type and select "Matrix Grid: How vs. What" in the search bar. Figure 5-8 shows a typical performance-potential 9-box configuration. We will not cover both configuration screens since they are identical.

**Note** While the configuration screens are named for performance-potential and How vs. What, the system is flexible enough to make any kind of matrix grid your organization needs by relabeling one or both of the configuration screens. Just know that you are limited to two reports.

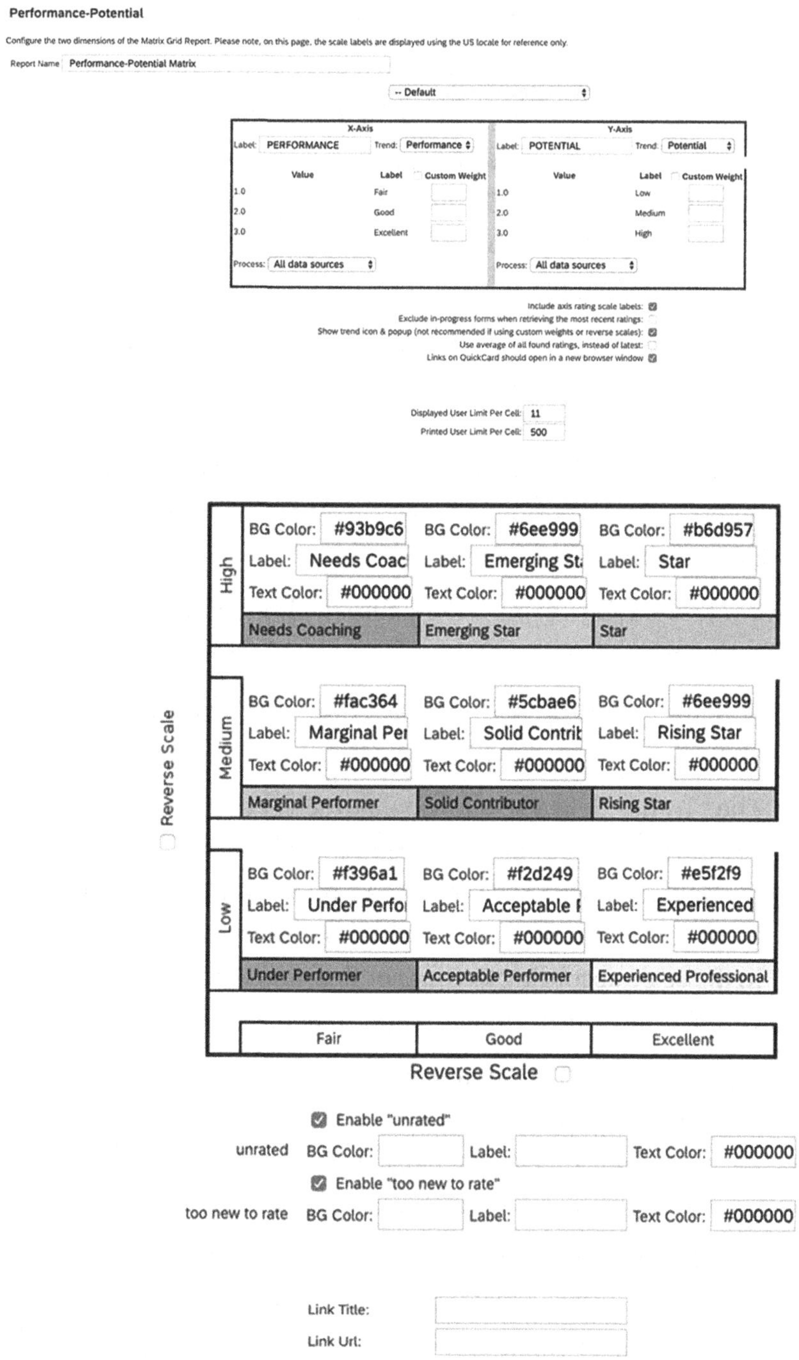

**Performance-Potential**

Configure the two dimensions of the Matrix Grid Report. Please note, on this page, the scale labels are displayed using the US locale for reference only.

Report Name: Performance-Potential Matrix

-- Default

| X-Axis | | | Y-Axis | | |
|---|---|---|---|---|---|
| Label: PERFORMANCE | Trend: Performance | | Label: POTENTIAL | Trend: Potential | |
| Value | Label | Custom Weight | Value | Label | Custom Weight |
| 1.0 | Fair | | 1.0 | Low | |
| 2.0 | Good | | 2.0 | Medium | |
| 3.0 | Excellent | | 3.0 | High | |
| Process: All data sources | | | Process: All data sources | | |

Include axis rating scale labels: ☑
Exclude in-progress forms when retrieving the most recent ratings: ☐
Show trend icon & popup (not recommended if using custom weights or reverse scales): ☑
Use average of all found ratings, instead of latest: ☐
Links on QuickCard should open in a new browser window ☑

Displayed User Limit Per Cell: 11
Printed User Limit Per Cell: 500

| | Fair | Good | Excellent |
|---|---|---|---|
| High | BG Color: #93b9c6<br>Label: Needs Coac<br>Text Color: #000000<br>Needs Coaching | BG Color: #6ee999<br>Label: Emerging St<br>Text Color: #000000<br>Emerging Star | BG Color: #b6d957<br>Label: Star<br>Text Color: #000000<br>Star |
| Medium | BG Color: #fac364<br>Label: Marginal Per<br>Text Color: #000000<br>Marginal Performer | BG Color: #5cbae6<br>Label: Solid Contrit<br>Text Color: #000000<br>Solid Contributor | BG Color: #6ee999<br>Label: Rising Star<br>Text Color: #000000<br>Rising Star |
| Low | BG Color: #f396a1<br>Label: Under Perfo<br>Text Color: #000000<br>Under Performer | BG Color: #f2d249<br>Label: Acceptable I<br>Text Color: #000000<br>Acceptable Performer | BG Color: #e5f2f9<br>Label: Experienced<br>Text Color: #000000<br>Experienced Professional |

☐ Reverse Scale (vertical)

Reverse Scale ☐

☑ Enable "unrated"
unrated BG Color: Label: Text Color: #000000
☑ Enable "too new to rate"
too new to rate BG Color: Label: Text Color: #000000

Link Title:
Link Url:

***Figure 5-8.** The Matrix Grid Configuration Screen*

To configure the matrix grid, follow these steps:

1. The dropdown at the top of the screen indicates the language selection for which you are editing the screen. Select your desired language, and the screen will automatically repopulate for the selected language. If your organization requires multiple languages, you will need to repeat this step and the following ones for each desired language.
2. The "Report Name" field allows you to adjust the wording of the report name to fit your organization's terminology. For example, if your organization only uses a performance -potential matrix grid which is commonly known as a "9-box," you may want to relabel the report name to "9-Box." This will automatically change the navigation label as well for end users.
3. The X-Axis box allows you to configure the horizontal dimension of your matrix.
    a. With the "Label" field, you can change the label that shows along the bottom of the X-axis in the end user screens.
    b. The "Trend" field also allows you to select one of the scales you configured in the "Matrix Grid Rating Scales" configuration screen. This will control not only how many boxes appear along this axis but also the labels for each point in the scale according to your configurations in the "Matrix Grid Rating Scales" configuration screen.
    c. If you would like to normalize the distribution of scores along this axis with a custom weighting, check the "Custom Weight" checkbox and enter a percentage weight next to each rating value.

---

**Note** Entering values here will control how, for example, a five-point performance scale is converted to a three-point scale on a 9-box. If, for example, a 100% was entered for the 1 rating, all employees would land on the 1 rating. If 50% was entered on the 1 rating, then anyone with a 1–2.5 on the five-point scale would land on the 1 rating. A common example would be a 20/60/20 distribution that would land most scores as a 2 rating.

---

d. The "Process" dropdown allows you to select one of your configured processes or the employee scorecard (employee profile) or all available data sources to populate your report. Select one of the options as appropriate.

---

**Note** Understanding the source of your matrix grid report is fundamental to proper configuration. The ratings that drive the score on each dimension and thus the placement within the grid can come from two sources:

1. *The employee profile (e.g., the live profile or scorecard; additionally, there is an option to include or exclude any in-progress calibration sessions on the live profile on the "Manage Calibration Settings" screen)*
2. *A form (e.g., a performance form or the Talent Review Form and possibly a calibration session included in the route map of the form as mentioned earlier – this depends on how the process was set up using the Processes and Forms configuration screen)*

   *If "All data sources" is chosen, then the system will take the latest score from the employee scorecard and all processes that are active in the system. While this option gives the latest information, it can also become very confusing to end users. We generally recommend selecting your latest configured process and then communicating to managers/decision makers when the system will be switched to the next process. It is important to create sample data and test that your configuration gives the expected result. Many times, source selection can get confusing and cause unexpected results in the report. In our experience, a misconfiguration in this area is usually the culprit!*

---

4. Repeat the preceding X-Axis box steps for the Y-Axis box.
5. The "Include axis rating labels" checkbox will make the labels visible that were configured for the rating scales in the "Matrix Grid Rating Scales" configuration screen.

6. The checkbox for "Exclude in-progress forms when retrieving the most recent ratings" does literally what it says. Check this box as needed.

---

**Note** We generally recommend not checking this box. It is often helpful for managers and HR resources to look at how employees are stacking up in the middle of the process in order to help finalize ratings.

---

7. The "Show trend icon & popup" is really deprecated and refers to an old popup that has since been replaced by the trend view on the employee talent card. We typically just leave this checked as it no longer has an effect.
8. The "Use average of all found ratings, instead of latest" checkbox comes into play when someone performs a report across multiple years. Normally the system takes the latest score, whereas in this case it would average all found ratings. Check this box as needed.

---

**Note** The user will have the option to select the date range to search when they run the matrix grid report. By default, the system will use one year prior to today's date in this field; and then subsequent to that, it will use the last date range the user ran on the report. There is no option to change this behavior. We typically recommend not checking the box mentioned in the preceding step as it can become confusing to the end user. Typically, users are interested in the latest information on an employee to make succession decisions rather than an average. Furthermore, they can click the employee talent card and view their trend over time if such information is needed.

---

9. The "Links on Quickcard should open in a new browser window" refers to an obsolete option called the quick card. This is no longer relevant.

10. The "Display User Limit Per Cell" field will limit how many maximum employees will fit in each cell of your matrix. The highest value you can enter in this field is 5000. A display message will appear telling the user that the maximum is exceeded in the event that they run the report where the maximum is exceeded.

---

**Note** We don't recommend showing a large number of users per cell as this can cause performance issue with the system and can also become cumbersome for the user to visualize.

---

11. The "Printed User Limit Per Cell" acts in the same manner, but with the printed version of the report.
12. The "Reverse Scale" checkboxes alongside each axis will flip the order of the scale on each axis, respectively (e.g., from ascending to descending).

---

**Note** We recommend not using reverse scales – as a convention, most organizations assume the upper right-hand corner box is the best possible rating.

---

13. The "BG Color" fields within each cell allow you to set the background color of that cell. Enter the html color hex code for the color you would like in each cell.

---

**Note** You can use a reference site like the W3Schools website as a reference for what codes correspond to what colors: `www.w3schools.com/colors/colors_picker.asp`.

---

14. Similarly, the "Text Color" fields allow you to pick the color of the text that will appear in each box. Enter another html hex code for each cell.

**Note** You should try to pick a text color and background color for each that contrast well to help meet accessibility guidelines and to make for an easy-to-use system. The US General Services website which outlines accessibility guides provides a great accessible color palette builder here: `https://accessibility.digital.gov/visual-design/color-and-contrast/`.

15. Enter text for each label according to your currently selected language within each "Label" field.

16. If you wish to allow users to see who among their selection criteria for the report is unrated as an extra area to the right of the matrix grid, select the "Enable unrated" checkbox. Similarly, check the "Enable too new to rate" to see employees who were selected for this rating as well to the right. Similar to cell background colors, labels, and text colors, choose colors for these boxes or leave them blank.

**Note** We recommend use of both of these options (unless "too new to rate" is not an option in your performance review cycle, in which case we only recommend using "Enable unrated" – see Volume 1, Chapter 6 for more information on "too new to rate"). Selecting these options can be very helpful for identifying employees who may have been overlooked during the process. For example, a manager reviewing their team's ratings could realize on the report that they never performed a talent review for an employee appearing in this area.

17. Add a link to the matrix grid report by filling out the "Link Title" and "Link Url" fields. Entering values into these fields will show an "i" icon in the upper right-hand corner of the report that will open the link when clicked.

**Note** We recommend using this link as a reference point to documentation on your organization's policies and/or a user guide for managers on criteria for 9-box placement.

## Matrix Grid Icon Configuration Screen

The matrix grid icon configuration screen (Figure 5-9) is used to display icons on the matrix grid report when employees have talent data populated in the fields configured on this screen. For example, if an employee is male or female, you can choose to display the male or female symbol by their name on the report. The configurations you make here will control the icons that appear throughout the Succession module such as in the Succession Org Chart.

**Admin Center > Matrix grid report icon reconfiguration**

**Edit Matrix grid report icon reconfiguration**

Here is the matrix grid report ("9-box") icon configuration. The icons are displayed to the left of each employee name and you can adjust the order of the icons. You can have up to 8 icon sets, but for best usability 4 or fewer are recommended. If you use multiple matrix grid reports, the same icon configuration will apply to all of them.

Add A New Field

| Field Name | Field Icons | Actions |
|---|---|---|
| Diversity Candidate | | Take Action |
| Future Leader | | Take Action |
| Reason for Leaving | | Take Action |
| Impact of Loss | | Take Action |
| Risk of Loss | | Take Action |
| Retirement Date | | Take Action |

Save Changes Reset

***Figure 5-9.*** *The Matrix Grid Report Icon Configuration Screen*

Follow these steps to perform configurations on this screen:

1. Click the "Add A New Field" button to call up the "Add Field" popup (Figure 5-10). Select the field for which you would like to add an icon and click "OK." The list of fields here represents all talent fields from your data model that have not yet been assigned a set of icons. For more information on the data model, see Volume 1, Chapter 2.

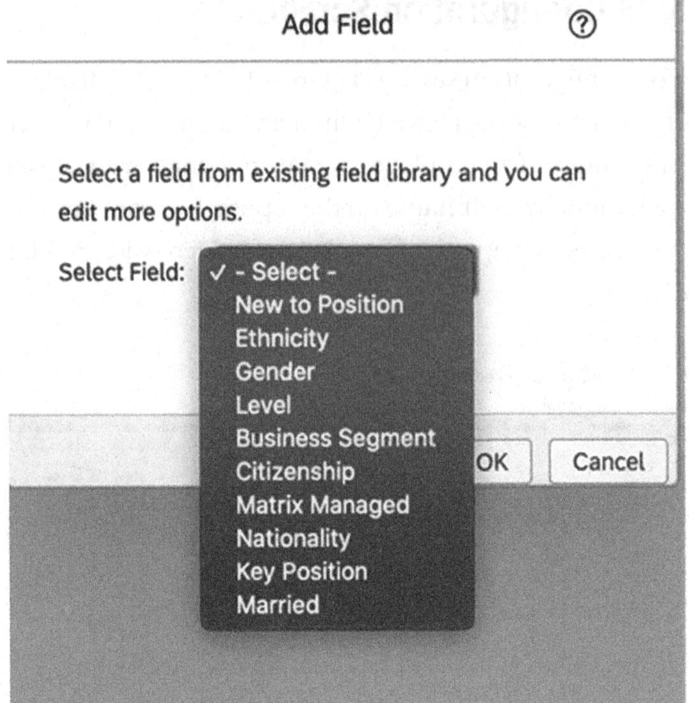


***Figure 5-10.*** *The Add Field Popup*

2. The Edit Field popup will appear (Figure 5-11). This popup will read the picklist ID associated with the field and list all items within the picklist.

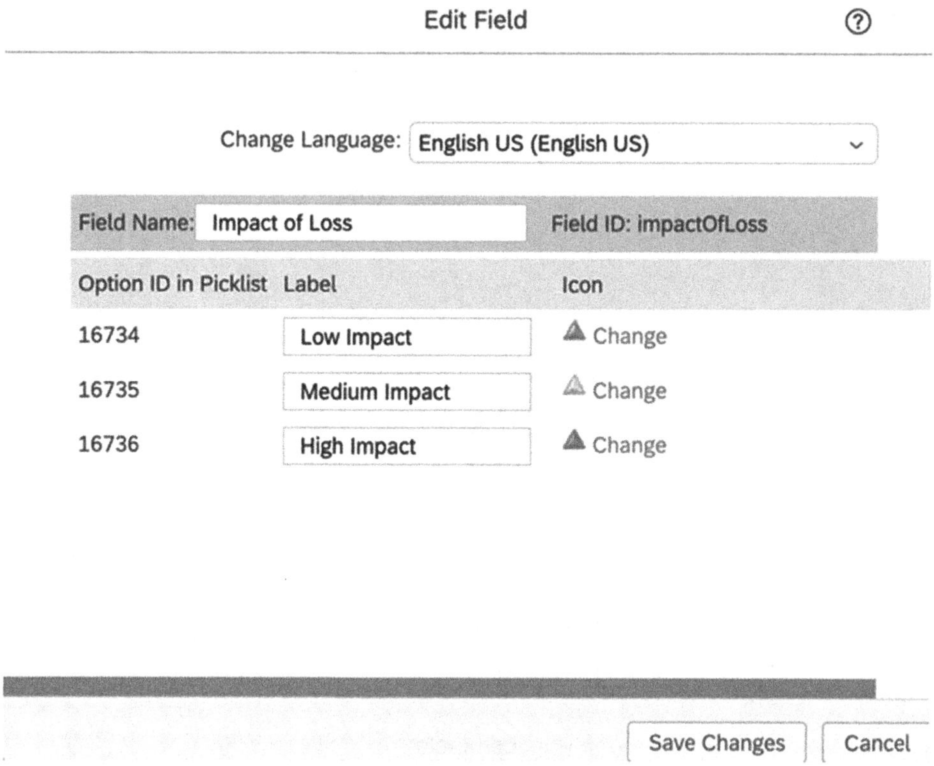

Edit Field

Change Language: English US (English US)

Field Name: Impact of Loss Field ID: impactOfLoss

| Option ID in Picklist | Label | Icon |
|---|---|---|
| 16734 | Low Impact | Change |
| 16735 | Medium Impact | Change |
| 16736 | High Impact | Change |

Save Changes Cancel

***Figure 5-11.** Edit Screen for the "Impact of Loss" Category Field*

---

**Note** The picklist ID in the system must match the technical field name of the field in the data model in order to show in the preceding screen. If the picklist does not match, an error screen will appear instead, and you will not be able to conduct configurations. You can edit the list of possible values for the field in the picklist center (Figure 5-12). For more information on configuring talent fields which includes assigning picklists, please see Volume 1, Chapter 2.

---

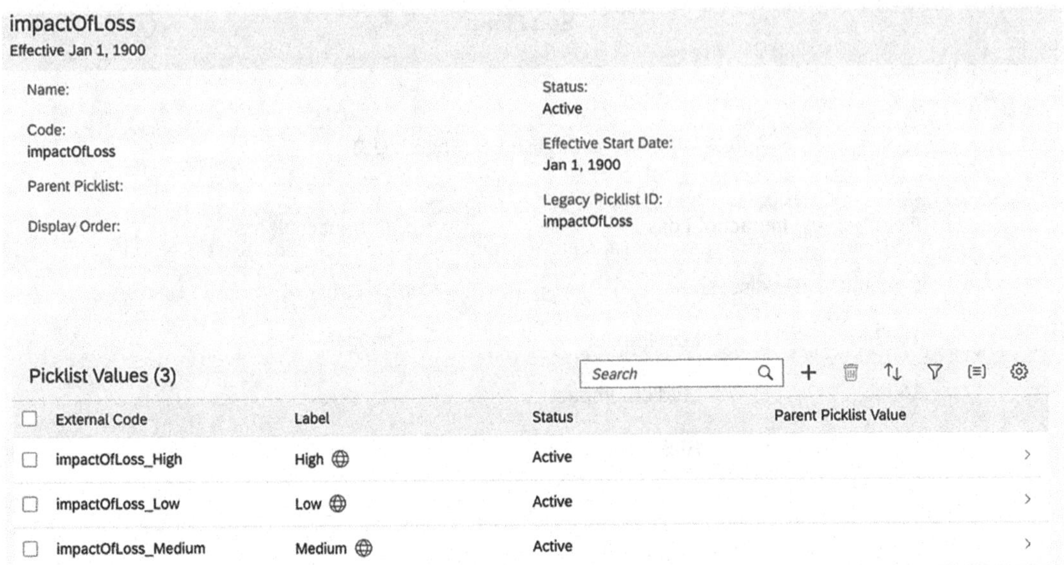


***Figure 5-12.** Picklist Center Screen Showing the Picklist ID impactOfLoss Matches the Technical Field Name impactOfLoss*

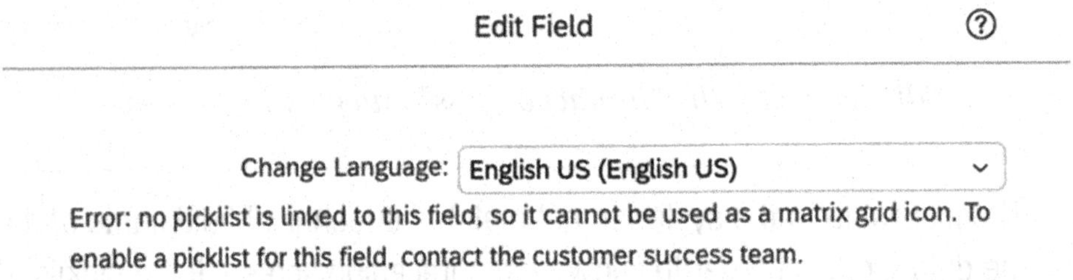

Edit Field

Change Language: English US (English US)

Error: no picklist is linked to this field, so it cannot be used as a matrix grid icon. To enable a picklist for this field, contact the customer success team.

***Figure 5-13.** Error Shown for Field Category When No Picklist Is Configured*

3. So long as your picklists are properly configured, you can then choose an icon for each by clicking the "Change" button on the "Edit Field" screen (Figure 5-13). The list of standard icons from the system will display for you to choose. You must choose from the list of standard icons – you cannot upload a custom icon. Click Save Changes when you are finished, and you will be returned to the main screen.

4. Repeat the preceding steps for all desired field icon assignments.

5. If you do not wish to show an icon and instead see the text of the picklist, simply delete the entry for the category field by clicking "Take Action" and then "Delete."

---

**Note** We recommend using icons for all talent fields so that they display on all available screens. This will allow for an optimized visualization experience. When icons are not used, the text may not display on some of the overview screens such as on the Succession Org Chart.

---

6. To make edits to existing configurations, click "Take Action" and select "Edit." The "Edit Field" popup will appear, and you can repeat step 2 to complete the configuration for the field.
7. To change the order in which the fields appear, click "Take Action" and select the up or down arrow for the fields. When you have the desired order, click "Save Changes."

## Matrix Category Configuration Screen in Provisioning

Another way to configure the icons shown on the matrix grid icon configuration screen is to access the XML configuration directly in Provisioning. To do this, log in to provisioning and choose the desired company and then select "Matrix Category Configuration" (see Figure 5-14). When you're finished making your edits directly to the XML, click "Save Content."

---

**Note** You should not have to perform this step in Provisioning if you use the matrix grid icon configuration screen. You can compare the following code segment to the screenshot of the Impact of loss configuration to understand how the XML and the config screen correspond to one another.

---

**Edit the matrix category configuration**

Use this page to edit the matrix grid report (9-box) category configuration in XML format.
Note that this configuration can also be changed through the UI in admin tools with the "Edit matrix grid report icon configuration" tool.

Save Content | Delete | Obtained from the Database

```
<?xml version="1.0" encoding="UTF-8"?>
<!DOCTYPE Classifier SYSTEM "classifier_1_0.dtd">
<Classifier>
  <Category id="minority" name="Minority">
    <label lang="ar_SA" value="مرشح التنوع."/>
    <label lang="de_DE" value="Bewerber aus Minderheitengruppe"/>
    <label lang="en_US" value="Diversity Candidate"/>
    <label lang="es_ES" value="Candidato de diversidad"/>
    <label lang="fr_FR" value="Candidat issu de la diversité"/>
    <label lang="ja_JP" value="多様性を持つ候補者"/>
    <label lang="ko_KR" value="다양성 후보자"/>
    <label lang="pt_BR" value="Candidato de diversidade"/>
    <label lang="ru_RU" value="Кандидат, способствующий диверсификации"/>
    <label lang="zh_CN" value="候选人多样性"/>
    <label lang="zh_TW" value="候選人多樣性"/>
    <Level id="is minority">
      <ExactEvaluator value="true"/>
      <Icon alt="" title="Minority" url="/ui/sm/img/org_icons
/sap_ui5_icon_DiversityCandidate02_Purple.png">
        <label lang="ar_SA" value="مرشح التنوع."/>
        <label lang="de_DE" value="Bewerber aus Minderheitengruppe"/>
        <label lang="en_US" value="Diversity Candidate"/>
```

*Figure 5-14. The Matrix Category Configuration Screen in Provisioning*

A code sample for the XML configuration is shown in the following for the "impactOfLoss" category. Similar structures for each category would be placed in the ... areas of the XML sample:

```
<?xml version="1.0" encoding="UTF-8"?>
<!DOCTYPE Classifier SYSTEM "classifier_1_0.dtd">
<Classifier>
...
   <Category id="impactOfLoss" name="Impact of Loss">
    <label lang="ar_SA" value="تأثير الخسارة."/>
    <label lang="de_DE" value="Verlustfolgen"/>
    <label lang="es_ES" value="Impacto de pérdida"/>
    <label lang="fr_FR" value="Impact de la perte"/>
    <label lang="ja_JP" value="喪失の影響"/>
    <label lang="ko_KR" value="손실의 영향"/>
    <label lang="pt_BR" value="Impacto da perda"/>
    <label lang="ru_RU" value="Последствия потери"/>
    <label lang="zh_CN" value="离职影响"/>
    <label lang="zh_TW" value="離職影響"/>
    <Level id="impactOfLoss01">
      <ExactEvaluator value="16734"/>
      <Icon alt="Low" title="Low" url="/ui/sm/img/icons/triangle_grey.gif">
        <label lang="ar_SA" value="تأثير منخفض."/>
```

```
      <label lang="de_DE" value="Niedrig"/>
      <label lang="en_GB" value="Low"/>
      <label lang="en_US" value="Low Impact"/>
      <label lang="es_ES" value="Baja"/>
      <label lang="fr_FR" value="Faible"/>
      <label lang="ja_JP" value="低"/>
      <label lang="ko_KR" value="낮음"/>
      <label lang="pt_BR" value="Baixa"/>
      <label lang="ru_RU" value="Низкий"/>
      <label lang="zh_CN" value="低"/>
      <label lang="zh_TW" value="低"/>
    </Icon>
  </Level>
  <Level id="impactOfLoss02">
    <ExactEvaluator value="16735"/>
    <Icon alt="Medium" title="Medium" url="/ui/sm/img/icons/triangle_
    yellow.gif">
      <label lang="ar_SA" value="،طسوتم ريثأت"/>
      <label lang="de_DE" value="Mittel"/>
      <label lang="en_GB" value="Medium"/>
      <label lang="en_US" value="Medium Impact"/>
      <label lang="es_ES" value="Media"/>
      <label lang="fr_FR" value="Moyen"/>
      <label lang="ja_JP" value="中"/>
      <label lang="ko_KR" value="중간"/>
      <label lang="pt_BR" value="Média"/>
      <label lang="ru_RU" value="Средний"/>
      <label lang="zh_CN" value="中"/>
      <label lang="zh_TW" value="中"/>
    </Icon>
  </Level>
  <Level id="impactOfLoss03">
    <ExactEvaluator value="16736"/>
    <Icon alt="High" title="High" url="/ui/sm/img/icons/triangle_red.
    gif">
```

```
        <label lang="ar_SA" value="عالية التأثير،"/>
        <label lang="de_DE" value="Mittel"/>
        <label lang="en_GB" value="High"/>
        <label lang="en_US" value="High Impact"/>
        <label lang="es_ES" value="Alta"/>
        <label lang="fr_FR" value="Élevé"/>
        <label lang="ja_JP" value="高"/>
        <label lang="ko_KR" value="높음"/>
        <label lang="pt_BR" value="Alta"/>
        <label lang="ru_RU" value="Высокий"/>
        <label lang="zh_CN" value="高"/>
        <label lang="zh_TW" value="高"/>
      </Icon>
    </Level>
  </Category>
...
 </Classifier>
```

## Matrix Grid Retirement Eligibility Configuration Screen

Some organizations may like for the retirement eligibility icon to appear automatically if someone is approaching retirement. This can be very helpful during succession planning discussions to help identify employees who may be leaving soon due to retirement.

---

**Note** End users cannot manually edit this field. It will only turn on automatically based on the Date of Birth and Hire Date fields. Please ensure these fields are included in Talent Profile prior to configuration. For more information, see Volume 1, Chapter 2.

---

To configure the Retirement Eligibility feature, follow these steps:

1. Ensure the retirement eligibility icon has been configured (see the "Matrix Grid Icon Configuration Screen" section in this chapter) and the Date of Birth and Hire Date fields have been included in Talent Profile.

2. Type and select "Matrix Grid Reports: Retirement Eligibility" in the search bar.

3. The Retirement Eligibility Settings screen will appear as shown in Figure 5-15.

**Retirement Eligibility Settings**

Retirement Eligibility Settings

| | | | | |
|---|---|---|---|---|
| Age: | 60 | Year | 0 | Month |
| OR | | | | |
| Tenure: | 25 | Year | 0 | Month |
| | | | Save | Cancel |

***Figure 5-15.*** *The Retirement Eligibility Settings Configuration Screen*

4. Enter the age threshold and the tenure threshold and select "and" or "or" in the dropdown as per your organization's policy. Selecting "and" will require both criteria to be met before the icon appears, whereas "or" will show the icon if either condition is met.

5. Click "Save."

## Running and Using the Matrix Grid Reports

Now that we've completed configuring the matrix grid, it is time to see it in action! In the introduction, we mentioned several places where the matrix grid can display. The main reports where we can see matrix grid information are the "Performance-Potential Matrix" and the "How vs. What Matrix."

**Note** Remember that the standard names of these reports can be changed based on your configurations! We will reference the standard names in the following navigation steps. In the event you changed the names, click the custom name you have identified.

Using the example of our model company, these reports are where the regional president and the current SVP of Sales of the facility could look to find high potentials in their teams in the event they do not already have successors identified for the vacant SVP of Sales position or to simply check if their current nominations are still performing well at a high rate of potential.

## Prerequisites for Running the Reports

Aside from the configurations already covered in this chapter, there are a couple of additional configurations that may need to be performed.

1. Ensure that divisions, departments, and locations are loaded for your company. In a basic talent implementation, these are automatically populated as you load the fields in the user data file.
2. If you would like to use any dynamic groups, be sure to add the groups prior to attempting to run the report. To do so, click the picture icon for the logged-in user and choose "Settings." On the menu to the left, choose Groups. Click "Create New Group" to add a group. An example is shown in Figure 5-16.

Settings

- Password
- Start Page
- Sub Tab Configuration
- Notifications
- Change Language
- Compensation Number Format
- Forms
- Accessibility Settings
- Proxy
- Groups
- Mobile
- Privacy Statements
- Outlook

Groups

Create New Group   Import Static Groups   Items per page 50   Page 1 of 1

| Group Name | Static or Dynamic | Membership | Show/Hide ↓ | Last Modified | Acti |
|---|---|---|---|---|---|
| Sandbox Germany | Dynamic | 35 | ✓ | 2019-06-13 | |
| Edit Candidate Profile Group - DO NOT CHANGE NAME | Dynamic | 9 | ✓ | 2018-03-01 | |
| Mentees | Dynamic | 34 | ✓ | 2017-01-09 | |
| Mentors | Dynamic | 14 | ✓ | 2017-01-09 | |
| Comp Philippines Group | Dynamic | 10 | ✓ | 2015-10-20 | |
| Comp Taiwan Group | Dynamic | 12 | ✓ | 2015-10-20 | |
| Comp Australia Group | Dynamic | 61 | ✓ | 2015-10-20 | |
| Comp Germany Group | Dynamic | 122 | ✓ | 2015-10-20 | |
| Comp France Group | Dynamic | 65 | ✓ | 2015-10-20 | |

***Figure 5-16.*** *The Dynamic Groups Screen*

# Running the Reports

To run either report, follow these steps:

1. Navigate to Succession ➤ Performance-Potential Matrix or Succession ➤ How vs. What Matrix.

2. The screen shown in Figure 5-17 will load for the report you selected.

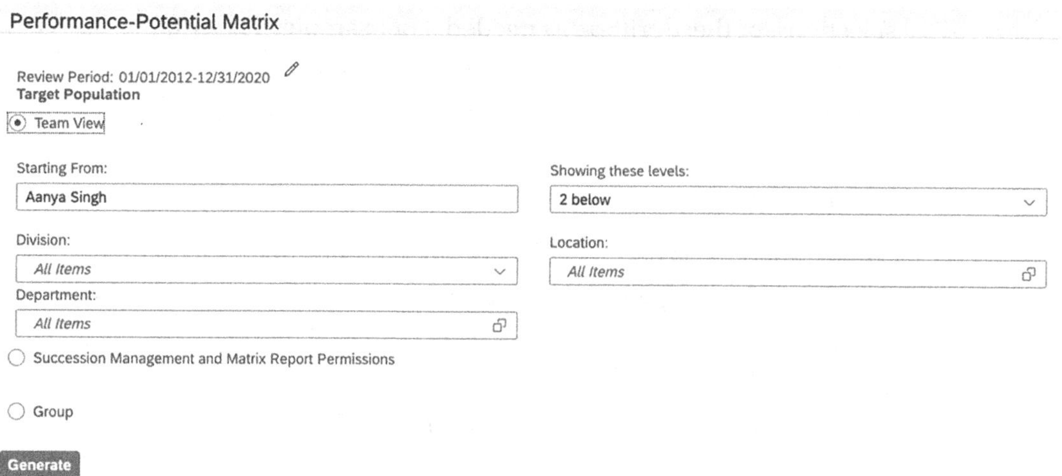


***Figure 5-17.*** *The Performance-Potential Matrix Report*

3. Select the review period date range by clicking the pencil icon. If you choose multiple years, remember the settings you chose during configuration will affect whether the latest rating or the average is shown as a result.

4. Next, select the target population. First, choose either Team View, Succession Management and Matrix Report Permissions, or Group from the radio button:

    a. Team View: Use this option to show team members starting from a specific manager and down. Fill in options for how many levels below the manager to include in the selection criteria as well as divisions and departments and locations to choose from (division, department, and location configuration is performed as part of platform configuration). For example, if our regional president had access to look for high-performing employees across all regions within operations, he could choose the CEO in the Starting From field, all levels, and choose the entire operations division.

    b. Succession Management and Matrix Report Permissions: This option will give you all results for which you have permission to view (see the "Permissions" section earlier in this chapter). The only extra selection criteria that appear when this option is selected are division, department, and location. Enter selections for these criteria as needed. For example, if an HR admin is assisting our regional president in finding high-performance and high-potential candidates and has access to the entire company, they may choose this option and select the operations division to refine criteria.

    c. Group: This option lists all of the dynamic groups that have been made in the system. You cannot add dynamic groups here; only select what has already been created. Dynamic groups can be helpful for making ad hoc groupings, for example, if an HR admin keeps track of certain users that cannot be defined by normal selection criteria by earmarking them using a dynamic group.

5. After entering your selection criteria, click "Generate" to run the report.

---

**Note** Often, the matrix grid report will return no results or confusing results. We recommend following these steps to help troubleshoot:

1. *Check the date for which the report is being run – are you running for the current year or last year?*
2. *In the configuration screen, make sure the data sources are correct and that you have data in the employee profile and processes you have chosen in the configuration within the year chosen in the selection criteria for the report.*
3. *Check that you have appropriate role-based permissions to view the people you are trying to view in the selection criteria.*
4. *Is the "All data sources" data source selected in the matrix grid report configuration screen? Or is the "Use average of all found ratings, instead of latest" checked? This could explain why unexpected ratings are showing from other processes or averaging of ratings is occurring across multiple years.*

---

## Using the Reports

After following the instructions in the previous section to run the report, the report will show per your configurations as in Figure 5-18.

---

**Note** This is a read-only report. To edit the placement of a candidate, the data from the data source selected in the configuration must be edited. To edit data related to the icons that appear next to each employee, the Talent Profile data for the employee must be edited on the Talent Profile screen.

---

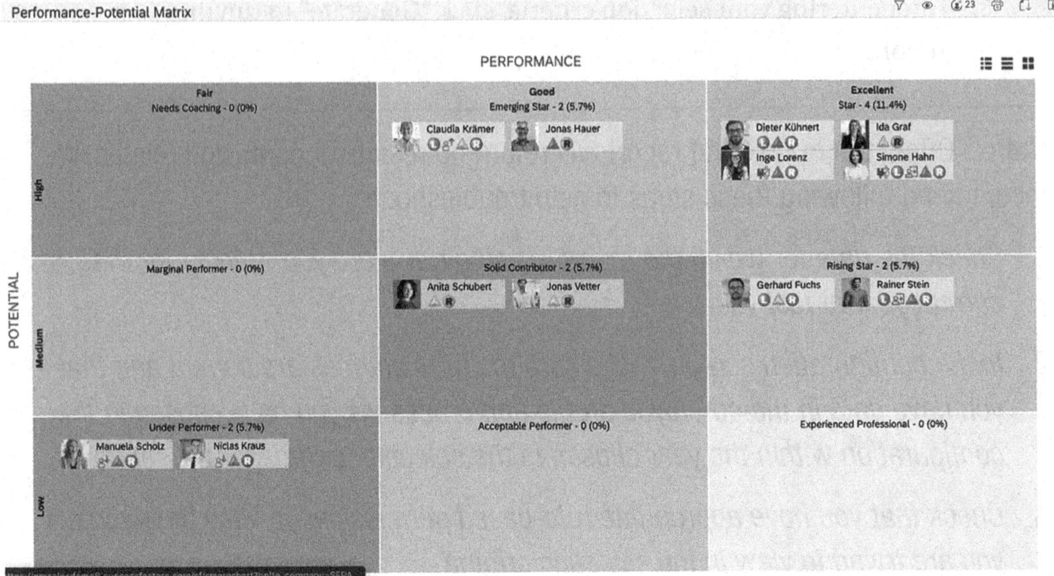


***Figure 5-18.** The Performance-Potential Matrix Report*

We will review the functionality of each icon starting from top to bottom and left to right as they appear in the preceding screen:

1. Click the filter icon to reopen the selection criteria screen covered in the last section.
2. Click the eye icon to open display options. This will add/remove the appearance of different icons configured per your icon configurations.
3. Click the person icon to open an area to the right of the matrix showing those employees within the selection criteria who are either too new to rate or unrated per your configurations.
4. Click the print icon to open a print preview screen where you can print the matrix.
5. Click the download icon to download an Excel report of the matrix and talent category details about each.
6. Click the "i" icon to open the link you may have added as part of your matrix configuration (this will not appear if no link was added).

7. Click the display both name and photo icon to show all employees with both a photo and information to the right of the photo (this is currently selected in the preceding figure).

8. Click the display name only icon to remove the photos and only show names. This option can be helpful to visualize more employees in each cell.

9. Click the display photo only icon to only show photos for the employees on the matrix. This option can also be helpful to visualize more employees in each cell.

10. Click a matrix cell to expand that cell and show more employees within it (if applicable).

11. Click an employee name/photo to show the talent card for that employee. We will cover talent card configuration in the next chapter. Multiple talent cards can be opened at once to allow for side-by-side comparison of employees.

# Talent Review Form

The Talent Review Form is a special type of stand-alone performance form designed to work with matrix grid information. It provides a form where performance and potential changes to employee data can be made dynamically using a matrix grid layout.

---

**Note** While the stand-alone Talent Review Form is included as part of Succession Management, it may not be right for all organizations. One of the most important decisions in designing your Talent Management and Succession process is deciding how talent data will be kept fresh – whether in a form such as this Talent Review Form, as part of a large comprehensive performance form, or simply with Talent Profile data. The most important fact to gain from this section is that the only way to have a potential rating included as part of a form is to include the Performance Potential Summary section in the form. Otherwise, the only data source for the matrix grid will be the potential field on the Employee Talent Profile. Similarly, in order for objective-competency ratings to appear in Talent Profile, the employee must have been rated on a form that includes the Objective Competency Summary section (though the section could be hidden).

---

For the sake of our model company example, the president and the SVP of Sales would have used a Talent Review Form (or alternate comprehensive performance form and/or calibration method) for assigning 9-box placement to potential successors as part of an annual review process. This way, the talent data is refreshed in the system on a regular basis and at the ready for when a succession nomination or movement needs to take place.

## Prerequisites for Configuring the Talent Review Form

Since the Talent Review Form runs on the Performance module, the required prerequisite configurations are the same. Please see Volume 1, Chapters 6 and 7 for these prerequisites.

Unlike other performance forms, the Talent Review Form must also have the matrix grid configurations completed prior to use. This is because the form will use the rating scales, defined axis configurations, cell colors, and labels from the configurations.

## Configuring the Talent Review Form

Like a performance form, the Talent Review Form is configured in the Manage Templates screen. Follow these steps to configure the form:

---

**Note** Often the Talent Review Form is not already available in a customer instance or SuccessStore. In this event, download a copy from a demo system from Provisioning and upload via Provisioning in the target instance. Alternatively, you can simply create one from scratch by creating a performance form and adding a Performance Potential Summary section or Goal Competency Summary section depending on the type of matrix you would like to edit. These sections could also be added to an annual performance review form to make one comprehensive form instead of a separate Talent Review Form.

---

1. Type and select "Manage Templates" in the search bar to access the Manage Templates screen.

2. Select the Talent Review Form by clicking its name.

---

**Note** The following sample form includes an Introduction section, a Performance Potential Summary section, and a comments section. Since the Introduction and comments sections are already covered in Volume 1, Chapter 7 on Performance Management, we only cover the Performance Potential Summary section here. The Goal Competency Summary section type provides the same configuration options, except using those fields as input instead and also providing an option to see calculated ratings from Goals and Competency sections, so it is not covered separately.

---

3. Click the Performance vs Potential section. The screen will load as shown in Figure 5-19.

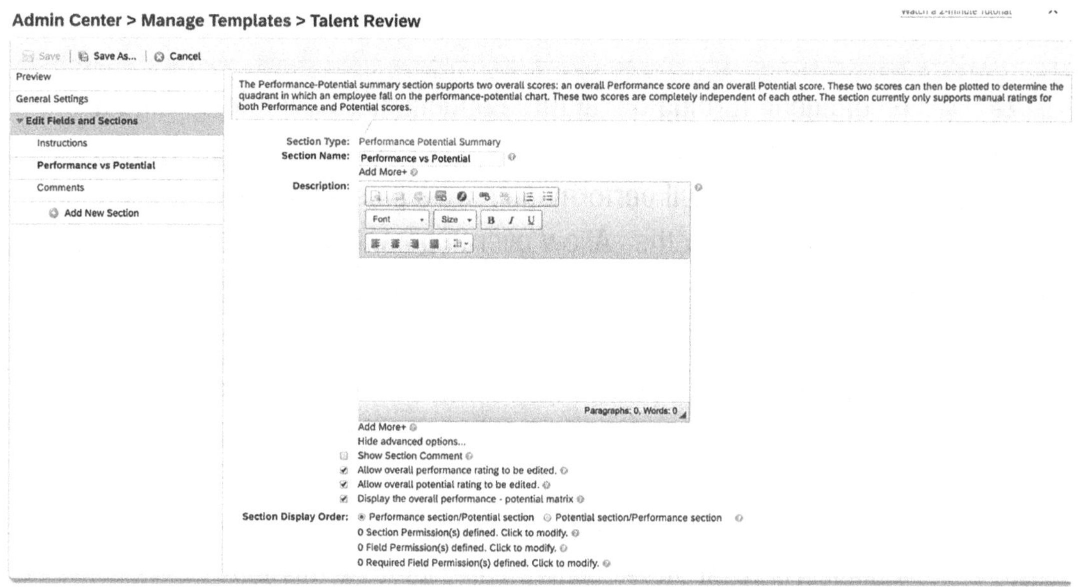


***Figure 5-19.*** *The Performance Potential Summary Section Configuration Within a Talent Review Form*

a. Enter a text value for the Section Name such as "Performance vs. Potential" or "9-Box."

b. Optionally, enter a description or instructions for the end user specific to the section.

c. Click "Show advanced options..." to see the items listed in the following.

d. The "Show Section Comment" box acts like all other such boxes in other sections where the evaluator can add comments specific to the section. Select this box if you wish to make these comments available

e. Check the "Allow overall performance rating to be edited," "Allow overall potential rating to be edited," "Display the overall performance - potential matrix" as needed. These will make the performance and potential editable on the form within this section and also provide a visual matrix grid where the subject employee can be dragged and dropped into the desired cell.

---

**Note** We recommend turning on all three options here if implementing a stand-alone Talent Review Form. If a comprehensive performance form is being used that includes a full performance cycle plus a potential rating, then you would likely only turn on the "Allow overall potential rating to be edited" and hide the other options.

---

f. The radio button for "Section Display Order" simply controls in which order the performance field and the potential field are shown above the matrix.

g. The remaining options are for permissions. See Volume 1, Chapters 6–10 for more details on how these permissions work.

# Launching and Managing the Talent Review Form Process

The Talent Review Form must be assigned a route map and be launched and managed like any other performance form. See Volume 1, Chapters 6–10 for detailed instructions on how to create and associate a route map, launch a form, and manage the process. You may also want to include a calibration session at the end of such a route map. You can reference Volume 1, Chapters 14 and 15 for details on setting up a calibration session.

# Using the Talent Review Form as an End User

After the Talent Review Form has been launched, it will follow the route map as will any other performance form. Once the form reaches the end user as part of a route map step, the form will appear in the user's Performance Inbox and on the home page "To-Do" section within the "Review Performance" tile.

Follow these steps to use the form:

1. Navigate to Performance to load the Performance Inbox and click the Talent Review Form for the employee. The form will load and you will be able to view the Performance vs. Potential section as shown in Figure 5-20.

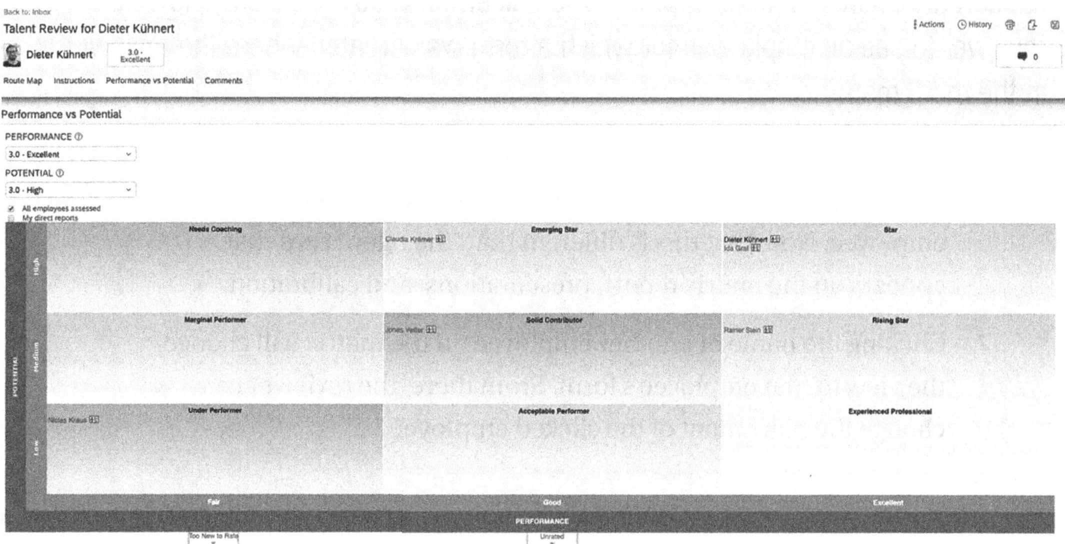


*Figure 5-20.* *Talent Review Form – Performance vs Potential Section*

2. Click the "?" icon next to either Performance or Potential to view the rating scale.
3. You can manipulate the employee's placement on the matrix grid by either dragging and dropping from one cell to another or by entering values in the Performance and Potential dropdowns. Select values in the dropdowns first to place the employee, and then try dragging and dropping to change the ratings.
4. The "Too New to Rate" and "Unrated" boxes show at the bottom - you can drag and drop the employee in and out of these areas as well. Make sure to click the down arrow to expand the boxes first.
5. The reviewer also has the option to only view the one employee being reviewed, all employees who have been assessed, or just direct reports. Switch between these three modes by unchecking both boxes or checking one or the other (both checkboxes cannot be checked at the same time).

---

**Note** It is most useful for managers to use the "My direct reports" option. An HR admin may choose the "All employees assessed" since the employees they support are likely not direct reports. The "All employees assessed" allows the reviewer to see all employees for which a form was created where the reviewer is in the route map.

---

6. Clicking the business card icon will open up the biz card for that employee. Note that this is different than the talent card that appears on the matrix report, presentations, and calibration.
7. Clicking the name of another employee on the matrix will change the view to that employee's form. From there, the reviewer can change the placement of the clicked employee.

**Note** This feature of immediately switching forms can become a bit confusing for end users. Be sure to cover this in your change management/training sessions! The name and the picture of the employee being edited will switch at the top of the form to cue the reviewer as to whose form they are on.

8. When you are finished with your ratings, click "Finalize Form" to move to the next step in the route map for the employee being rated.

You've now completed reviewing the employee! Data will now appear in the matrix grid report for this employee (given that this form is included as your data source and this current date is included in your selection criteria). If you have chosen not to include in-progress forms, then you must make sure the route map is completed prior to results showing up in the report.

## Optional Calibration Step

We'd also like to touch on Calibration at this point as well. Some organizations treat these calibration sessions as the finalization of their matrix grid placements in the process. In this scenario, you would configure your route map so that subsequent to each manager reviewing their employees, there is a calibration step where groups of managers and/or other participants come together to collectively attend a calibration session and agree on finalized placement of the individuals. In this scenario, the ratings the managers entered for performance and potential and/or goals and competencies could potentially be overridden by the calibration session.

In Volume 1, Chapters 14 and 15, we outlined all of the configuration options for calibration sessions which should guide you in setting up the Talent Review Form (or a large performance form that includes both performance and potential and/or objectives and competencies) as a data source within the calibration session. We urge you to keep in mind that calibration sessions can also be used to decide on values for the Talent Profile/Succession Data Model fields that appear through Succession Management as well (we will cover these in more detail as the next chapters progress). Thus, it is worth mentioning that Calibration can be used as a comprehensive tool for conducting a talent review than spans beyond just applying a bell curve to performance ratings! We have found these additional capabilities of Calibration to be very useful in designing a talent review process with real-life companies.

# Conclusion

At this point in reading both volumes of the book, you have enough information to configure the Performance Potential Summary and Objective Competency Summary sections on a stand-alone Talent Review Form or comprehensive performance form that includes the Performance Potential Summary section as one of many sections in an annual performance cycle. This section should help you understand how data is populated into the matrix grid report and appears in other features of the Succession Management module we will be covering in the next two chapters.

CHAPTER 6

# Core Succession Management

In the last chapter, we focused on the 9-box and Talent Review Form. These functionalities provided us basic information about who in the organization we might want to consider for succession planning. Now we focus on the core functionality of Succession Management: nominating employees to positions. We will start with the basic configuration of talent cards which are found throughout the module. We will then jump into configuring nominations which is important as it will be used throughout the module. After that, we can put the nomination setup to use with nominating employees as covered in the "Succession Org Chart" section.

## Talent Cards

Talent cards are configurable popups that provide additional talent details on employees. They are configurable so that information most relevant to your organization is displayed. There are multiple places where talent cards appear: the Succession Org Chart, the Lineage Chart, the Position Tile View, MDF Talent Pools, the matrix grid report, Calibration, and Presentations. This section will teach you how to configure the talent cards and view them as an end user.

## Prerequisites for Configuring Talent Cards

In order to configure talent cards, you will first need permission:

1. Type and select "Manage Permission Roles" in the search bar.
2. When the screen loads, click the role you wish to modify. Then click "Permission...:"




S. Traynor et al., *SAP SuccessFactors Talent: Volume 2*, https://doi.org/10.1007/978-1-4842-6995-4_6

3. The "Manage Talent Card Configuration" permission can be found under the Manage Talent Card section of the permission settings as seen in Figure 6-1. Click "Done."

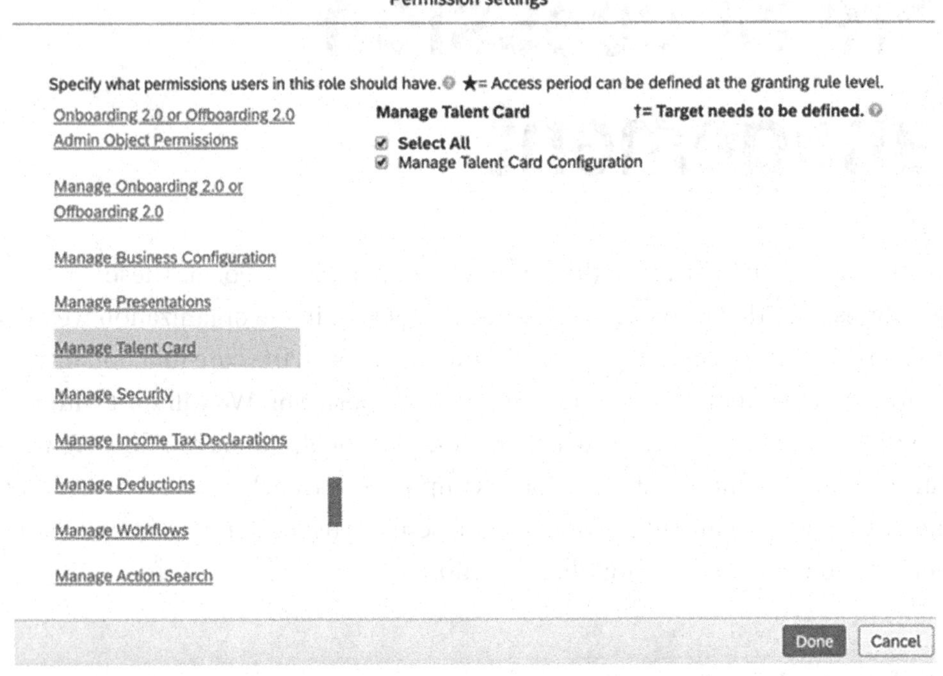


***Figure 6-1.*** *Manage Talent Card Configuration Permission*

# Configuring Talent Cards

To configure the talent cards, follow these configuration steps:

1. Access the Manage Talent Cards configuration screen by typing and selecting "Manage Talent Cards" in the search bar. You will see the screen as shown in Figure 6-2.

Admin Center > **Manage Talent Cards**

| Talent Card | Description | Date Modified |
|---|---|---|
| Succession Talent Card | Customize the talent card for position tile view. | 04/13/2017 |
| Calibration Talent Card | Customize the talent card in calibration new 9-Box. | 09/03/2015 |
| Presentations Talent Card | Customize the talent card for people in org-chart and 9 box matrix. | 09/03/2015 |

***Figure 6-2.*** *Manage Talent Cards Configuration Screen*

**Note** You will see that there are in fact three talent cards that can be configured. The configuration options on each of these screens are the same, so we will only cover the Succession Talent Card configuration. The Succession Talent Card configuration will appear for talent cards in the Succession Org Chart, the Lineage Chart, the Position Tile View, MDF Talent Pools, and the matrix grid report. Calibration Talent Card will show in calibration sessions only. Presentations Talent Card will show within presentations only. We recommend configuring all three types consistent with one another unless differences are specifically requested by senior leadership for a presentation or calibration sessions.

2. Click Succession Talent Card to begin configuration of the card. The screen in Figure 6-3 will appear.

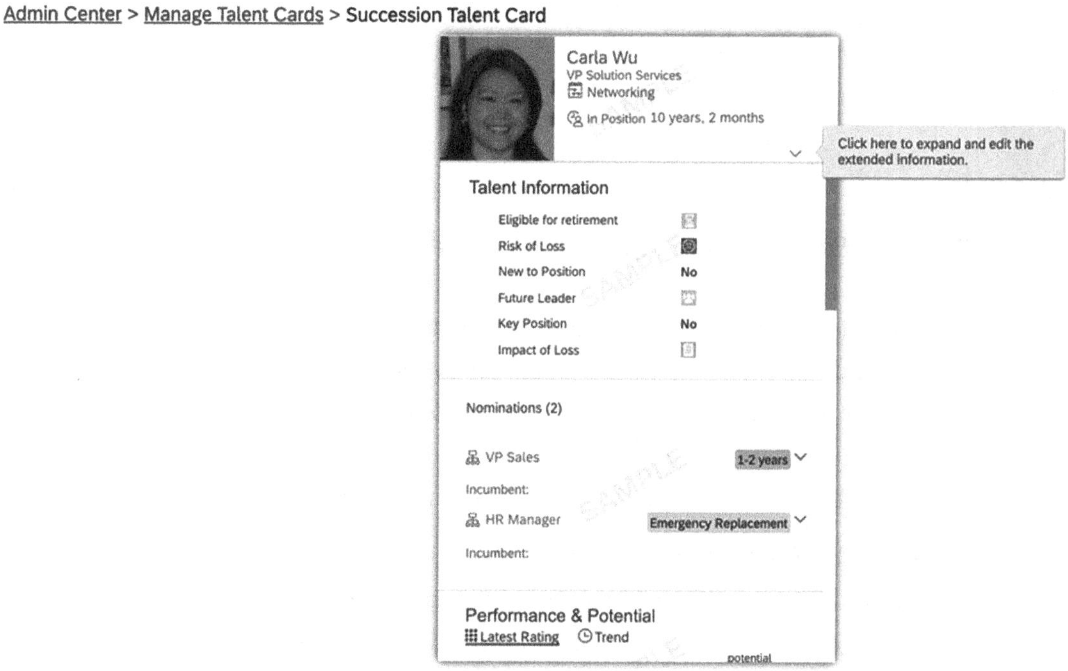

Admin Center > Manage Talent Cards > Succession Talent Card

***Figure 6-3.*** *Succession Talent Card Configuration Screen*

3. Click the down arrow to expand and edit the extended information area. Then click "Edit." The area will appear as shown in Figure 6-4.

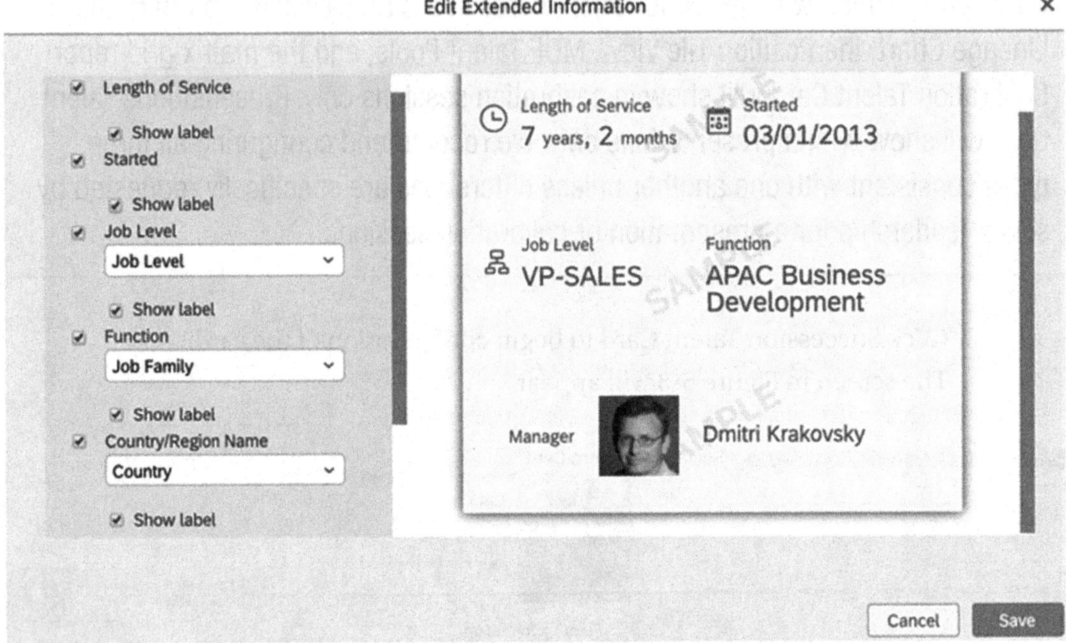


***Figure 6-4.** The Edit Extended Information Screen*

4. Check the box next to each area of the section you would like to show and whether or not you would like to show the label of that area. For Job Level, Function, and Country/Region Name, choose the talent field from the data model whose values you would like to associate with the area. When you are finished, click "Save."

5. Click "Edit" on the Talent Information section (or "Add a New Section" and select Talent Information if the section is not already showing on the talent card). The popup will load as shown in Figure 6-5. Click the checkboxes next to the fields you would like to show and choose the talent field from the data model whose values you would like to associate with that field.

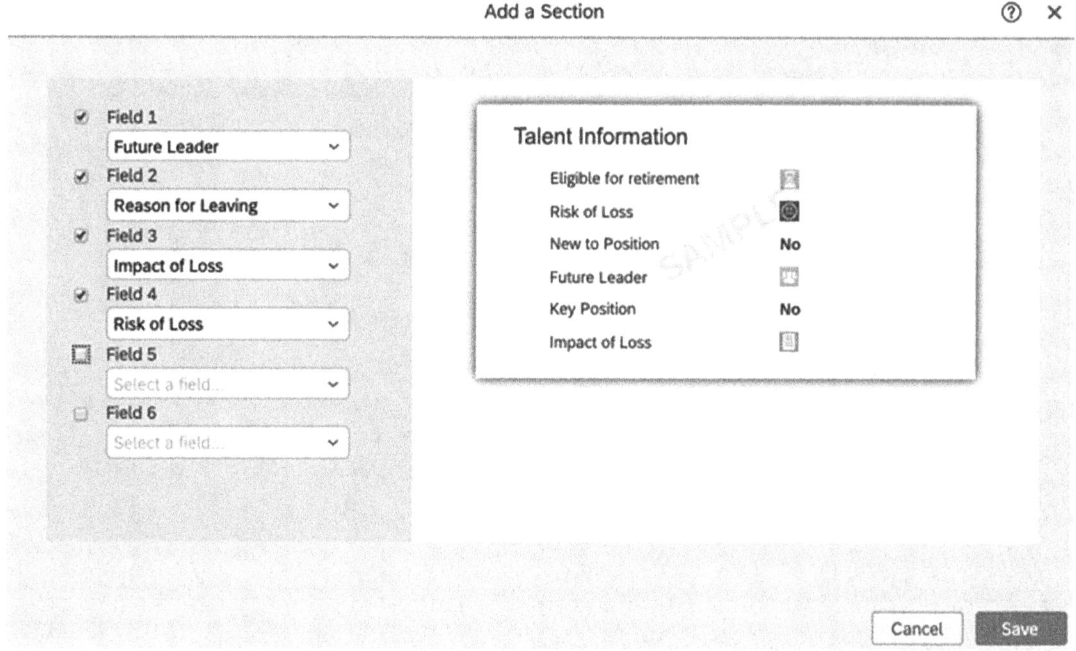


***Figure 6-5.*** *The Talent Information Section Screen*

6. Click "Edit" on the Performance & Potential section (or "Add a New Section" and select "Performance & Potential" if the section is not already showing on the talent card). The popup will load as shown in Figure 6-6. Choose whether you would like to use the employee profile ratings or the matrix grid configuration. Repeat this step for the Competency & Objective section as shown in Figure 6-7.

---

**Note** We recommend using the matrix grid admin configuration for consistency if you give managers access to the matrix grid report and have performed these configurations. The Employee Talent Profile should only be used in simple implementations where this is the only available data source. Since it is not recommended, we do not cover it in detail – for more information on the legacy Overview Scorecard Portlet mini 9-box in the Employee Talent Profile, see SAP note 2091458.

---

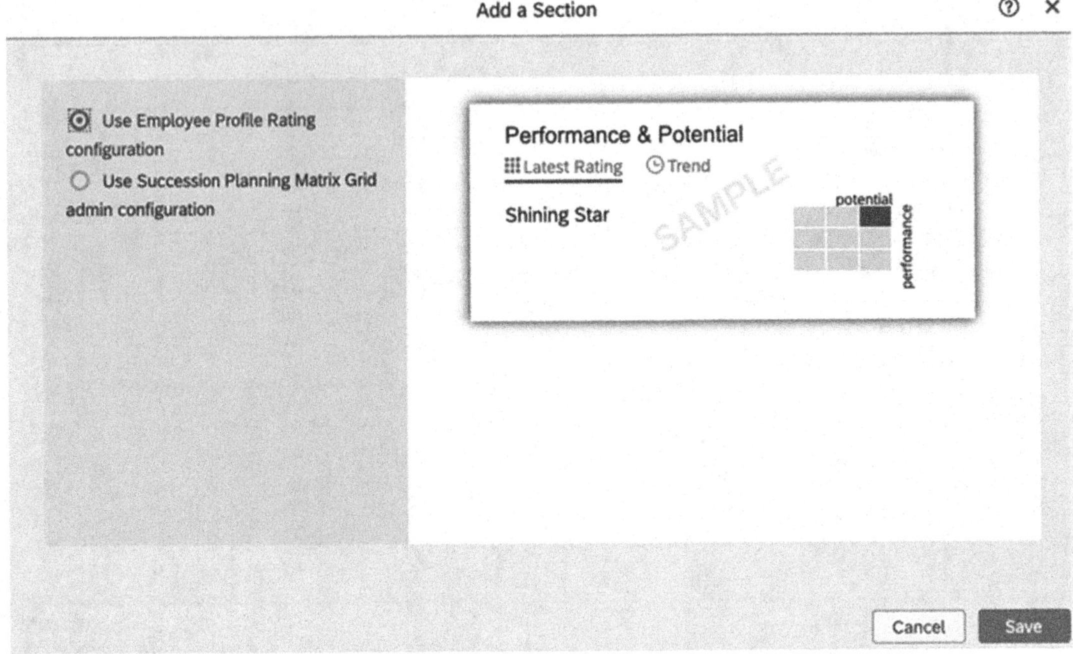


*Figure 6-6.* *The Performance & Potential Section Screen*

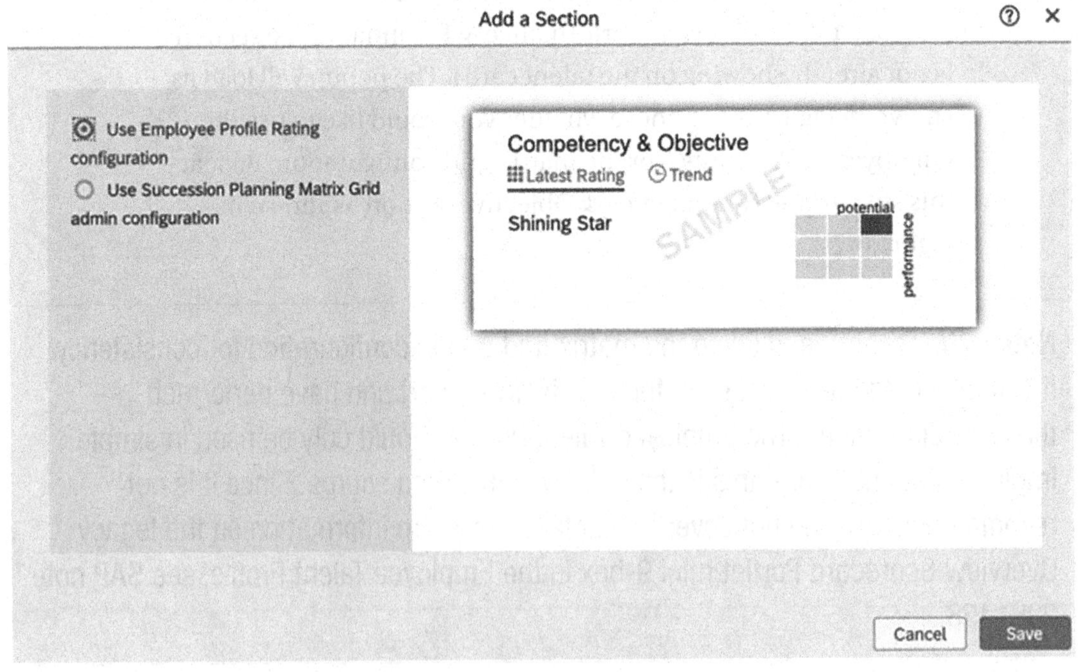


*Figure 6-7.* *The Competency & Objective Section Screen*

7. Add/edit any background elements from the data model you would like to include by clicking Edit for the section or clicking "Add a Section," then choosing "Custom Section," and selecting the specific background element as shown Figure 6-8. Choose the fields you would like to display. You are limited to two headers and two subtitles regardless of the structure of the background element defined in the data model.

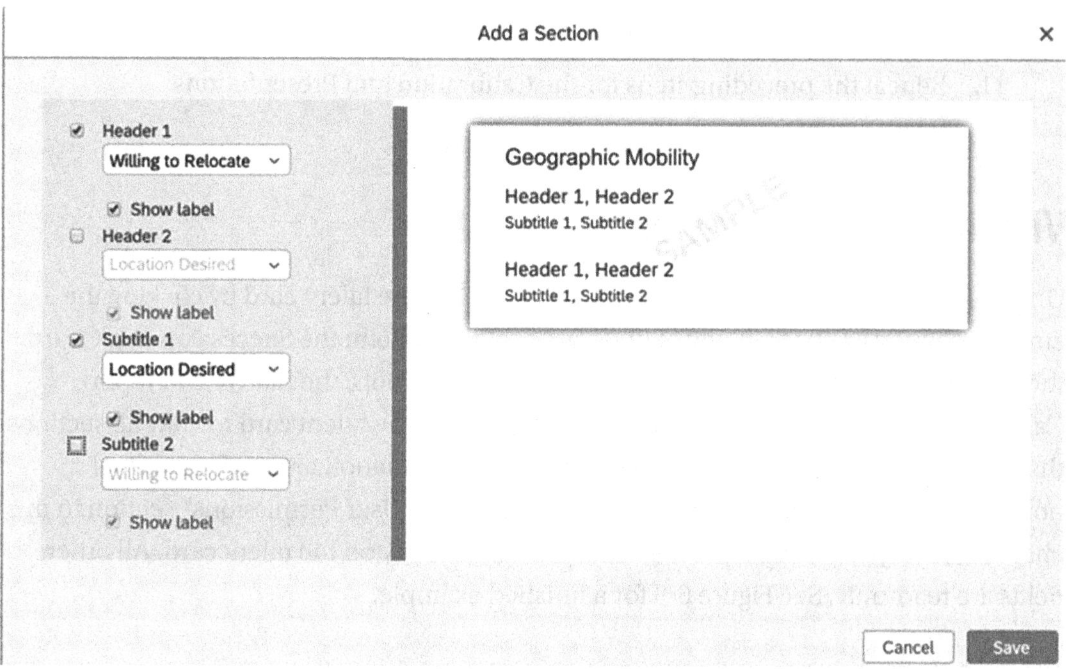


***Figure 6-8.** The Add/Edit a Custom Section/Background Element Screen*

8. Add a badges section if desired by clicking "Add a Section" and choosing badges and then clicking "Add." There are no configuration options for badges other than adding them. The section will display any badges awarded to the employee.

**Note** Badges can be a fun, free way to allow managers and other employees to reward one another for great work or positive attitudes. However, due to the open nature of the functionality, we find most companies to not use them.

9. Click "Move Up" or "Move Down" on any section to change the order as needed.
10. Click "Delete" to remove any section as needed.
11. Repeat the preceding steps for the Calibration and Presentations talent cards.

## Viewing Talent Cards as an End User

Once talent cards have been configured, you can view the talent card by clicking the employee name or photo in any of these areas of the system: the Succession Org Chart, the Lineage Chart, the Position Tile View, MDF Talent Pools, the matrix grid report, Calibration, and Presentations. You can scroll through the talent card to view all sections that have been configured. If you have succession nomination and/or Talent Pool nomination permissions assigned (see the "Set Up End User Permissions" section in this chapter), then you can add and edit nominations directly on the talent card. All other fields are read-only. See Figure 6-9 for a finished example.

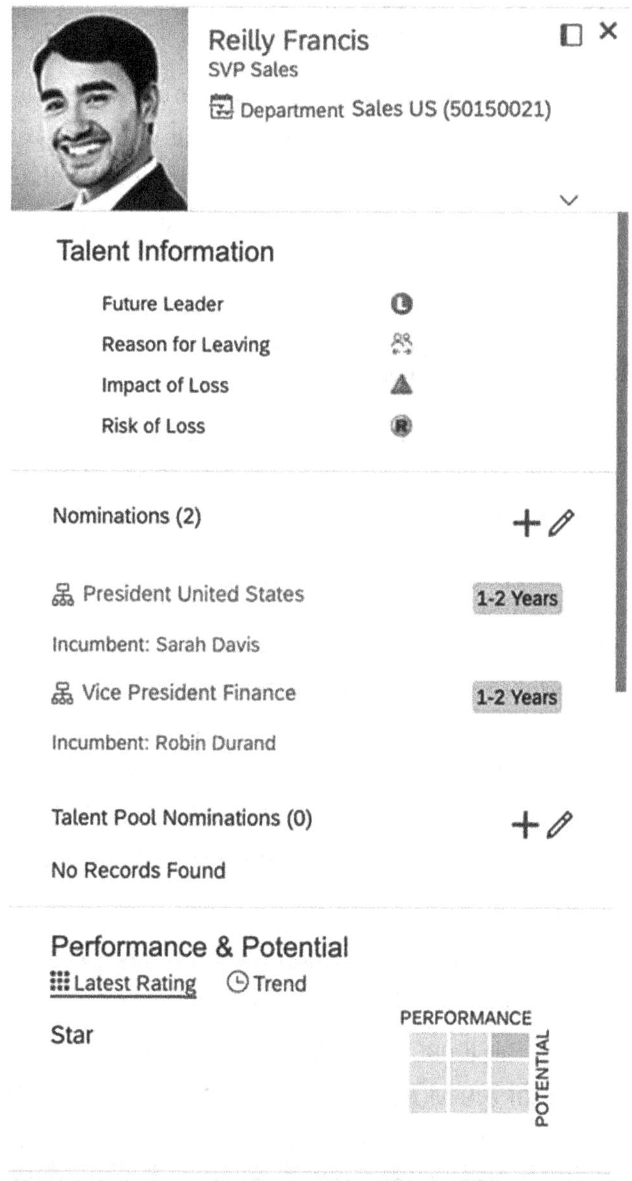


***Figure 6-9.** Example Talent Card*

Now that you understand how to configure and view the talent card, we can continue the example of our model company. Once the SVP of Sales and President have identified potential star candidates to succeed the SVP of Sales using the matrix grid reports, they can click the employee's name or picture to open the talent card. Using the talent card, they can view more information on the candidate and nominate the candidate immediately.

## Nomination Configuration

The main concept behind succession planning is to nominate specific individuals for specific positions and develop them into successors. This concept is central to the Succession Org Chart which we will cover in the next section. It is also important for Talent Pools. Thus, we now focus on setting up how nominations will work in the system across the features of succession planning.

## Understanding Nomination Methods

One of the most important decisions in succession planning configuration is choosing your nomination method. SuccessFactors allows you to choose between position-based and role-person-based nomination methods. We recommend MDF position-based nomination be used for organizations that have position data and practice position management. In brief, position management is the practice of separating individual employee data from their job-related information such as required skills, classifications, and so on down to the individual role level. The two are treated as separate data objects. A common way to think of position management is to treat the position as the "seat" and the employee as the one occupying the seat. The seat can be filled or vacant depending on if someone is in the seat. SAP SuccessFactors Employee Central as well as legacy on-premise SAP is typically implemented using position management.

---

**Note** Within the position-based nomination method, there is a legacy position nomination method as well as an MDF position–based method. Since there is not much sense in choosing the legacy position-based method as it does not take advantage of the power of the MDF, it is not covered. We also recommend the MDF position–based nomination method over the role-based method wherever possible. The role-person–based nomination method should really only be chosen when your organization has no position data available at all. Even then, however, SAP offers a special MDF Position Sync feature that attempts to create position hierarchy based on the employee hierarchy. We will not cover this feature in detail as it is rarely used and the requisite lengthy explanation will distract you, the reader, from the more common scenarios.

---

The role-person-based nomination method (also known as incumbent-based) accommodates organizations that are transitioning to SuccessFactors and have not yet achieved the level of position data needed for position-based nomination. In this method, you are essentially nominating people to replace a specific employee, rather than the position that person occupies. The nominations are really set up against a person-job code relationship, and if the job code is changed, the nomination data is dropped.

## Choose a Nomination Method and Activate Reporting

Now that we have a basic understanding of what the different nomination methods mean, let's go ahead and set one up in the system so we can get started!

1. Log into Provisioning for your organization and click "Company Settings."
2. Scroll down to "Succession nomination method" and choose your method as shown in Figure 6-10.
3. Check the box next to "Use formless nomination approval workflow" as seen in Figure 6-10 (note only the role-person nomination method can use the form-based nomination approval workflow). Also check the box next to "Ultra Organization Chart" (not pictured)
4. Click "Save."

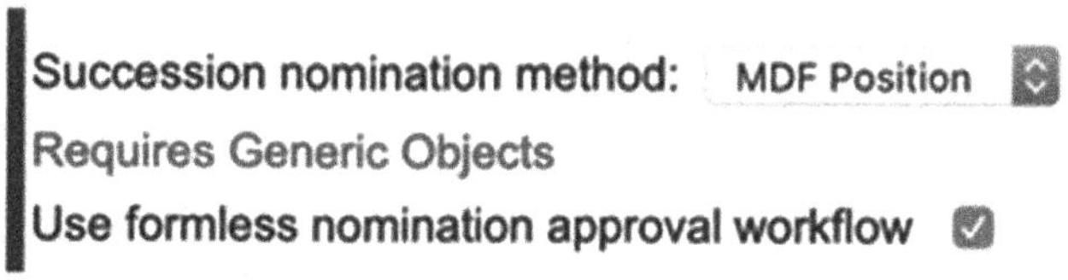

Succession nomination method: MDF Position
Requires Generic Objects
Use formless nomination approval workflow

***Figure 6-10.*** *Succession Nomination Method Selection in Provisioning*

---

**Note** You should also have the MDF activated as well as role-based permissions prior to choosing MDF positions. You may also want to turn on reporting at this point as well since it is specific to the nomination method. Select the "Succession (MDF Position based nominations)," "Succession History (MDF Position based nominations)," and "Inclusive Succession (MDF Position based nominations)" checkboxes. We do not cover reporting in detail in this chapter since the ad hoc reporting and dashboard concepts are consistent with other modules. We simply need to turn on the access to the data.

## Readiness Rating Scale

The readiness rating scale must be configured so that when nominating someone, the user can choose how ready the nominee is for the position. This is done similar to Performance Management. Follow these steps:

1. Type and select "Rating Scales" in the search bar.
2. Click the "Create New Rating Scale" button. The screen will appear as in Figure 6-11.
3. In the Name field, type exactly "Readiness" (the name must always be Readiness for all implementations).
4. Choose the number of levels in your scale. Then enter a score, label, and description for each level of the scale and click "Save."

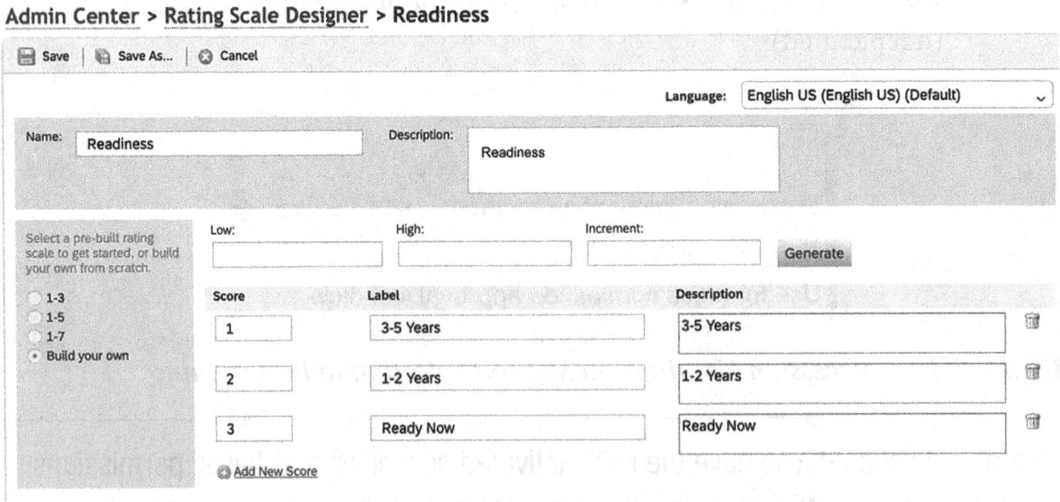

***Figure 6-11.*** *Readiness Rating Scale Configuration*

**Note** We recommend the lowest score be the least ready and highest be most ready. You will also need to define this in your Succession Org Chart XML, and the two must match EXACTLY. We will cover the org chart XML in the "Succession Org Chart" section.

## Nomination Setup Screen

Prior to using this screen, be sure to follow these steps to configure the nomination setup screen:

1. Type and select "Nomination Setup" in the search bar.
2. Select configuration options per Table 6-1.
3. Click "Save."

***Table 6-1.*** *Nomination Setup Screen Options*

| Option | Description |
|---|---|
| Hide Succession nomination history entries prior to this date (leave blank to show all entries) | We recommend leaving this blank so that all history shows. If you have cutoff periods in your review cycle where data has become stale or have transitioned to a new process, this tool can come in handy to hide old data that is no longer relevant. |
| Enable ranking of successors | By checking this box, whenever a successor is nominated, the system will allow the user to also enter a ranking number which will serve as a secondary sort for the successors on a position. |
| Allow ranking across readiness | Checking this box will allow users to sort by ranking first rather than readiness first. This box only appears if the preceding box is checked. |

(*continued*)

***Table 6-1.*** *(continued)*

| Option | Description |
|---|---|
| Allow reports to launch future role competency assessments, if they have the appropriate form creation privileges. | If your organization uses competency assessments, you can click this box to allow. Users will see an "Evaluate Readiness" option when choosing a readiness level. If this box is checked, you will need to pick a form template identifying the readiness template for each configured locale. |
| Filter Current Nominations portlet data by Succession Planning permissions | By default, if you have permission to view a person, you will see all nominations to the position. If this checkbox is checked, the user will only have permission to view nominations for positions to which the user also has succession planning permissions. |
| Show the # of hidden nominations in Current Nominations portlet | If the preceding checkbox is checked, this checkbox will appear. When checked, it will give users a warning popup telling how many positions were hidden due to security restrictions. |
| Hide pending nominations on the scorecard portlets from all users | If you have chosen to segregate nominations and approvals, this checkbox would hide the nominations that have not yet been approved when users view the employee scorecard on Talent Profile. |
| Allow succession planners with recruiting candidate search permissions to nominate external candidates | If you have implemented recruiting and users have permission to perform recruiting candidate searches, checking this box would allow them to perform an external candidate search based on the recruiting external candidate database for nomination. |
| Automatically remove nominated successor if that user becomes incumbent | If you are using MDF positions, you can check this option to have the nomination hidden when the successor occupies the position. The nomination will still be present but recorded as a "succeed" that is only not shown on the Succession Org Chart so that any history reporting is not removed. When you check the checkbox, the system will not retroactively hide nominees. |

*(continued)*

*Table 6-1.* (*continued*)

| Option | Description |
| --- | --- |
| Apply target population to Talent Pool Nominations Permissions | If you check this box, you will need to define target permissions for Talent Pool nomination permissions. We go into more details on this setting in the Talent Pools section later in this chapter. |
| In "Add Nomination" dialog, show separate fields for "Position" search and "Incumbent" search (recommended for better performance with extremely large number of users and positions) | If you check this box, users searching for nominees will get a popup box with a radio that lets them choose between positions or nominees. This is recommended for companies with large numbers of positions who are experiencing slowness in nomination searches without this feature. Note that this can only be used for the MDF position nomination method. |

Now that our nominations are set up, we'll be able to look in detail at the features that use nominations, starting with the Succession Org Chart which is the most common way nominations are created.

# Succession Org Chart

Now that we've set up the ability to perform nominations, let's dig into how to nominate some of those talented people into specific positions. The Succession Org Chart allows users to view talent and nomination information in the form of a position-based organizational chart. We like to think of the Succession Org Chart as the pinnacle of SuccessFactors Talent. It gives a sort of bird's-eye view of your organization and where each position and person are in terms of succession planning at whatever levels you choose. It is the feature that raises the most eyebrows from executives in sales demonstrations - and for good reason. The visualizations it renders are the culmination of a lot of data and a lot of hard work keeping that data up to date! However, we like to think SAP SuccessFactors makes that work a bit easier and fun. Let's take a more detailed look!

## Prerequisites for Configuring and Using the Succession Org Chart

Before we can configure or use the org chart, we need to make sure we have some key system settings in place as well as permissions. Let's take a look at them in the following.

### Activate Org Chart

Now that we have a basic understanding of what the different nomination methods mean, let's go ahead and set one up in the system so we can get started!

1. Log into Provisioning for your organization and click "Company Settings."
2. Scroll down to "Succession nomination method" and choose your method.
3. Check the box next to "Ultra Organization Chart."
4. Click "Save."

---

**Note** The "Ultra Organization Chart" applies to all org charts in the system, not just Succession. You can choose to turn off the Succession Org Chart feature by checking the box next to "Turn off Succession Organization Chart."

---

### Set Up MDF Position Object and Grant Configuration Permissions

If you are using the MDF position-based nomination method, it is a good idea to set up your position data. The permissions and process for setting up the MDF position in the system are covered in the next chapter in the "Position Tile View" section. We intentionally split the configuration between these two sections to show how the same data can be viewed in different ways and the same config affects the two areas of the system similarly.

## Load MDF Position Data

Now that our prerequisites are complete and the MDF object has been defined, we can begin loading any legacy position data you may have. Follow these steps to import this data:

1. Type and select "Import and Export Data" in the search bar.
2. In the "Select action to perform" field, select "Download Template."
3. In the "Select Generic Object" field, choose "Position."
4. Reference Table 6-2 for the other field choices.

***Table 6-2.*** *MDF Import Template Option Descriptions*

| Option | Description |
|---|---|
| Include Dependencies | Choosing "Yes" will download a zip file with .csv templates for the parent object and any child objects per the MDF object definition. The zip file would then have to be uploaded via zip file option on the import screen as well. Choosing "No" will download just one .csv file for the position object. |
| Include Immutable IDs | Will download the entity id and record id if "Yes" is chosen. |
| Exclude Reference Objects | Includes or excludes reference object .csv templates in the .zip file if "No" or "Yes" is chosen, respectively. |
| Key Preference | Selecting "Business Key" will use the set of fields the MDF uses to create a unique identifier. "External Code" can be a manually set key based off of this one entered field. |
| Hide External Code | Will hide this field from the downloaded .csv file. Note this cannot be selected if your key preference is set to "External Code." |
| Identity type | Defines whether "User ID" or "Assignment ID" is used to reference employee identity. The assignment ID is a newer concept introduced for Employee Central to simplify global assignments. If you have not implemented Employee Central, then use user ID. |

5. Click "Download."
6. Open the file in an editor and add your legacy data.
7. In the "Select action to perform" field, select "Import Data."
8. In "Select Generic Object," choose "Position."
9. Click "Choose File" and find the file on your local computer.
10. Reference Table 6-3 for all other field options.

***Table 6-3.*** *MDF Import Option Descriptions*

| Option | Description |
|---|---|
| File Encoding | Refers to the character encoding on the file. Note when you save your local .csv file using your editor, but sure to select this here as well. We recommend UTF-8 as it handles international languages the best. |
| Purge Type | "Incremental Load" will only add new objects or replace old. "Full Purge" will delete any existing objects that do not exist in the upload. |
| Suppress Redundant Date-Effective Records | Choose "Yes" or "No"; we recommend "Yes" so there is no redundant data in the system. |
| Key Preference | See the previous table and choose the same option as in the template export. |
| Use Locale Format | Defines formatting for dates and so on based on locale. If you choose "No," the sample date format of MM/DD/YYYY is shown at the bottom of the screen. If you choose "Yes," you will be prompted to choose the locale preference. |
| Enable Decimal Round Option | If you had a field for which you defined decimal rounding in the MDF, this option would enable the rounding. |
| Identity Type | See the previous table and enter the same value selected for the template. |

11. Click "Import."

The system will create a job to import the data. You can check the progress of the job and check the error logs by typing and selecting "Monitor Jobs" in the search bar.

# Configure the Succession Org Chart

Now that we have our basic system settings and permissions set up and our position data defined and loaded, it is time to define how our Succession data is structured and visualized. This is accomplished with the Succession Org Chart XML.

## Understanding Fields Within the Succession Org Chart XML and Ensuring Picklists Are Configured

Before you can understand how to edit the Succession Org Chart XML, there are some key concepts to cover. One of the more confusing concepts in Succession Management is understanding the mapping between Succession Data Model XML keys and the Succession Data Model. While usually these technical field names match in the XML, it is not always the case. For example, addressLine1 in the data model equates to the addr1 key in the Succession Org Chart XML, and lastReviewDate maps to last_review_date. These subtle differences can become very frustrating when creating your XML if you are not familiar with them. In addition, you can only visually display items that are not text in the latest version of Succession Org Chart (v12). To clarify these nuances, please reference Table 6-4.

***Table 6-4.*** *Data Model to Succession Org Chart Field Mapping and Field Types*

| Succession Data Model Field | Succession Org Chart Key | Field Type |
|---|---|---|
| addressLine1 | addr1 | text |
| addressLine2 | addr2 | text |
| benchStrength | benchStrength | picklist |
| businessPhone | biz_phone | text |
| businessSegment | businessSegment | picklist |
| Citizenship | citizenship | picklist |
| City | city | text |
| competency | competency | Follows matrix grid config using competency scale configured there |

(*continued*)

***Table 6-4.*** *(continued)*

| Succession Data Model Field | Succession Org Chart Key | Field Type |
|---|---|---|
| Country | country | text |
| custom01–custom15 | custom01–custom15 | text |
| sysOverallCustom1 | customrating1 | Follows matrix grid config using custom1 scale configured there |
| sysOverallCustom2 | customrating2 | Follows matrix grid config using custom2 scale configured there |
| dateOfBirth | dateOfBirth | text (date format) |
| dateOfPosition | dateOfPosition | text (date format) |
| Department | department | Automatic list from system departments loaded in user data file |
| Division | division | Automatic list from system divisions loaded in user data file |
| Email | email | text |
| empId | empId | text |
| Ethnicity | ethnicity | picklist |
| Fax | fax | text |
| firstName | firstName | text |
| Function | function | picklist |
| futureLeader | futureLeader | Boolean (true/false) |
| Gender | gender | Hardcoded enumeration as M, F |
| hireDate | hireDate | text (date format) |
| impactOfLoss | impactOfLoss | picklist |
| jobCode | jobCode | text |
| keyPosition | keyPosition | Boolean (true/false) |

*(continued)*

***Table 6-4.*** *(continued)*

| Succession Data Model Field | Succession Org Chart Key | Field Type |
|---|---|---|
| lastName | lastName | text |
| lastReviewDate | lastReviewDate | text (date format) |
| Level | level | picklist |
| location | location | Automatic list from system locations loaded in user data file |
| managerId | managerId | text |
| Married | married | Boolean (true/false) |
| matrix1label | matrix1label | text (from matrix grid configuration) |
| matrix2label | matrix2label | text (from matrix grid configuration) |
| matrixManaged | matrixManaged | Boolean (true/false) |
| Mi | mi | text |
| Minority | minority | Boolean (true/false) |
| Nationality | nationality | picklist |
| newToPosition | newToPosition | Boolean (true/false) |
| objective | objective | Follows matrix grid config using objective scale configured there |
| performance | performance | Follows matrix grid config using performance scale configured there |
| potential | potential | Follows matrix grid config using potential scale configured there |
| reasonForLeaving | reasonForLeaving | picklist |
| reviewFreq | review_freq | text |
| riskOfLoss | riskOfLoss | picklist |
| serviceDate | serviceDate | text |
| Ssn | ssn | text |

*(continued)*

***Table 6-4.*** *(continued)*

| Succession Data Model Field | Succession Org Chart Key | Field Type |
|---|---|---|
| State | state | text |
| talentPool | talentPool | picklist |
| Title | title | text |
| userId | userId | text |
| Username | username | text |
| zipCode | zip | text |

We recommend configuring picklists for each Succession Data Model field you choose to include in your org chart configuration labeled as such in the preceding table. This will ensure you can make icon associations for them in your XML configuration. You will need to type and select "Picklist Center" in the search bar to maintain these picklists prior to XML configuration. You have likely already done this as part of the Succession Data Model configuration outlined in Volume 1, Chapter 2. Picklists are important because you can associate picklists with color gradients and/or icons in your Succession Org Chart configuration.

## Editing the Succession Org Chart XML in Provisioning

Now that our picklists are set up, we can begin XML configuration! Follow these steps to access and edit the XML in Provisioning:

1. Log in to Provisioning and select your company.
2. Click "Edit Org Chart Configuration" under "Succession Management."
3. Make your edits to the XML (we recommend cutting and pasting an offline editor) to display the icons and gradients you would like to make available on your org chart.
4. Click "Save."

Figure 6-12 shows a sample XML file with each element collapsed to show the highest-level structure of the file. You can see each high-level element is either a gradientOption, iconSetOption, textOption, or keyPositionOption. Since we are using the latest Succession Org Chart (v12), the textOptions will be ignored (only in prior versions were these used). The only allowed gradientOptions are "readiness" and "benchStrength." All other non-text fields from the prior table can be configured as iconSetOptions. The keyPositionOption must be last in the order of the XML.

---

**Note** We recommend at a minimum configuring the XML to include the gradientOption for readiness and benchStrength as well as the keyPosition. The rest of the configuration is a matter of identifying which picklist and Boolean fields from the preceding table you wish to surface as icons and which icon goes with each field value.

---

```
<?xml version="1.0" encoding="UTF-8"?>
<OrgChartConfig>
  <view>regular</view>
  <maxwidth>1000</maxwidth>
  <gradientOption index="1" key="readiness"> ••• </gradientOption>
  <gradientOption index="2" key="benchStrength"> ••• </gradientOption>
  <iconSetOption index="3" key="riskOfLoss"> ••• </iconSetOption>
  <iconSetOption index="4" key="impactOfLoss"> ••• </iconSetOption>
  <iconSetOption index="5" key="reasonForLeaving"> ••• </iconSetOption>
  <iconSetOption index="6" key="futureLeader"> ••• </iconSetOption>
  <!-- ••• -->
  <iconSetOption index="9" key="minority"> ••• </iconSetOption>
  <iconSetOption index="10" key="newToPosition"> ••• </iconSetOption>
  <textOption index="1" key="performance"> ••• </textOption>
  <textOption index="2" key="potential"> ••• </textOption>
  <textOption index="3" key="matrix1label"> ••• </textOption>
  <textOption index="4" key="jobCode"> ••• </textOption>
  <textOption index="5" key="hireDate"> ••• </textOption>
  <textOption index="6" key="division"> ••• </textOption>
  <textOption index="7" key="department"> ••• </textOption>
  <textOption index="4" key="dateOfPosition"> ••• </textOption>
  <!-- ••• -->
  <keyPositionOption indicator="boolean" key=""> ••• </keyPositionOption>
  <SMFormId>4</SMFormId>
</OrgChartConfig>
```

*Figure 6-12.* *Collapsed View of the Succession Org Chart XML*

Figure 6-13 shows the end result of having each of these gradientOption and iconSetOption elements configured as well as the keyPositionOption. You can see that each icon is accounted for as an icon in the display options and that each gradient is an associated color. For example, the "SVP Sales" position is shown with a green mark to the left because it has an overall bench strength of "Ready Now" because there is a nominee with a readiness level of "Ready Now" for that position (also shown in green).

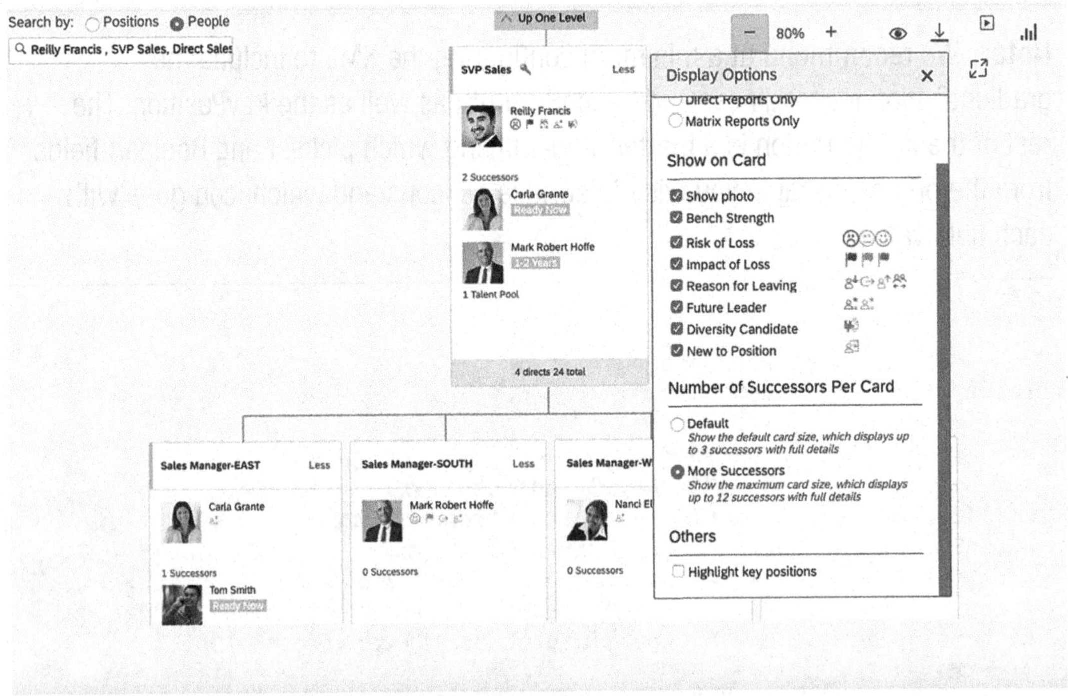


***Figure 6-13.** Resulting Visualization from the Succession Org Chart XML*

The next subsections illustrate examples of how to configure each type of highest-level XML elements shown in the preceding example. Follow Table 6-5 for guidance on how each element in the XML should be treated.

*Table 6-5. Succession Org Chart XML Element/Attribute Descriptions*

| Element/ Attribute | Description |
|---|---|
| index= | Unique incremental number. Use "1" for readiness and "2" for benchStrength. For the remaining icons, use an incremental number in the order in which you would like to see the icons appear. |
| key= | Fill in the Succession Org Chart field key from the mapping table provided in this chapter. |
| Type | Always "readiness" for readiness and "titleGradient" for benchStrength. Always "iconset" any iconOption. |
| Label | The default text label the user will see. See the example gradientOption in the next subsection for how to provide localized labels. |
| Value | Enter the picklist value. Make sure the corresponding value field has also been filled out in the Picklist Center screen. For readiness levels, the highest value is the most ready. Use "M" or "F" for gender or "true" or "false" for the Boolean fields. |
| Index | Used only for gradientOption. Single digit number that corresponds to a color table that SAP maintains here: `https://help.sap.com/viewer/55e0a1102eda4d83a5638a3526003bd0/2005/en-US/6dadf9f3ebc34b51a65102c6dba07081.html`. |
| image | Used only for iconOption. Identifies the icon image that will appear for each value of the field. SAP maintains a table of image values and corresponding images here: `https://help.sap.com/viewer/55e0a1102eda4d83a5638a3526003bd0/2005/en-US/523be343cf874f10a633c5089ac65117.html`. |

## Example gradientOption Element XML Configuration for readiness

```
<gradientOption index="1" key="readiness">
  <type>readiness</type>
  <label>Readiness</label>
  <gradientset>
    <gradient>
      <label>3-5 Years</label>
      <label lang="en_US">3-5 Years</label>
      <value>1.0</value>
```

```
        <index>3</index>
      </gradient>
      <gradient>
        <label>1-2 Years</label>
        <value>2.0</value>
        <index>2</index>
      </gradient>
      <gradient>
        <label>Ready Now</label>
        <value>3.0</value>
        <index>1</index>
      </gradient>
    </gradientset>
  </gradientOption>
```

---

**Note** In the preceding example, we include only one localized label for "3–5 Years" for the en_US locale for the sake of brevity. Repeat this pattern for each label and locale you wish to localize. This applies to gradientOption, iconOption, and keyPositionOption.

---

## Example iconOption Element XML Configuration for riskOfLoss

```
<iconSetOption index="3" key="riskOfLoss">
  <type>iconset</type>
  <label>Risk of Loss</label>
  <iconset>
    <icon>
      <image>sap_ui5_icon_RiskOfLoss01_high</image>
      <label>High</label>
      <value>3.0</value>
    </icon>
    <icon>
      <image>sap_ui5_icon_RiskOfLoss01_medium</image>
      <label>Medium</label>
```

```
      <value>2.0</value>
    </icon>
    <icon>
      <image>sap_ui5_icon_RiskOfLoss01_low</image>
      <label>Low</label>
      <value>1.0</value>
    </icon>
  </iconset>
</iconSetOption>
```

### Example keyPosition Element XML Configuration

```
<keyPositionOption indicator="boolean" key="">
  <label>Highlight key positions</label>
  <keypositionset/>
</keyPositionOption>
```

### Other Optional settings

If you would like to show custom managers in the Succession Org Chart, replace the second line of the XML with the following:

```
<OrgChartConfig configurableDisplay="true">
```

## Org Chart Configuration Screen

We wrap up our org chart configuration with the Org Chart Configuration screen. To access the screen, follow these steps:

1. Type and select "Org Chart Configuration" in the search bar.
2. Click the "Succession org chart" tab. The screen will load as shown in Figure 6-14.

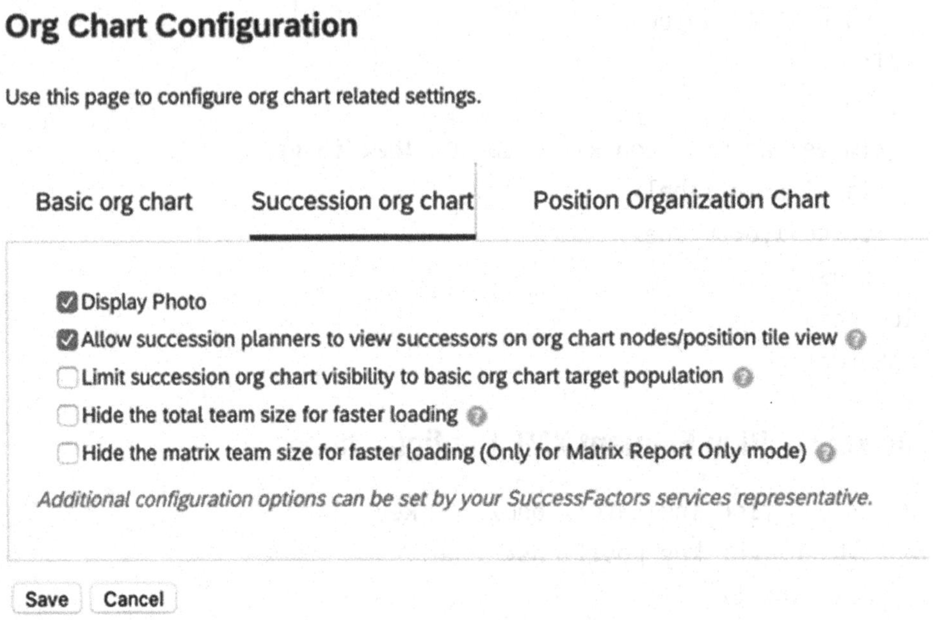

**Org Chart Configuration**

Use this page to configure org chart related settings.

Basic org chart Succession org chart Position Organization Chart

☑ Display Photo
☑ Allow succession planners to view successors on org chart nodes/position tile view
☐ Limit succession org chart visibility to basic org chart target population
☐ Hide the total team size for faster loading
☐ Hide the matrix team size for faster loading (Only for Matrix Report Only mode)

*Additional configuration options can be set by your SuccessFactors services representative.*

Save Cancel

***Figure 6-14.*** *The Org Chart Configuration Screen*

3. Make recommended selections as shown in Table 6-6 and click "Save."

***Table 6-6.*** *Org Chart Configuration Fields*

| Field | Description |
|---|---|
| Display Photo | We recommend checking this box so that the photos show unless your organization has not loaded any photos on the employee profiles or has disabled the ability for employees to load their own photos. |
| Allow succession planners to view successors on org chart nodes/position tile view | When you check this box, the system will also use the "Succession Planning" permission to determine who can see succession information rather than just the "Succession Management and Matrix Report Permissions" (see the subsection later in this chapter on setting up end user permissions). We recommend checking this box unless you have a scenario where you want to limit visibility for some people who can nominate – for example, if a manager can nominate for their employees but you do not want them seeing other nominations within that same span of control. |

(*continued*)

*Table 6-6.* (*continued*)

| Field | Description |
|---|---|
| Limit succession org chart visibility to basic org chart target population | Checking this box will limit visibility to the permission setting "Organization Chart Navigation Permission" under "General User Permission" within the "Permissions" screen when creating your role-based Permissions. We have not come across a scenario where organizations have needed this since you can already define the population with the "Succession Management and Matrix Report Permissions." It may be useful if you want these permissions to exactly mirror one another. |
| Hide the total team size for faster loading | If your organization is very large, you may have issues when viewing the top few levels of the organization because the system attempts to count all of the reports underneath each position. For example, the CEO of a 300,000-employee organization would show x number of direct and 299,999 total reports. If you are experiencing long wait times for the org chart to load at these levels, we recommend checking this option so that this calculation is not performed prior to loading the screen. |
| Hide the matrix team size for faster loading (Only for Matrix Report Only mode) | Similar to the preceding scenario, if you use matrix reporting and choose the "Matrix Report Only" visualization option, you may check this box to improve screen load time. |

# Load Legacy Successor Data

Once we have finished all of our configurations and have loaded position data, we can load any legacy successor data from a prior system. Follow these steps to access the import screen, download the template, and upload any legacy data:

1. Type and select "Import Successors" in the search bar. The Import Successors screen will load as shown in Figure 6-15.

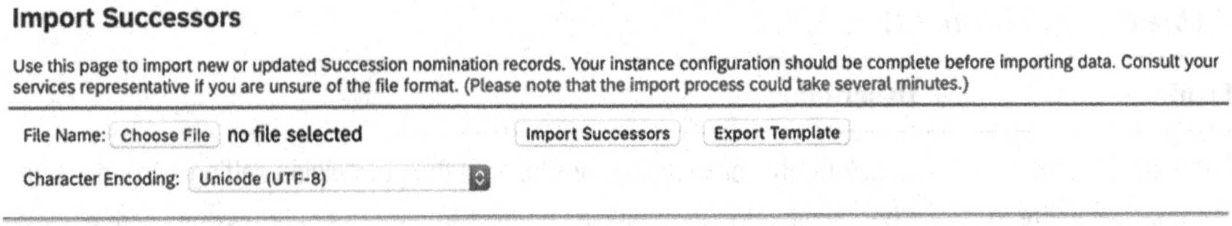

**Import Successors**

Use this page to import new or updated Succession nomination records. Your instance configuration should be complete before importing data. Consult your services representative if you are unsure of the file format. (Please note that the import process could take several minutes.)

File Name: Choose File no file selected Import Successors Export Template

Character Encoding: Unicode (UTF-8)

***Figure 6-15.*** *Import Successors Screen*

2. Click "Download Template."

---

**Note** The template will change dynamically based on the configurations you have made, so the template isn't necessarily transferable between organizations.

---

3. Fill out the template on your local machine using Table 6-7 as a guide (this assumes you've followed our recommended configurations thus far).

***Table 6-7.*** *Fields Within the Successor Import Template*

| Field | Description |
|---|---|
| GENERIC_POSITION_CODE | Enter the "code" field value for the MDF position object you wish to nominate the successor. |
| OLD_GENERIC_POSITION_CODE | If using the TRANSFER action, enter the source position code from which the nominee will be transferred. |
| POOL_CODE | Enter the "code" field value for the MDF Talent Pool object you wish to nominate the successor. |
| OLD_POOL_CODE | If using the TRANSFER action, enter the source Talent Pool code from which the nominee will be transferred. |
| READINESS | Enter the value of the readiness level – for example, the "value" field in the picklist and in the Succession Org Chart XML. |
| SUCCESSOR_USERID | Enter the USERID from the Succession Data Model/Employee Data file for the employee. |

*(continued)*

*Table 6-7.* (*continued*)

| Field | Description |
|---|---|
| NOTE | Enter any comments on the nomination you want to appear in the comments section. |
| RANK | Assuming you have chosen to include a ranking in your nomination setup, enter the numerical readiness ranking for the candidate. |
| ACTION | Values can be ADD, UPDATE, TRANSFER, or DELETE. Leaving the field blank or using ADD or UPDATE performs the same function: The system will look for an existing record to update; if none is found, then it adds the record. DELETE will remove the record. For TRANSFER, you need to define the target and source nomination to move the record. |

4. Choose your file encoding (we recommend UTF-8 as it handles localized languages the best).
5. Click "Choose File" and select the file you have edited with your successor data.
6. Click "Import Successors." You will receive an email with the details of the import when it is complete. Repeat the preceding steps to resolve any successor data that did not load per the email.

# Set Up End User Permissions

We've put in a lot of work setting up our Succession Org Chart. We are almost there! The final step is to set up permissions for our users. In order to properly view the Succession Org Chart, you will need permission to view the MDF positions, the Succession data, and the org chart screen itself. We cover permissions for the MDF position object in the next chapter under the "Position Tile View" section as this pertains to the MDF configurations done there as well. Follow these steps to grant access to the Succession Org Chart screen and the Succession data:

1. Type and select "Manage Permission Roles" in the search bar.
2. When the screen loads, click the role you wish to modify. Then click "Permission...:"
3. Click "Succession Planners" (Figure 6-16) and choose from the following options in Table 6-8 as needed.

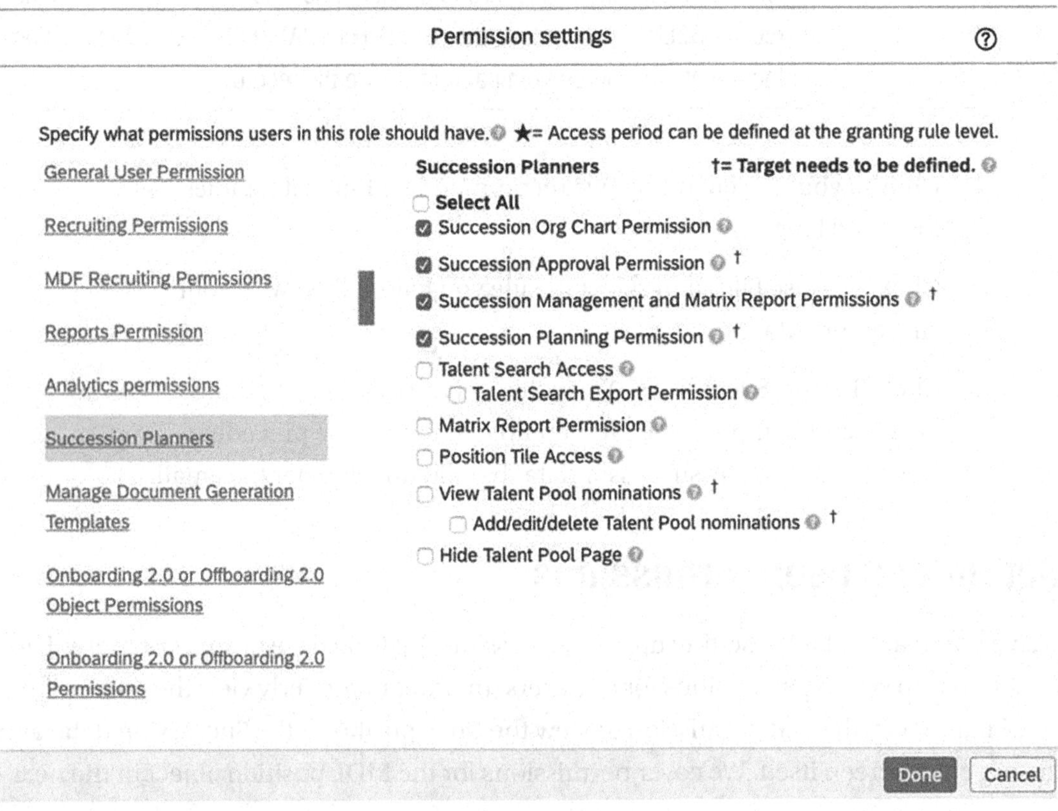


***Figure 6-16.*** *Succession Org Chart Permissions*

***Table 6-8.*** *Succession Org Chart Permission Options*

| Option | Description |
|---|---|
| Succession Org Chart Permission | Gives access to the Succession Org Chart screen. |
| Succession Approval Permission | Allows users to approve nominations. Nomination approval in the system is simplistic – you can effectively eliminate the approval process by always giving the Succession Planning Permission and Approval Permission together. If approval is not given for the same user and employee population, then the user's nomination will have to be approved by a user that does have approval over that population. Be sure to define your target populations on the role when selecting this in the preceding text. (Note that you can optionally set up pending approval emails in the system. This requires setting up a "Send Pending Nomination Emails" batch job in Provisioning and setting up the "Succession Email Approver" email template on the "E-Mail Notification Templates Settings" screen.) |
| Succession Management and Matrix Report Permissions | Allows user to see this defined population in the org chart. |
| Succession Planning Permission | Allows user to nominate successors for this defined population. |

4. Optionally, if you would like to see recommended successors in the position card, go to "Career Development Planning" and select "Recommend Successors."

5. Optionally, if you have implemented the SuccessFactors LMS and would like to be able to assign learning from the org chart, go to "Learning" and select "Learning Access Permission." Click "Done." Be sure to save your role on the main screen as well.

## Using the Succession Org Chart

The time has arrived to start using our Succession Org Chart! Follow these steps to step through the Succession Org Chart:

1. In the search box, type and select "View Succession Org Chart." The org chart will appear starting with the position of the logged-in user.
2. To select another user or position, click the radio button indicating you would like to search via position or person. Enter and select the person or position name in the search box. The org chart will appear as shown in Figure 6-17.

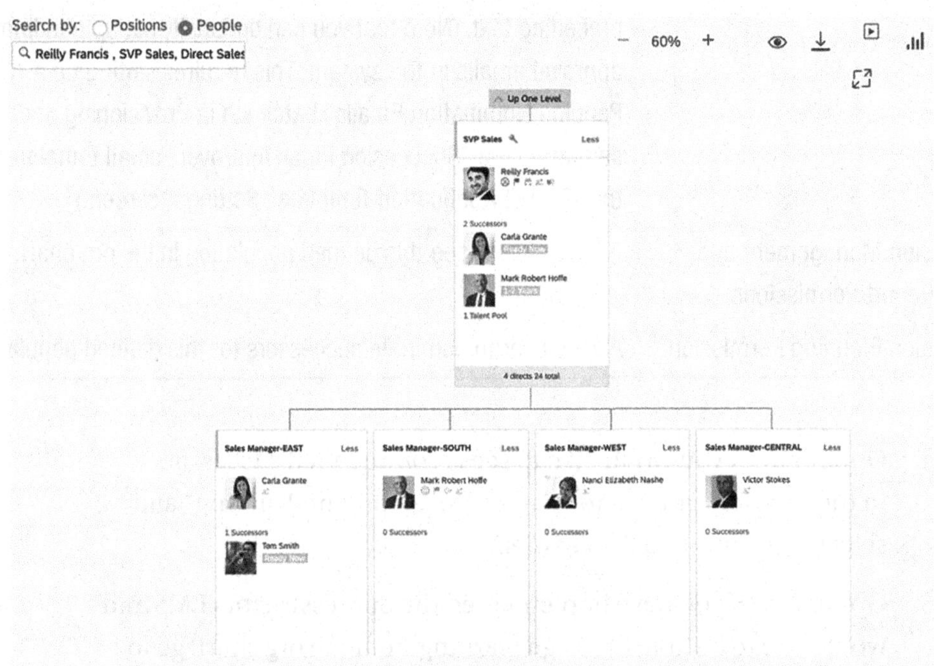


***Figure 6-17.*** *The Succession Org Chart*

3. If you have filled in any of the talent fields for a person and set up the icons in the org chart XML such as riskOfLoss, the icons will appear next to the individual. You can mouse over the icons to see the text descriptions configured as well in a small popup in case you are not familiar with what each icon means.

**Note** A common frustration/misconception of customers is editability of the talent fields here. Users must navigate to the Talent Profile of the employee to edit the values in these fields. You can navigate to the Talent Profile of the employee by clicking their name or picture to open the position tile and then clicking the name or picture again to open the talent card for the employee. Then click the name or picture again on the talent card to open the Talent Profile in a new window. From there, you can scroll down to the Talent section of the profile and make edits given that you have the proper permissions on Talent Profile.

4. If you are not able to see any of your icons, click the eye icon in the upper right-hand corner to pull up the display options. Here you can choose whether to show all reports, only direct reports, or only matrix reports. You can also check the box next to each configured icon to control whether or not it is displayed on the main screen. You can also select whether to show 3 or 12 successors for each position. In addition, there is an option to highlight only key positions (all other positions will become grayed out).
5. To show or hide the icons and nominees for a single position, toggle the "More" or "Less" link in the upper right-hand corner of the position.
6. You can navigate up or down the org chart by clicking the "Up One Level" at the top of a position or the number of reports at the bottom of the position.
7. If the org chart becomes cluttered, you can close the direct reports for a position that is already displaying direct reports by clicking the number of reports at the bottom of the position again.
8. You can also move around the org chart by clicking and dragging the mouse.
9. To zoom in or out, click the "+" or "-" icon in the upper-right hand corner of the screen.
10. To hide the menu bar at the top and get more room for the org chart, click the box with two arrows icon in the upper right-hand corner of the screen.

11. To download a copy of the chart on-screen, click the down arrow icon in the upper right-hand corner of the screen. You will have the option to download in .pdf or .jpg format.

12. To open the position card, click anywhere on the screen. The position card will pop up as shown in Figure 6-18.

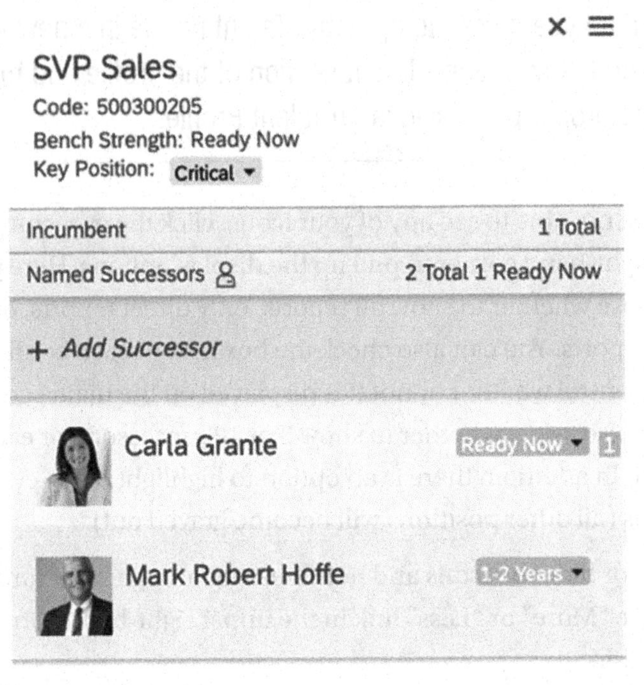


*Figure 6-18.* Position Card

a. Click the menu hamburger icon in the upper right-hand corner to either edit the MDF position object, delete the MDF position object, view the nomination history (which displays nomination actions taken on the nominee), create a job requisition, view the Lineage Chart, view the job role details, or hide the position. If you are using the Recruiting module, you can add a "Create Requisition" menu item here as well. All of these options are dependent on your configurations and permissions. MDF position-related configuration and permissions are covered in the "Position Tile View" section in the next chapter. Nominations are covered earlier in this section and the "Nomination Setup Screen" section of this chapter. The Lineage Chart is covered in the "Lineage Chart" section of the next chapter. Job role permissions are covered in Volume 1, Chapter 3:

   i. If you hide a position, a new icon will appear in the upper right-hand corner of the org chart with a profile and a lock indicating the number of hidden positions. You can click this icon to unhide all hidden positions.

b. To change the key position value, select it from the dropdown.

c. You can toggle between viewing the incumbent, the named successors, or Talent Pools to which the position is associated via job code by clicking the respective bar. Click any of the employee names or photos to open the talent card for any of these people. Talent card configuration is covered earlier in the "Talent Cards" section of this chapter. Note that you can nominate the person to a position from their talent card or nominate someone to that employee's position as well. Additionally, you can nominate a successor by clicking "+ Add Successor" from the Named Successors bar (the popup will display as shown in Figure 6-19). You will notice as you add successors here with various readiness levels, your bench strength on the position card and the corresponding color to the left of the position will adjust to the best readiness level among your nominees. Finally, you can also click "Manage Pool" from the specific Talent Pool bar you have chosen to open the Talent Pool screen for that pool (see the "Talent Pool" section in the next chapter).

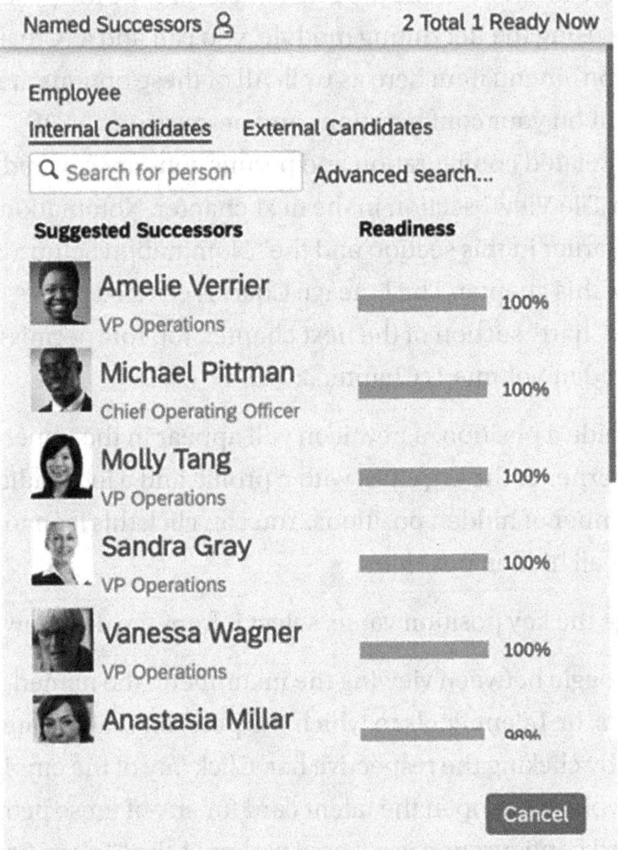


*Figure 6-19. Nomination Popup*

---

**Note** You will notice in the figure that your search options such as whether to search by position or person separately, the ability to search for external candidates, and whether suggested successors will appear on the nomination screen will all display or hide based on your nomination setup configurations covered earlier in this chapter. Clicking the "Advanced search…" in the popup will open Talent Search in a popup – Talent Search is covered in a previous section in this chapter.

---

It is very gratifying to see from these steps how the Succession Org Chart brings together many of our configurations across this chapter and many others into one centralized location! Circling back to our model company, we can see the powerful visualization and quick access to view and edit data the Succession Org Chart provides to our President as they attempt to evaluate the succession situation at their organization. They can quickly see that the SVP is a high risk of loss and impact of loss by the icons shown on their position. They are able to nominate the SVP to their own position as well and assign a readiness level. They can also see which regional sales managers are being considered for the SVP position and what their readiness level is! Based on this quick information, the manager can have informed conversations with the SVP about their development and how to best fill their position given that they have successfully succeeded her.

# Conclusion

At this point in our Succession Management journey, we've seen how to identify our top talent using the 9-box and Talent Review Form in Chapter 5. Now we've also seen how to nominate those employees to specific positions using an org chart-style visualization. In the next chapter, we will wrap up by covering a multitude of other features that allow us to organize and nominate our employees and also other ways to visualize this and other talent data.

CHAPTER 7

# Succession Management Additional Features

In this final chapter on Succession Management, we walk through the remaining features of the Succession Management module (SCM). These features allow you to view and organize your talent and Succession data in many helpful ways. We start with Talent Search which allows you to find employees by searching on any of their talent fields. We then cover Talent Pools which allow you to organize these employees into logical groupings. Next, we cover the Position Tile View which offers an alternate way to view positions outside of the Succession Org Chart. We then cover the Lineage Chart which shows succession planners' "what if" scenarios of succession. Finally, we conclude with Succession Presentations which help planners make quality presentations using real-time talent management data. We continue to utilize the model company example described in Chapter 5 to bring a practical example to each functionality.

## Talent Search

Talent Search allows end users to search for employees through any talent field within their span of security permissions. In addition, users can download search results, compare employees, make succession and Talent Pool nominations, and more! This section will show you how to configure the functionality and run it as an end user.

## Prerequisites for Configuring Talent Search

Prior to being able to configure and run Talent Search, the following settings and permissions must be set. Additionally, be sure your Employee Talent Profile has been configured in the data model. For more information, see Volume 1, Chapter 2.




S. Traynor et al., *SAP SuccessFactors Talent: Volume 2*, https://doi.org/10.1007/978-1-4842-6995-4_7

## Provisioning Settings Required for Talent Search

Follow these steps to turn on Talent Search in Provisioning. These must be completed prior to security and other configuration settings:

1. Log in to Provisioning and select your company instance.
2. Navigate to Company Settings and click the checkbox next to "Succession Talent Search" as shown in Figure 7-1. Click Save.

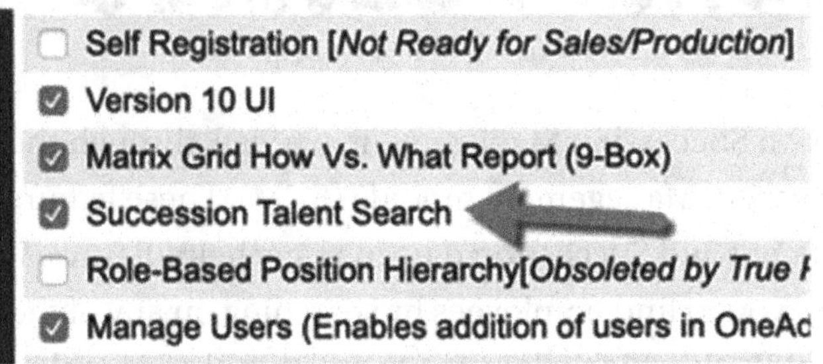


***Figure 7-1.*** *Succession Talent Search Provisioning Setting*

3. If you would like to use the option keyword search that performs a quick search across all available fields rather than just individual field keyword searches, follow these additional steps:
   a. Add Read permission for all fields you would like to make searchable within the data model XML. See Volume 1, Chapter 2 for more information.
   b. In Provisioning, go to Search Index and generate an index (even as a partner, you will not have permission to access this and need to contact SAP to index for the first time).

## Permission Settings Required for Talent Search

Follow these steps to ensure you have the proper permissions for Talent Search:

1. Type and select "Manage Permission Roles" in the search bar.
2. When the screen loads, click the role you wish to modify. Then click "Permission...:"

3. Ensure the following permissions shown in Figure 7-2 are active on your assigned roles to enable Talent Search configuration: Manage System Properties ➤ Talent Search Management.

Permission settings

Specify what permissions users in this role should have. ★= Access period can be defined at the granting rule level.

Manage Question Library
Manage Recruiting
Manage MDF Recruiting Objects
Manage Succession
Intelligent Service Tools
Manage System Properties
Manage User
Manage Pay Scale
Manage Apprentices
Manage Time
Manage Time Off

Employee Central Feature Settings
Platform Feature Settings
Cross Talent Feature Settings
Performance Management Feature Settings
Process Guide Setting
Handout Builder
Show Me Author
Text Replacement
To-Do Admin
Welcome Portlet Admin
Org Chart Configuration
Talent Search Management
Variance Report
Data Inspector
View Provisioning Access
Control Provisioning Access
View Job Analyzer Salary Section
View Job Analyzer Gender Check Section
View Job Analyzer Skills Section

Done Cancel

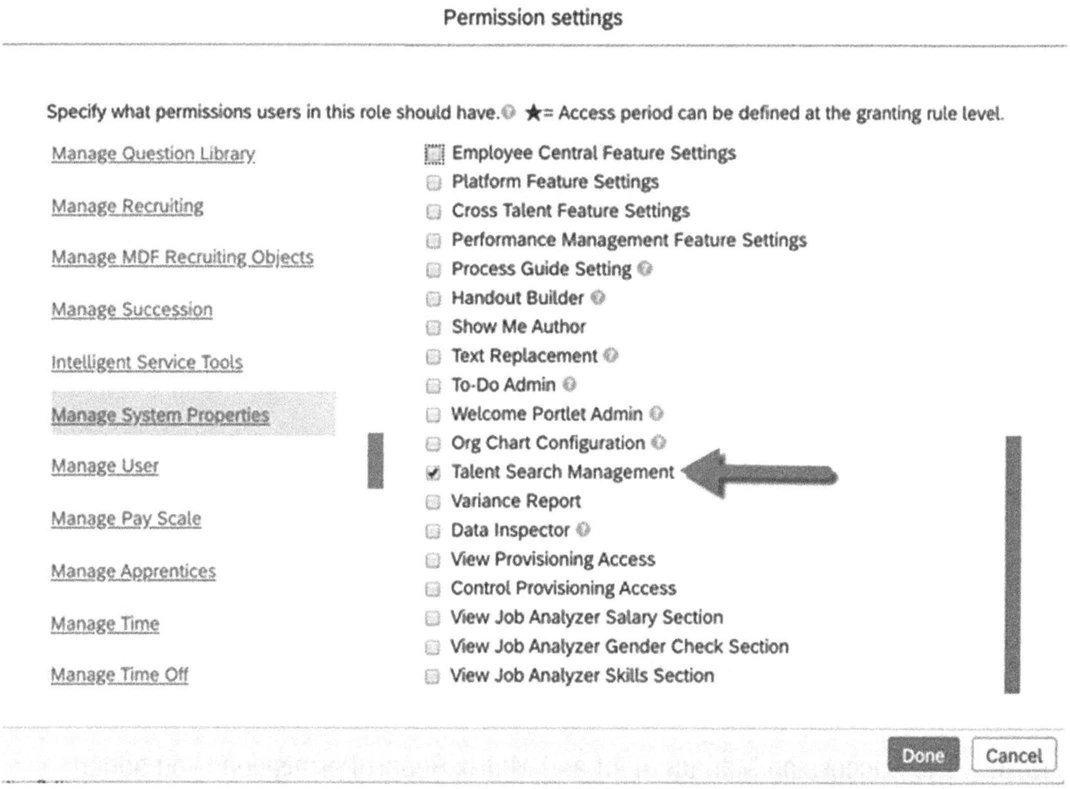

***Figure 7-2.** Permissions to Enable Talent Search Configuration*

4. Ensure the following permissions shown in Figure 7-3 are active on your assigned roles to enable Talent Search as an end user: Succession Planners ➤ Talent Search Access. Talent Search Export can optionally be added if you would like to be able to download an export file of your search results. Click "Done." Be sure to save your role on the main screen as well.

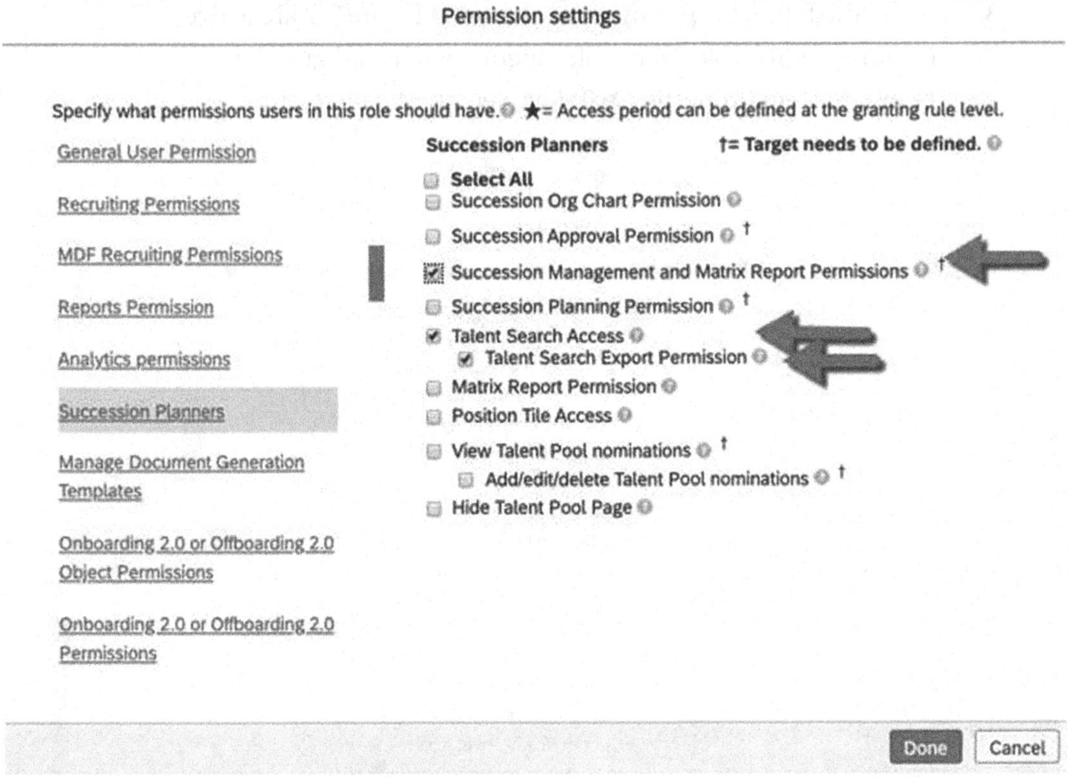

Permission settings

Specify what permissions users in this role should have. ★= Access period can be defined at the granting rule level.

General User Permission
Recruiting Permissions
MDF Recruiting Permissions
Reports Permission
Analytics permissions
Succession Planners
Manage Document Generation Templates
Onboarding 2.0 or Offboarding 2.0 Object Permissions
Onboarding 2.0 or Offboarding 2.0 Permissions

Succession Planners    †= Target needs to be defined.

Select All
Succession Org Chart Permission
Succession Approval Permission †
Succession Management and Matrix Report Permissions †
Succession Planning Permission †
Talent Search Access
Talent Search Export Permission
Matrix Report Permission
Position Tile Access
View Talent Pool nominations †
Add/edit/delete Talent Pool nominations †
Hide Talent Pool Page

Done Cancel

***Figure 7-3.*** *Permissions to Enable Talent Search as an End User*

---

**Note** The Succession Management and Matrix Report Permissions you added in Chapter 5 also needs to be enabled. The assigned user groups associated with this permission will determine which employees you can search.

---

# Configuring Talent Search

Now that all prerequisite configurations and permissions have been assigned, we can access the Talent Search Settings configuration screen. Follow these steps to complete configurations:

1. Access the Talent Search Settings configuration screen by typing and selecting "Talent Search Settings" in the search bar. The screen will load as shown in Figure 7-4.

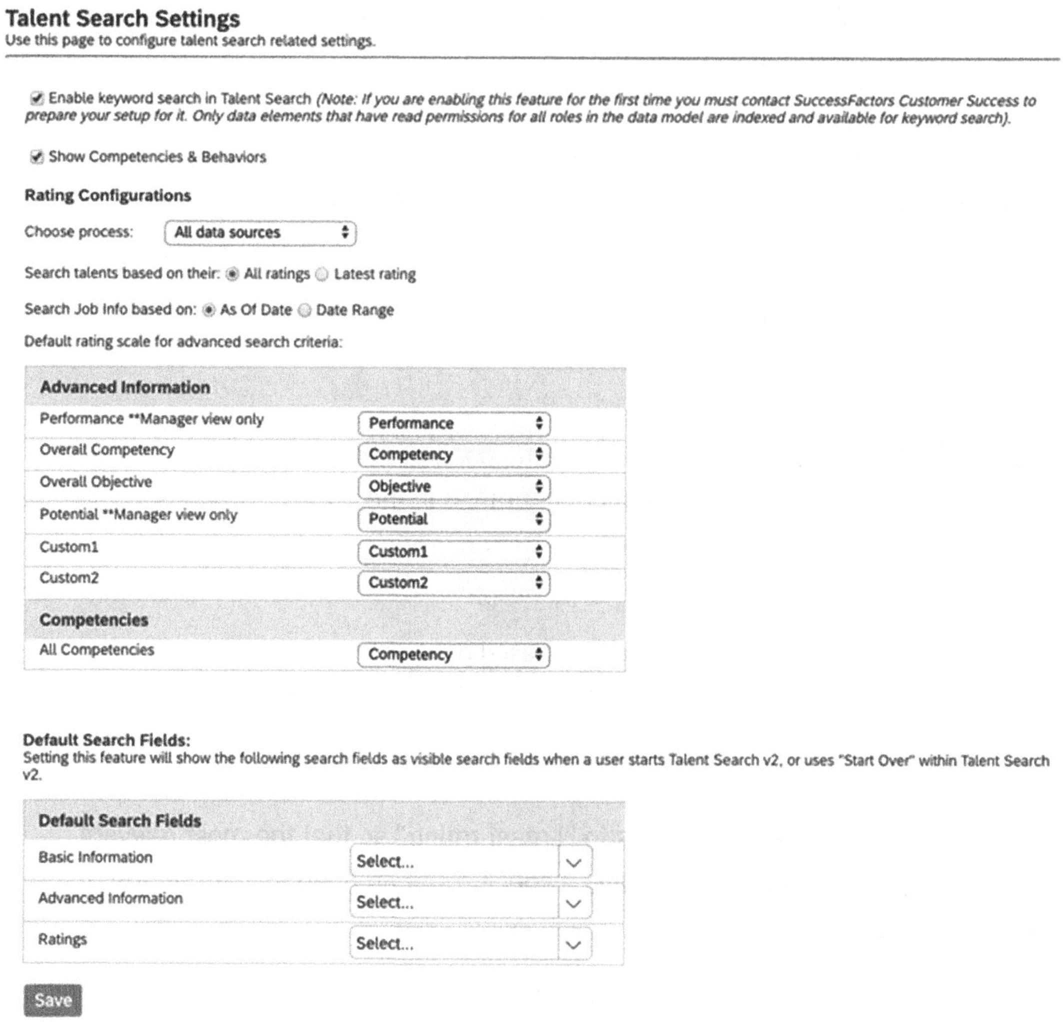

**Talent Search Settings**
Use this page to configure talent search related settings.

☑ Enable keyword search in Talent Search *(Note: If you are enabling this feature for the first time you must contact SuccessFactors Customer Success to prepare your setup for it. Only data elements that have read permissions for all roles in the data model are indexed and available for keyword search).*

☑ Show Competencies & Behaviors

**Rating Configurations**

Choose process: All data sources

Search talents based on their: ◉ All ratings ○ Latest rating

Search Job Info based on: ◉ As Of Date ○ Date Range

Default rating scale for advanced search criteria:

| Advanced Information | |
|---|---|
| Performance **Manager view only | Performance |
| Overall Competency | Competency |
| Overall Objective | Objective |
| Potential **Manager view only | Potential |
| Custom1 | Custom1 |
| Custom2 | Custom2 |
| **Competencies** | |
| All Competencies | Competency |

**Default Search Fields:**
Setting this feature will show the following search fields as visible search fields when a user starts Talent Search v2, or uses "Start Over" within Talent Search v2.

| Default Search Fields | |
|---|---|
| Basic Information | Select... |
| Advanced Information | Select... |
| Ratings | Select... |

Save

***Figure 7-4.** The Talent Search Settings Screen*

2. Check the "Enable keyword search in Talent Search" if you would like to enable the simple keyword search we have mentioned earlier in this section.

---

**Note** We recommend turning on this option as it can save end users time having to build their queries. In addition, users may not know where in the data model structure a particular field is located. This can allow the users to still search without as much knowledge of these structures.

---

3. Check "Show Competencies & Behaviors" if you wish to include competencies in your search.

---

**Note** We recommend turning this option on if your organization uses competencies as it is the only way to include competencies in the search.

---

4. For the "Choose process" field, select either "All data sources" or one of your configured processes.

---

**Note** We recommend you mirror the same configurations you selected for your data sources during the matrix grid configuration in the previous chapter for the sake of consistency for the end users.

---

5. Select a value for "Search talents based on their" field. "All ratings" will include all ratings, whereas "Latest rating" will only include the latest.

---

**Note** We recommend setting this to "Latest rating" so that the most relevant ratings appear unless resources have a specific search need to search through historical scores.

---

6. Select a value for the "Search Job Info based on" field. Selecting "As Of Date" will offer one date field where the employee must have held the job when performing a job search, whereas "Date Range" will offer two date fields where employees can hold the job anytime in between those dates.

---

**Note** We recommend using the Date Range option as it allows for more flexibility.

---

7. Select a value for each type of advanced information search default rating scale. These allow you to select from any settings in the matrix grid configurations or the performance rating scales.

---

**Note** We recommend these settings match what you have configured in the matrix grid configurations unless you have not performed such configurations.

---

8. Select any default search fields you would like to appear when the page first loads or when the user clicks "Start Over."

---

**Note** We don't recommend setting any default fields here.

---

9. Click "Save."

## Running Talent Search

Now that all configurations and permissions have been set up, we are ready to run a talent search! Follow these instructions to conduct a talent search:

1. Type and select "Talent Search" in the search bar to load the Talent Search screen as shown in Figure 7-5.

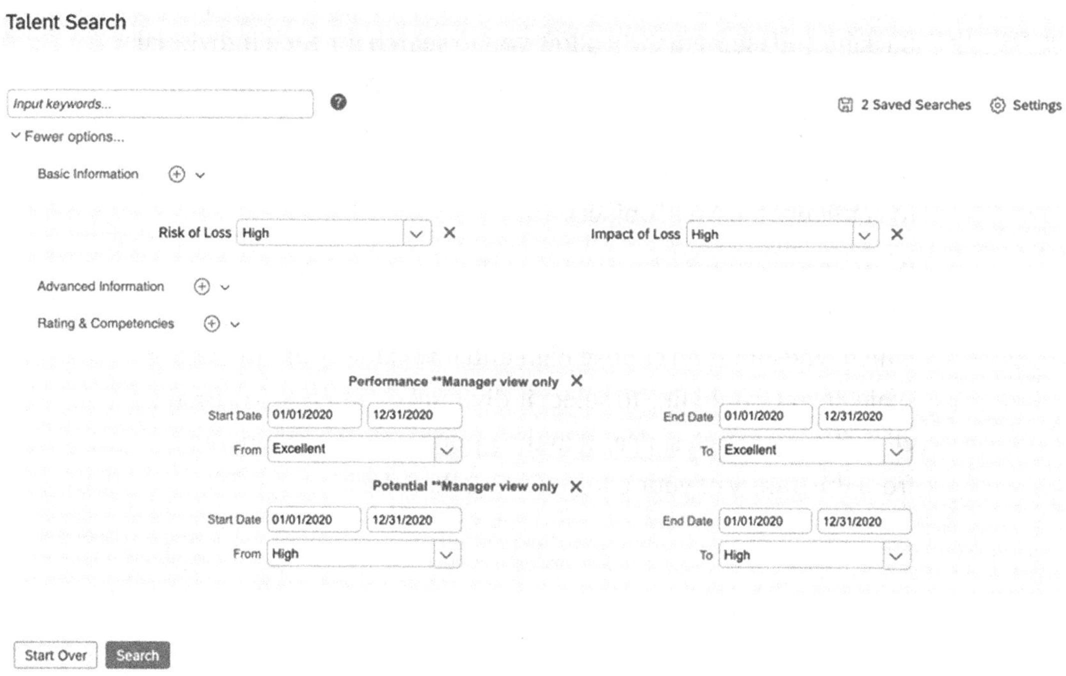

Talent Search
Input keywords...
2 Saved Searches
Settings
Fewer options...
Basic Information
Risk of Loss High
Impact of Loss High
Advanced Information
Rating & Competencies
Performance **Manager view only
Start Date 01/01/2020 12/31/2020
End Date 01/01/2020 12/31/2020
From Excellent
To Excellent
Potential **Manager view only
Start Date 01/01/2020 12/31/2020
End Date 01/01/2020 12/31/2020
From High
To High
Start Over
Search

***Figure 7-5.*** *The Talent Search Selection Criteria Screen*

2. If the keyword search has been configured, the first field you will see is a field to search by keyword. This field performs a quick search across all available fields rather than just individual field keyword searches. It is useful for quick searches, but is not as precise as picking fields individually. Enter a keyword here, or optionally click "More options..." to expand the screen to search fields individually. If you use quotes around groups of words, it will treat those words with AND logic, whereas not using quotes will use OR logic.

3. If you are searching by fields individually, click the "+" icon next to the type of information you would like to search:

    a. Basic Information: This area lists all of the basic fields in your data model XML. Enter the search text next to each field selected.

    b. Advanced Information: This area lists the background elements from your configured data model regardless of permissions set in the XML, as well as your Talent Pools (see the next section for more information on Talent Pools). You will need to choose "As Of Date" or Date Range depending on your configuration options. Background elements will allow you to search for each individual field within the background element. Talent Pool will allow you to select from a list of Talent Pools as well as other fields you may have configured in the MDF object (see the next section for how to configure the MDF object).

    c. Rating & Competencies: This area allows you to select performance, potential, objective, and competency ratings. Select which type and then choose high and low values from the rating scale. If you would like to select individual competencies, then click "Competencies..."; and in the popup, select a competency from the library of your choice and click "Select."

4. Prior to running you search, click the "Settings" icon to choose from the following:

   a. Which role to run: You can choose which permission role to run for the query. For example, if you are a manager and an HR admin, you may have roles for both. The HR admin role would return results for all employees for whom you are the HR responsible individual, whereas the manager role would return results for all employees for whom you are the manager.

   b. Check the checkbox "Make All Criteria Optional" to make the search inclusive, whereas unchecking the box makes the search exclusive.

5. You can also call up saved searches by clicking the "Save" icon.

6. If you want to clear your screen back to the default search criteria, click "Start Over."

7. When you are ready to execute your search query, click "Search." A results screen will display similar to Figure 7-6.

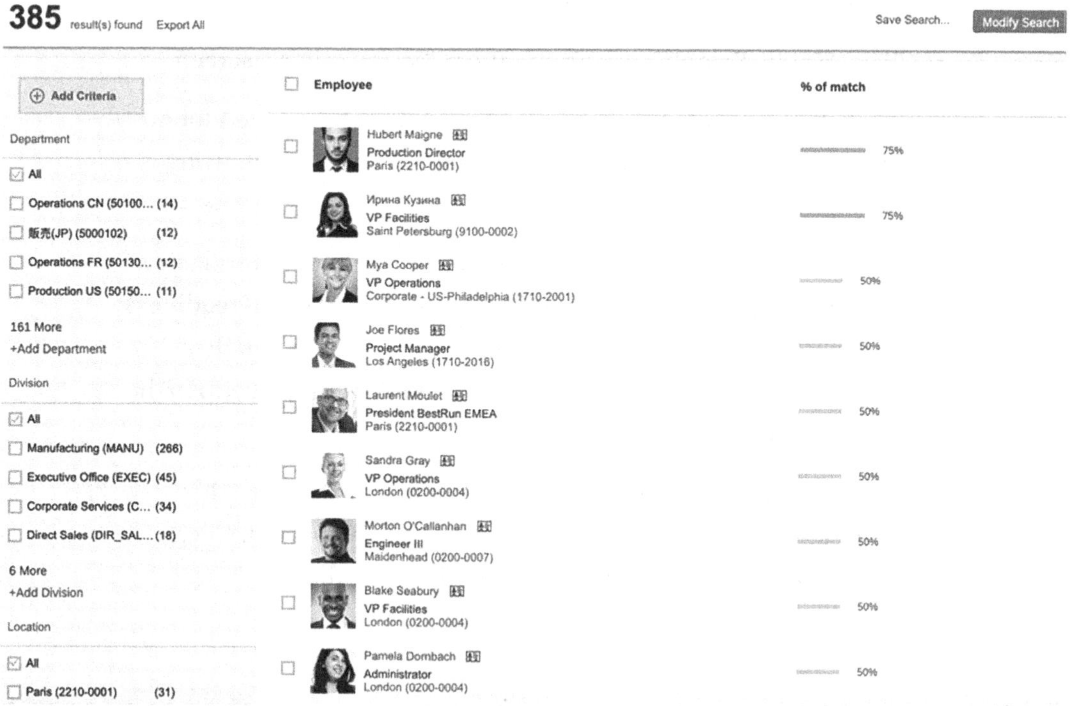

***Figure 7-6.*** *The Talent Search Results Screen*

8. The results screen shows a list of employees along with a calculated percentage match to the criteria you defined in the prior screen. To the left is filter criteria to refine the current search results:

    a. Click the name of an employee to open the quick card for the employee.

    b. Click the percentage to show details of how the employee matched the search.

    c. Click "Add Criteria" to add additional filter criteria.

    d. Check the boxes next to the criteria on the left to immediately refine the search.

    e. Click Export All to open the Export popup. You can enter a name for the export file and which fields to include. Click "Export" to generate the .xls export.

    f. Click "Save Search" to list these search criteria in your saved searches on the selection criteria screen.

    g. Click "Modify Search" to return to the selection criteria screen.

    h. Check the box next to each employee you want to select. A menu will appear at the top of the selection screen with the following options:

        i. Add to pool: Select this option to open a popup that will allow you to select from existing Talent Pools. You can add readiness levels, notes, and so on based on your Talent Pool MDF configuration. Click "Nominate" to add the employee(s) to the Talent Pool.

        ii. Export: Will open the same Export popup as "Export All" except only the selected employees will be exported. Click "Export" on the popup to download the .xls file.

iii. Compare: This will open a popup which shows a side-by-side comparison of the selected employees for each of the fields in your selection criteria as shown in Figure 7-7. You can click "Configure Fields" to bring up another popup that will allow you to add any additional fields you might want to consider on the fly (very cool)! You can also click "Print" to open a print preview page that can be sent to a printer.

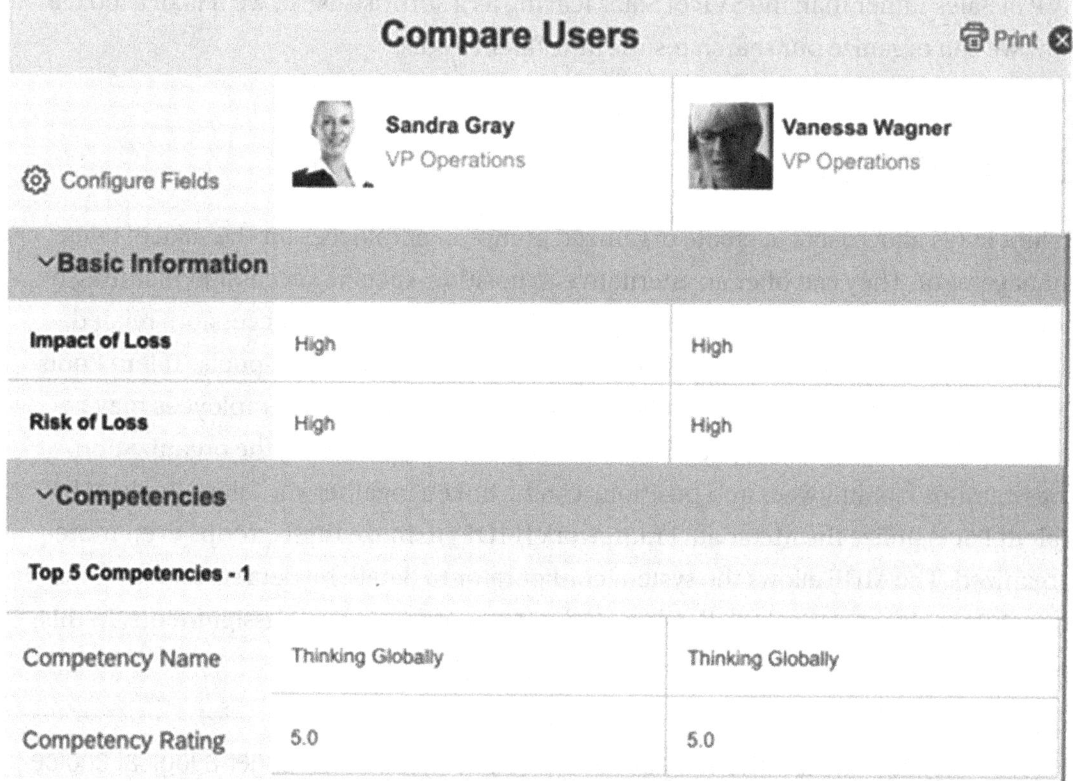


*Figure 7-7. The Compare Users Popup*

iv. Nominate: Type a position title or number in the "Nominate employees for" field to nominate the selected employees for that position. Select a readiness level and ranking (depending on your succession nomination configurations; see the next section), as well as any notes in the "Notes" field for each employee. Click "Nominate" to finish.

Now that we've walked through all of the steps to run Talent Search, let's revisit our model company example. For the sake of our example, this functionality could allow an HR admin or president to perform a periodic search of employees with a high risk of loss and high impact of loss who also land in the highest performance and potential cell of the 9-box (see example in the preceding figure). In this way, the HR admin or VP can identify that the SVP of Sales in our example may be on their way out of the company! They can then proactively work with the SVP of Sales to cultivate their talent via a development plan for the President position while they search for a successor for the SVP of Sales rather than the SVP of Sales leaving as a surprise. Next, we'll take a look at how we can organize our search results into Talent Pools.

# Talent Pools

Talent Pools allow users to create organized groups of employees for the sake of talent management. They can offer an alternative to position-specific succession planning by allowing more general groupings. They can also be used for non-succession-related needs like development plans, rotation programs, or high-potential pools. Talent Pools can also be associated with positions so that, for example, if many employees may be qualified for our model company SVP of Sales position throughout the organization, these groups of employees and positions can be linked together via Talent Pools! MDF Talent Pools utilize the Metadata Framework (MDF) to make these groups even more organized. The MDF allows the system configurator to detail the data structure of the Talent Pool object, as well as allowing for detailed permission role assignments. In this section, we will cover how to configure and use Talent Pools.

---

**Note** Legacy Talent Pools will not be covered as they are no longer a logical choice for configuring the system and are in an end-of-maintenance phase from SAP.

---

## Prerequisites for Configuring and Using Talent Pools

Prior to being able to configure and use Talent Pools, ensure the requirements and steps in this section are completed.

---

**Note** We assume the MDF is turned on in provisioning prior to these configuration steps as well.

---

### Upgrade Center

In the event Talent Pools are not activated in your system, follow these steps to activate:

1. Type and select "Upgrade Center" in the search bar.
2. Select "New MDF Pool-based Succession Planning" from the list and follow the on-screen instructions.

### Configurator Permissions

Prior to configuring Talent Pools, ensure your assigned permission role has the Administrator Permissions ➤ Metadata Framework permissions as shown in Figure 7-8 (Configure Object Definitions, Manage Data, Configure Business Rules, Access to non-secured objects, Import Permission on Metadata Framework, Admin access to MDF OData API, Manage Configuration UI, Manage Positions, Manage Sequence).

---

**Note** Unlike other sections, we separate configurator and user permissions. This is because the MDF structure should be defined prior to the user permissions since the user permissions are dependent on the MDF configuration.

---

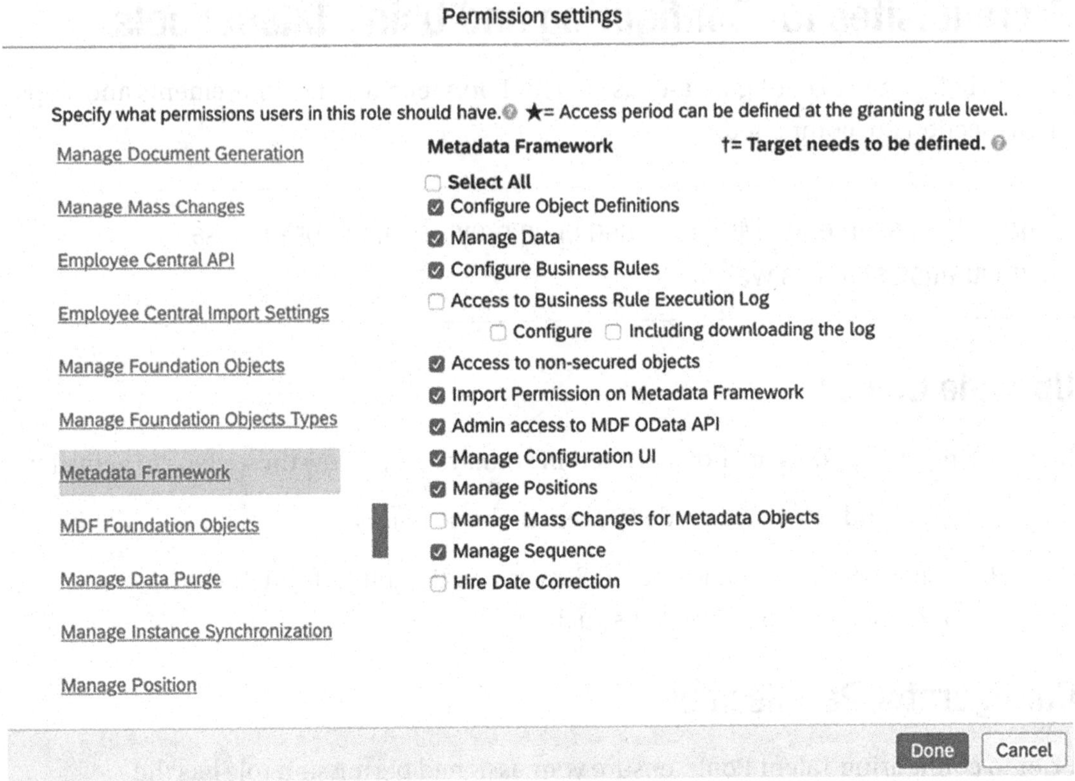

Permission settings

Specify what permissions users in this role should have. ★= Access period can be defined at the granting rule level.

Manage Document Generation
Manage Mass Changes
Employee Central API
Employee Central Import Settings
Manage Foundation Objects
Manage Foundation Objects Types
Metadata Framework
MDF Foundation Objects
Manage Data Purge
Manage Instance Synchronization
Manage Position

**Metadata Framework** **†= Target needs to be defined.**

- [ ] **Select All**
- [x] Configure Object Definitions
- [x] Manage Data
- [x] Configure Business Rules
- [ ] Access to Business Rule Execution Log
  - [ ] Configure
  - [ ] Including downloading the log
- [x] Access to non-secured objects
- [x] Import Permission on Metadata Framework
- [x] Admin access to MDF OData API
- [x] Manage Configuration UI
- [x] Manage Positions
- [ ] Manage Mass Changes for Metadata Objects
- [x] Manage Sequence
- [ ] Hire Date Correction

Done Cancel

***Figure 7-8.*** *Administrator Permissions ➤ Metadata Framework Permissions*

In addition, ensure "Talent Pool Field Configuration" is selected under "Manage Succession" as shown the Figure 7-9.

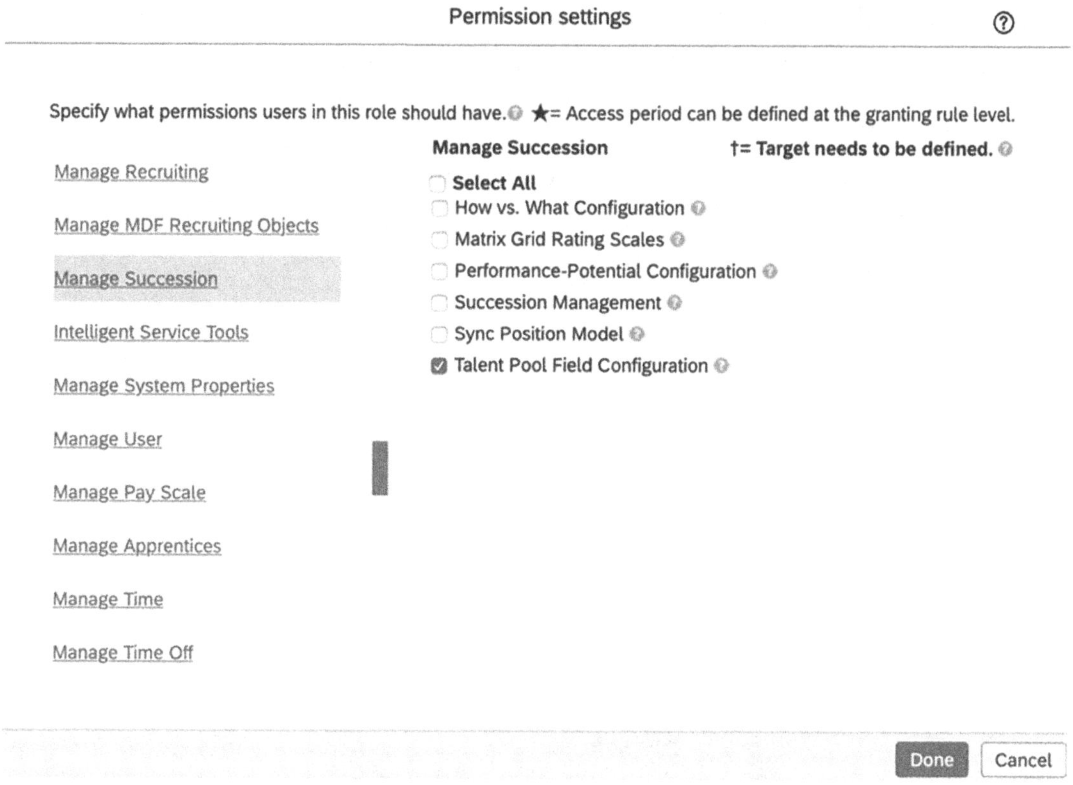

Permission settings

Specify what permissions users in this role should have. ★= Access period can be defined at the granting rule level.

Manage Recruiting
Manage MDF Recruiting Objects
Manage Succession
Intelligent Service Tools
Manage System Properties
Manage User
Manage Pay Scale
Manage Apprentices
Manage Time
Manage Time Off

**Manage Succession** †= Target needs to be defined.

- [ ] Select All
- [ ] How vs. What Configuration
- [ ] Matrix Grid Rating Scales
- [ ] Performance-Potential Configuration
- [ ] Succession Management
- [ ] Sync Position Model
- [x] Talent Pool Field Configuration

Done Cancel

***Figure 7-9.*** *Talent Pool Field Configuration Permission*

## Configuring Talent Pools via MDF

Now that you have permission, you can begin defining the data structure of Talent Pools.

---

**Note** This section will cover some of the steps we recommend for configuring the Talent Pool object definition. It should not be considered a comprehensive guide to all MDF object definition options. The MDF is a very large and powerful tool that can take up the contents of an entire book! In our following example, we only add security to the object and add a single field from our model company to help filter through Talent Pools.

---

Defining the data structure of a Talent Pool is completed via the MDF "Configure Object Definitions." Follow these steps to complete the configuration:

1. Type and Select "Configure Object Definitions" in the search bar.
2. In the "Search" field, select "Object Definition." In the next dropdown, select "Talent Pool." The Talent Pool object definition will appear as in Figure 7-10.

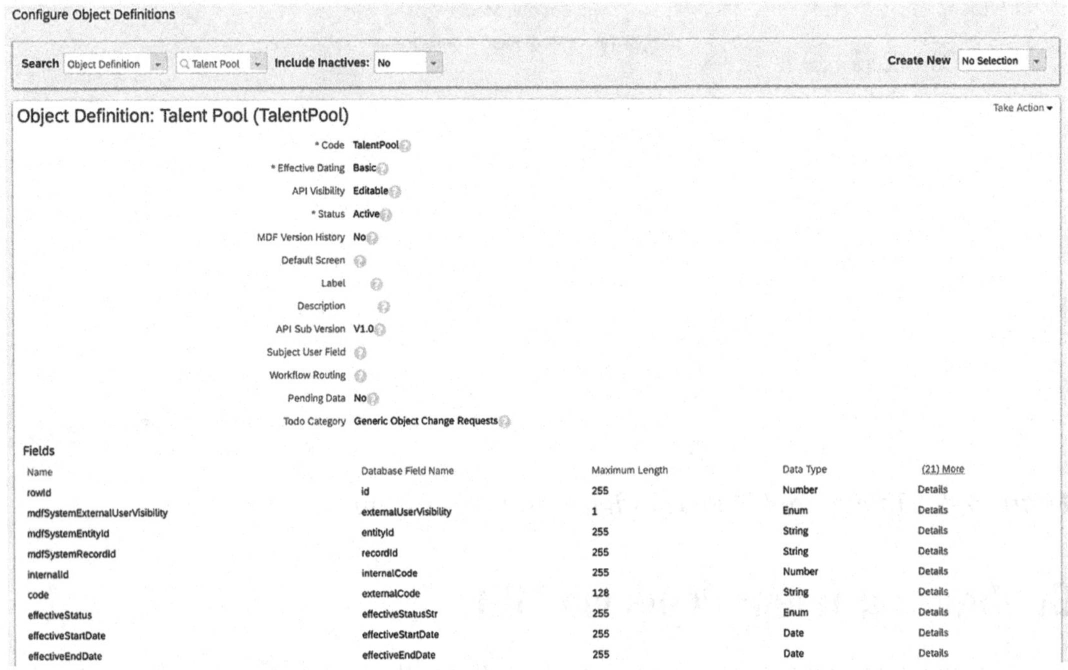


***Figure 7-10.** The Talent Pool Object Definition Screen*

3. Select the "Take Action" dropdown and select "Make Correction." The fields will become editable.
4. Scroll to the end of the "Fields" section and add a field by entering "cust_ExecutiveLevel" in the "Name" field, "2" in the "Maximum Length" field, and "Number" in the Data Type field. Click "Details" next to the fields. A popup will appear.
   a. In the popup, scroll down to the "Label" field and type "Executive Level." Click Done.

5. Back on the main screen, scroll down to the "Searchable Fields" section and type "cust_ExecutiveLevel" in the "Name" field. Then scroll down to the "Security" section and select "Yes" for the "Secured" field and "Miscellaneous Permissions" for the "Permission Category" field. Scroll to the bottom and click "Save."

## Permissions for Users

Now that the MDF has been configured where the Talent Pool object has been set to secured, we can modify any user permission roles we wish to give access to Talent Pools. Follow these steps to add the Talent Pools permission to the role(s):

1. Navigate to "Manage Permission Roles" using the search bar.
2. Click the role you which to edit. Then click "Permissions...:"
3. On the "Permission settings" screen, click "Miscellaneous Permissions" and scroll to "Talent Pool." Check the checkboxes next to "View Current," "View History," "Create," "Insert," "Correct," "Delete," and "Import/Export" as shown in Figure 7-11. Click "Done."

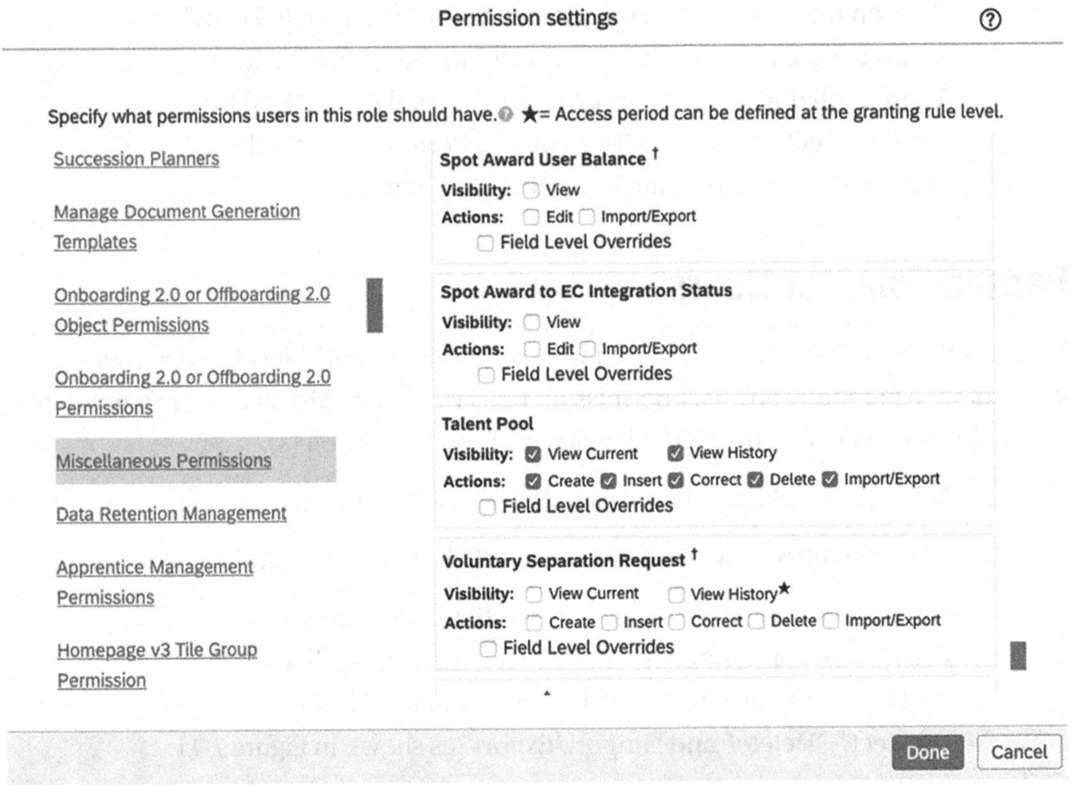

Permission settings

Specify what permissions users in this role should have. ★= Access period can be defined at the granting rule level.

Succession Planners
Manage Document Generation Templates
Onboarding 2.0 or Offboarding 2.0 Object Permissions
Onboarding 2.0 or Offboarding 2.0 Permissions
Miscellaneous Permissions
Data Retention Management
Apprentice Management Permissions
Homepage v3 Tile Group Permission

Spot Award User Balance †
Visibility: View
Actions: Edit Import/Export
Field Level Overrides

Spot Award to EC Integration Status
Visibility: View
Actions: Edit Import/Export
Field Level Overrides

Talent Pool
Visibility: View Current View History
Actions: Create Insert Correct Delete Import/Export
Field Level Overrides

Voluntary Separation Request †
Visibility: View Current View History★
Actions: Create Insert Correct Delete Import/Export
Field Level Overrides

Done Cancel

***Figure 7-11.** Permission Settings for Talent Pool User Permission Role*

4. You can further refine which Talent Pools an end user can access. For the sake of our example, we will use the new field we created, cust_ExecutiveLevel, to allow different users access to different Talent Pools. We will grant this specific role access to Executive Level 2 for use of the HR admins as shown in Figure 7-12 and assume another role will be created for Level 1 for use of the executive team only. On the Permission Role Detail screen, click "Edit Granting" and scroll down to "Talent Pool" and select the radio button for "Restrict target population to:" Check the first checkbox and enter "Executive Level," ">=", and "2". Click "Done."

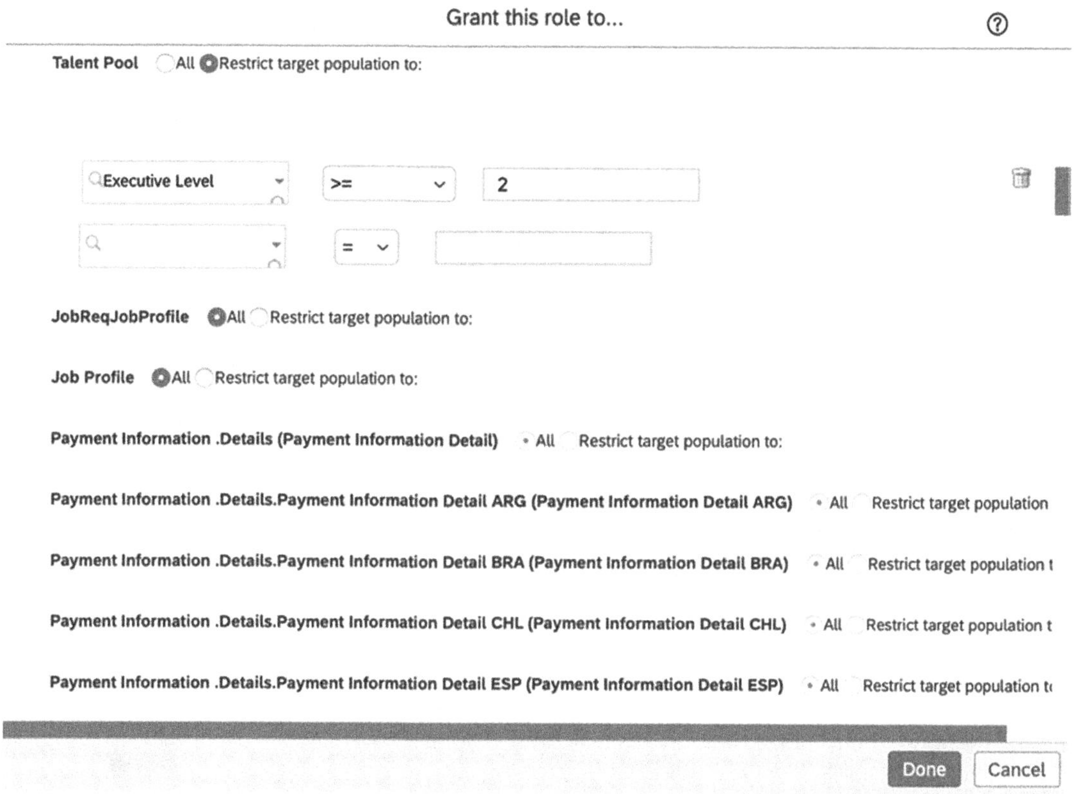

Grant this role to...

Talent Pool All Restrict target population to:

Executive Level >= 2

=

JobReqJobProfile All Restrict target population to:

Job Profile All Restrict target population to:

Payment Information .Details (Payment Information Detail) All Restrict target population to:

Payment Information .Details.Payment Information Detail ARG (Payment Information Detail ARG) All Restrict target population

Payment Information .Details.Payment Information Detail BRA (Payment Information Detail BRA) All Restrict target population t

Payment Information .Details.Payment Information Detail CHL (Payment Information Detail CHL) All Restrict target population t

Payment Information .Details.Payment Information Detail ESP (Payment Information Detail ESP) All Restrict target population t

Done Cancel

***Figure 7-12.*** *Defining the Target Population of Talent Pools to Executive Level 2 or Below*

5. It is important to remember the preceding permissions give the user access only to view and edit the Talent Pool objects, not the permission to view the actual nominations within Talent Pools! To add permission to view nominations, in the "Permission settings" screen, click "Succession Planners" and check the boxes next to "View Talent Pool nominations" and "Add/edit/delete Talent Pool nominations" as shown in Figure 7-13 and click "Done." Be sure to save your role on the main screen as well.

---

**Note** By default, this will give nomination access to all employees. To make this permission specific to a target population, click "Apply target population to Talent Pool Nominations Permissions" in the "Nomination Setup" screen and then define a target population as you would with any other permission role. We will cover this screen in more detail in the next section.

---

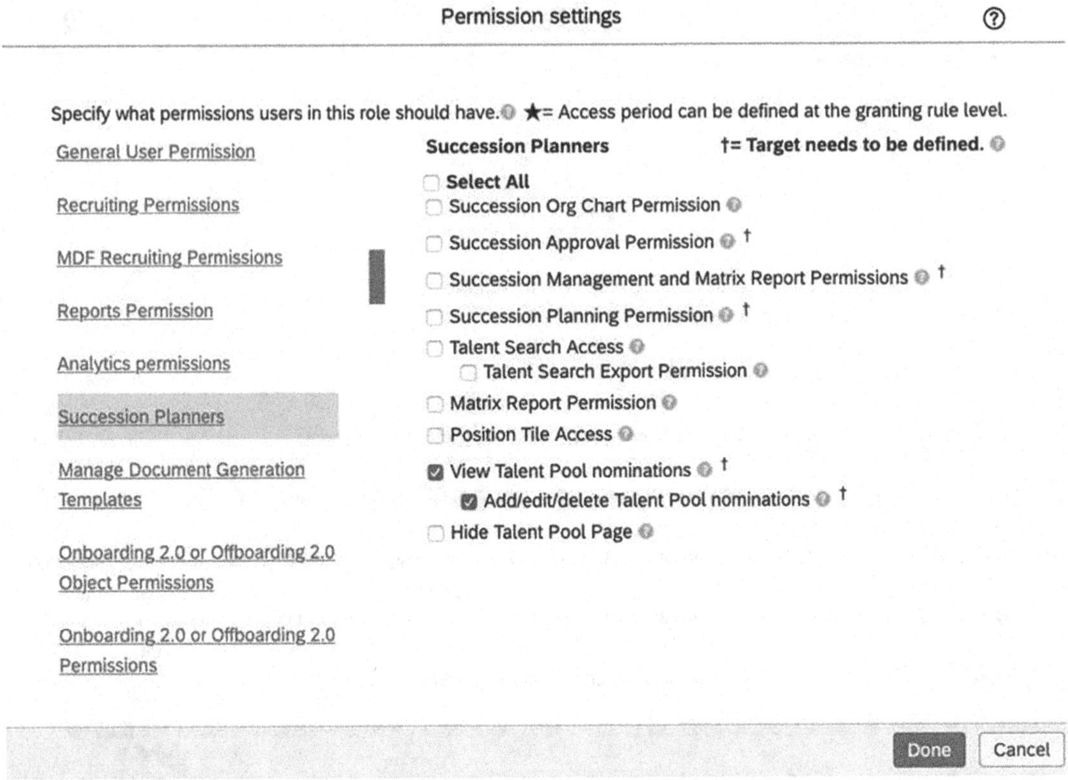

***Figure 7-13.*** *Permissions for Viewing and Editing Talent Pool Nominations*

6. For some organizations, it may make sense to allow managers to see nominations from Talent Profile and talent cards even if they don't have the permissions set in steps 1 and 2. If you want to enable this feature, log into Provisioning, select your organization, and click "Company Settings." Click the checkbox next to "Viewing Talent Pool Nominations in People Profile and Talent Card Without Having the Talent Pool Object Level Permission."

## Configure Talent Pool Nomination Fields

The "Manage Talent Pool Field Settings" configuration screen controls which employee fields can show as columns or be used as filter criteria within Talent Pool nominations. Follow these steps to configure the Talent Pool fields:

1. Type and select "Manage Talent Pool Field Settings" in the search bar. The configuration screen will show as in Figure 7-14.

**Admin Center > Manage Talent Pool Field Settings**

Save | Cancel

You can select fields from the list. The selected fields can be used as filters and display options in the Talent Pools page.

| Field Name | Include Field |
|---|---|
| First Name | ☑ |
| Last Name | ☑ |
| Job Title | ✓ |
| Division | ☑ |
| Department | ☑ |
| Location | ☑ |
| Risk of Loss | ☑ |
| Impact of Loss | ☑ |
| New to Position | ☑ |
| Future Leader | ☑ |
| Key Position | ☐ |
| Retirement Date | ☐ |
| Reason for Leaving | ☐ |
| Customizable Field 1 | ☐ |
| Customizable Field 2 | ☐ |
| Customizable Field 3 | ☐ |
| Customizable Field 4 | ☐ |
| Customizable Field 5 | ☐ |
| Customizable Field 6 | ☐ |
| Customizable Field 7 | ☐ |
| Customizable Field 8 | ☐ |
| Customizable Field 9 | ☐ |
| Customizable Field 10 | ☐ |
| Customizable Field 11 | ☐ |
| Customizable Field 12 | ☐ |
| Customizable Field 13 | ☐ |
| Customizable Field 14 | ☐ |
| Customizable Field 15 | ☐ |
| Readiness | ✓ |

***Figure 7-14.** The Manage Talent Pool Field Settings Screen*

2. The screen will show all of the standard Talent Pool fields from your data model. Check the box next to each field you wish to add as a potential column or filter and click "Save."

---

**Note** "Job Title" and "Readiness" are always selected by default.

---

## Using Talent Pools

Now that we have finished configuring our Talent Pool setup, it's time to create some Talent Pools and nominate some employees! Follow these steps to view Talent Pools, create a Talent Pool, nominate employees, and organize our view of those employees within a Talent Pool:

1. In the search bar, type and select "View Talent Pool."
2. Click "+" to create a new Talent Pool. A popup will appear as shown in Figure 7-15. Enter "GenManagers" for the "Code" field, "Active" for the "Status" field, today's date for the "Start Date" field, "SVP of Sales" for the "Name" field, "Yes" for the "Enable Readiness" field, and "3" for the "Executive Level" field. When you are finished, click "Save."

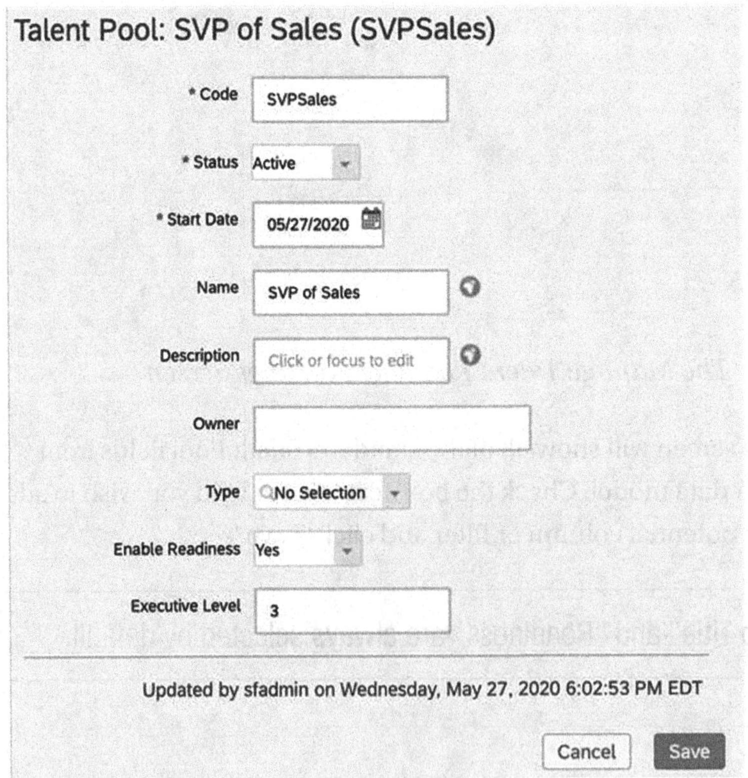


***Figure 7-15.*** *The Create Talent Pool Screen*

**Note** The fields that appear here are entirely up to your MDF configuration. You may want to hide some of these extra fields if they don't make sense for your implementation or add others. For the sake of our example, we only want to show that the custom "Executive Level" field has appeared that helps us with an extra level of security. Also note that any field with the globe icon can be translated into multiple languages depending on which languages have been activated in your instance.

3. You will then be taken to a confirmation screen that shows the information you just entered for the new Talent Pool MDF object as shown in Figure 7-16. You can change the information by clicking "Edit" or "Manage." Click the "x" to close and return to the main Talent Pool screen as shown in the following figure.

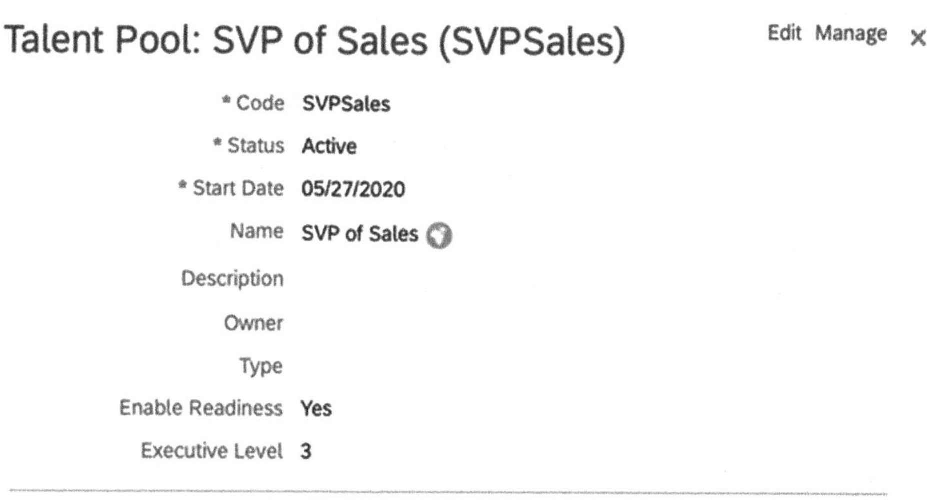


***Figure 7-16.*** *Talent Pool MDF Object Information Screen*

4. Repeat steps 2 and 3 for all Talent Pools you would like to create.

5. After creating your Talent Pools, they will appear on the main screen as shown in Figure 7-17. You can filter and sort them by code or name by clicking the funnel icon in the upper right-hand corner. Enter your criteria in the "Code" or "Name" field and click "Filter." Click "Reset" to clear the filters. You can also click the "Sort By..." next to the funnel icon to change the sort field and the order (ascending or descending).

Talent Pools    Sort By Name

SVP of Sales
Owner:
3

*Figure 7-17.* *Talent Pools Filtered by Name "SVP of Sales"*

6. Click the three dots next to any Talent Pool name to edit the Talent Pool MDF object information or delete it.

7. Click the name of the Talent Pool to view and edit the Talent Pool nominations within the Talent Pool. The screen will refresh showing any current nominations as seen in Figure 7-18.

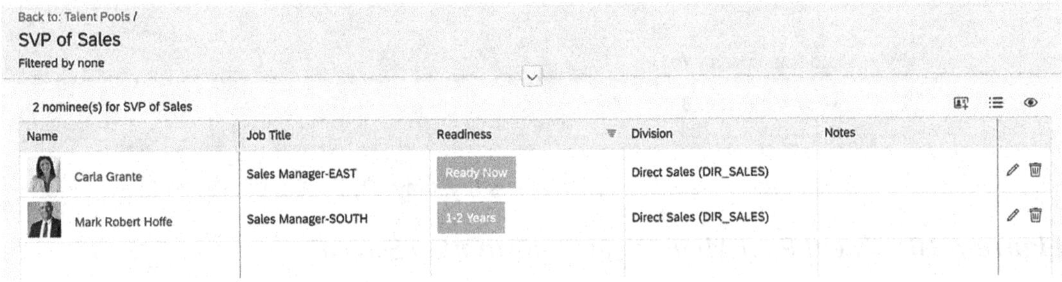

Back to: Talent Pools /
SVP of Sales
Filtered by none

2 nominee(s) for SVP of Sales

| Name | Job Title | Readiness | Division | Notes |
|---|---|---|---|---|
| Carla Grante | Sales Manager-EAST | Ready Now | Direct Sales (DIR_SALES) | |
| Mark Robert Hoffe | Sales Manager-SOUTH | 1-2 Years | Direct Sales (DIR_SALES) | |

*Figure 7-18.* *Talent Pool Nominations Screen*

8. To add an employee to the Talent Pool, click the business card icon. In the popup, type and select the name of the employee in the search bar. Click the "Next" button. Enter a readiness level and any notes and click "Submit." You will be returned to the screen as shown in the preceding figure with the newly added employee showing.
9. Repeat step 8 for any more nominations you would like to make.

---

**Note** So long as you have appropriate permissions, you can also make nominations from any talent card such as in the Succession Org Chart, Calibration, or Presentations, as well as from Talent Search. See those sections in this chapter for more details. These other areas are more commonly used to nominate employees because they offer more contextual information about the employees rather than simply typing their names.

---

10. Click the menu icon to edit the Talent Pool MDF object properties.
11. Click the eye icon. A popup will display as shown in Figure 7-19 to control which columns are displayed for each employee in the list of nominees. You will notice these are the talent fields you selected during configuration. Click the checkbox next to each field you would like displayed as a column and click "OK." You will return to the main Talent Pool nominations screen.

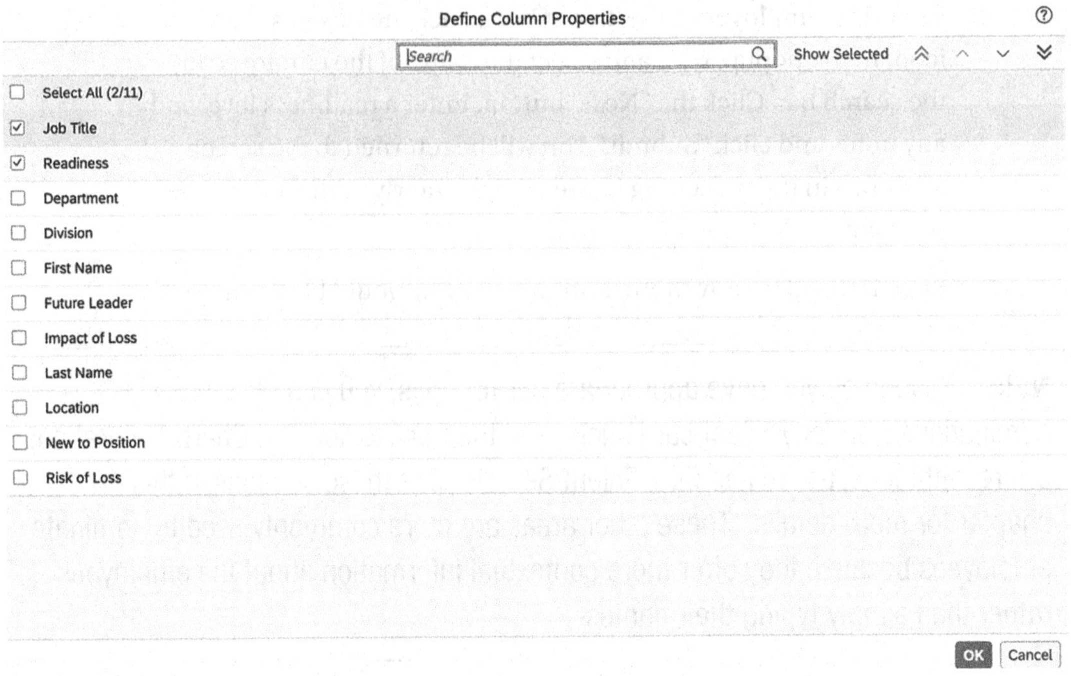

Define Column Properties

Search | Show Selected

- [ ] Select All (2/11)
- [x] Job Title
- [x] Readiness
- [ ] Department
- [ ] Division
- [ ] First Name
- [ ] Future Leader
- [ ] Impact of Loss
- [ ] Last Name
- [ ] Location
- [ ] New to Position
- [ ] Risk of Loss

OK Cancel

***Figure 7-19.*** *Defining Columns to Display on the Talent Pool Nominations Screen*

12. You can click the title of any column to sort by each column in ascending or descending order.

13. Click "Adapt Filters." A popup will display showing the current filters. To add any of the fields from your configuration that are not yet being used as filters, click "More Filters." In the new popup, check the boxes next to the fields you wish to add and click "OK." You can remove fields by unchecking the boxes next to each. Each field shows a dropdown with all of the valid values for the nominees in the Talent Pool. Choose the values you wish to use to filter the list of nominees and click "Go" to apply the filters. You will return to the main nominees list with the filters applied. The filters will show in the filter bar at the top of the screen. Click the up or down arrow to toggle the filter bar open or closed.

14. Click the pencil icon next to any nominee to edit the readiness or notes for the nominee in a new popup. Click Submit when completed.

15. Click the trash icon next to any nominee to remove the nominee from the Talent Pool. Click "Confirm" on the popup to proceed with the removal.

For the sake of our model company example, we can easily see how Talent Pools could be used to electronically capture an active list of potential SVPs of Sales across the organization based on up-to-date talent data rather than maintaining manual offline lists based on out-of-date information. The Talent Pool screens allow users to organize their lists, and the MDF allows any needed data about Talent Pools to be captured. We can even use those MDF fields for enhanced security. Within our example, we could rest assured that the president of the United States can access Talent Pools at their level and lower, but not higher (say at the global senior leadership team level). We also understand that users could make nominations from a variety of areas in the system so that nominees are organized into Talent Pools whenever the idea or discussion occurs in the system or even proactively using Talent Search. In this manner, at the advent of a succession event, our users are well prepared to determine a list of highly qualified successors and prepare them for their new potential positions!

---

**Note** We can even map Talent Pools to job profiles directly when creating them using Job Profile Builder. When in the "Roles" tab of Job Profile builder, select a role and go to the "Mapped Talent Pools" tab. For the sake of our example, we could ensure the SVP of Sales Talent Pool is always associated with the job profiles as well so the pool shows up whenever viewed on the Succession Org Chart or Position Tile View. See Volume 1, Chapter 2 for more information on Job Profile Builder.

---

# Position Tile View

The Position Tile View allows users to view positions from a different angle than the traditional org chart. Rather than viewing positions and their incumbents in a hierarchy, users can search by a variety of filters across all of the positions in the organization for which they have security access. The results are presented in a list of tiles that is sorted alphabetically. We are able to define what filters are available to the users with the MDF position object definition. This can be a very useful tool if you have added fields to your MDF position object definition that are key in differentiating positions in your organization. Let's take a look!

## Prerequisites for Configuring and Using the Position Tile View

Prior to starting our configurations, there are a few steps we need to take to ensure the system is ready. Let's take a look at these in the following.

---

**Note** As with the "Succession Org Chart" section in the prior chapter, we assume MDF positions are being used per our recommendations for your Succession Org Chart. The Position Tile View cannot be used without MDF positions.

---

### Provisioning

Before the Position Tile View permissions will appear in the system, we need to turn them on in Provisioning. Log in to Provisioning and select the company for which you would like to make the change, click "Company Settings," and check the box next to "Position Tile View" as seen in Figure 7-20. Click "Save."

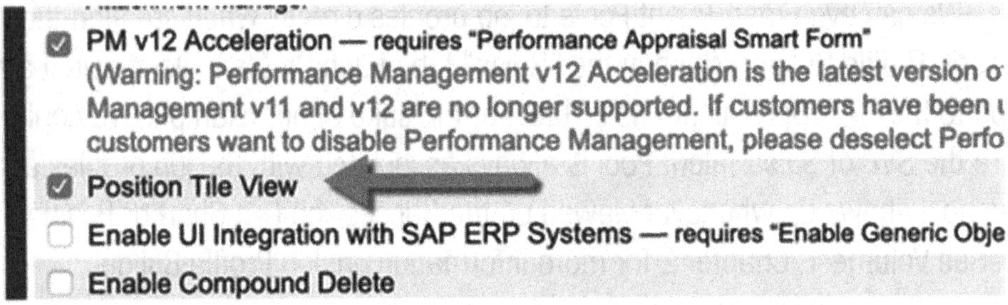

***Figure 7-20.*** *Provisioning Settings for the Position Tile View*

### Configurator Permissions

Like Talent Pools, we will need to define the MDF position object prior to using the Position Tile View. See "Configurator Permissions" in the "Talent Pools" section of this chapter for more details.

## Configuring the Position Tile View

Once we have appropriate permission, we can configure the MDF position object. In the following steps, we will add a field and make it searchable so that we have an additional meaningful field by which and based on which we can filter our positions and set additional security permissions. Follow these steps to complete the configuration:

---

**Note** If your implementation is part of an Employee Central (EC) implementation, you may have already configured the position object or may want to work closely with the EC team to ensure you are building a cohesive solution as this is an important touch point between Succession Management and Employee Central!

---

1. Type and select "Configure Object Definitions" in the search bar.
2. In the "Search" field, select "Object Definition." In the next dropdown, select "Position." The Position object definition will appear as in Figure 7-21.

***Figure 7-21.** Position Object Definition*

3. Click "Take Action" ➤ "Make Correction."

4. Scroll to the end of the "Fields" section and add a field by entering "cust_ExecutiveLevel" in the "Name" field, "2" in the "Maximum Length" field, and "Number" in the Data Type field. Click "Details" next to the fields. A popup will appear.
   a. In the popup, scroll down to the "Label" field and type "Executive Level." Click Done.
5. Back on the main screen, scroll down to the "Searchable Fields" section and type "cust_ExecutiveLevel" in the "Name" field. Then scroll down to the "Security" section and select "Yes" for the "Secured" field and "Miscellaneous Permissions" for the "Permission Category" field. Scroll to the bottom and click "Save."

---

**Note** While we don't cover all of the available fields here and just try to show how a field is added and edited, at a minimum, you will need to make the code, effectiveStatus, effectiveStartDate, effectiveEndDate, and positionCriticality fields required. The Incumbent field should be included as well but can be optional since a position can be without an occupant. Job code should also be included if you wish to associate job classifications. You should also use this screen to ensure a proper picklist is created for your positionCriticality field. The picklist name MUST be EXACTLY "PositionCriticality."

---

## Configuring End User Permissions

Now that the MDF has been configured where the Position object has been set to secured, we can modify any user permission roles to whom we wish to give access to Positions Follow these steps to add the Position Tile permission to the role(s):

1. First, we will grant permission to the Position Tile View screen. On the "Permission settings" screen for your role, click "Succession Planners" and check the box next to "Position Tile Access" as seen in Figure 7-22.

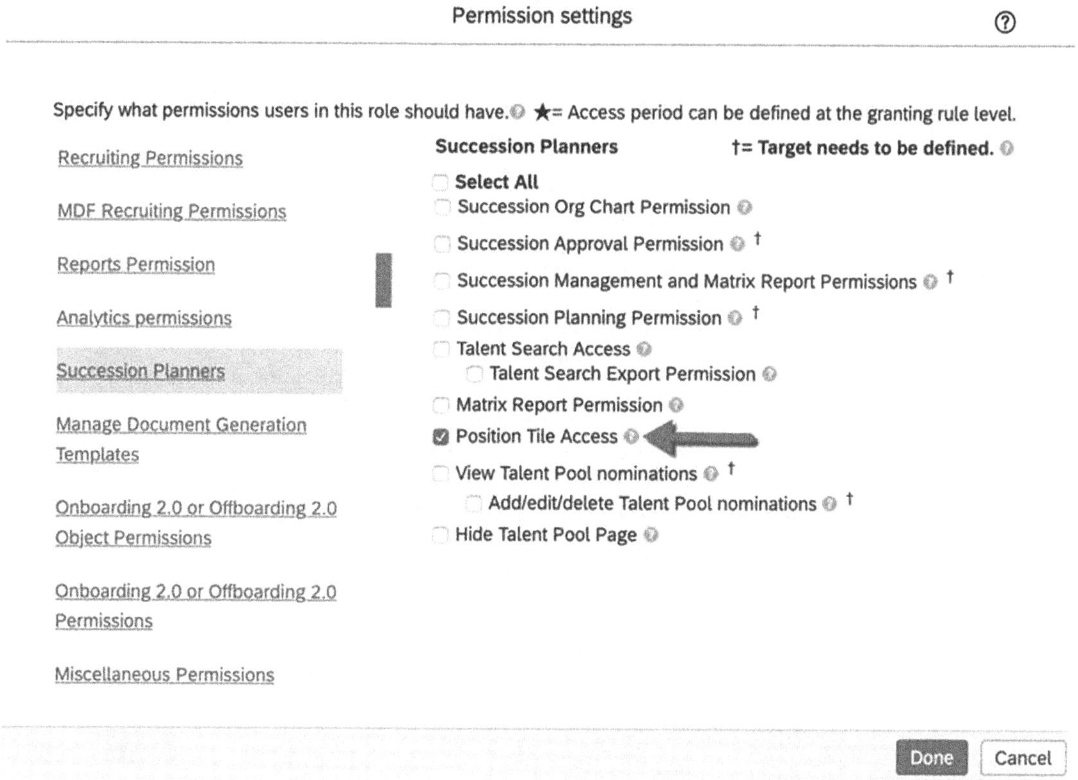

***Figure 7-22.*** *Position Tile Access Permission*

2. Next, we will grant permissions to the position objects so that some positions will populate on the screen. On the "Permission settings" screen, click "Miscellaneous Permissions" and scroll to "Position." Check the checkbox next to "View Current," "View History," "Create," "Insert," "Correct," "Delete," and "Import/Export" as shown in Figure 7-23. Click "Done."

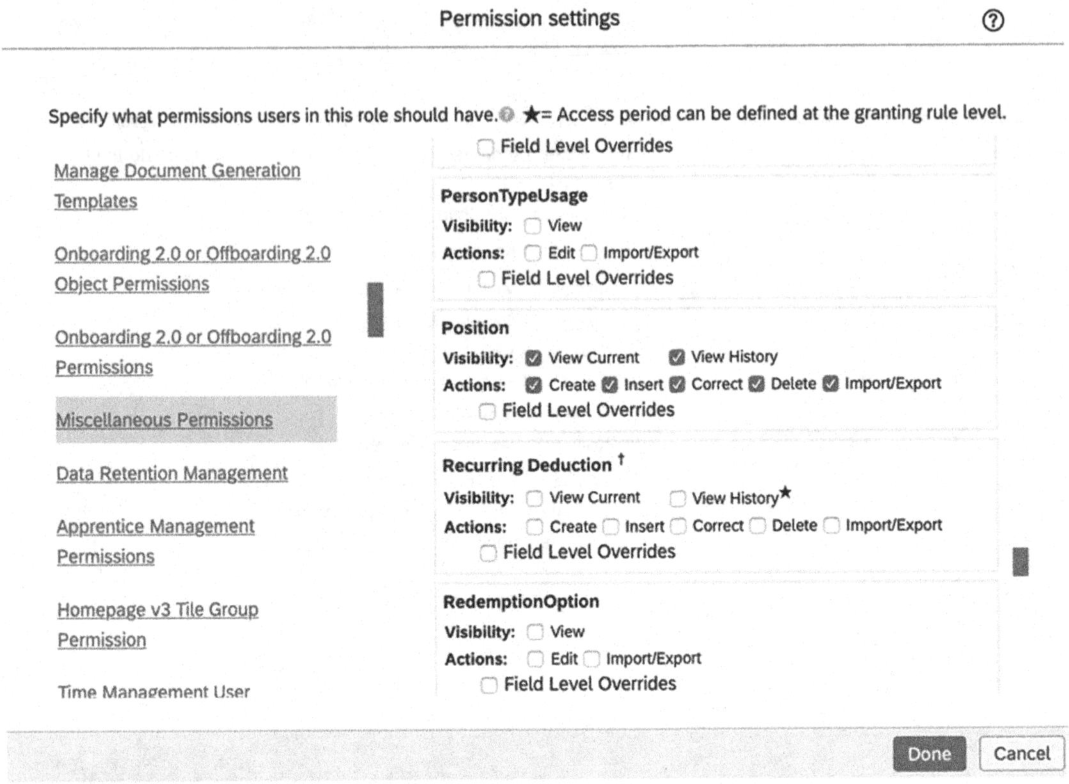

Permission settings

Specify what permissions users in this role should have. ★= Access period can be defined at the granting rule level.

Manage Document Generation Templates

Onboarding 2.0 or Offboarding 2.0 Object Permissions

Onboarding 2.0 or Offboarding 2.0 Permissions

Miscellaneous Permissions

Data Retention Management

Apprentice Management Permissions

Homepage v3 Tile Group Permission

Time Management User

Field Level Overrides

**PersonTypeUsage**
**Visibility:** View
**Actions:** Edit Import/Export
Field Level Overrides

**Position**
**Visibility:** View Current View History
**Actions:** Create Insert Correct Delete Import/Export
Field Level Overrides

**Recurring Deduction** †
**Visibility:** View Current View History★
**Actions:** Create Insert Correct Delete Import/Export
Field Level Overrides

**RedemptionOption**
**Visibility:** View
**Actions:** Edit Import/Export
Field Level Overrides

Done Cancel

***Figure 7-23.*** *Granting Position Permissions*

3. You can further refine which Position an end user can access. For the sake of our example, we will use the new field we created, cust_ExecutiveLevel, to allow different users access to different positions. We will grant this specific role access to Executive Level 2 for use of the HR admins as shown in the following figure and assume another role will be created for Level 1 for use of the senior leadership team only. On the Permission Role Detail screen, click "Edit Granting" and scroll down to "Position" and select the radio button for "Restrict target population to:" Check the first checkbox and enter "Executive Level," ">=", and "2." Click "Done." An example is shown in Figure 7-24.

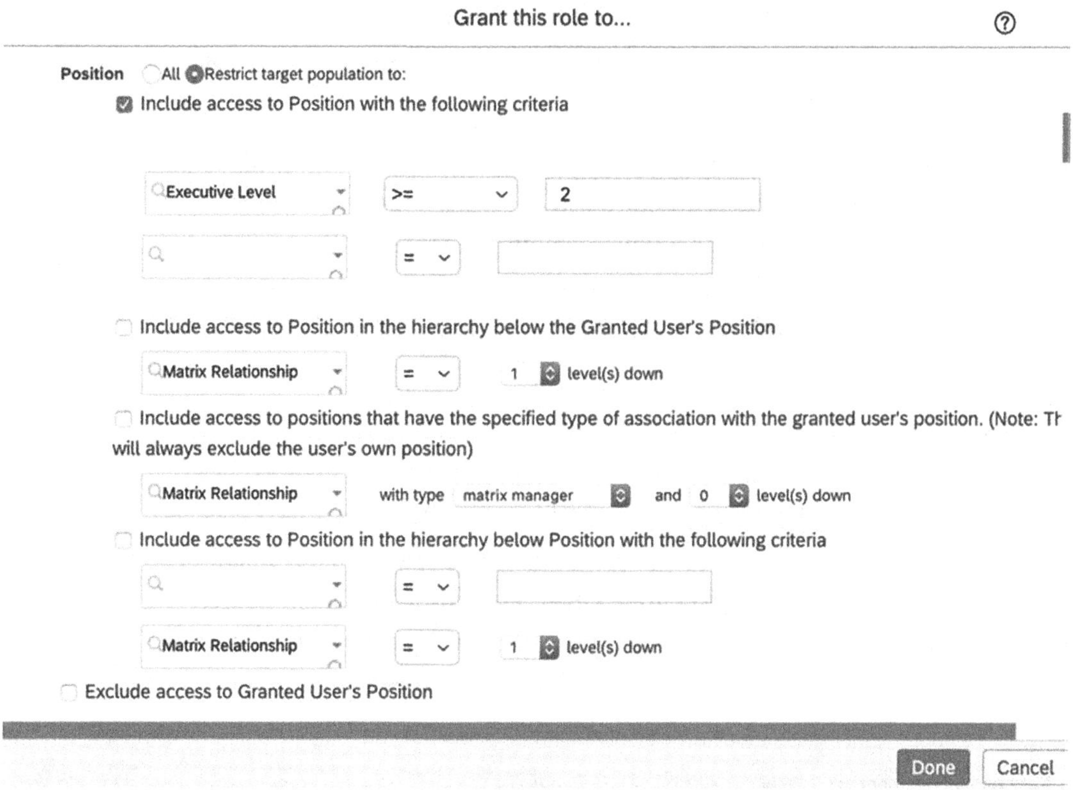

Grant this role to...

Position ◯ All ◉ Restrict target population to:

☑ Include access to Position with the following criteria

Executive Level >= 2

=

☐ Include access to Position in the hierarchy below the Granted User's Position

Matrix Relationship = 1 level(s) down

☐ Include access to positions that have the specified type of association with the granted user's position. (Note: Th will always exclude the user's own position)

Matrix Relationship with type matrix manager and 0 level(s) down

☐ Include access to Position in the hierarchy below Position with the following criteria

=

Matrix Relationship = 1 level(s) down

☐ Exclude access to Granted User's Position

Done Cancel

***Figure 7-24.*** *Refining Position Access to Executive Level 2 and Below*

4. It is important to remember the preceding permissions give the user access only to view and edit the position objects, not the permission to view the actual nominations within the positions! To add permission to view and make nominations, select the "Succession Planning Permission" as well from step 1.

5. When you are finished with all permission role changes, click "Save."

# Using the Position Tile View

Now that the Position Tile View has been activated and configured and we have security access, we can visit the screen and start using it. Follow these steps to use the screen:

1. In the search bar, type and select "Position Tile." By default, the screen will load with results of all of the positions for which you have security access in alphabetical order by position name.

The positions show as tiles with the position name at the top and the incumbent, if any, just below. Any named successors to the position are shown as well.

2. Click the "+" icon to add a position. Note the fields here will vary depending on your configuration of the MDF position object. Enter the start date as today's date and the title as "Regional Manager - Misc US Territories," set "Status" to "Active," and set "Executive Level" to "3." Click "Save." Then click the "x" on the confirmation screen.

3. Click the funnel icon or "Add Filters" to open the filters pane on the right-hand side of the screen. Scroll to the bottom and click "Add" to add filter criteria. You will notice the "Executive Level" is present since we added this as a searchable field on our position object! Select the "Executive Level" and enter "3." Click "Search" and the system will pull up our position! Click clear filters to show all available positions for your security again. See Figure 7-25.

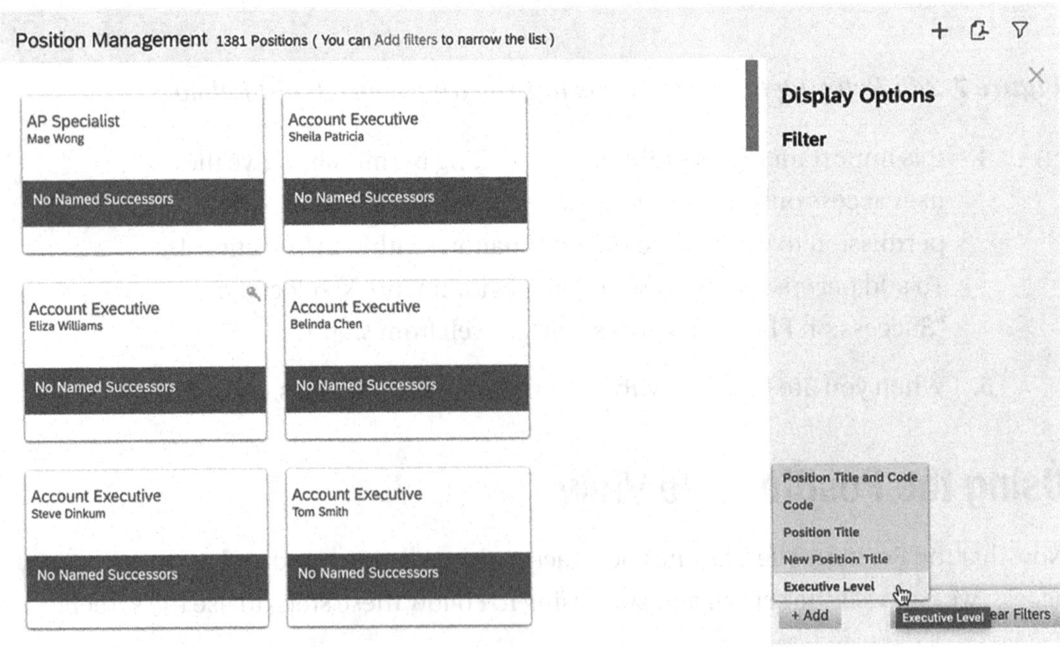


*Figure 7-25.* *Position Tile View*

4. Click the tile of any position to bring up the position card. This works the same ass the Succession Org Chart where you can view incumbent talent cards, set the position as a key position, or nominate successors. You can also click the menu icon to edit the position, delete it, show nomination history, or view the Lineage Chart. Click the "x" to close the position card.

---

**Note** If you have implemented recruiting, you can also create a requisition from here as well!

---

5. You can also click the download icon to download an output of the positions on-screen if you have created a BIRT report for this screen.

---

**Note** Downloading a printable version of this screen requires building a BIRT report and uploading it to Provisioning. The report can be uploaded in the "Import/Update/Export – BI Publisher Template/BIRT Template" section of Provisioning. We will not cover authoring a BIRT report in this book.

---

# Lineage Chart

After you have made multiple nominations against various positions up and down the org chart via the Succession Org Chart or the Position Tile View, the Lineage Chart feature will start to become very useful! The functionality allows the user to visualize what a specific succession scenario might look like, not only in terms of the direct replacement but also those below that replacement.

## Prerequisites for Accessing the Lineage Chart

The Lineage Chart has no specific configuration screen or permissions for itself. The chart is simply based off of the same configurations and permissions used for the Succession Org Chart. Since we have already detailed these in prior sections, we will not cover them again. To enable the Lineage Chart, it must be activated in Provisioning. Log into Provisioning and access your company. Click "Company Settings" and check the box next to "Succession Lineage Report" as seen in Figure 7-26. Click Save.

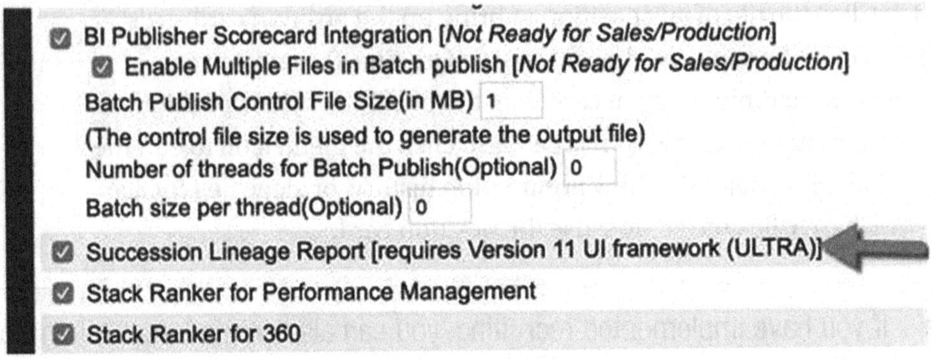

***Figure 7-26.*** *Turning on Succession Lineage Report in Provisioning*

## Using the Lineage Chart

To use the Lineage Chart, follow these steps:

1. Type and select "View Succession Lineage Chart" in the search bar.
2. On the screen that appears, type the employee for whom you want to start the lineage in the new search bar that appears.
3. When the employee appears, you can click the business card icon to open the talent card for the employee.
4. Click the name of the employee to see all the text descriptions of the talent field icons showing for that employee (these are pulled from the Succession Org Chart configuration XML; see the "Succession Org Chart" section of Chapter 21 for more details).
5. Click the bottom bar showing the number of nominations to vexpand and show tiles for those nominees.
6. Repeat step 5 for all levels of the lineage you would like to view.
7. Click and drag the mouse to move your view of the lineage. You can also use the "+" and "-" to zoom in and out. An example final output is shown in Figure 7-27.

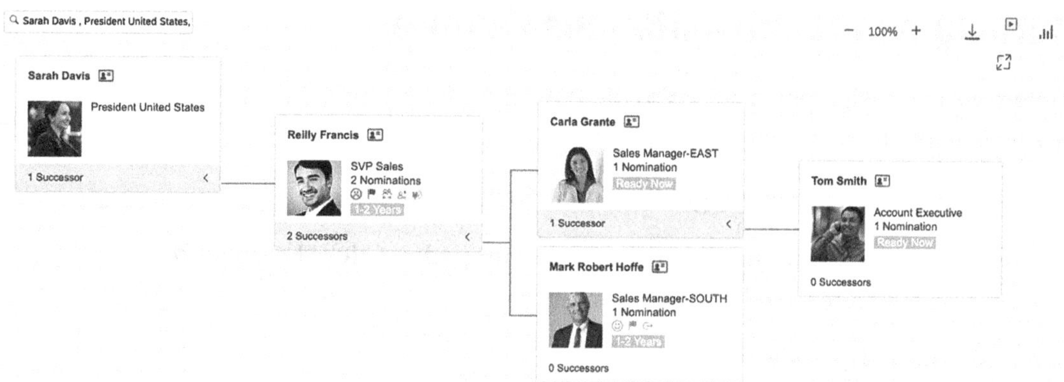


*Figure 7-27.* *Example Lineage Chart*

8. Click the down arrow icon to download the chart as a PDF or JPEG.

For the sake of our example model company, you can see how the President would find this tool very useful. They can not only see who might replace the SVP but also easily visualize who is lined up to replace those replacements as well! The example in the preceding figure shows a visualization of our model succession scenario quite nicely! The President can be confident that if the SVP moves into their position, there will be a regional sales manager ready now to take the SVP's place and an account executive to take that regional manager's place in turn.

# Succession Presentations

Now that we've toured the entire set of configurations and features of Succession Management, we have one final feature left to cover: Presentations. Presentations are commonly used to present succession data in a guided way to senior executives during a succession meeting. This feature is popular with organizations who are new to online succession planning and have traditionally performed succession planning via manually building PowerPoint presentations to the senior leadership team. The feature makes a nice bridge between leveraging traditional PowerPoint format and taking advantage of the up-to-date information available in the system. Minimal configuration is required to activate Presentations. The features within Presentations once it is activated will adopt your configurations from the previous sections of this chapter.

## Turning on the Presentations Feature

Before we can assign permissions to the Presentations feature, it needs to be activated. To activate the feature, follow these steps:

1. Type and select "Upgrade Center" in the search bar.
2. Find "Presentations" in the optional upgrades. Click "Learn More & Upgrade Now."
3. Click "Upgrade Now."
4. Click "Yes" and "OK."

## Granting Access to Presentations

As with almost all features, we need to add permission to access the screen for end users. Follow these steps to add permission to your permission role:

1. Type and select "Manage Permission Roles" in the search bar.
2. When the screen loads, click the role you wish to modify. Then click "Permission...:"
3. Click "Manage Presentations" and then select the checkbox next to "Manage Presentation" as seen in Figure 7-28. Click "Done." Be sure to save your role on the main screen as well.

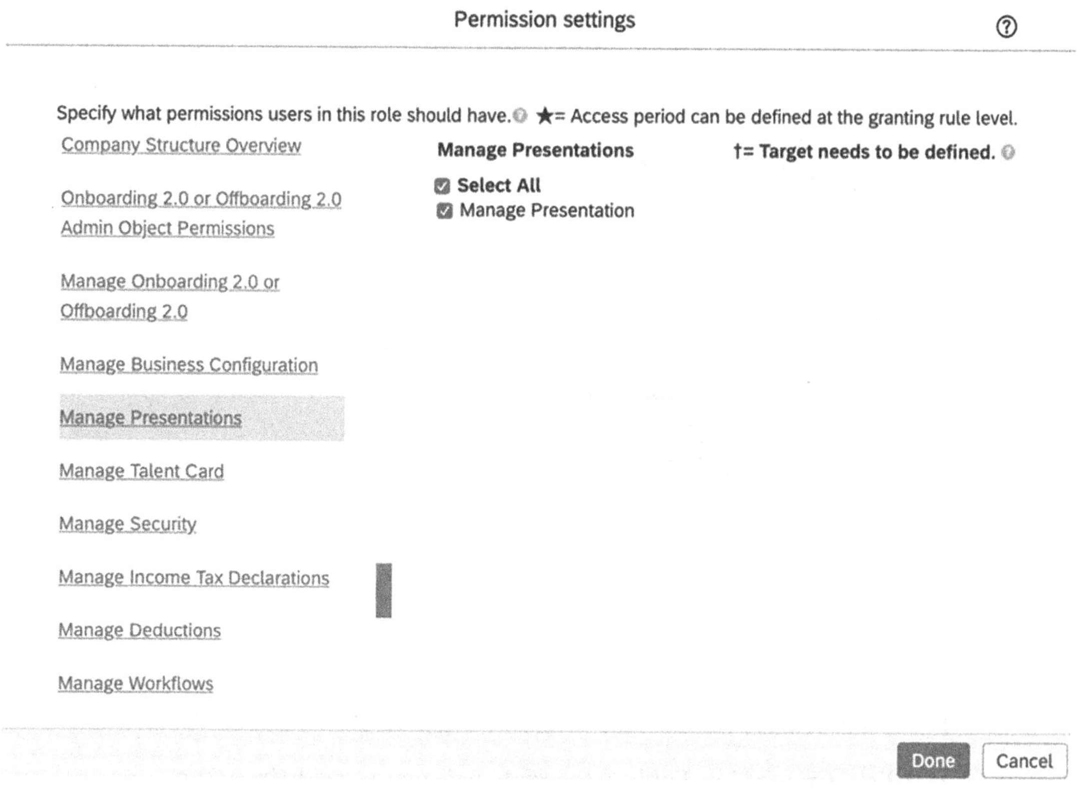

Permission settings

Specify what permissions users in this role should have. ★= Access period can be defined at the granting rule level.

Company Structure Overview

Onboarding 2.0 or Offboarding 2.0 Admin Object Permissions

Manage Onboarding 2.0 or Offboarding 2.0

Manage Business Configuration

Manage Presentations

Manage Talent Card

Manage Security

Manage Income Tax Declarations

Manage Deductions

Manage Workflows

Manage Presentations

†= Target needs to be defined.

Select All

Manage Presentation

Done Cancel

***Figure 7-28.*** *Manage Presentation Permission*

---

**Note** The preceding permission will only grant access to the Presentations screen itself. It is important to remember that the data the user can see within the presentation is based on the target-based permissions we've already covered in this chapter for positions, employees, and nominations.

---

## Using Presentations

Now that we have set up with permissions, let's get started using the Presentations feature. Follow these steps:

1. Before you can access Presentations for the first time, you will need to accent the End User Licensing Agreement (EULA). Type and select "Accept EULA" in the search bar.

2. Click "Accept EULA" and read the EULA.
3. Click Accept.
4. Type and select "Presentations" in the search bar. The screen will appear as in Figure 7-29.

***Figure 7-29.*** *Presentations Main Screen*

5. From this screen, you manage any existing presentations you have.
   a. Click "Create New Folder" to create a directory aside from the default "Presentations," "Archived," and "Trash" folders. A popup will appear for you to enter the folder name. Click "OK" when done.
   b. You can delete or edit the name of any folder you have created by mousing over the folder name and clicking the trash can or pencil icons, respectively (you cannot delete the default folders).
   c. If you place a presentation in the "Trash" folder, it will not be deleted immediately. Mouse over the "Trash" folder to see the "Empty Trash" option which can be clicked to delete the presentations within.
   d. To access a folder and see the presentations within it, click the name of the folder.

e. To create a presentation, click the "+" sign.

i. Type a presentation name in the popup that appears and click "OK." You will see the Presentations edit screen load as shown in Figure 7-30.

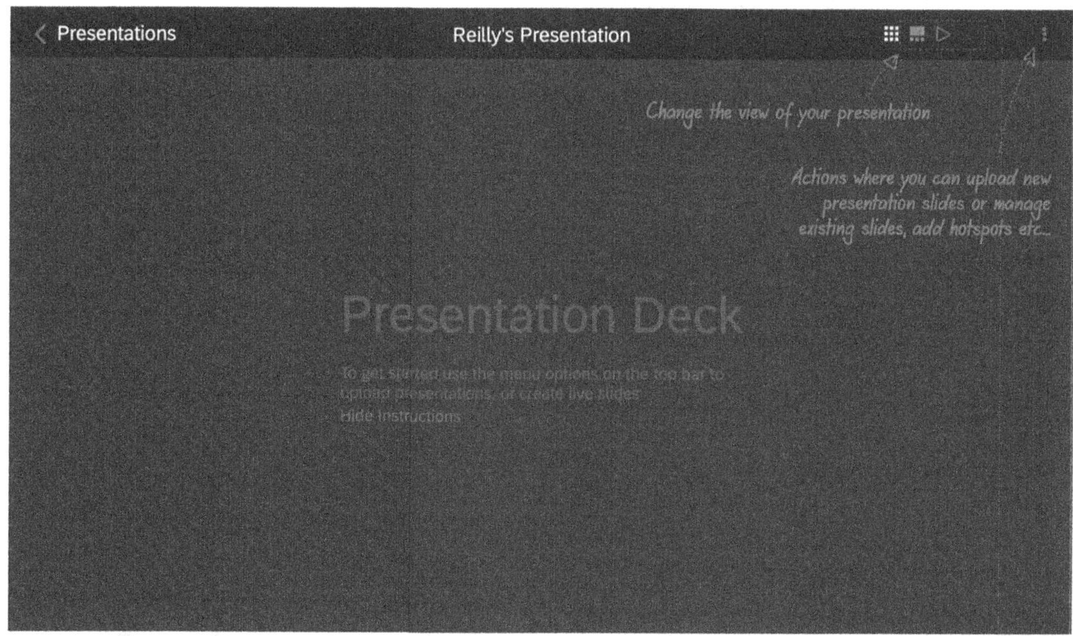


***Figure 7-30.*** *Presentations Edit Screen*

ii. Click the three dots menu icon in the upper right-hand corner. The menu will give you the option to upload a PowerPoint or PDF to start from, add a live slide, edit the presentation details (which is just editing the name), print the presentation, or delete the presentation. If you have a slide selected, you can also create a customized slide (if the slide you are on is an uploaded slide), edit the slide that you selected when you created it, and edit the slide contents (which simply allows you to edit hotspots).

1. Click "Add a Live Slide". Select your type of live slide based on Table 7-1.

***Table 7-1.** Available Live Slides*

| Live Slide Name | Description | Sample Screenshot |
| --- | --- | --- |
| Performance-Potential Matrix | Creates a 9-box showing live data based on your matrix grid configurations. Requires you to select a particular team or group as well as date parameters as you would in the matrix grid report. | 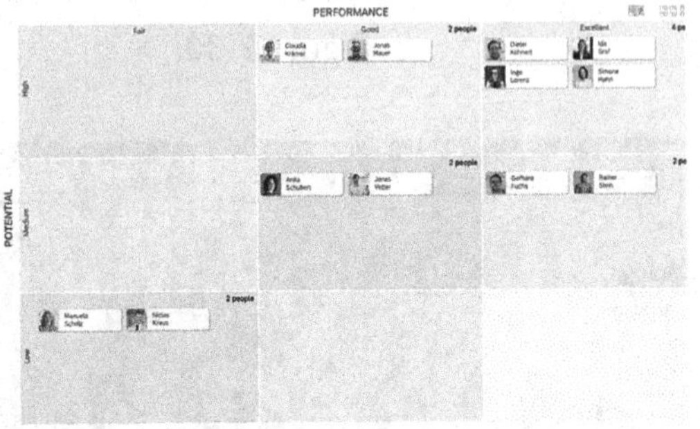 |
| How vs. What Matrix | Same as in the preceding but for objective-competency configurations. | 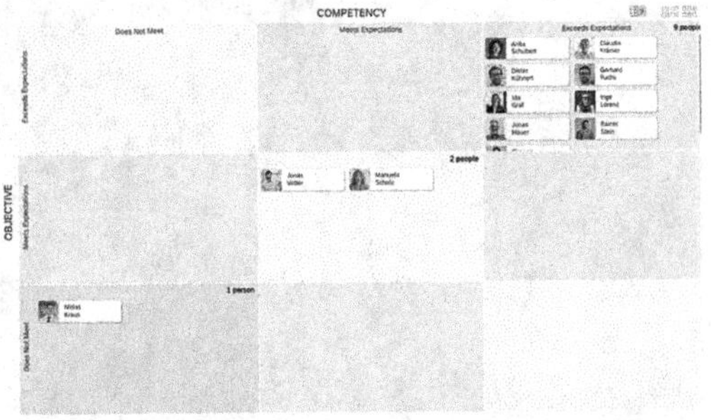 |
| Succession Org Chart | Displays an area of the Succession Org Chart starting from a particular person or position you specify. You can optionally choose to include matrix reports and/or only show key positions. | 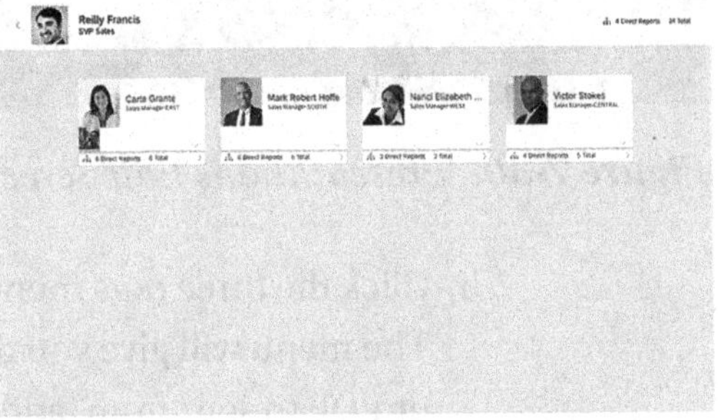 |
| Team View | Displays the talent cards for a particular team starting from a manager of your choosing. The only difference with the previous slide is the exclusion of succession nominee information. | 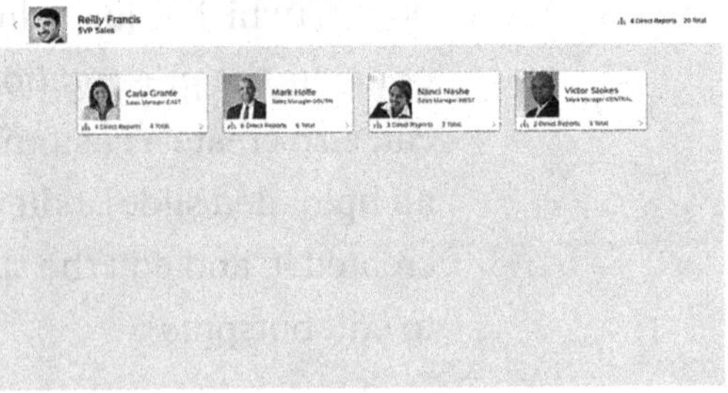 |

*(continued)*

*Table 7-1.* (*continued*)

| Live Slide Name | Description | Sample Screenshot |
| --- | --- | --- |
| Talent Pools | Select one or more Talent Pools to which you have access to view on the slide. | 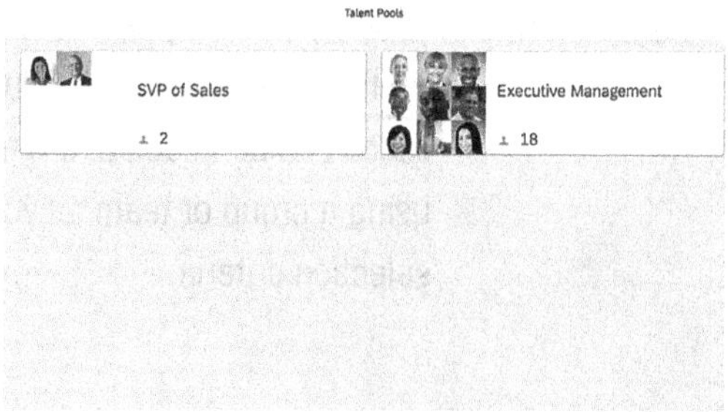 |
| People Grid | Used to compare a static set of individuals on one slide. Select the orientation of one to four grids and add the individuals you prefer to each grid. | 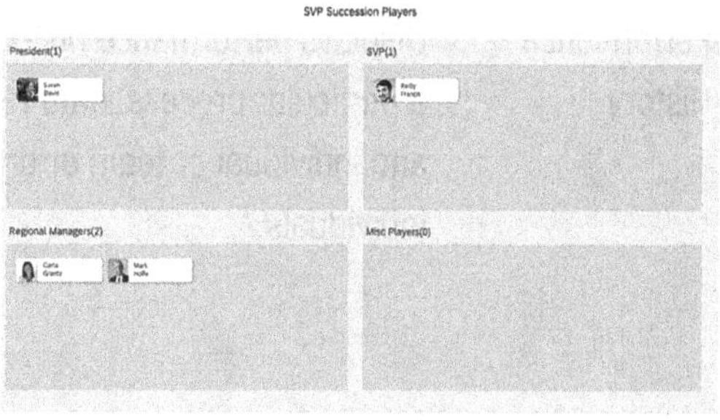 |
| Compensation Review | If you have implemented the Compensation Management module, you can use this slide to present any relevant compensation fields for whatever team or group you choose. | 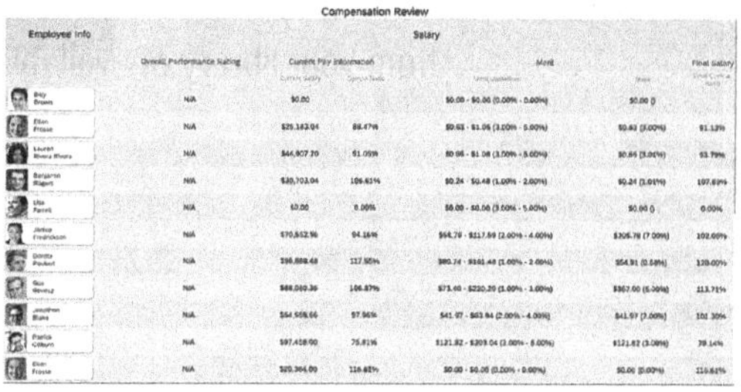 |
| Position Tile | Allows you to run a search query for positions based off of your available MDF searchable fields and shows the tiles for those positions. |  |

(*continued*)

***Table 7-1.*** *(continued)*

| Live Slide Name | Description | Sample Screenshot |
|---|---|---|
| People Profile | Allows you to display the Talent Profile for an individual. Multiple slides can be added at a time using a group or team as your selection criteria. | 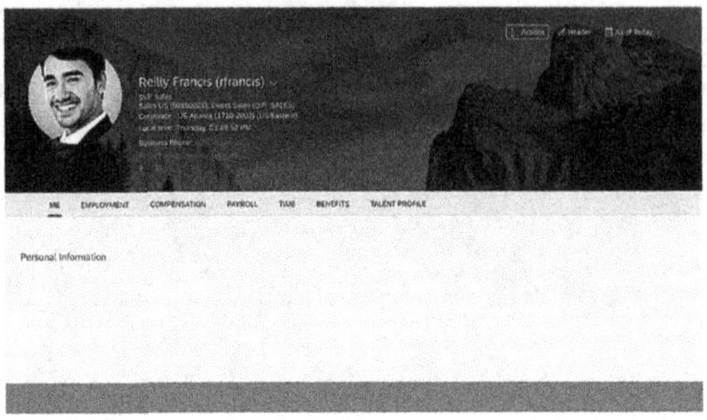 |
| Performance History | Displays performance history for a particular process, date range, and individual or team or group of individuals. | 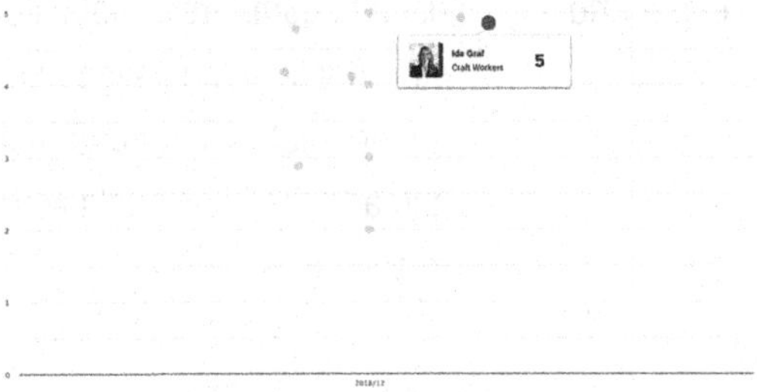 |
| Analytics | Displays up to four analytics tiles from your library of available tiles. | 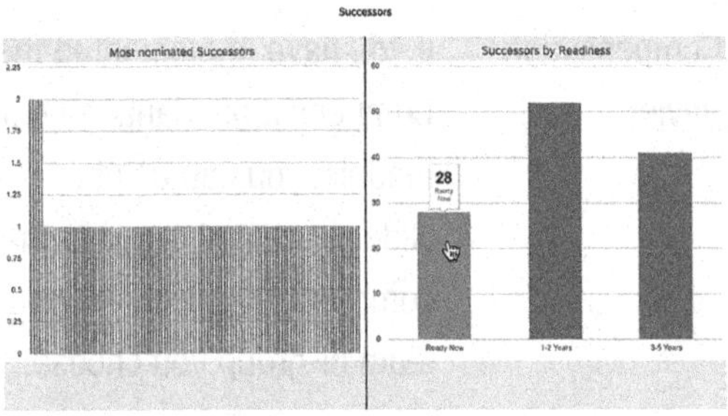 |

2. Printing the presentation will give you options on how you want each type of slide included in your presentation to be formatted prior to final printing. Click "Print."

3. Editing the slide contents introduces the concept of hotspots which simply let you click the area of the hotspot in presentation mode to either open a link or a talent card for a particular individual. After selecting this option, click the square icon in the upper right-hand corner of the slide you are editing and then click and drag over the area of the slide you wish to make a hotspot. Then choose the link or individual you would like to show when

clicking the hotspot from the menu that appears. Click "OK" to finish the hotspot. Then click "Done" when you are finished editing all slides.

4. Creating a custom slide allows you to choose one of your static uploaded slides to overlay with live talent information using a drag and drop editor as shown in Figure 7-31. Selecting this option will prompt you to find an employee whose info you want to enter prior to bringing you to the editor shown in the following figure. The concept from SAP is to use this to replace the pixel-perfect talent card.

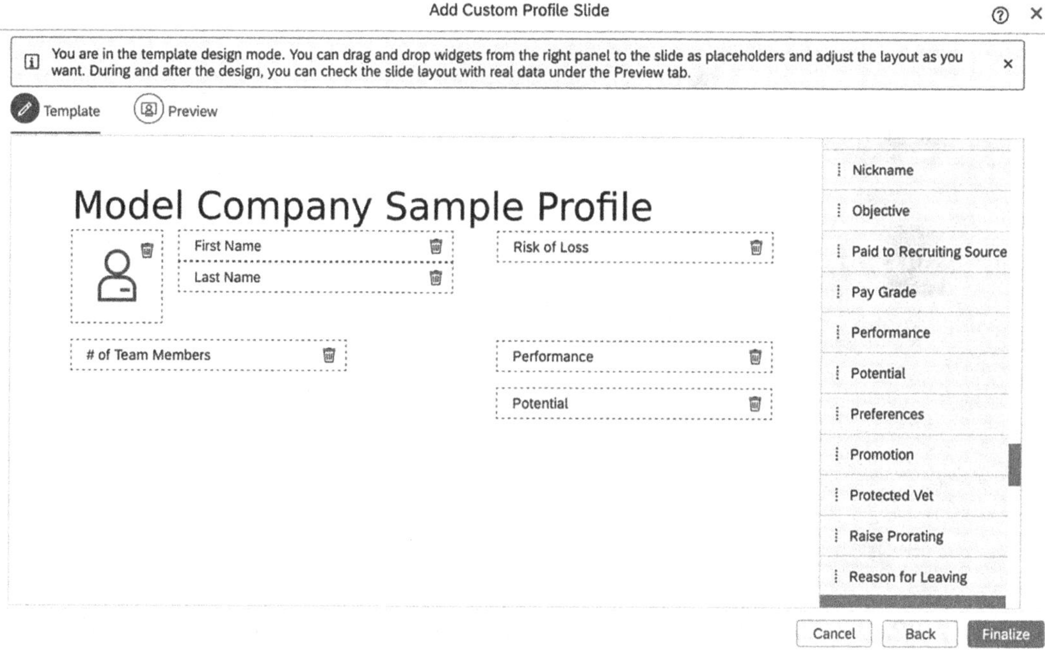


***Figure 7-31.** Editing a Custom Slide*

---

**Note** Many users begin creating their presentations offline using PowerPoint or by creating a PDF. Often, presentations are a combination of "live" slides that are created in the tool and access real-time data and these uploaded slides which include text and images created offline.

---

iii. Once slides are added to the presentation, the three view mode icons at the top toggle between seeing all slides as small icons, seeing a large preview of each slide as they are selected from a scrolling list on the bottom, or viewing them in presentation mode.

1. In presentation mode, you can progress through your slides by clicking the left or right arrow, click your hotspots, or click any individual shown on a live slide to view their talent card as shown in Figure 7-32.

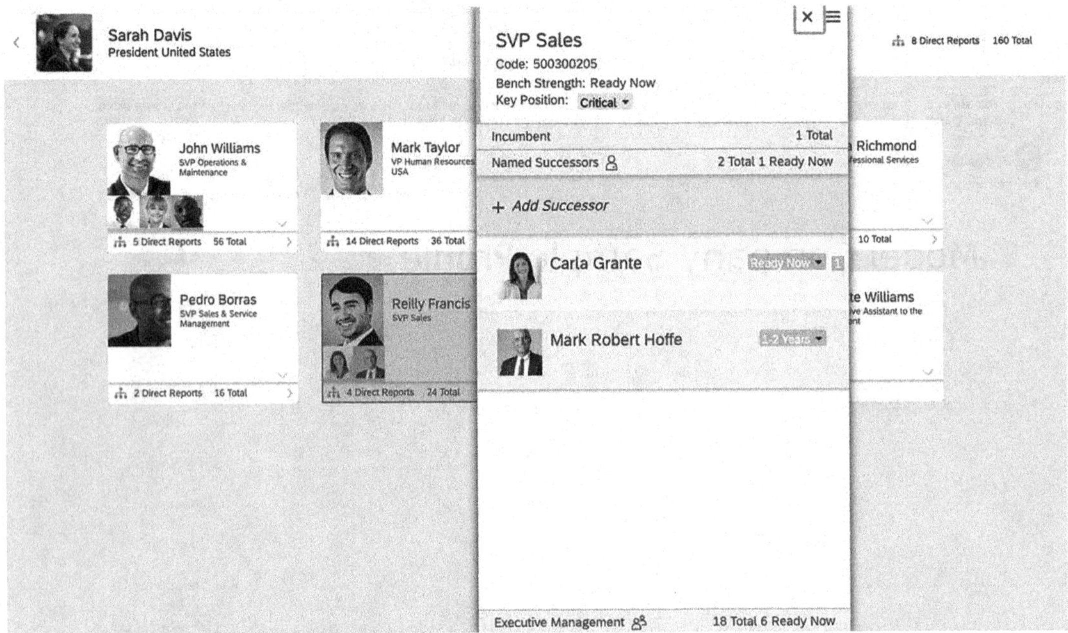


***Figure 7-32.** Presentation of Succession Org Chart Live Slides Showing a Talent Card*

2. To exit presentation mode, click the down arrow in the upper left-hand corner of the screen (it will only appear when you mouse over it!).

iv. To return to the main screen, click "Presentations" in the upper left-hand corner of the screen.

f. To share a presentation, click the molecule icon.

i. A new popup will appear to let you search by name or by group (see the " Running and Using the Matrix Grid Reports" section of Chapter 5 for reference on how to create groups).

ii. Enter and select the name or group. Repeat as necessarily until you have all individuals and groups with which you would like to share.

iii. Optionally check the box to email the individuals with whom you are sharing. You can also customize this email by clicking the "Customize Email" button. (You can edit and activate this email template in the "E-Mail Notification Templates Settings" screen).

iv. Click "Done" to share the presentation.

g. Click the three dots menu icon on a presentation to edit the title, copy it, move it to another folder, or delete it. Selecting delete will only move the presentation to the "Trash" folder.

h. Click the "SHARED WITH ME" tab to view presentations others have shared with you. You can only view and copy a presentation which has been shared with you.

For the sake of our model company, our president, as well as any supporting HR admins, now has access to a tool that frees them up from the manual processes involved with creating a presentation to their senior leadership team. They can quickly put together a presentation for these executives that illustrates the situation with the SVP and regional managers with factual up-to-date information presented in an organized and guided manner rather than having to have a difficult conversation or attempting to use potentially out-of-date spreadsheets as a reference.

# Conclusion

We hope you have enjoyed this tour of configuring and using Succession Management! At this point, you should now have a solid understanding of what each of the features is and how to configure and grant access to them. In addition, we've stepped through recommended settings based on real-world experience and also touched based periodically on how our model company would take advantage of all the features of the module. With this system and practical application knowledge, you should be well on your way to empower any organization with this robust succession tool!

# CHAPTER 8

# Conclusion

Congratulations on completing the second volume of our total run through of the Talent Management modules and functions of SAP SuccessFactors! Let's take a look back and review what we've learned across both volumes so we can understand how these modules work together to provide a comprehensive talent management solution.

In Volume 1, we began with the Talent Profile and Job Profile Builder. We showed you how to store, organize, and display employee and job-related data talent management data for use across the various modules of SuccessFactors Talent. We then took a deep dive into the Goal Management and Performance Management modules to show you how to set goals and measure employee success achieving them.

In this volume, we started with a deep dive of the Development module. Chapters 1, 2, 3, and 4 looked at various employee development features. In Chapter 1, you learned how to configure a development plan including creating a basic plan from SuccessStore and directly editing the XML. Similarly, Chapters 2 and 3 showed you how to configure the career worksheet so that employees can view suggested roles and target specific roles for development through integration with Job Profile Builder. In Chapter 4, we learned how to set up administrators and participants for three different types of standard mentoring programs or how to create a custom one tailored to your organization's needs to bring employees together to enhance their careers. Overall, these chapters showed you how the system helps employees set development goals, work with their managers to achieve those goals, tie the goals to specific learnings, target specific roles and career paths, and find help outside of direct managers through mentoring.

Finally, in Chapters 5, 6, and 7, you explored the Succession Management module. Chapter 5 introduced you to configuring and using the 9-box and Talent Review Form and showed how they could be integrated into Calibration. Chapter 6 explored how nominations work and how the Succession Org Chart can be configured to draw on a variety of data to help decision makers make key position nominations. In Chapter 7, we explored other helpful tools like Talent Search, Talent Pools, the Position Tile




S. Traynor et al., *SAP SuccessFactors Talent: Volume 2*, https://doi.org/10.1007/978-1-4842-6995-4_8

View, the Lineage Chart, and Presentations. In summary, you saw how the Succession Management module can draw on data across the Talent Management suite to identify top talent and assist decision makers with key position succession decisions.

After reviewing the chapters across both volumes, we hope you can now recognize the high-level business processes the features and modules of SAP SuccessFactors support. Furthermore, we hope you can see how the modules integrate to make for a cohesive solution. Indeed, when properly implemented and used, SAP SuccessFactors can help employees and organizations set and track business and development goals collaboratively while providing rewarding career opportunities that help both the business and employees succeed. In the next section, we will cover how to actualize this potential business value through an implementation of a fully productive system.

# Realizing Business Value and Next Steps

In our review, we walked through each chapter to paint a high-level picture of the business value presented by each module and functionality. Throughout the book, we've also brought in real-world experience as well as model companies to give recommendations on making configuration decisions. Furthermore, we've pointed out how each module ties into the others to build into a cohesive solution.

The art of implementation consulting is understanding what the customer wants while juggling those desires with what is practical and typical. This is accomplished by being able to draw on the knowledge of what is possible and what others have done while not losing sight of how to provide real long-term value. Hopefully after reading this book, you have gained a significant amount of that required knowledge based on our technical and real-world input. The key now will be understanding business priorities and realizing them into business value using the product. The first step in setting and realizing those priorities is planning a system rollout.

# Planning Your Rollout

By understanding the capabilities of the complete Talent Management suite and how the modules work together, you can plan how you would like to roll out your organization's implementation. Typically, we see individual modules within the Talent Management suite rolled out one at a time rather than a "big bang" approach. We have purposefully laid out our chapters in order of how we recommend (and often see) customers roll out each module and functionality. This is not to say it is the only way we recommend rolling out the Talent Management suite. For example, many organizations need time to create a job catalog before implementing Job Profile Builder, so they may implement Goal Management and Performance Management without any linkage to Job Profile Builder. They may even implement Development and Succession without Job Profile Builder and go back to add integrated features in smaller waves once the job catalog is complete. Events like a contract ending with a legacy performance appraisal system often drive timelines - but we find in these scenarios that a bit of forward thinking with knowledge of the entire suite can avoid rework later when other modules are implemented. A final rollout plan should consider the priorities of the business as well as time-to-value considerations.

## Implementation

After developing a rollout strategy and timeline, it is time to begin your first module implementation! Whether you are a partner or a customer, you should be sure to familiarize yourself with the SAP Activate implementation methodology. At a high level, the methodology takes an agile approach. Typically, implementations see three iterative cycles where customer requirements are gathered in a workbook and the system is configured, demonstrated to business stakeholders, and then reconfigured based on feedback prior to final launch. Normally, configurations are completed in a test instance and then moved to a separate productive instance once all testing is completed and signed off by business stakeholders. The implementation process can be challenging, but in our experience, the Talent Management modules are among the most straightforward to implement with SAP SuccessFactors.

## Life After Go-Live

Once an implementation is completed, the system has really only started its life being useful. It is important to note that as a cloud product, SAP SuccessFactors is not static. As of writing this book, SAP conducts major releases twice a year.

Releases are put into test instances that reside in test data centers first prior to moving to customer productive instances so that customers have a chance to explore the release prior to rollout to production. These releases typically contain product enhancements across all modules. It is important to check the product release schedule details for dates and specifics on what new functionality and changed functionality will be included in each release. SAP also provides a road map for their vision of where each product module will be taken in the upcoming years. We recommend checking each of these periodically to align your ongoing system maintenance and deployment strategy so that you take advantage of the latest technology enhancements and adjust the course of your system as business priorities change.

In our experience, once the system is live, there is a constant cycle of working with business stakeholders to update the system with new and relevant features periodically and communicating those released changes to users. As an ever-evolving product, it is exciting to see what is coming next for SAP SuccessFactors!

## Final Thoughts

Thank you for joining us on our journey through the various functions and modules of SAP SuccessFactors! We hope your reading experience has been a positive one and that you will enjoy implementing and administering SAP SuccessFactors just as much. If you are new to the technology, then we wish to welcome you to the community and the exciting career opportunities it brings. If you are an experienced professional, then we hope you learned something new. If you are just evaluating, we hope you consider this comprehensive product. We wish you well on your talent management adventures and hope to meet you out in the field!

# Index

## A, B, C






S. Traynor et al., *SAP SuccessFactors Talent: Volume 2*, https://doi.org/10.1007/978-1-4842-6995-4

## D



## E, F, G, H, I



## J, K



## L



## M

## N



## O



## P, Q



## R



## S

## T



## U, V, W, X, Y, Z